REASSERTING INTERNATIONAL ISLAM

A Focus on the Organization of the Islamic Conference and other Islamic Institutions

REASSERTING INTERNATIONAL ISLAM

A FOCUS ON THE ORGANIZATION OF THE
ISLAMIC CONFERENCE AND OTHER ISLAMIC INSTITUTIONS

SAAD S. KHAN

Foreword by
JOHN L. ESPOSITO

OXFORD
UNIVERSITY PRESS

OXFORD

UNIVERSITY PRESS

Great Clarendon Street, Oxford OX2 6DP

Oxford University Press is a department of the University of Oxford.
It furthers the University's objective of excellence in research, scholarship,
and education by publishing worldwide in

Oxford New York

Athens Auckland Bangkok Bogotá Buenos Aires Cape Town
Chennai Dar es Salaam Delhi Florence Hong Kong Istanbul Karachi
Kolkata Kuala Lumpur Madrid Melbourne Mexico City Mumbai Nairobi
Paris São Paulo Shanghai Singapore Taipei Tokyo Toronto Warsaw

with associated companies in Berlin Ibadan

Oxford is a registered trade mark of Oxford University Press
in the UK and in certain other countries

ISBN 0 19 579411 7

Typeset in Times
Printed in Pakistan by
New Sketch Graphics, Karachi.
Published by
Ameena Saiyid, Oxford University Press
5-Bangalore Town, Sharae Faisal
PO Box 13033, Karachi-75350, Pakistan.

To
my
FATIMA
with love

Contents

List of Charts

Foreword

The 20th century brought many challenges to the Muslim world. In politics and international relations, Muslim societies struggled amidst the emergence of modern Muslim nation states. At the same time, concerns that nationalism would undermine the transnational identity and reality of Islam, the *ummah*, led many Muslims to address this concern ideologically and institutionally. The writings and ideas of Muhammad Abduh, Rashid Rida, Muhammad Iqbal and many others were accompanied by attempts to create an Islamic organization to represent and seek a modern institutional expression of Islamic unity or pan-Islamic sentiment.

The challenge of Gamal Abdul Nasser's Arab nationalism/socialism and the desire to contain his influence in the Arab world and the broader Muslim world became a catalyst for Saudi Arabia's support for the creation of an Islamic alternative to promote Islamic unity and solidarity. The shock of the 1967 Arab–Israeli war, the ignominious defeat of Arab forces and massive loss of territory, especially Jerusalem, and the subsequent arsonist attack on al-Aqsa mosque in 1969 proved major catalysts for the creation of the Organization of the Islamic Conference (OIC) in 1969. The OIC was to promote Islamic solidarity and cooperation and promote peace and justice in the Islamic world.

Despite its noble goals and the fact that its summit conferences bring together the heads and foreign ministers of Muslim states, the OIC and its activities remain relatively invisible. Saad Khan has provided the first exhaustive study of the OIC in this book. His comprehensive and critical analysis reveals its history and organization and analyzes and evaluates its projects and activities. Khan identifies the sources of unity and in particular disunity, its symbolic strength but substantive weaknesses, that have plagued the OIC and its effectiveness (more accurately, ineffectiveness) throughout the years. He does not shrink from raising critical issues and conclusions:

The primary objectives of the Organization, that is, the Islamic solidarity, has been the casualty of this wide variety of factionalisms. The Organization tends to be coherent in such emotive issues such as saving a particular Muslim community from ethnic cleansing as in Bosnia, Kashmir and Philippines, that is to say when one of the parties to the conflict is non-Muslim. In a conflict between two Muslim parties, the sympathies and prejudices of individual member states come to the fore, ripping apart the chances of a common stand.

Both critics and defenders of the OIC will benefit from the critical questions and issues that Saad Khan raises in this perceptive and comprehensive study. The significance of this volume is enhanced at the dawn of the 21st century. Muslim states will be forced to define and redefine their roles in a global community of contending currents and forces. They will need to balance national and regional interests with the realities and demands of international politics, economics and globalization.

Today, as throughout Islamic history, Islamic ideals of unity and solidarity are challenged to move beyond rhetoric and symbols. Will the OIC receive the political and financial support and resolve required to achieve its goals? Will it achieve the recognition and stature necessary for it to become a respected, effective international player/organization? If future possibilities are affected by past and present realities, Saad Khan's critical study is and will be a required reading.

John L. Esposito
University Professor and Director
Center for Muslim–Christian Understanding
Georgetown University
Washington, D.C.

Preface

Since the advent of Islam, around one and a half millennium ago, its polity has recognized some sort of central authority, for the fast expanding and vastly multiplying needs of the growing Muslim community. Though the Muslim world, save for the first century of the Islamic history, has never been a single political entity; the institution of the Caliphate continued to portray a semblance of spiritual and temporal unity of the Muslims all over. The Islamic Caliphate can be understood as a rough equivalent of early Roman Catholic Papacy, except that the former was vested with greater political authority in the areas under its direct rule. Rather, the Caliphate is more akin to the position that the *Vilayat-e-Faqih,* or the supreme spiritual leader, in Iran enjoys today. (The supreme leader, Ayatollah Khaminei at present, is in many ways, more powerful than the President, in the post-Islamic revolution Iran). Thus, the abolishment of Caliphate in 1924, necessitated the creation of an alternative arrangement to fill the void. The Muslim political leadership as well as the intelligentsia, apparently felt that international Islamic organizations could play the role of homogenizing the thinking and policies of Muslim political units and acting as the collective spokesman for their interests.

The World Muslim Congress, established in 1926, was the first non-governmental Islamic organization in the 20th century, while the OIC, established in 1969, turned out to be the first inter-governmental organization of the Muslim states. For whatsoever reasons, the past quarter of a century saw a mushroom growth of Islamic organizations, both inter-governmental and non-governmental, working in virtually every area, such as politics, culture, education and research, maritime cooperation, propagation of Islam, and so on. Quite many of these institutions came up under the framework of the OIC. Depending upon their nature of work and autonomy enjoyed, they are known as specialized organs, subsidiary organs or affiliated institutions. This book is devoted to the study of the OIC and over thirty other institutions, both within and outside the OIC framework.

If we discount the now-virtually-defunct Non-Aligned Movement, the OIC becomes the largest inter-governmental organization of the world, after the United Nations. There are a number of smaller Islamic institutions as well that are significant in their own right. Yet, very little research has so far been done on the OIC or other Islamic organizations. The very reference to the OIC, for instance, in the ever-expanding ocean of documented knowledge is conspicuous by its absence. One may find sufficient literature on the prominent regional organizations of the developed and the developing world in encyclopaedias, reference books, reputed research journals and the website; the academic apathy towards the Islamic organizations is astonishing, nay, alarming. This book is a humble attempt to fill this lacuna.

My interest in the subject dates back to the time when I was a student at the International Relations Department at the university, and against better advice, I took a thesis on the OIC when. The first finding of my research turned out to be the realization that there was an acute scarcity of information on the OIC. In fact, most of the work on the scope of pan-Islamism and on the analysis of Islamic organizations, appears to have been written to score polemical rather than academic points. Since there were limitations on the scope as well as length of the thesis, I later decided to write a book on Islamic organizations that would meet the demands of objective scholarship. That is why I have avoided entangling myself in the irrelevant rhetorical debates on the notion of pan-Islamic unity. However, a discussion on the *'ummah'* concept in Islam has been given in the introductory chapter for building up the necessary conceptual framework.

In fact, it is a book on 'International Islam', a term that signifies the Islamic factor in international relations between the Muslim states themselves or between the Muslim and the non-Muslim states. Given that conference diplomacy is one of the most important determinants in international politics, it was thought prudent to look at the prominent Islamic organizations and analyse their role free of rhetoric and free of malice. Thus while the better part of the book deals with the establishment, objectives and activities of the various organizations, the question of the reassertion of international Islam per se, prospective political scenarios in the 21st century and the probable role of Islam as an international political ideology thereunder, comes in the concluding chapter.

The selection of the Islamic organizations for inclusion in this treatise, therefore, had a definite criterion. The position of the OIC in the Muslim world, a crude equivalent of the UN's position in the whole world, warranted a close study. Otherwise, all the international Islamic inter-governmental organizations that had a pan-Islamic agenda in the area of any issue and had a membership drawn from more than twenty states, found their place in the book. Not coincidentally, most such organizations and institutions had come up under the OIC framework. Such inter-governmental organizations of the Muslim states which had regional cooperation, not Islamic solidarity, on their expressed agenda, have not been dealt with in this work. For instance, the Islamic Shipowners Association with membership from twenty Muslim countries has been included while the Arab League and the Economic Cooperation Organization (ECO), with the exclusive Muslim states' memberships of twenty-two and ten respectively, have not been addressed here. The Islamic Non-Governmental Organizations that have been included in this book, also owe their inclusion to the nature of their goals and scope of activities.

During the three year research, three major sources were relied upon. The first source was direct correspondence with the OIC, its organs and other Islamic institutions, soliciting response to the author's questionnaires and requesting their latest activity reports. This primary source material proved to be extremely helpful in assessing the objectives, performance, and constraints of the organizations concerned. Positive response from a number of Islamic bodies was an encouragement, but my answer to a lack of response by an institution was 'persistence'. Some organizations finally responded to my third or fourth letter or facsimile message, while a few never did. In fact, the OIC General Secretariat falls in this last category.

The second source was press clippings. In Islamabad, I was granted permission to review the relevant record at the Press Information Department and later at the National Archives of Pakistan. Besides these two institutions, some other institutions and libraries, especially the Reference Sections in the offices of leading national dailies, also had very well-maintained subject-specific files containing press clippings on an Islamic organization, institution, country or a problem. Obviously, the news items on organizations carried the coverage of meetings and conferences, statements of leaders and the like.

Lastly, the third major source of information was the text of resolutions or declarations adopted by the organizations. In this respect, some foreign diplomatic missions based in Islamabad were particularly helpful in providing the copies of OIC resolutions concerning their respective countries. All the sources have been acknowledged in the footnotes.

A major problem, which arose as a corollary of this method of research, was that it was relatively easier to surmise, through resolutions and statements, what was decided by the OIC or any other institution, but it was difficult to verify whether and to what extent, the decisions were implemented. This sometimes results in loss of continuity as bits of information are collected from different sources and then put together to make sense. So the reader may discern, at quite a few places, small gaps or jumps in this treatise. But such lacunas are to be found in all the publications on the OIC including, not surprisingly, the OIC General Secretariat's own.

Now, a note on the format and content of this book is in order. The book consists of two parts; the first part is exclusively devoted to the OIC. The first four chapters deal with respectively, the emergence, structure, bureaucracy and an analysis of the Charter of the OIC. The next three narrate its political history and the eighth one deals with the problems and weaknesses of the OIC. The second part has six chapters, one each on the specialized committees, specialized organs, subsidiary organs, affiliated universities, and affiliated institutions, of the OIC, and finally, the Islamic international non-governmental organizations (outside the OIC framework). The concluding chapter, after defining international Islam, gives a brief summary of the points made in the book and the conclusions made therefrom. The chapter argues that the post-cold war world is characterized, from the Muslim world's viewpoint, by uncertainty, instability and confusion. As the contours of a new-world order hint at the emergence of multiple centres of power, the reaction of and implications for the Muslim world, can only be guessed at. Thus the chapter takes an organizational approach to address the fundamental conundrum of whether the Muslim states, under the influence of so many Islamic organizations, are moving towards politico-economic union.

Given that in the infrastructure there is not much to be desired, since the Muslim states have been successful in creating platforms for cooperation in virtually every field; there can hardly be two opinions on whether cooperation, consultation and co-ordination are primary steps for confidence building, that may eventually lead to economic or political unions between nation states. So when the fifty-five Muslim states move into a new millennium, they are not as disjointed and disunited a group as they were, say, in the 1960s. The voting behaviours of the Muslim countries at the UN General Assembly and other world fora, bear testimony to it since the coefficients of agreement have increased considerably in the past few decades. Standing at the vantage point of the turning to the third millennium, with history as a guide, what predictions can be made about the future? Can this plethora of institutions bridge the gap between the thinking of the Muslim states or are they simply good-for-nothing white elephants? The concluding chapter argues that these questions merit serious consideration from present day scholars, though, history would be the final judge. At the end of the book there are some useful annexures. Relatively unfamiliar terms have been explained in the glossary while the frequently used acronyms are included in the consolidated list of abbreviations.

In the end I wish to acknowledge the cooperation received from a number of persons and institutions. Though the list is long, I cannot help but mention the names of Dr Khalil Saeed (Head of the OIC mission in Islamabad); Dr Mohammed el Syed Selim (Director of the Asian Studies Center at the Cairo University); Khalid Mohsin (Director at the Press Information Department); Mohammed Ramzan (Deputy Director at the National Archives); Abrar-ul-Haq (Senior Librarian at the FST Institute); and Nasir Zaidi (Incharge of *The News* library). The help given and concern shown by my immediate family and my close friends, has now become a part of my sweetest memories. My profound gratitude is due to all those who gave me their guidance, inspiration or encouragement ungrudgingly. And praise be to God, the merciful, who enabled me to accomplish the task.

As noted earlier, it has been my endeavour to make this book one of the most up-to-date reference volume on the subject. I have reason to hope that it will be a contribution to the field and of value to both students and scholars alike.

Saad S. Khan
No. 622, G-9/1,
Islamabad, Pakistan

NOTE: The author shall welcome the opinions, comments and suggestions of the readers on his personal Email address <saadskhan@yahoo.co.uk>

Abbreviations

AJK	Azad (liberated) Jammu & Kashmir
AH	After *Hijrah* (used for the Islamic lunar calendar)
AL	Arab League (*see* LAS *below*)
APHC	All Parties *Huriyyat* (freedom) Conference (in the Indian-held Kashmir)
ARMM	Autonomous Region of Muslim Mindanao (in South Philippines)
ASG	Assistant Secretary General
BMAC	Babri Mosque Action Committee
CBM	Confidence Building Measures (*see* CSBM *below*)
CD	Conference on Disarmament
CG	(OIC) Contact Group
CIS	Commonwealth of Independent States
COMCEC	The OIC Standing 'Committee on Commercial and Economic Co-operation'
COMIAC	The OIC Standing 'Committee on Information Affairs and Culture'
COMSTECH	The OIC Standing 'Committee on Science and Technology'
CSBM	Confidence and Security Building Measures
DG	Director General
ECO	Economic Cooperation Organization
ECOWAS	Economic Cooperation Organization for West African States
EEC	European Economic Community
EICFM	Extraordinary (session of) Islamic Conference of Foreign Ministers
EU	European Union
FAO	Food and Agriculture Organization
FCO	Financial Control Organ (of the OIC)
FIS	Islamic Salvation Front (in Algeria)
G-7	Group of Seven (most industrialized nations)
GATT	General Agreement on Trades and Tariff (now replaced by the WTO)
GCC	Gulf Cooperation Council
IAS	Islamic Academy of Sciences
ICA	Islamic Cement Association
ICAC	Islamic Civil Aviation Council
ICCI	Islamic Chamber of Commerce and Industry

ICDT	Islamic Centre for Development of Trade
ICE	Islamic Council of Europe
ICECS	Islamic Commission for Economic, Cultural and Social Affairs
ICFM	Islamic Conference of Foreign Ministers
ICIC	Islamic Committee for the International Crescent
ICJ	International Court of Justice
ICPICH	International Commission for Preservation of Islamic Cultural Heritage
ICRC	International Committee of the Red Cross
ICTVTR	Islamic Centre for Technical and Vocational Training and Research (renamed IIT)
ID	Islamic Dinar (basic monetary unit of the IDB)
IDB	Islamic Development Bank
IFOR	International Force (in Bosnia)
IFSTAD	Islamic Foundation for Science, Technology and Development
IGO	Inter-Governmental Organization
IHK	Indian-Held Kashmir
IICJ	International Islamic Court of Justice
IIIT	International Institute of Islamic Thought
IILC	International Islamic Law Commission
IINA	International Islamic New Agency
IIT	Islamic Institute of Technology
ILO	International Labour Organization
IMF	International Monetary Fund
IO	International Organization
IPU	Islamic Postal Union (proposed)
IRCICA	Research Centre for Islamic History, Art and Culture
IRTI	Islamic Research and Training Institute
IS	Islamic Summit (Conference)
ISBO	Islamic States Broadcasting Organization
ISESCO	Islamic Educational, Scientific and Cultural Organization
ISTU	Islamic States Telecommunication Union (proposed)

ISF	Islamic Solidarity Fund	PFLP	Popular Front for the Liberation of Palestine
ISSF	Islamic Solidarity Sports Federation		
IULA	Islamic Union of Legislative Assemblies	PLO	Palestine Liberation Organization
IWA	Islamic Women Association	POW	Prisoner of War
JKLF	Jammu Kashmir Liberation Front	PPP	Pakistan People's Party
LAS	League of Arab States (*also called* Arab League)	RA	*Radi-Allahu Anhu* (May Allah be pleased with him)
LDC	Least Developed Countries	RNC	Republic of Northern Cyprus (*same as TRNC below*)
LDMC	Least Developed Muslim Countries		
MILF	Moro Islamic Liberation Front	SAARC	South Asian Association for Regional Cooperation
MNLF	Moro National Liberation Front		
MWL	Muslim World League	SAW/SAAW	Initials of the Arabic version of PBUH
NAM	Non-Aligned Movement	SESRTCIC	Statistical, Economic and Social Research and Training Centre for Islamic Countries
NATO	North Atlantic Treaty Organization		
NGO	Non-Governmental Organization		
NIEO	New International Economic Order	SFOR	Stability Force (in Bosnia)
NPT	Non-Proliferation Treaty	SG	Secretary General
NWFZ	Nuclear Weapons Free Zone	TRNC	Turkish Republic of Northern Cyprus
NWO	New World Order	UAE	United Arab Emirates
(N)NWS	(Non-) Nuclear Weapon States	UAR	United Arab Republic (now Egypt)
OAPEC	Organization of Arab Petroleum Exporting Countries	UN	United Nations
		UNDP	United Nations Development Program
OAS	Organization of American States	UNESCO	United Nations Educational, Scientific and Cultural Organization
OAU	Organization of African Unity		
OECD	Organization for Economic Cooperation and Development	UNIDO	United Nations Industrial Development Organization
OIC	Organization of the Islamic Conference	UNMOGIP	United Nations Military Observer Group in India and Pakistan (on Kashmir)
OICC	Organization of Islamic Capitals and Cities		
		UNPROFOR	United Nations Protection Force (in Bosnia)
OISA	Organization of Islamic Shipowners Association	UNSCOM	United Nations Special Commission (in Iraq)
OPEC	Organization of Petroleum Exporting Countries	USSR	Union of Soviet Socialist Republics (former)
OSCE	Organization of Security and Co-operation in Europe	WAMY	World Assembly of Muslim Youth
PBUH	(PBUH) Peace Be Upon Him	WHO	World Health Organization
PDPA	Peoples' Democratic Party of Afghanistan	WMC	World Muslim Congress
		WMD	Weapons of Mass Destruction
PFC	Permanent Finance Committee (of the OIC)	WSIC	World Society of Islamic Call
		WTO	World Trade Organization

Introduction: Some Conceptual Frameworks

The Organization of the Islamic Conference (OIC) is the largest organization of the Muslim world, comprising fifty-five sovereign Muslim states.[1] In addition there are about twenty observers including sovereign states, non-sovereign states[2] and international organizations. The Organization has brought together such diverse states as Indonesia and Lebanon, Maldives and Albania etc., on the basis of the common bond of Islam, thus making it the largest, if not the only, religious association of the nation-states in the world.

Significance of the Islamic Organization

No serious student of international affairs can overlook or ignore the OIC. Besides its unique character of religion being the sole bond, its significance stems out of three factors. Firstly, the OIC is the principal spokesman of the largest religion of the world and can veritably claim to represent about three-fourths of the followers of Islam who live in the OIC member states. The preceding statement can be disputed on two grounds; one, the Christians too have similar claims about theirs being the largest religion; and two, as the OIC is an association of the Muslim governments which are mostly not representative of their peoples, it cannot be said to represent 75 per cent of the Muslims of the world.

Regarding the first objection, it is our submission that numerical superiority of either religion cannot be conclusively proved. According to a recent survey, Muslims constitute more than one-fourth (25.88 per cent) of the world population, thus outnumbering other religions. In Africa (58.88 per cent) and Asia (27.91 per cent), Islam respectively predominates and is the single

largest religion. In all the other continents, Islam is the second largest religion.[3] Here the pitfall is that the statistics about religious composition are highly unreliable and have wild discrepancies. In the Muslim minority states, the governments usually downplay the percentage of Muslims and exaggerate the population of non-Muslims. The reverse is true in the case of Muslim majority states. Even if the government statistics about religious composition are correct, the minority refuses to accept them, making the figures highly controversial, for obvious reasons. The Muslim population in Uganda is anywhere between 13 to 40 per cent,[4] in the Central African Republic between 11 to 40 per cent[5] and in China, between 1.2 to 15 per cent.[6] Due to the high polarization among various religions, it is well nigh impossible to verify the accuracy of such figures, hence the whole debate becomes subjective. For instance, it is also argued that if the sole criterion for labeling someone as a Muslim is that he says he is a Muslim and so on, then the numerical superiority of the Muslims over the other religions is convincingly established because the Muslim peoples generally believe in Islam while a significant proportion of putative Christians does not profess the religion at all and openly says so.[7] Instead of going into such emotional and parochial arguments, it is better to leave the Muslims and Christians believing about the following of their religion what they like to believe.

This brings us to the second objection about the OIC's credentials on representation. Here we shall argue that though the constituent governments do not necessarily represent their peoples but OIC, as an organization, usually does so. During the cold war, many member countries were aligned with the USA or the USSR, this did not deter the OIC from maintaining a strictly radical anti-imperialist posture. To quote one example, in the first extraordinary ICFM (Islamabad, January 1980), strong worded resolutions of condemnation were adopted against both the superpowers, the USSR for its invasion of Afghanistan and the USA for escalating the Iran hostage crisis, at the same time.[8] Similarly, in the Bosnia, Kashmir, and Philippines crises, the OIC has represented the sentiments of the Muslim masses irrespective of what the individual Muslim governments' policies were about the issues.

Secondly, the OIC membership is spread across ten geographical regions in four continents; Asia, America, Africa and Europe:

1. Arabian peninsula: Saudi Arabia, Yemen, UAE, etc.
2. South Asia: Pakistan, Bangladesh, Maldives.
3. Iran and the Caucasus: Iran, Azerbaijan.
4. Central Asia: Uzbekistan, Turkemanistan etc.
5. Far East: Indonesia, Malaysia, Brunei.
6. North Africa: Libya, Algeria etc.
7. West Africa (Sahel region): Guinea, Senegal, Gambia etc.
8. Horn of Africa: Mozambique, Djibouti etc.
9. Europe: Turkey, Albania, Bosnia, North Cyprus.[9]
10. South America: Suriname, Guyana.

We have included Turkey in Europe, though it is as much a part of Asia as of Europe. The better part of its land and people is in Asia, but politically and culturally, Turkey is drifting towards Europe. It is a NATO partner, currently striving to gain entrance into the European Union in order to become a full fledged member of the Euro-Club. Hence, it is safe to place Turkey among the European members of the OIC. By granting membership to Suriname and observer status to the Republic of Guyana, the OIC has now got a foothold in the American continent as well. So the OIC is not simply an Afro-Asian organization any more.

And thirdly, the OIC has a huge outfit of subsidiary and specialized organs, numbering about forty-eight. Such an expanded structure is only rivaled by the United Nations, and to a large extent, the European Union. The Organization can boast of several organs and committees, working for cooperation in economic, educational, scientific, research oriented and political fields.

OIC: The Theoretical Foundations

The reason why Islam is the only religion that has cobbled together such an association on religious basis, can be traced to the traditional concept of *ummah,* i.e., the feeling of affinity, that of belonging to the same community, among the Muslims. But this does not imply that the OIC is a religious body in the strict sense of the word. The OIC's foundations lie in the modern concept of sovereign nation-state system as well. A cursory glance at the Charter testifies to the strictly secular character of the OIC. Therefore, to formulate a conceptual framework, we will have to analyse the classical Islamic concept of *ummah* and its scope and then the modern concept of international organizations. Finally, we will merge the two concepts into a wider canvas.

The *Ummah* Identity and OIC

Abdullah al Ahsan is not alone in believing that 'it was the *ummah* identity consciousness of modern Muslims that lead them, in 1969, to form a political institution, known as the Organization of the Islamic Conference (OIC).'[10] Though the term '*ummah*' has been widely and extensively used in all the texts on the topic of the Muslim world, including the literature of the OIC, it is all the more difficult to translate it, or to define it in simple terms.

Ummah means a 'community or a nation,' but not in the modern sense of nation. According to a scholar,

> The Arabic word the Quran uses *ummah* is often treated today as synonymous with nation. Yet if there is one thing the Islamic *ummah* is not, it is a nation, in either Roman or the modern sense. What was significant about the *ummah* of Muslims in history was that it transcended national and tribal loyalties rooted in the accident of birth, and was a community of believers, bound together in a brotherhood more vital than that of blood.[11]

This term's association with the word '*umm*' (mother, source) seems plausible, and acceptable to the native Arabic speakers. R.B. Serjeant proposed that '*ummah*' referred to a 'confederation around a religious nucleus', well before the dawn of Islam.[12] But the term is so extensively used in the Quran, that it gives a clear picture of what Islam means *ummah* to be, rendering all pre-Islamic contexts of *ummah* irrelevant for us.

The term in the Quranic context: The word appears sixty-four times (thirteen of which in plural form) in the Quran. The primary meaning of the word, as the Quranic commentator Mohammad Asad puts it, is 'a group of living beings having certain characteristics or circumstances in common.'[13] In the Quran, we find *ummah* used in the following contexts; the whole human community was a single *ummah* (*ummatan wahidatan*) in the beginning because mankind originated from a single source (10:19); all the prophets followed divine guidance, therefore, they belonged to one *ummah* (21:92); and followers of each prophet constituted an *ummah* (10:47). The Quran also uses the word *ummah* to mean a belief (43:22–23) or a person exemplar of an ideological group (16:20). Thus the Quran declares *ummah* to be a group of persons distinct from the mass because of ideology or conviction. In this way, the holy book draws a clear line between *qawm* (nation or community in a general sense) and *ummah* (the particular group within that nation) in different verses. For instance: 'Among the folk of Musa (*qawm*), there have been people (*ummah*) who would guide others in the way of truth and act justly in its light.' (7:159) At another place, the Quran says: 'When he (Musa) arrived at the wells of Madyan, he found there a large group of men (*ummah*), who were watering (their herds and flocks)...' (28:23)

Now by the first verse we saw that *ummah* was that specific section of the *qawm* which was acting justly and guiding others, and in the second verse we see that the people Musa found were an *ummah*, because (a) all the men were of the same profession (herdsmen) and (b) were doing the same thing (watering).

So the Quranic concept of *ummah* can be explained as a committed ideological group amongst the people (*nas*) doing the same right thing or believing in the same just belief, for the same righteous cause.[14]

The Prophet's (PBUH) interpretation of *ummah*: The Quran says, 'Verily, the believers are but brothers' (49:10). The Prophet Mohammad (PBUH) thus declared, 'In relation to one another, the Muslims are like a building. Every unit reinforces and is reinforced by others.' Anas ibn Malik reports the Prophet (PBUH) said, 'None of you truly has faith, if he does not desire for his brother Muslim, that which he desires for himself.'[15] Abdullah ibn Umar quotes the Prophet (PBUH) as saying, 'The Muslim is the brother of Muslim: he shall not do him wrong or let wrong be done to him; if he comes to his brother's need, Allah shall come to his needs; ...and if he shields a Muslim, Allah shall shield him on the day of resurrection.'[16]

The Prophet Mohammad (PBUH) laid the foundations of his new state at Madina on this concept of brotherhood. His companions who had fled from Mecca in *Hijrah* (migration of the Muslims to Madina), had been deprived of all their belongings by the pagans at Mecca. Through his pronouncement of *Mu'akhaat* (fraternity), he declared that each *Mohajir* (Muslim migrated from Mecca) was a brother of one *Ansar* (Madenite Muslim). Thus each *Ansar* was supposed to help his *Mohajir* brother until the time when the latter became financially well-established in the new city. The Prophet's (PBUH) emphasis on this fraternal relationship continued till his farewell sermon at the last pilgrimage (*Hujjat-ul-Wida*), just a couple of months before his death, when he summarized his teachings and re-emphasized the Islamic concepts of equality, fraternity and justice.

The Prophet (PBUH), did not destroy the fabric of tribal identities. In times of crisis, he used to summon the chiefs of different Muslim clans in order to confer with them. Even when Muslim troops were marching towards the final liberation of the holy city of Mecca from pagans (AD 630), each of the tribes was being led by its chief holding the standard of the tribe. Thus the Holy Prophet's (PBUH) vision of *ummah* did not entail the destruction of tribal identities (*asa'biyah*) but changed the hierarchies of a person's loyalties. This was perhaps the first major experiment of unity in diversity.[17]

The *ummah* in the political sense: The above view of Prophet Mohammad (PBUH) about *ummah* has led the historian M.A. Shaban to argue that *ummah* was 'a political not a religious concept.'[18] This confusion has arisen due to misinterpretation of the Madina Charter, a pact between the Prophet (PBUH) and the Jews of Madina, whereby the authority of the former, especially in matters of dispute, was accepted, and the both sides, the Muslims and the Jews, undertook to defend Madina jointly in case of an external attack. Shaban, in his analysis of the Madina Charter, believes that the members of the new commonwealth, both the Muslims and the Jews, belonged to the same *ummah*, as long as they accepted the authority of the Prophet (PBUH). 'Thus the citizens were one *ummah* (political community) with different *din* (way of life)'.[19]

Shaban's analysis does not stand the test of close scrutiny, and other scholars like R.B. Serjeant and Frederick Denny have pointed out that the Jews did not belong to the single community, referred to as '*ummah*' in the Madina Charter. Nevertheless, even if we accept Shaban's view of *ummah* being a community of Muslims and non-Muslims, under the suzerainty of the former, we come closer to the present structure of the OIC, which is an association of the Muslim-majority states, not just the Muslim majorities of those states.

The *ummah* concept after the Prophet's (PBUH) death: An institution of Caliphate was established after Prophet Mohammad's (PBUH) death. The Caliph or *Khalifa*, literally 'the deputy' (of the Prophet [PBUH]), became the embodiment of the Muslim central authority, and under him the *ummah* ranks swelled. Parinder notes that 'after Mohammad [PBUH], the spread of Islam across much of the ancient world led to *ummah* being enlarged from Arabic people to all Muslims and this has created a strong sense of community which has characterized Islam.'[20]

True, the Muslim world did not remain a single political entity for long. The Caliphate degenerated into a dynastic monopoly. In AD 756, less than one and a half century after the establishment of the Islamic state, a relatively short span in the history of nations, the first infringement on the temporal authority of a Caliph was witnessed when an Omayyad prince Abdul Rahman became the ruler of Andulasia (now Spain). By the tenth century, three separate dynasties had assumed the mantle of Caliphate, namely, the Abbasides of Baghdad, the Fatimides of Egypt and the Omayyads of Spain. The famous Muslim traveller, Ibne Batuta of Morocco, passed through twenty-two independent Muslim kingdoms during his travels (1325–54).[21] But all this had, in no way, eroded the *ummah* affinity or the respect to the symbol of Islamic unity, the Caliph. Many independent Muslim rulers and Sultans got the sanction of the Caliph to legitimize their ascendancy to the throne. The famous Muslim scholar Maulana Maududi writes:

> Differences on the basis of nationality, race, and tribal conflict did crop up now and again…But the idea that the Muslims of the world constitute one *ummah* remained intact…A Muslim from any part of the world could go to any Muslim land without any restrictions, move freely in that country, stay there as long as he wished, engage in any trade, get married without difficulty or secure a high position in the court. Islamic history is replete with instances where a Muslim went out of his land and stayed in another Muslim country for decades. He might have studied in one country, engaged in business in another, become a minister or a commander in-chief in the third one, and yet he may go to another country, settle and get married there.[22]

Thus the Islamic 'Ummah' concept was never held hostage to the quarrels and tensions among the believers. An expert of Islamic history, H.A.R. Gibb has aptly remarked:

> There were plenty of obstacles: fanatics who vindicated their convictions of being the only true heirs of Mohammed by rebellion and slaughter, partisans of rival claimants to the government of the community, disputes over principles and details of legal development. But it is precisely through these experiences that the concept of *ummah* gained in clarity and significance.[23]

Today with more than fifty Muslim sovereign states, having a diverse range of cultures, languages, races and conflicting national interests, the concept of *ummah* seems to be as intact as ever. And it is in this *ummah* concept, that we can trace the tremendous potential of the Organization of the Islamic Conference.

Organizational Framework

Any organization that draws its membership from more than one nation is called an international organization which can be either an inter-governmental organization (IGO) or a non-governmental (NGO) one. Since the Second World War, there has been a mushroom growth of international organizations. Today, there are thousands of IGOs and NGOs working on the international level. The reasons for this growth are manifold. Neither an unorganized world without law and cooperation, nor a *Pax Romana* (a despotic empire dominating all other countries) is an appealing idea. A loose supremacy of international regimes through multinational bodies, based on sovereign equality of members, seems to be the only viable option today.

The world is rapidly turning, if has not already turned, into a global village where isolation is simply out of the question. Postal, communications and meteorological fields have been to be of international dimension since the last century. Now human rights, health, environment and a lot more issues have also shifted to the realm of international concern. The need to evolve common and integrated strategies on these issues has become all the more imperative. The functions of international organizations (IOs) can thus be summarized as:

1. They are important actors on the world scene, like the nation-states, in their own right.
2. They are vehicles for changing the hierarchical and stratified world system into a more equal and just system.
3. They are tools for greater cooperation among equal states and for eliciting financial support and technical assistance from more developed states.
4. They lessen dependency and promote inter-dependency.
5. They are fora for evolving common strategy on common problems.
6. They are instrumental in bringing peace, harmony and friendship in global scenarios.[24]

Regional Organization: International organizations can be general (like OAU, British commonwealth etc.) or specialized (like UNIDO, ILO etc.).[25] In terms of membership, international organizations can be universal or regional. Presently, the United Nations alone can claim to enjoy near universal membership. So, all the other organizations can be bracketed as regional organizations.

The trickiest matter in the concept of regional organizations is the definition of 'region' itself. Today region is not taken in the geographical sense alone. The NATO and G-7 are regional organizations, though in both the cases, member states are not contiguous geographically. Common security interests in the former and economic interests in the latter appear to have brought them together. In the case of the Arab League, the SAARC and the European Union, the shared culture and the geographical unity may have convinced the states to embark upon economic cooperation also.

The proponents of regional organizations argue that (a) most problems are regional in nature and need regional solutions; (b) it is easier to have implementation, or if the case so demands, sanctions machinery within a region; and (c) regional organizations can work more effectively because of greater likelihood of reaching a decision, greater affinity among the peoples, and cheaper and productive solutions.

The UN Charter has legitimized the regional arrangements but the framers of the Charter of the world body appear to have envisaged the dominating security aspect of this phenomenon, though presently most of the regional organizations are primarily oriented towards economic spheres. The UN Charter imposes certain restrictions on regional organizations. Article 102 makes the registration of every pact, treaty or any other form of diplomacy (including the establishment of an organization) with the UN Secretariat, mandatory. Article 51 allows the right of 'collective' self defense. Article 52 bars the regional organizations from working at cross purposes with the UN Charter. Article 53 and 54 further legitimize 'enforcement' actions under collective arrangements, provided that they are under the authority and sanction of the UN Security Council.[26]

Chart 0.1: International Organizational Tree

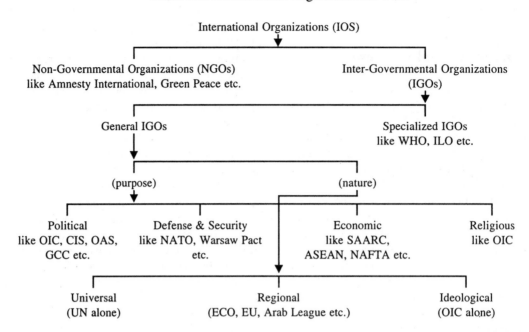

Note: The categories shown in this Chart are not mutually exclusive. So the OIC is a political, economic and religious organization at the same time. Likewise the GCC is an economic as well as a political outfit, and so on.

Coming back to our topic, the OIC is an IGO of general (economics, political) orientation and it is certainly not a universal organization. Then is it a regional organization? With the above discussion on regional organizations, we can say that if an IGO established out of a perception of common interests is a regional organization, then the OIC can also be labelled as such. But unlike other regional organizations, the OIC has a religion, Islam, as the least common factor among the member states. Since it seems bizarre to declare common religion as constituting a region, Noor Ahmad Baba coins another term, i.e., ideological organization, for it. According to his argument, the UN is the only universal IGO and the OIC is the only ideological IGO.[27] All the other IGOs are thus regional organizations.

To wind up our discussion of the conceptual framework of the OIC in the context of organizations, we can say that regional organizations, legitimate under the UN Charter, are gaining added significance today, because of greater commonality of interests, and consequently, greater potential for cooperation. The OIC is a regional organization in the modern sense except that the least common factor among the members is the religion. Hence, the OIC can be described as an ideological organization as well.

Harbinger for a Change?

We have been seen above that the feeling of affinity, that of belonging to one single community, had been born concurrently with the dawn of Islam. All the religions give their followers a set of rituals as well as guidance towards leading a life of piety. But Islam inherently gives a good dose of emotional attachment to one Allah, the holy book and to a universal brotherhood. This is not to deny that other religions also inculcate feelings of goodwill for each other amongst their followers, but there is nothing like the Islamic concept of *ummah* in them. For centuries, the *ummah* consciousness among the Muslims was embodied in the institution of Caliphate. It is precisely for that reason that the abolishment of the institution by the Kemalist regime of Turkey in March 1924 was resisted by the Muslim public all over the world. At that time, most of the Muslim regions were under colonial subjugation and a unified stand on the issue was therefore out of the question.

In the first two decades after the end of the Second World War, most of the colonies found independence though under the framework of the modern nation-state system. During that time the modern concepts of nationalism became the major challenge to the traditional concept of *ummah*. Now if the very idea of returning to the colonial domination was an anathema to the new nationalist leadership, they were equally unwilling to sacrifice their hard won independence at the altar of universal theories of *ummah*.

By the end of 1960s, however, they did lay the foundation of an institution, the OIC, which was envisaged as being capable of responding to any political or economic threat to the *ummah* without trespassing into the jealously-guarded sovereign status of the member states.

So finally there was a blend of the classical and modern concepts of unity in the form of the OIC and later its subsidiary organs. The statutes of all these institutions define their foremost objective as the integration of Muslim states in the respective fields. Can they actually translate their stated aims into reality? In other words, is the very establishment of the plethora of Islamic institutions a new beginning, as far as the future place of Muslim states in the world system is concerned? The answers to these questions, whatever they might be, will have far-reaching implications for the world.

Change can only come about if a nation has a vision of its future and a will to achieve success. If the sharp and volatile battle lines of Europe, based on the narrow concepts of ethno-nationalism, could not retard her progress towards integration in a European Union, with a single currency and a unified visa system, it would be parochial and unscholarly to dismiss the notion of the Muslim world's integration as impractical. Equally

unconvincing and implausible is the notion that Muslim states may soon be forming a Commonwealth, on the pattern of the EU. So, the OIC may eventually turn out to be the Islamic version of the League of Nations (LON), which was a failure in its own reference, but upon whose debris, the foundations of a new, more powerful and more effective organization, the United Nations, were laid. Still, whatever the shape and scope of any future political or economic arrangement between Muslim states, or of a distinct Islamic grouping in the international system, the OIC shall be remembered as one of its building blocks.

NOTES and REFERENCES

1. So far the Organization has been joined by fifty-seven sovereign Muslim States. With the merger of the Arab Republic of Yemen and the Democratic Republic of Yemen into a single State in May 1990, the OIC membership was reduced by one, whereas Zanzibar withdrew soon after joining. Very few Muslim states like Tanzania, Ethiopia and Eritrea are still outside the OIC. The proportion of Muslims in these three states is highly disputed and many statistics show them as Christian majority states.

2. The Turkish Republic of Northern Cyprus, under the tutelage of Turkey, and the Pakistan-backed State of Azad (Liberated) Jammu and Kashmir are non-sovereign states.

3. This research has been conducted by *Mu'tamar al-Alam al-Islami*, that puts the number of Muslims in the world at 1.38 billion. See Ibrahim Qureshi, *World Muslim Minorities*, (Karachi: WMC, 1993), pp. 391–99. The figures about the share of Muslims in the world population has been taken from that book, and included in our Annexure 2.

4. See AIOU publication, *Modern Islamic World*, (Islamabad: 1985), vol. 2, p. 82, which gives the former figure while M.A. Kettani, *Muslim Minorities in the World Today*, (Lahore: Services Book Club, 1990), p. 163, gives the latter figure.

5. See Qureshi, ref. 3, p. 65 and also Kettani, ref. 4, p. 182.

6. Qureshi, ref. 3, p. 80. Also see Barbara Pillsbury, 'Muslim Population of China: Quest for identity', *Jimma* (Vol. 3, No. 2), 1981, p. 36, for a discussion about the number of Muslims in China.

7. In France, for instance, 86 per cent of the people used to go to the Church thrice a day, just seventy-five years ago. Now 11 per cent of them go to Church

once a week. It is just one indicator of the growing irrelevance of religion in public life.

8. The resolution of condemnation for the Soviet Union was opposed by five radical Arab states (see Chapter 5) on the plea that it would aggravate the Afghan crisis. The other resolution accusing the United States for the escalation of the Iran-hostage crisis was opposed by eight conservative Arab-African member states who had objection on referring to the US by name. Here our argument is that OIC maintains a radical non-aligned posture, no matter what the polices of individual member states happen to be.

9. Bosnia in Europe and Guyana in America enjoy an observer status at the OIC. The Republic of North Cyprus, in the Mediterranean, is also represented as observer.

10. Abdullah Ahsan, *Ummah or Nation? Identity Crisis in Muslim Society*, (Leicester: Islamic Foundation, 1992), p. 6.

11. John Williams, ed., *Themes of Islamic Civilisation*, (California: 1971), pp. 8–9.

12. R.B. Serjeant, *Haram and Hawtah*, (Cairo: *Dar al-Ma'aref*, 1962), pp. 41–58.

13. Mohammad Asad, *Introduction to Koran*, (Gibraltar, *Dar al-Andulus*, 1980), p. 177.

14. See Ahsan, ref. 10, pp. 9–28, for a detailed discussion on the concept of *ummah*.

15. Bukhari, Book 2, Bab 9.

16. Ibid., Book 46, Bab 3.

17. See Martin Lings, *Muhammad: His life based on earlier on earlier sources*, (London: G. Allen and Unwin, 1983) and also see Shibli Naumani, *Seerat-un-Nabi* (Urdu), vol. 1–2, (Lahore: Services Book Club, 1985), for a detailed account of *Mu'akhat* and the conquest of Mecca.

18. Ahsan, ref. 10, p. 21.

19. Ibid., p. 19.

20. Geoffrey Parinder, *A Dictionary of non-Christian Religions*, (London: 1971), p. 292.

21. Mohammad bin Abdullah (1304–69), popularly known by his surname Ibne Batuta, was born in Tangiers, Morocco. At the age of twenty-one, he set out for far off lands. For the next twenty-nine years, he travelled across Africa and Asia. He is the most renowned traveler of the Orient, much like Marco Polo in the Occident. On his return, he was appointed *Qadi* (Judge) in Tangiers. On the bidding of the King, he wrote a fascinating account of his adventures. His travelogue is now available in many languages.

22. Abul A'la Maududi, *Unity of Muslim World*, Khurshid Ahmad (ed.), (Lahore: Islamic Publications, 1967), pp. 14–15.

23. H.A.R. Gibb, 'The Community in Islamic History', *Journal of American Philosophical Society*, no. 107, April 1963, p. 173.

24. Haider Mehdi, *Organization of the Islamic Conference*, (Lahore: Progressive Publications, 1987), pp. 6–7.

25. See the list of abbreviations for the unknown acronyms.

26. See Stephen G. Goodspeed, *The nature and function of international organization*, (New York: Oxford University Press Inc., 1967) pp. 567–642, for a thorough discussion on the phenomenon of regionalism and regional organizations and the provisions of the UN Charter regarding it.

27. Noor Ahmad Baba, *OIC: Theory and Practice of Pan-Islamic Cooperation* (Karachi: Oxford University Press, 1994), pp. 6–8.

PART-1

1 The Emergence of OIC

We have seen in the preceding chapter, that the Islamic concept of *ummah* had a wide appeal among the Muslims and that the institution of Caliphate was an embodiment of the spiritual unity of the Muslims. As long as the Caliphate endured (AD 632–1924) in one form or another, the Muslims had something to look towards as a semblance of their '*ummah*-hood'. But as the institution of Caliphate showed signs of weakness and decay, in the latter days of the Ottoman dynasty, the Muslims got confused. Meanwhile, the Ottoman Caliph, Sultan Abdul Hamid (1876–1909) increasingly emphasized his claims of being the Caliph and also got this embodied in the Constitution, in 1876. Since the Caliph's pan-Islamism was believed to be aimed at securing loyalty of his Muslim subjects in order to sustain his moribund empire, and not for any genuine desire to provide temporal and spiritual leadership to the Muslims; a parallel non-official brand of pan-Islamism, propounded by the famous thinker Jamal-ud-Din Afghani (1838–97) started gaining popularity about the same time. 'Pan-Islamism' does not have a stereotype definition and different people have different visions about it. Afghani lived in an era when imperialism was rapidly engulfing vast areas in Asia and Africa. He fully comprehended the exploitative nature of colonialism, so he called upon the Muslims to unite and fight against the 'Western imperialists'. Afghani was in favour of the liberation of all of the East, and approved of accepting the fruit of Western progress in science and technology. He wanted the Muslims to return to the fundamentals and strictly follow the precepts of Islam, and wanted the Muslim rulers to unite in some sort of a confederation.[1]

So by the end of the First World War, two types of pan-Islamic theories were in vogue: the Caliph and his supporters' version, aimed at sustaining the institution of Caliphate, and the populist ideas of Muslim reformers who had long-term pan-Islamic objectives.

Eventually, Turkey's Grand National Assembly, after much wrangling between the pro-Caliph and the republican lobbies in it, decided to abolish the institution on 3 March 1924. Even the supporters of the popular version of pan-Islamism took it as a blow to their pan-Islamic ideals and, as we shall see below, embarked upon a search to find an alternative arrangement to fill the vacuum. The efforts in this direction went on unabated in the 45-year interregnum between 1924 and 1969, till the OIC was established. We can thus infer that the OIC is the 20th century version of the institution of Caliphate, and its emergence has to be understood in this perspective. To quote Noor Ahmad Baba:

> Every idea is dynamic and shapes itself in relation to changing socio-political realities. Therefore, the same idea can have different practical expressions at different places and at different times. This is true of the idea of Islamic unity and brotherhood enshrined in the Quran and *Hadith* as well. This idea, even though an integral part of the socio-political philosophy of Islam and its historical ethos, has differently influenced the practical situation in the Muslim world in different historical phases. The most recent manifestation of the unifying thrust of Islam is the OIC.[2]

Baba thus traces the origin of the OIC to the thinking of Afghani, Abduh, and Iqbal and argues that the institution of the OIC is an improved version of the institution of Caliphate in harmony with the demands of modern times.[3]

As the level of political consciousness at the mass level among the Muslims was rather low in 1924, so the first initiative in the search for a new symbol of Islamic *ummah* identity was taken by the *ulema* who met in conferences. These moots, in turn, resulted in the formation of some non-governmental Islamic organizations. Finally, following the period of decolonization in the fifties and sixties, several Muslim states became the protagonists in the drive to unite the Muslim world. We will thus take a look at the pan-Islamic conferences and the role of Islamic organizations in preparing the ground for an Islamic Summit, and finally discuss the special efforts of some Muslim countries in this regard. The Pakistani, the Saudi and the Malaysian initiatives took quantum leaps towards the goal of convening an Islamic Summit. But as we shall see, it was the 'Israeli' initiative (*sic*) that ultimately led to the calling of the summit and the formation of the OIC.[4]

The Initial Attempts

The first initiative to find a replacement was taken within days of the abolishment of the Caliphate. A group of prominent *ulema* met at Cairo and concurred that the deposed Ottoman Caliphate was not compatible with the Islamic precepts about Caliphate and hence the allegiance (*ba'yah*) paid to it was not valid by Islamic law. The *ulema* decided to call a conference of the Muslim representatives to decide upon whom to vest the mantle of Caliphate. In pursuance of this decision, the Rector of Al-Azhar University appointed a permanent Secretariat (Administrative Council) of Great Islamic Congress for Caliphate. The Egyptian government headed by Saad Zaghlul Pasha remained unenthusiastic about this affair.

Mecca Conference (July 1924): In the meantime, the rebel leader of Arabia, Sharif Hussain, who had led the rebellion against the Ottoman rule, declared himself the ruler of Hijaz and the Caliph of the Muslims, at Mecca. But his credentials for the office were not recognized by the Muslim world at large so he invited leading Muslim scholars of the world to this holy city, in his bid to rally support for his claims. The conference took place during the *Hajj* season when a number of Arab *ulema* were already present in the Hijaz region. The conference agreed on a Charter specifying Muslim unity as its ultimate goal and indicated Arab unity as a basis for future union of all Islamic states. To this end, it promised to promote the Arabic language. The Charter did not mention the Caliphate and all efforts by Hussain to extract a categorical recognition of his Caliphate

were resisted. Things became worse for Sharif Hussain, and within months he was ousted by Abdul Aziz of the Al-Saud clan, who replaced him as the ruler of Hijaz. Hussain fled to Cyprus and gave up his claims to the Caliphate.[5]

Cairo Convention (May 1926): By this time King Fuad of Egypt had started eyeing the prized post of Caliph. To this end he encouraged the afore-mentioned Al-Azhar initiative to hold a convention to study the Caliphate issue, with the possibility of nominating a Caliph. The convention was attended by Muslim delegates from thirteen states including British India, Dutch East Indies (Indonesia), Egypt, Hijaz (Saudi Arabia), Iraq, Malay State of Johore, Morocco, Palestine, Poland, South Africa, Tunisia, and Yemen.[6] Like the Mecca conference two years earlier, here again the delegates declared unity of Islam as their goal but disagreed on the desirability of the reinstatement of the Caliphate or its mechanism. Rather, the convention recognized the difficulties in the appointment of a Caliph after the emergence of Muslim sovereign nation-states. In its final declaration, it exhorted the Muslims 'not to neglect the Caliphate and work for its establishment'. It proposed a grand assembly of Muslim representatives of the world who would 'discuss measures with a view to establish a Caliphate fulfilling all the conditions prescribed by the *Shari'ah*'. However, no such conference could be held as the idea did not have the blessing of Muslim governments. The Cairo Convention never met again.

Mecca Convention (June 1926): King Abdul Aziz had formally proclaimed himself the ruler of Hijaz in January 1926. He sponsored an international Islamic conference in the following June in order to legitimize his rule, and remove the misconceptions about his clan's *Wahabi* activism. He was also afraid that other Islamic conferences might challenge his rule over the two holy places of Hijaz, if a consensus were reached for the high post of Caliph. He made it clear in the beginning that the conference was not meant to discuss any political issues or the rule of Hijaz. The conference thus confined itself to discussions on the economic welfare of Hijaz and the administration of *Hajj*. The issue of Caliphate was adroitly omitted from the agenda, ostensibly under Turkey's new republican government's protest that identified any reference to Caliphate as 'use of religion in politics'. Turkey had not attend the Cairo conclave, but sent a delegation to the Mecca Convention.

While carefully avoiding all controversial issues, the conference arrived at two decisions: to entrust King Abdul Aziz with the responsibility for the administration of *Hajj*, and to constitute itself as a permanent body *Mu'tamar al-Alam al-Islami* (World Muslim Congress) that would meet annually at Mecca during *Hajj*, with a wider scope to consider all Islamic issues.[7] By virtue of the first decision, King Abdul Aziz had got all his objectives, and he never called a Congress again, neither was he interested in joining any international body. Although the convention had elected Shakib Arsalan as its Secretary General, the *Mu'tamar* remained dormant. Its Secretariat at Mecca served as no more than a meeting place for Muslim scholars during *Hajj*. So it was only five years later that the second *Mu'tamar* convention could be held.

Al-Quds Convention (July 1931): The Grand *Mufti* of Palestine, Amin al-Hussaini, convened the second *Mu'tamar* convention in Jerusalem (Al-Quds) on 26 July 1931. The British administration maintained a close watch because of which the conference thought it prudent to be mild in criticism of the colonial administration. It also did not announce the restoration of the Caliphate of the last Ottoman Caliph, as was being feared, but did discuss political issues confronting the Muslim world, contrary to the pledge Hussaini had earlier given to the British High Commissioner that the conference would confine itself to religious issues alone. The delegates deliberated upon the condition of Muslim world in general and matters pertaining to the Muslim holy shrines in Palestine.[8] The convention gave unqualified support to the Palestinian struggle against the Zionist movement. It also succeeded in creating an executive council of the *Mu'tamar* consisting of twenty-five members. Mufti Amin Hussaini became the President, and the prominent Persian politician Syed Ziauddin Tabatabai was appointed as the Secretary of the Central Bureau. In 1934, the

Mu'tamar was instrumental in bringing to an end the Yemen–Saudi Arabia war.[9]

Geneva Convention (1935): Due to the joint efforts of Mahmud Salim, an Egyptian journalist and lawyer and a former participant of the Al-Quds convention, and Shakib Arsalan, this Muslim Congress took place and was attended by delegates from Soviet Union, Palestine, and North Africa. Arsalan had given a pledge to the Swiss authorities that political issues would not be taken up and the goals of the conference would be to foster the spirit of cooperation, bonds of fraternity and Islamic virtue among the Muslims living in different parts of the world. But here again the discussion veered into the realm of politics. The delegates condemned Zionism and talked about the effects of colonialism on the enslaved Muslim lands. The conference did not produce any concrete results.[10]

Muslim Parliamentary Congress on Palestine (Cairo; 1939): This inter-parliamentary conference for the defence of Palestine was attended by delegates from various Muslim and Arab lands. Some Christian nationalists were also invited to make common cause with them on Jerusalem. The conference decided to side with the Axis powers in the World War, hoping to 'get rid of colonialism and imperialism'.[11]

Post-War Efforts

After the Second World War the efforts towards pan-Islamism were renewed. Two more *Mu'tamar* conferences were held at Karachi in 1949 and 1951, respectively, which proposed various projects in education, commerce, and social welfare. Suggestions were made regarding the establishment of two relief organizations, the Inter-Islamic Volunteer Corps and the Red Crescent Society. On the initiative of the Pakistani Finance Minister, Ghulam Mohammad (later Governor-General), the first ever Islamic Economic Conference was held in 1949 at Karachi. This was followed by another at Tehran in 1950, with the aim of seeking ways and means to foster economic cooperation among Muslims.[12]

At the same time, several Muslim states started taking the idea of a pan-Islamic bloc seriously. As early as 1946, Egypt attempted to set up a worldwide Islamic League. Pakistan's leader Mohammad Ali Jinnah visited Cairo to discuss the project.[13] Around the same time, Saudi King Abdul Aziz also toyed with the idea of a pan-Islamic league and started consultations with other Muslim leaders. In 1949, Jordan's King Abdullah initiated a project to unite Muslim states in a Union of the Fertile Crescent. The project ended with his untimely assassination. The idea was revived in 1952 by Pakistan's Foreign Minister Zafarullah Khan but came to naught. At the unofficial level, a prominent Muslim activist of Pakistan, Chaudhry Khaliquzzaman, founded a 'Muslim People's Organization' in 1949 which made several abortive bids to set up a bloc of Muslim states in the following years.[14] In April 1953, a gathering of religious leaders at Maidan, Indonesia, also made a call for the establishment of a Commonwealth of Muslim states.[15]

General Islamic Congress: The first tangible result of the efforts was the establishment of the General Islamic Congress with its headquarters in Cairo. Though the Congress was short-lived, but being the first-ever Islamic association of sovereign states, it became a precursor to the OIC. In 1955, King Saud of Saudi Arabia, Anwar Sadaat of Egypt and Ghulam Mohammad of Pakistan decided to establish this Congress. Its Charter was ratified in March 1956.[16] It was the time when President Nasser had not yet become disillusioned with the pan-Islamic ideas and was fervently talking of Islamic solidarity:

> As I ponder over the hundreds of millions of Muslims, all wedded into a homogeneous whole by the same faith, I come out increasingly conscious of potential achievements and cooperation, naturally not going beyond their loyalty to their original countries but which will ensure for the brethren-in-Islam unlimited power.[17]

Nasser's right-hand man Anwar Sadaat (later, President of Egypt) was appointed the Secretary General of this Islamic Congress in Cairo. Sadaat admitted in an interview with Majid Khadduri in

1958, that the idea of restoration of the institution of Caliphate had become impractical due to the divergent politics of sovereign Muslim states. He said that an international Islamic organization like the Congress would be instrumental in solving the problems of the Muslim world. His office identified colonial subjugation of many Muslim countries, economic backwardness of Muslims and ideological differences among different sects, as the major problems of the Muslims.[18] Actually, the Islamic Congress never got off the ground and its activities remained limited to the educational and cultural fields. No other Muslim state joined it and when it became paralysed in 1958 due to the Saudi-Egypt conflict, Pakistan also withdrew.

Nevertheless, the efforts for an Islamic Summit conference continued to gain momentum. In 1957, King Hussain of Jordan called for a world conference on Palestine. In 1960, President Soekarno of Indonesia proposed an Afro–Asian inter-governmental conference with permanent headquarters in Jakarta. In 1962 and 1964, the 5th and 6th *Mu'tamar* conferences were held, respectively, at Baghdad, Iraq; and Mogadishu, Somalia. The latter conference renewed the call for an association of Islamic countries, which was also echoed in the address of Somali leader Abden Abdullah Osman to the moot.[19]

In the meantime, Muslim World League (*Rabita al Alam al Islami*) was established at Mecca in 1962. At its annual conference at Mecca (April 1965), a joint resolution called for an Islamic Summit. This resolution was strongly endorsed by King Faisal and the Nigerian statesman Sir Ahmadu Bello in their speeches to the Conference.[20]

Reasons for Increase in Islamic Appeal

It would be worthwhile here, to understand why this Islamic appeal was gaining wider acceptance. Five major reasons can be enumerated. First of all, decolonization had resulted in the emergence of a large number of sovereign states. Before the Second World War, most of the Muslim states were not masters of their own house. The Muslim leaders of that era like Ahmad Sanousi, Omer Mokhtar, and Mohammad Ali Jauher might not have been less committed to Islamic solidarity than were Faisal, Bhutto, or Ahmadu Bello, decades later; but the former corps of leaders had emancipation from the colonial yoke, as their immediate objective. However, after decolonization the newly independent countries were eager to demonstrate their independence in a different style.

Secondly, the new states were liberated mostly after long, and bitter struggles so the post-independence leadership was nationalist in orientation. This nationalism found expression in Third World unity and Islamic solidarity theories.

Thirdly, there was an economic motive as well. During the colonial period most of the largely mono-culture economies of the colonies were closely integrated with, and dependent upon, those of the imperialist powers. Hence this technical and economic dependency of the South had made the neo-exploitative relationship more rewarding for the North. It was thus realized that (a) economic independence was essential for political independence; (b) this could be achieved through economic cooperation within the South; and (c) the Muslim world, bound by a common religion, had a potential for cooperation and for creating a joint forum to negotiate with the North.

Fourthly, many of the liberation movements, military ones like in Algeria, as well as political ones like in Pakistan, had used Islam as a slogan to motivate anti-imperialist struggle. The decolonization left the secular leadership at the reins of power and the marriage of convenience with the Islamist allies was broken. This led to a crisis of identity in most of the ex-colonies. The secular nationalists in power started a two-pronged policy of brutally suppressing the Islamist opposition internally on the one hand and externally, stressing their Islamic credentials abroad on the other.

And finally, the establishment of Israel, believed to have taken place through active connivance of the Western powers, was a cause of resentment in the Muslim world. Not only the masses, but the leadership as well believed in conspiracy theories. King Faisal, once dubbed Communism as a Jewish conspiracy. Many leaders, with whom the idea of the Muslim world's economic cooperation never found favour, did talk of Islamic solidarity in the Israeli context.

In this scenario, the idea of pan-Islamism found three protagonists in the Muslim world, viz. Pakistan, Saudi Arabia, and Malaysia.

Pakistani Initiative

Pakistan came into being as a separate Islamic state on 14 August 1947, on the demand of the Muslims of the Indian subcontinent. Pakistan thus always stressed the Muslim world as its constituency. The founder of Pakistan, Mohammad Ali Jinnah, was always forceful in his support for the Palestine cause. Pakistan hosted the 3rd and 4th *Mu'tamar* conferences (1949 and 1951), the first-ever Islamic economic conference (1950) and the conference of religious scholars (1952). Also in 1952, Pakistan made the first serious effort to convene an inter-governmental Islamic conference, but failed.[21] This did not deter Pakistani leader Ghulam Mohammad from his bid to form an Islamic Congress with King Saud and Anwar Sadaat in 1955. Pakistan was so enthusiastic about its neo-pan-Islamism that King Farouk of Egypt ridiculed it by saying, 'Do you know Islam was born on 14 August 1947 [referring to Pakistan's date of independence]?'[22] Many aspersions were cast on Pakistan's motives. Reaffirming that the only 'ulterior' motive that Pakistan had, was service to the cause of Islam, the Pakistani Foreign Minister Zafarullah Khan, in an interview on 2 May 1952, described the allegations against Pakistan as 'mischievous'.[23]

This attitude by fellow Muslim countries helped dampen Pakistan's zeal. Many Pakistanis started questioning the wisdom of hankering after other Muslim countries for the 'elusive' goals of pan-Islamism at the expense of Pakistan's prestige. This public thinking, coupled with the fact that Pakistan's pan-Islamic efforts were being spurned or misconstrued by its Muslim 'brothers', led Pakistan to adopt a very low profile on Islamic issues since the mid-fifties. An editorial of the leading Pakistani daily *Dawn* speaks of the prevalent mood:

The time has come for Pakistan's intelligentsia to realise that Pakistan is not adding to its prestige by running after other countries which are economically and otherwise in a far less stable position than Pakistan itself and which can be of little help to us. If we concentrate on building up our resources and our strength...the day will come when many will be candidates for our friendship without our chasing them. Let us not forget that we in Pakistan constitute a Muslim world in ourselves. We say to our nation to give up slogans and be realists.[24]

In the mid-1950s, Prime Minister Huseyn Shaheed Suhrawardy completely reoriented Pakistan's focus from West Asia arguing that the sum of many zeroes is also a zero. By 1958, a military government under General Ayub Khan, whose fascination with the West never failed him, assumed power in Pakistan, thus making Islam temporarily irrelevant to the country's foreign policy.

Saudi Initiative

As Pakistan was getting more and more disillusioned with pan-Islamism, the initiative passed on to Riyadh where the crown prince Faisal was becoming increasingly powerful. He took over as prime minister in 1962 and two years later ascended the Saudi throne when the royal family deposed his incompetent elder brother King Saud. Apart from the religious bent of Faisal's own personality, one should not forget that Saudi Arabia is a religious monarchy. The Saudi ruling dynasty was a follower of the teachings of the 18th century puritanical reformer Abdul Wahab. Under the al-Saud rule, Saudi Arabia became a theocracy with no written constitution except the Holy Quran. The monarchy enjoyed the prestige of being the custodian of Islam's two holiest shrines. It is in this backdrop that we should see King Faisal's pan-Islamic initiatives.

Beyond the religious orientation of the king and the kingdom, their political motives better explain the Saudi emphasis on Islam, which became a question of survival for the ruling dynasty. After the 1956 Suez war, President Gamal Abdul Nasser of Egypt, had adopted an aggressively radical policy. This socialist radicalism had so much

public appeal in the Arab world that Iraq, Syria, Yemen, all fell one after the other into the radical camp. Saudi Arabia, the bulwark of conservative countries (ringleader of reactionary states and an agent of imperialism, according to Egypt) was alarmed. And as Nasser made no secret of his desire to see radical governments all over the region, Saudi Arabia decided to resist the domino effect.[25]

On the political front, Riyadh had taken major steps to counter the Nasserite designs during King Saud's rule. It had entered into friendship agreements with the conservative monarchies of Jordan and North Yemen, in an apparent attempt to cobble up an anti-Egypt regional alliance. Then in February 1957, Saudi Arabia renewed the contract for the US military base on its soil for another five years, getting a pledge from the latter to equip and train its 15,000-strong army in return. Saudis also won a security guarantee from Washington through the Eisenhower doctrine.[26] When Faisal came to the helm of affairs, he took the battle to the ideological front also. He employed the strategy of using Islam against Nasser's socialism. Referring to Nasserite criticism, the King said:

> They say we are opposed to socialism. As Muslims we believe in God, and Koran is our law. If they claim that socialism does not conflict with the teachings of Islam, why do they ask us to abandon the substance and run after the shadow? If, however, it does conflict with Islam, let them say so frankly and reveal their aim.[27]

Re-emphasizing Saudi Arabia's Islamic credentials, Faisal argued:

> We can, under no circumstances, forget the Islamic nature and sanctity of this country which distinguishes if from all its Arab sister states...We glorify Islam and serve it before everything else. We consider Islam to be our stronghold to which we accept no substitute.[28]

Faisal took up the idea of the Commonwealth of the Muslim states from the 6th *Mu'tamar* Conference (Mogadishu, December 1964) attended by delegates from thirty-three countries. In April 1965, addressing the conference of Muslim World

League at Mecca, he undertook the initiative for an Islamic Summit saying:

> We are at one with our Muslim brothers everywhere. We try with all our power to unite the Muslims, bring them nearer, and do away with any disagreement or influence that might mar their relations. (So) we support the call for an Islamic Summit...[29]

King Faisal took up this mission with a missionary zeal and visited Iran (December 1965); Jordan (January 1966); Sudan (March 1966); Pakistan (April 1966); Turkey (August 1966); and Morocco, Guinea, Mali; and Tunisia (September 1966) in order to garner support for the proposed Islamic Summit. The radical Arab regimes became suspicious of his motives, so the King reiterated, 'We have no other intention but to promote Islam, support the religion of God and bring all Muslims together to enable them to discuss among themselves the affairs of their religion and life'.[30]

Whatever opposition was there to Faisal's idea of an Islamic Summit within the Arab leadership, evaporated with the Arab defeat in 1967 in the Arab–Israel war. Most of all, the loudest voice against this idea, that of President Nasser of Egypt, was silenced. After the debacle Nasser became 'a gloomy, broken man—a living corpse'.[31] For the three years that he lived after the war, he had shed the socialist rhetoric, and became increasingly devoted to Islam.[32]

On 22 August 1967, the Arab leaders met at Khartoum to assess the post-war situation and decided to provide ample annual subsidies to the front-line states; Egypt, Syria, and Jordan which had lost vital sources of revenue. Nasser saw that those who helped him in this hour of grief were the 'conservative' monarchies of Saudi Arabia, Libya, and Kuwait, and not the 'progressive socialist' Eastern bloc of Europe. As the Arab and Muslim states supported each other, there was a thaw in their relationships and the conflicts over ideological outlook were temporarily consigned to the back burner.[33]

Precisely in these years, Malaysia started a new initiative.

Malaysian Initiative

Prime Minister Tunku Abdul Rahman had been thinking about a Commonwealth of Islamic states as early as 1959. In 1961, he publicly expounded this idea while speaking at Shahjehan Mosque near London. As a follow-up, he wrote letters to different Muslim heads of state seeking their support but received a disappointing response.[34] Seven years later, in the summer of 1968, Tunku felt that the time was ripe, so he sent the Malaysian Lands and Mines Minister, Abdul Rahman Qaucub, to several Muslim countries with the proposal for the first ever inter-governmental Islamic conference and to explain its aims and objectives.

After much delay, the conference was finally inaugurated by Tunku Abdul Rahman on 21 April 1969. It was attended by 100 delegates and observers from twenty-three countries including Muslim delegations from Singapore, Thailand, and Philippines. Though it was not a summit, its significance lay in the fact that it was the first-ever inter-governmental conference on Islam. Unlike the *Mu'tamar* and *Rabitah* conferences, where the delegates and scholars came in their private capacity, the delegations in the Kuala Lumpur moot were representing their governments, and three countries were being represented by ministers. Ostensibly, it was a religious conference but was not a get-together of *ulema*.[35]

An interesting situation arose when a three-member delegation of the Palestine Liberation Organization (PLO), led by Abu Hasham arrived at Kuala Lumpur on 24 April and sought permission to participate in the Conference. The Conference rejected their request on the plea that their entry would give this, otherwise a religious gathering, a political colour. The PLO delegation was highly critical of the decision and the Muslim press also joined the chorus of criticism saying that Al-Quds was 'more of a religious issue than a political one. And even if strictly religious issues are to be discussed, why should the Palestinian Muslims not join the discussions'. The delegation met Tunku Abdul Rahman on 26 April and was granted entry on his intervention. Seeing this, the Pakistani delegation led by Allauddin Siddiqui, Vice Chancellor of the Punjab University, tried to raise the Kashmir issue, drawing a parallel between the Kashmir and Palestine crises and insisting that both the problems posed equally grave threats to the *ummah*. However, Pakistan accepted the decision to defer a formal discussion on Kashmir problem till the next conference (that was never held).

The Conference discussed religious issues in three areas including the family laws, trade cooperation, and the sighting of moon (*Ruet-i-Hilal*), to devise a mechanism for the *Eids* to be celebrated throughout the world on the same day. Several calls to establish an Islamic news agency and a broadcasting network, and to enhance trade cooperation among the Muslim countries, were made. It was decided to hold this conference annually, preferably at the summit level. A couple of countries even offered to host the following year's conference. By any standards, the Kuala Lumpur conference was a great success. However, the kaleidoscope of events turned so rapidly in the next few months that it took everybody by surprise and by September 1969, the Organization of the Islamic Conference was established. Tunku resigned from the Premiership of Malaysia to join the OIC as Secretary General (1970). So the Kuala Lumpur moot was never held again. No need to emphasize that this conference was a significant milestone in the road towards the inception of the OIC. Had the Al-Quds (Jerusalem) arson not taken place in 1969, the OIC might have emerged anyway, though after the fifth or sixth Kuala Lumpur conclave.

The Al-Quds Tragedy: On 21 August 1969, the third holiest shrine of the Muslims, the Al-Aqsa Mosque at Jerusalem, was set to fire by an arsonist. This was considered as the biggest assault on Islam since the abolishment of the Caliphate. Though the Tel Aviv government denied any hand in the incident, her subsequent behaviour, including a mere symbolic punishment to the culprit, left no doubt as to who was behind this rash and highly provocative act. This incident demonstrated how very vulnerable the Muslims were, and how emboldened Israel had become after her 1967 victory.

This incident plunged the Muslim world into 'shock, anguish, and indignation'. The Grand Mufti

of Jerusalem and the President of *Mu'tamar*, Amin al Hussaini, cabled to all Muslim heads of state the same day and requested them to hold an emergency Islamic Summit conference since, according to him, 'the real danger posed by Zionism and their malafide intentions have been exposed'. King Hussain of Jordan also wrote to the Arab leaders on the same day to have a summit. Accordingly, the conference of Arab League foreign ministers met in Cairo on 25 August.[36] There was a sharp disagreement on the proposal of holding an Islamic Summit, as Jordan and the PLO were in favour of an Arab summit while Morocco and Saudi Arabia were insistent on calling an Islamic Summit. The latter view prevailed as it was felt that Arab Summits had achieved nothing tangible in the preceding quarter of a century. And that Al-Quds was a problem for the whole Muslim world, not of the Arab countries alone. Saudi King Faisal and Moroccan King Hassan became the sponsors of the proposed summit and it was decided that the latter would host the summit in Rabat, Morocco.[37]

The Formative Years

Hectic preparations for the Rabat summit got underway and emissaries of King Hassan conveyed his invitations to thirty-five Muslim heads of state. Moroccan foreign minister Ahmad Laraki became the chairman of a seven-member preparatory committee. No agenda was fixed because the host, Morocco, feared that the smallest disagreement would wreck the conference. The foreign ministers' preparatory meeting took place on the morning of 22 September (that is, only a few hours prior to the inaugural session of the summit meeting), that too to discuss procedural matters only.[38]

Though the conference deliberations largely remained focussed on the Jerusalem tragedy and the problem of Palestine, a proposal to create a permanent mechanism for the Islamic Conference was also taken up at this first ever Islamic Summit. The move was strongly resisted by the radical states of UAR, Libya, and Algeria etc. who feared it could become another pro-West bloc in the Middle East, since the conservative states were to dominate the organization by the sheer weight of their numbers. For altogether different reasons, Turkey and Indonesia also expressed strong reservations, so the decision about drafting a Charter was deferred. The summit ended after making an earnest call for greater cooperation among the Muslim states and decided to convene a foreign ministers' conference shortly, to consider the establishment of a permanent organization and, if a decision were reached on the matter, take measures for the establishment of its Secretariat.[39]

Establishment of the Secretariat: In pursuance of the decision of the Summit, the 1st foreign ministers' moot was held at Jeddah (March 1970). It was attended by delegates from twenty-two Muslim states. This conference was to examine the results of the Rabat summit and to decide on the establishment of the secretariat. On the first issue, the conference reiterated the demands for the restoration of occupied Arab territories and pledged full support to the just struggle of the Palestinians and the liberation of Jerusalem. On the second issue, decision to establish a permanent secretariat at Jeddah was supported by all but five participating states. Malaysia was asked to nominate the first Secretary General. Again the secular states, Turkey and Indonesia, opposed the establishment of an Islamic Secretariat. The UAR (now Egypt) called it 'useless and irrelevant to the *Arab* struggle'. Thus the issue of drafting of the Charter proved to be more thorny and was once again left to future conferences.

The 2nd Islamic foreign ministers' conference (Karachi; December 1970) went further and elected Tunku Abdul Rahman as its first Secretary General on Malaysia's recommendation. Each member was asked to contribute $10,000 initially and the first budget of $450,000 was approved. The proposals for establishing an Islamic bank, a news agency, and Islamic cultural centres were discussed and committees formed for the purpose. Basic principles and objectives of the conference were agreed upon and the member states were asked to send proposals about the shape of the new organization.[40]

The 3rd ICFM scheduled for September 1971 at Kabul could not take place because Afghanistan backed out from its pledge to host the meeting at the last moment, citing the clash of dates with the UN General Assembly session as the reason. The OIC Secretary General believed that the drought in Afghanistan was the cause for the continued postponement. In fact, King Zahir Shah never showed any interest in the OIC, so the Kabul conference was never held. However four conferences, one each on the establishment of an Islamic News Agency (Tehran; April 1971), Islamic Cultural Centres (Rabat; June 1971), drafting of the Charter (Jeddah; June 1971), and on the proposed Islamic Bank (Cairo; February 1972) were duly held and the reports presented on the eve of the 3rd ICFM that eventually took place at Jeddah (February 1972).

The 3rd ICFM was a watershed since it was here that the discussion on, and the approval of, the Islamic Charter took place. There were heated debates on the different articles of the Charter. Sierra Leone criticized Article II (A/5) concerning the liberation of Palestine, on the grounds that the Charter should not be problem-specific but rather of a general nature. Guinea too argued that once Palestine was liberated, the said clause would become redundant. On the insistence of some Arab states, that Palestine had a unique significance for the Muslim world, the name of Palestine was not removed but a sixth objective, viz. to support all just liberation struggles of the Muslim peoples, was added elsewhere. Similarly, Article VI (1) provoked a controversy as it was not clear whether ICFM would elect the Secretary General or would simply designate a member state to nominate one, as happened when Tunku Abdul Rahman was appointed. Another heated debate occurred over Article XII (A) which said, 'this Charter shall not contain any matter which contradicts the UN Charter or infringes the rights of member states and their obligations towards it.' Most countries were of the view that the Islamic Charter should have nothing to do with the UN Charter, so the para was removed. Article XII now pertains to the interpretation of the OIC Charter alone.

The final point of discord arose when five secular Muslim states made the point that their constitutions did not allow them to become party to such a religious Charter. So they requested that the OIC membership not be made conditional upon the ratification of the Charter as they were not able to subscribe to its Islamic clauses. Mauritania and Saudi Arabia said that the organization should be strong and confident of itself, so there should be no room for a member to wriggle out of its obligations towards the OIC on the plea that it had not ratified the Charter. So the view was rejected, and Syria and Chad ratified the Charter while the remaining three did not. Strangely enough Indonesia, Lebanon, and Turkey are still OIC members without ratification of the Charter, for all practical purposes, except that they cannot get their national elected as the Secretary General.[41]

The 3rd ICFM is thus important as it formally established the Organization in its present form. It also took decisions in principle, to set up the Islamic Development Bank, Islamic News Agency, and Islamic Cultural Centres in non-Muslim states. It designated Jeddah as the seat of the General Secretariat of the new Organization, which it named in the three official languages of the Conference, as the 'Organization of the Islamic Conference' (English), *'Organization de la Conference Islamique'* (French), and *Munazzamah al-Mu'tamar al Islami* (Arabic). In all, thirty-one states signed the Charter and by the fall of 1972, the necessary number of ratifications had been deposited at the General Secretariat, and technically speaking, it came into existence thereupon. Needless to say, the OIC had been in *de facto* existence for the preceding three years also.

NOTES and REFERENCES

1. Noor Ahmad Baba, *OIC: Theory and Practice of Pan-Islamic Cooperation*, (Karachi: Oxford University Press, 1994), pp. 14–18.
2. Ibid., p. 24.
3. Mufti Mohammad Abduh, an Egyptian, was a disciple of the Afghan intellectual Jamal-ud-Din Afghani, and a prominent thinker in his own right. Dr Mohammad Iqbal was an Islamist poet-philosopher of the India–Pakistan subcontinent in the first half of the 20th century.
4. It is a big debate whether the OIC would have been established through the momentum of these conferences, or the stimulus provided by the Israeli desecration of Al-Aqsa mosque, was necessary.
5. Mohammad el-Selim and Mounir el-Sayed, 'The OIC: A general profile', in Mohammad el-Selim (Ed.), *The OIC in a Changing World*, (Cairo: Cairo University, 1994), p. 12.
6. For a comprehensive account of this conference, see Arnold Toynbee, *Survey of International Affairs: 1925*, vol. 1, (London: Royal Institute of International Affairs, 1927), pp. 81–91. Also see Selim, op. cit., p. 13.
7. For details, see 'Proclamation of Sultan Abdul Aziz B. Saud as King of Hijaz and the Islamic Congress at Mecca' in Toynbee, op. cit, pp. 308–19. Also see Selim, op. cit., p. 14.
8. Selim and Mounir ref. 5, p. 14.
9. See *Mu'tamar al-Alam al-Islami: A brief history*, (Karachi: WMC, n.d.), pp. 2–7. It needs to be mentioned that *Mu'tamar* when it appears alone, refers to the *Mu'tamar al-Alam al-Islami* (World Muslim Congress) and the word *Rabita* usually refers to *Rabita al-Alam al-Islami* (Muslim World League).
10. Selim and Mounir, ref. 5, p. 15.
11. Ibid., p. 17.
12. Sisir Gupta, 'Islam as a factor in Pakistan's foreign relations', *India Quarterly*, (New Delhi), vol. 18, no. 1, pp. 40–41.
13. Selim and Mounir, ref. 5, pp. 18–19.
14. Ibid.
15. Khalil al Hamidi, *'Tehrik-e-Islami Key Asraat'* (Urdu), (Lahore: Idara-e-Maarif, 1990), p. 108.
16. Selim and Mounir, ref. 5, p. 19.
17. President Gamal Abdul Nasser, *The philosophy of revolution*, (Cairo: Ministry of Information, 1954), pp. 70–72.
18. See Vernon McKay, 'Impact of Islam on relations among African states', in J. Harris Proctor (Ed.), *Islam and International Relations*, (London: Pall Mall Press, 1965), p. 186. Sadaat talked of this Congress in a nostalgic tone when he addressed the 2nd Islamic Summit (Lahore; 1974). See the text of Sadaat's speech in *Lahore Islamic Summit*, (Islamabad: Ministry of Information, 1974), p. 83.
19. Haider Mehdi, *OIC: A Review of its Political and Educational Policies*, (Lahore: Progressive Publishers, 1987), p. 14.
20. Ibid., p. 15.
21. Gupta, ref. 12, pp. 240–41.
22. S.M. Burke, *Pakistan's Foreign Policy: A Historical Analysis*, (London: 1973), p. 67.
23. *Dawn*, Karachi, 3 May 1952.
24. Ibid., 4 May 1952.
25. Baba, ref. 1, pp. 40–41.
26. Ibid., p. 42.
27. Ministry of Information, Kingdom of Saudi Arabia, *King Faisal Speaks*, (Jeddah, n. d.), quoted in ibid.
28. Ibid.

29. For the text of the speech, see *The Islamic Review* (London), vol. 53, no. 7, 1965, pp. 5–6.

30. See *King Faisal Speaks*, ref. 27, pp. 53–54.

31. Anwar Sadaat, *In Search of Identify: An Autobiography*, (New York: Harper and Row, 1979), p. 136. Sadaat recalls that Nasser's voice was that of a person, who belonged to a dark, hollow and distant past and adds that 'His pride, his most treasured asset, had been hurt as never before'.

32. Nasser's ideas about Islam have always been a subject of debate. Nasser was probably unsure of his ideas himself. Commenting on the Baghdad Pact he had said, 'I do not believe in mixing religion with politics...Although Pakistan is an Islamic country, UAR is an Islamic country, I do not find anything in this to justify a pact between them...if there were an Islamic pact, a Jewish pact, a Christian pact, that would not make the world wonderful'. But on the other hand, on his visit to Pakistan, he talked of the Islamic bonds of unity that united the two nations. He explained Pakistan's support to Palestine as being based on the urge of Islamic comradeship felt by the former. Likewise, he once described his differences with Iraq as hostility between 'Islamic values' and 'atheist Communism', see P.J. Vatikiotis, 'Islam and Egypt's Foreign Policy', in Proctor (Ed.), ref. 18, pp. 120–23. During his heyday, Nasser's arrogance led him to be ruthless to Islamists at home and a scholar of Syed Qutb's calibre was sent to the gallows. But in March 1970, he convened an international *ulema* conference and talked of Islamic fraternity in glorious terms in his inaugural address. In September 1970, when Nasser died, his senior advisor and a 'closet Islamist', Hassan Tohamy (later OIC Secretary General), told a Pakistani

diplomat 'Now that the citadel of unbelievers has fallen, things are going to be different'. See Iqbal Akhund, *Memoirs of a Bystander*, (Karachi: Oxford University Press, 1997), p. 184.

33. Baba, ref. 1, pp. 52–53.

34. See Tunku Abdul Rahman's interview with *The Impact International* (London), vol. 2, no. 5, 1971, pp. 4–5.

35. The information that follows has been taken from the Press Information Department (PID), Ministry of Information, Government of Pakistan, Islamabad, file no. 914.046, consisting of press clippings of 1968–69.

36. See *Keesing's Contemporary Archives, 1969–70*, p. 23689, for the immediate developments leading to the convening of the Summit. Also see Baba, ref. 1, pp. 54–55.

37. Saudi Arabia and Morocco have theocratic monarchies. The former's King is called *Khadim al Harmain Sharifain* (Custodian of the two holy shrines) and the latter's is called *Ameer-ul-Momineen* (Leader of the faithful). King Faisal was assassinated in 1975. King Hassan, however, survived several coup and assassination attempts and ruled his kingdom till his death in 1999, when he was succeeded by his son King Mohammad VI.

38. Baba, ref. 1, pp. 63–69.

39. Chaudhri Nazir Ahmad, *Commonwealth of Muslim States*, (Lahore: Ferozsons, 1972), pp. 48–56.

40. For detailed accounts of these ICFMs, see ibid., pp. 157–89, Also see Chapter 5 of this book.

41. Noor Ahmad Baba gives a very interesting account of the debate on the adoption of the Charter and the disagreements that arose. See Baba, ref. 1, pp. 81–85.

2 OIC: The Structure

The OIC has a three-tier structure. On the top, there are four principal organs, namely, the Conference of Kings and Heads of State, Islamic Conference of Foreign Ministers, the General Secretariat and, since 1981, the International Islamic Court of Justice.[1] Then on the second level, there are specialized committees like the three standing committees (one each on economic cooperation, science and technology, and cultural and information affairs, respectively), Permanent Finance Committee and Al-Quds Committee etc. On the third tier, there are a number of specialized and subsidiary organs like Islamic Bank, Islamic News Agency, ISESCO, etc. In addition, there are several independent institutions, affiliated with the Organization. They include Islamic Chamber of Commerce and Industry (ICCI), Islamic Shipowners Association (OISA), Islamic Cement Association (ICA)0 and some others. In this chapter, we shall introduce the four principal organs of OIC. Part II of this book deals with the specialized and the subsidiary organs, and the affiliated institutions.[1]

The Conference of Kings and Heads of State

The Conference of Kings and Heads of State, commonly known as the Islamic Summit, is the highest authority of the OIC Conference. Article III of the OIC Charter declares it to be the first of the principal organs of the OIC. Originally, Article IV ordained the holding of the summit 'when the interest of Muslim nations warrants it'. But at the 3rd Islamic Summit (Taif; 1981), on Pakistan's suggestion, it was decided that the summit would be convened after every three years. Now the amended Article IV reads:

> The Conference of Kings and Heads of State and Government is the supreme authority in the Organization. The Islamic Summit conference shall convene periodically, once every three years or whenever the interest of Muslim Nations warrants it, to consider matters of vital importance to the Muslims and coordinate the policy of the Organization accordingly.

To date, eight regular and one extraordinary Islamic Summits have taken place. (See chart 2.1)

Chart 2.1
List of Islamic Summit Conferences
(Dates and Venues)

1st Islamic Summit	22-25 Sep. 1969	Rabat	(Morocco)
2nd Islamic Summit	22-24 Feb. 1974	Lahore	(Pakistan)
3rd Islamic Summit	25-28 Jan. 1981	Mecca/Taif	(Saudi Arabia)
4th Islamic Summit	16-19 Jan. 1984	Casablanca	(Morocco)
5th Islamic Summit	26-29 Jan. 1987	Kuwait	(Kuwait)
6th Islamic Summit	09-11 Dec. 1991	Dakar	(Senegal)
7th Islamic Summit	13-14 Dec. 1994	Casablanca	(Morocco)
8th Islamic Summit	09-12 Dec. 1997	Tehran	(Iran)
9th Summit (scheduled)	December 2000	Doha	(Qatar)
1st extraordinary Islamic Summit	23 March 1997	Islamabad	(Pakistan)

Working: The Islamic Summits are held in one of the member countries and a pledge to host the next Islamic Summit is usually made in the previous summit. Each summit elects a Chairman who is, by convention, the head of state of the host-state. Three or more Vice-Chairmen are also elected giving equitable representation to the Asian, African, and Arab blocs.

The summit conference opens with a recitation from the Holy Quran. Then the formality of elections takes place, and the outgoing Chairman hands over charge to the newly elected one, who thereafter conducts the business of the conference. The opening speech by the leader of the host country is followed by the customary speeches of the leaders of the delegations. On the following days, general debate takes place. This debate is usually not confined to the agenda set by the preparatory committees, but covers a wide spectrum of issues concerning the Islamic world. This debate is the most interesting part of the Islamic Summit, especially when compared to the mundane activity reports presented by the heads of the committees. For example, the presidents of Turkey, Senegal, and Pakistan, the *ex-officio* chairmen of the OIC standing committees on economic cooperation, cultural and information affairs, and science and technology, respectively, present their committees' reports. The Secretary General of the OIC presents the report of the progress and activities of the Organization since the previous summit, and informs the leaders about the pace of the implementation of Islamic Conference resolutions. Usually the UN Secretary General is also invited to attend and make a speech at the summit. The delegations from the Republic of North Cyprus, *Azad* (free) Kashmir, and Southern Philippines are also invited but these delegations cannot take part in voting. Past practice has been that Kings, Presidents, and Prime Ministers, not only discuss the problems confronting the *ummah* and the OIC affairs, but also use this forum to defend their countries' position on some controversial issue or to attack a rival country.[2] The scores of resolutions to be adopted are finalized by the Foreign Ministers' preparatory meeting that precedes every summit. So almost all the resolutions are adopted verbatim on the concluding day of the Conference. (In the Dakar Summit, in a surprise departure from the usual practice, all the resolutions were adopted on the opening day, and the rest of the days were utilized for debate and discussion.)

The summit conference concludes after adopting a final declaration and issuing a communiqué, which contains the summary of all the decisions taken. The declarations are usually named after the venue of the conference, like 'Rabat Communiqué', 'Lahore Declaration' etc. There appears to be a growing tendency to adopt a greater number of resolutions; the 1st summit adopted one resolution, the 2nd summit seven, the 3rd summit twenty-eight, the 4th summit forty-two and finally the 8th summit approved 142 resolutions.

A Declining Graph: The 1st Islamic summit (Rabat; 1969) was a pure reflex to the instigation provided by the arson at the holy mosque at Jerusalem (21 August 1969). This Summit was a new beginning in the intra-Islamic relationship. The Arab victory of October 1973 provided the impetus for another summit (Lahore; 1974), that was the zenith of OIC's political history. After seven long years, the 3rd Islamic Summit (Taif; 1981) took place to mark the advent of the 15th century of the Islamic calendar. Though politically, the Taif summit did not produce many tangible results, it did take a number of decisions in the economic sphere, including measures to enhance economic cooperation and establishment of new organs and committees, and some in administrative affairs. Three years later, except for the re-entry of Egypt and the introduction of voting in the OIC procedure, the 4th Islamic Summit (Casablanca; 1984) had nothing significant to its credit.

After Casablanca, the precipitous downward trend started, and the 5th Islamic Summit (Kuwait; 1987) was a non-event. In August 1990, with the Iraqi invasion of Kuwait, the Muslim world faced one of the gravest challenges in recent history, more serious than that of the 1973 war, that warranted the convening of a special summit of the Islamic Conference. Not only that no extraordinary summit of the OIC was convoked but the scheduled triennial Dakar Summit was also postponed indefinitely. Thus the OIC was decisively marginalized and the prestige of the institution of Summit Conference received an irreparable blow. Finally, when the 6th summit was eventually held (Dakar; 1991), it was a non-starter *ab initio* as all but five Arab leaders stayed away. At Dakar, Saudi Arabia and Iran pledged to host the next two Islamic summits. However, demonstrating the utmost apathy, the host country Saudi Arabia expressed its regrets about holding the 7th summit, just when the time arrived. Hence a two day pseudo-summit was held at an alternative venue (Casablanca; 1994).

Next, a one-day special summit conference of the OIC was held in Islamabad, Pakistan, on 23 March 1997. The single-item agenda of the moot was 'Preparing the Islamic *ummah* for the 21st century'. The session was convened by Pakistan as a part of its Golden Jubilee celebration.

The 8th summit (Tehran; 1997) fared better. It was well attended despite US attempts at Iran's isolation. It remains to be seen if the 142 or so decisions taken by the Tehran summit have a concrete outcome.

An Evaluation: The Organization of the Islamic Conference itself, came into being by virtue of an Islamic Summit in 1969. It was felt that instead of having an organ like the UN Security Council, the OIC should have a get-together of the top leaders for effective and prompt decision-making. As the governmental structure is highly centralized in most of the Muslim countries, it was visualized that the assembly of the Kings/Presidents would be the most viable mechanism for decisive action. After debating the vital issues confronting the nation, the leaders, needing no sanction from back home, would make decisions that would be firm, resolute, and unambiguous; and it was further taken for granted, that the decisions of the summit would promptly be implemented.

Today the institution of the Islamic Summit is anything but what the framers of the OIC Charter had envisaged. It has been relegated to a secondary position *vis-à-vis* the ICFM. The summits are badly organized and poorly attended. The resolutions are derided, decisions seldom implemented, and befitting media coverage not accorded. One thing that still goes to the credit of this institution is that it has acquired a unique symbolic value as a show of fraternity of the Islamic community. Unless the Islamic Conference limits the agenda of the summits and stakes its prestige on the implementation of its resolutions, the Islamic Summit will go no further than remaining a talk shop on Islamic issues.

Islamic Conference of Foreign Ministers

The Islamic Conference of Foreign Ministers (hereinafter referred to by its acronym ICFM) is the second principal institution of the OIC. Though the Charter envisages its role to be subordinate to the Conference of Kings and Heads of State, the ICFM has, through convention, arrogated the initiative to itself. It is the *de facto* decision-making body of the Islamic Conference. Not only that the ICFM has held its yearly sessions regularly (twenty-five annual sessions in around thirty years), but has also held emergency sessions on seven occasions so far, to consider the grave situations in Palestine and Bosnia etc. It is this institution which has given life to the Organization. But for the ICFMs, the Islamic Conference might have been an inactive organization. Article V (1) of the OIC Charter says:

a) The Islamic Conference shall be convened once a year or whenever the need arises at the level of Ministers of Foreign Affairs or their officially accredited representatives. The sessions shall be held in any one of the Member States.

b) An extraordinary session may be convened at the request of any Member State or at the request of the Secretary General, if approved by two-thirds of the Member States. The request may be circulated to all Member States in order to obtain the required approval; and

c) The Conference of Foreign Ministers has the right to recommend the convening of a Conference of Heads of State or Government. The approval can be obtained for such a Conference by circulating the request to all Member States.

In all, the Islamic foreign ministers can meet in five ways:

1. First of all, there are the regular annual sessions of the ICFM. So far twenty-five such sessions have been held. (See chart 2.2 for detail.)

Chart 2.2
List of Islamic Conference of Foreign Ministers
(Dates and Venues)

1st ICFM	23-25 Mar.	1970	Jeddah	(Saudi Arabia)
2nd ICFM	26-28 Dec.	1970	Karachi	(Pakistan)
3rd ICFM	29 Feb-4 Mar.	1972	Jeddah	(Saudi Arabia)
4th ICFM	24-26 Mar.	1973	Benghazi	(Libya)
5th ICFM	21-25 June	1974	Kuala Lumpur	(Malaysia)
6th ICFM	12-15 July	1975	Jeddah	(Saudi Arabia)
7th ICFM	12-15 May	1976	Istanbul	(Turkey)
8th ICFM	16-22 May	1977	Tripoli	(Libya)
9th ICFM	24-28 Apr.	1978	Dakar	(Senegal)
10th ICFM	08-12 May	1979	Fez	(Morocco)
11th ICFM	17-22 May	1980	Islamabad	(Pakistan)
12th ICFM	01-05 June	1981	Baghdad	(Iraq)
13th ICFM	22-26 Aug.	1982	Niamey	(Niger)
14th ICFM	06-11 Dec.	1983	Dhaka	(Bangladesh)
15th ICFM	18-22 Dec.	1984	Sana's	(N. Yemen)

16th ICFM	06-10 Jan.	1986	Fez	(Morocco)
17th ICFM	22-25 Mar.	1988	Amman	(Jordan)
18th ICFM	13-16 Mar.	1989	Riyadh	(Saudi Arabia)
19th ICFM	31 July-5 Aug.	1990	Cairo	(Egypt)
20th ICFM	04-08 Aug.	1991	Istanbul	(Turkey)
21st ICFM	25-29 Apr.	1993	Karachi	(Pakistan)
22nd ICFM	10-11 Dec.	1994	Casablanca	(Morocco)
23rd ICFM	09-12 Dec.	1995	Conakry	(Guinea)
24th ICFM	14-19 Dec.	1996	Jakarta	(Indonesia)
25th ICFM	15-17 Mar.	1998	Doha	(Qatar)

2. As noted above, the Charter provides for an extraordinary session of Islamic Foreign Ministers, if and when the situation so warrants. The emergency sessions of ICFM, commonly known as EICFMs meet on those issues, on which there is a fundamental consensus within the Muslim world. The seven EICFM sessions held so far, had respectively Afghanistan, Palestine, Palestine, Iran-Iraq war, Bosnia, Bosnia, and Kashmir as their top agenda. See chart 2.3 for the dates and venue of EICFMs.

Chart 2.3
List of EICFMs (Dates and Venues)

1st EICFM	27-28 Jan.	1980	Islamabad	(Pakistan)
2nd EICFM	11-12 July	1980	Amman	(Jordan)
3rd EICFM	18-20 Sep.	1980	Fez	(Morocco)
4th EICFM	26 Sep.	1980	New York	(USA)
5th EICFM	17-18 Jun.	1992	Istanbul	(Turkey)
6th EICFM	01-02 Dec.	1992	Jeddah	(Saudi Arabia)
7th EICFM	07-09 Sep.	1994	Islamabad	(Pakistan)

3. Since 1980, the OIC has initiated the annual coordination meetings of Foreign Ministers at New York. At the beginning of the annual session of the UN General Assembly in September every year, the Islamic Foreign Ministers assemble in New York to coordinate the Muslim countries' policies for the General Assembly session.
4. In the intervals between the regular OIC conferences, meetings of the bureaux of the Summit and ICFMs are convened to consider pressing issues confronting the Muslim bloc. Several meetings of the joint bureaux of the Summits/ICFMs have been held on Palestine, Bosnia etc.
5. Finally, the various ministerial Contact Groups of the OIC, like those on Kashmir, Bosnia, and

South Philippines, provide the forum where the OIC foreign ministers get the opportunity to meet each other.

Functions and Powers: The ICFMs run the business of the OIC on the guidelines set by the Islamic Summit. The ICFM approves the convening of an emergency or regular Summit and/or Foreign Ministers' Conference. It appoints the Secretary General of the OIC and, on his recommendations, four Assistant Secretary Generals. It accepts or rejects the request of a country to join or withdraw from the OIC. The ICFM can expel or suspend a member for violating the Charter and is authorized to discuss and approve the OIC budget. The major functions of the ICFM are defined in Article V (2) of the Charter, as:

a) To consider the means of implementing the general policy of the Conference.
b) To review progress in the implementation of resolutions adopted at previous session.
c) To adopt resolutions on matters of common interest in accordance with the aims and objectives of the Conference set forth in this Charter.
d) To discuss the report of the financial committee and approve the budget of the Secretariat General.
e) To appoint the Secretary General.
f) To fix the date and venue of the coming Conference of Foreign Ministers.

Working: The ICFM meets in one of the member countries and elects the foreign minister of the host country as its Chairman. Usually a few vice-chairmen are also elected. The conference is formally opened by the President or the Prime Minister of the host country. Then the OIC Secretary General presents the annual report. Two-thirds of the member states in any session form the quorum. The decisions and resolutions (including those on admission/suspension of a member or convening of an Islamic conference) are adopted by a two-third majority, on the basis of one member state, one vote. The ICFM, however, prefers to work on consensus basis. The conference discusses the huge agendas item by item. Now the ICFM agenda is usually anywhere between fifty to ninety-five items, divided into four categories, namely, political, economic, cultural, and financial and administrative affairs. For most of the time, the ICFM concentrates on the political issues while the other three categories are dealt with by the concerned sub-committees. The ICFM itself approves the following year's budget for the OIC and determines the allocations for the subsidiary organs. The ICFM also discusses the implementation of past decisions and adopts new resolutions on a wide range of issues.[3]

The ICFMs sometimes hear firsthand accounts from the victims. For the first time, a Filipino Muslim girl and her maimed brother were produced before the 4th ICFM (Benghazi; 1973).[4] The ministers were moved by the harrowing tales of torture perpetrated by the Philippines army, related by these children. Since then this practice has been followed several times, like in the 2nd EICFM (Amman; 1980), the conference listened to the two expelled Palestinian mayors of occupied West Bank about the Israeli policies of Judaisation of Jerusalem.[5] At other times, the ICFMs have evaluated the reports of OIC fact-finding missions like those on Bulgarian Muslims and the situation in occupied Kashmir, instead of summoning the representatives of the 'victim' Muslim communities. Yet another practice has also sneaked into the working of ICFM, that of inviting a chief guest. President Izzetbegovich of Bosnia and Prime Minister Erbakan of Turkey, among others have attended ICFM/EICFMs on special invitation.

An Evaluation: The ICFM is the most successful institution of the OIC. One has very little to complain against this institution *per se*. The Charter has assigned a lot of responsibilities, which it has always fulfilled diligently, and as noted above, it has become more important than the institution of the Islamic Summit. The general role of this institution has been to adopt resolutions to express the common concern of the Muslim world on issues confronting the Muslims. The ICFM has maintained a radical anti-imperialist posture by 'habitually' condemning both the erstwhile superpowers, in addition to India, Bulgaria, Philippines and others, for what the OIC believes, are excesses against their Muslim minorities. Many a times the resolutions have had significant impact,

with the concerned state sending messages of clarification. Moreover, the ICFMs, especially its coordination meetings at New York, have largely been instrumental in evolving a common strategy of the Muslim countries on all world fora, on the issues where a fundamental consensus exists among the Muslim states themselves.

The General Secretariat

Two things give permanence to an international organization: building and staff. The two then constitute the Permanent Secretariat. The General Secretariat is the third principal body of the OIC. Patterned on the UN Secretariat, it is the executive and administrative organ of the Organization. The Secretary General heads the Secretariat. We have given a separate account of the OIC bureaucracy, i.e., the Secretary General and staff in the next chapter. Hence this section is confined to the administrative structure of the Permanent Secretariat.

The Secretariat was established following the decision of the 1st ICFM (Jeddah; 1970). It is temporarily located at Jeddah, 'pending the liberation of Jerusalem', which the Charter says will be its permanent Headquarters. Initially many states insisted on locating the Secretariat at the holy city of Mecca, but due to administrative reasons, and proximity with diplomatic missions, it was decided that the Secretariat should be in Jeddah.[6] The first Secretary General, Tunku Abdul Rahman, offered space for the Secretariat at Kuala Lumpur and suggested that he would work without pay and hire the services of Malaysian government officials, as long as the building and financial resources for the proper functioning were not made available.[7] However, King Faisal provided a building in Jeddah soon afterwards. After the receipt of the first tranche of members' contributions, the Secretariat started functioning in that premises.

The Secretariat carries out the duties entrusted to it by the Conference under the Charter, as described in the rules and regulations of the Organization and as instructed within the framework of action plans adopted by the Conference, and under the overall supervision of the Secretary General. It assists subsidiary organs and specialized bodies in carrying out their tasks and coordinates their programmes. It supervises the implementation of resolutions and recommendations of the Summits and the ICFMs. Article IV of the Charter delineates the functions of the Secretariat as:

1. The Secretariat General shall work to promote communication among Member States and provide facilities for consultations and exchange of views as well as the dissemination of information that may have common significance to these States.
2. The headquarters of the Secretariat General shall be in Jeddah pending the liberation of *Baitul Maqdis* (Jerusalem).
3. The General Secretariat shall follow up the implementation of the resolutions and recommendations of the Conference and report back to the Conference. It shall also directly supply the Member States with working papers and memoranda through appropriate channels, within the framework of the resolutions and recommendations of the Conference.
4. The General Secretariat shall prepare the meetings of the Conference in close cooperation with the host States in so far as administrative and organizational matters are concerned.
5. In the light of the agreement on immunities and privileges to be approved by the Conference...it shall enjoy, in the Member States, such legal capacity, immunities and privileges as may be necessary for the exercise of its functions and the fulfilment of its objectives.

The Secretariat is divided into four main sections headed by Assistant Secretary Generals (see the chart) and each section is subdivided into departments headed by Director Generals.[8] The functions and responsibilities of the sections are as detailed below.

1. Secretary General's Office: This office is looked after by a cabinet headed by a director. It has to (a) perform all work of the office of Secretary General; (b) coordinate the meetings and conferences; and (c) follow up the activities of the organs. This office is divided into seven sections:

i. **Department of Administration and Finance** deals with personnel matters, prepares and executes the budget, and manages the accounts.
ii. **Department of Protocol and Public Relations** deals with protocol matters and handles contacts concerning privileges and immunities of the OIC.
iii. **Department of Coordination** coordinates the activities of the Secretariat with subsidiary and specialized organs.
iv. **Department of Conferences** plans and coordinates all arrangements for meetings and conferences.
v. **Da'wa Department** coordinates the activities of various organizations in the field of *Da'wa* (Preaching of Islam) to avoid overlapping or duplication.
vi. **General Services Unit** is responsible for the centralization of correspondence to ensure proper liaison.
vii. **External Offices** at Geneva, New York, and Islamabad coordinate the diplomacy with that of the United Nations.

2. Section of Political Affairs: This section headed by an ASG seeks to harmonize political actions of the member states and looks after the implementation of political decisions.

i. **Department of Muslim Minorities:** It collects data and statistics on Muslim minorities, promotes contacts with them and looks after their interests.
ii. **Department of Legal Affairs:** It provides legal counsel to the OIC Secretariat and its organs examines international draft treaties and prepares legal texts of conventions to be signed within the OIC member states.

3. Section of Science and Technology and Economic Affairs: Under an ASG, this section draws up plans and undertakes development studies to foster economic, technical, and trade cooperation in priority fields designated by the Islamic Conference. It consists of two departments:

i. Department of Economic Affairs: It seeks to speed up the economic progress of the Muslim countries, and to protect their natural resources.

ii. Science and Technology Department: Its functions are to promote development of Science and Technology in the Muslim world and to ensure implementation of decisions in this regard.

4. Section of Cultural, Social, and Information Affairs: Headed by the third ASG, it consists of two departments:

i. Department of Social and Cultural Affairs: It promotes cooperation among members in the cultural and sports fields through publications, meetings and other cultural frameworks.

ii. Information Department: It keeps the public informed about the OIC activities, disseminates information about Islamic history and culture, and works to bring the Muslim peoples closer.

5. Section of Al-Quds Al-Sharif: The post of the fourth ASG was established by the 3rd Islamic Summit (Taif; 1981) and designated as ASG (Al-Quds Al-Sharif). As the name indicates, the primary task of this section is to coordinate the activities of the OIC towards the liberation of Palestine. It also looks after the Islamic Bureau for Boycott of Israel and the Islamic Bureau for Military Coordination with the Frontline States against Israel.

International Islamic Court of Justice

The idea of an Islamic court is as old as the Organization of Islamic Conference itself. The 3rd Islamic Summit (Taif; 1981) finally decided to set up the IICJ by virtue of its resolution no. 1/3-PIL(I.S), on a suggestion by Kuwait.[9] The Iran–Iraq war had started a few months before the 3rd summit and all the OIC initiatives to bring about a settlement, were being frustrated as both sides had refused to accept cease-fire unless the other side was branded as the aggressor. Both sides had agreed to cooperate with any Islamic Commission that would adjudge the apportionment of blame for initiating the war. It was in this context that the OIC decided to add a judicial organ in its system. It took several years to draft the Statute that was finally approved by the 5th Islamic Summit (Kuwait; 1987), by virtue of which, the Islamic Court of Justice is the highest judicial authority and the fourth principal organ of the OIC and it 'works independently in accordance with the Islamic *Shari'ah* and the OIC Charter'. The Court is not yet in operation, as the necessary numbers of ratifications have not been deposited.

Competence of the Court: The jurisdiction of the Court is to:

1) Deal with all cases, whose referral to it is agreed to by its member states, as well as all such cases stipulated in the Charter or in the treaties and conventions in force.
2) Look into the disputes that may arise among the member-states.
3) Arbitrate in order to resolve differences that may arise from the interpretation of the OIC Charter.
4) Give advisory opinions on legal issues on the request of Islamic Summit, ICFMs or the OIC organs.
5) Issue *fatwas* on important matters.

Functions: As provided by the statute, the Court has three types of functions. The judicial function involves the settling of disputes among the member states or among the various organs of the OIC, and resolving questions and disagreements regarding the interpretation and/or implementation of the OIC Charter. Such cases can be presented before the Court by the Islamic Summit, the ICFM, or any member or non-member state. The consultative function of the Court involves providing legal opinion or issuing religious edict on a controversial problem. The member states cannot seek the legal opinion; the request has to come through the Islamic Summit, the ICFM, or any of the technical organs of the OIC competent to do so, like the Islamic Fiqh Academy, Islamic Development Bank etc. The third function of the Court is arbitral. It can attempt to resolve a dispute through mediation, conciliation or arbitration, depending upon which of the three options, the parties to the dispute agree on. Only the Islamic Summit, the ICFM, and the parties to the dispute are authorized to invoke the Court's attention to a conflict. One cannot fail to notice that the competence of the Court to take *suo moto* notice of a conflict is limited. Similarly, any third party is debarred from referring a case before the Islamic Court.[10]

However, once the Court is established, it may expand its scope through practice and convention. For instance, a major omission in the statute is that it does not authorize the IICJ to constitute War Crimes tribunals. But, had the Court been in existence in 1997, and if either of the warring factions in Afghanistan had invoked Article 46 of the Statute to draw the Court's attention to mass graves in Afghanistan, the Court would have been obliged to constitute war crimes tribunals to investigate the massacres. This, in turn, could have added a new convention for the IICJ.

Selection of Judges: The judges of the Islamic Court are elected by the ICFM for a four-year term, renewable only once. Each member state has the right to nominate up to three candidates, one of whom may be its citizen. Should two candidates get equal votes, the older nominee is selected. One state cannot be represented by two judges on the bench. Five qualifications need to be satisfied for a person to be eligible for contesting the election. He should be: a Muslim known for his high Islamic morality, a subject of a member-state, less than forty years of age, an expert of Islamic *Shari'ah*, and be qualified for appointment to the highest judicial position in his country.

Composition and Administration: The Islamic Court of Justice will be composed of eleven judges, expert in Islamic jurisprudence, elected by the ICFM from amongst the nominees of the member states.[11] The sole source of law for the Islamic Court would be *Shari'ah*. The Court would be located in Kuwait. The official languages of the Court would be Arabic, English, and French. The Court shall have an independent budget and the member states would bear the Court's expenses through mandatory contributions. The jurisdiction of the Court is optional. No state can refuse to honour the Court's judgment once it has agreed to the Court's competence in the first place.

The Islamic Court: The 3rd Islamic Summit had called for a committee of experts from the member states to frame a statute for the proposed Court. Accordingly, a meeting of experts was convened for this purpose by the Secretary General in January 1983. The committee failed to agree on the statute and consequently the matter was referred to the 4th Islamic Summit (Casablanca; 1984), which decided to constitute a fresh committee of legal experts under King Hassan of Morocco. Consequently, the statute could only be adopted as late as 1987.

Since then the OIC has time and again, in its Summits and various Ministerial conferences, urged the member states to ratify the statute, pointing to the successful experience of Europe with the European Court of Justice and the separate Euro Court for Human Rights. Still, as against thirty-seven ratifications required for the Court to come into operation, so far only eight ratifications have been deposited, and no more countries appear to be enthusiastic about ratification. Hence, it is unclear how long it will take for the International Islamic Court of Justice to formally come into existence.[12]

The OIC Structure: Some Loud Thinking

It cannot be over emphasized that the OIC has not lived up to expectations. There needs to be some rethinking of the structure and working of the Organization, especially its principal bodies.

First of all, the OIC should have a permanent decision making organ and a regular debating forum. In other words, it needs to have the counterparts of the UN Security Council and the General Assembly in its structure. Without belittling the significance of the institutions of the Islamic Summit Conference and the ICFM it has to be recognized that an institution in session just for four days in one or in three years, fails to respond to the challenges posed by the growing needs of a community of fifty-five nations.

It may well be argued that an institution on the pattern of the Security Council where all member-states are equal but 'some are more equal than the others', does not suit an Islamic organization. To circumvent this problem, the OIC can create a Permanent Islamic Committee for Political Affairs

(PICPA) at the General Secretariat, comprising the accredited envoys to the OIC, of all the fifty-five member states. Instead of keeping high chairs for certain members, the committee can have rotating chairmanship for a one-month term each to conduct business. The Committee can have regular weekly sessions, and special sessions on matters of urgency, to consider developments concerning the Muslim world globally. Provided that necessary secret balloting procedure is adopted for decision-making and full media coverage is accorded to its meetings (ruling out allowance for any closed door sessions), the proposed Committee can drastically improve the effectiveness of the OIC. This will reduce the workload of the annual ICFM sessions and also obviate the most common criticism of the OIC that it has no mechanism to constantly monitor the political developments, oversee the implementation of decisions, and to offer a swift reaction to the urgent problems.

Likewise, for a debating forum, the model of the European Parliament with necessary adjustments, appears to be more pertinent to the needs of the Islamic Conference, than that of the UN General Assembly. Since elitism does not go well with the Islamic law (*Shari'ah*), the weightage in representation to be given to each of the member state will have to be determined on some complex formula taking into account the area, population, and the assessment of the country's contribution to the OIC budget etc. Other thorny issues such as the functions and scope of the proposed Islamic Parliament can also be worked out in due course.

And, finally, a discussion on the rationale of the establishment of the Islamic International Court of Justice (IICJ) appears to be in order. One of the stark realities of the present day international political system is that no nation-state easily compromises its sovereignty and that the international judicial organs do place limitations on a state's sovereignty. We have seen that only a few states such as Jordan, Kuwait, Libya, Qatar, Saudi Arabia and some others have ratified the IICJ Statute whereas the Statute requires at least two-thirds of the OIC members (i.e., thirty-seven) to ratify it for the Court to start functioning. One cannot fail to notice that this condition is unrealistic. It would be better to go ahead with the establishment of the Court with the few

ratifications already received. Once the Court starts functioning, it may gradually acquire prestige, and more and more Muslim states would shed their misapprehensions and would find themselves obliged to ratify its Statute, so as to manage to get their judges elected to the Court.

Even the United Nations employs this trick. A pertinent example is the recently concluded Chemical Weapons Convention (CWC), negotiated and finalized by the Geneva-based Conference on Disarmament (CD) which has an extremely intrusive mechanism for verification and inspection of the suspected production sites. Taking into account the anticipated reservations by the nation-states, the required number of ratifications for the Convention to come into force was settled as one-third of the total UN membership, i.e., sixty-two. The sixty-second ratification was deposited on 29 October 1996,[13] and the convention came into effect 180 days later on 29 April 1997. Though hardly any state, possessing or suspected to be in possession of chemical weapons, has ratified the CWC but with the passage of time, as more and more countries adhere to it, the moral force of the convention may become so strong that no country, whether party to the convention or not, will dare employ chemical weapons in a war. The same is true of a host of other UN-sponsored treaties and conventions, especially those pertaining to disarmament and ecological affairs, where the Entry Into Force (EIF)-related provisions are considerably lax.

As for the binding jurisdiction of the Islamic Court's judicial awards, we can again draw an analogy with the relevant provisions of the International Court's statute. It will be interesting to note that neither the ratification of the statute of the International Court of Justice (ICJ) at Hague is mandatory, nor are the decisions binding on the UN member states so, except when the country decides to accept the same of its own free will. Since, the Statute of the ICJ is an integral part of the UN Charter, any country that joins the United Nations, *ipso facto* accepts the ICJ as the supreme judicial body.

As for the ICJ jurisdiction, Article 36 of the ICJ statute talks about the 'Optional clause of compulsory jurisdiction', by virtue of which any member state can give a voluntary declaration about acceptance of the ICJ jurisdiction. Ratification of the ICJ statute alone does not entail compulsory jurisdiction of the Court. So far only one-third of the UN members have given a general declaration to accept the ICJ's jurisdiction. Interestingly, a few others have accepted the Court's jurisdiction in specific areas only. Nevertheless, once a declaration to accept ICJ's jurisdiction (wholly or partially) is given, it cannot be rescinded. Another irony with the ICJ is that so far none of the five permanent members of the UN Security Council has given a general declaration to accept the Court's jurisdiction, still all five have one judge each on the ICJ panel.[14]

Had the framers of the ICJ Statute preferred to wait for the unequivocal support from the whole or, at least, two-thirds of the UN membership for the Court to come into operation, the world would have been without the highest judicial organ till now. The importance of the ICJ, and the respect its awards and advisory opinions enjoy today, need no elaboration. Similarly, the Islamic Court of Justice, once it comes into existence can get a niche in the world's judicial order in no time. Just to give a hypothetical example, the advisory opinion of the International Court of Justice on the legality or otherwise of the possession of nuclear weapons, released on 6 July 1996, states that the possession of nuclear weapons is legal and permissible under international law and a country has the right to deploy them in self-defense. Now had the Islamic Court been in existence; the Islamic Conference would definitely have sought its legal opinion on the possession of nukes. Since the Islamic Court is to work in the light of *Shari'ah* alone (which outlaws any instrument of war that threatens the lives of non-combatants), it could not but have declared the production, possession or proliferation of nuclear arms as illegal, immoral and a threat to humanity; the IICJ would have scored a point in the eyes of the world at large.

In any case it is very difficult to ignore a Court's directive or opinion, once a Court is in operation. Article 94 of the ICJ Statute also grants the right to any party to move the UN Security Council to take necessary measures to give effect to an ICJ judgment, which had been given in its favour but

not carried out by the other party.[15] Nevertheless, this Article has never been invoked since there is no known instance of an ICJ judgment not having been implemented. This is so because respect according to the International Court involves the reputation of the international community and no state wants to lose face by flouting international legality.

A case in point is the European Human Rights Court's order to Turkey to pay $50,000 compensation to six Kurdish ex-deputies for their illegal confinement for fourteen days.[16] Turkey is not a partner in the European Union and is very sensitive over Western criticism of its track record on human rights, especially in relation to the Kurdish trouble, which it considers, is its internal affair. The judgment was nonetheless implemented. So, the gist of our argument is that the non-establishment of the Islamic Court of Justice, reflects the lack of foresight on the part of the OIC leadership. For the organization to play a dynamic role, it is imperative that its principal judicial organ be set up without the unwarranted delay.

Concluding Remarks

Summarizing our discussion, two more points on the OIC structure, pertaining to its over-centralization, need mention. The OIC consists of four principal organs, five specialized organs, thirteen specialized committees, two contact groups, ten subsidiary organs, four affiliated universities and ten affiliated institutions. This makes a total of forty-eight. We have argued elsewhere that the member state that chairs a particular OIC committee or hosts the headquarter of a subsidiary organ, acquires undue clout in the conduct of affairs of that particular committee or institution. From Chart 2.4, we can see that in two of the principal organs, namely the Islamic Summit and the ICFM, the chairmanship is held through rotation. Each time, the country that hosts the conference becomes the chairman. Likewise, the two OIC contact groups, one each on Bosnia and Kashmir, are chaired by rotation. Seven of the OIC specialized committees are headed by the Secretary General of the Islamic Conference.[17] Two of the

Chart 2.4
Concentration of OIC Organs

S. No.	Location of the organ / Chairmanship by the Head of State COUNTRY	Principal Organs	Specialized Organs (chairmanship)	Specialized Committees (chairmanship)	Contact Groups	Subsidiary Organs	OIC sponsored Universities	Affiliated Institutions	Total
1.	Bangladesh					1	1		2
2.	Egypt							1	1
3.	Guinea			1					1
4.	Iraq		1	1					2
5.	Kuwait	1							1
6.	Libya							1	1
7.	Malaysia						1		1
8.	Morocco		1	1		1			3
9.	Niger						1		1
10.	Pakistan			1				1	2
11.	Saudi Arabia	1	3			5		4	13
12.	Senegal			1					1
13.	Turkey			1		2		1	4
14.	Tunisia					1			1
15.	Uganda						1		1
a.	By rotation	2			2				4
b.	Chaired by OIC Secretary General			7					7
c.	HQ not decided							2*	2
		4	5	13	2	10	4	10	48

* The two OIC affiliated institutions whose headquarters are yet to be decided are the Islamic Women Association (IWA) and the Islamic Union of Legislative Assemblies (IULA). There is a strong likelihood that the two would respectively be located at Tehran, Iran, and Kuala Lumpur, Malaysia.

affiliated institutions, IWA and IULA (see Chapter 13) are not yet in operation, so the question of chairmanship or of headquarter city does not arise. This leaves us with thirty-five organs or committees. As seen from the Chart 2.4, thirteen of these organs are either located in Saudi Arabia or are chaired by its representative. The corresponding figures for Turkey, Morocco, and Pakistan are four, three, and two, respectively. Thus, twenty-two of the thirty-five OIC organs are dominated by four member states alone.

Moving on to Chart 2.5, same trend is observable in respect of playing host to the Islamic Summit and Foreign Ministerial conferences. Eight regular and one extraordinary Islamic Summits, and twenty-five regular and seven extraordinary ICFMs have been held so far. This sums up to forty-one. Pakistan and Morocco top the list by hosting seven conferences each, followed by Saudi Arabia and Turkey with a score of six and three, respectively. Thus twenty-three of the forty-one conferences were held in the same four countries. One conference was held at New York, USA, while the remaining seventeen took place in fourteen member states. With more than half of the OIC activity concentrated in four leading

Chart 2.5
The Venues of OIC Conferences

S. No.	Country (Venue)	Islamic Summits	Extraordinary sessions of Islamic Summit	ICFMs	Extraordinary sessions of ICFM	Total
1.	Afghanistan*			–		–
2.	Bangladesh			1		1
3.	Egypt			1		1
4.	Guinea			1		1
5.	Indonesia			1		1
6.	Iran	1				1
7.	Iraq			1		1
8.	Jordan			1	1	2
9.	Kuwait	1				1
10.	Libya			2		2
11.	Malaysia			1		1
12.	Morocco	3		3	1	7
13.	Niger			1		1
14.	Pakistan	1	1	3	2	7
15.	Qatar			1		1
16.	Saudi Arabia	1		4	1	6
17.	Senegal	1		1		2
18.	Sudan*			–		–
19.	Tunisia*			–		–
20.	Turkey			2	1	3
21.	USA				1	1
22.	Yemen			1		1
	Total	8	1	25	7	41

* Afghanistan, Sudan, and Tunisia had volunteered to host the 3rd, 21st and 22nd ICFMs respectively, but due to certain circumstances the conferences could not be held on schedule and at the agreed venue. The three conferences were held, after much delay in each case, in Saudi Arabia, Pakistan, and Morocco, respectively.

member states; thirty-seven member states have never organized an OIC conference while forty have no OIC organ on their soil. In all, there are thirty-two OIC member states who neither hosted a conference, nor chaired an OIC Permanent Committee, nor got their national elected to the post of Secretary General and nor have any OIC institution located on their soil. They can, at best, be categorized as passive members. As the OIC revolves around a core membership of twenty-three, most of the remaining thirty-two do not pay their dues regularly and many even do not participate in all the conferences at the appropriate level. There is a need to affect the devolution of responsibility and de-concentration of the OIC organs into a wider bracket, so as to bring the majority of the member states into the mainstream. Failing which, the OIC may not become capable of acting as a united bloc on the international stage.

NOTES and REFERENCES

1. Though the total number of OIC organs is forty-eight but quite a few of them have not started functioning yet, like the International Islamic Court of Justice, Islamic Civil Aviation Council, and Islamic Women Association etc. It may be pointed out at the outset that this and the following two chapters increasingly refer to the OIC Charter and declarations. The Charter is included in Annexure 1 and all the nine final declarations of the Islamic Summits in Annexure 3. The charts 2.1, 2.2 and 2.3 have been taken from the *Guide to the OIC*, (Jeddah: OIC Secretariat, 1995), pp. 20–21, 21–23 and 24, respectively.

2. The same is true for the ICFMs also where occasional verbal duels between Iraq and Kuwait, Iran and Saudi Arabia, Uganda and Sudan and so on, are witnessed. Likewise, the ICFMs also invite the Republic of North Cyprus and the autonomous South Philippines as observers, and Azad Kashmir as guest.

3. See Abdullah Ahsan, *OIC: Introduction to an Islamic political institution*, (Herndon: IIIT, 1988), pp. 24–25, for a thorough discussion on the working of the ICFM. The ICFM developed the practice of splitting up into four commissions to cover the increasingly crowded agenda, since the 5th ICFM in 1974.

4. *Dawn*, Karachi, 19 April 1973.

5. *Pakistan Times*, Islamabad, 13 July 1980.

6. Chaudhri Nazir Ahmad, *Commonwealth of Muslim States*, (Lahore: Ferozsons, 1972), pp. 150–59.

7. Noor Ahmad Baba, *OIC: Theory and Practice of Pan-Islamic Cooperation*, (Karachi: Oxford University Press, 1994), p. 73.

8. The details about the OIC Secretariat structure have been taken from the OIC Guide, ref. 1, pp. 27–34.

9. Ibid., pp. 37–8.

10. Mounir el-Sayed and Mohammad el-Selim, 'The OIC: A general profile', in Mohammad el-Selim (Ed.), *The OIC in a changing world*, (Cairo: Cairo University 1994), pp. 35–36. The article gives an account of the functions of the IICJ as well as of the criteria for the judges.

11. Ahsan, ref. 3, p. 28.

12. The 8th Islamic Summit (Tehran; December 1997) through its resolution no. 49/8-P(IS) expressed concern over the lack of ratifications received for the IICJ, commended the states which have ratified the statute and appealed to those, which have not, to do so at the earliest. Through a separate resolution, the Summit established an experts committee to study why the requisite number of ratifications has not been received for the IICJ and some OIC-sponsored agreements.

13. *The News*, Islamabad, 30 October 1996.

14. See J. G. Starke, *An Introduction to International Law*, (London: Bulterworth, 1984), pp. 472–81, for a thorough understanding of the scope and working of the ICJ.

15. See Sir Zafarullah Khan, *The forgotten years: A memoirs*, (Lahore: Vanguard, 1991), p. 192. It may be added that Sir Zafarullah, an ex-Foreign Minister of Pakistan, remained the Chief Justice of the ICJ and President of the UN General Assembly also.

16. *The News*, Lahore, 27 November 1997.

17. As for the remaining six committees, they are headed by the Vice-President of Iraq (Committee on Sahel), the King of Morocco (Al-Quds Committee), and the Presidents of Gambia (Peace Committee), Pakistan (COMSTECH), Senegal (COMIAC) and Turkey (COMCEC), ex-officio.

③ OIC Bureaucracy

One of the biggest charges against huge international organizations, as well as against national government machineries, is the inefficiency and red-tapism of the bureaucracy. It is particularly true of the UN. The bloated UN bureaucracy is known for corruption, wastage of funds, and inefficiency.[1] The financial mismanagement scandals at the UN secretariat have become a challenge for the Secretary Generals. So far no organization chief has been successful in sorting out this mess. The UN staff is estimated to be 25,000 around 14,000 at the New York Secretariat alone. If we include the employees of the UN organs and agencies also, the strength of the UN personnel becomes 51,000.[2]

The OIC bureaucracy is very limited and in 1989, was further cut to size when the Secretary General terminated the services of twenty-six employees including a deputy director at the Jeddah secretariat as part of measures to reduce Secretariat expenditure. A few months later he sacked another 130 for the same reason. In fact, the Organization cannot afford to have a large bureaucracy because of non-payment of mandatory dues by the member states, which sometimes makes it difficult for the Secretariat to pay the salaries and allowances to the existing staff in time.[3]

Though the exact figures about the numerical strength of staff at OIC General Secretariat and all the subsidiary organs is not available but it is evident that their numbers are far less than those of other similar organizations and their organs. The OIC General Secretariat now has around a hundred officers and a lower staff of about half that number. The strength of staff at the three OIC Permanent Missions for Coordination with the United Nations at New York, Geneva, and Islamabad is eight, five, and two, respectively. In the subsidiary organs, the IFSTAD had a meager staff of thirteen, the SESRTCIC has twenty, while IINA has twenty-six full-time employees. The Islamic Development Bank (IDB), one of the most active of OIC organs has a relatively large staff of 685, which comes from the OIC member states, except fifty who are Muslim nationals of non-member states. The break-up of this staff comprises 238 professionals, twenty-four special category staff, 340 general service staff and eighty-three manual workers. Compared to other such financial institutions like World Bank, Arab Bank, and the IMF etc., this too is a modest number.[4]

The General Secretariat at Work

The rules and regulations regarding the employment of the OIC employees are based upon the 'Personnel Regulations of the Organization of the Islamic Conference', approved by the 19th ICFM (Cairo; 1990).[5] The terms and conditions for hiring an employee are more or less similar to those in other international organizations but the emoluments paid to the OIC officials are considerably lower than their counterparts in sister organizations. The OIC officials enjoy the status of international diplomats in performance of their duties.

Functions: According to Article VI of the OIC Charter, the functions of the Secretariat include providing facilities for consultation and exchange of views among member states, dissemination of information, follow up of the implementation of resolutions of the summits and the ICFMs and reporting back to the conference, supply of working papers to the member states and preparation for meetings. Considering the severe financial constraints, the OIC staff is quite efficient in organizing meetings, documentation of resolutions, co-ordination between the OIC organs and supplying the working papers. The Secretariat officials also undertake such functions as collection of statistics and preparation of publications.

Under Article 6 of the Regulations, the officials are expected to hold the interest of the Organization supreme, and Article 7 debars them from taking instruction from any quarter except the Organization. Article 20 expects them to be loyal to Islam and to the Muslim *ummah*.

Service Structure: The OIC General Secretariat has a five-tier hierarchy with a sixteen-grade structure.[6]

i. **Elected posts:** The Secretary General is the chief executive of the OIC and is elected by the Islamic Conference of Foreign Ministers for a four-year renewable term. The ICFMs also elect four of his Assistants for the same tenure on his recommendations. The Secretary General and Assistant Secretary Generals take an oath under Article 20 of the Regulations to 'discharge their duties to the true religion (Islam) and to the Muslim *ummah* with honesty, sincerity and loyalty'.
ii. **Principal posts:** The Director Generals and Directors of various sections within the OIC Secretariat or of its subsidiary organs fall under this category. They are subdivided into grades D1 and D2. Usually they are appointed on a four-year initial contract, renewable yearly at the end of term till the seventh year.
iii. **Professional posts:** These posts are reserved for professionals and are divided into four grades (P1 to P4).
iv. **Administrative posts:** The next in status are the administrative posts (A1 to A4) like the administration and accounts officials, security officers, and librarians etc.
v. **Support posts:** The manual workers and other lower staff (S1 to S4) are hired on a permanent basis from amongst the locals. The first year of service, for all the categories except the first one, is a probation period.

Composition: Although there is a convention that only Muslim citizens of member states are appointed as officials as far as the General Secretariat is concerned, but the subsidiary organs have their own rules. Islamic Development Bank (IDB) also inducts Muslims from the non-Muslim states, while the Islamic Foundation for Science, Technology and Development (IFSTAD) hires the services of 'Muslim and non-Muslim citizens of OIC member states and Muslims of the non-

Muslim states'.[7] Though the OIC purports to be an equal opportunity employer for both sexes, there is only one woman in the OIC General Secretariat system, that too in the OIC Permanent Mission at New York. However, there are quite a few women in some subsidiary organs of the OIC.

Appointments: Except for the Assistant Secretary Generals (ASGs) who are elected by the ICFM on his recommendation, the Secretary General has the exclusive authority to appoint the staff. Article VI (2) of the OIC Charter asks him to nominate the staff (a) from the OIC member states, (b) paying due regard to their competence and integrity, and (c) in accordance with the principle of equitable geographical distribution. Article 15 of the OIC Personnel Regulation adds a few more conditions for the prospective appointees including, that the candidate should be Muslim by faith belonging to a Muslim country (spouse should also be Muslim in case of married persons). Annexure 2 of the Regulation lays down the specific requirements (qualifications, experience and age etc.) against each category of posts. Thus one can distinguish four kinds of appointments. Firstly, political appointments like the Secretary General, ASGs and the Director Generals of various organs; secondly, contract-based appointments much like those at the United Nations whose officials are initially hired on contract, renewable at the end of term; thirdly, borrowed officials including experts and professionals, lent by the member governments on deputation (often, even the ASGs are on lease from their home governments, for the duration of their tenure); and finally, permanent employees who consist of locally hired support staff.

Promotion and Transfers: The staff members who have served for at least four years in the same capacity are eligible to be promoted to the next grade, provided that (a) there is a vacancy, (b) the official meets the qualifications for the next grade as laid down in the Regulations, and (c) the official has consecutively received at least 'very good' remarks in the annual performance reports. An official may be transferred within the General Secretariat or from the Secretariat to a subsidiary

organ or vice versa, usually for a two-year period at a time, on the discretion of the OIC Secretary General, in consultation with the Director General concerned (See Articles 24–31 of the Regulations).

Disciplinary measures: Any official found guilty of dereliction of duty or corruption, as well as the one who receives 'unsatisfactory' grade in performance reports in two consecutive years is liable to receive disciplinary action initiated against him by a three-member disciplinary committee. On the recommendation of the committee, the OIC Secretary General may, in his discretion, (a) withhold his annual increment for one year, (b) withhold the same permanently, or (c) dismiss him from service, and where applicable, refuse to renew his contract, depending upon the nature of the offence (See Article 73 and 74 and Article 71; paras 'e' to 'g').[8]

Remuneration and perks: The Secretary General gets a fixed monthly salary of US$7,300 whereas the ASGs get $4,000 per month. The range of salaries for the D category ($2,656–3,402), P category ($1,626–2,999), A category ($1,263–2,153) and S category ($303–736) depends upon the exact grade within the category, the seniority, as well as the number of increments received. In addition, the staff is entitled to house rent (25–35 per cent of basic pay), transport allowance (a car in case of very senior officials), free health care (including that for the immediate family), one month paid leave each year, gazetted holidays on the Muslim festivals of *Eid-ul-Fitr, Eid-ul-Adha* and the OIC foundation day, and several other fringe benefits as detailed in Articles 42–48 of the Regulations. Married employees also receive a monthly family allowance depending upon the number of family members and an educational allowance of $2,700 per child per annum. The Secretary General is authorized to award a bonus equal to two-month salary to outstanding staff-members only.[9]

Immunities and Privileges: The Charter gives the OIC staff absolute freedom in performance of their duties and asks them not to take directions from their home countries. Article VI (3) says:

In the performance of their duties, the staff shall not seek or receive instructions from any government or authority other than the Conference. They shall refrain from taking any action that may be detrimental to their position as international officials responding only to the Conference. Member States undertake to respect this quality and the nature of their responsibilities, and shall not seek to influence them in any way in the discharge of their duties.

The Charter gives diplomatic immunities to the OIC officials by virtue of sub-clause (c) of Article VI (8):

The Staff of the Conference shall enjoy the immunities and privileges necessary for the performance of their duties as may be decided by the Conference.

In addition, the staff enjoys diplomatic immunity under the Agreement on Privileges and Immunities of the Organization (APIO) as well as under any special agreement that may be in force between the OIC and the state concerned. In return, the OIC officials are expected not to violate the laws of the land. The Secretary General of the OIC alone has the discretion to waver the immunity of an OIC diplomat working with the Secretariat or any subsidiary organ.[10]

In Pakistan, there was a controversy when Mr Sharifuddin Pirzada, after retiring as the OIC Secretary General, retained the two cars imported by him duty free during his tenure. He had sought permission for this privilege from the then President of Pakistan on the grounds that he needed a small office and two cars in Islamabad, for his duties as the OIC chief. Now the Central Board of Revenue (CBR) of Pakistan was of the view that since Mr Pirzada had relinquished the office, he was no longer entitled to retain those cars unless he paid the customs duty. The case went to the Federal Ombudsman of Pakistan who ruled on 18 July 1991 that Mr Pirzada had the status of a diplomat of an international organization settled in Pakistan after retirement, hence, he could not be required to pay the customs duty on his cars.[11]

Chart 3.1: The OIC Structural Chart

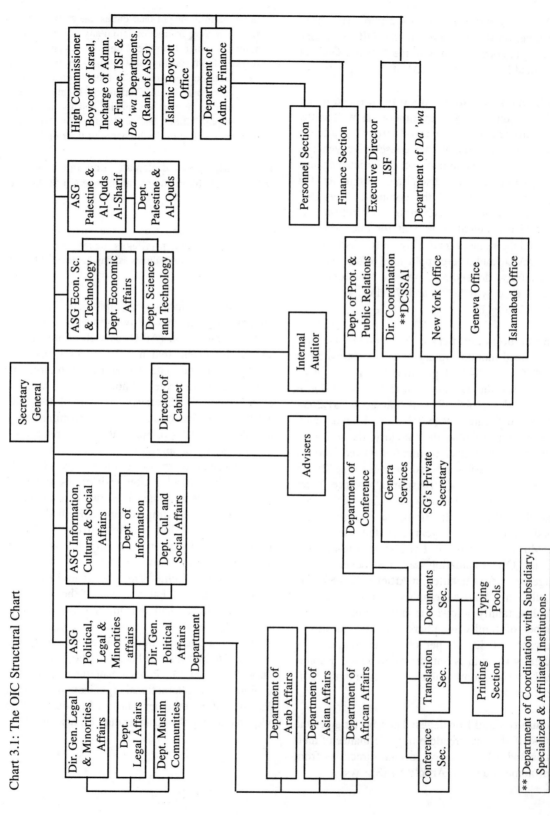

** Department of Coordination with Subsidiary, Specialized & Affiliated Institutions.

Key: ASG = Assistant Secretary General, Dept. = Department, Dir. Gen. = Director General, Sec = Section / SG = Secretary General

Chief Executive

As the Secretariat of the OIC is patterned on that of the United Nations, its chief executive too is designated as the Secretary General, and is responsible for the overall functioning of the Organization. He is the ultimate authority at the General Secretariat, he appoints and sacks employees and nominates, and in other cases recommends, the names to the ICFM for nomination to senior posts in the OIC and its organs.[12] He represents the OIC at international fora, presents reports at Islamic summits and the ICFMs, takes decisions on day to day running of the Organization and is the *ex-officio* chairman of some of the OIC committees and commissions.

The Secretary General is elected by the foreign ministers' conference for a four-year term, renewable once. He is assisted by four Assistant Secretary Generals (ASGs), also elected by the ICFM on his recommendation for four-year renewable terms. Their designations are ASG Political Affairs; ASG Science, Technology, and Economic Affairs; ASG Information and Cultural Affairs; and ASG Al-Quds Al-Sharif. The last mentioned post was created by virtue of a decision of the 3rd Islamic summit (Taif; 1981). Earlier, the Director (Co-ordination) on Palestine used to look after this department and enjoyed the status of an ASG. It may be added that the ASG (Political Affairs) is also responsible for Muslim minorities and legal affairs.

The Secretary General's cabinet is responsible for administration and finance affairs of the Secretariat as well as the departments of protocol, public relations, *Da'wa*, conferences and external offices. The Secretary General is assisted by a Director of Cabinet and several advisers in addition to the heads of these departments.[13] In the Secretary General's absence, the senior most ASG officiates, since there is no post of Under Secretary General in the OIC. Likewise, in case of his death, resignation, or dismissal, the senior most ASG is supposed to take over till the election of a new Secretary General but such an eventuality has so far never arisen. If all, or more than one ASGs are of the same seniority, then the eldest ASG is considered to be the most senior one also.[14]

The framers of the Charter of the United Nations had visualized the role of its Secretary General as that of a Prime Minister. But no such role had ever been envisaged for the OIC chief so he is fundamentally weaker than his counterpart at the UN. But as has been pointed out elsewhere also, the conventions and precedents, rather than the text, are more responsible for shaping the structure of an organization. In the UN, powerful Secretary Generals like Trigvie Lie and Dag Hammerskjold brought prestige to the office. As for the OIC, it had many Boutrous Boutrous Ghalis and no Dag Hammerskjold, so the office could never emerge as a powerful or a potent one.

It has been argued in the last chapter that the OIC declined after 1990, when it was decisively marginalized in conflict resolution during the Iraq–Kuwait crisis; the office of the Secretary General also faced the same trend. Before that date, there used to be several contenders for the post and hence intense lobbying and hobnobbing before elections, but in 1992 and 1996, there was only one candidate, elected unopposed. It may be noted that never has voting taken place for the Secretary General's election. Rather, the candidates likely to be defeated used to withdraw after persuasion by other countries, and unanimous election of the consensus candidate brought him to office. So far seven persons have been elevated to this august post:

Chart 3.2: OIC Secretary Generals

1.	H.E. Tunku Abdul Rahman	Malaysia	1 Jan. 1971–31 Dec. 1973
2.	H.E. Hassan Tohami	Egypt	1 Jan. 1974–31 Dec. 1975
3. i.	H.E. Dr. Amadou Karim Gaye	Senegal	1 Jan. 1976–31 Dec. 1977
ii.	H.E. Dr. Amadou Karim Gaye	Senegal	1 Jan. 1978–31 Dec. 1979
4.	H.E. Habib Chatti	Tunisia	1 Jan. 1980–31 Dec. 1984
5.	H.E. Sharifuddin Pirzada	Pakistan	1 Jan. 1985–31 Dec. 1988
6. i.	H.E. Dr. Hamid Algabid	Niger	1 Jan. 1989–31 Dec. 1992
ii.	H.E. Dr. Hamid Algabid	Niger	1 Jan. 1993–31 Dec. 1996
7.	H.E. Dr. Izzuddiene Laraki	Morocco	1 Jan. 1997–

The 2nd ICFM at Karachi had appointed Tunku Abdul Rahman as Secretary General for three years but when the Charter was approved, the tenure was fixed for two years and Tohami stayed for the two-year tenure. Gaye held the post for two consecutive terms of two years each. During Chatti's two year term, the 3rd Islamic summit at Taif decided to make the tenure of Secretary

General four year non-renewable. Mr Chatti, who had one year left in his tenure automatically got three. When his term was drawing to a close, he propounded a strange logic—that since the tenure of Secretary General was made four years in January 1981, he would count his four years from that date rather than January 1980, when he took office. Pakistan and Bangladesh, the two leading contenders for his successor did not accept his logic but since no consensus candidate was emerging (both the countries had refused to withdraw their candidature), the 4th Islamic summit (Casablanca; 1984) extended Chatti's tenure by one year. So Mr Chatti served for five years, followed by Mr Pirzada who served for a term of four years. Later, during Dr Gabid's tenure, the 6th OIC summit again amended Article VI (1) of the OIC Charter, making the re-election of Secretary General possible, once. Dr Gabid got re-elected for another term. Now minus the incumbent Secretary General, the six OIC secretary generals served for 3, 2, 2+2, 5, 4, and 4+4 years respectively. So there is absolutely no consistency in the tenure of the office.

All the seven Secretary Generals had a distinguished political career in their home countries. Three of them served as Prime Ministers, one as Deputy Prime Minister, and the remaining three as Ministers for Foreign Affairs. As for their academic and professional backgrounds; two were doctors, two were lawyers, two were diplomats, and one was an economist. Of the first six Secretary Generals, two each represented the Arab, African, and Asian blocs within the OIC; the seventh (incumbent) Secretary General belongs to an Arab country (Morocco).

Following are brief life-sketches of each of the OIC Secretary Generals:

Tunku Abdul Rahman: Tunku was born on 8 February 1903 in the town of Alor Star in Kedah state, Malaysia, and got his early education from there. He went to UK for higher studies in 1920 and studied at Inner Temple (London) and St. Catherine's College (Cambridge). In 1931, he returned home and joined Kedah Civil Service. He returned to UK in 1947 but was called to the Bar two years later and was appointed Deputy Public Prosecutor at the Malayan Federal Legal Department.[15]

In 1951, he resigned and joined politics. He became the President of his United National Malays Organization (UNMO) the same year. He was nominated unofficial member of the executive and legislative councils in 1952. He won the 1955 general elections and became the chief minister and home minister of Malaya. In January 1956, he visited London to negotiate the demand for immediate self-government which was granted.

In August 1957, he took over as Prime Minister and foreign minister of independent Malaya. In September 1963, he presided over the formation of Malaysia, and then Singapore's withdrawal, two years later. He resigned in September 1970 following serious ethnic riots between the Chinese and Malays in the wake of 1969 elections in which Chinese had made significant gains. He was succeeded by Tun Abdul Razzak.

Tunku had propounded the idea of a Commonwealth of Islamic States, way back in 1961. He also presided over the first ever International Islamic Conference in Kuala Lumpur (April 1969). At the 1st ICFM (Jeddah; March 1970), it was decided that the first OIC Secretary General would be from Malaysia. The Kuala Lumpur government was asked to send its nomination, which accordingly designated Tunku, so the 2nd ICFM (Karachi; December 1970) confirmed his appointment. After serving for three years as the OIC chief he retired and was appointed the first President of the newly established Islamic Development Bank (IDB).[16]

Hassan Mohammad El-Tohami: Tohami was born in 1924 in lower Egypt. After completing his basic education, he joined Military College, Cairo. He became the vice president of Cairo's Islamic Conference in 1959. He joined the Foreign Ministry in 1961 and was appointed ambassador to Austria. In 1969, he was appointed Secretary General to Egypt's Presidency by President Nasser. He remained a minister of state (1970–71) and adviser to President Sadaat on religious affairs (1971–74). He was elected to the office of the OIC Secretary General by the 4th ICFM (Benghazi; 1973) and served for two years (1974–75) in that capacity. He was again taken in as minister in

Egyptian cabinet and led the delegation to Fez (May 1979) where his country's membership of OIC was suspended by the 10th ICFM. He also served as the Deputy Prime Minister of Egypt.[17]

Dr Amadou Karim Gaye: Dr Gaye was born on 8 December 1913 at St. Louis, Senegal. His primary education (1922–35) was in *Ecole Primaire* at St. Louis. He studied veterinary medicine from *Ecole Nationale Veterinaire* (France) during 1941–45. For the eleven years till 1957, he served as a veterinary inspector in Senegal. In 1949, he also became General Councilor. He was elected a deputy in Senegal's National Assembly, a position he held till taking over office at the OIC.[18]

Dr Gaye was very active in politics and was Under Secretary for Propaganda in *Union Progressive Senegalaise* (UPS) during 1960–70. During the same period, he served in the cabinet in various capacities including as Minister for Education (1959), Planning (1959–60), Technical Co-operation (1961–65), Armed Forces (1965–8), and finally Minister for Foreign Affairs (1968–72). He served as Chairman of the UN Economic and Social Council (ECOSOC) from 1972–75. Amadou Karim Gaye was elected Secretary General at a special ICFM held on 5 November 1977, at Jeddah, Saudi Arabia, to elect Tohami's successor. The five-hour long session was presided over by the foreign minister of Sudan. After stormy canvassing and consultations, his main rival Omer Arteh Ghalib, the foreign minister of Somalia, withdrew.[19] Gaye took over on 1 January 1976 for his first two-year term. The 8th ICFM (Tripoli; May 1977), re-elected him for another term. Dr Gaye had tried his best to organize the 3rd Islamic summit that was eventually held after his retirement.

Habib Chatti: Chatti, a journalist, diplomat, and politician was born in 1916 at Msaken, Tunisia. He was educated at Sadeki College (Tunis). He first worked as a journalist in *La Presse de Tunisie* and *Tunis-soir* and later took over as Editor of *Az-Zohra* (1943–50) and *As Sabah* (1950–52). He was imprisoned by the French government in 1952–53 for his criticism of the colonial administration.[20]

Chatti was head of Press and Public Relations Office and member of National Council of Habib Borguiba's *Dastour* Party (1954–55) and the Director of *Al-Amal*. He later became the member of politburo of the Neo *Dastour* Party and also the Vice President of the Constituent National Assembly of the newly independent Tunisia, in 1956. His illustrious diplomatic career includes ambassadorial assignments to Lebanon (1957–59), Turkey (1959–63), UK (1962–64), Morocco (1964–68), and Algeria (1969–72). Chatti served as Director to the President's cabinet in 1972–74 and finally as Foreign Minister of Tunisia in 1974–77. He also served as Chairman of the Executive Council of the Arab League for some time.

On 7 October 1979, a special session of Islamic foreign ministers was convened at New York to find a successor to the outgoing Secretary General, Dr Amadou Gaye. Besides Chatti of Tunisia, Pakistan's Finance Minister Ghulam Ishaq Khan (later President of Pakistan) and Bangladesh's Foreign Minister Shamsudoha Choudhry were the other contenders.

On 8 October, a four-member committee comprising Morocco, Saudi Arabia, Turkey, and Cameroon, was formed to arrive at a consensus for the post. Pakistan's Foreign Minister Agha Shahi insisted that it was Asia's turn (Dr Gaye and Habib Chatti both belonged to Africa). Bangladesh was equally adamant on this point; while some states, Kuwait being prominent, argued that there were no geographical distinctions in Islam. At long last, Pakistan and Bangladesh agreed to withdraw, on the assurance that the next turn would definitely go to Asia. The OIC had for the first time, recognized the reality of the existence of geographical groupings within the Islamic body.[21]

So finally, Chatti was elected as a consensus candidate. His two-year term as Secretary General commenced from 1 January 1980. But when the 3rd Islamic summit met (Taif; 1981) it amended the Charter to increase the Secretary General's term from two to four years. His extended term was drawing to a close in late 1983, but as the 14th ICFM (Dhaka; December 1983) came to a deadlock on the issue of succession, Chatti manoeuvred to get another year on technical grounds, understandably with the blessings of King Hassan of Morocco.

During Chatti's tenure two Islamic summits, four ICFMs, and four extraordinary sessions of ICFM were held. Several serious challenges to the Islamic world including the Iran–Iraq war, Soviet invasion of Afghanistan, and Israeli invasion of Lebanon and PLO's subsequent expulsion therefrom, emerged during his term in office. Habib Chatti died at the age of 74, on 7 March 1991, after an unsuccessful open-heart surgery in Tunis.

Sharifuddin Pirzada: Born on 12 June 1923 at Burhanpur (India), he was educated at the University of Bombay (now called Mumbai). Pirzada joined politics in the early 1940s and served as a Secretary to Pakistan's founder Quaid-i-Azam Mohammad Ali Jinnah (1941–44); Secretary of Bombay City Muslim League, and Chairman of the Publicity Committee of the party's provincial chapter (1945–47). In 1947, when the subcontinent got its freedom and was partitioned into India and Pakistan, his family, like most Muslims, decided to migrate to Pakistan. After settling in Karachi, he took over as the Managing Editor of *Herald* in 1947.

Pirzada has had long associations with all of Pakistan's four military regimes. He remained Foreign Minister (1966–68) and Attorney General (1968–71) of Pakistan. In 1977, he became the Chairman of UN Human Rights Sub-committee on Minorities. He also became the member of International Law Commission, and Chairman, Experts Committee for Drafting Statute of the IICJ. He again remained Law Minister and Attorney General of Pakistan (1977–84) in the third military government.[22] The 15th ICFM (Sana'a; December 1984) elected him as the Secretary General against Mr Shamsudoha (Foreign Minister of Banglades) who had to withdraw, in the face of an imminent defeat. He held the office for four years. On 1 January 1989 his successor Dr Gabid took charge from him.

Since his retirement from OIC, he has been very active in the legal profession in Pakistan. The Supreme Court of Pakistan has also sought his opinion while hearing some constitutional petitions. He was inducted in the caretaker cabinet as foreign minister in April 1993, for a brief stint. Later in 1999, he became a civilian member of the ruling council of the military regime, as Law Adviser. He is the author of several books on the life of M.A. Jinnah, the founder of Pakistan.

Dr Hamid Al-Gabid: Dr Gabid was born in 1941 in the town of Tanout, Niger, then a part of Algeria. He got his early education in Niger. Then he proceeded to *Lycee El Biar* at Algiers, from where he obtained his High School Certificate (*Baccalaureat*). Afterwards he got an LL.B degree from the University of Abidjan, Ivory Coast. He holds a Diploma in Public Administration from the International Institute of Public Administration (IIAP), Paris, and another from the International Monetary Fund's Institute at Washington. He was awarded a Ph.D. for his thesis on the Banking system by the University of Paris (Sorbonne).[23]

He returned to his country and joined the Ministry of Finance, first as Director (1972–74) and then as its Secretary General (1974–75). He then became the Resident Executive Director of the Islamic Development Bank (1975–79). In 1979, he was back in his country and got his first political assignment as Secretary of State in the Ministry of Foreign Affairs (1979–81). During the next couple of years, he also served as the Minister of Commerce, then as Minister of Transport, and for a brief stint as the Finance Minister. In 1983, at the age of 42, he became the Prime Minister of Niger. He ruled the country till 1988 under difficult economic conditions.

He was first elected at the 17th ICFM (Amman; March 1988) to succeed Sharifuddin Pirzada, w.e.f. 1 January of the following year. In 1991, the 6th Islamic summit amended the Charter to give him another term and he got the second mandate in 1992. Dr Gabid is to date, the longest serving Secretary General of the OIC, and at the age of 48, the youngest one to assume this office. His tenure saw two Islamic summits, seven ICFMs, and two extraordinary sessions of Islamic foreign ministers' conference. The Gulf war, break up of the Soviet Union, and Bosnian and Chechnyan tragedies took place during his tenure. Similarly, the OIC membership was enlarged; Palestinians reached an understanding with Tel Aviv and the southern Philippines problem got resolved. Dr Gabid met with the Pope in Vatican to initiate a Muslim–Christian dialogue and brought about large-scale economic and financial reforms in the OIC. Just before his retirement in late 1996, he made a bid for the Secretary Generalship of the United Nations but lost to Kofi Annan of Ghana. He has been awarded the prestigious King Faisal Prize and numerous other international decorations.

Dr Izzuddiene Laraki: Laraki was born in 1929 in Fez, Morocco. After getting his basic education there, he moved to Paris to study in the Faculty of Medicine where he obtained his Ph.D. in 1957. After his return to Morocco he worked in the Ministry for National Education (1958) and the Ministry of Public Health (1959). In 1960, he joined the Avicenne Hospital as Director and Head of Respiratory Surgery Department. He also became professor in 1967 at the faculty of medicine in Rabat.[24] He later became the Chairman of the Faculty.

Laraki started taking active interest in politics from a very early age. He has adhered to the *Istiqlal* Party since 1942. As a companion of Syed Allal El Fassi, the popular leader of *Maghreb*, Laraki took part in the independence movement of Morocco. He became a member of the executive committee of the *Istiqlal* Party in 1977. He joined the cabinet as Minister for National Education and Cadres Training on 10 October, the same year. He was elevated to vice-premiership on 13 March 1986. Just a few months later, on 30 September 1986, King Hassan appointed him Prime Minister. In this capacity, he represented Morocco at the 5th (Kuwait; 1987) and the 6th (Dakar; 1991) Islamic Summits as well as several sessions of the Al-Quds Committee. He thus enjoys friendly relations with several Muslim statesmen.

Dr Laraki is a scholar with numerous research publications to his credit, both in the literary and the scientific fields. He holds senior offices at the Moroccan Writers Union and the Academy of the Kingdom of Morocco (AKM). In early 1996, he was elected President of the Board of Directors of the Al Akhawayne University, a post he still holds. Laraki is married and has three children.

In October 1996, Morocco announced that it was nominating Laraki to contest for the top slot of the OIC. Consequently, the 24th ICFM (Jakarta; December 1996) unanimously elected him successor to Dr Hamid Al-Gabid, for a four-year term. He was the only contender. Laraki claims that OIC is a very active organization and since its inception has taken giant leaps towards the goal of Islamic solidarity. He has vowed to make it more responsive to the problems of Islamic world during his tenure.[25]

An Assessment

In the final analysis one may make a few observations about the OIC bureaucracy. Firstly, there is a tradition that elected offices in the OIC are filled through consensus. We have seen that all the Secretary Generals have been elected unopposed. The same is true of the elections of the ASGs who are, by convention, nominated unanimously by an ICFM. The only time that an election took place was in late 1996 for the ASG seat reserved for Asia; Pakistan, Iran, and Indonesia were the three contenders. Pakistan's Additional Foreign Secretary Khalid Saleem, defeated his two rivals by a comfortable majority and took up his new assignment on 1 July 1997, on a four year deputation from Pakistan's Foreign Ministry.[26]

The second point relates to the appointments of the staff. Though a quota on the basis of equitable geographical distribution is maintained at the OIC Secretariat, most of the OIC organs are staffed by the locals only. And in violation of the laid down rules, the posts are not always properly advertised, so, except at the IDB, merit is usually compromised. Fouad A. Hameed Al-Khateeb, an ex-ASG from Saudi Arabia, once publicly admitted that 'the OIC could become more effective if a rational recruitment policy is applied for the Secretariat as well as the subsidiary organs' instead of accepting mediocre officials of member-states on deputation.[27] It also needs to be noted that the Secretary General has been granted unduly wide powers in the matter of appointments. There is at least one incident when there was a serious row between a Secretary General (Tunku Abdul Rahman) and a member state (Pakistan) on the matter of appointment of an official against the seat reserved for the latter.[28]

Finally, the OIC bureaucracy is characterized by the perennial shortage of manpower and finances. We have already noted that the OIC offices are poorly staffed and its officials grossly under-paid. Many a time, different OIC organs have defaulted on payments to their staff for ten months or so, in a row. Given these circumstances, the output of the OIC Secretariat and its various subsidiary organs is really commendable.

The 8th Islamic summit (Tehran; December 1997) has constituted a permanent experts committee for administrative and financial affairs that will consider the administrative problems of the Organization and the non-payment of contributions by the member states. It will also make recommendations for a more equitable upward revision of salaries of the OIC employees.[29]

NOTES and REFERENCES

1. See Dale Van Atta, 'The folly of UN peace-keeping', *Readers Digest*, Asia Edition, Hong Kong, November 1995; and part two of the same article, 'The United Nations is out of control', *Readers Digest,* December 1995, for an interesting account of the corruption, inefficiency and financial mismanagement in the UN bureaucracy.

2. The figures are good for 1992. See, *Basic facts about the UN*, (New York: UN Secretariat, 1993), pp. 20–26.

3. The Secretary General's actions were a corollary of the mandate given to him by the 18th ICFM (Riyadh; March 1989) to restructure the Secretariat to reduce expenditure. See the report of *Saudi Gazette*, Riyadh, 11 June 1989.

4. The information about the strength and functions of the OIC General Secretariat staff was provided to the author by the OIC permanent mission in Islamabad. The information about the employees of the subsidiary organs has been taken from their annual activity reports. For instance, see the *20th Annual Report of the Islamic Development Bank*, (Jeddah: IDB, 1996), p. 163, for information about IDB employees.

5. A copy of *Personnel Regulations of the OIC*, (Jeddah, 1990), copy of the resolution no. 1/19-ORG, by virtue of which the 19th ICFM approved the Regulations and the Report of the seventh session of the Committee of Seven (Vide No. 7MC/6-90/REP/FINAL; dated 16 July 1990) on which the regulations are based, were provided to the author by the Permanent Mission of the OIC in Islamabad. The same regulations were in force, as of mid-1999 and the given information is based on this source.

6. See, *Personnel Regulations*, op. cit., Article 10 (Para 2) and its Annexure 2.

7. This is how the IFSTAD used to define the talents of the Muslim world (IFSTAD has now been dissolved). See Abdullah Ahsan, *Ummah or Nation: Identity crisis in the Muslim world*, (Leicester: Islamic Foundation. 1992), p. 110.

8. Also see Chapter 12: 'Disciplinary Measures' in the *Personnel Regulations*, ref. 5.

9. Ibid., see Annexures 3 and 4 of the Regulations.

10. Ibid., see Article 8.

11. See, *The News*, Islamabad, 19 July 1991. Also see *Pakistan Times*, Islamabad, 14 February 1991.

12. On the insistence of the then Secretary General Tunku Abdul Rahman, the framers of the OIC Charter made the election of ASGs subject to the recommendation of the Secretary General. Tunku argued that smooth running of the OIC could be jeopardized if the ICFMs would elect the ASGs directly without reference to the OIC Secretary General.

13. See, *Guide to the OIC*, (Jeddah: OIC Secretariat, 1995), pp. 27–29.

14. Noor Ahmad Baba, *OIC: Theory and Practice of Pan-Islamic Cooperation*, (Karachi: Oxford University Press, 1994), p. 212.

15. For a brief life sketch of Tunku Abdul Rahman, see *Encyclopaedia Britannica*, (Chicago: 1977), vol. 1, p. 16.

16. Inamullah Khan (ed.), *World Muslim Gazetteer: 1985*, (Karachi: WMC, 1987), p. 55.

17. See, *Africa's Who's Who*, (London: African Books Ltd., 1981), p. 1096.

18. Ibid., pp. 449–50.

19. *Keesing's Contemporary Archives, 1975*, p. 27294.

20. *Who's Who*, ref. 17, p. 264.

21. See, *Pakistan Times*, 7, 9, and 10 October 1979.

22. See, *The International Who's Who*, (London, Europpa Publications Ltd., 1992), p. 1289. Pirzada's bio-data also appears in the *Introduction of Speeches and Statements of the OIC Secretary General Sharif Pirzada*, (Karachi, n. p., 1989).

23. See, *Dr. Hamid Al-Gabid: A profile*, (Jeddah: OIC Secretariat, 1993), pp. 1–8.

24. The life sketch of Laraki has been prepared from *Who's Who*, ref. 22, p. 933 and the SESRTCIC/OIC website on the internet (http://www.sesrtcic.org). His bio-data also appears in *The Muslim World*, (Karachi: WMC), vol. 34, no. 34, 17 May 1997, p. 1.

25. *The News*, 16 December 1996.

26. Ibid., 24 July 1997.

27. Baba, ref. 14, p. 213.

28. Tunku appointed a person settled in Britain, of Pakistani origin but then holding British nationality, as Director against the vacancy reserved for Pakistan without consulting Islamabad which naturally annoyed the latter. See, *Nawa-e-Waqt* (Urdu), Islamabad, 28 November 1973.

29. See, resolution no. 2/8-97/AF (IS) of the 8th Islamic summit (Tehran; 1997).

4 Analysis of the Islamic Charter

The Charter or Statute of an international organization is one of the most sacrosanct documents of international law. A Charter evinces the minimum common denominators on which a certain number of sovereign states, the signatories to that Charter, agree. It also reflects the nature and orientation of the international organization concerned. It is not unusual for a Charter to be ambiguous, so that different states could interpret it in different ways; and moreover, a gulf between theory and practice of a Charter is not rare either. In fact, it is the conventions developed by an organization that accentuate certain articles of the legal document, overshadowing certain others. The analysis of a Charter makes an interesting study with respect to international organizations.

The Charter of the OIC is a unique document in many ways. First of all, it is the constitution of the only *religious* inter-governmental organization of the world. We shall come to the religious character of the OIC a little later, suffice it to say here that the emphasis on Islam in the Charter, which also recurs in all the OIC documents, declarations, and agreements, distinguishes it from other Charters. In this way, the Charter purports to reflect certain values and thus tries to develop an 'Islamic vision' of international relations. Needless to say, the tenets of the religion brought by Prophet Mohammad (PBUH) one and a half millennium ago, do not necessarily correspond with the present day Geneva and Hague conventions. But as we shall see below, disrespect to international legality was never the intention of the framers of the OIC Charter.[1] The OIC argues that its values do not contradict international legality and that there is no conflict between its Islamic and international identities, since cherishing universal fraternal sentiments is itself an Islamic teaching.

Another observation regarding the Islamic Charter is that it is very ambiguous. This is a consequence of the diversity within the Organization which is composed of 55 nation-states, spread over four continents and with a population exceeding one billion. This composition includes monarchies and democracies, secular states and theocratic ones, land-locked states and archipelagoes; the only common factor being that a significant population within each member state adheres to the Muslim faith. The Charter is thus a short document consisting of a preamble and just fourteen articles. This is a compromise between the 55 states. The Charter has a very deficient legal framework and the Organization has to violate or circumvent its own Charter, more often than not, to formulate a decisive response to a challenge, like punishing a prodigal member-state, etc. Likewise, the Charter is very vague in defining the membership criterion, so that virtually any developing state can apply for membership.[2] And a final observation regarding the OIC Charter characteristics, is the gap between the letter and practice. There are certain things that the OIC effects regularly but they have no mention in the Charter, and yet others that the Organization shies away from, but they are stipulated under the Charter. First of all, we shall discuss the nature of the OIC, then move on to the philosophy of the OIC Charter, and finally analyse the Charter.

Nature of the Organization

International organizations aim primarily at cooperation in one or more of four areas, namely, politics, economics, security, and religion. As for the last category, the OIC is the only inter-governmental organization that operates under this head. The establishment of the OIC was a culmination of a long struggle for a Pan-Islamic organization and in the end, was a direct response to a religious stimulus, i.e., the arson and desecration of the third holiest shrine of Islam, the Al Aqsa Mosque at Jerusalem. The immediate prelude to the OIC, the Islamic conferences at

Kuala Lumpur (April 1969) and Rabat (September 1969) were convened basically to discuss religious issues. Its religious character remained dominant in the formative years of the OIC.

In the face of vehement opposition by a host of Muslim states, the organization gradually started veering into the political field. The first step in this direction was taken when the PLO delegations were, after considerable wrangling, admitted in both the above conferences. The 3rd ICFM (Jeddah; 1972), for the first time discussed a wide gamut of political issues. By the time the 2nd Islamic Summit conference (Lahore; 1974) took place, the OIC had become a political organization in the true sense of the word. The 3rd Islamic Summit (Taif; 1981) added a new dimension to the activities of the OIC by approving the Plan of Action for enhancing economic cooperation among the Islamic countries. In the following half a decade, a number of subsidiary organs emerged within the OIC framework in the field of economic cooperation. Around the same time, the OIC took upon itself to work for the preservation of Islamic cultural heritage and for undertaking research on Islamic history, art, and culture.

Perusing the list of forty-eight of the OIC's specialized and subsidiary organs and affiliated institutions, one finds a noticeable omission. There is not one institution in the field of defence cooperation. Although the OIC has time and again emphasized that the security of any one Muslim country is the vital concern of the whole Muslim world, but in the absence of a formidable military apparatus under the OIC framework, such pronouncements cannot have a tangible effect on the ground realities. As a corollary, the Conference has no coercive implementation machinery, peacekeeping mechanism, or a collective security system. And the member states have to invite other international and regional organizations for such purposes. Thus at this juncture, we have determined that the OIC is a religious, political, economic, and cultural institution of sovereign states and the one thing it is not, is a defence arrangement. So we have to look at the Charter in this light.

Philosophy of the OIC Charter

As for the *raison d'etre* of the emergence of the OIC, there are two schools of thought. One school believes that the OIC is a sequel to the institution of the Caliphate, albeit in a different form, and is the outcome of the psychological and emotional need of the Muslims, if not a religious obligation, to have some sort of a symbolic central authority. The same was vested in the person of the Caliph till the institution of Caliphate got abolished in 1924; then the struggle to find an alternative, led to the emergence of the OIC in 1969.[3] The Organization thus is mandated to look after the interests of the Muslim World, to act as its principal spokesman, to protect the rights of Muslim communities and to promote cooperation in the Muslim states in all fields including politics, security, trade, maritime activities, aviation, sports, and others.

The second school considers any connection between the Caliphate and the OIC as bigoted and parochial and does not see Islam *per se* as the basis of the Organization. Instead, the exponents of this school trace the foundations and activities of the OIC in the correlation of a number of factors. For instance, they argue that the world is rapidly transforming into a global village and because of the new interdependence, no country can live in isolation politically or economically. Consequently, there is a mushroom growth of international organizations, especially regional ones. The states form them or join them, to enhance political standing and to explore avenues of economic and trade partnerships. Thus the Afro-Asian states lying in the contiguous land mass between the Far East in Asia and Morocco in North West Africa, the majority of which happen to be Muslim-majority countries, have established a number of regional organizations, the OIC being one of the most prominent. Since, in pursuit of national interests, the states try to gatecrash into the maximum number of international organizations, the impressive membership of the OIC has its roots in the economic motives of member states. The ex-Soviet Muslim republics, for that matter, are still being ruled by secular former Communist elite but have joined the Islamic Conference, to enhance their bargaining position against a possible blackmail by Moscow, which still considers itself their big brother.[4] Similarly, Turkey which has always been a very active member in the Islamic Conference is waging a relentless struggle to join the European Union as well. Thus the Islamic Conference is a modern inter-governmental organization, not much different from other regional organizations in orientation and scope.

Even a cursory glance at the OIC Charter testifies that the truth lies somewhere in the middle. The emergence of the Islamic Conference was actually a synthesis between the two ideas of the traditional *ummah* concept and the modern nation-state system. The first three paragraphs of the Preamble of the Charter indicate the Islamic nationhood as the basis of the Organization while the latter three emphasize the commitment of the signatories towards universal peace and progress. Again, in Article II of the Charter, one discerns a clear Islamic tinge in the list of the OIC objectives but Part B of the same article, which speaks of the principles under which the OIC is to operate, suggests the OIC's respect for the modern nation-state system. The principles appear to be borrowed from the UN Charter, thus indicating that the OIC does not aim at establishing a trans-national Islamic confederation but is content with trying to promote cooperation, while giving due respect to the existing boundaries.[5]

An Analysis of the Charter Provisions

The Charter names thirty Muslim countries as the founder members of the Organization and begins with the convictions of the member states that led them to found the Organization and approve the Charter. It states that the member states are *convinced* that:

> 'their common belief constitutes a strong factor for…solidarity between Islamic peoples'; *resolved* to 'preserve the Islamic spiritual, social and economic values' which is an 'important factor of achieving progress for mankind'; *reaffirm* their 'commitment to the UN Charter and fundamental human rights' because their purposes provide 'the basis for fruitful cooperation amongst all people'; *determined* to

'consolidate the bonds of prevailing brotherly and spiritual friendship among their people….' and are *endeavoring* to 'increase human well-being, progress and freedom everywhere and resolved to unite their efforts in order to secure universal peace which ensures security, freedom and justice for…people…throughout the world'.[6]

It becomes clear that the member states have purportedly closed ranks since the common faith (Islam) is a 'strong factor for solidarity' and the OIC wants to further consolidate the *existing* 'brotherly and spiritual friendship' among them. The preamble specifies that the 'Islamic values' are important factor for achieving the progress of the whole mankind and that the principles of fundamental human rights provide the basis for cooperation among all people. In view of these things, the Charter announces, the member states are endeavouring to ensure freedom, security, justice, toleration and non-discrimination 'for their people and all people' of the world. At no point does the preamble suggest that geographical contiguity, cultural affinity, or, for that matter, shared economic interests, might have brought the member countries on a single platform.

This predominantly Islamic character of the preamble and its reference to the common faith of the peoples highlights an inherent contradiction. Abdullah Ahsan points out that the OIC is not an organization of Muslim peoples but of Muslim states; obviously a state represents its whole population, Muslim and non-Muslim. Herein lies the problem, Ahsan believes, that either the OIC presupposes cent per cent population of the member states to be Muslim, or ignores a significant segment of their populace.[7] Another problem is discussed by Noor Ahmad Baba, who argues that by reaffirming the commitment to the UN Charter, the Islamic Conference has not only accepted a subservient status for its own Charter but has also arrogated for itself permanent underdog status *vis-á-vis* the United Nations.[8]

These two flaws in the preamble have led a few Muslim countries with secular constitutions not to ratify the Charter on the one hand; and have given the members a backdoor to wriggle out of their responsibility as a Muslim state under the garb of commitment to UN Charter on the other.[9] For instance, no Muslim state sent its troops to save the Bosnian Muslims from the 1994–95 carnage, because such military activity needed the permission of the UN Security Council which was not forthcoming. Thus the obligation to 'promote Islamic solidarity and protect Muslim communities' was coming into conflict with the 'commitment to the UN Charter', leaving the member states to chart their own course, according to their interpretation of the OIC Charter.

Name, Objectives, and Principles

Article I declares the name of the organization to be the Organization of 'The Islamic Conference'.[10] This is so because back in 1969, the countries that gathered to discuss an Islamic issue and to demonstrate their Islamic solidarity, thereby chose to qualify themselves as 'Islamic'. As was explained at the outset, the Islamic Conference is a synthesis between the objectives of Islamic solidarity and the principles of modern state system; this very fact is reflected in Article II of the Charter that defines the objectives and principles of the OIC. One finds that the objectives of the OIC are 'Islamic' (and Article IX of the OIC Charter itself qualifies the objectives enumerated in Article II as Islamic) and the principles are 'secular'.

Though the Organization does not subscribe to the traditional concept of the Islamic jurisprudence that the world is divided into a *Dar al Islam* (The Muslim world) and a *Dar al Harb* (The enemy world), but it has in its Article II, developed two separate sets of rules, one for relations among the member-states and the other for relations with non-member states. The Article II (A) defines its objectives by exhorting the members to unite with each other, 'make efforts' for eradicating colonialism, and 'support' the liberation of occupied lands. It is silent on whether the efforts are to be violent or non-violent. At no point does the Charter rule in or rule out military means to achieve the ends. But reading together all the relevant paras in the preamble and the text of the Charter, thus noting the OIC's desire to promote peace and its commitment to the UN Charter, one gets the impression that offensive military

measures by the OIC or any of its member state are absolutely forbidden. When the OIC Charter talks of exerting all means, say, for restitution of occupied lands and safeguard of holy places, it does not violate the international legality which allows the use of military force in self-defence and to deter aggression.[11] The collective security measures against Iraq are a case in point. On the other hand, part B of the same Article, which exclusively deals with relations among member states, completely outlaws threat or use of force.[12] This is so because the OIC believes in the existence of a special notion of fraternity among all the Muslim states.

Objectives: The OIC Charter has enunciated seven goals of the Organization. These are: (a) to promote Islamic solidarity among member states; (b) to consolidate cooperation among member states in the economic, social, cultural, scientific, and other vital fields of activities, and to facilitate consultation among its member-states in international organizations; (c) to eradicate racial discrimination, and to eliminate all forms of colonization; (d) to take necessary measures to support international peace and security founded on justice; (e) to strengthen the struggle of all Muslim peoples with a view to safeguarding their dignity, independence, and national rights; and (g) to create a suitable atmosphere for the promotion of cooperation and understanding among member-states and other countries.

The first objective of the Organization, to promote Islamic solidarity is a self standing objective of the OIC. The second objective with its multiple aims further spells out the possible areas of cooperation and also mandates the Organization to carry out consultations among the member states. The Islamic conferences at various levels, held under the OIC auspices, are in realization of this objective. The third objective is a reflects OIC's endeavour to achieve Afro-Asian solidarity by trying to eliminate colonialism, imperialism, racism and discrimination. However, it does not emphasize non-alignment since such a reference could have led to the exclusion of a number of Muslim countries, which were at any given time, allied with either super power. But in practice, the OIC did maintain a strictly non-aligned posture throughout the cold-war era, irrespective of the foreign policy inclinations of the individual member-states.[13] Support of international peace and security 'based on justice' is another aim of the OIC. The Charter talks of 'justice' alone while the UN Charter, in this context, refers to 'justice and international law'. The framers of the OIC Charter did have optimum respect for international legality but, as Hassan Moinuddin notes, the OIC believes that the writ of law sometimes conflicts with the demands of justice.[14] This very belief led the OIC to reject some of the UN Security Council resolutions regarding Palestine, Bosnia etc., where it believed the world body resolutions were favouring the aggressor, or treating the aggressor and the victim on equal terms.

The fifth objective obliges the OIC to coordinate efforts to safeguard the holy places and help the Palestinians to liberate their lands. Referring to a problem by name, quite unusual for the Charters of international bodies, evinces the commitment of the OIC to the Palestine cause, which was originally its *raison d'etre*. Most of the detractors of the OIC criticize it for its failure to liberate Palestine, but we see from the text that the Charter has asked the OIC to 'help' the Palestinians to liberate their land, and not to take-up arms itself for this liberation. Another point that needs to be mentioned is that by 'holy places', the OIC means Islamic holy places alone, though the text suggests that the Organization is committed to safeguard the holy places of any religion, threatened by its opponents. But in such cases, one has to look into the intentions of the framers, rather than wording of the text, to guess the aim of the document. The next point brackets all the struggles of the Muslim peoples, other than the Palestinians, for safeguarding their independence and rights, and obliges the OIC to strengthen the same.[15] And the final objective of the OIC is to create an atmosphere of cooperation and understanding among the member states and the non-member states. This reinforces the OIC commitments for international peace and harmony, delineated earlier in the preamble.

Principles: In order to realize the objectives, Article II mentions five principles, namely, (a) total equality among the member states; (b) respect of the right to self-determination, and non-intervention in the domestic affairs of the member states; (c) respect of the sovereignty, independence, and territorial integrity of each member state; (d) settlement of disputes that may arise, by peaceful means such as negotiation, mediation, reconciliation or arbitration, and (e) abstention from the use of or the threat to use force against the territorial integrity, national unity or political independence of any member state. The principles emphasize several elements of the UN Charter. Thus the OIC does not have a trans-national confederation of the Muslim states on its present agenda, as it respects the existing reality of the Muslim countries as being separate, sovereign, political units.

Structure and Functions

Article III describes the structure of the Islamic Conference as consisting of four principal organs; the Islamic Summit Conference, the Islamic Foreign Ministers' Conference (commonly known as the ICFM), the General Secretariat (and its subsidiary organs) and the Islamic International Court of Justice (IICJ). The last mentioned organ was included in the said Article in 1981 when the decision to set up the IICJ was taken. The following three Articles, respectively, define the functions of the first three principal organs of the OIC. As for the IICJ, its composition and functions are given in its statute, separately adopted by the 5th Islamic Summit (Kuwait; 1987). In any case, the Court is not yet in operation since the necessary number of ratifications have not so far been deposited.

Summit and the ICFM: Article IV of the OIC Charter declares the Conference of Kings and Heads of State (Islamic Summit) as the supreme authority of the Conference that usually meets once every three years to discuss issues of vital concern to the Muslims. Article V which deals with the ICFM, is more detailed. It says that the ICFM meets annually, and if the request of any member state or that of the Secretary General to the effect is supported by a two-thirds majority, it also meets in emergency sessions. It is mandated to adopt resolutions on matters of common interest, implement the general policy of the Organization, review the progress regarding the previous decisions, finalize and adopt the OIC budget, vote to fill in the elected offices of the OIC, and approve the convening of an Islamic summit conference, the next ICFM etc. Its resolutions are adopted by the two-thirds majority and two-thirds of member-states in any session which form the quorum.

In the first thirty years of the OIC's existence, the ICFM has met in twenty-five regular and seven emergency sessions and it has developed a number of conventions. For instance, all resolutions are adopted through consensus rather than two-thirds majority.[16] Usually, the posts of Secretary General and his Assistants are also filled through unanimity. Though the ICFM is authorized to consider any matter that concerns one or more member states, but it has usually refrained from discussing matters concerning 'one' member state, like civil wars, the human rights situation, domestic political turmoils etc., except when the government concerned has no objection to the matter being taken up—which happens rarely. But the ICFM does consider issues that fall under the domestic jurisdiction of non-member states, like condition of Muslim minorities, development of nuclear weapons and the like. There is no provision in Article V, that would explicitly allow the ICFM to consider problems that do not directly concern the member states, yet in practice this may happen.

OIC Chairmanship: The last clause of Article V requires the ICFM to develop basic procedures to run its business, including the appointment of a Chairman for each session, which will also hold good for the Summit conferences. The host country, by convention, assumes the Chairmanship.

The chairman of an ICFM or that of the Islamic Summit retains office till the next conference of the kind. The Islamic Summit Chairman is also deemed as the Chairman of the OIC. Since the Charter says no more on the subject, there is an aura of ambiguity surrounding the office and functions of the Chairman OIC. One question is whether the head of state or the head of

government of the host state is to be the Chairman of the Islamic Summit. The convention is that the King, President, or the Prime Minister of the host state becomes the Summit Chairman, depending on whether the state has a totalitarian monarchy, a presidential or a parliamentary form of government. So, among others, King Khalid of Saudi Arabia, President Abdou Diouf of Senegal, and Prime Minister Zulfikar Ali Bhutto of Pakistan, have held this post. At the 8th Islamic Summit (Tehran; 1997) there was initially some confusion over whether the Iranian President Khatami or the supreme spiritual leader Ali Khaminei, was becoming the OIC Chairman. The controversy was resolved in favour of the former.

Another question arises as to whether it is the person or the office of the head of the host State that is elected as Chairman. King Khalid of Saudi Arabia died during his tenure as the OIC Chief and his successor King Fahd was accepted as the new Chairman. But the matter usually turns out to be thornier. For instance, Kuwait was annexed by Iraq, when the Amir of Kuwait was still the OIC Chairman. Had President Saddam Hussain of Iraq, therefore become the Chairman of the OIC during the period of occupation? Much earlier Z.A. Bhutto, the first ever directly elected leader of Pakistan, was overthrown and imprisoned by the military in a *coup d'etat*, while he was still the OIC Chairman. While in prison he still believed that he was the OIC Chairman since the Islamic Conference had elected his person to the office. Two years later, when the decision to execute him was made public, several Muslim leaders made clemency pleas to the Pakistan's military government on his behalf, referring to Mr Bhutto as the OIC Chairman.[17] It was after Bhutto's death that the military ruler Gen. Zia came to be accepted as the new OIC chairman.

Another irony is that the OIC chairmen themselves, are often unsure of their role. Hence, the office has become symbolic, with the Chairman occasionally making general statements on the OIC's behalf expressing concern about some Islamic issue. On its part, at the conclusion of the Chairman's three-year tenure, the OIC passes resolutions commending his 'wisdom, sagacity, and statesmanship' for 'excellently running the OIC'.

General Secretariat: Article VI of the Charter describes the structure and functions of the executive organ of the Organization, viz. the General Secretariat. As per clause 1, it is to be headed by a Secretary General, elected by ICFM for a four-year renewable term, who in turn, according to clause 2, appoints the staff of the Secretariat, 'paying due regard to their competence and integrity, and in accordance with the principle of equitable geographical distribution'. The practice is that only Muslim persons of the member states are employed at the Secretariat. Clause 3 requires the staff to place the interests of the Organization supreme; forbids them from taking instructions from anywhere except the Conference and expects the member states to undertake not to influence their nationals working at the OIC in any way. Clause 5 designates Jeddah as the location of the OIC headquarters 'pending the liberation of Jerusalem'. Clause 8 confers the status of international diplomats on the OIC staff and states that the Conference itself and its employees in the member states and the accredited representatives of member states at the Conference, shall enjoy such 'immunities and privileges as may be required in the exercise of their functions' and in the light of the 'agreement on immunities and privileges' concluded by the Conference. The remaining three clauses (4, 6, and 7) dilate upon the duties and responsibilities of the Secretariat, that include securing communication among the member states, dissemination of information, following up the implementation of the resolutions of the Conference, supply of working papers to the member states and preparation of the OIC meetings in collaboration with the host states on administrative matters.

A notable omission in this Article is the absence of a definition of the role and powers of the OIC Secretary General, except in the matter of appointment of staff. A former UN Secretary General, Perez de Cuellar, had once termed the UN Charter, '*Une Charte piegee*' (booby-trapped Charter), which left him without any power to enforce a decision and made all major decisions subject to veto.[18] The OIC Secretary General is much weaker than his counterpart at the United Nations, since he has virtually no power to make a decision, enforce one, or even to convene an emergency ICFM, which requires the support of two-thirds of the member states. He is even careful not to make statements on behalf of the OIC, as its policy could change suddenly without his opinion being sought.

Finance

Article VII deals with financial matters, and like all other international organizations, places the burden of expenses on mandatory contributions from member states 'according to their national incomes'. A formula to apportion the share of each state has been worked out and is revised every few years. At present, the basic contribution to the Secretariat budget (that obviously excludes contribution to its specialized organs and affiliated institutions, which have their own independent formulas) is $94,000 per annum. The Less Developed Muslim Countries (LDMCs) are obliged to pay this amount; Pakistan and Oman have been assessed to pay four times this amount, Kuwait, eighteen times, Saudi Arabia, twenty times the basic contribution and so on. Paragraph 2 of this article vests the ICFM with the authority to approve the rules of procedure for financial affairs, under which the Secretariat is to administer the money. Para 3 establishes the Permanent Finance Committee of the OIC that meets at the Secretariat to draft and supervise the budget.

Membership

The Charter lays down the conditions and procedure for membership to the OIC in Article VIII. The vague wording of this Article has created some legal problems as we shall see. One finds two separate sets of criteria for membership in Article VIII; one for the founder members and one for the states that join the Organization later on. For the first category, the Charter says that the OIC 'is made up of states which took part in' the Rabat Islamic Summit and the first two ICFMs 'held in Jeddah and Karachi, and are signatories to the present Charter'. The number of member states that attended the Rabat Summit, the first ICFM, and the second ICFM, stood at twenty-five, twenty-two and twenty-three, respectively. In all, there were twenty-seven Muslim countries that had participated in, at least, one of these three moots. Since the Charter was adopted by the 3rd ICFM (Jeddah; 1972) three more states became signatories to the Charter, qualifying themselves as founder members according to the second criterion above. Thus the names of the thirty states appear at the beginning of the Charter. For future membership, Article VIII goes on to state:

> Every Muslim State is eligible to join the Islamic Conference on submitting an application expressing its desire and preparedness to adopt this Charter. The application shall be deposited with the General Secretariat, to be brought before the Foreign Ministers' Conference at its first meeting after the submission of the application. Membership shall take effect as of the time approval of the Conference by a two-third majority of the Conference members.

Thus there are five conditions for membership; the applicant should be a State; it should be a *Muslim* state; desirous to join the Islamic Conference; prepared to adopt its Charter; and its application should be approved by two-thirds majority at the next ICFM.

For the sake of comparison, let us examine the UN Charter. By virtue of its Article IV, the UN Charter lays down four more or less similar conditions for membership: that the applicant country should be (i) a sovereign state; (ii) peace-loving; (iii) willing to accept the Charter obligations and (iv) able to carry out these obligations. The fifth condition, which the Charter does not lay but is followed in practice, is that a positive recommendation should come from the UN Security Council and the General Assembly should approve it by a two-thirds majority. Interestingly enough, four of the fifty-one founder members of the UN were not sovereign states at that time. British India (now India and Pakistan) and Philippines were colonies of Britain and the USA, respectively. They were inducted as prospective independent states but the same could not be applied to Ukraine and Bylorussia, which were for all practical purposes, provinces of the then USSR, but were granted separate voting rights as sovereign states.

The ambiguity in the UN Charter on membership questions led to many more quizzical situations. The super powers used the veto freely to deny membership to the newly-independent states suspected of being allies of the other side of the divide. Till 1955, the pro-US West Germany and South Korea were not UN members. Their mere observer status did not bar them from being the members of several UN Committees. As for China, the UN Credentials Committee gave its seat to Taiwan on technical grounds.

Except for India, which was expelled at the first Islamic Summit, the OIC has never rejected any member state that is 'desirous' to join the Islamic Conference. And the decision to induct new members has always been taken unanimously, rather than by two-thirds majority. As for the 'preparedness to adopt its Charter', we have earlier noted, the OIC has shown some flexibility towards the Muslim states that have secular constitutions. The real problems lie in the definition of *Muslim* state and, more interestingly, the definition of *state* itself. The very absence of these definitions has resulted in elasticity in the rules and regulations of the OIC regarding membership.

Problem of definition of a Muslim state: The Charter lays down that *Muslim* states are eligible to become its members, but it is silent on the criterion for a state being deemed Muslim. Hence one has to look elsewhere for the definition. The obvious protocol would be to label the Islamic states (where Islam is the state religion and Islamic laws are in force) as Muslim states. But such a definition would lead to secular states with Muslim majority (like Turkey with 99 per cent Muslim population), being characterized as non-Muslim states, which would be grossly unfair. An alternative solution, more plausible at the first glance, is to deem any state, where Muslims constitute more than 50 per cent of the population, as a Muslim state. The closer we come to this definition, the more blurred it becomes. Firstly, there is the problem of the high unreliability of the statistics regarding religious composition in many developing states. And secondly, such a rigid criterion would lead to the exclusion of many borderline cases like Bosnia (with 47 per cent Muslims) from the definition of Muslim state.

Hence, we need to look for a more comprehensive and scholarly definition. A noted scholar on Islam, M. Ali Kettani, gives the definition of a Muslim state as one 'that is a member of the OIC'.[19] This of course is not helpful, so we should search for the answer in the conventions adopted by the OIC itself, regarding the induction of new member states. We discern four criteria:

i.   Islamic states (Iran, Pakistan, Saudi Arabia etc.)
ii. Secular states with Muslim majorities (Indonesia, Turkey etc.); even if the head of state may occasionally be a non-Muslim (Chad, Nigeria etc.)
iii. Countries where Muslims and non-Muslims are almost equal but the Muslims have a significant share in government (Kazakhstan, Lebanon etc.)
iv. Non-Muslim majority countries, provided that:
     a) the Muslims are the single largest community, or form a substantial minority; and
     b) the head of state is a Muslim or has converted to Islam (Gabon, Uganda etc.)

There can hardly be two opinions regarding the first two criteria for defining a Muslim state. But the latter two criterions are controversial, even if the state concerned is itself willing to be identified as an OIC member. For instance, coming to the third criterion, the OIC has admitted Kazakhstan, a secular state with barely over 50 per cent Muslims. The country has around 38 per cent ethnic Russian population and 12 per cent other non-Muslim minorities including Ukrainians, Bylorussians, and Armenians. The country has a presidential form of government. Traditionally, the president is a Kazakh Muslim while the Prime Minister is usually an ethnic Russian belonging to the Christian Orthodox Church. Similarly, in Lebanon, another member of the OIC, an estimated 57 per cent of the people are Muslims but under the pre-Second World War arrangement brokered by the French colonial administration, the posts of President, Prime Minister, and the Speaker are always held by a Maronite Christian, a *Sunni* Muslim, and a *Shiite* Muslim, respectively. Now since the OIC has also inducted the country as a full member, sometimes an unwelcome situation is created. For instance, the incident at the 3rd Islamic Summit (Taif; 1981) where Lebanon was being represented by the Christian President. When

in the inaugural session, the Muslim leaders assembled in the Grand Mosque of Mecca for prayers, the Lebanese President was stopped because under the Islamic law, non-Muslims cannot enter the holy *Ka'aba* or the surrounding holy mosque (*Masjid al Haraam*).[20] Because of the inherent contradictions within the OIC Charter, and between the Charter and the practice, such unpleasantries are unavoidable.

And finally, Albania can be enumerated in this category which till 1939 had a 75 per cent Musim majority but after half a century of Communist dictatorship, when especially during Enver Hoxha's rule, religion as well as its practice and teaching were banned, it is uncertain how many people still profess Islam. But since the people are of Muslim origin and have not accepted another religion, they can be counted as Muslims. Most of the Albanian Muslims do not follow the Islamic religious rituals strongly but it is the cultural Islam that characterizes them as Muslims, since in Europe, religious following is calculated through taking into account the dominant culture in the lives of people.[21]

Countries like Gabon and Uganda fall under the fourth category. Uganda submitted its request for membership during the rule of President Idi Amin, a Muslim, though the different estimates put the figure of Muslims in the country at 20 to 40 per cent. The application was accepted in 1974, all the same. Gen. Amin was overthrown in a *coup d'etat* in 1979, in spite of which Uganda has retained the OIC membership. In the case of Gabon, President Robert Bango had converted to Islam, and assumed the name Omer Bango. Gabon too got OIC membership on President Omer Bango's request. (The most flattering statistics put the figure of Muslims in Gabon at 10 per cent, Christians about 25 per cent and the rest following the indigenous religions.)

Bosnia is another example, where 47 per cent Muslims constitute the single largest community and the President, Vice President, and one of the two co-Prime Ministers, are usually Muslims. Suriname is a notable exception in this category, where there are 35 per cent Muslims but there has never been a Muslim President. There were a few other factors that led to the admission of Suriname as a member and Guyana as an observer, the foremost being that their Muslim populations are well-treated and are well-represented in the state structures. Unlike all the other Caricom states, Suriname and Guyana have mostly voted with the Muslim bloc at the UN General Assembly on issues like Palestine, Kashmir, and Bosnia. If their decision to join the OIC was driven by economic diplomacy, the latter was no less keen to get a foothold across the Atlantic. Then there are a couple of countries, Trinidad & Tobago in the Carribean and Fiji in Oceana, which have significant Muslim populations, and did have at least one Muslim President and Muslim Prime Minister, respectively, but have never shown any interest in joining the OIC.

The impressive membership of the OIC, is a manifestation of its flexibility. This is how the OIC has opened its doors to several former Communist Muslim states in Asia and Europe and it has resulted in the OIC becoming a very diverse and large organization.

Problem of sovereign states: The term *state* in the OIC Charter, appears to denote the sovereign actors on the international scene. But as early as in 1974, the OIC had granted Palestine, or more specifically the PLO, the status of a full member, though, Palestine did not exist as a state at all. In another strange move, the OIC accepted the membership request of Zanzibar in 1992 which, since its union with the mainland Tanzania in 1964, was not a sovereign state any longer. However, the OIC did not recognize or admit Chechenya and Tartaristan, the two Muslim republics that had seceded from the Russian Federation, though Moscow did not recognize the secession (in fact, these two states never made a formal request to join the OIC). This fact alone highlights another contradiction in the Islamic Conference—that apparently it does not want to annoy a powerful country.

Problem of Muslim minority representations: This fact also merits attention that there is no allowance for the representation of Muslim communities at any level in the OIC political set up. So the OIC takes notice of a major crisis that afflicts any of the Muslim minority communities only when a member country raises the issue, like Turkey in the case of Bulgarian Muslims, Pakistan in the case of Indian Muslims, and so on. In cases where no Muslim state is willing to raise a certain issue like that of the persecution of the Ulghar Muslim population in Xingjiang, China, no action is taken. The idea of giving some kind of half membership/observer status to all the persecuted Muslim minorities has never been discussed formally. In February 1990, the then Secretary General did issue a statement, that starting from the forthcoming 6th Islamic Summit, the OIC would invite representatives of persecuted Muslim minorities in India, China and elsewhere, but nothing came out of it. Observer status was granted to the Muslim communities of Philippines and Cyprus as an exception, so the practice did not get institutionalized.

Problem of domestic backlash: Sometimes, the OIC membership becomes a major domestic political issue in many cases. For instance, the decision by President Sali Berisha of Albania in 1992 to join the OIC met with severe criticism at home where the opposition dubbed this move political suicide. He was accused of throwing the lot of his *European* country with the Orient. The President, however, defended his decision on different grounds saying that Albania had joined the OIC for economic, not religious, motives.[22] But actually, Berisha was trying to enlist OIC support for the security of the ethnic Muslim Albanian population of Kosovo (a province of Serbia). He feared that the Bosnia war may spread to Kosovo, since he was a vocal critic of the Western response to the genocide in Bosnia, he could not bank upon Western support, were this to happen. In hindsight, it appears that his gambit paid off.

The decision of Nigeria (1986) and Zanzibar (1992) to join OIC, met with such a hostile reaction from the non-Muslim population at home that both of them tried to withdraw from the OIC. But more of this in the following pages.

Observer Status

The problem of admission or otherwise of 'half-members' in the OIC, was debated threadbare at the time of the drafting of the Charter and finally, it was decided that the Organization would only consist of full members. But as the time passed, more and more delegations started to attend the conferences under different labels like observer, guest, and invitee. Some of them later got a permanent observer or permanent guest status. There is no provision for observer status in the OIC Charter as such. However, the closest provision to the grant of observer status is Article IX, which actually talks about the cooperation between the OIC and other Islamic organizations:

> The General Secretariat shall act within the framework of the present Charter with the approval of the Conference to consolidate relations between the Islamic Conference and the *Islamic organizations of international character* [emphasis added] and to bolster cooperation in the service of the Islamic objectives approved by this Charter.

One way to 'consolidate relations', which Article IX obliges the Islamic Conference to do, is through participating in each other's conferences on reciprocal basis. Thus, many leading Islamic organizations like the Muslim World League, World Muslim Congress and others, attend the OIC conferences as observers. The same is true of all the organs set up within the OIC framework. However, there is no clause in the OIC Charter, that can be twisted to legally justify the grant of observer status to a nation-state or to a non-Muslim organization. Yet, the practice has been that the OIC has conferred observer and guest status on states and international and regional organizations with equal liberality.

The distinction between observer and guest is rather blurred. It appears that a guest is a little 'less privileged' than an observer. For instance, immediately after the disintegration of the Soviet Union, the six former Soviet Muslim Republics were reluctant about joining the OIC. At the 6th Islamic Summit (Dakar; December 1991), Azerbaijan and Turkemanistan applied for an observer status and Kirghizia applied for a guest status.[23] By 1995, all the six republics had joined the OIC. At other times, it so happens that a particular state after attending two or so OIC conferences as observer, requests a permanent observer status. At present, three states Guyana

(South America), Central African Republic (Africa), and Bosnia (Europe), besides the Republic of North Cyprus (TRNC) and Autonomous Region of Muslim Mindanao (ARMM) in Philippines enjoy observer status. The OIC does not recognize the last two as sovereign states, since the goal of the OIC is the territorial integrity of Cyprus and of Philippines with adequate safeguards for the Muslim majority areas. Consequently, the OIC has actually given observer status to the Muslim 'communities' of Cyprus and Philippines. But for these five, all other observers are organizations.

The exact number of observers has fluctuated over time since a state/organization can attend a few OIC conferences as observer, and then never again turn up at all, while another state may become a full member after remaining an observer for some period. As early as 1977, the 8th ICFM requested the Secretary General to study the problem of the increasing number of observers and guests, and make recommendations to resolve it. Nothing came of it and the numbers continued to swell. By 1985, there were twenty observers at the OIC. The 21st ICFM (Karachi; 1993) was attended by thirty-four delegations as observers or guests.[24] The extraordinary Islamic Summit (Islamabad; 1997) was attended by fifty delegations in this capacity. As in the case of granting membership, the Islamic Conference has followed a certain loose criterion in inviting states or organizations as observers or guests. The observer states can be divided into three categories:

i.   Muslim countries, which do not want to join the OIC immediately, are invited to join as observers. And most of them after getting acquainted with the OIC, join as full members. Kazakhstan, Mozambique, Nigeria, Albania, to quote a few examples, remained observers before applying for membership.

ii.   States with a considerable Muslim population, that cannot qualify for full membership, become observers. For instance Guyana, with 20 per cent Muslims and a non-Muslim regime cannot qualify for OIC membership by any standard, is enjoying an observer status. Similarly at the 21st ICFM (Karachi; 1993), Croatia was invited as an observer because there is a substantial population of Muslims in Croatia and of Croats in Bosnia; and both countries were allied against Serbian aggression.

iii. Non-sovereign states like the Ankara-backed Republic of North Cyprus and the Pakistan-backed State of Azad (free) Jammu and Kashmir have not been granted full membership, though both governments have repeatedly applied for it. The former attends as observer and the latter as guest. The Islamic Conference wants the solution of Cyprus and Kashmir problems in accordance with the UN resolutions which, in both cases, call for the eventual reunification of Cyprus and Kashmir.

The following criteria have roughly been applied for granting observer status to organizations:

i. Islamic non-governmental organizations discussed earlier like MWL, WMC etc.
ii. All OIC subsidiary and affiliated organs, IDB, IINA, ISESCO etc.
iii. Regional organizations exclusively composed of OIC member-states like the ECO, Arab League.
iv. International organizations, mainly the United Nations and its specialized and affiliated organs.
v. Liberation movements of the Muslim world like MNLF and, prior to being accorded full membership, the PLO.

Withdrawal

The OIC Charter recognizes the right of any member state to withdraw at its own discretion, and discusses the conditions for withdrawal through Article X:

1) Any member State may withdraw from the Islamic Conference by sending a written notification to the Secretariat General, to be communicated to all Member States.
2) The State applying for withdrawal shall be bound by its obligations until the end of the fiscal year during which the application of withdrawal is submitted. It shall also settle any other financial dues to the Conference.

One cannot fail to notice that not only is the withdrawal accepted in principle but also there is no provision linking the withdrawal with an acceptance by the ICFM or the OIC Secretariat.

So, theoretically speaking, a member state ceases to be a member as soon as the notification 'informing' the decision is communicated to fellow OIC members, with or without the consent of the latter. The only condition is that the withdrawing member has to fulfil its financial obligations for the running financial year. In practice, however, four countries have tried to withdraw at one time or another, namely, Syria, Sudan, Nigeria, and Zanzibar. In all the four cases, the OIC rejected the withdrawal applications.

The above clause makes another interesting contrast with the UN Charter where once a state becomes a member, it cannot withdraw. The framers of the UN Charter thought that the provision for withdrawal could be used in future for blackmail by the member states.[25] When in mid-1960s Indonesia announced its withdrawal in protest over the Malaysia affair, the UN statement simply expressed regret over Jakarta's decision but made no mention of termination of Indonesia's membership. The name and flag of the country continued to be on the UN rolls and when three years later Indonesia rejoined, there was no formality because in the UN's eyes, Indonesia had never withdrawn. Similarly, after the 1965 Indo-Pak war, the then Pakistani Foreign Minister Zulfikar Ali Bhutto (later Prime Minister) threatened that Pakistan would withdraw from the UN if the resolutions on Kashmir were not implemented.[26] This threat drew an indifferent reaction from the UN because no country, legally speaking, can withdraw from the UN, and later the Pakistani President Ayub Khan disowned the threat saying that the Pakistani statement had actually been miscommunicated.

A brief resumé of the theory and practice regarding withdrawal, at the United Nations, has been provided since the OIC attitude over this issue may be better understood in this light. The first time, the OIC had to face the threat of withdrawal was in January 1984, when there was a serious row between Syria and Morocco because the latter had issued visa to a delegation of Israelis who wished to attend a Jewish Congress at Morocco. King Hassan of Morocco was the Chairman of the OIC's Al-Quds Committee, so Syria withdrew from the Committee in protest.[27] As King Hassan was also the Chairman of the OIC at that time, there was confusion about whether Syria had also withdrawn from the OIC to protest King Hassan's Chairmanship. Syria later clarified that its membership with the OIC and all its organs, except the said Committee, would remain unaffected.

On 1 October 1992, Sudan announced that it was quitting the OIC, to protest the OIC decision to alter the venue of the 21st ICFM which had been scheduled for Khartoum.[28] The OIC Secretariat had expressed dissatisfaction over the security arrangements in the city of Khartoum for the OIC ministers and without seeking the consent of the government of Sudan, had postponed the 21st ICFM which the country took as an insult. Its decision to withdraw was, however, not accepted. Sudan was ultimately convinced to revoke its decision and Sudan did attend the 21st ICFM belatedly held at Karachi, Pakistan, in April 1993. The cases of withdrawal of Zanzibar and Nigeria are complex ones and merit longer discussions.

Nigeria: The case of Nigeria is interesting since the Muslims form a bare majority, one-fourth of the population is Christian, and the rest follow indigenous religions. Traditionally, the Christian minority has been politically active and has a very strong representation in the upper strata of military-political hieararchy. Nigeria had retained an observer status at the OIC since the seventies but was not regular in attending the OIC moots. In 1985, Gen. Ibrahim Babangida assumed power through a military coup. One of the steps taken by the new regime, in its search for legitimacy, was applying to the OIC for full membership. The request was granted when the 16th ICFM (Fez; January 1986) admitted Nigeria as the 44th member of the Islamic Conference.[29]

Nigeria's membership was taken as a big achievement by the OIC. Mali, Mauritania, Pakistan and other Muslim states welcomed the biggest African Muslim country into the OIC fold. As soon as the OIC Secretariat issued the statement saying that the matter of Nigeria's membership stood closed, a controversy erupted as Commodore Ebitu Ukiwe, a Christian and the No. 2 in the Nigerian government claimed that he was unaware of Nigeria's membership to the OIC since the matter had never been discussed by the ruling council. As late as on 5 February, President

Babangida broke his silence, publicly confirmed the OIC membership, and formed a twenty-member experts' panel to examine the membership issue. To allay the minority apprehensions, he added that there was no question of Islam being imposed as the state religion.

There was a strong reaction from the Christian minority which accused the government of betrayal for joining the OIC without prior public debate. The country plunged into street violence during 7–14 February 1986, which was described as the most serious national crisis since Babangida's assumption of power. In order to appease the Christians, the government cancelled the lecture by the visiting 'Nation of Islam' Chairman, Louis Farrakhan (the most prominent leader of the Muslims in the United States), scheduled for 9 February. This proved to be too small a concession for the angry minority. The simmering resentment again led to the breaking out of furious Christian–Muslim riots in the second week of March which resulted in huge loss of life and property from both sides.[30] While the Christians were demanding unconditional withdrawal from the OIC, the demands of Muslim agitators also radicalized and they began to insist that Nigeria should become a full-fledged Islamic republic through the promulgation and enforcement of *Shari'ah* laws. The controversy never cooled down.

In 1990, President Babangida started his democratization reforms. He allowed a few political liberties, a two party system, and a controlled parliamentary system. Now he needed domestic political support, for which he started pacifying the Christian minority. Thereupon, in 1991, a very strange situation emerged when instead of withdrawing, Nigeria announced that it was never a member of the OIC. The claim was rejected by the OIC Legal Affairs Department and so was her withdrawal. Nigeria did attend the 6th Islamic Summit (Dakar; December 1991) but, along with Mozambique, only as an observer. The OIC continued to reaffirm that Nigeria was still a member and Nigeria itself started attending the OIC conferences again with the 21st ICFM (Karachi; 1993). The 23rd ICFM (Conakry; 1995) declared again that Nigeria was a full OIC member.[31] Nigeria did not contest or deny it. It has thereafter continued to actively take part in the OIC activities.

Zanzibar: In the latter half of 1992, Zanzibar applied for the OIC membership. Despite the OIC being an association of sovereign states, the 6th EICFM (Jeddah; December 1992) admitted Zanzibar as the fifty-first OIC member. Ever since its union with mainland Tanganyika to form the United Republic of Tanzania in 1964, howsoever coercive such a decision might have been, Zanzibar was no longer a sovereign state.[32]

As soon as Zanzibar's membership was made public, there rose a storm of protest by the Christians, both in Zanzibar and in mainland Tanzania. Most of the opposition parties in the parliament were equally critical. However, on 10 January 1993, President of Zanzibar, Salmin Amour (*ex-officio* second Vice-President of Tanzania) reaffirmed that Zanzibar was and would remain an OIC member and asked the opposition to keep religious and political issues separate. He further stressed that Zanzibar's decision would not affect its union with the mainland. On 28 January, President of Tanzania, Ali Hassan Mwinyi, a Muslim, came out in full support of Zanzibar's membership of the OIC, which he said, was for economic, not religious, considerations.[33]

Ignoring the statements of Mwinyi and Amour, the parliament formed a committee to investigate the issue which on 19 February declared Zanzibar's membership to be illegal. President Amour reacted by warning the parliament to desist from criticizing the OIC membership issue as 'it would be like shaking a match box'.[34] In a strong reaction, fifty-eight MPs dubbed his remarks as an insult to the parliament and demanded an unconditional apology from Amour or to face blocking of annual estimates of his (Tanzanian Vice-President's) office. The Prime Minister of Tanzania, John Malecela, a Christian, came to his rescue by asking the parliament not to take such a rash step. Malecela said Tanzania would investigate the possibility of the United Republic joining the OIC.[35] The crisis further deepened when Tanzania's strongman, and former President, Julius Nyerere, joined the chorus by rebuking Zanzibar, for what he called, violating the Tanzanian Constitution.

Finally, Zanzibar had to eat the humble pie. In an address to the parliament on 13 August 1993, President Amour announced his decision to withdraw from the OIC.[36] The same was formally notified to the OIC Secretariat on 21 August. The OIC refused to accept the withdrawal of Zanzibar. The annual lists of members issued by the OIC Secretariat in December 1993 and December 1994 still showed Zanzibar as an OIC member. In December 1995, for the first time the Secretariat dropped Zanzibar's name from its list suggesting that the OIC had tacitly accepted the decision of Zanzibar, though, no formal statement to this effect was ever issued by the OIC Secretariat.[37]

To sum up, the OIC does not accept the decision of a member state regarding withdrawal, irrespective of what the Charter says. It is highly unlikely if the OIC would ever accept a withdrawal in future.

Expulsion and Suspension

There is no provision in the OIC Charter that would allow it to expel or suspend any member state. Here again there is a fundamental difference between the OIC and the UN Charters. Conversely, the latter has a provision for the suspension/ expulsion of a member-state. The United Nations has never invoked its powers to expel a member, not even against the pariah states of North Korea and Iraq, against which collective security measures were taken. On its part the OIC has expelled Egypt and suspended Afghanistan, though legal justification for these measures cannot be derived from the Charter.[38]

Egypt: There was a reorientation in the Egyptian political thinking after the 1973 war on account of the realization that as long as the US guaranteed the security of Israel, no effort to annihilate it could succeed. President Sadaat's regime was also seriously concerned about the heavy toll that the unabated confrontation was taking on Egyptian economy. Finally, he made up his mind to adopt the 'Egypt First!' policy at the expense of the wider Islamic and Arab causes. In violation of all the intra-Arab agreements and understandings, Sadaat made a surprise visit to Israel in 1977 and addressed the Israeli Knesset. Thus began Cairo's solo flight in search of peace which culminated on 16 September 1978 when Egypt and Israel agreed in principle to make peace, at Camp David (USA); and in March 1979, the final peace deal was signed. By 26 January 1980, with the opening of border posts in the Sinai desert, the normalization process began.[39]

These developments were received with shock in most of the OIC member states who accused Egypt of betraying the Islamic and Palestinian cause as well as backtracking from all its commitments to Arab and Islamic States. It was decided that instead of letting the Muslim unity be torn asunder for one betrayal, a strong stance should be taken. Consequently, Egypt was expelled from all Islamic and Arab organizations, and all aid to it was stopped, diplomatic relations were broken and trade agreements revoked. On 5 December 1978 President Sadaat wrote to King Hassan that the OIC should concentrate on the situation in East Jerusalem instead of criticizing Egypt–Israel border talks.

In the aftermath of the Egypt–Israel treaty, the 10th ICFM took place with the treaty at the top of its agenda. In sheer defiance of the bellicose mood of the conference, a high-powered uninvited Egyptian delegation, led by the former OIC Secretary General Hassan Tohami arrived at Fez, which was obviously not allowed in. Many of the member states had made it clear that they would withdraw if the Egyptian team was allowed to join the ICFM.[40] The delegation said that Egypt had not violated the OIC Charter in any way and that any decision to expel Egypt would be illegal since the Charter does not allow expulsion of a member state. The conference, however, noted that Egypt had violated Article II (A/5) of the Charter which had declared the support to the Palestine cause to be an objective of the Islamic Conference.[41] It said that Egypt had made a mockery of the OIC's commitment to the Palestine cause and of the profusion of OIC declarations on the Jerusalem question. The conference condemned the agreement, which had 'neither solved the Palestine problem, nor determined the future status of Jerusalem'. The resolution to expel Egypt was moved by Syria and Libya. It was supported by thirty-four states while six African states, Niger,

Upper Volta, Senegal, Gambia, Gabon, and Guinea-Bissau abstained. Sudan, Somalia, and North Yemen had voted reluctantly in favour.[42] Egyptian Foreign Ministry reacted by issuing a statement that 'expulsion of one pillar of Islam will weaken the OIC and sabotage the path of unity'.[43] In January 1981, the 3rd Islamic Summit at Taif reaffirmed all the ICFM resolutions about the Middle East situation, condemned Egypt for Camp David and made a call for an end to the illegal Israeli occupation of the Arab lands.

For the next few years, the OIC continued to reaffirm all its resolutions on the Palestine problem and the condemnation of the Camp David, while Egypt never let go an opportunity to emphasize that it had neither violated the OIC Charter, nor betrayed or harmed the Palestine cause in any way. Gradually, many Muslim states began to feel that Israel had become emboldened by neutralizing Egypt. Following the Israeli invasion of Lebanon, it was the Palestinian leadership that became the protagonist of Egypt's readmission. In December 1983, Palestine, Chad, and Sudan made a call for Egypt's re-entry.[44] By the time of the Casablanca Islamic Summit (January 1984), tempers had cooled down and there was new thinking on the wisdom of keeping Egypt, which had given the largest number of sacrifices against Israel, out of the Islamic Conference. At the said Summit, the proposal to invite Egypt to join the OIC was propounded by Guinea and was supported by Jordan, Malaysia and later, very strongly by Pakistan. Five states spoke in strong opposition to the move while South Yemen criticized Egypt's re-entry on technical grounds—that it was not on the Summit agenda. Finally the matter was left to voting. Egypt's re-admission was decided by 32–6 votes with three abstentions. Though the resolution implied that Egypt would have to accept the 3rd Islamic Summit resolutions, which meant a virtual renunciation of the Camp David accord, the final Summit communiqué did not mention this. While welcoming the OIC moves to re-admit it, Egypt had declared that it would accept no prior conditions.

In a letter to the then OIC Chairman, King Hassan of Morocco, Egyptian President Hosni Mubarak made clear that the Camp David accord was already dead for all practical purposes. 'The treaty does exist formally but in politics one must not stick to forms but look at basics,' he added. On 30 January 1984, Egypt accepted the offer of re-entry and thanked the Muslim world. The Egyptian leader termed the 4th Islamic Summit as 'a unique epic which our people cherish and to which they respond with gratitude and loyalty.' President Ahmad Sekou Toure who had led the OIC goodwill mission to Cairo, comprising Guinea, Malaysia, Pakistan, and the OIC Secretary General, praised Hosni Mubarak for the reorientation in Egyptian foreign policy that 'is in total conformity with the ideas espoused and defended by the Muslim peoples.' In his turn President Mubarak said, 'Egypt is working within the OIC framework to honor its commitments.' Responding to a question by the press corps, he denied that there was anything in the OIC Charter that infringed on Egypt's sovereignty.[45] Addressing a function in Cairo a few days later, Mubarak declared that Egypt belonged to the Islamic family and down the ages, it had been in the vanguard of all Islamic movements. He said Egypt had no grudge and no malice against its Muslim brothers and that Egypt 'will march with the Muslims...on the path of liberty and honor.'

Egypt formally joined OIC on 2 April and immediately, in conformity with the OIC resolutions, broke off diplomatic relations with the thirteen states which had moved their embassies in Israel, from Tel Aviv to Jerusalem.[46] At the 15th ICFM (Sana'a; December 1984), the Egyptian delegation led by its foreign minister Esmet Abdul Muguid (later Secretary General of the Arab League) participated as a full member for the first time since the 9th ICFM (Dakar; April 1978). Syria, Iran, and Libya strongly resisted the Egyptian entry at Sana'a but their objections were overruled.[47]

Afghanistan: Afghanistan's case is different from Egypt's because Afghanistan was never expelled from the OIC whereas Egypt was. The first ever extraordinary session of ICFM (Islamabad; January 1980) had decided to suspend the membership of the Soviet-installed, puppet Kabul regime; while the country continued to be represented on the OIC fora by the opposition Afghan Mujahideen leadership. At the 11th ICFM, six of the

Mujahideen leaders participated as part of the Iranian delegation. Later the *Mujahideen* leadership was accorded observer status in their own right. Finally when the *Mujahideen* formed their own interim government in February 1989, it was given full membership at the OIC, despite strong opposition by Dr Najibullah's regime. In Spring 1992, the Mujahideen captured Kabul and formed their own government headed, for an initial stint of two months, by Sibghatullah Mojaddedi and then by Professor Burhanuddin Rabbani. The power-sharing formula was brokered by the OIC. So after twelve years, the *de facto* and the *de jure* government in Afghanistan was finally the same.

In fact, all the three agreements, namely, Jalalabad Accord, Peshawar Accord, and the Islamabad Accord, were directly or indirectly concluded under the aegis of the OIC, with active help from the three member states of Pakistan, Iran, and Saudi Arabia. Each of these agreements between the Mujahideen factions was violated, each faction accusing the other of breaking the fragile peace. The air of mutual distrust and hostility continued to persist. In December 1994, the refusal of President Rabbani to step down when his extended mandate of two years expired, plunged the country into an abyss of chaos and civil war. The crisis in leadership was far from resolved when ultimately on 26 September 1996, the student militia, known as the Taliban, captured Kabul and formed a cabinet. The taliban were in full control of three-fourths of the country forcing Rabbani to take refuge in a northern province where he cobbled together a new a alliance to fight them.

The Taliban regime was looked at with suspicion by most of the regional states for its radical agenda of spreading the Islamic revolution and for its treatment of women and policies on education. Most stupefying of all was the enigma of the personality of the new leader, Mullah Mohammad Omer, a 32-year old radical cleric, who neither took oath as President, nor moved out of his mosque-cum-residence at Qandhar to the capital Kabul, and has never been seen on the media. Omer prefers to be called *Ameer-ul-Momineen* (leader of the faithful), and not President, which he believes is a Western term.

Hence in the absence of clarity as to the person of president, and since the ousted Rabbani regime still claimed to be the legitimate government of Afghanistan, the 24th ICFM (Jakarta; December 1996) again suspended Kabul's membership and declared its seat vacant.[48]

Meanwhile, the situation took another turn when some powerful members of the OIC, Pakistan, Saudi Arabia, and the UAE, extended recognition to the Taliban government, raising alarm over the strategic concerns in Iran and the Central Asian states. The afore-mentioned members tried to get the OIC to recognize the Taliban but failed to muster sufficient support. An interesting situation arose when Pakistan accorded full protocol to the Taliban Prime Minister Mullah Rabbani (not related to the ousted President Burhanuddin Rabbani) when he came to attend the extraordinary Islamic Summit (Islamabad; March 1997) and seated him next to the Iranian President Rafsanjani.[49] Mullah Rabbani, however, had to attend the Summit as an observer. He later visited some Muslim countries in his bid to win the OIC seat but to no avail.

A few months later, it was Iran's turn to respond when it accorded full military protocol to the ousted President Rabbani, who came to attend the 8th Islamic Summit (Tehran; December 1997) in a direct affront to the Taliban. The latter boycotted the Summit, spurning the offer to take part as an observer again. Meanwhile, the ousted President's delegation tried to physically occupy Afghanistan's vacant seat at the Summit, but Pakistan did not let them do so.[50]

Consequently, Afghanistan's membership again remains suspended, which the new Islamist Kabul regime resents as much as the earlier Communist regime used to do. Mullah Omer calls the OIC decision a violation of the Charter which does not provide for expulsion or suspension of a member state.

Provisions related to the Charter

The last four Articles of the OIC Charter relate to the Charter itself.

Amendment: Article XI of the Charter stipulates that the Charter can be amended 'if approved and ratified by a two-third majority of the member states'. Unlike the UN Charter which has not been amended, except when the number of non-permanent members of the UN Security Council was increased from six to ten, the OIC Charter has been amended no less than four times, though, the amendments related to administrative matters alone, like the time frame for Islamic Summit conferences and the tenure of the Secretary General or the ASGs. The Articles thus affected are Articles III, IV, V, and VI.

The 6th Islamic Summit (Dakar; 1991) in its final declaration noted that

> the numerous changes and developments that have taken place on the international scene require readaptation of the [OIC] Charter...so as to enable it to effectively benefit from the experience gained by the Organization in various fields since the adoption of the Charter...to respond to the requirements of the coming phase.

Save for the amendment made by the 6th Summit itself, regarding the tenure of the Secretary General (Article VI), it has not been amended after 1991. The afore-mentioned Para of the Dakar declaration still remains a policy guideline for the OIC, in that it recognizes the necessity to make further amendments in the Charter.[51]

Interpretation: Article XII says that any dispute that may arise 'in the interpretation, application or implementation' of the Charter is to be settled peacefully through 'consultations, negotiations, reconciliation or arbitration'. These are the same elements that appear in Article II (B) regarding the settlement of inter-State conflicts among the member states. The 5th Islamic Summit (Kuwait; 1987) approved the statute of the Islamic International Court of Justice that, inter alia, mandated the Court to interpret the Charter. So when the necessary number of ratifications gets deposited and the Court becomes operational, this Article would become redundant, since the Court is to become the arbiter in deciding what a particular provision of the Charter actually means. Any agreement to amend the Charter would definitely precede negotiations and consultations, but its interpretation would be at the discretion of the IICJ.

The Article XII is also important because it is one of the articles that evoked a heated controversy at the time of the drafting of the OIC Charter. Iran was insisting on inserting in para (b) of this Article a stipulation that the Charter 'shall not contain any matter which contradicts the UN Charter or infringes on the rights of the member states and their obligations towards it.' Saudi Arabia, supported by Morocco, Algeria, and Guinea, strongly opposed the Iranian suggestion saying the new Organization has to be confident of itself, so its Charter obligations cannot be made subject to those of the UN Charter. This latter view won the support of the majority.[52] As for the reference to the UN Charter in the preamble, it was stressed that all the OIC members were already members of the United Nations also, so there was nothing wrong in reaffirming the commitment to a Charter that each member state was already a party to.

Language: Article XIII designates Arabic, English, and French as the three official languages of the Islamic Conference. All the subsidiary and the affiliated organs have the same three official languages. Arabic was the national language of sixteen of the thirty founder states of the OIC. Although, there is no country in the OIC that has English or French as the native language, but since a number of Muslim countries had remained colonies of Britain and France, no less than four of the remaining fourteen founder states had English as the official language and seven had French. Now the Arabic speaking states have become a minority in the OIC; twenty-two out of fifty-five. But Arabic has a special significance for the Muslims since the Quran was revealed in this language. That is why, if there is a dispute over the meaning of a particular word in an OIC document or declaration; the meaning in its Arabic text is given preference.

Ratification: The final Article says that the Charter would go 'into effect as of the date of deposition of the instruments of ratification with the General Secretariat by a simple majority of the States participating in the 3rd Islamic Conference of Foreign Ministers'. It should be borne in mind that it was the 3rd ICFM (Jeddah; February 1972) that had approved the Charter. Though the exact date

is not known but it appears that the requisite number of ratifications (i.e., sixteen) were deposited by the end of 1972. In conformity with Article 102 of the UN Charter, the OIC Charter was registered with the UN Secretariat on 1 February 1974. Technically speaking, the OIC came into existence then, but the OIC usually calculates its age from 1969, and sometimes, from 1970. The date when all the legal formalities for the OIC to come into existence were completed, is seldom ever mentioned, if at all known.

Reflections on the OIC Charter

The Charter of the Islamic Conference is a short and vague document which is conspicuous by the inconsistencies between its theory and practice. Whatever the OIC wants to do, it justifies it by twisting some ambiguous Article from the Charter. When it wants to do the opposite, all it has to do is to twist the same Article in the reverse direction to suit its ends. Exceptions have been made many times, only to add exceptions to these exceptions. At the time of admitting a new member, rejecting a withdrawal notice, or suspending a membership, no reference to the Charter is made, even in the discussions. The only time that Article II (A/5) was alluded to as being violated, was on Egypt's expulsion. A few years later, the Organization revoked its decision, then again no talk was heard about the Charter.

This had led to a number of contradictions in the Organization's practice. For instance, Egypt was expelled for signing the Camp David Accord, as this was considered violative of Article II (A/5). But a few years later, Palestine was not castigated when it signed the Oslo agreement with Israel in 1993. In 1990, Iraq's invasion of Kuwait was condemned, (without giving it any benefit of doubt) as violative of Article II (B/4) regarding the non-use of force and peaceful resolution of disputes. This Article was not invoked when the same Iraq had attacked Iran ten years earlier. North Cyprus was granted observer status while Azad Kashmir was given only a guest status in the name of Article II (A/1) which calls for the promotion of Islamic solidarity. This Article was never applied to Chechenya, so to speak. It appears that the application of this Article is toned down proportionate to the strength and power of the non-Muslim state concerned.

Similar is the fate of Article II (A/6) pertaining to support for the struggles of Muslim peoples. The OIC never fails to condemn India and Philippines for committing atrocities against the Muslims; despite the fact that their track record on human rights is better than that of many Muslim states. It is as if when Muslims are being persecuted by or in a Muslim State, then all the relevant clauses of Article II (A) about extending support to them vanish, while Article II (B) concerning non-interference in the domestic affairs of other states becomes operative. That is to say that if the Afghan government's membership can be suspended twice, it becomes all the more imperative to suspend the membership of Algeria's ruling junta and to grant the Islamic Salvation Front (FIS), the right to represent Algeria where the military, which torpedoed the thumping victory of the FIS in the first and only transparent multi-party elections in the country, does not have even a semblance of legitimacy. We can go on and on like this. Apparently, all but four of the Charter Articles have been violated at one time or the other, by the Organization itself or by the majority of its member states.

The Charter has several equally convincing positive aspects also. It has accentuated a set of principles and values that have their basis on the notion of justice, which neither contradict international legality nor compromise the religious precepts. The Charter has its own ideological limitations which influence the position of the Organization when approving or disapproving something. When the OIC approach appears to be in conflict with that of the United Nations, it does not mean that it is defying international law since it is surreal to take the Security Council regulations to be always synonymous with international legality. The OIC Charter is itself a legal document and a new perspective on international legality, adhered to by fifty-five law-abiding states. If a police van breaks a traffic signal, all the cars are not supposed to follow it blindly since a policeman is as prone to error as any human being. This is the thinking of the OIC when it refuses to recognize the legitimacy of certain UN resolutions on Israel and Serbia, and demands a more equitable solution founded on the spirit of justice.

The Charter's emphasis on Islam, notwithstanding, it has been acceded to by states like Turkey, Albania, and Central Asian Muslim states without undermining their secular character. Its underlying spirit of fostering peace and development in the world is the same as that of many other international organizations. Thus the convictions of the member states have led this Charter to be instrumental in protecting the rights of oppressed communities, resolving conflicts, and managing crises, albeit in the Muslim world alone, and certainly not in equal degrees (as we shall see in the next three chapters). As the Dakar declaration has admitted, it is time that the OIC Charter is readapted to benefit from the rich experiences of the Organization, so that its legal deficiencies will not lead it to fail in expectations, as it has in the past. The OIC Charter can become complementary to the United Nations Charter if it is strong and clear enough to spur the Organization to act decisively for the realization of its objectives within the area of its mandate. The world body would then find the Islamic Conference to be sharing a considerable portion of its burden. Cooperation, not competition or suspicion, will be the harbinger for a better tomorrow.

NOTES and REFERENCES

1. Hassan Moinuddin, *The Charter of the Islamic Conference*. (Oxford: Clarendon Press, 1987), p. 16 and p. 76.
2. Dr Mohammad el-Syed Selim (ed.), *The OIC in a changing world*, (Cairo: Cairo University, 1994), pp. 4–6.
3. The events leading to the establishment of the OIC have been discussed in Chapter 1 while the debate on the ideological orientation of the OIC has been dealt with in the introductory chapter, hence need not be repeated here.
4. Russian Federation was understandably feeling queasy over the decision of its 'near abroad' to join the Islamic Conference and even tried to dissuade the Central Asian states from doing so, but received an emphatic 'No'.
5. See Mohammad Selim and Mounir el Sayed, *The OIC: A General Profile*, in Selim (ed.), ref. 2, pp. 25–26.

6. The OIC Charter appears in Annexure 1 and the readers may consult it, wherever a reference to any Article of the Charter is made in this chapter.

7. Abdullah Ahsan, *Ummah or Nation? Identity crisis in the Muslim society*, (Leicester: Islamic Foundation, 1992), pp. 108–11.

8. Noor Ahmad Baba, *OIC: Theory and Practice of Pan-Islamic Cooperation*, (Karachi: Oxford University Press, 1993), pp. 82–83. Here the author summarizes the debate about the inclusion of this clause.

9. Initially, Indonesia, Lebanon, and Turkey refused to ratify the OIC Charter on the plea that their secular Constitutions do not allow them to become party to a religious Charter. They continued to enjoy all the benefits of the membership, except that they could not get their nominee elected to the post of Secretary General. Now since Turkey has got one Assistant Secretary General while Indonesia too made an abortive bid to win the post of ASG, it is unclear whether they have ratified it or not. The legal affairs department of the OIC remains tight-lipped on the issue and neither confirms nor denies that these states have also ratified the Charter. See Ahsan, ref. 7, p. 113 and also Baba, ref. 8, p. 136.

10. During the research, this author failed to find out who suggested this name and why, and whether there had been any debate on the suggested names of the new organization at the time of drafting of the Charter. Later on, however, suggestions to change its name did come up. As early as 1974, the then Secretary General suggested that the name of the OIC be changed to 'Organization of Solidarity in Islamic (Peoples and) States (OSIS/OSIPS).

11. Ola Abdel Aziz Abouzeid, 'The policy of the OIC towards international issues that concern the Muslim world', in Selim (ed.), ref. 2, pp. 51–54 and 61–63.

12. The Dakar declaration of the 6th Islamic Summit, for the first time extends the refrainment from threat or use of force against non-Member states also. See para (5) of the Declaration. It, however, did not rescind any of the earlier OIC resolutions that exhort the member-states to liberate the Palestinian lands (present-day Israel) by 'all means including *Jihad*'.

13. Abouzeid, ref. 11, pp. 56–56, give a detailed analysis of the objectives of the Islamic Conference. Also see Selim and Sayed, ref. 5, pp. 22–26.

14. Moinuddin, ref. 1, p. 14, 16, 19, 22, 27 and 76.

15. Several African member states had objected to the reference of Palestine problem by name on the plea that the Charter should be of general nature and not problem-specific. Once Palestine is liberated, they argued, this clause would become redundant. Their viewpoint was rejected by the majority of the Muslim states, however, the sixth objective calling for strengthening the struggles of all Muslim peoples for safeguarding their rights and dignity was added, for the purpose of accommodating their objection. See Mohammad Selim, 'The OIC and the Palestine Problem' (in Arabic), *Shu'an Arabiyyah*, December 1988, p. 201. Also see Baba, ref. 8, pp. 80–83.

16. Still, negative votes or dissenting opinions are freely allowed. There have been a number of incidents when the resolutions were not carried through consensus. The pro-USSR Muslim states always opposed any resolution condemning the Soviet Union for any reason whatsoever. Similarly, the American allies never favoured any resolution condemning the United States by name. This dissension is accepted as their right.

17. See for example, Sajjad Bokhari, *Zulfiqar Ali Bhutto: Wiladat se Shahadat tak* (in Urdu), (Lahore: Fiction House, 1993), p. 284.

18. Iqbal Akhund, *Memoirs of a Bystander*, (Karachi: Oxford University Press, 1997), p. 440.

19. M. Ali Kettani, 'Muslim minorities in the world today', (Lahore: Services Book Club, 1990), p. 160. Kettani is so rigid in this definition that he terms Uganda with 20 per cent Muslims as a Muslim state (p. 163) while Nigeria, which according to his research has 60 per cent Muslims as a Muslim minority state (p. 164 in ibid.) since Nigeria was not a full member of the OIC at that time.

20. Ahsan, ref. 7, p. 110.

21. The same holds good for the ex-Soviet Muslim states where the majority of the Muslims do not practice all the Islamic rituals but are conscience of being Muslims. If one asks a Kazakh if he is a Muslim; the most likely answer would be 'of course, I am a Kazakh', since for him, his Kazakh and Muslim identities are synonymous.

22. *Dawn*, Karachi, 10 January 1993.

23. *Pakistan Times*, Islamabad, 26 October 1991.

24. Selim and Sayed, ref. 5, p. 27.

25. Stephen S. Goodspeed, *The Nature and Function of International Organization*, (New York: Oxford University Press, 1962), pp. 110–13.

26. Altaf Gauher, *Ayub Khan: Pakistan's first military ruler*, (Lahore: Sang-e-Meel, 1994), pp. 359–407, gives a good description of the general frustration in Pakistan over the UN's inaction regarding Kashmir.

27. *Keesing's Contemporary Archives, 1984*, p. 32949.

28. *The Nation*, Lahore, 2 October 1992.

29. Baba, ref. 8, p. 172.

30. 'Facts on File', 1986, p. 197.

31. *Keesing, 1995*, p. 40883. Also see *Keesing, 1991*, p. 38260.

32. The tiny island of Zanzibar's 650,000 population is almost entirely Muslim. It was traditionally ruled by Arab *Sultans*, who had suzerainty on mainland Tanganyika also, until it became a British protectorate. It got independence in December 1963. The following

month John Okello invaded the island with 600 mercenaries and overthrew the government. Zanzibar was immediately merged into Tanganyika and the new republic came to be known as Tanzania. See Kettani, ref. 19, pp. 171–73.

33. *Keesing, 1993*, p. 39299 and 39342.

34. *The News*, Islamabad, 20 February 1993.

35. *Dawn*, 21 August 1993. Also see *Keesing, 1993*, p. 39619. It may be added that Zanzibar has 98 per cent Muslims whereas the combined population of Tanzania has 55 per cent Muslim composition. See Kettani, ref. 19, p. 163.

36. *Dawn*, 16 August 1993.

37. *Keesing, 1995*, p. 40883.

38. The absence of precise rules delineating the conditions under which a member state could be expelled has made the decision quite arbitrary. Speaking at a seminar on international leadership, Pakistani's ex-Prime Minister Benazir Bhutto claimed that during her rule, a group of religious scholars in some Muslim countries embarked upon a plan to pressurize their governments to get Pakistan expelled from the OIC since it was being ruled by a woman. See, *The News*, Lahore, 27 November 1997.

39. See Sadaat, *In Search of Identity*, (New York: Harper and Row, 1979), wherein the Egyptian President explains the reasons why Egypt decided to make a separate peace deal with Israel. Also see. P. J. Vatikoties, *Arab and Regional Politics in the Middle East*, (New York: St. Martin's Press Inc., 1984), for the developments leading to the accord and its aftermath.

40. *Morning News*, Karachi, 8 May 1979.

41. Selim and Sayed, ref. 5, pp. 27–28.

42. Baba, ref. 8, pp. 118–19.

43. 'Facts on File', 1979, p. 360.

44. *Dawn*, 10 December 1983.

45. 'Facts on File', 1984, p. 53.

46. *Keesing, 1984*, p. 32894.

47. Baba, ref. 8, p. 170.

48. *The News*, 20 December 1996.

49. Ibid., 24 March 1997 and 25 April 1997.

50. Ibid., 5 December 1997.

51. See the last paragraph of the Dakar declaration.

52. Selim and Sayed, ref. 5, p. 25.

5 Political History I: Islamic Conferences

One thing in which the Organization of the Islamic Conference has so far been most successful is the organizing of Islamic conferences. Since they have been held more or less regularly, it is no mean achievement in itself. We can divide the conferences into three categories:

i.   The Conference of Kings and Heads of States of Islamic countries, commonly known as the Islamic Summits
ii. The Islamic Conferences of Foreign Ministers or ICFMs (both regular and extraordinary)
iii. Other Conferences at the Ministerial or Experts level including the conferences of OIC information ministers, finance ministers, etc.

In the order of significance, however, the ICFMs have taken precedence over the Islamic Summits. Though the Charter defines the latter as the supreme authority of the Organization, the former has gradually become the *de facto* decision-making body because of four reasons: (a) Islamic Summits are supposed to take place every three years which is a long interval. The ICFMs are, however, held annually and also much more regularly than the Summits which may be convened after a five to seven years' gap; (b) The ICFMs also meet in extraordinary sessions when the situation so demands while the same is not true of the Islamic Summits; (c) The turn-out in the Islamic Summits is not very encouraging as a large number of Heads of State stay away and this lack of interest translates into lack of concrete results, whereas at the ICFMs, almost all the delegations are represented at the appropriate level;[1] (d) the practical duration of an Islamic Summit is usually three days, most of which is consumed in the customary speeches, statements, and (if some head of state is not present in person) messages. On the other hand, an ICFM remains in session normally for five days and, after the two or three formal opening speeches in the plenary session, there is sufficient time to deliberate on the agenda.

Before entering into a discussion on Islamic conferences, one should establish their significance in the context of the OIC. Firstly, the holding of Islamic conferences has been the major contribution of the OIC. This has brought the Muslim leaders together and in many cases, worked out a common stand, thus giving more than a semblance of unity in the Islamic world. Secondly, the Islamic Summit Conference and the Foreign Minister's Conferences are two of the three existing principal constituent organs of the OIC. In the absence of permanent bodies, like the Security Council and the General Assembly in the UN system, these conferences held more or less regularly are the OIC brand of permanent institutions. Thirdly, the Islamic Summits, ICFMs and other ministerial organizations have at times taken momentous decisions and adopted seminal resolutions. They are, in no way, mere gatherings of the Muslim leaders but have become indispensable institutions in their own right. Finally, the name of the Organization also suggests that it has been established, so as to enable the Islamic world (leadership) to confer (with each other). This has been made possible only through the regular holding of Islamic conferences by the Organization of the Islamic Conference. Thus, this chapter recounts the history of the Islamic conferences.

Regular Islamic Summits

Although the conferences of Kings and Heads of States of Islamic countries have not been held at regular intervals, this section has been marked as such in order to distinguish them from the extraordinary summit conference. Initially, there was no set time frame for the holding of the Islamic Summit Conference.

The first three Islamic Summits were held in response to the Al-Quds arson, Arab–Israel war of 1973, and the advent of the 15th century of the Islamic calendar, respectively. In the Taif Summit (1981), that was held after a long gap of seven years, it was realized that without a definite time frame, it would not be possible to hold regular Summits. Article IV was thus amended to provide for an OIC Summit Conference after every three years. Usually at the concluding session of a Summit Conference, one of the member states offers to host the next conference. So far eight Islamic Summit Conferences have been held. The 9th Islamic Summit is scheduled for Doha, Qatar, for December 2000. (See Chart 2.1 in Chapter 2)

1st Islamic Summit (Rabat): The 1st Islamic summit was held at Rabat, Morocco, during 22–25 September 1969. It was basically convened to discuss the sacrilege of the third holiest shrine of Islam at Jerusalem. Earlier on the morning of 22 September, the foreign ministers of the participating nations met to formulate an agenda. Conservative states like Saudi Arabia, Morocco, Iran, etc. wanted the agenda to be limited to the Al-Aqsa mosque incident only. While the UAR supported by Algeria, Sudan, and Libya pressed for a broader agenda involving the whole question of Palestine, occupied territories and refugees et al. As a major concession to the radicals, the latter view carried the day.[2]

In all, thirty-six countries were invited, of which twenty-five attended. Only ten were led by the heads of states. Prominent among the participants were King Faisal of Saudi Arabia, King Hassan of Morocco, Reza Shah of Iran, President Houari Boumeddienne of Algeria, and President Yahya Khan of Pakistan.[3] The radical states like Iraq and Syria boycotted the conference, dubbing it 'an imperialist ploy to divide the Muslim world'. Earlier, Iraq had set three pre-conditions for its participation: that the conference would have a clear-cut agenda, that it would pledge unequivocal support to the Palestinian struggle, and that all the

participating Muslim nations would agree to sever diplomatic relations with Israel. At the time, Iraqi demands were deemed as asking for too much. Since the assurances were not forthcoming, Iraq stayed away.

Though the conference was convened to discuss a religious issue, two peripheral issues, viz. admission of the PLO and expulsion of India dominated the proceedings.

The Al-Fatah group of Yasser Arafat had launched an armed struggle against Israel since early 1965 and was desperately seeking international legitimacy. So an uninvited PLO delegation arrived at Rabat and was kept waiting while the conference debated whether to let them in. In Chapter 1, it was described how the PLO had eventually managed to get into the Islamic Conference in Kuala Lumpur (April 1969); the story was not much different at Rabat. Several countries, including Iran and Turkey which were on friendly terms with Israel, opposed the PLO's entry on the grounds that the admission of PLO would politicize an otherwise 'religious' conference, and secondly, that since the PLO was not a sovereign state, it could not be admitted on technical grounds. On the other hand, Pakistan and UAR questioned the logic of discussing the Al-Quds issue, with the exclusion of the first victims—the Palestinians. President Boumeddienne recalled that Algeria's National Liberation Front (FLN) delegation was admitted to the Non-Aligned Summit at Bandung, Indonesia, in 1955, though Algeria was not yet a sovereign state. He thus forcefully pleaded the case of PLO, after which the PLO delegation was admitted, as an observer, in accordance with King Hassan's compromise formula.[4]

The second major controversy occurred regarding the credentials of India to attend the conference that ultimately led to her expulsion. India had earlier herself requested an invitation to the Rabat conference, citing the presence of sixty million Muslims in India and their concern about the Al-Quds arson. However, the seven-member preparatory committee had rejected her request, as India did not have a Muslim majority. India did not give up efforts and pursued all available channels to elicit an invitation. Saudi King Faisal was sympathetic to Indian pleadings and he talked to President Yahya of Pakistan to allow an Indian Muslim delegation at Rabat to which the latter agreed reluctantly. And late in the day, an invitation was duly forwarded to New Delhi.[5]

As the delegation led by India's powerful Minister for Industrial Development Fakhruddin Ali Ahmad (later President of India), a Muslim, had not arrived, the Indian ambassador to Morocco, Gurbachan Singh, a Sikh, took the seat to represent India for the time being. Meanwhile, in another development within India, the death toll in furious anti-Muslim riots in the city of Ahmadabad had risen to one thousand in the past five days. On seeing a Sikh at the Islamic Summit, President Yahya Khan was furious. He asked the delegates to expel India whose hands were red with the blood of Indian Muslims in Ahmadabad. Yahya claimed that he had never agreed to an Indian government delegation; instead, he had wanted a representative delegation of Indian Muslims to apprise the Conference of the victimization by the Hindu majority.

The participants were left bewildered as they saw the Pakistani delegation walking out in protest. In New Delhi, the External Affairs Ministry reacted to the incident by regretting 'the false propaganda by the Pakistani President against India' and claimed that the Ahmadabad disturbances were an internal affair of India. The statement further dismissed the idea of a non-official delegation of Indian Muslims, as Pakistan was demanding, in a conference of sovereign states, as frivolous. All the same, the conference at Rabat was paralysed as Yahya stayed out in his villa outside Rabat. As it was not easy to offend India, several Muslim leaders called on Yahya at his villa, trying to persuade him to show flexibility. 'More Muslims have been killed in Ahmadabad in the last two days than in Jerusalem in the last several years', Yahya told them. Entreaties by four monarchs (King Faisal of Saudi Arabia, King Hassan of the host country, Reza Shah of Iran, and King Hussein of Jordan) failed to move the Pakistani President, and instead, the last two joined him in the boycott. Nonetheless, it was not easy to convince all the leaders present, to agree to expel India. At this moment, a prominent Pakistani politician and member of its delegation Zulfikar Ali Bhutto (later President and then Prime Minister

of Pakistan) quipped that if India with 10 per cent Muslims was to be admitted as a full member, the conference would have no locus standi to reject Israel, with 11 per cent Muslims, as a full member of the Islamic Conference if such a request were made by Tel Aviv.[6] Two days were wasted in this controversy and finally the Indian delegation, which was unwilling to sit as an observer only, was expelled and Pakistan returned to the conference.

To add insult to injury, as soon as India was expelled, its flag was removed from the venue. Although Iraq and Syria had also boycotted the Summit, their flags had continued to flutter on the conference hall throughout the four days. Similarly, when one Mosque each was named after all the participating states of the Rabat summit, no mosque was named after India. Thus for India, the expulsion was an abject humiliation. At home, the Rabat fiasco became a political issue and the New Delhi government had to face a lot of embarrassment. Ahmad claimed that Indian delegation had participated in the conference so that Pakistan 'would not use the forum to mislead the Muslim leaders against India.' India later recalled its ambassadors from Rabat and Amman in protest.[7] (Since the Rabat summit, Pakistan considers the OIC as its constituency whereas India re-oriented its foreign policy emphasis towards the Non-Aligned Movement).

Those two issues created so much heat in the conference that they took most of the time and attention of the delegates. Even in the media, the real issues before the conference were shrouded in the coverage of these controversies.[8] When the problems of admission of the PLO and expulsion of India were settled, the Conference held threadbare discussions on the Al-Quds issue, for which it had been convoked it the first place, and felt the need to take a united stand. Libya called for severing of diplomatic relations with Israel, and the UAR and Sudan urged military help for Palestine. Both these resolutions were rejected. But the Conference did condemn the act of arson on the Al-Aqsa mosque in the strongest possible terms and called upon the world community to take note of this heinous crime. This conference did not deliberate on any political issue other than Palestine but in later conferences, not only was the

the scope extended but much stronger resolutions than those proposed by Libya and Sudan became the norm. However, the need to have a common forum, felt during the debate on the Jerusalem issue, led the Muslim leadership to resolve to work together for common causes of the Muslim *ummah*. Consequently it was decided to set up a permanent secretariat of the Organization and to draw up a Charter.

So, in spite of some unpleasant situations, the 1st Islamic Summit was a resounding success in the following ways:

- The dream of an Islamic Summit was fulfilled and provided a platform on which for the first time countries as diverse as Turkey and Iran on the one hand and UAR and Jordan on the other, were gathered.
- The conference created a lot of goodwill among the Muslim states. President of Mauritania, Mokhtar Daddah, whose appearance in Rabat was as unthinkable as Nasser's in Tel Aviv, just a few weeks ago, embraced King Hassan at the Rabat airport on the eve of this Summit.[9]
- The 1st Summit laid the groundwork for the establishment of the Organization of the Islamic Conference (OIC) which is today the largest association of the Muslim states.
- In spite of the boycott by most of the radical states, they carried the day all the same. Admission of the PLO, expulsion of India (that too on religious grounds) and condemnation of Israel, all of which would have seemed like a joke a few weeks earlier, now actually took place. Hence, the Summit was a major milestone in the history of Pan-Islamism.

2nd Islamic Summit (Lahore): The 2nd Islamic Summit, but technically speaking, the 1st OIC Summit, was held at Lahore on 22–24 February 1974. It was originally scheduled for December 1973 in response to the Arab–Israeli war but was postponed due to the pressing engagements of key Arab leaders in the post-war developments. In the war of October 1973, Arabs had made significant gains against Israel and after nearly three weeks of war, the latter had failed to dislodge the Egyptian forces from the Eastern bank of the Suez canal. Arab success was not confined to the battlefield only; they are still reaping the political and monetary fruit of the war. Politically, the Arabs were united as never before and their oil embargo

had shaken the Western world. And monetarily, as a corollary, the oil prices shot up resulting in the huge influx of petro-dollars. The prosperity in the Arab world seen today, might never have come, had the oil prices remained at $2.50 a barrel. Moreover, the war proved to be a morale booster for the Arab and the Muslim peoples, in so far as it shattered the myths of invincibility of Israeli forces and the impossibility of Arab unity.

The OIC Charter, that was approved in March 1972, did institutionalize the Summit Conference but stopped short of giving a precise schedule for the same. As noted above, the 1974 Islamic Summit was called to discuss the aftermath of the war and the oil-embargo, since it was felt that the situation 'was grave enough to warrant a conference of Kings and heads of state of the Islamic Conference'. King Faisal of Saudi Arabia and Prime Minister Zulfikar Ali Bhutto of Pakistan, were the architects of this conference. King Faisal financed the whole event as it was difficult for Pakistan alone to do so.

The Summit venue at a non-Arab state had an added significance, as it showed, symbolically, that on the Palestine issue the whole Muslim world stood united. The encouraging turn-out was the consequence of two perceptions: one, the Rabat summit had already shown that an Islamic Summit was neither an exercise in futility, nor an 'imperialist ploy'. Hence, all the Muslim states had shed their misgivings; and two, Pakistan had, in its own right, a standing in the Islamic world.[10] It had mobilized enough diplomatic resources to make the Summit a success because Pakistan was using the event, partly to restore the national pride damaged by the East Pakistan debacle and partly to regain the initiative in international affairs, if not also to tilt the diplomatic balance in South Asia in its own favour. So there were no boycotts and all the radical states actively participated in the conference this time, as opposed to in 1969. It was rather unprecedented that thirty-eight members (including the PLO), as against thirty-one who were invited, turned up, i.e., a 122 per cent success rate (*sic*), which raised the spirits of the participants and stimulated the mood of the conference.

In all, twenty-five heads of state and five heads of government led their delegations while eight states were represented at a lower level. The conference was also attended by the Grand *Mufti* of Palestine, Amin al Hussaini and His Beatitude Muawad Elias IV, Patriarch of Antioch and All Orient. It was, in fact the last major event graced by the former's presence. The highly revered Grand *Mufti* died on 4 July. Notable absentees were King Hassan of Morocco, King Hussein of Jordan, and King Reza of Iran.[11]

On the very first day of the conference, Pakistan recognized its breakaway province of Bangladesh, ostensibly 'in the larger interest of Muslim unity'. Several Muslim states friendly to Pakistan recognized it on the same day.[12] Besides, Pakistan did not raise the Kashmir issue at the conference, though the Pakistani Prime Minister alluded to it in veiled terms, since it did not want to embarrass some of its guests, that were on good terms with India. Afghanistan, however, tried to create an unpleasant situation by raising the issue of its border dispute with Pakistan, but was stopped by Algeria. The Summit Conference noted with pride, the successful initiatives taken by the OIC in the dispute settlement between Pakistan and Bangladesh and between Morocco and Mauritania. The Black September bloodbath was not an event of the distant past but Amman recognized the PLO as the sole representative of the Palestinians. The Summit also marked the resumption of diplomatic relations between Jordan and Syria, Jordan and Tunisia, and Iran and Iraq. The OIC also granted membership to Bangladesh along with Cameroon, Gabon, Gambia, Guinea-Bissau, Uganda, and Upper Volta.

Iran, which was facing criticism for increasing oil prices, announced a $1 billion aid package for the most affected developing countries through the World Bank, on the eve of the Summit. (Uganda, however, stressed that the money should have been deposited in the Islamic Development Bank instead, for disbursement among the Muslim LDCs.) In another move, a message by Iraqi President Hassan al-Bakr was read out by President Idi Amin, in which the former assured the OIC of Iraq's full cooperation in the Organization's efforts to resolve its conflict with Iran, to avoid the spilling of Muslim blood.

In the backdrop of the solemn vows about Islamic solidarity being made by the leaders, which was no doubt the finest hour in the OIC history, the much talked about 'Faisal–Bhutto' plan is said to have been floated. According to this plan, it is believed, the Caliphate was to be revived, and King Faisal, the custodian of the two holy shrines of Islam, was to assume the mantle of Caliph of Islam and Z.A. Bhutto was to be the Chairman of the Caliph's executive council for the Muslim world. As a corollary to this hypothetical plan was the theory that the violent and untimely deaths of the two leaders was an imperialist conspiracy to remove the two from the scene by those who had got wind of this plan. (During his research, this author failed to find any evidence to the effect that any such plan had ever existed. So one can, with reasonable certainty, dismiss this theory as baseless.)

As the conference was being held in response to the Arab-Israeli war, Israel was the main item on the agenda. The members resolved to shun all kinds of relations with Israel and resolved to work for the liberation of Palestine by all means. The PLO was recognized as the sole legitimate representative of the Palestinian people and its chief Yasser Arafat was accorded the full protocol of a head of state.[13] This alone shows how mature the Organization had become since the last Summit where the admission of PLO was being resisted and the very idea of breaking diplomatic relations was being laughed at. Libya reminded the leaders that the 4th ICFM (Benghazi; 1973) had through its resolution no. 1, asked member states to open offices where volunteers for war against Israel would register their names, and lamented that this, like many other resolutions, had not been implemented by any member state. Besides the observations of the Muslim leaders on the Palestine problem, the speech of Patriarch Muawad IV was also widely hailed when he said, 'Is Jerusalem not the goal of this long journey on the path to liberty which we are all engaged in together? Are we not, Muslims and Christians alike, dedicated to Jerusalem, in hope, determination and sacrifice?' He told the conference that the Pope, Paul VI, was equally concerned about the Jerusalem situation and was struggling against its Judaization.[14]

The issue of Filipino Muslims also came under discussion and the concern of the OIC over the Mindanao situation was conveyed to Manila. The

Manila regime denied persecution and killing of Muslims and expressed willingness to negotiate the issue with the OIC. This ultimately led to the signing of the Tripoli agreement two years later. The Islamic Summit also supported the freedom struggles of the African people and decided to break off diplomatic relations with the racist regimes of South Africa, Rhodesia, and Portugal.

The conference devoted a lot of its time to economic issues and noted the effects of increase in oil prices on less developed countries. Colonel Qaddafi of Libya proposed a three-tier oil price structure: a low price for Muslim states, relatively higher for the third world, and highest for the rest of the world. Although, this proposal did not find favour with most of the oil producing states but several measures to alleviate the effect of the oil crisis on less developed countries were approved. The final declaration made special reference to the speeches of the Presidents of Libya and Algeria, and constituted an eight-member committee consisting of Algeria, Egypt, Kuwait, Libya, Palestine, Saudi Arabia, Senegal, and the UAE to give recommendations for greater economic cooperation.[15] The African bloc was most vocal in the calls for greater economic aid. Idi Amin, the President of Uganda, stressed the need for a fund to help the least developed countries (LDCs) and many leaders called upon the rich countries to give 15 per cent of their earnings to the poor countries. It was pointed out that by 1974, almost $20 billion of Arab money was deposited in European Banks. In the preceding year alone five countries, viz. Saudi Arabia, Iran, Kuwait, UAE, and Iraq, had earned $46.8 billion by oil exports. This single year's income was large enough to support all the LDMCs without incurring domestic financial strains.

The conference failed to agree on a definite mechanism for transfer of money from the rich Muslim states to poor ones. It, however, declared that the member states of the Conference would extend their support and solidarity to one another in mobilizing of their resources for development purposes, and called upon all developing countries to unite their efforts in order to establish new international economic relations which would be more equitable and more balanced. The Summit's resolutions in the economic sphere later proved to be hollow words, as nothing tangible came out of it.

The Summit, inter alia, decided to establish the Islamic Solidarity Fund, with an initial capital of $26 million, approved in principle the establishment of Islamic universities and noted the progress achieved on the proposed Islamic Bank. The Secretary General, Hassan Tohami, proposed the change of name of the OIC to 'Organization of Solidarity of Islamic States (OSIS)' or 'Organization of Solidarity of Islamic Peoples and States (OSIPS)'. No action was taken on this suggestion.

The Summit concluded after approving the Lahore Declaration wherein the heads of the participating Governments proclaimed their conviction that their common faith was an indissoluble bond between their peoples. They expressed their determination to preserve and promote solidarity among Muslim countries and to respect each other's independence and territorial integrity. Through a separate resolution, the conference congratulated, and paid glowing tributes to Prime Minister Zulfikar Ali Bhutto and the Pakistani leadership for making the Summit a success.

The 2nd Islamic Summit was a big success and if we survey all the nine Islamic Summits held so far in retrospect, we feel that the spirit of Lahore has never returned. It was Lahore that gave birth to Islam as a political force which was played up by another international press as well. Daily *L'Ardennaise* of France opined that after Bandung, the Islamic conference of Lahore had demonstrated the birth of a new political bloc on the international chessboard. Daily *La Croix* thought that the OIC was a powerful religio-political bloc holding petroleum riches. Daily *Jeune Afrique* went a step further by calling it new world power.[16] *Karier* of Austria viewed the reconciliation of Pakistan and Bangladesh alone worth a hundred brotherly embraces. Singapore's *The New Nation* accorded Lahore a memorable place in world history because Jordan had recognized the PLO as the sole representative of Palestine.[17] Pakistan's arch-rival India was the lone critical voice terming the Summit as a conspiracy to divide the Non-Aligned Movement. But the Indian Premier, at the same time, also demanded representation of Indian

Muslims in the Islamic Summit, thereby tacitly accepting the importance of the moot.[18] It was during this conferences that the Islamic world was called 'the fourth world' and, for the time, people started believing that the goal of a commonwealth of Islamic states was only a matter of time, though the idea as such, never came under discussion there.[19]

The prevailing optimism, was expressed in the concluding speech made by the Chairman of the Conference, Z.A. Bhutto. He said:

> As I survey this splendid gathering, I recall that as a young student twenty-six years ago, I was asked to address the student body of a University, almost wholly non-Muslim, on the Islamic Heritage. After making a youthful attempt at defining it, I spoke of Muslim unity against exploitation and of Muslim revival and sketched a plan for a Muslim commonwealth. I ventured to predict that a movement in this direction would take shape in the next twenty years.
>
> There have been periods in my life when, like all of us, I have been assailed by doubts whether this vision of mine would be fulfilled. Today, despite all difficulties in our path, I bow my head in gratitude to Allah for making me witness to a scene which should dispel those doubts.
>
> I trust that we will not fritter away the historic opportunities now presented to us. For long centuries, we have hoped for a turning point. That turning point has arrived. The break of a new dawn is not now a forlorn hope. Poverty need no longer be our portion. Humiliation need no longer be our heritage. Ignorance need no longer be the emblem of our identity.[20]

3rd Islamic Summit (Mecca/Taif): The 3rd Islamic Summit was held on 25–28 January 1981 in Saudi Arabia. The initiative to convene this Summit was taken by the then Secretary General, Dr Amadou Gaye, back in 1978. There were the customary delays and finally the Islamic Summit took place on the eve of the advent of the 15th century according to the Islamic (lunar) calendar; to be precise, it recommended on the 19th of Rabi-I, in the year 1401 AH. Dr Gaye, the architect of this Summit, had retired by then. Since Mecca is Prophet Mohammad's (PBUH) birth place and Rabi I, the month of his birth, the choice of venue

and date of the Summit itself speaks of the sanctity being awarded to the conference.

The inaugural session was held at the Holy Mosque in Mecca al-Mukarramah where the Muslim leaders, most of them in *Ahraam*, assembled and performed the *tawaaf*. The *Imam* of *Masjid al-Haram* led the prayers for the solidarity of the Islamic *ummah*. The aura lent the conference a profound solemnity.[21] The Mecca Declaration was adopted in the inaugural session. The rest of the proceedings took place at the nearby resort of Taif. This is the reason why in different texts, this conference is referred to as Taif Summit or as Mecca Summit, which sometimes causes confusion.

Taif was beautifully decorated for the conference. Besides a rosewood conference auditorium and a marble mosque, opulent buildings for housing the delegates had been constructed. The lavish outlay of around $4 billion on the arrangements, made it the most expensive international conference of the world.[22] In all thirty-eight member states, twenty-eight of which were represented by their heads of state, took part in the conference. The membership of the OIC then stood at forty-two, with the addition of four new entrants since the previous Summit. The memberships of Egypt and Afghanistan had been suspended earlier, while Iran and Libya boycotted the conference because Iran said it could not sit at the same table with Iraq, and Libya had broken diplomatic relations with Saudi Arabia since the latter had allowed an airbase to the United States on its soil.[23]

The major political issue under discussion was the Iran–Iraq war that had erupted a few months ago. The President of Pakistan, who was the Chairman of the OIC Peace Committee, admitted his and the Secretary General's failure, despite what he called, 'doing everything possible to stop the war'. Habib Chatti accepted that Iran's lack of confidence in the OIC was a challenge to the authority of the OIC and an impediment in the negotiations. The Conference expressed the deep concern of the Islamic *ummah* over the internecine conflict and reaffirmed the desire of the OIC to accelerate efforts to bring about peace in the Gulf. The membership of the Ummah Peace Committee, which earlier consisted of Pakistan, Palestine, and the OIC Secretary General, with a mandate to mediate between Iran and Iraq, was expanded with the addition of Bangladesh, Gambia, Guinea, and Turkey. The Summit also confirmed the mediation offer, made by the extraordinary session of Islamic foreign ministers, held at New York in September 1980, to bring an end to the war. On the recommendation of the said foreign ministers meeting, the 3rd Islamic Summit accepted the proposal of an 'Islamic peace force' in principle. No practical steps were taken then or ever thereafter for the purpose but the proposal stands as a policy guideline.[24]

The second major issue before the Islamic Summit was the Soviet invasion of Afghanistan. On the one hand, the illegal occupation of a Muslim state by a non-Muslim power; and on the other, the enormous loss of (Muslim) lives, comparable to that in the ongoing Gulf conflict, in the Afghan imbroglio, entailed a decisive response on the part of the Muslim world. The Summit deliberated at length the implications of the Soviet occupation, and called for an immediate and unconditional withdrawal of Soviet troops from the Afghan soil. It also formed a three-member committee on Afghanistan. In the meantime, French President Giscard d'Estaing proposed a 'conference of eight' on Afghanistan (that would have included the big five and three most affected regional powers, excluding Afghanistan). His announcement surprised the Muslim leaders who were deliberating on Afghanistan, despite which the French President had not cared to inform them about his proposals in advance.[25] It was indeed very undiplomatic, if not rude, on the part of the latter. On its part, the Conference abstained from condemning the Soviet Union and instead, called for greater efforts for a peaceful and negotiated settlement of the war, entailing the restoration of sovereignty, territorial integrity, and the non-aligned character of Afghanistan.[26]

The third major political issue was obviously that of Palestine, on which the Conference reaffirmed its earlier resolutions, and reassured the Palestinians of the OIC's unflinching support for their just cause. The military employment of means to liberate Jerusalem was not ruled out though political means were stressed. The special post of Assistant Secretary General (*Al-Quds Al-Sharif*)

was established to coordinate the efforts of the Islamic *ummah* for the cause of Al-Quds. Confirming the condemnation of the Camp David agreement and affirming that UN Security Council resolution 242 did not offer a sound basis for settlement of the Palestine issue, the Summit rejected any solution implying an acceptance of *fait accompli* on the status of Palestine and Jerusalem. The Summit called upon the members to utilize their resources to undermine the Israeli economy. An Islamic Boycott Bureau was also created for the purpose. Among other things, the conference discussed the political situation of the Southern Philippines, Eritrea, and the horn of Africa pledging full moral support to all just liberation struggles in the Third World, especially where Muslims were one of the concerned parties.

Nevertheless, the real significance of this conference, as opposed to the previous Summit, lies in its economic, and not in the political, decisions. The conference realized that without economic cooperation, it would be well-nigh impossible to have greater cooperation in the political fields since in this age political, economic, and religious issues could not be placed in separate watertight compartments.

The Islamic Summit took a giant leap forward by approving an 'Economic Plan of Action' which aimed at greater integration of the economic structure of the Islamic world. The Plan of Action contained a number of recommendations for fostering close economic cooperation in ten major sectors, namely, Food and Agriculture, Trade, Industry, Transport, Communication and Tourism, Financial and Monetary Questions, Manpower and Social Affairs, Energy, Science and Technology, Population and Health, and Technical Cooperation. It recognized that the primary responsibility for economic development in the Muslim countries rested upon themselves and thus placed emphasis on self-reliance and the maximum utilization of the indigenous potential and resources. The plan gave policy guidelines for cooperation in the fields of economics, science and technology, and information.[27] Three standing committees were established for the purpose:

- Standing Committee for Commercial and Economic Cooperation (COMCEC)

- Standing Committee for Information and Cultural Affairs (COMIAC)
- Standing Committee for Scientific and Technological Cooperation (COMSTECH)

The three committees are respectively headed by the President of Turkey, the President of Senegal, and the President of Pakistan, *ex-officio*. In addition, the Islamic Summit approved the establishment of various commissions and committees for the same purpose. Besides expanding the OIC infrastructure, this plan of action serves as a blueprint for the direction of activities of the older organs like ISESCO, IFSTAD, and the IDB etc.

In the administrative sphere, the 3rd Islamic Summit amended the Charter. The term of the Secretary General, earlier 'two years renewable once', was made four years non-renewable. A similar amendment was made by the 12th ICFM (Baghdad) five months later, with regard to the term of office of ASGs which was likewise made four years non-renewable. The Summit also elevated the post of Director Coordination on Palestine to ASG (*Al-Quds Al-Sharif*). Similarly, Article IV of the Charter was also amended so that the Conference of Kings and Heads of State was to be 'convened periodically, once every three years'.[28] In another major move, the Conference approved the establishment of the International Islamic Court of Justice which the OIC considers its fourth principal organ. An amendment was made in Article III in this respect. The Summit also established Islamic Fiqh Academy at Mecca 'to achieve the theoretical and practical unity of the Islamic *ummah* and to strengthen the link of Islamic community with the faith.'[29] The 3rd Islamic Summit concluded with a note of optimism and a general euphoria about the future prospects of the OIC.

4th Islamic Summit (Casablanca): The 4th Summit was held at Casablanca, Morocco, on 16–19 January 1984. From 15 January, the historic city took on a deserted look as the government had closed the airport as well as all the commercial centres to the general public. Police checkposts appeared all over the city and army helicopters were wheeling overhead, providing absolute

security to the guests. The conference was attended by forty-two member states including Palestine, twenty-five of which were represented by their heads of state. In addition, Prof. Burhanuddin Rabbani (later President of Afghanistan), a leader of Afghan resistance movement and Nur Masauri (now Governor of autonomous South Philippines), the leader of MNLF, were leading their delegations, and participated as observers. Brunei Darussalam was admitted as the forty-fifth member; so the three absentees included, as in the Taif summit, Afghanistan and Egypt, the suspended members, and Iran which boycotted the converence. The Speaker of the Iranian parliament, Hashmi Rafsanjani (later President), had said that Iran would attend the Summit if the venue were shifted from Morocco. That the heads of state of Algeria, Iraq, Jordan, Lebanon, Libya, and Syria were conspicuous by their absence, was another unhappy circumstance.

The outgoing OIC Chairman, King Fahd of Saudi Arabia, inaugurated the conference. Then in accordance with the customary practice, the conference elected the head of state of the host country, King Hassan of Morocco, as its Chairman. Kenan Evren (Turkey), Abdou Diouf (Senegal), and Yasser Arafat (Palestine) were elected as the three Vice-Chairmen.[30] The preparatory meeting of the Islamic Foreign Ministers had finalized a 19-item agenda. However two issues, viz. the re-admission of Egypt and the tenure of the Secretary General, not initially included in the agenda, dominated the whole conference.

After the formal opening speeches, the issue of Egypt's re-entry came up in the very first session when Guinean President Ahmad Sekou Toure raised it. By the time of this conference, tempers had cooled over the issue of the Camp David Treaty. Some members were openly questioning the wisdom of keeping a major Islamic country out of the OIC. There was a general feeling that Egypt's isolation from the rest of the Muslim world had emboldened Israel. The latter's air raid on Iraqi nuclear installation and land invasion of Lebanon etc. were being cited to justify this view. Libya's was the strongest voice resisting the move on the plea that re-admission of Egypt before its renunciation of Camp David accord would be a negation of the OIC Charter. However, Malaysia insisted that even if Egypt were not re-admitted, the pros and cons of the proposal should be discussed. This suggestion found favour with many member states who thought that this issue was more important than many items on the agenda.

In the beginning, Saudi Arabia, Sudan, and Syria were also among those opposing discussion on this issue, though for reasons different from those of the radical states. Before the Islamic Summit, these three countries had agreed amongst themselves that the issue should be deferred until the Arab League session and if the League decided to re-admit Egypt into its fold, then the same move would be supported in the following OIC moot. Pakistan took strong exception to this contention and made it clear that the OIC would not be allowed to become a rubber stamp of the Arab League, and that an organization representing the whole Muslim world could not be held hostage to a much smaller regional organization's decisions. Hence, the OIC decided to discuss the issue in its own right and thus began one of the most interesting and emotional debates in the OIC history. Libya walked out in protest.[31]

The debate on Egypt took so much time that the conference had to be extended by one day. Morocco, Pakistan, Jordan and some other states spoke in favour of Egypt's re-admission. It was noted that Egypt, as a front-line state, had made the largest number of sacrifices in the wars against Israel. So much so that a joke was going around 'about the Arab determination to fight Israel to the last Egyptian'. It was argued that without Egypt, the OIC was incomplete. The logic of denying Egypt its sovereign right to defend its national interests, when many other states had gone farther in pursuance of their security and economic interests, albeit in a different way, was questioned. On the other hand, Libya, Algeriathe Arab and Tunisia were of the view that Egypt had betrayed the Islamic and the Arab cause, and had caused irreparable damage to Islamic unity, therefore, it had to be punished.

The heat and fury generated by the issue brought a host of other problems like cleavages in the Muslim world and the Arab versus non-Arab controversies into the debate. A large number of leaders invoked the famous *Hadith* of the Holy Prophet (PBUH) that there was no distinction between an *Arabi* and an *Ajami* or between a white and a black. The Libyan Prime Minister Abdul Salam Jalloud, while agreeing that Islam accepted no discrimination on the basis of colour, racethe Arab or language, said that there were two groups in the contemporary Islamic world; the leftist progressive states and the rightist conservative ones. The Pakistani President refuted this idea and stressed that 'Islam needs no other 'isms' as it has a monolithic ideological basis.'[32]

Finally, the matter was left to voting, the first and the last time the practice has taken place in the OIC. The Conference decided to re-admit Egypt with thirty-two votes in favour, and three abstentions. Six countries including Algeria, Libya, South Yemen, Syria, Tunisia, the Arab and Upper Volta boycotted the voting. Although the text of the resolution adopted on the issue implied that Egypt would have to renounce the peace accord before re-admission, the final communiqué of the Summit made no such mention (See Chapter 4 for a detailed account of Egypt's re-entry). It is worth noting that Palestine, the arch enemy of Israel and the Camp David Accord, was the protagonist of the move for Egypt's re-admission.

The second major issue, as noted earlier, was the tenure of Secretary General Habib Chatti whose four-year term had expired on 21 December, the preceding year. Chatti was claiming that since the 3rd Islamic Summit had increased the tenure of his office to four years, his term should be counted from the date of the 3rd Summit. As the report of the OIC Secretariat on the legality of Habib Chatti's claim was ambiguous, the Islamic Summit took upon itself to pass a verdict. Had the Conference decided against Chatti, a special ICFM session to elect his successor would have had to be convened. The Conference, however, decided in his favour and entitled him to stay for another year. On Pakistan's request, 31 December of that year was declared to be the last day of his tenure.

On the political side, the Conference reiterated the customary polemics about Jerusalem and the Palestine problem. The Conference supported the Fez peace plan propounded by the Arab leaders while rejecting the Reagan plan as 'unjust and unacceptable'.[33] The Summit renewed its commitment to upholding the Arab and Islamic character of the Al-Quds (Jerusalem) and condemned the alliance between the US and Israel as 'a source of tensions and a threat to world peace and security'.

In another resolution, the Islamic Summit condemned US for air attack on the Syrian border. The Conference expressed its deep concern over the unabated Iran–Iraq war and decided to resume efforts for a cease-fire. Sekou Toure, the President of Guinea, strongly urged the need for sending a goodwill mission to Tehran to bring her back into the OIC mainstream. Iran had boycotted this and the preceding Islamic Summit. One effect of Iran's boycott was the slight tilt of the Summit's resolution on the Gulf war towards Iraq. As Iraq had by then accepted all the OIC resolutions on cease-fire, the Conference expressed satisfaction that at least one party (Iraq) was willing to comply. So the other party (Iran) was asked to reciprocate the gesture. The Summit made a fervent appeal to both sides to withdraw their troops to internationally recognized borders.

The civil war in Lebanon, since the break-up of the PLO and the consequent factional fighting in 1983, was the subject of discussion in most of the private meetings. The Conference debated the Cyprus issue, and heard the report of President Rauf Denktash of Turkish Republic of Northern Cyprus on the latest situation in the island. The UN Secretary General Perez de Ceullar also attended the Summit. He discussed his peace plan on Cyprus with the Turkish President Kenan Evren and President Rauf Denktash.[34] The Conference took notice of the racist policies in South Africa and Namibia and expressed solidarity with their peoples. The Islamic Summit also supported Comoros' claims over Mayotte islands and warned France not to take any rash action. The Conference noted with satisfaction that a Muslim, Amadou Mokhtar M. Bow, from the Third World, had assumed the office of the Director General of UNESCO. In the interest of the principles of universality and equality, on which the UN and the UNESCO were based, it appealed to the United States to reconsider its decision of withdrawing from UNESCO.

The Conference heard the report of the Pakistani President, the *ex-officio* Chairman of COMSTECH, and appreciated the organization's plan of action on Science and Technology. It heard another report

on the drought conditions in the Sahel region and approved measures for helping the people of the region. In another major move, the 4th Islamic Summit approved the Islamic Charter of Human Rights and asked the members to adhere to it.[35]

The progress on the OIC's Plan of Action on Economic Co-operation, approved in the 3rd Islamic Summit was reviewed; the draft statute of the IICJ was given to another committee of Muslim legal experts for in-depth study; and the member states were requested to be efficient in the payment of contributions to OIC's subsidiary organs on Cultural and Information affairs. In his concluding speech the Secretary General recounted the major challenges to the Muslims and lamented that the situation had somewhat worsened since the previous Summit. The Conference concluded after approving the draft communiqué containing nineteen resolutions in all.

Casablanca was the last point in the upward journey of the OIC Summits. Since then, this principal organ of OIC is on the decline and the successive Conferences of Kings and Heads of State of the Islamic countries are marked by increasing irrelevance and indifference, by the public and the media.

5th Islamic Summit (Kuwait): Kuwait was the venue of the 5th OIC Summit conference during 26–29 January 1987. In all, forty-four members attended the conference including twenty heads of state. Egypt attended an Islamic Summit after thirteen years whereas the membership of Afghanistan still stood suspended. Iran not only boycotted the Summit again this time but also launched a major military offensive code-named Karbala-5 against Southern Iraq. The battle of Basra (January 1987) was one of the most fiercely fought battles in the eight-year war. This move by Iran, was interpreted by analysts as a calculated move to intimidate the OIC Summit participants, meeting in nearby Kuwait. Way back in 1974, the King of Iran had stayed away from the Lahore Islamic Summit because of his annoyance over Pakistan being given preference over Iran as the summit venue. In 1981, the Gulf war was too recent and Iran was under the illusion that it could be won on the field, and she was arrogant enough not to sit on the same table with Iraq. So Iran boycotted all the conferences including the Islamic Summit where Iraq was to be an equal member. Iran had a different reason for shunning the 4th Summit (Casablanca; January 1984) as it was critical of King Hassan of Morocco's soft line towards Israel. Finally in 1987, Iranian President decided not to land at Kuwait because by supporting Iraq financially, Kuwait had become her *de facto* ally.

The OIC was concerned about Iran's persistent absence for one reason or the other and this time, just before the conference, hectic efforts were made to convince Iranian President Ali Khaminei to attend. Iran was insistent that it was ready to attend the Summit provided that the venue was shifted to a 'neutral' country, preferably Pakistan. The Iranian demand was turned down. So when Sharif Pirzada, the OIC Secretary General, leading a delegation, visited Tehran to make a last ditch effort to elicit an assurance of Iran's participation, his request was politely but firmly rejected.[36]

King Hassan and King Fahd were the other prominent (and regular) absentees. Hassan had stayed away fearing that Syria's Hafiz al Asad would raise the matter of his meeting with the Israeli Premier Shimon Peres. Two active members, viz. Malaysia and Senegal were also represented by Foreign Ministers. On the other hand, Uganda turned up after a long absence, i.e. the first time since the overthrow of Field Marshal Idi Amin.

There was another unpleasantry at the beginning of the Summit. A radical militant Islamic group in Lebanon called *Al-Jihad* was threatening to sabotage the conference as it believed that the OIC had become an impotent talkshop. So the Group dubbed the Muslim heads of states as 'Western imperialist agents'. *Al-Jihad* warned the leaders of suicide attacks against them, in case any one of them dared attend the Summit. Despite the foolproof security arrangements by the Kuwait administration, fire erupted in three oil wells just north of Kuwait city after explosions rocked the site on 19 January. The Kuwait regime, desirous of making the Summit a success, played down the incident, ruling out sabotage as the cause, but the incident cast doubts on the success of the Summit.[37] On 23 January, while the foreign ministers were in session for the preparatory

meeting, another bomb rocked Falika Island, 25 km. north-east of Kuwait city, apparently planted there by a gunboat.[38]

The Kuwaitis had made lavish arrangements to show traditional Arab hospitality for the 21,000 guests associated with the Summit. Over fifty royal palaces were constructed and roses were imported from Europe to adorn the streets of Kuwait city; the total expenses incurred might have been around $900 million while the food bill alone was $20 million. On the forenoon of 26 January, Sheikh Jabber al-Ahmad al-Sabah, the Amir of Kuwait, opened the Conference at the newly built magnificent $400 million Convention Hall, being guarded at that time by 4000 elite commandos, as per schedule.[39] Subsequently, the Amir was unanimously elected as the Chairman of the summit conference. The Islamic Summit again brought bitter rivals closer. King Hassan met the PLO chief Yasser Arafat, while President Asad of Syria met Mubarak of Egypt for the first time after the latter's taking office. President Mubarak had announced that in the spirit of fraternity and goodwill, he would not respond to Hafiz al-Asad's hard hitting speech against his country in the summit conference. The Syrian leader had earlier blasted Egypt for 'strengthening its ties with Israel at the cost of Arab unity'.[40]

The Summit passed resolutions in support of Palestinian freedom fighters and Afghan Mujahideen and wished them success in their struggles. With a volley of condemnation for the Israeli policies as well as the unlimited support to Israel by the US, the Conference described the Israeli legislation on Golan Heights as null and void. It hailed the steadfastness of the Lebanese people and called for Israeli withdrawal. One of the achievements of the Summit was to have worked out an agreement to end the factional fighting around Palestinian refugee camps in Lebanon. Giving details, the Algerian Foreign Minister Ahmad Talib el-Ibrahim said that the agreement stipulated a cease-fire and immediate lifting of siege of the refugee camps.

The Conference discussed the Gulf war and, in view of the prevailing situation, postponed the OIC peace mission to Tehran and Baghdad but called on both sides to agree to a cease-fire. In the absence of the Iranians, the Iraqi Vice President lashed out at Iran, which he dubbed as the villain in the conflict, in his lengthy speech.[41]

With the change of leadership in Moscow, positive feelers were emanating from Kremlin. The Soviet Presidium sent a message to the Islamic leadership, expressing its willingness to withdraw its troops from Afghanistan as soon as an acceptable formula was reached. While hoping that such a step would remove a big obstacle in Moscow's relations with the Muslim World, the Summit expressed the hope that the ongoing UN-mediated talks would be successful. (The Geneva negotiations on the Afghan problem were in the final stages at that time.)[42] In one resolution, US air raids on brotherly Muslim state of Libya were condemned in unequivocal terms; yet in another, both the parties in the Libya-Chad dispute were urged to settle the conflict in accordance with the Charter, resolutions, and principles of the Islamic Conference. In a resolution sponsored by Kuwait, international terrorism was condemned in all its forms and manifestations. In another resolution, sponsored by Syria, the OIC Summit called for defining terrorism and drawing a line between terrorism and just liberation struggles. In addition, the Conference called upon the Muslim states to pool their resources in the field of aviation. An important resolution called for drafting an international covenant prohibiting attack on the nuclear installations of developing states.

The 5th Summit also approved the Statute of the IICJ; decided to hold a conference of information ministers of the OIC states at Saudi Arabia; constituted a ten-member committee to look into the sorry state of affairs in the IINA; and asked the member states to help their African brothers in implementing OAU's plan for Africa's economic revival for 1986–87.[43] The Summit adopted the Kuwait Declaration as well as thirty-two resolutions in the political and four each in economic and cultural fields.

6th Islamic Summit (Dakar): Senegal had the honour of hosting the 6th Islamic Summit at its capital Dakar, from 9 to 11 December 1991. It was the first gathering of the Muslim leadership in the new political landscape of the world, in the backdrop of the disintegration of the Soviet Union.

We have seen above that the 5th Islamic Summit was marred by an unwelcome beginning due to Iran's behaviour and the Islamists' threats. The Dakar Summit was a failure *ab initio*. Scheduled for January 1990 but delayed till mid-year, when the Kuwait crisis deteriorated, it was again postponed indefinitely by the Riyadh-led Arab bloc. Though the Iraqi occupation of Kuwait was no less serious a challenge for the Islamic *ummah* than the Ramadan war of October 1973, seventeen years back, warranting an urgent Islamic Summit, President Abdou Diouf had to acquiesce to the postponement of the Summit due to the Arab pressure. The Summit was thus a non-starter.

Just about half the number of states were being represented by their heads of state. Only five out of twenty-one Arab heads of state, namely, King Hussein (Jordan), Yasser Arafat (Palestine), Chadli Benjadid (Algeria), Jabber al-Sabah (Kuwait), and Ilyas Harawi (Lebanon) were there in person. President Abdou Diouf was furious at the poor response. 'We give more importance and respect to Arab countries than they give us', he remarked.[44] The absence of the Arab leadership contrasted with the substantial presence of non-Arab leadership, and the fact that the Summit was taking place in a black African country for the first time, gave the Conference a highly non-Arab character. Although Senegal is not a rich country, it had left no stone unturned in making the conference a memorable event. The 3000 delegates and thousands of other guests, media men etc. enjoyed Senegal's hospitality. The conference hall alone had been built at a colossal cost of $135 million, the major chunk of which was borne by the Saudi monarch, King Fahd.

Still, there is the positive side of the picture. After a long time, all the OIC members (forty-six at that time) were participating in the Summit. The presence for the first time of the Presidents of Iran and Indonesia in an Islamic Summit was widely hailed. It was no less encouraging that the Iranian delegation was most active in all the deliberations. At the same time, the Black African Muslim countries were equally enthusiastic to make the first Islamic Summit in West Africa a big event. Similarly, the presence of Azerbaijan (which was admitted as a full member) and Albania and Kazakhstan as observers, in the first post-cold war

Islamic Summit raised the hopes that the newly independent Muslim republics would join the larger Muslim community in the near future. (By 1996, all eight former Communist republics of Central Asia, Caucasus, and Europe had joined the OIC.)

The Summit was being held in the wake of the Gulf war of 1991, the most divisive conflict in recent Muslim history, so the cleavages were still wide enough. Iraq had boycotted the Summit calling it a 'theater to peddle suspect US policies against Iraq'.[45] The delegations of Saudi Arabia and Kuwait turned a cold shoulder to Jordan and Palestine who had backed Iraq in the war. So, poor attendance was not the only discouraging factor; as one analyst notes:

> One...could not help taking note of the lack of spirit of warmth and cordiality that should have animated the participants of such a summit. There was an air of going through the formalities and of fulfilling obligations rather than of an enthusiastic endeavour to infuse life into an organization that reflects the aspirations of a billion Muslims to forge closer links.[46]

For the first time, an Islamic Summit took note of the grave situation and massive human rights violation in the Indian occupied Kashmir. Recognizing the Kashmiris' right of self-determination, the Summit called for a peaceful resolution to the Kashmir crisis 'in accordance with the UN resolutions.' Many Muslim leaders reiterated the Pakistani line regarding the 'state sponsored repression' against the 'predominantly Muslim population of Kashmir, fighting for their right of self-determination'. Hence, taking note of the grave human rights violations against the Kashmiri Muslims, the resolution also requested the Secretary General, once again, to send a fact-finding mission to Occupied Kashmir. (Since such a request earlier had been rejected by New Delhi, the OIC fact-finding mission had to base its report on secondary sources, including Pakistan-based Kashmiri resistance groups and international human rights agencies.)[47]

On the political side, the Summit expressed full solidarity with Libya and also took note of the problems of 300 million Muslims constituting minorities in non-Muslim states. In another move,

the Summit upheld the OIC verdict of 1989 on Salman Rushdie as 'apostate'. On the Gulf crisis, many Arab leaders blasted Iraq for its misadventure in Kuwait, as that was apparently their only pastime since the previous year. King Hussein and Yasser Arafat urged the leaders to 'overcome' the Gulf war. Hence no resolution of condemnation of Iraq was adopted this time, though, unconditional release of Kuwait's POWs was demanded from her. The conference went on to support all the UN resolutions concerning Iraq.

The 6th Islamic Summit would also be remembered for the historic controversy that related to the deletion of the word '*Jihad*' from the text of the resolution on Palestine, on the plea that modern Arabic language had witnessed tremendous change in vocabulary and usage that had made *jihad* irrelevant. Though a detailed analysis of the meaning of *jihad* and the OIC's opinion about it, is outside the scope of this chapter but many political observers questioned the credentials of the OIC Summit as an intellectual body comprising experts on linguistics and Arabic-English lexicon.[48]

This decision, a momentous departure from OIC's earlier stand on the Jerusalem issue, was received with surprise and shock in the Muslim world. PLO Chief Yasser Arafat stormed out of the Conference in protest. 'What would I tell the martyrs of the Palestine cause: that the blood of Muslims was spilled in vain?', an emotional Arafat asked. He was later persuaded to return when the Summit expressed support for the inalienable rights of the Palestinian people to self-determination, to return to their homeland, and establishment of the Palestinian State. Iranian President Hashmi Rafsanjani was most vocal in all-out support for the Palestinian resistance movement 'Intifada', launched in the Gaza strip and the occupied West Bank since 9 December 1987. The Summit, while lauding the Palestinian determination, gave cautious support to the ongoing peace process.[49] Moreover, the Islamic Summit, in a resolution designated the liberation of Jerusalem as 'the greater Islamic cause of the present generation', and through another resolution asked the members to 'oppose all the attempts to repeal the 1975 UN General Assembly resolution equating Zionism with racism'. The irrelevance of the OIC became apparent when just weeks later the said resolution was actually repealed, with some Muslim states abstaining or even favouring the repeal.[50]

The 6th Islamic Summit adopted a resolution propounded by the Pakistani Prime Minister Nawaz Sharif on the creation of an Islamic Common Market and directed the COMCEC to take necessary actions in this regard. In response to the earnest pleadings by the African Muslim states for financial aid, Saudi Arabia announced that it would write-off the debts of the least developed Muslim countries (LDMCs), a gesture which was appreciated by the African bloc in the OIC. The Kingdom also announced a contribution of $10 million to ease the OIC budgetary deficit that stood at around $49 million at that time.[51]

The Summit concluded a day ahead of schedule on 11 December as most of the delegates had left on 11 December, before waiting for the concluding session the following day. One major reason for this attitude was that the OIC had changed its practice of adopting the resolutions on the last day. In Dakar, all the twenty-two resolutions were adopted on the first day and debate followed later.[52] So the leaders had no interest in staying. From all angles, the 6th OIC Summit appears to have been a debacle and a point of nadir for the Organization of the Islamic Conference or at least for the institution of the Islamic Summit. The twenty-two months' delay, extremely poor turnout, lack of interest by the leaders, the resolutions on *jihad* and Iraq, all point in this direction.

7th Islamic Summit (Casablanca): The 7th Islamic Summit which was held in Casablanca, the third in the Kingdom of Morocco, on 13–14 December 1994 fared no better than the Dakar Summit. Saudi Arabia, the would-be host, demonstrated the utmost indifference by expressing regrets on its inability to organize the Summit, and the venue had to be shifted to Morocco. It was the shortest regular Islamic Summit to date, lasting just a couple of days.

After the Dakar debacle, nobody took this Summit seriously and it was given astonishingly, but not unexpectedly, marginal coverage by the media. Except on the issues of Kashmir and Bosnia, the Summit passed very lukewarm resolutions; though the long final communiqué

comprised no less than 182 articles.[53] This time again, Iranian President Hashmi Rafsanjani announced that he would boycott the Summit in protest against King Hassan's decision to entertain the Israeli delegation at the Middle East and North Africa (MENA) economic conference. Iran's supreme spiritual leader Ali Khamenai (former President) feared that the 'Summit would be swayed by traitors to take a position in favour of Israel'.[54] However, on the Middle East problem the Conference reiterated its earlier resolutions regarding Palestine but had some cautious words of approval and support for the US-sponsored Middle East peace process. King Hussain of Jordan stormed out in protest when Jerusalem was referred to as a Palestinian territory.[55]

This was the first Summit to be attended by the leaders of Azad (free) Kashmir as well as of the Indian-occupied Kashmir. India had allowed Mir Waiz Omer Farooq to proceed to Morocco for attending the Summit. A jubilant Pakistan credited its 'successful' foreign policy which forced Delhi to allow the Kashmiri leaders to attend the OIC moot. The Conference adopted the Pakistani resolution on Kashmir, verbatim, calling for plebiscite in Kashmir in accordance with the UN resolutions. India was called upon to respect human rights and the right of self-determination of the Kashmiri people.[56] Moreover, in the final resolution on Kashmir there was no reference to the Simla agreement implying that the OIC did not consider Kashmir as simply a bilateral issue. (India rejected the OIC resolution.)

The Conference also discussed Afghanistan and expressed concern over the ongoing civil war. Afghanistan's *de facto* president, Burhanuddin Rabbani represented Afghanistan who appealed for greater economic aid for his country. The Afghan opposition alliance Supreme Coordination Council for Islamic Revolution in Afghanistan (SCCIRA) criticized the OIC decision to allow Rabbani to represent Afghanistan.[57]

On the question of Bosnia, the OIC was very forceful in its condemnation of Serbian aggression. The Summit called for lifting of the 'unjust and unwarranted' arms embargo against the Bosnian government. The Summit, which was also addressed by Alija Izzetbegovich, the President of Bosnia, approved a meager amount of $0.3 million as aid to Bosnia. The Chechnyan crisis was not discussed at all in the formal sessions; though it came up in the private meetings among the leaders. Otherwise, the Conference affixed a tacit stamp of approval on the Russian claims of the civil war in Chechenya being her domestic affair.[58]

Iraq asked the OIC to support her in the face of severe UN-imposed sanctions against her. She failed to get passed a resolution to the effect that Iraq was fully complying with all the UN resolutions. On the other hand, the Summit showed the first signs of a softening Saudi stance towards Iraq when the Saudi Foreign Minister expressed the hope that Iraqi isolation would end by the next Summit (Tehran; 1997).

The speeches of the Muslim leaders had all the customary OIC rhetoric. Many speakers recalled the famous *Hadith* of Prophet Muhammad (PBUH) that the Muslims were like a single body and a pain in one part of it makes the whole body uncomfortable.[59] Scores of proposals were made in the speeches. King Hassan called for the establishment of an Islamic equivalent of the Vatican for the propagation of Islamic views. Pakistan's Benazir Bhutto stressed the need for a Collective Security System for the Islamic countries, what she called 'partnership for peace'.[60] The Conference adopted a Code of Conduct for Combating Terrorism. Through a similar resolution, the member states pledged to refrain form supporting activities of Muslim extremist groups working against their governments.[61] Saudi Arabia and Iran rejected Oman's suggestion to include 'Islamic' extremism, by name, in the said resolution. The Summit also included in its discussions the situation in Somalia, Azerbaijan, Cyprus, etc. and discussed issues relating to economic cooperation in the Islamic world. Commenting on the 7th OIC Summit one analyst aptly remarked, 'OIC has now been stripped of the rhetoric, that used to cause ripples in the calm waters of US diplomacy'.[62]

8th Islamic Summit (Tehran): The session of 'Dignity, Dialogue and Participation', was the theme of the 8th Islamic Summit Conference held at Tehran during 9–12 December 1997. The strength of the OIC stood at fifty-five at that time; all but one member state participated. The Taliban-

led government of Kabul, at very unpleasant terms with Tehran, boycotted the Summit to protest against the OIC decision of the twenty-fourth ICFM to keep Afghanistan's seat vacant.[63] In all, the Summit was attended by twenty-seven Presidents, seven Prime Ministers, three Crown Princes and four Vice Presidents / Deputy Prime Ministers. After the thaw achieved at the Islamabad Summit (see the next section), the presence of the Saudi Crown Prince Abdullah and the Iraqi Vice-President Taha Yaseen Ramadhan among the galaxy of Muslim leaders at Tehran, did not come as a surprise. President Hosni Mubarak, who had been highly critical of, what he calls, Iranian support of Islamic terrorism in his country, could not be persuaded to attend personally.[64] Similarly, the UAE sent a low key delegation to show its resentment over its territorial dispute with Iran. The Summit was preceded by a two-day Foreign Ministers' preparatory meeting and a two-day experts' meeting.

As it was the biggest diplomatic gathering in post-revolution Iran, the host country left no stone unturned in according hospitality to the 5000 or so foreign guests. A conference centre, a blend of modernist and Islamic architecture, was built from scratch within six months. Iranian parliament approved 250 billion Rials ($80 million) for sprucing up the Summit's meeting rooms.[65] Tehran's imperial palaces and posh hotels, largely untouched since the Islamic revolution, were refurbished to accommodate thousands of guests. A huge square carpet—weighing one ton, containing 282 million knots and valued at $1 million—was moved to one of the venues to welcome the dignitaries. King Fahd of Saudi Arabia, gave a drapery of the Holy *Kaaba* as a gift to the Summit. Richly embroidered with Quranic verses in gold and silver, the cloth hung over the area where the presiding board of the 8th Summit met. A four-day public holiday was declared in Tehran and the bustling city of ten million came to a halt in the unprecedented security arrangements. Huge portraits of Iranian leaders, flags of Muslim states and welcoming banners adorned the whole city.

Opening the Summit, Iran's paramount religious leader Ali Khaminei talked about the bonds of Islamic unity and the misunderstandings created by, what he called, the enemies of Islam.[66] Criticizing the Western military presence in the Persian Gulf, he opined that a powerful OIC 'can on the one hand use the medium of Islamic power and dignity to force the aliens to dispense with this intervention and on the other hand eliminate the pretexts for this improper presence (in the region)'. He launched a blistering attack on Western countries and appealed to the *ummah* to take the initiative. 'So far, the enemy has always held the initiative, and we have, at most, complained,' he deplored, while terming the Middle East peace process as 'unjust, arrogant, contemptuous and illogical'. He said the OIC could be a symbol of true unity of the Muslim countries in facing challenges and protecting their common interests. 'It can speak on behalf of its members, make demands, carry out requisite measures, and enjoy their financial, economic, and political backing...Whenever measures and activities for an enormous task and a common objective require coordination, the Organization can act as the coordinator. Where needed, it can engage in arbitration, and when beneficial, it can offer advice and consolation,' he said. Khaminei also proposed that the OIC should establish the inter-parliamentary union of the Islamic countries and translate the idea of the common Islamic market from a farfetched dream into a reality.

His long discourse, listened to in pin drop silence, dwelt at length on crises in the Muslim world including famine in Afghanistan, the food and medicine crisis in Iraq, spate of gruesome massacres in Algeria, and so on. He proposed the establishment of an Islamic army and an Islamic arbitration tribunal and called for the OIC being granted a sixth veto power in the UN Security Council. His speech was followed by the statement of Iran's new moderate President, Dr Mohammad Khatami, who was also elected the Chairman of the Summit Conference. The President said that dialogue between civilizations was necessary. He thus called for greater understanding of the West but warned against imitation of Western culture. While rejecting the US-sponsored New World Order, Khatami stressed the need for an 'Islamic Human Order'. He said that Muslim countries were mature enough to guard their security interests on their own.

The top agenda item of the Islamic conference was the Al-Quds problem and the Palestine. Though there was some wrangling over the texts of resolutions between Iran and some Arab states, as the former opposes the peace process, but the final draft of the six resolutions related to the Palestine–Israel problem condemned 'Israeli crimes, expansionism and threats' to the Muslim world.[67] The resolutions reiterated support for a Palestinian state with Jerusalem as its capital and called for a halt to the building of Jewish settlements in the occupied lands. The Palestinian leader Yasser Arafat, while lashing out at Israel for 'trampling on the sentiments of the Muslims...in a flagrant manner', asked the OIC leadership to counter the Israel-Vatican accord of 10 November 1997. He requested the leaders to use their contacts in the Vatican to apprise the Pope of its implications and to convince him to withhold the ratification.[68] Speaking at the Summit, Syria's hard-liner President, Hafiz Al Assad, termed the 'Zionist aggression against the Arab lands as the most serious danger facing the Muslim world'. 'Any dissension in our ranks is a source of strength for Israel and an opening of infiltration into...Muslim countries', he warned.[69] Turkey's joint military exercises with Israel were unequivocally criticized by most of the members.[70] On Iran's insistence, Turkey's reference by name was omitted from the resolution 'expressing deep concern about the fact that some member states...are establishing military cooperation with Israel'.

Turkey's President Suleiman Demirel's departure from the Summit a day earlier was construed as a mark of protest over the said resolution, though, Demirel tried to dispel the impression in his talk with the journalists on arrival at the Ankara airport. Rather he expressed pleasure that the two OIC resolutions disapproving Turkey's policies did not refer to it by name. He dubbed the allegations about tensions within the Muslim countries as 'mere fabrications'. Like Turkey, the *de facto* ruling military junta of Algeria also had a reason to be upset since some leaders of the Islamic Summit heard the delegation of the Islamic Salvation Front (FIS) which asked the OIC to persuade the Algerian rulers to 'halt the state-sponsored terrorism and murder sprees' that were resulting in 'unquantifiable human losses'.

The Summit 'deplored the continuation of conflict and violence in Afghanistan, and expressed support for an intra-Afghan dialogue and formation of a broad-based government'. In a resolution jointly tabled by Pakistan and Iran, the OIC Secretariat was asked to accelerate its efforts for mediation among the Afghan warring factions and a call was made to provide economic and material assistance to the war-torn country. As a big snub to India, the Summit underlined its support for the right of self-determination of the Kashmiri people. The OIC Contact Group on Kashmir, which held several meetings in the sidelines of the Summit condemned the atrocities, including genocide, arson and rape, being perpetrated by the Indian occupation forces against the Kashmiri Muslims.[71]

The Summit stressed its solidarity with the Muslim people of Bosnia and Herzegovina and underscored its confidence that the Ministerial Contact Group on Bosnia would continue to pursue the process of peace and reconstruction. The conference also called for rejection of the aggression of the Republic of Armenia against the Republic of Azerbaijan and complete withdrawal of Armenian forces from all occupied territories, and early and peaceful resolution of the Armenian-Azerbaijani conflict. Iraq raised the question of its sovereignty and lashed out at Turkey for its incursions in northern Iraq 'on the behest of the United States'. Turkey justified her incursions calling them 'inevitable clean-up operations, as long as there was power vacuum in the region'.[72]

The Islamic Summit adopted 142 resolutions in all. Other resolutions dealt with nuclear-weapon free zones in the Middle East and South Asia, Disarmament, security of the non-nuclear weapon states, support to sovereignty and territorial integrity of Iraq, salute to the steadfastness of the Syrian, Lebanese, and Palestinian peoples, structural reforms at the UN and the Security Council expansion, the UN sanctions against Iraq, Sudan, and Libya, and the desecration of the Babri mosque in India. The conference also concerned itself with the image of Islam and the hostile propaganda against it, and adopted resolutions on Islamic human rights, support to Muslim minority communities, support for women and family, and

status of women in Islam, besides the one condemning terrorism in the name of Islam. Addressing the assembly of Muslim leaders, the Arab League Secretary General, Esmet Abdul Muguid, supported the 'veto right for 1.3 billion Muslims'. He painted a gloomy picture of the Iraqi and Libyan peoples' sufferings, expressed sympathy with them and demanded immediate lifting of 'oppressive' sanctions as 'Iraq and Libya were fully willing to comply with the UN resolutions'. In his statement, the UN Secretary General, Kofi Annan, called for 'sacrifices and compromises needed to attain peace'. He rejected the demand to consider the OIC's claims for a seat in the UN Security Council as the sixth veto power.[73]

While torrential rains, followed by snow, tumbled over Tehran (causing flooding of the venue, a short power shut off and a delay in the second session), a flurry of meetings continued in the sideline of the Conference. President Khatami held talks with Saudi Prince Abdullah and Kuwaiti Amir Jaber al Ahmad al Sabah to bring about a new beginning in Iran–Arab relations. He also met the Turkish leader, Suleiman Demirel, and both leaders hailed the close Turkey–Iran ties. Khatami explained to Arafat the reasons for the Iranian reluctance to endorse peace talks with Israel. He received a call from Egyptian Foreign Minister Amr Moussa who said that the two countries should agree to disagree as a basis for settling disputes. The most significant of Khatami's parleys was his meeting with Iraqi Vice-President Taha Ramadhan—the first high level contact between the two countries since 1980. The two leaders discussed their disputes in a cordial atmosphere and agreed to hold further talks.[74] President Khatami said that Iran and Iraq were brothers and assured the Iraqi leader that 'your pains...resulting from great power aggressions are...our pains too'. He referred to the United States saying 'if we look at the twenty years just passed between us, we can see who our real enemy was'.

The Tehran Islamic Summit was a diplomatic coup in the true sense of the word. Frustrating the attempts made at the Extraordinary Islamic Summit (Islamabad; 1997) to scuttle the Tehran moot, Iran broke out of its diplomatic isolation. Considering Iranian diplomatic gains as American losses and vice versa, even the Western media called this Summit 'a signal of the collapse of American prestige'.[75] Though Israel's stubbornness in the Middle East peace process may be a contributing factor, the shrewd Iranian diplomacy led the Arabs to say a big 'No' to the US-sponsored Middle East Economic Conference and instead, assemble at Tehran, which the United States dubs the 'capital of world terror.' In the conference, Iran mended fences with several Arab states, while retaining her opposition to the Middle East peace process, and largely succeeded in polishing the country's tarnished image. In the end, the Tehran moot approved the request of Qatar's Amir Shiekh Hammad bin Khalifa al-Thani to host the 9th Islamic Summit at Doha, in December 2000.

Extraordinary Sessions of the Islamic Summit

An extraordinary session of the Conference of Kings and Heads of State of the Muslim countries can be convened 'whenever the interest of Muslim Nations warrants it, to consider matters of vital importance to the Muslims' according to Article IV of the OIC Charter. It may be pointed out that the first three Islamic Summits can, in a way, be called extraordinary Summits since they were held in response to particular circumstances; it was at the Taif Summit that an amendment was made in the said Article calling for regular triennial Summit Conferences. Since 1981, only one special session of the Islamic Summit Conference has been held.

Special Islamic Summit (Islamabad): A one-day extraordinary session of the Islamic Summit was held in Islamabad on 23 March 1997 with a single-item agenda, 'Future of the Islamic *ummah* in the twenty-first Century'. The request by Benazir Bhutto's government to host this Summit to mark Pakistan's golden jubilee celebrations had been approved by the 23rd ICFM (Conakry; 1995). Attended by 104 delegations, including all the fifty-four member states at that time; the Summit was opened by Mr Farooq Leghari, the then President of Pakistan. In all, eleven Presidents, ten Prime Ministers or Deputy Prime Ministers, four Vice-Presidents and three Crown Princes represented their countries, while the remaining delegations were led by Foreign Ministers, or parliament Speakers etc.

The beautiful city of Islamabad presented a festive look on Pakistan's Republic Day. Welcoming banners and buntings and rows of imported flowers on the main streets of the town enthralled the visitors. The city's administration had announced a lighting competition whereby most beautifully decorated buildings in each category: offices, commercial plazas etc., were to be awarded prizes. As night fell, thousands of Islamabad's buildings lit up with brilliant illuminations. The city was literally glowing with light and jubilation. The government had booked 2300 rooms in Islamabad's leading hotels while many important guests were housed in the Ministers' official residences and the houses of prominent citizens who had voluntarily lent their mansions for the purpose. Though all Pakistani embassies had stopped issuing visit visas for Pakistan between 15 to 28 March 1997 as part of the stringent security precautions, unlike the other Islamic Summits held elsewhere, the lives of the ordinary citizens of Islamabad remained largely unaffected. There was some checking at the entry and exit points of Islamabad, but on the whole the security personnel were less visible on the streets of the city. The Summit cost around $500 million to the national exchequer.

The leaders of the fifty-four Muslim states reviewed the Joint Services Pakistan Day Parade. Smartly turned out contingents of Pakistani armed forces marched past the Saluting Dais followed by the mechanized columns. After watching an impressive fly-past display by the Pakistan Air Force and a performance by the military bands, the leaders were taken to the newly built OIC Convention Centre. The Centre, built at a cost of $16 million, was completed in just nine months, and was also meant to be a befitting monument marking Pakistan's golden jubilee.[76]

In the first session, President Leghari's inaugural speech was followed by the statements of President Yasser Arafat of Palestine, President Suleiman Demirel of Turkey, and President Yahya Jammeh of Gambia, representing the Arab, Asian, and African states in the Islamic Conference, respectively.[77] Yasser Arafat's speech was particularly important since he was the only survivor of the 1974 Islamic Summit, held in Pakistan. In a fiery speech, he informed the audience that Israel had terminated the Middle East peace process. He condemned Israel and invited the Muslim leadership to do the same. In a marked departure from his earlier stance on Kashmir, this time he toed the Pakistani line by backing the Kashmiris' right of self-determination.[78] The Summit was also addressed by the OIC Secretary General Dr Izzeddienne Laraki, representative of the UN Secretary General, Hazem al Beblawi, and the representatives of over thirty member states, besides the leaders of Kashmir, South Philippines, and Bosnia. The second and concluding marathon session, that started in the afternoon, went four hours beyond its scheduled time because of the large number of leaders wishing to speak. A sumptuous dinner hosted by the President of Pakistan awaited the dignitaries after a hectic day.

As is usually the case, different leaders raised their voices about the issues that concerned them most. Algeria decried the FIS-led insurgency, Azerbaijan talked of Nogorno–Karabagh dispute, while Iran lamented the 'external interference' in Afghanistan. But on the specific issues confronting the Muslims, there was a unanimity; like on the condemnation of Israel, the support for the struggles of Kashmiri, Bosnian, and Palestinian Muslims, and the call for economic assistance to Albania, which was beset by a political turmoil at that time.[79]

The host state, Pakistan, outlined a future economic agenda for the Muslim *ummah*. The Conference reiterated its resolve to work for an Islamic Common Market and pledged to progressively eliminate all obstacles in the way of intra-Islamic trade with a special focus on reduction of tariff barriers. Another issue that evoked widespread emotion among the participants was the 'onslaught of the Western media against Islam.' At a time when the combined power of airwaves and print machines 'creates' reality there is a picture of distorted Islam that it creates. The leaders called for effective measures to counter this media challenge. On the fate of the OIC itself, the Muslim leaders were categorical that it was needed far more today than in the year 1969 when its birth was prompted by the Israeli attack on the

Al-Aqsa mosque. However, questions were raised about the ability of the OIC in its present organizational state, to meet the present challenges. There was consensus on the need for reform and revitalization of the OIC.

Finally, the OIC members declared, in the Islamabad Declaration, their resolve to promote and protect the rights of Muslim minorities, strengthen joint Islamic action in the humanitarian field to alleviate the sufferings of refugees and displaced persons, cooperate in all efforts to eradicate the phenomenon of terrorism which 'constitutes a violation of the teachings of the glorious Islamic religion', and advance scientific and technological cooperation by 'harnessing our human and material resources to create Islamic institutions of higher learning throughout the Islamic world and by sharing expertise through all other means.' The leaders emphasized the need for forging a common vision of mankind's peace, progress and prosperity and called for a global society founded on equality and justice.

It is noteworthy that back in 1995, when the then Prime Minister of Pakistan Benazir Bhutto had decided to host this Islamic Summit, the opposition parties had lambasted her for this 'sheer wastage of money' for no specific purpose. They questioned what gains the Prime Minister had in mind, save her personal popularity, while organizing a special OIC Summit in Pakistan.[80] In February 1997, the general elections brought her nemesis, former opposition leader Nawaz Sharif, to power. The few weeks old government of Mr Sharif was not enthusiastic about the Summit, and did not try to make any political gain out of it. Since the government gave scant coverage to the event in the state-controlled media, the emotional excitement over the Islamic Summit, that had characterized the public response during the 1974 Summit, was missing this time.

Nevertheless, Pakistan got into the world limelight by this Summit, and won support over Kashmir from the assembly of Muslim leaders at its 50th anniversary, which were no mean accomplishments for the host state. In the city of Islamabad (literally: the city of Islam), the Conference felicitated Pakistan and its people on their 50th anniversary; paid glowing tributes to the sagacious leadership of Quaid-e-Azam Mohammad

Ali Jinnah; hailed the progress made by Pakistan in different fields, and saluted the historic contribution made by Pakistan to all Islamic causes. Several leaders were more fulsome in praise for Pakistan; President Col. Yahya Jammeh of Gambia termed Pakistan the 'embodiment of Muslim world unity.' The Foreign Minister of Brunei talked of the 'historic debt that the Muslims owe to Pakistan' for her support to Muslim causes. The Syrian representative complimented Pakistan by maintaining that it was 'a nation born in Islam that no one can defeat.'[81]

The Summit had several other redeeming features. Sworn enemies had a chance to meet each other. The Iranian and Iraqi delegations exchanged pleasantries for the first time in years. In the corridors of the conference, Iranian President Hashmi Rafsanjani and Saudi Crown Prince Abdullah had several meetings that led to the breaking of ice in the theretofore antagonistic relationship between the two states. Saudi Crown Prince Abdullah and Anwar Ibrahim, Deputy Prime Minister of Malaysia, showed themselves as the rising stars of the Muslim world. All these developments were to be accentuated a few months later at the Tehran Summit.

At one time, the Summit found itself facing a serious crisis when some members proposed to scuttle the oncoming Tehran Summit, by suggesting that the Islamabad conference should be turned into the regular 8th Islamic Summit. The Iranian delegation, led by the then President Rafsanjani, threatened to boycott if the proposal was adopted. But the matter was resolved by dexterous handling by the host Pakistanis. A minor clash occurred between Sudan and Uganda when the latter's Deputy Prime Minister Eriya Kategaya hurled a rejoinder to Sudanese President Omar Hassan's accusatory speech against Uganda.

The Islamabad Summit was also criticized for granting a tacit recognition of Israel's right to exist, by giving support to the Middle East peace process and for its failure to discuss the problems of the Iraqi people, created by the UN embargo. The hawks in the Pakistani establishment lamented that Islamabad had failed to convince the Summit to recognize the Taliban government as the legitimate claimant to Afghanistan's vacant seat at the OIC.[82] (Pakistan had accorded full protocol to Taliban-

backed Prime Minister Mullah Rabbani on his arrival in Islamabad. He was seated next to the Iranian President at the Pakistan Day parade but attended the Islamic Summit as an observer.) The Summit largely went unnoticed by the world media. The BBC termed it as 'nothing more than rhetoric'. It is the 'habit of Muslim states to come together after every crisis to express solidarity and do nothing', it added.[83]

Islamic Conferences of Foreign Ministers

The annual conferences of foreign ministers of the OIC member countries commonly called the Islamic Conference of Foreign Ministers (ICFMs) constitute the most important institution of the OIC. The ICFMs have given permanence to the Organization. To date, twenty-five regular and seven extraordinary ICFM sessions have been held (See Charts 2.2 and 2.3 in Chapter 2). The number does not include special ICFM sessions, say, to elect a new Secretary General, the annual co-ordination meetings of Islamic Foreign Ministers at the UN or the various commissions and contact groups whose meetings bring together a number of OIC Foreign Ministers.

As the ICFMs have a heavy agenda of seventy or more items each time and usually last longer than the OIC summits, hence, it would not be possible to relate the detailed proceedings of each of the thirty-two ICFMs, as we have tried to do with the Islamic Summits in the last section. Therefore, we shall confine ourselves to a brief summary of each of the ICFM decisions.[84]

1st ICFM; 23–25 March 1970; Jeddah (Saudi Arabia): In accordance with the resolution of the Rabat Summit Conference, the foreign ministers of Muslim States met in Jeddah to review the implementation of Islamic Summit decisions and to consider the feasibility of establishment of an Islamic Secretariat.[85] The Conference decided that the Foreign Ministers of the member states of the Islamic Conference would regularly meet once a year for the following purposes:

a) Reviewing the progress achieved in the implementation of the Summit decisions; particularly those related to the Al-Quds issue;
b) Discussing matters of common interest and making recommendations for common actions;
c) Deciding the date and place of the Islamic Summits.

The Conference also decided, despite strong opposition from the radical Arab states, to establish a Secretariat with its headquarters in Jeddah, pending the liberation of Jerusalem. Whereas the Rabat moot had laid the foundation of Summit Conference as a principal organ of the OIC, the two other principal organs, namely, the ICFM and the Secretariat came into being during this meeting.

2nd ICFM; 26–28 Dec. 1970; Karachi (Pakistan): Pursuant to the decision of the 1st ICFM, the 2nd ICFM was hosted by Pakistan. The Conference reaffirmed the resolutions of the Rabat Summit and the Jeddah ICFM which had drawn attention to the dangerous situation in the Middle East; demanded the immediate withdrawal of Israeli forces from all occupied Arab territories; demanded the restoration of the legitimate rights of the people of Palestine to their usurped homeland; and reaffirmed its support to their struggle of national liberation.[86] The Conference elected Tunku Abdul Rahman as the first Secretary General of the OIC on Malaysia's recommendation. Tunku resigned from the Malaysian Premiership and announced that he and his staff would work without pay, till the Organization became financially strong.

The meeting adopted the first budget of $450,000 (for the year 1971) of the newly born organization. Each member was asked to deposit an initial sum of $10,000. Besides conducting preliminary discussion on the objectives, principles, and rules of procedure of the new body, it also took up the proposals regarding the establishment of an Islamic News Agency, and a Muslim Bank or a Federation of Banks of the Islamic countries.

The conclave condemned Portugal's aggression against Guinea, a Muslim country. It also expressed concern over the Black September massacre of Palestinians and asked Jordan and the PLO to adhere to the Cairo agreement.

3rd ICFM; 29 Feb.–4 March 1972; Jeddah (Saudi Arabia): Initially planned for Kabul in September 1971, this ICFM was postponed because of Afghan King Zahir Shah's government's lack of interest. Still, the year 1971 saw a number of expert committee meetings, contemplating the establishment of an Islamic Bank, a news network and cultural centres etc. in different Muslim countries. The belated Conference that took place in Jeddah, examined the developments in the Middle East and the struggle of the Palestinian people and denounced the Zionist movement 'as racist, aggressive and expansionist, in contradiction with all noble human ideals, and constituting a constant threat to international peace.'[87]

The 3rd foreign ministers' conference was an historical event since it approved the draft of the Charter of the Islamic Conference whose purpose was defined as that of consolidating Islamic solidarity and promoting cooperation in the economic, cultural, scientific and other fields among the Muslim countries in general and the participating countries in particular. The 3rd ICFM further approved the project for the establishment of an International Islamic News Agency and an Islamic Bank and decided to create the department of Cultural Affairs in the Islamic Secretariat, to be headed by an Assistant Secretary General.

The Conference declared its full support for Pakistan; its territorial integrity, national sovereignty and independence. Pakistan was not satisfied as unequivocal condemnation for Indian aggression against Pakistan and its role in the latter's dismemberment was not issued. A committee comprising Morocco, Algeria, Tunisia, Somalia, Iran, and Malaysia was constituted to try to bring about a rapprochement between Islamabad and Dhaka but the ruling junta of the seceding East Pakistan refused to receive the delegation. The ICFM urged all the peace loving nations who respected moral values to support the Muslim nations in maintaining the peace and security of the Islamic territories and peoples, and to uphold the principle of non-interference in their internal affairs and principles of the UN Charter. The Conference also expressed its determination to give moral support to the legitimate struggle of the

African people and that of the Muslims of Southern Philippines.

4th ICFM; 24–26 March 1973; Benghazi (Libya): Libya, in its capacity as Chairman ICFM, wanted to have the Philippines' Muslims crisis as item no. 1 on the agenda. After the minority view of Indonesia and Malaysia, that it was an internal affair of the Philippines, was overwhelmingly rejected, the ICFM passed strong resolutions expressing concern over the plight of Moro Muslims and urged Manila to solve the dispute peacefully. A mission comprising Libya, Somalia, Senegal, and Saudi Arabia was sent to Manila to discuss the problem with the Marcos-led government.

The Conference discussed the Palestinian problem, the situation in the Middle East, the Zionist threat to the Red Sea Basin, support for liberation movements in Africa, the Eriterian issue, the situation of Muslim minorities and economic problems of the developing world, and other questions.[88] The Conference decided to set up new Islamic Cultural Centres in Africa particularly in member states, as early as possible and to hold a conference of Islamic (Cultural) Centres in Europe at London, and follow it up with similar conferences in other key areas in the world. A Jihad Fund was attached to the Secretariat, and the Conference also decided to set up a Permanent Committee of economic experts selected from member states within the Secretariat, to be convened at the Secretary General's invitation.

The 4th ICFM expressed anxiety over the continued detention of Pakistani POWs from the war of 1971 by India, especially when the peace agreement between the two States had already been signed in July 1972. Pakistan had already released all the Indian POWs unconditionally. The meeting accepted the request of the Secretary General Tunku Abdul Rahman to be allowed to retire, and appointed Egypt's Hassan Tohami in his place.

5th ICFM; 21–25 June 1974; Kuala Lumpur (Malaysia): The 5th Conference endorsed the Declaration and the Action Programme for the establishment of a New International Economic Order (NIEO) adopted by the United Nations' General Assembly at its sixth extraordinary session

held in New York, and requested all member countries to play an active role in the implementation of this declaration and the Action Programme; recommended to extend observer status to the OAU at the OIC; and decided to set up a fund estimated at $2.5 million earmarked to furnish capital investment needs for the establishment of a telecommunication system for the IINA.[89]

The Malaysian Prime Minister, Tun Abdul Razzak stressed the need for greater economic cooperation. Libyan Foreign Minister Abdul Ati al-Obiedi lamented that the resolutions of the past four ICFMs had not been implemented. He suggested that the ICFMs should adopt no new resolutions until the earlier ones were implemented. Meanwhile, the ICFM rejected the request of Brunei Peoples Party, a pro-independence anti-Sultan group, for membership.

The Conference reaffirmed that the PLO was the sole legitimate representative of the Palestinian people and condemned all countries which extended military, economic, or human support to Israel and called upon them to discontinue this support immediately. It is not out of place to mention here that the year saw several tangible achievements by the OIC on the West Asian problem. They included the granting of observer status to the PLO by the United Nations and two other resolutions, passed by the UN General Assembly, affirming the inalienable right of Palestinians' self-determination, and equating Zionism with racism.

Citing the Indian nuclear test of 18 May 1974, Pakistan raised the issue of nuclear proliferation which was taken up by the OIC for the first time. Without explicitly condemning India as a threat to world peace, as Pakistan was demanding, the Conference expressed concern over the nuclear proliferation and declared the firm support of the member countries of the Islamic Conference to the political independence, territorial integrity and state sovereignty of the non-nuclear weapon states. The Conference noted that the report of the four-member OIC Mission to Philippines was critical of the atrocities being committed against the Muslims, and that Manila had not responded to the five proposals of the Mission. It urged the Philippines government to find a political and peaceful solution through negotiations with Muslim Leaders, particularly with the representatives of the Moro National Liberation Front (MNLF), in order to arrive at a just solution to the problem of the Filipino Muslims, within the framework of the national sovereignty and territorial integrity of the Philippines.

6th ICFM; 12–15 July 1975; Jeddah (Saudi Arabia): The Conference commenced with the recitation of *Fatiha* and a one minute silence, in memory of the late King Faisal and all the martyrs who laid down their lives in the cause of Islam.[90] Inaugurating the ICFM, the new Saudi monarch King Khalid said that the best tribute to the late King's memory was to work for Islamic solidarity and the liberation of Al-Quds. The ICFM was in a buoyant mood due to the previous year's diplomatic victories against Israel including the latter's expulsion from the UNESCO. In a significant resolution, the Conference decided to try to expel Israel from the UN General Assembly. This caused a stir and the United States and the European Community formally made known to the OIC on 15 July, that they would withhold all financial contributions to the UN budget, were the OIC move to succeed. (The strong reaction by the US deterred many prospective supporters of the OIC motion, and consequently the Muslim states failed to garner the requisite two-thirds support at the UN General Assembly to expel Israel. The motion was, therefore, withdrawn in October that year, for the time being.)

The resolutions of the 6th ICFM covered all the issues that concerned the Islamic world in the political, economic, and social spheres. It passed resolutions on Jerusalem, the Middle East, Western Sahara, support to African Liberation movements, and security of non-Nuclear nations. In the economic field, the 6th ICFM passed a significant resolution on Exploitation of Developing Countries by the Developed Ones. The Resolution recommended the member states to adopt a common front against any pressure to which any Islamic country may be exposed, in its efforts to safeguard its sovereignty and control over its natural resources. It declared the readiness of Islamic countries to engage in a constructive dialogue with the developed countries which should deal with the problems of development and related issues in a comprehensive and integrated manner so as to usher in a new equitable International Economic Order.

The 6th ICFM gave full support to Morocco for retrieving its legitimate rights in the Spanish enclaves of Coata and Melulba. The Conference also considered the serious difficulties encountered by the member states in their balance of payments due to the global inflation, and recommended that the question of setting up of an Islamic fund for economic adjustment be seriously considered by the member states.

7th ICFM; 12–15 May 1976; Istanbul (Turkey): All matters of interest to the Islamic world in the political, economic, and cultural spheres were discussed by the appropriate committees of the conference which presented their reports to the plenary session for adoption. However, the problem of Eritrea was left for the African community to decide. Similarly, the Western Sahara question was excluded from the agenda on the request of Algeria, Morocco and Mauritania who were discussing it among themselves.[91]

In the political sphere, the Conference hailed the struggle of the Palestinian and Arab peoples in the occupied Palestine lands; decided to establish a 'Jerusalem Fund' for sustaining the heroic resistance of the Palestinians in Jerusalem and other occupied territories; condemned Israeli operations in the occupied Arab territories and reaffirmed its 1975 resolution for expulsion of Israel from the UN; reiterated the commitment of the Islamic countries to denounce racism in Southern Africa, Namibia, Zimbabwe, and Occupied Palestine; and called upon the Islamic countries to extend greater moral and material assistance to the liberation movements in these territories. However, the Conference took no action on the demand of an Eastern Turkistani Muslim delegation to send a protest note to Beijing over the victimization of the Muslims in the Xinjiang province of China. The ICFM also expressed its concern over the danger of introduction of nuclear weapons in the region of Africa, Middle East, South Asia and the Indian Ocean, and called for the establishment of Nuclear Weapons Free Zones in these regions.

Turkey, the host, was keen to muster Muslim support for the rights of ethnic Turk Cypriot Muslims. The Conference supported the equality of Cypriot Turks with the Greek majority in Cyprus. Though the Conference did not accord observer status to the Muslim Cypriot delegation, it agreed to strengthen its participation in all future conferences.[92]

In the cultural domain, the moot decided to set up an Islamic Research Centre for History, Art and Culture at Istanbul and a Statistical Research Centre at Ankara. It adopted a recommendation calling upon the member states to issue special stamps on Jerusalem and Palestine and transfer the net proceeds to Palestine.

8th ICFM; 16–22 May 1977; Tripoli (Libya):
The 8th Conference passed various resolutions on matters of interest to the Islamic countries such as the Middle East problem, struggle of the oppressed people of Palestine, support to liberation movements in Africa, establishment of Nuclear Weapons Free Zones in Africa, the Middle East, and South Asia, and making the Indian Ocean free of military bases, strengthening the security of Non-Nuclear Weapons States and the rights of the Muslim minorities and communities in some countries. The Conference re-elected Dr Gaye as the OIC Secretary General for another two-year term. It also agreed to set up an International Red Crescent Society with headquarters in Benghazi, Libya.[93]

The 8th ICFM granted observer status to MNLF as a special case, formed a four-member committee on the Philippines crisis and called for a Fund for assisting Filipino Muslims. The ICFM expressed regret that the Tripoli negotiations had broken down on 5 March 1977, that were to finalize the modalities for granting autonomy to South Philippines under the Tripoli agreement, concluded in the previous year (see the next Chapter for details about Philippines-MNLF conflict). It decided to coordinate its efforts with those of the OAU to achieve a just and equitable solution of the Eriterian crisis within the framework of Afro-Asian brotherhood. The Conference rejected the 'farce' referendum in Mayotte islands of Comoros, conducted by the French administration, and declared all such future actions null and void.

In the economic sphere, the Tripoli Conference decided to set up a number of expert's groups to suggest measures to intensify economic cooperation among Islamic states. These expert's groups were set up in the field of promotion and expansion of trade, planning and development, technical cooperation, exchange of manpower, and development of links in telecommunication, tourism, etc.

9th ICFM; 24–28 April 1978; Dakar (Senegal):
The Conference affirmed the commitment of Islamic states to support the Arab cause and pledged to extend political, material, and military support to the Arab front line states and to the PLO. It condemned Israel for its aggression on the Arab land and declared Zionism and Apartheid as twin forces of racism. It urged the member states to make all possible efforts for the establishment of Nuclear Weapons Free Zones in Africa, the Middle East, and South Asia.[94] The non-compliance of the OIC-brokered Tripoli agreement by the Marcos regime of the Philippines was seriously noted and was disapproved of.

Pakistan ended its silence on the Kashmir conflict, and its delegation leader drew parallels between the Kashmiri struggle for freedom and that of other oppressed Muslim communities (Pakistan had to wait till 1990 for the Kashmir dispute to become a formal agenda item in a meeting of the Islamic Conference). A landmark achievement of the 9th ICFM was the decision to set up a new department at the OIC Secretariat for the Muslim communities in the non-Muslim states, for which an initial budget of $475,000 was approved.

In the economic sphere, the Conference reviewed the current international economic situation, with special emphasis on the relations between the developed and developing countries. It called for the establishment of a new international economic order, which would ensure a more balanced relationship among states. The Dakar Conference approved a number of recommendations formulated by the expert's groups set up by the 8th ICFM. In the cultural field, the Conference approved a programme of celebrations to mark the advent of the 15th *Hijrah* Century.

10th ICFM; 8–12 May 1979; Fez (Morocco): The 10th ICFM considered the current international issues and passed resolutions on the Middle East problem, the status of the holy city of Jerusalem, support to the Palestinian people for restoration of their inalienable rights and for the establishment of the independent sovereign state of Palestine in their own homeland. It condemned repeated Israeli aggression against southern Lebanon and denounced Zionism, racism, and Apartheid.[95]

At the same time the Conference condemned Egypt for betraying the Islamic cause by signing the Camp David accord, and suspended its membership from the OIC and its organs, and asked the members to break diplomatic relations with Cairo, whose membership of all other joint economic ventures with the Muslim/Arab countries was also cancelled.[96] Six African members, Gambia, Guinea, Guinea-Bissau, Niger, Senegal, and Upper Volta, abstained form voting in motions censuring Egypt. The ICFM also passed a resolution on cooperation between the OIC and the OAU. It adopted another resolution concerning measures to counter propaganda against Islam and Muslims.

In the economic field, the Conference reaffirmed the commitment of the Islamic countries to forge closer economic cooperation between the member states and work collectively for the realization of the new world economic order. The Fez Conference approved the establishment of the Islamic Chamber of Commerce, Industry and Commodity Exchange (ICCI&CE) with its Headquarters at Karachi. It also approved the charter of the Islamic Science Foundation (the idea for the establishment of this important institution was initially put forward by Pakistan); and called for steps to reserve the Islamic heritage in Timbuktu (Mali), Kairawan (Tunisia), and Fez (Morocco).

11th ICFM; 17–22 May 1980; Islamabad (Pakistan): In the second consecutive meeting in Islamabad in five months, the issue of the recent Soviet invasion of Afghanistan remained dominant; and Pakistan, the second most affected country of this region, made full use of this forum to castigate Moscow.[97] On 15 May, Kabul offered to guarantee Soviet withdrawal if Pakistan, Iran, and the USA gave the assurance that the territories of Iran and Pakistan would not be used for infiltration into Afghanistan. Iran remained silent while Pakistan spurned the offer as a gimmick to divide the 11th ICFM.

Afghan opposition was not invited. Yet eight Afghan leaders attended the conference as part of the Iranian delegation. A very harsh resolution against the USSR for its invasion of a Muslim country was adopted, to which Libya, Syria, PLO, and South Yemen lodged strong objection. These states, dependent upon the Soviet Union for military hardware procurements, argued that the Soviet involvement in Afghanistan should not be seen in isolation. Rather, Moscow should be given allowance for its positive role in the Middle East, where it was a 'dependable friend'. The ICFM formed a three-member ministerial committee comprising Pakistan, Iran, and the OIC Secretary General, to seek ways and means for a comprehensive solution of the Afghan crisis. Another committee comprising Saudi Arabia, Gabon, and Pakistan was formed to administer the disbursement of the $25 million donation announced by Saudi Arabia, Malaysia, etc. for the Afghanistan Fund. Besides the customary large number of resolutions on political issues like Palestine, Eritrea, and Somalia, the Conference approved several measures for enhancing economic and cultural cooperation and the setting up of some new organs within the OIC framework. A notable decision in this regard is the establishment of the *Waqfs* for the Islamic Solidarity Fund and the Al-Quds Fund, with $100 million each of initial capital.

The Conference again gave full support to Iran over its hostage crisis with the US. True to its non-aligned moorings, the Conference asked the member states to guard against the establishment of foreign military bases on their soils. The resolution on Somalia expressed concern over Soviet and allies' presence in the horn of Africa; condemned the aggression against the Democratic Republic of Somalia; deplored the presence of foreign troops in a Muslim country and called for their immediate total and unconditional withdrawal. This resolution also met with opposition from seven states including Algeria, Mali, and North Yemen etc.

12th ICFM; 1–5 June 1981; Baghdad (Iraq): There was nothing new in this meeting as it was simply an extension of the Taif Summit held three months earlier. As the war between Iran and Iraq had erupted the previous year, Iran took strong exception to the venue and boycotted the meeting.[98] The Iran–Iraq war was on the top of the agenda this time. The Conference asked both sides to agree to a cease-fire. The Conference expressed regret over the failure of the OIC peace initiative of the preceding March. That the Iraqi President Saddam Hussain's hard-hitting speech against Iran was incorporated in the final communiqué, cast further doubts on the OIC's neutrality in the conflict. The ICFM amended the Charter to make the Assistant Secretary General's term four year non-renewable instead of two years renewable once. The Conference expressed concern over the presence of the forces of the super powers, in the Persian Gulf. It adopted several harsh resolutions regarding the Palestine and the Afghanistan crises.

13th ICFM; 22–26 Aug. 1982; Niamey (Niger): In the wake of the Israeli invasion of Lebanon in June 1982, the 13th ICFM condemned Israeli aggression and reiterated earlier resolutions demanding Israel's unconditional withdrawal from all occupied Arab lands, and decided to form an international commission to investigate the Israeli war crimes. Even Saudi Arabia criticized the US for its unqualified support to Israel. Iran, which was attending an OIC meeting after a long boycott, called for an oil embargo and sanctions against the USA.[99]

In the backdrop of unpleasant verbal duels between Ali Akbar Vilayati and Saadoun Hammadi (foreign ministers of Iran and Iraq), the Conference urged all the members to use their good offices to bring an end to the war. The Conference demanded unconditional Soviet withdrawal from Afghanistan, approved the statute of Islamic *Fiqh* Academy, approved the establishment of Islamic Universities in Niger and Uganda, and pledged $210 million for the drought stricken people of Sahel.

14th ICFM; 6–11 Dec. 1983; Dhaka (Bangladesh): The Conference endorsed the establishment of the Turkish Republic of Northern Cyprus (TNRC) and gave full support to Ankara in this regard. The Iran–Iraq war, described by General Hussain Irshad, President of Bangladesh, as the 'gaping wound in the body politic of Islam' was discussed and regret was expressed over the unabated military conflict between two brotherly Muslim countries. On Iran's objection, the reference to the UN resolutions in the OIC call for immediate cease-fire in the Gulf was removed. However, no joint attitude towards the war could be evolved.[100]

The Conference condemned the security arrangement between Israel and the USA as jeopardizing the chances of a Palestinian homeland. In a similar vein the Israeli air attack on Iraqi nuclear installation was strongly condemned. The meeting also stressed the need for a 'new, fairer and more opportune' Information Order to project a more unified image of Islam. In this regard, different ideas to activate the IINA and the ISBO also came up for consideration. The 14th ICFM also approved the Islamic Charter of Human Rights, which was adopted by the 19th ICFM, six years later.

15th ICFM; 18–22 Dec. 1984; Sana'a (N. Yemen): The top item in the agenda for Sana'a moot was the long awaited election for the post of Secretary General. Although it was clear that Pakistan's Sharifuddin Pirzada would win overwhelmingly, it was quite a job to convince Mr Shamsud Doha of Bangladesh to withdraw, since unopposed election of a consensus candidate had been a tradition in the OIC.[101]

The 15th ICFM adopted the traditional resolutions on the Iran–Iraq war, the Afghanistan crisis, and the Palestine issue. The Conference endorsed the draft bye-laws of the Islamic Cement Association (ICA) and the Islamic States Telecommunication Union (ISTU) and welcomed the offers made by Turkey and Pakistan to locate the head offices of these two institutions in the two countries, respectively. It also called upon those member states that had not ratified the Islamic Civil Aviation Council (ICAC) Statute, to do so. It was Egypt's first conference after resuming full membership of the OIC. Libya, Syria and Iran tried to keep the Egyptian delegation led by its Foreign Minister Esmet Abdul Muguid (later Secretary General of the Arab League) out of the conference, but with the intervention of other delegates, Egyptians finally made their way in.

16th ICFM; 6–10 Jan. 1986; Fez (Morocco): The primary issue under consideration was the sharply deteriorating US–Libya relations and the Conference gave full support to Libya. The declaration condemning 'the aggressive escalation and constant provocation on the part of international imperialism and Zionist entity', tacitly implied that the escalation in tensions with the United States was actually a Zionist conspiracy.[102] The Conference also condemned the US sanctions against Libya and asked the members 'to counter them'. The threat to Libya was declared a threat to all Muslim countries. (It is a separate matter that no action was taken in April by any member state when the US Air Force actually started bombing Tripoli.)

Israeli air raid on the PLO headquarters in Tunis killing seventy people, was also condemned. Regarding the war in Afghanistan, the Conference reiterated its earlier demands for immediate Soviet withdrawal, praised the *Mujahideen* for their 'heroic struggle', deplored the attempts to spread the war into the Pakistani territory, and appreciated 'the restraint exercised by Pakistan in the face of massive air raids and bombing' by the Soviet troops. In another move, the moot decided to renew dialogue with the Philippines government for autonomy to Muslim majority regions, in response to the request to this effect by the MNLF leadership. It was in this conference that the ICFM accepted Nigeria as a member, which hitherto had an observer status.

17th ICFM; 22–25 March 1988; Amman (Jordan): The conference was held in the wake of a bloody clash between the Iranian pilgrims and the Saudi forces in Mecca on the eve of *Hajj* which resulted in 401 persons killed and another 568 injured from both sides. Saudi Arabia used this forum for Iran bashing and the Kingdom's Foreign Minister Prince Saud al-Faisal announced that Saudi Arabia would limit the number of Iranian

pilgrims from the following year. Iran continued to insist that Iranian pilgrims were demonstrating against American–Zionist imperialism, and Saudi forces' 'unprovoked firing to please their American mentors' had led to the massacre of hundreds of Iranians. Saudi Arabia denied firing and insisted that the Iranians had died due to a stampede.[103] The Saudis managed to get approved a resolution that supported the Kingdom's 'right to adopt all measures to ensure the pilgrimage in safety and security'. The Iranian team led by *Hujjat-ul-Islam* Mohammad Ali Tashkiri walked out of the meeting in protest.

Apart from this nibbling, the ICFM considered the report of the OIC fact-finding mission on Bulgarian Muslims, that stated that all Turkey's complaints were genuine. The Bulgarian Minister in charge of Religious Affairs, Lynbomir Popov, strongly denied victimization of Muslims in his country and termed the findings of the report an 'attempt to mislead the OIC and to place its prestige at the service of self seeking pan-Turkish objectives.'

The Conference observed that the Palestinians had launched a self-rule movement, named *Intifada*, in the occupied areas three months back, and praised the valour and resilience of the Palestinian people. Bahrain's Mohammad bin Khalifa noted that had it not been for the disunity in the Muslim world, Israel would not have dared to persist with its aggressive designs. The ICFM unanimously elected Dr Hamid Al Gabid, a former Prime Minister of Niger, as the new Secretary General of the OIC, for a four-year term commencing from 1 January 1989.

18th ICFM; 13–16 March 1989; Riyadh (Saudi Arabia): This ICFM was being held in the background of three major events. The first one was the Soviet withdrawal from Afghanistan and the formation of an Afghan Interim Government (AIG) by the *Mujahideen*. The ICFM hailed the Soviet troop pullout and recognized the interim government. Eulogizing the heroic struggle of the Afghan people against foreign intervention, the ICFM hoped that a better future awaited the Afghan people.[104] The second event was the end of the Gulf war. The ICFM congratulated Iran and Iraq over the cease-fire, and appealed for an early release and return of the POWs from both sides. Finally, the third encouraging factor was that the *Intifada* uprising had gained momentum and a Palestinian state was proclaimed in November 1988. The OIC gave formal recognition to the Palestinian government-in-exile.

In another resolution, the Bulgarian government was asked to fulfil its international obligations with respect to the Muslim minority. (Sofia dismissed the resolution as an interference in its domestic affairs.) The ICFM declared Salman Rushdie, the author of 'Satanic Verses' as apostate, and urged joint action that included the banning of the book and the publishers, if they did not stop printing it, and finally banning the entry of its author in any Muslim state. The Conference declared that blasphemy could not be justified on the basis of freedom of expression and announced that Islamic states would make effective and coordinated efforts to ensure respect for Islam and its noble values. The ICFM stopped short of endorsing Imam Khomeini's *fatwa* of death sentence for Salman Rushdie as many of the member states, notably Saudi Arabia, believed that the *fatwa* had tarnished the image of Islam as a tolerant religion.

19th ICFM; 31 July–5 Aug. 1990; Cairo (Egypt): The membership of the OIC had declined by one, to forty-four, since the last ICFM, because North and South Yemens had united. The conference expressed pleasure over the reunification of Yemen. Then following the presentation by the Secretary General of his report on Afghanistan, the interim *Mujahideen* government was given the seat of Afghanistan; prompting the *de facto* Kabul regime of Dr Najibullah to lodge a strong protest.[105]

The ICFM passed a resolution on the Kashmir crisis which had taken a serious turn by then. It was the first time that Kashmir had figured on the OIC agenda. Since 7 January 1989, an *Intifada*-type uprising had started in the Indian-held parts of Kashmir. The occupation forces were accused of being ruthless in trying to quell the insurgency. On 19 May 1990, Mir Waiz Maulvi Mohammad Farooq, the highest Muslim religious authority of Kashmir, was assassinated for which the Muslims blamed the Indian government's secret services. His funeral procession the following day, was indiscriminately fired upon by the Indian police resulting in the killing of 107 unarmed mourners. The Pakistani Prime Minister Benazir Bhutto, a known hawk on the Kashmir issue, visited a score of Muslim countries to personally request the leaders to support the Pakistan-sponsored resolution at the ICFM. The 19th ICFM expressed serious concern over the wanton killings of Kashmiri Muslims by the Indian troops, and called for a peaceful solution to the dispute.

The Conference was also concerned over the Iraq–Kuwait dispute. While the Conference was still in session, the Iraqi forces seized Kuwait on 2 August. The sessions had to be frequently adjourned thereafter, as the Arab Foreign Ministers held separate meetings to discuss the Kuwait crisis. A resolution, tabled by some Arab states condemned, what it called, Iraqi aggression against Kuwait and demanded unconditional withdrawal of Iraqi forces from the oil-rich Sheikhdom. Iraq, Jordan, Sudan, Mauritania, and Palestine did not support the resolution of condemnation, while Libya, Pakistan, and Djibouti had serious reservations over its text.

20th ICFM; 4–8 Aug. 1991; Istanbul (Turkey): Again, a host of issues including Palestine, Kashmir, Lebanon and economic and cultural cooperation in the Muslim world, were discussed. The ICFM debated the UN sponsored peace conference on the Middle East. Saudi Arabia and Egypt strongly supported the proposed conference. Syria had serious reservations about it but Iran was more vocal in questioning the wisdom of participation in a UN sponsored conference. 'The UN cannot but help Israel', declared Ali Akbar Vilayati, the Iranian Foreign Minister. The ICFM also urged greater efforts for peace in war-ravaged Afghanistan and in South Philippines.[106]

In this first post-Gulf war ICFM, the Iraqi delegation had come to garner sympathy over the 'destruction and genocide' caused to Iraq. The moot began with the Turkish President Turgat Ozal's opening speech blasting Iraq 'for its adventurism in Kuwait', to which the Iraqi delegation listened with mute silence. The meeting passed a resolution which 'sympathized with the Iraqi people' but blamed 'the Iraqi government for this ordeal'. There was strong opposition to the latter part of the resolution by the Arab League chief and some member states, but even on the first part, the ICFM did not take any measures to alleviate the sufferings of the Iraqi people, which it accepted as genuine. The Iraqi delegation leader termed the OIC position as 'a calamitous and scandalous event.' On Kashmir, the Conference renewed its call for the holding of a UN-sponsored plebiscite in the Indian-held areas. It appealed to India to allow the OIC fact-finding mission to investigate large-scale killing and torture of the Muslims in Kashmir by the Indian security forces. Taking the advantage of the fact that it was on home ground, the Turkish Cypriot (TRNC) leadership again requested full membership of the OIC, like the PLO had. But the decision was deferred with a pledge to strengthen the participation of TRNC in the OIC at all levels.

21st ICFM; 25–29 April 1993; Karachi (Pakistan): This ICFM was held in the wake of two extraordinary ICFMs on Bosnia, the previous year, whose strong-worded resolutions had been ignored. The Conference was presided over by the Pakistani Foreign Minister Farooq Leghari (later President of Pakistan); Uganda, Palestine, and Tunisia were elected as Vice-Chairmen. It was the first time that Albania as well as all the six ex-Soviet Muslim republics were attending an OIC moot.[107]

On Bosnia, the Conference pledged $210 million for aid as against $260 million requested by Bosnia, and called for freezing all Serbian assets. In a departure from the standard procedure, the ICFM sent a message to the UN Security Council, while still in session, requesting it to authorize immediate use of force against the Serbs. Saudi Arabia announced that King Fahd would donate another $20 million for Bosnia in addition to the contributions made by the Saudi public. A Pakistani spokesman made it clear, however, that the ICFM was concerned with the political aspects of the Bosnian crisis, so it did not discuss the sending of arms consignments to Sarajevo at all. The ICFM also discussed the Kashmir crisis, expulsion of 400 Palestinians by Israel, nuclear-free zones and a host of items relating to economic cooperation in the OIC member states. *Fatiha* was offered for the departed soul of President Turgat

Ozal of Turkey, who had died on 18 April due to cardiac arrest.

Pakistan's acting Prime Minister Balkhsher Mazari called for an end to distrust and suspicion in the *ummah*. He used this forum to defend Pakistan over the presence of non-Pakistani Islamic 'fundamentalists' there, who had come to fight the Afghan war in their tens of thousands in the early 1980s, but were now a source of constant tension with some Arab states. The Conference stressed the need for convening a UN sponsored conference to define terrorism because it was felt that peace-loving states like Pakistan and Sudan were accused of being terrorism-sponsoring countries whereas a 'rogue state' like Israel could go scot-free.

Item 25 of the eighty-four-item agenda was the subject of wrangling between the Iraqi and Kuwaiti delegates which called for discussion on the 'consequences of Iraqi aggression on Kuwait and its non-compliance with UN resolutions'. Iraq said that it had already complied with the UN resolutions and that there was no need for using offensive language against Iraq when the theme of the 21st ICFM was 'Islamic Unity and Cooperation for Peace'.

22nd ICFM; 10–11 Dec. 1994; Casablanca (Morocco): Originally scheduled for Tunis in April 1994, the ICFM had to be postponed as the Tunisian government expressed regrets for its inability to host the conference at the last moment. Finally, it was held just before the 7th Islamic Summit at Casablanca, Morocco. To date, it is the only regular ICFM that has also served as the preparatory Foreign Ministers' meeting for an Islamic Summit.[108] It was a very brief meeting lasting only two days and hence had a very limited agenda: primarily Bosnia, Kashmir, and Palestine. The Conference reaffirmed its support to the ongoing peace process in the Middle East. It recalled the Simla agreement and asked India and Pakistan to resolve the Kashmir dispute, which had resulted in the killing of about 30,000 people in the preceding five years, in accordance with the UN resolutions.

23rd ICFM; 9–12 Dec. 1995; Conakry (Guinea): For the first time, an ICFM officially recognized the presence of groups within the OIC. Saudi

Arabia, Mali, and Pakistan were asked to give opening speeches respectively on behalf of Arab, African, and Asian members. The 23rd ICFM accepted the Pakistani request and recommended the convening of an extraordinary session of the Islamic Summit in Islamabad in March 1997, to coincide with Pakistan's golden jubilee celebrations. The Conference accepted the request of membership by Kazakhstan, the last remaining ex-Soviet Muslim state outside the OIC.[109]

The ICFM took serious note of the problems of the Indian Muslims and called upon all the member states to extend economic and humanitarian assistance to the Kashmiris, fighting a war of liberation. The ICFM condemned the burning of the holy Muslim shrine of Chirar Sharif in the Indian Held Kashmir (IHK) and also called upon Delhi to honour its pledge on the reconstruction of the Babri Mosque. The Conference gave an earnest call to the member states to desist from fratricidal conflicts in the Muslim *ummah*.

24th ICFM; 14–19 Dec. 1996; Jakarta (Indonesia): The primary item on the agenda was the election of a new Secretary General; the lone contender, Izzeddienne Laraki of Morocco, was unanimously elected for a four-year term beginning 1 January 1997.[110]

Indonesia and Malaysia emphasized the need for a greater stress on economic cooperation in the Islamic world, upon which, they believed, depended the success of the OIC. But the Arab states were bent upon giving priority to the political issues, primarily the Al-Quds problem. The ICFM declared Israel as the sole party responsible for the impasse in the peace process and condemned it for its policies undermining the peace in the Middle East. The members were asked to freeze normalization of relations with Israel.

The Conference called for a peaceful resolution of the Kashmir conflict, projection of a favourable image of Islam, and major reforms in the organization. It decided to help in the reconstruction of Southern Philippines. Nur Masauri, the MNLF Chairman and the new governor of the autonomous Muslim region of South Philippines (ARMM), said he was not disappointed with the absence of specific pledges

for money, because 'the things work initially that way in the OIC'.

25th ICFM; 15–17 Mar. 1998; Doha (Qatar): The Conference discussed the stalled Middle East peace process. Holding Israel wholly responsible for the past one year deadlock, it urged the Muslim countries to respect the Islamic boycott of Israel. The Conference again assured the 'extension of full support to Palestinian brothers in their struggle'. The OIC hailed the 23 February Iraq–UN accord on weapons inspection and expressed the hope that Iraq would comply with the UN resolutions. The Secretary General called upon the international community to respect Iraq's sovereignty and to meet its humanitarian needs.[111]

The third major issue before the conference was the rump Yugoslavia. The foreign ministers called upon the international community 'to restore security and calm' in Kosovo and 'to intervene to ensure that it does not become another Bosnia'. The meeting was also attended by Rajab Boya, the Grand *Mufti* of Kosovo, who requested full support from the OIC for Kosovo's independence bid as, according to him, the mere restoration of autonomy (revoked since 1989) was not enough. The OIC condemned the genocide of Kosovar Muslims, decided to remain seized of the matter and mandated the OIC's New York Mission to constantly monitor the situation and recommend further action to the OIC, if any further repression of Muslims was carried out in Kosovo.

On the question of Jammu and Kashmir, the ICFM called for its peaceful settlement and condemned the 'gross and systematic human rights violations' of Kashmiri Muslims. The Conference reiterated that the Indian occupied Kashmir was a land under 'foreign occupation' and that the armed liberation struggle of Kashmiris was not terrorism. Any political process or sham election, short of a UN-sponsored plebiscite was rejected, and Islamic and other philanthropist organizations were asked to mobilize funds for humanitarian aid to the Kashmiri Muslims. The ICFM also approved a Pakistan-sponsored resolution condemning 'state terrorism', an obvious reference to the excesses of Indian forces in occupied Kashmir and the bomb blasts at public places and trains and sniper firing incidents on mosques within Pakistan, which the latter says are carried out by infiltrators sent by Indian intelligence agencies to settle scores over Pakistan's alleged support to Kashmir Liberation Front guerillas. India has consistently refuted all Pakistani allegations.

26th ICFM; 1–5 July 1999; Ougadougou (Burkina Faso): The meeting was held at a time when hostilities had broken out over the disputed State of Kashmir between world's two new nuclear powers, India and Pakistan. The meeting expressed deep concern over the fighting, and urged both sides to exercise restraint. The moot once again called for the resolution of the Kashmir dispute in accordance with the UN resolutions asking India to accept their validity as Pakistan already does. It also supported the territorial integrity of Pakistan.

The ICFM had a seventy-five-point agenda. The meeting called for immediate lifting of sanctions on Iran and Libya; urged members to help ease the plight of the Iraqi people; called for an end to the civil war in Afghanistan, urged the international community to speed up the implementation of the Dayton peace accords on Bosnia, and lastly, called for the establishment of NWFZs in the world, excluding South Asia, reference to which was dropped on Pakistan's request. The ICFM also observed the silver jubilee celebration of the establishment of the Islamic Development Bank (IDB), whose President also addressed the ICFM to mark the occasion.

Extraordinary Sessions of Islamic Conference of Foreign Ministers

The extraordinary sessions of Islamic Conference of Foreign Ministers (EICFMs) are held in accordance with Article V (1-b) of the Charter, at the request of any member state or that of the Secretary General, provided that 'the request is approved by two thirds of the members'.

Hence, there is no consistency in the frequency of EICFMs. So far, seven EICFMs have taken place; four in 1980 alone, two in 1992, and the last one in 1994. The subject-wise categorization is as follows: Two each on Palestine and Bosnia-Herzegovina, and one each on the Iran–Iraq war, the Afghanistan crisis, and the Kashmir dispute.

The venue was twice Pakistan and once each Jordan, Morocco, Saudi Arabia, Turkey, and New York in the United States.

It is important to note that the EICFMs are not necessarily single-item-agenda moots. Once the Foreign Ministers get together, the discussion extends to other issues as well as the problem for which the meeting was actually convened. However, the EICFMs last only for one day or, at best, two. Secondly, a serious crisis in the Islamic world does not *ipso facto* imply that the EICFM would be convened. For instance, when Iraq annexed Kuwait in 1990, the strong Arab bloc opposed the EICFM, and Pakistan, Iran, and Turkey failed to muster up two-thirds signatures to arrange an EICFM to consider the crisis, despite their utmost endeavours. A brief account of the seven EICFMs is given below.

1st EICFM; 27–28 Jan. 1980; Islamabad (Pakistan): Article V(1-b) was first invoked by Bangladesh in early 1980, on the plea that the invasion of a Muslim country (Afghanistan) by a superpower (USSR) was such a grave situation that it warranted an EICFM. The request was concurred with by most of the Muslim countries and 26 January was announced as the date of the 1st EICFM. The five-member Steadfastness Front objected to the date as it coincided with the beginning of Israeli troop withdrawal from the Sinai, in accordance with the Camp David accord. Pakistan extended the date by one day so Algeria, Libya, and the PLO turned up, bringing the total to thirty-six.[112]

The EICFM demanded immediate and unconditional withdrawal of the Soviet troops from Afghanistan and called for respect to the sovereignty and territorial integrity of the country and non-interference in its internal affairs. The EICFM refused to recognize the puppet Kabul regime of Babrak Karmal and decided to suspend Afghanistan's OIC membership, give full support to *Mujahideen;* and to boycott the forthcoming Moscow Olympics in protest against the Soviet invasion.

The Conference expressed serious concern over the presence of the Soviet Union's and its allies' troops in the horn of Africa. The Conference also deliberated on the US hostage crisis in Iran and warned the United States against escalation of the crisis by reaffirming 'the vital stakes of the Islamic Conference and countries in the sovereignty, territorial integrity and independence of Iran'. Moscow, which was unhappy about the holding of an EICFM on the problem of its invasion of Afghanistan, hailed the resolution against the United States.

2nd EICFM; 11–12 July 1980; Amman (Jordan): The 2nd EICFM was convened on the request of the PLO to discuss the Jerusalem question. The Conference warned Israel not to flout its international obligations by moving the capital from Tel Aviv to Jerusalem. It also warned the world community against moving their diplomatic missions to Jerusalem.[113] For the first time, the Conference listened to two expelled mayors Mohammad Hilham and Fahd Kawasmeh of the occupied West Bank, to get first hand knowledge of the atrocities being committed on the Palestinians.

The Conference rejected any partial or piecemeal solution of the Palestine crisis and declared the Camp David accord as a 'conspiracy against the future of Jerusalem'. Iran suggested that the Islamic countries should break diplomatic relations with all the countries who have relations with Israel. The Secretary General was asked to prepare list of such countries within six months and present the same to the ICFM. The member states were given 180 days to implement this decision.

3rd EICFM; 18–20 Sept. 1980; Fez (Morocco): As Israel had ignored the 2nd EICFM's stern warnings and had annexed East Jerusalem, the 3rd EICFM, the second in two months, was convoked which termed the Israeli action as hostile to the Muslim world, and called for *jihad* against the Israeli annexation of Jerusalem.[114] It also decided to establish an Islamic Boycott Bureau like the Arab Boycott Bureau for an effective boycott of Israel, which was to serve such purposes as blacklisting of firms dealing with Israel, etc. The EICFM expressed concern over Israeli threats to Iraqi nuclear installations and gave full support to the Iraqi nuclear programme. The Conference also

expressed concern over the escalation of tensions between Iran and Iraq.

4th EICFM; 26 Sept. 1980; New York (USA): Just a couple of days after the conclusion of the Fez moot, the Iran–Iraq war started. The Islamic Foreign Ministers, who had arrived in New York to attend the OIC's coordination meeting at the beginning of UN General Assembly's annual session, met in an emergency session to consider the situation arising out of the war in the Gulf. The Conference urged both sides to agree to an immediate cease-fire and resolve the disputes through peaceful means.[115] The 4th EICFM expressed serious concern over the spilling of Muslim blood in the fratricidal conflict. The OIC decided to initiate all-out efforts to mediate between Iran and Iraq. The OIC mediator, the President of Pakistan, left for Tehran and Baghdad immediately and met President Banisadr (Iran) on 28 September and President Saddam Hussain (Iraq) on 29 September respectively, to convey the concern of the OIC and its members over the outbreak of the war.

5th EICFM; 17–18 June 1992; Istanbul (Turkey): The 5th EICFM was convened on the initiative of Tunisia, Iran, and Turkey, to discuss the alarming situation in Bosnia, since her declaration of independence on 29 February. The Conference decided that the OIC would support all UN efforts for a peaceful settlement of the conflict. It asked the latter to invoke Article VII of its Charter for tougher measures if the 'sanctions do not force Serbia to stop aggression'.[116] The EICFM warned against the spread of bloodshed into the Muslim majority Serbian province of Kosovo and also appealed to the members not to recognize Serbia unless Serbia recognized the sovereignty of Bosnia.

Iran, Turkey, and Pakistan expressed willingness to contribute troops for any UN-sponsored military action in Bosnia. Turkish Foreign Minister Hikmet Cetin went further, and declared that his country was ready to spill blood if necessary. The Bosnian Foreign Minister Haris Siladjic (later Prime Minister) who had called for immediate military intervention said he was satisfied with the wording of the resolutions on

Bosnia. The Conference requested the Islamic Bank to finance the reconstruction of Bosnia. It passed two other resolutions on the situations in Jerusalem and Lebanon. It also accepted the membership application of Turkemanistan, an ex-Soviet Muslim republic of Central Asia.

6th EICFM; 1–2 Dec. 1992; Jeddah (Saudi Arabia): As the war escalated in Bosnia, another EICFM was held to consider other ways and means to resolve the crisis. The conference began with a call by King Fahd to the UN to fulfil its obligations; the UN negotiators on Bosnia, Cyrus Vance and Lord Owen, were attending on special invitation.[117] In his speech, President Alija Izzetbegovich of Bosnia, who also attended the conclave on a special invitation, made a fervent appeal for provision of defensive weapons to his country.

The final communiqué of the 6th EICFM, called for lifting of the 'unjust and uncalled for' arms embargo on Bosnia and Herzegovina 'which is in urgent need of weapons for its legitimate self-defense'; and renewed the OIC's offer of financial and military support to the UN in its operations in Bosnia. Four new members viz. Albania, Kirghizistan, Tajikistan, and Zanzibar were formally inducted into the OIC during this conference.

7th EICFM; 7–9 Sept. 1994; Islamabad (Pakistan): As Tunisia had expressed regrets on holding the ICFM in 1994, Pakistan decided to convene an extraordinary session of ICFM and succeeded, at last, in getting the support of two-thirds of the members. The EICFM discussed a number of issues confronting the Muslim world, especially Kashmir. It called for respecting human rights in Kashmir and supporting the inalienable right of the self-determination of the Kashmiri people.[118]

The Conference condemned the Israeli policies in the Middle East, supported the sovereignty and territorial integrity of Bosnia, expressed its concern over the war between Armenia and Azerbaijan, called for a just and equitable solution of the problem of Nogorno-Karabagh, expressed its desire for an end to the Afghan civil war, and finally reaffirmed its call for a just trial of the two Libyan

Lockerbie suspects by Scottish judges at the International Court of Justice (ICJ) in the Hague.

Specialized Ministerial Conferences

Besides the Islamic Summit and Foreign Ministers' Conferences, several other types of conferences are also held, under the auspices of the OIC. The basic aim of these specialized ministerial conferences is to explore avenues of cooperation in the Muslim countries in various fields. These conferences are held on the decisions of, and are meant to be complementary to, the Islamic Summits and the ICFMs. Ministerial conferences take decisions on the issues under consideration with a view to enhance intra-Muslim world cooperation; and try to work out a common stand for the Muslim *ummah* on each issue.

Conferences of OIC Finance Ministers: The first ever OIC specialized ministerial meeting was that of the Ministers of Finance. The finance ministers of the OIC member states met in Jeddah in December 1973 and laid the groundwork for the Islamic Development Bank (IDB) by issuing a Declaration of Intent to establish the Bank. Ghulam Ishaq Khan of Pakistan was elected Secretary of the said meeting.[119] Since then, several meetings of the OIC Finance Ministers or experts have been held. One such economic conference on the experts level was held in Ankara (4–6 November 1980).[120] The finance ministers/experts conferences have dealt with economic cooperation between the OIC member states, OIC's financial organs, OIC budgetary problems, and a host of similar issues. Lately, one meeting of OIC Finance Ministers was scheduled to be held on 2 November 1993 at Banjul, Gambia.[121] No meeting of the OIC finance ministers appears to have been held after 1994, save in the context of the Board of Directors' meetings of the Islamic Development Bank.

Conferences of OIC Information Ministers: The Islamic International News Agency (IINA) has been in operation since 1979. In the last week of October that year, a conference of Islamic news agencies was held in Ankara, Turkey, to deliberate upon ways and means of making the newly born

IINA an effective source of news. As things turned out, the IINA could not take off. Far from making a niche in the highly competitive news world, the IINA even failed to sustain its existence and by 1985, it could not pay its staff their salaries and was a defaulter in everything including electricity bills. This problem came up for discussion at the 5th Islamic Summit (Kuwait; 1987) which formed a ten-member committee to look into IINA affairs. The Summit also decided to convene the 1st conference of the Information Ministers of the OIC member states during 1987.[122] Saudi Arabia offered to host this conference which was belatedly held in October 1988 at Jeddah. This meeting approved the famous OIC Plan of Action on Information.

The 2nd conference of the OIC Information Ministers was held at Cairo, Egypt, in January 1992; the third one took place at Damascus, Syria, in May 1995;[123] and the fourth in the series was convened at Dakar, Senegal, in December 1997. The Dakar meeting called for embracing modern technologies to counter the distorted image of Islam projected by the Western media, and to stem the tide of Western culture sneaking into the electronic media in Muslim countries. It considered the drafting of an Islamic code of ethics in the field of information, greater exchange of television programmes among member states and a new range of new technologies and communication links. The Conference decided to hold the 5th OIC information ministers' conference at Tehran, Iran, by the end of 1998.[124] The purpose of these conferences is to work out a common strategy of the Muslim ummah to counter the global information challenge.

Conference of the OIC Ministers of Religious Affairs: The first ever conference of the OIC Ministers for Islamic (or Religious) Affairs was held in the late seventies. Shortly thereafter, the second conference of OIC Ministers for *Awqaf* and Religious Affairs was held at the holy city of Mecca, Saudi Arabia, in March 1980.[125] After a long interval, the third such ministerial conference met at Cairo, Egypt, on 21 January 1993. The Conference called for immediate establishment of the International Islamic Court of Justice and an Islamic army.[126] All these conferences have also

called for the implementation of *Shari'ah* in the Muslim countries.

The Islamic Affairs Ministers of the OIC also set up an Islamic Affairs Supreme Council to consider the Islamic issues at the experts level. This Council duly held its meeting in July 1996 at Cairo. Meanwhile, the OIC Secretariat's Department of *Da'wa* (Islamic Call) has also set up a similar body named Committee on Coordination of Joint Islamic Action in the Field of *Da'wa*. The tenth session of this committee was held at Kuala Lumpur, Malaysia, in January 1996. It was inaugurated by Prime Minister Mahatir Mohammad and was attended by the Presidents of one hundred Islamic organizations in the field who discussed matters pertaining to the preaching of the Islamic religion in the world. The last session of this Committee to date, was held in May 1998 in Tehran, Iran.

OIC Ministerial Conference for Industry, Food and Agriculture: The first conference of OIC Ministers of Food and Agriculture was supposed to be held in Egypt in 1979, in pursuance of the decision by the 9th ICFM (Dakar; 1978) but could not be held due to Egypt's expulsion from the OIC. Mali was accepted as an alternate venue but the 11th ICFM (Islamabad; 1980) noted with concern that the conference did not take place due to poor response by the member states. Finally, the OIC Food and Agriculture Ministers meeting took place at Ankara, Turkey, in 1981.[127] The meeting approved proposals to improve agricultural production and security of food supplies in the Muslim countries. The Ministers agreed to set up a research centre at Turkey to study agrohydrology and called for a study on setting up agricultural research centres. The IDB offered a $300 million initial fund for the promotion of agricultural trade.[128]

During the same year, Pakistan hosted the OIC Ministerial conference on trade cooperation. Sudan offered to host the second OIC conference on Food and Agriculture but it appears that it could not be held on schedule, though ministerial consultations on industrial cooperation did take place at Islamabad (February 1982), attended by thirty-one Muslim countries and eleven specialized OIC agencies. The second such meeting was held in

Istanbul (November 1984). The OIC meetings on industrial development considered a number of measures for enhancing industrial cooperation within the OIC membership. The 4th Islamic Summit (Casablanca; 1984) urged the holding of more ministerial conferences on agriculture and industry but very few could be held.[129] In response, the second conference of Ministers for Food and Agriculture probably took place at Rome in 1985. The third in the series took place in October 1988 while the fourth is still awaited.

Other Conferences: There are various other conferences that were held under the OIC auspices. The first conference of OIC Ministers of Culture was held at Dakar in 1989. The first education conference was held at King Abdul Aziz University (Jeddah) in 1977. The first Islamic conference on *Zakat* was held at Kuwait at the end of April 1984. In May 1984, the first conference of architects and town-planners from Islamic states was held at Lahore, Pakistan, which called for the establishment of an International Islamic Architects Council. Similarly, the Islamic Society of Statistical Sciences holds its conferences on the subject; the last Islamic conference on Statistics and Science was held at Lahore in September 1994. In addition, the OIC has held a large number of expert meetings on Muslim minorities, problems of women etc. in collaboration with other organizations like the WMC, Call of Islam Society etc.

NOTES and REFERENCES

1. Since the 3rd Islamic Summit (Taif; 1981), this article has been amended and now the summit conference takes place triennially.
2. Noor Ahmad Baba, *OIC: Theory & Practice of Pan-Islamic Cooperation*, (Karachi: Oxford University Press, 1994), pp. 64–65.
3. For a detailed account of the 1st Islamic Summit, see Shamim Akhtar, 'The Rabat Summit Conference', *Pakistan Horizon,* (Karachi: Pakistan Institute of International Affairs), vol. 22, no. 4, October–December 1969, pp. 336–341. Also see 'Facts on File', 1969, p. 624.
4. Keesing's Contemporary Archives', 1969–70, p. 23689, gives details about the controversy over PLO's admission.
5. The committee consisted of Iran, Malaysia, Morocco, Niger, Pakistan, Saudi Arabia, and Somalia. See Syed Najibullah, 'Rabat—The Untold Story', *Pakistan Observer,* Dhaka, 2 November 1969, for details about the expulsion of India.
6. Ibid. Also see Akhtar, ref. 3.
7. See *The New York Times* report on the Rabat Summit, in the clippings file no. C-811/66-11 (on Rabat Islamic Summit), in the records of National Archives of Pakistan, Islamabad.
8. *Los Angeles Times,* 26 September 1969. Also see, *Holiday,* 5 October 1969.
9. *Chicago Tribune,* 22 September 1969. Also see, *Los Angeles Times,* op. cit., 26 September 1969.
10. Egypt, one of the front-line states, and Iran, were the other two contenders for the honor of hosting the summit. But King Faisal and many other leaders favored Pakistan as the venue. King Reza of Iran thus stayed away in protest.
11. For a detailed account of the conference, see Mehrunnisa Ali, 'The Second Islamic Summit conference', *Pakistan Horizon,* (Karachi: PIIA), vol. 27, no. 1, January–March 1974, pp. 29–50.
12. Keesing's Contemporary Archives, 1974, p. 26689.
13. See 'Facts on File', 1974, p.139. The 2nd Islamic Summit conferred a permanent member status on the occupied state of Palestine, at par with all other member states. Prior to this, the PLO had an observer status.
14. This and other quotes from the speeches have been taken from *Lahore Islamic Summit 1974,* (Islamabad: Ministry of Information, Directorate of Films and Publications, 1974).
15. Baba, ref. 2, pp. 99–100 and 102–3.
16. See International Press on the Islamic Summit in *The Lahore Islamic Summit,* ref. 14, pp. 155–63.
17. See 'Karier', 4 March 1974, and *The New Nation,* 28 February 1974.
18. See Ali, ref. 11.
19. This caption 'The Fourth World' was first used by *Sun* of Sri Lanka in its editorial on the Second Islamic Summit.
20. For the full text of Mr Z.A. Bhutto's speech, see *Lahore Islamic Summit 1974,* ref. 14, pp. 32–45.
21. Baba, ref. 2, p. 129. The conference was opened by King Khalid who was indisposed and spoke briefly. The full text of this speech was read out by Crown Prince Fahd (now King).
22. See, *Financial Times,* London, 31 January 1981.
23. For a detailed account of the 3rd Islamic Summit, see SGM Badruddin, 'The Third Islamic Summit Conference', *Pakistan Horizon,* (Karachi: PIIA), vol. 34, no. 1, January–March 1981, p. 44–58.
24. 'Facts on File', 1981, p. 63 and 83.
25. Keesing, 1981, pp. 30881–82.
26. Baba, ref. 5, pp. 132–33.

27. Ibid., pp. 133–35

28. Ibid.

29. Ibid., p. 134.

30. For a detailed account of the 4th Islamic Summit, see Sabiha Hassan, 'Casablanca Islamic Summit', *Pakistan Horizon,* (Karachi: P11A), vol. 37, no. 1, January–April 1984, pp. 74–88.

31. Ibid.

32. Ibid.

33. Former US President Ronald Reagan (1981–89) had floated a Middle East peace plan known as Reagan Plan. It was unacceptable to the Muslim leadership since it did not recognize the national rights of the Palestinians. It did not accept the PLO as the sole spokesman of the Palestinian peoples either. Consequently, several key Arab leaders met at Fez, Morocco, to draft alternative proposals. The latter is known as Fez Peace Plan. Also see 'Facts on File', 1984, p.53.

34. Kessing, 1984, p. 32823.

35. Baba, ref. 2, pp. 166–69.

36. See *Dawn*, Karachi, 23 December 1986, and 8 January 1987.

37. *The Muslim*, Islamabad, 17 January 1987.

38. *Pakistan Times*, Islamabad, 23 January 1987.

39. *Saudi Gazette*, Riyadh, 27 January 1987.

40. Baba, ref. 2, p. 175.

41. Ibid., pp. 176–77.

42. 'Facts on File', 1987, p. 84.

43. Baba, ref. 2, p. 177.

44. See Mushahid Hussain, 'The Dakar Summit', *Frontier Post,* Peshawar, 29 December 1991. According to *The Muslim* (9 December 1991), one major reason for the poor response of the Arab leaders was the Israeli delaying tactics for the peace talks which were postponed form 4 December to 9 December, so that many key Arab leaders would become occupied with this affair. This, the paper believes, was a deliberate attempt by Israel to sabotage the Islamic summit.

45. Keesing, 1991, 38699. Also see *Tehran Times*, Tehran, 18 November 1991.

46. Maqbool Ahmad Bhatty, 'Reflections on the Islamic Summit', *The Nation,* Lahore, 21 December 1991.

47. Baba, ref. 5, p. 191. Also see Hussain, ref. 73.

48. See 'What's a few million between brothers', *The Muslim*, 21 December 1991.

49. Baba, ref. 2, p. 190.

50. Ibid.

51. *Kuwait Times*, Kuwait 11 December 1991.

52. *Jang* (Urdu), Rawalpindi, 10 January 1992.

53. See Ayaz Ahmad Khan, 'Casablanca Diplomacy Must Be Followed Through', *The Muslim*, 28 December 1994, for a brief account of the Seventh Islamic Summit. Also see 'Facts on File', 1994, p. 971.

54. See *The News*, 14 December 1994, and 15 December 1994.

55. See *Frontier Post*, Lahore, 24 December 1994.

56. *Mir Waiz*, literally the principal preacher, is the highest religious authority of the state of Jammu and Kashmir. It is a hereditary position and enjoys a lot of respect among the Kashmiris. *Mir Waiz* is also the *ex-officio Imam* of the Grand Mosque of Srinagar, the summer capital of the Indian-Held Kashmir. See *Pakistan Times*, 21 December 1994.

57. Ibid., 18 December 1994. Also see, *The Muslim*, 15 December 1994.

58. Ibid., 14 December 1994.

59. Riaz A. Syed, 'Casablanca Islamic Summit: A major foreign Policy Breakthrough', *Pakistan Times,* 24 December 1994.

60. Keesing, 1994, p. 40339. Also see Khan, ref. 53, and *Dawn*, 13 December 1994, and 16 December 1994.

61. Keesing, 1994, p. 40339.

62. Editorial of *The Muslim*, 24 December 1994.

63. The pro-Iran ousted President Burhanuddin Rabbani arrived at Tehran leading a delegation. He even tried to physically occupy the Afghanistan's seat at the Preparatory Meeting of Experts, in the absence of the *Taliban*. He was, however, forced to withdraw on Pakistan's insistence. See, *The News*, 5 December 1997. Also see, *Asas* (Urdu), Islamabad, 5 December 1997.

64. The diplomatic relations between Iran and Egypt were broken at the time of latter's signing of Camp David agreement in 1978. Since then a war of attrition between the two countries has continued unabated. Nevertheless, one reason for Hosni Mubarak's absence could be his concerns for personal safety. Since an abortive assassination attempt against him at Addis Ababa, Ethiopia, during an OAU summit, he has been particularly careful in going abroad. At the 8th Islamic Summit, Mubarak was represented by his Foreign Minister Amr Moussa. Also see *The News*, 7 December 1997.

65. Saad. S. Khan, 'Tehran Summit: Not just a gathering', *The News*, 7 December 1997. Also see *The Muslim World*, (Karachi: WMC), vol. 35, no. 18, 22 November 1997, for details about Summit preparations. Also see the reports of *The News*, 6 December 1997 and 9 December 1997, and that of *The Muslim World*, vol. 35, no. 21, 13 December 1997, p. 2, about summit arrangements.

66. See, *The News,* 10 December 1997. The full text of the speeches made by Ayatollah Ali Khaminei and President Khatami were provided to the author by the Iranian diplomatic mission at Islamabad.

67. Copies of all the resolutions approved by the Eighth Summit were provided by Ambassador Khalil Saeed, head of the OIC Mission in Islamabad, to the author.

68. *The News*, 10 December 1997.

69. Ibid.

70. Ibid., 8 December 1997. It is noteworthy that Prime Minister. Necmettin Erbakan had announced the cancellation of any joint military activity with Israel during his brief one-year stint in power. He was however, forced to resign by the Turkey's powerful military, his party dissolved and he banned from politics. His successor, Mesut Yilmaz, was not strong enough to dabble in the decisions of the military.

71. Ibid., 12 December 1997. India rejected the OIC resolution on Kashmir and asked the OIC leadership not to be misguided by Pakistan. The puppet head of the Indian occupied part of Kashmir, Farooq Abdullah, unleashed a vitriolic diatribe against the OIC for raising the issue of Kashmiri Muslims. 'The OIC has never helped the Muslim community of India, the second largest in the world, in natural calamities', he said.

72. Ibid., 8 December 1997.

73. Ibid., 10 December 1997 and 12 December 1997.

74. Ibid., 11 December 1997.

75. See Robert Frisk, 'Islamic conference signals the collapse of American prestige', *The Independent,* carried by *The News,* 5 December 1997, under special arrangement.

76. See Saad. S. Khan, 'OIC Summit Arrangements', *Communicator,* Islamabad, Spring 1997, p. 20.

77. *Dawn,* 24 March 1997.

78. Ibid.

79. See Nasim Zehra, 'Summit Talking', *The News,* 1 April 1997. Also see the text of Islamabad Declaration.

80. See Gen. Aslam Beg, 'OIC, Bhutto to Nawaz Sharif', *The News,* 25 March 1997. Also see M.A. Niazi, 'A Unique Summit' in ibid., 29 March 1997.

81. Zehra, ref. 79. Also see *The Nation,* Lahore, 24 March 1997.

82. Beg, ref. 80. Also see Jamil-ur-Rehman 'Islamabad Declaration', *The News,* 29 March 1997, and the editorial comments of *The Nation,* 24 March 1997 about the summit.

83. Quoted by the '*Nawa-i-Waqat*' (Urdu), Lahore, 25 March 1997.

84. Most part of the account of the first ten ICFMs has been taken from the Press Release of the Press Information Department (PID), Government of Pakistan, Islamabad, issued on the occasion of the holding of 11th ICFM (Islamabad; May 1980) in Pakistan. This release can be seen in file no. 914.046/ 1980, at the record and research section of the PID. In addition, the yearbooks of 'Keesing's Contemporary Archives' and 'Facts on File' also give a brief picture of the proceedings of all the ICFMs. For preparing this section of Chapter 5, I have also gone through a number of newspapers of the dates when any OIC moot was in progress. These newspapers give daily coverage to the conference decisions of the preceding day. Among the English dailies in Pakistan, *Pakistan Times* and *Dawn,* and since 1990 *The News* also, are rich in information. For researchers, these papers can be seen in the research sections of National Archives of Pakistan (Islamabad), Press Information Department (Islamabad) and Pakistan National Library (Islamabad). One may also consult the newspapers of other Muslim countries for details about ICFMs, provided he knows the relevant dates. Readers, who are interested in the ICFMs proceedings in greater detail, are highly recommended to go through Noor Ahmad Baba, *OIC: Theory & Practice of Pan-Islamic Cooperation,* (Karachi: Oxford University Press, 1994). In addition the OIC General Secretariat publications on the Resolutions and Declarations of Islamic Conferences are helpful in knowing the decisions taken by the respective ICFMs or summits. The accounts given here of all the ICFMs are concise yet comprehensive, since almost all sources mentioned above have been exhausted.

85. See PID Press Release, ref. 84. Also see Baba, op. cit., pp. 70–72. Also see Chaudhri Nazir Ahmad, 'Commonwealth of Muslim States', (Lahore: Ferozsons, 1972), pp. 157–163; Keesing, 1969–70, p. 23689; Facts on File, 1970, p. 305.

86. See PID Press Release, ref. 84. Also see Baba, ibid., pp. 72–76. Also see Nazir, ref. 85, pp. 164–70; Keesing, 1971–72, p. 24482.

87. See PID ref. 84. Also see Baba, ibid., pp. 76–85; and Nazir, ibid., pp. 175–188.

88. See PID, ref. 84. Also see Baba, ibid., pp. 85–89.

89. See PID, ref. 84. Also see Baba, ibid., pp. 105–9; Keesing, 1974, p. 26689.

90. See PID, ref. 84. Also see Baba, ibid., pp. 109–112; Keesing, 1975, p. 27294. The architect of the OIC, King Faisal was killed by one of his nephews on 25 March 1975. It is difficult to guess the motives in the closed Saudi system. It is believed that the assassin wanted to avenge his brother's death ten years earlier who had led a procession to condemn the opening up of the first television station in the Kingdom, which he thought was un-Islamic. His procession was fired upon by the police resulting in his death. Today many conspiracy theories enjoy credence like, that the prince was an American agent etc. But the motives of King Faisal's assassination may remain shrouded in mystery.

91. See PID, ref. 84. Also see Baba, ibid., pp. 112–214; Keesing, 1976, p. 27900; Facts on File, 1976, p. 373.

92. The Turk Cypriot Community got an observer status only after November 1983, when Turkey formally announced the establishment of the Turkish Republic of Northern Cyprus.

93. See PID, ref. 84. Also see Baba, op. cit., pp. 114–115; Keesing, 1977, p. 28556.

94. See PID, ref. 84. Also see Baba, ibid., pp. 115–118.

95. See PID, ref. 84. Also see Baba, ibid., pp. 118–119; Keesing, 1979, p. 29953; Facts on File, 1979, p. 360.

96. Likewise, Egypt was also expelled from the Arab League its eighteen specialized bodies and eleven authorized ministerial councils.

97. See Baba, ref. 2, pp. 121–126; Keesing, 1980, p. 30242; Facts on File, 1980, p. 395. Just five months ago, Islamabad was the venue of the first-ever extraordinary session of ICFM (January, 1980) on Afghanistan. See EICFMs in the next section. Pakistan's obsession with Afghanistan crisis is understandable since the influx of 3.5 million refugees took a heavy toll on Pakistan's economy and law and order situation. As the war went on, tensions between Islamabad and Moscow rose. So with tens of thousands (believed-to-be Pakistani) religious fanatics fighting along with the Mujahideen inside Afghanistan and massive Soviet retaliatory bombing of Pakistani territory, Pakistan and ex-USSR were virtually at war with each other.

98. See Baba, ref. 2. pp. 157–160; Keesing, 1981, p. 31014.

99. See Baba, ibid., pp. 161–163 and the newspaper reports of 23–27 August, 1982.

100. See Baba, ibid., pp. 163–166. Also see Keesing, 1984, p. 32824.

101. See Baba, ibid., pp. 170–172. Also see Keesing, 1986, p. 34718.

102. See Baba, ibid., pp. 172–175. Also see Keesing, 1986, p. 34260; Facts on File, 1986, p.2.

103. See Baba, ibid., pp. 178–180. Also see Keesing, 1988, p.36305, and Facts on File, 1988, p. 297.

104. See Baba, ibid., pp. 180–83. Keesing, 1989, p. 36537; Facts on File, 1989., p.229. As per Geneva agreement (14 April 1988), the last batch of Soviet troops vacated Afghanistan by 15 February 1989. While the agreement between Iran and Iraq to end the war was reach end on August 9, 1988 and the cease-fire took affect on August 20, 1988.

105. See Baba, ibid., pp. 183–86; Keesing, 1990, p. 37668. When the *Mujahideen* toppled the Kabul regime in spring 1992, Dr Najibullah took refuge in the UN Mission in Kabul. He was arrested from there on 26 September 1996, when *Taliban* forces captured the city and formed their government. He was later publicly hanged by the radical student militia.

106. See Baba, ibid., pp. 186–89; Keesing, 1991, p. 38260.

107. See Baba, ibid., pp. 193–99. See *Dawn*, 28–30 April 1993, and *The News* of the same dates.

108. See, *The News*, 11, 12 December 1994; and *Dawn* of the same dates.

109. See, *The News*, 13, 14 December 1995; and *Dawn* of the same dates.

110. See, *The News*, 18, 19, 20 December 1996.

111. See, *The News* 16–20 March 1998; and *Dawn* of the same dates.

112. See Baba, ref. 2, pp. 119–121; Keesing, 1980, p. 30241; Facts on File, 1980, p. 67; *The Muslim*, 29 January 1980 and *The Pakistan Times*, 29 January 1980. The Steadfastness Front was formed by five hard-line Arab States, namely, Algeria, Libya, PLO, Syria and S. Yemen to counter Camp David agreement. Syria and Yemen continued their boycott while the PLO said that it was participating as an observer only but it later took part in the voting also.

113. See Baba, ref. 2, pp. 126–129; Also see *Pakistan Times*, 13 July 1980. The OIC warning had a very positive affect and ten countries that had shifted their diplomatic missions to Jerusalem, moved them back to Tel Aviv. Costa Rica, a small Latin American state, did not comply immediately, so the OIC member states broke off relations with her.

114. See Baba, ibid., pp. 126–129. Also see 'Facts on File', 1980, p. 736 and 775; *Pakistan Times*, 20 and 21 September 1980.

115. See, *Pakistan Times*, 26 September 1980.

116. See Baba, ref. 2, pp. 192–193. Also see Keesing, 1992, p. 39970 and 39987 and *Pakistan Times*, 19 June 1992.

117. See Baba, ref 2. pp. 192–93. Also see Keesing, 1992, p. 39038; *Pakistan Times*, 3 December 1992.

118. See Keesing, 1994, p. 40211; *Dawn*, 10 September 1994; *The News,* 10 September 1994.

119. See, *Pakistan Times*, 16 December 1973.

120. See, 'Facts on File', 1980, p.865.

121. *Dawn*, 13 October 1993.

122. Baba, ref. 2, p. 177.

123. *Dawn*, 22 May 1995 and *Pakistan Times*, 27 May 1995.

124. See, *The News*, 30 November 1997 and 5 December 1997.

125. See, *Dawn*, 25 March 1980, and *The Muslim*, 15 March 1980.

126. Keesing, 1993, p. 39299.

127. Abdullah Ahsan, *Ummah or Nation: Identity Crisis in Muslim Society*, (Leicester: Islamic Foundations, 1992), pp. 131–33.

128. Baba, ref. 2, p. 169 and 174.

129. See Ministry of Information, *Pakistan's Role in OIC*, (Islamabad: Directorate of Films and Publications, n. d.), p. 13.

⑥ Political History II: Crises Management and International Issues

The quintessence of a discourse on an international organization is usually a discussion on its effectiveness. In this respect, we shall analyse the role of the OIC in international conflicts concerning the Muslim world and its policies towards contemporary global issues. This is a litmus test for the existence of the OIC which has been criticized, in some cases quite unjustly, for its timid response, if not the lack of it, to several serious challenges. We will analyse the OIC policies and activities in five areas, namely, Islamic causes, conflict resolution, Muslim minorities, domestic political turmoils, and policies towards contemporary issues. The definition of the scope of each of these headings is tricky and thus sheerly arbitrary. We have termed the conflicts between a Muslim and a non-Muslim state, especially when the former is at the receiving end, as Islamic causes. In such cases, the role of the OIC is not to mediate between the belligerents for bringing about an amicable solution but to throw its full weight, except in the Iraq–US dispute of 1990–91, behind the Muslim State. This is so because the OIC believes the security and territorial integrity of any one Muslim State (or community) to be the concern for the whole Muslim world. Moreover, it traditionally treats such a crisis in a particular Muslim country as a cause to fight for, and thus a rallying point, for all Muslim states; Palestine, Bosnia, and Cyprus are notable examples in this category.

When two Muslim sides are locked in a conflict, the OIC presents its services for mediation and good offices to bring about a peaceful resolution of the fratricidal dispute, usually without taking sides. The OIC role in the Iraq–Iran war and the Pakistan–Bangladesh conflict, constitutes its conflict resolution activities. The same is true of the civil wars in Afghanistan, Somalia, and Tajikstan where all the warring factions belong to the Muslim faith. Here the problem is that the above two categories are not mutually exclusive. For instance, as long as the Soviets were occupying Afghanistan it was an Islamic cause but thereafter it became a civil war where the former *Mujahideen* warlords found themselves at each others throats in the quest for power. Now the OIC role fell into the second category, i.e., mediation in the conflict. The reverse was the case in the Gulf crisis where the OIC was supposed to perform conflict resolution as long as the nibbling was confined to Iraq and Kuwait. But with the involvement of the US, it became an Islamic cause, because Iraqi civilians became the victims of the horrors of war and the post-war US-led punitive measures against Baghdad. Such dual-nature cases have been placed in one or the other category depending upon the direction of the OIC activity. Again a case can also be built to classify the Muslim minority problems, especially the Kashmir and South Philippines crises, as Islamic causes but we have studied the OIC policies *vis-à-vis* the Muslim minorities in a separate section.

Considering the magnitude of this topic, it is not possible to recapitulate the OIC policies in all disputes and crises, hence we have identified a few case studies for each of the five sections. Otherwise, the OIC policies towards Palestine alone, for example, constitute so vast a topic as to warrant a whole volume. An attempt has been made to give a very brief background of a dispute before narrating the OIC's involvement in the developments, and the impact of its decisions, on the situation. Reproduction of the texts of OIC resolutions and the speeches made during its fora, has been carefully avoided.

Islamic Causes

The OIC has, in a plethora of resolutions, declarations, and statements, reaffirmed that the security of any one Muslim state was a cause of concern for the whole Muslim world. The first, third and fourth objectives of the OIC require it to promote Islamic solidarity, endeavour to eliminate colonialism and take measures in support of international peace and security, respectively. The sixth objective further obliges the OIC to effectively strengthen the struggles of Muslims for safeguarding their dignity and independence. Read together, they leave no room for doubt that the OIC is entrusted with the task of defending any Muslim entity, under the threat of extinction or aggression.

The OIC practice has shown that it considers a conflict between a Muslim state and a non-Muslim state, when the latter is predominant in military terms, as the concern of the whole Muslim world. There is not one instance of the OIC playing an active part in a conflict where neither party is Muslim, the OIC's statutory commitment to fight against imperialism, colonialism, and racism everywhere in the world, notwithstanding. Instead, the field is left open for other regional organizations, with the OIC confining itself to occasional adoption of a non-committal resolution supporting the efforts of a particular organization over the issue. Likewise, if the aggressor happens to be a Muslim state, the OIC keeps silent and inactive. The case of the Iraqi invasion of Kuwait is an exception.

Palestine (1948) and Afghanistan (1979) were physically occupied by non-Muslim states whereas over Northern Cyprus (1974) and Bosnia (1992), the danger of physical extinction through incorporation into larger non-Muslim states was looming large. As for Pakistan (1971) and Azerbaijan (1991), territorial annexation was not within the gamut of possibilities, but aggression by a stronger hostile neighbour had in each case left a portion of the country concerned, in enemy hands. Then, the disputes of Iran (hostage crisis), Iraq (UN arms inspection), and Libya (Lockerbie affair) with the US are of comparatively smaller magnitude but do fall in the same category and

hence a study of the OIC's position here is relevant.

The Palestine, Afghanistan, Cyprus, Bosnia, and Azerbaijan crises are our case studies here; the Indian invasion of East Pakistan and the UN stand-off with Iraq will be dealt with in the next section in the context of the OIC role in respect of Bangladesh and Kuwait respectively. As for Iran and Libya, it has been the OIC position to express solidarity with the governments and peoples of these states. Though the OIC had repeatedly called upon Iran to release the United States hostages, it also continued to warn the United States against any misadventure, affirming time and again 'the vital stakes involved of all the Muslim states in the sovereignty, political independence and territorial integrity of Iran.'[1] In response to the Western criticism of the Islamic revolution in Iran, the OIC always reiterated its respect of 'the right of the Muslim people of Iran to choose whatever system they prefer for their political and social life.[2] When the US hostages were released in January 1980, the OIC expressed satisfaction over the diffusion of the crisis.

Similarly, in the US–Libya Gulf of Sidra crisis (1986), while the OIC asked Libya to show flexibility, it accused the United States of 'aggressive escalation and constant provocation', at the same time.[3] Years later, it was the Lockerbie affair, where the OIC again believed that the Libyan stand was justified, and several resolutions were adopted expressing solidarity with the Libyans who were suffering under an UN-imposed embargo throughout the decade-long stand-off.

The OIC did not spare the other super power, the Soviet Union, either. Aside from the Soviet (mis)adventure in Afghanistan, the OIC never hesitated to condemn the presence of Soviet troops in the horn of Africa, reiterating its commitment to the sovereignty and independence of Somalia.[4] In the case of Chechenya, the OIC has been less fulsome in adopting resolutions over the loss of Muslim lives in its war with Russia. However, the problem did figure in bilateral discussions of Muslim leaders in several Islamic conferences.[5] The OIC institutions in the economic and cultural fields, especially the IDB, have been providing financial help to displaced persons in Chechenya for humanitarian purposes.

As neither the scope of the discussion nor the space available permit a detailed discourse on all such issues, we shall move on to our five case studies. It may be made clear at this point that our purpose here is not to make value judgements as to which side was at fault in these conflicts. Wherever there seems to be a tilt in favour of one party, it is purely for deliberative purposes, in order to elucidate the OIC point of view or to present the rationale of OIC's action or inaction.

(i) The Problem of Al-Quds and Palestine: The problem of Al-Quds (Jerusalem) is the *raison d'être* of the emergence of the OIC and it has remained its single dominant obsession.

In fact, the fifth objective of the OIC mandates it to support the struggle of the Palestinian people and to coordinate efforts to safeguard the holy places (in Jerusalem). It is indeed very unusual for any international organization to allude to a specific problem in its Charter since crises diffuse and problems get resolved, but the organization is usually there to stay. An objection was raised on this ground at the time of drafting of the OIC Charter also, but was overruled by the majority. The OIC's association with the problem is so long that, at times, it started being identified with the Palestine problem alone.

The permanent headquarters of the OIC are to be located in the holy city of Jerusalem; the Secretariat at Jeddah, according to the OIC, is a temporary arrangement pending the liberation of Jerusalem. One of the four Assistant Secretary Generals of the Organization has the exclusive designation of ASG (Al-Quds Al-Sharif). At least seven of the OIC organs/specialized committees exclusively deal with the Palestine issue while statutes of most of the rest, require them to promote the cause of Palestine in their respective fields of activities. The State of Palestine is *ex-officio* permanent member of the Governing Boards of Islamic States Broadcasting Organization (ISBO), Islamic Heritage Commission (ICPICH), Organization of Islamic Capitals and Cities (OICC), and so on.

The issue has remained the top agenda item in all the OIC conferences. It is difficult to count how many times the names of Palestine, Al-Quds, or in this connection, Israel, appear in the literature of the OIC. It was the OIC, which recognized the Palestine Liberation Organization (PLO) as the sole legitimate representative of the Palestinian people, even before the Arab League did so. Again, it was the OIC that gave political and material support to Palestine and gave Yasser Arafat a head of state protocol, when the West treated him as no more than a ringleader of a terrorist outfit. And it was this Organization that internationalized the Middle East problem in the true sense of the word. What is baffling is why the OIC has always been criticized, not the least by the Palestinians themselves, for not doing enough for the Palestine cause. The following discussion will attempt to find an answer.

For the Muslims, the Al-Aqsa mosque at Jerusalem is the third holiest shrine after the holy Ka'aba at Mecca and the Prophet's mosque at Medina. The Prophet Muhammad (PBUH), the Muslims believe, started his famous journey to the seven heavens, called *Mairaj*, from there. Since Caliph Omar's conquest, Jerusalem had largely remained in the hands of the Muslims till Britain assumed its mandate in the aftermath of Turkey's defeat in the First World War.[6] The founder of the Zionist movement, Theodore Herzl, advocated the idea of a Jewish state to be situated either in Palestine or in Argentine. The Balfour Declaration (1917) gave a pledge on Britain's behalf to establish a Jewish home in Palestine. During the British mandate (1922–48), the Jewish population in Palestine rose eleven-fold due to immigration, greatly disturbing the demographic balance in their favour. During the Second World War, terrorist activities of Jewish para military organizations, especially Irgun, created terror among Palestinians, a large number of whom started fleeing. The State of Israel was proclaimed in May 1948 a day prior to the termination of the British mandate. The war of 1948 failed to dislodge Israel. In 1967, in a pre-emptive strike, Israel attacked several Arab countries, capturing the Sinai desert of Egypt, Golan Heights of Syria, and the West Bank of River Jordan. The Arab East Jerusalem also fell into Israeli hands.

Setting aside their ideological rivalries several Arab states started coming together in this hour of grief. When, with the apparent connivance of Tel Aviv, the holy Al-Aqsa Mosque of Jerusalem was set ablaze, the Muslim states held a summit meeting at Rabat, that called this arson a 'grievous event' that 'has plunged the Muslims throughout the world into the deepest anguish'. This was the beginning of the OIC's association with the Palestine cause as the same Summit laid the foundation of the Organization itself. Now, as the OIC has already crossed its thirtieth year of existence, we can distinguish three distinct phases in OIC's Palestine policies (a) 1969–72; (b) 1973–90; (c) 1991–onward.

(a) First Phase (1969-72): At this point, it should be borne in mind that when the OIC was established, the right of Israel to exist started to be taken as a settled issue. If there were any illusions about Israel being there to stay, they were removed by the 1967 war. Many Muslim countries had established diplomatic relations with Israel as with any state in the Middle East. As for the anti-Israel rhetoric by the leadership of some frontline Arab states, that was simply reflective of their frustration and humiliation. A close look at the Arab Summit declaration showed that 'no-recognition, no-negotiation, no peace' was neither a denial of Israel's existence nor of its right to exist.[7] It was simply an instrument to pressurize a *de facto* existing state to surrender its expansionist designs and be content with the pre-1967 territory, for winning peace and *de jure* status as a state, in the Middle East. If the Arabs were following the textbook rule of 'defiance in defeat', its reverse, 'magnanimity in victory' did not exist in the Israel's political dictionary. This is where the roots of the Middle East problem lie.

If the existence of Israel was a settled affair by 1969, the rights of Palestinians had practically become a non-issue. Neither the declaration of the Islamic Congress formed in Cairo (1956) referred to the Palestine problem, nor did the Charter of Muslim World League founded at Mecca (1962) allude to it. If there were some affirmations about the liberation of Al-Quds, they were political polemics of individual leaders, rather than substantive policy statements. In late 1964, the PLO had come into being and had started military operations from 1 January 1965, but nobody was taking it seriously.

So we notice a strange paradox in this state of affairs. The Palestine issue could be tackled effectively only by concerted efforts of the Muslim states, but neither the 1967 war nor their concern about neo-colonialism by the West was enough to bring them together. Only the Al-Quds issue itself was sufficiently strong and grave to impel the Muslims to unite. Still, and this brings us back to square one, no Muslim country was willing to look at Al-Quds and the Palestinian problem as an issue, let alone a serious one.

Finally it was Israel that itself provided the spark which helped the Muslims out of this ironical situation, and led to the 1st Islamic Summit (Rabat; 1969). Given the state of affairs, it is no surprise that this Conference did not condemn Israel for the 1967 war or the Al-Aqsa arson; it did not even hold Israel directly responsible for the act of sacrilege.[8] The Conference expressed 'deep anguish' over the incident of 'profanation of holy places *that have taken place under the military occupation by Israel* of Al-Quds' (emphasis added). Note that Israel is not being accused of aggression or of being behind the arson. The Conference called upon the four big powers to prevail upon Israel to withdraw from areas occupied in 1967, and affirmed support to the Palestinians for 'the restitution of their usurped rights' through peaceful means alone. It was with difficulty that the PLO delegation could be allowed in, otherwise the conference was nearly wrecked as some states insisted on keeping the (political) Palestine problem divorced from the (religious) Al-Aqsa incident, for which it had been convened in the first place.

The 1st ICFM (Jeddah; 1970) went a step further by unequivocally holding Israel responsible for the 1967 'aggression and continued illegal occupation' of Arab lands. It decided to observe 21 August as Al-Quds Day every year. And it entrusted the Muslim states with: one, extending moral and material support to the Palestinian struggle, and two, facilitating the representation of the Palestinian liberation movement in Islamic countries (the PLO was not mentioned by name). In a very important resolution, the ICFM denounced the Zionist movement as 'racial, aggressive and expansionist'.[9] The 2nd ICFM (Karachi; 1970) merely reiterated the resolutions of the previous conference. It, however, pointed out that Israel's continued occupation of Arab lands was a violation of the UN Charter.[10] It endorsed the Cairo Agreement of September 1970 stressing the need for coordination between the PLO and Jordan against Israel. The Black September massacre was just three months old at the time; how did the Muslim leadership manage to bring together Palestine and Jordan so soon, is beyond the scope of our discussion at the moment. The 3rd ICFM (Jeddah; 1972) decided to set up an office within the General Secretariat to support the Palestine cause. It was the first OIC conference that condemned a particular Israeli action—its military incursions in Lebanon in this case. Also for the first time, specific economic measures were suggested for support of Palestine, namely, the creation of a Palestine Fund, and economic boycott of Israel.[11]

During this first phase, the OIC's gradual shift towards a hardline stance on the Palestine issue is noticeable. The OIC had clearly wedded the Al-Quds and the Palestine issues into a single problem and identified it to be the core issue of the Middle East conflict. Most of the OIC decisions had been successfully implemented; contributions were received for the Palestine Fund and re-directed to the PLO, economic boycott of Israel as far as Muslim states were concerned was nearly universal, and the OIC resolution equating Zionism with racism was soon to be adopted by the UN as well. The Muslim states had coordinated their policies towards the problem at all international fora including the UN, and had started 'condemning' the Israeli policies. Al-Quds Day was observed in most Muslim states on 21 August, every year, and is still being observed in many Muslim countries today. The PLO was soon able to set up offices in most of the Muslim states. The letter of the Chairman of the 3rd ICFM to the PLO Chief, assuring full support to the Palestinian struggle, further testifies to the emerging consensus in the Muslim states about PLO's credentials to represent the whole of Palestine.[12]

(b) Second phase (1973–90): The spectacular success of the OIC policy towards Palestine in the first phase, in so far as the implementation of its resolutions was concerned, however mild they were in their content, is not the only plausible explanation of the OIC's hard-line in the second phase. It may be recalled that the OIC Charter was approved in the 3rd ICFM in March 1972 and by the year's end, necessary ratifications had been deposited with the General Secretariat. Hence, by 1973 the OIC had formally come into being. The Arab–Israeli war, later that year, shattered the myth that the Israeli forces were invincible and boosted the sagging morale of the Arab public. The unprecedented unity shown by Muslim states in the subsequent oil embargo, suggested that there were some common denominators on which all the Muslim states could see eye to eye.

The 4th ICFM (Benghazi; 1973) declared *jihad* (holy struggle) for the liberation of Al-Quds, and the name of the Palestine Fund was changed to 'Jihad Fund for Palestine'—a name considered and turned down by the previous ICFM, due to the objections raised by the donors such as Afghanistan.[13] This time, the Conference was in a different mood and declared 'jihad as the duty of every Muslim, man or woman, ordained by the *Shari'ah* and glorious traditions of Islam' and called upon 'all Muslims, living inside or outside the Islamic countries, to discharge this duty by contributing each according to its capacity, in the cause of Allah Almighty, Islamic brotherhood and rightousness'.[14] The ICFM also asked the Muslim countries to enlist volunteers for the holy war. In another bold resolution, the United States was identified as a super-power supporting Israel. The Conference also recommended the recognition of PLO as the sole legitimate representative of the Palestinian people. This was the beginning of belligerent posture of the OIC *vis-à-vis* Israel. And in no time, the OIC withdrew the tacit recognition it had been giving earlier to Israel. All Muslim states were asked to sever diplomatic relations with Israel and to establish them with Palestine (i.e. PLO). The OIC declared its support for the restoration of all lands and properties of the Palestinians (practically meaning more than half of Israel).

At the 6th ICFM (Jeddah; 1975) the OIC was more direct in calling for the liberation of the Arab lands occupied in 1948 and 1967.[15] In the previous year's resolutions the OIC had been calling for the liberation of Arab territories occupied in the 1967 war and the restoration of sovereignty of Egypt, Jordan and Syria over them. It implied that there was no room for Palestine in these lands. So, liberation of which land for the Palestinians had the OIC been harping about all these years? The official head of state protocol for Yasser Arafat, beginning from the 2nd Islamic Summit (Lahore; 1974) made it clear that the pre-1967 Israel was the actual Palestine whose struggle for liberation the OIC was supporting. But if there was still any doubt, the unequivocal resolution of the 6th ICFM had removed it.

Thenceforth, there was no country called Israel, as far as the OIC was concerned. There was a 'racist, aggressive and expansionist Zionist entity', to quote from the OIC jargon, that was in illegal occupation of Palestine since 1948 and that of territorial portions of three other Islamic states since 1967. The references to Jerusalem that had earlier meant the Muslim-dominated East Jerusalem, now started meaning the whole city. Now the OIC also started haranguing that it would not rule out military means to root out Zionism from *all* the occupied lands.

Now, if Israel was not a state, it had no right to be represented on the international bodies. The Muslim countries had successfully blocked Israel's induction into the international and regional organizations, except the United Nations and its bodies. All the Muslim member states of the UN had voted against Israel's application for membership, back in May 1949, but their number was small at that time. By the mid-seventies, Muslim states' representation in the UN General Assembly had increased manifold. In pursuance of the OIC decision, the Muslim states succeeded in getting an observer status for the PLO. Within months, Arafat was invited to address the UN General Assembly where he was received as a head of state. He even kept wearing the holster of his revolver during his hard-hitting speech.[16] The General Assembly gave a historic verdict supporting the inalienable rights of Palestinian people with ninety-three votes against eighteen. The OIC group succeeded in getting passed another resolution from the General Assembly on 10 November 1975 with seventy-five votes to thirty-five, equating 'Zionism' with 'racism'.[17] The

Israeli ambassador called it 'an evil deed...an obscenity...a day of infamy'.[18]

And for the next eighteen years, Israel, the US, and their allies continued to decry this 'anti-Semitic' resolution, often detracting the world's attention from the real issues in the Middle East.[19] Apparently, the OIC or the PLO had no strategic objectives in mind by this adoption. Apparently, they lacked the potency to harm Israel in any other way at that time. In any case, the OIC moved to the next item on its agenda, to expel Israel from the United Nations. The OIC bloc managed to expel Israel from the UNESCO but then Washington became agitated and declared that it would stop all its contribution to the UN budget if Israel was expelled from the world body. (The United States practically resigned from the UNESCO.) This deterred many third world countries from supporting this particular OIC-sponsored resolution. The OIC rescinded the resolution for Israel's expulsion from the General Assembly but contested Israel's credentials as a state at the UN's Credentials Committee on the grounds that an 'aggressive and racist entity' and a 'violator of all UN resolutions' could not be a member of the United Nations.[20] The Committee rejected the OIC point of view.

The 7th ICFM (Istanbul; 1976) reiterated the 6th ICFM resolution on Israeli expulsion from the UN and pledged to work for it when the situation became 'conducive'. It devised a common strategy for the exclusion of Israel from all international bodies in future.[21] After the decision of 10th ICFM (Fez; 1979) to this effect, the OIC again tried to expel Israel in 1980 but narrowly fell short of the requisite numbers and 'temporarily' dropped its plans.[22]

The UN was not the only forum for the OIC's political efforts in support of Palestine. The OIC group internationalized the issue employing all fora, all channels, and all means. There was not a single OIC conference that had not condemned Israel's policies in the harshest terms possible. The 6th ICFM had formed a nine-member Al-Quds Committee. Its membership was raised to fifteen and King Hassan of Morocco was made its Chairman at the 10th ICFM (Fez; 1979). Two years later, the 12th ICFM (Baghdad; 1979) made the Moroccon monarch the Committee's life

Chairman.[23] The Committee is mandated to study the situation of Al-Quds (Jerusalem), to follow the implementation of decisions taken by the OIC, and to contact other international bodies which can help in the protection of Jerusalem. The Committee meets on the request of its Chairman, King Hassan, or that of the OIC Secretary General, and presents annual reports to the ICFMs. King Hassan himself presents its report at the Islamic Summit Conferences. This Committee has played a truly pivotal role in internationalizing the Al-Quds issue and guiding the OIC reactions to Israel's policies. In response to Israeli settlement policies in the occupied areas and its military incursions and bombings in the neighbouring Muslim states the Committee has constituted two subsidiary committees; (i) Experts Committee for Devising Means Aimed at Combating the Dangers of Zionist Settlement in Palestinian Lands; and (ii) The Islamic Committee for Surveillance of the Actions of Zionist Enemy.[24]

In the eighteen-year period, from 1973 to 1990, the OIC closely monitored the Middle East situation and its policies were impulsive responses to Israeli actions. In 1979–80, the OIC faced two severe credibility tests and succeeded in passing both of them.

The first challenge was the Egypt–Israel peace process which culminated in the Camp David understanding (Sept. 1978) and the formal agreement in Washington (March 1979). This was apparently a major dent in the unity in the OIC ranks as one of the frontline states, exhausted by decades of hostility, had decided to go it alone, make peace with Israel, give it recognition, and in return, get back its part of Israeli occupied lands. The OIC states met at the 10th ICFM (Fez; 1979), which was aptly named the 'Session of Jerusalem and Palestine'. The Muslim states declared the Camp David Accord 'null and void' as it did not guarantee Palestinian rights, and legitimised the Zionist aggression.[25] The OIC, which had long been rejecting the UN Security Council resolution 242 as 'incompatible with Arab and Islamic rights and inconsistent with the basic parameters of peaceful conflict resolution in the Middle East',[26] reiterated its rejection of the Reagon Plan also, insisting that it would reject all future accords, plans and resolutions that did not ensure restitution

of occupied territories, guarantee Palestinian rights and restore Al-Quds back to Arab sovereignty. The most harsh resolutions of condemnation were adopted against the United States and Israel. Egypt was accused of being a traitor and made a pariah. It was charged with betraying all Islamic and Arab causes including the Al-Quds cause, and of violating the OIC decisions and the UN Charter.[27] It was expelled from the OIC, all its affiliated bodies and the Arab League. The Muslim States were directed to sever diplomatic relations, cancel all bilateral agreements, and withdraw all subsidies to Egypt. This was one of the harshest punishments ever meted out against a fellow country in the post-Second World War era by an international organization. The OIC thus managed to retain its unity as well as its tough posture against Israel. Egypt's isolation gave a clear warning to other Muslim states that could have contemplated embarking upon such a course. Most of the intended effects of the accord were nullified and within four years, Egypt itself was forced to concede that Camp David was a dead letter.[28]

The second major challenge before the OIC was the Israeli decision to declare Jerusalem as its permanent capital. In utter disregard of the UN Security Council resolutions 446, 452, and 465 as well as the declarations of the OIC, regarding the status of Jerusalem, Israel had started shifting its offices and moving foreign missions to this city.

The stated position of the Islamic Conference had been that Jerusalem was to be the capital of a free Palestine state and the headquarter of OIC itself, and that this was incontestable. The 11th ICFM (Islamabad; May 1980) gave any country that supported Israel's decision to alter the status of Jerusalem a stern warning of serious consequences. The Conference declared 1980 as the 'Year of Palestine and Al-Quds'. It also decided to observe a week to express solidarity with Palestine and to use it for propaganda about the significance of Al-Quds.[29]

The OIC largely succeeded in turning the general world opinion in its favour, so much so that history was re-written on 30 January 1980 when the UN Security Council, for the first time, condemned Israel for its decision with a 14–0 margin.[30] Even the US found itself compelled to abstain rather than veto the resolution.

Nevertheless, Israel went ahead with the plan and several countries, mostly Latin American, that were unaware of the gravity of the problem moved their embassies to Jerusalem. The OIC held an emergency ICFM session (Amman; July 1980) giving an ultimatum to these countries: to move back their embassies to Tel Aviv or face the music. The Conference requested a special UN session to consider the problem and decided to stiffen its economic boycott of Israel by asking the European Community member states to join in.[31] This had a very positive effect as a number of European states openly censured the Israeli decision, the Church also joined the chorus of condemnation against Israel, Switzerland refused to sign an agreement with Israel in the city of Jerusalem and, more significantly, the ten Latin American and one European states complied with the OIC ultimatum and withdrew their embassies back to Tel Aviv.[32]

Still, Israel was adamant and decided to go it alone by formally making Jerusalem its capital. So the OIC called another emergency session of ICFM (Fez; Sept. 1980) which noted with pride and satisfaction the successful outcome of the decisions taken by the previous ICFM emergency session, held two months earlier. It also took note of the UN Security Council resolution 478 of 20 August 1980, demanding Israel to move back its capital from Jerusalem, and requested the Council to take positive military action against Israel.[32] The special ICFM session decided to renew efforts to expel Israel from the UN. It also asked member states to withhold loans and contributions to the International Monetary Fund and the World Bank, unless they granted observer status to the PLO.[33] The meeting also noted that only two countries El Salvador and Costa Rica had not shifted their missions back to Tel Aviv. Following a later recommendation by the Al-Quds Committee, all the Muslim states, including Egypt, broke all kind of relations with these two states.[35] Consequently, Israel was forced to revert to Tel Aviv as its capital. Since then it has never again experimented any alteration in the status of Jerusalem. Thus the OIC won this crucial battle.

Once again, in March 1984, a resolution by the US Congress asking the government to shift its embassy to Jerusalem caused alarm in the OIC circles. A six-member OIC envoys committee led by the Ambassador Ejaz Rahim of Pakistan, met the US Secretary of State George Shultz, to discuss the matter. Shultz categorically assured the mission that the US had no intention of shifting its embassy.

Coming back to 1980, shortly after the two victories of that year, the OIC held its 3rd Islamic Summit (Taif; 1981) which in its final communiqué, called for holy *jihad* to salvage Jerusalem, to support the Palestinian struggle and secure Israeli withdrawal from all occupied territories. The Mecca Declaration, issued by the same Conference, while addressing this issue openly states that the OIC states are committed to exercising *jihad* using 'all' means at their disposal.[36] It may be emphasized that the Islamic concept of *jihad* (holy struggle for a just cause) is neither confined to, nor excludes, the military option. It is in this sense that the OIC takes it, as it obliges the Muslim states to employ military, political, diplomatic, and economic means to carry out their *jihad*.

In fact, the military *jihad*, was the least exploited option as far as the OIC was concerned. As seen above, the 4th ICFM (Benghazi; 1973) had created a Jihad Fund and asked Muslim states to enlist volunteers. Only Libya had opened offices for the purpose and had enlisted tens of thousands of motivated youth to fight for Jerusalem, in case the OIC decided so. But nothing happened till the 3rd Summit (Taif; 1981) which merely reaffirmed that the OIC did not rule out military option. A few months later, the 12th ICFM (Baghdad; 1981) established an 'Islamic Bureau for Military Coordination with Palestine' in order to foster military cooperation between Palestine (meaning the PLO) and the frontline Muslim states (Egypt, Jordan, Lebanon, and Syria) on one hand, and other Muslim states on the other. It also pledged to meet the PLO needs regarding military expertise and equipment, both qualitatively and quantitatively.[37] In September 1984, Lt. Gen. Fazl-e-Muqeem Khan of Pakistan, was appointed the Bureau's first Head. This was an addition to the two experts committees on Israel already in operation, referred to above. All these bodies in the military domain have kept a low profile as no tangible benefits came out of them for the Palestinian struggle.

The OIC record in the diplomatic *jihad* is, however, better. In a multi-pronged attack, the first objective of the OIC was to gain legitimacy for the PLO for representing the State of Palestine, which it managed in a very short time. The PLO became an observer at the United Nations, Yasser Arafat was accorded head of state status at his address to the General Assembly which also passed several resolutions in Palestine's support in the subsequent years with thumping majorities. The OIC's call for diplomatic isolation of Israel met with an equally encouraging response. Iran threw out Israeli staff and gave the premises of Israeli diplomatic missions to the PLO. Even the non-OIC states toed the line and in the first few years, Palestines' missions had been established in 106 states.[38] Israel was expelled from UNESCO, nearly expelled from the UN also and forced to back out from its decision regarding the status of Jerusalem.

The OIC's aggressive drive tried to convince the world that the Al-Quds issue was not an Islamic issue but a religious issue in the broader sense, and for this purpose it maintained a close liaison with the Vatican and the World Council of Churches.[38] The OIC never failed to stress the humanitarian dimension of the conflict, bringing round all 'anti imperialist' radical Third World states to its side. The OIC countered every Israeli move on the diplomatic front by invoking the UN Charter and the provisions of the international law against racism and colonialism, and thereby exploiting world concerns for peace and security. The OIC declared every plan or pact that did not guarantee Palestinian rights and the Arab-Islamic status of Jerusalem as null and void.[40]

On the political front, a separate division of the OIC Secretariat, headed by the Assistant Secretary General (Al-Quds Al-Sharif), was entrusted with devising the political strategy. The OIC in all these years continued to the support Palestinian struggle, condemn 'Israeli repression' and counter all Israeli 'designs'. For instance, it condemned Israeli air attack on Iraqi nuclear installations (1981), condemned its invasion of Lebanon (1982), decried the US–Israel security pact as jeopardizing regional security (1984), supported Tunisia's demand for reparations against Israeli air raids killing 70 people, censured the exodus of Ethiopian Jews to Israel, and castigated the Israeli action of shifting the 1200 Lebanese Muslim detainees to Israeli prisons (1985), criticized Israel's nuclear ambitions and took strong exception to the abortive attempt of hoisting the Israeli flag on Al-Aqsa Mosque (1986), expressed solidarity with Saudi Arabia over Israeli threats to its missile installations (1988) and finally, kept expressing full support to the Palestinians for their heroic 'steadfastness and sacrifices' in the 'Intifada' movement launched by them in the occupied Gaza strip and the West Bank, and continued condemning the Israeli repression as 'inhuman Zionist actions' (1987–onwards).[41] When on 15 November 1988, the 430-member Palestine National Council (also known as the Palestinian parliament-in-exile) declared the establishment of the State of Palestine, needless to say, recognition by the OIC followed promptly. Another major event of the same year was the closure of the PLO Mission at New York by the US government. The OIC deplored the American decision, termed it 'illegal' and decided to make efforts to influence the White House to reverse the same.

However, during this second phase, there was one occasion when the OIC completely failed to fulfil Palestinian expectations. That was the siege and later massacre in the Palestinian refugee camps in Sabra and Shatila in Lebanon during the Israeli invasion of June 1982. Though the reason for this inaction can only be speculated, this remains a blot on the OIC's performance on the issue.[42]

In addition to the above measures, the OIC took a number of measures that were purely symbolic. For instance, when the 10th ICFM (Fez; 1979) was swayed by King Hassan's passionate determination to offer prayers in Al-Aqsa Mosque in Jerusalem, the Conference considered a foot march of millions of unarmed Muslims to Al-Quds, led by the Kings and the Presidents of the Muslim states, to liberate the holy city of Jerusalem.[43] The 7th ICFM (Istanbul; 1976) asked the Muslim states to issue commemorative stamps on Jerusalem and contribute the revenues to the Jihad Fund. The 8th ICFM (Tripoli; 1977) recommended that such stamps were to be issued regularly. The 12th ICFM requested the Muslim countries to declare Islamic capitals as twin cities with the Al-Quds. The eighth meeting of Al-Quds Committee (Sept. 1983) submitted a plan whereby all Muslim countries were to teach history and geography of Palestine and Al-Quds at the school level. An experts committee for preparing school syllabi projecting Palestine in Islamic states was soon formed.

In the field of economic *jihad*, the OIC formed an Al-Quds Fund at the 7th ICFM (Istanbul; 1976) to finance the Palestinian struggle and to provide material support to the families of martyrs and those fighting. The initial amount of $60 million, to be raised by voluntary contributions, was revised by adding another $40 million, by the 10th ICFM (Fez; 1979). The 11th ICFM (Islamabad; 1980) dilated upon the need for a fixed income for the purpose and established the *Waqf* (Trust) of Al-Quds Fund, with an equal capital (i.e. $100 million), to be a consistent source of financial support for the Palestinian struggle and to reinforce the Al-Quds Fund.[44] It is difficult to verify precisely how much of this money was actually realized but there is no doubt that the PLO did receive substantial funding.

The other side of the OIC's economic war was attempts at the economic destruction of Israel. It urged the member states to utilize all their economic resources to weaken the Israeli economy; halt economic and financial support for Israel; and bring about changes in the position of neutral states in favour of Palestine (by using the economic leverage of the Muslim world). The 3rd Islamic Summit (Taif; 1981) established the Islamic Bureau for the Boycott of Israel, and asked the Muslim states to counteract US attempts aimed at nullifying the effects of this boycott.[45] This Bureau prepared and examined lists of companies that were Jewish-owned (even if the owner were a Moroccan or a Turkish Jew) and of companies that entered into any deal with Israel, on a monthly basis. The OIC officials claimed that no blacklisted company could ever get a contract in a Muslim state.[46] However, except for the oil embargo of 1973, the OIC met with little success as regards effective boycott of states which kept their contacts with Israel.

In the field of culture, the OIC made greater contribution. Muslim states usually responded enthusiastically to OIC decisions in this area like the ones mentioned earlier, such as issuance of stamps on the theme of Jerusalem and transferring the revenues to the PLO, declaring their respective capitals twin cities with Jerusalem making modifications in the school syllabi to stress the history of Palestine, and so on. The OIC's subsidiary organs, especially Islamic Historical Research Centre (IRCICA), Organization of Islamic Capitals and Cities (OICC), and some others have done a commendable job of research and publications on the Islamic heritage of Jerusalem. Likewise, most of the programmes made by the Islamic States Broadcasting Organizations (ISBO) play with the same theme. Unlike the offensive on political, diplomatic, or economic fronts, the OIC's activities in the cultural field do not have, save for the propaganda value, any effect on the ground realities in Al-Quds and Palestine.

In 1990–91, several developments on the world scene led to the slipping out of initiative on Palestine from OIC hands and, as we shall see later, a new phase dawned. It may be mentioned that the last major conference of this period was the 5th Islamic Summit (Kuwait; 1987) which reiterated its call for liberation of *all* Arab lands, declared the Palestinian struggle a 'legitimate struggle' and once again dubbed Israel's military operations as 'organized terrorism'.[47] The attitude of the following three ICFMs was the same. We can notice the OIC's persistence in not according any legitimacy to Israel or its actions.

(c) Third Phase (1991–onward): By the turn of the decade of the nineties, both the Palestinians and Israel had started feeling exhausted over the long-drawn conflict. The *Intifada* uprising had exacerbated the tensions in the Middle East and was posing the first serious challenge to Israel, in years. Still, three very important developments led the Palestinians to go their own way. First, as the disintegration of the Soviet Union became imminent, the Palestinians felt like orphans, the United States which had always dismissed the PLO as a terrorist outfit was assuming the role of a world policeman. The PLO felt cornered unless it came to terms with the US and, thereby, Israel.

Secondly, a little earlier, Iraq had captured Kuwait (Aug. 1990) and when the UN resolutions asked it to withdraw, President Saddam Hussein wisely and aptly drew the parallel with Israeli occupation of Arab lands; arguing that selective morality could not be applied in the same region. Israel can occupy alien lands and retain them for decades, and even resolutions of condemnation at the UN get vetoed, but if Iraq annexes Kuwait, a warning is issued within twenty-four hours to vacate Kuwait or face military attack, so ran his line of argument. He promised to withdraw if Israel did the same from the Arab lands. Wise arguments propounded by the weaker side hardly make a difference in the world of realpolitic. But in this case they did achieve something, they won the hearts of a large number of people in the Muslim world. It was only logical that the PLO started supporting Baghdad. As Iraq lost the Gulf War (Jan–Feb. 1991), the PLO and the Palestinians faced the wrath of a number of anti-Iraq Arab states. The financial position of the PLO weakened correspondingly.[48]

The third and the last factor, a corollary of the second, was the weakening of the OIC. We had argued elsewhere, that in the Kuwait conflict, several Arab states decided to settle old scores with Iraq and did not want the OIC to come in their way with its homilies about Islamic fraternity. The OIC was thus decisively and completely marginalized.

The PLO thus entered into Middle East peace negotiations in Madrid, starting October 1991. This resulted in the clandestine peace talks in Oslo that finally led to the exchange of letters between the Prime Minister of Israel and the President of Palestine on mutual recognition, dated 9 September 1993. Four days later, Declaration of Principles on Palestinian self-rule was signed at the White House in Washington D.C. The Cairo Agreement on Jericho and Gaza strip was signed on 4 May 1994. The status of Jerusalem was left to future negotiations.

For the OIC, this was the phase when everything previously done was undone. The 20th ICFM (Istanbul; 1991) virtually recognized Israel by supporting the peace process and a resolution to the effect even endorsed the proposal for a UN conference on Middle East where Palestine *and* *Israel* would be equal partners (emphasis added). Iran questioned the wisdom of supporting the UN, which, it said, could only benefit Israel. Other hard-line states also opposed the resolution, which was carried all the same. A few months later, the

6th Islamic Summit (Dakar; 1991) went a step further by dropping the call to *jihad* and, in protest, Arafat stormed out of the conference hall. Though both the above-mentioned conferences reiterated the 1975 resolution on Zionism and racism but the OIC had apparently lost its fecundity.[49] So in 1993, a US-sponsored resolution got approved by the UN General Assembly, rescinding the 1975 UN resolution equating racism with Zionism.

A cursory glance at the wordings of the OIC resolutions of this period shows that the OIC has recognized Israel as a reality but is withholding recognition as a quid pro quo for Israel's sincerity in the implementation of peace agreements. Gone are the days when member states vied with each other to table harsher resolutions against Israel. Morocco and Indonesia made an abortive attempt to bring the issue of recognition of Israel on the agenda of the 7th extraordinary ICFM (Islamabad; 1994). The PLO had to ask the OIC not to be hasty in recognizing Israel.[50] This prompted Iran to boycott the 7th Islamic Summit (Casablanca; 1994) saying it would be 'swayed by pro-Israel traitors'.[51]

Beginning from 1991, the OIC has been continuously supporting the Middle East peace process in which it has no direct role and is accusing Israel of deviating from it. Each Conference supports Arafat and the Palestinians who use this forum to condemn Israel for its 'obstinacy'. However, the OIC has taken a serious stand on Judaisation of Arab lands, meaning Jewish settlements in Arab lands and Jewish immigration in general, the deportation of 400 Palestinians by Israel (Dec. 1992), Al-Khalil mosque massacre of sixty-three Muslim worshippers by fanatic Jews (Feb. 1994), and the non-binding resolution of the US Senate recognizing Jerusalem as 'united capital' of Israel (June 1997). This latter resolution was denounced by the OIC as 'shameful' and 'provocative of Muslim feelings'.[52] Apart from these occasional outbursts, whatever developments have been taking place in the region since 1991, are outside the purview of the OIC.

The 8th Islamic Summit (Tehran; Dec. 1997), adopted seven resolutions related to the Middle East question. One dealt with the status of Palestine, another with that of Jerusalem, one each condemning Israel for its illegal occupation of the Golan Heights and southern Lebanon and for undermining the Middle East peace process, one inviting donations for the Al-Quds Fund, and one on censuring Turkey for initiating military cooperation with Israel.

A major diplomatic victory of the OIC regarding Palestine, after this Summit was the success of the UN General Assembly resolution upgrading the status of Palestine, that had been moved jointly by several Arab–Islamic countries. On 6 July 1998, the Assembly made a unique decision declaring Palestine a 'full member', without the right to vote or that to get elected to a UN committee, through a majority of 124 votes to 4. (Since 1988, the PLO Mission at the United Nations was already being known as the Permanent Mission of Palestine.)

Conclusion: The OIC has worked for the Palestine cause for over three decades. It would be a grievous error to believe that the OIC activities have had little or no bearing on the final outcome of the problem. At the time of inception of the OIC, the PLO had tried to make it a single objective-oriented organization. Luckily for the Palestinians, their point of view was rejected and a multi-dimensional OIC served their cause more purposefully. Yes, the OIC did not militarily attack Israel and remove it from the world map. No international organization has ever done such a thing. In any case, as Dr Mohammad el Selim, a noted scholar on the OIC, points out, the OIC Charter obliged the member states to *support* the liberation struggle of, not to fight themselves for, the Palestinians.[53] And that is exactly what the Muslim states were doing.

It has been argued above that the OIC in the first phase recognized Israel as a *de facto* state, in the second phase, it did not believe that Israel existed *de facto* or *de jure* and in the ongoing phase, it has tacitly recognized Israel as a *de facto* and *de jure* state. Here again, Dr Selim points out the irony that the OIC Charter talks about Palestinian rights and Arab lands, but leaves out the definitions.[54] This ambiguity, he believes, was necessary. Thus Libya could, even in the first phase, interpret Arab lands as the whole of Israel; while Turkey was free to interpret Arab lands as

those occupied in the 1967 war, even in the second phase.

This ambiguity helped in the successful foreign policy coordination of the Muslim states on Palestine under the OIC umbrella. Though Indonesia had been reluctant to allow a PLO Mission on its soil and Turkey expressed inability to break diplomatic ties with Israel, on the whole the Palestine policy of the OIC proved to be successful.

(ii) Afghanistan: For over a century, Moscow had considered Afghanistan to be under its legitimate sphere of interest and had been dabbling in its internal affairs. A series of domestic upheavals in the 1970s, finally led to a successful coup by some military officers, belonging to the pro-Communist Peoples Democratic Party of Afghanistan (PDPA) in April 1978. The new regime's innovative policies on women and education and its land reforms met with stiff resistance, mainly because of the traditional abhorrence of the largely illiterate and conservative population of Afghanistan for 'godless' communists. A substantial number of people crossed the porous Afghanistan-Pakistan border, regrouped themselves under religious leaders (whose authority had been challenged by the leftist regime at Kabul) and started launching cross-border guerrilla attacks. Matters were compounded for the Kabul government by the infighting between different ideological factions within the PDPA. As the fall of this unstable government became imminent, Soviet troops invaded Afghanistan on 27 December 1979, to save a communist set-up from collapse. President Hafizullah Amin was killed and Babrak Karmal, then the Afghan ambassador to Hungary and a former PDPA stalwart, was installed as the puppet President.[55]

The OIC, which had been indifferent to the developments in Afghanistan till this point, came into action when a non-Muslim power physically occupied a Muslim country. It became an Islamic cause for the OIC. At that time, hardly anyone could guess that the OIC engagement with the issue would go on for decades. Here again, we can observe three distinct phases in OIC's activities on Afghanistan. In the first phase (1979–88), the Organization gave full support to the Afghan opposition guerrillas to oust the Soviet forces. The OIC involvement in the second phase (1989–92), stemmed from its desire to root out the last vestiges of Soviet occupation, i.e., the Soviet-installed communist regime in Kabul. And finally, when this objective was achieved, the OIC saw its worst nightmares come true as the former Afghan Islamist warlords attacked each other ferociously. So, from 1992, the third phase of OIC activities began, during which it has been trying to mediate an end to the civil war.

First Phase (1979–88): As soon as Pakistan saw Soviet tanks trundling into Kabul, it requested the convening of an extraordinary ICFM session, with active support from several other Muslim states. The first ever extraordinary ICFM session in OIC history took place in January 1980 at Islamabad. It deliberated upon the situation arising out of the Soviet invasion of Afghanistan. The Conference outrightly rejected Soviet occupation of Afghanistan, condemned it in the strongest terms and dubbed it a violation of the OIC Charter and that of the UN. To quote the language of the OIC:

> ...[the Conference] denounces and deplores it as a flagrant violation of international laws, covenants and norms...condemns this aggression and denounces it as an aggression against Human Rights and a violation of the freedom of people, which cannot be ignored.[56]

The Conference decided to suspend the membership of the puppet regime of Babrak Karmal, though the request of the Islamic Alliance for the Liberation of Afghanistan, a grouping of six liberation organizations, for grant of an observer status was not acceded to.

The Conference called for an immediate, total, and unconditional withdrawal of Soviet forces and decided to withhold recognition to the 'illegal regime in Afghanistan', recommended a boycott of Moscow Olympics, scheduled for July 1980, made appeals to the world community to support Afghan resistance movements and urged the Muslim states to provide financial support to Pakistan so as to help it deal with the influx of refugees from Afghanistan.[57]

The session was highly cognizant of the fact that this Soviet intervention had given some western powers an excuse to pressurize some Muslim countries to provide military bases under the pretext of providing security. The Conference drew attention to the 'current attempts by certain Western powers to exploit this situation [Soviet invasion] for reintroducing imperialist intervention in the Islamic World'.[58] Meanwhile, the Soviet Union tried to win over some sympathy from the Muslim world, when on 4 February 1980, the Soviet foreign minister communicated an offer to Syria, that if and when the Israelis withdrew from the Occupied Arab lands, the USSR would also vacate Afghanistan.

The Afghanistan question naturally remained the top of the agenda at the regular 11th ICFM (Islamabad; May 1980) that was held in the same city a few months later. The Kabul regime's request for an invitation was rejected by the OIC on the grounds that the former could not be called the representative of the Afghan people as long as the Soviet troops were not withdrawn. The Kabul regime promptly offered Soviet withdrawal subject to positive guarantees by Pakistan, Iran, and the US, that they would not allow infiltrations into Afghanistan from Pakistan and Iran. While Iran and the US were sceptical about the proposal, Pakistan rejected it outright as a ploy to influence the forthcoming 11th ICFM to adopt soft resolutions.[59]

The 11th ICFM reiterated all the decisions of the previous OIC moot, condemned the Soviet Union and called for immediate withdrawal of foreign troops and restoration of the Islamic and non-aligned character of Afghanistan. It also called for full support to the frontline states, which were, in this case, Pakistan and Iran. (In a couple of years, the number of Afghan refugees in these two countries was to swell to 3.5 million and 2 million, respectively, becoming a serious economic burden for them.) The conference formed a committee comprising Pakistan, Iran, and the OIC Secretary General to 'seek ways and means for a comprehensive solution of the grave crisis' and offered the OIC's good offices for mediation between the rival sides. The committee first held talks with the leadership of the *Mujahideen* (literally: those waging *Jihad*), as the guerrillas came to be known. It also wanted to hold talks with the Kabul regime *without recognizing it;* a condition that Kabul would not accept. The committee then also considered sending a mission directly to Moscow.[60] Meanwhile, since a number of countries had already announced contributions for the Afghanistan Fund, another committee comprising Pakistan, Gambia, and Saudi Arabia was formed to administer the money.[61]

Two important points regarding these two ICFMs are noteworthy. One, that on both the occasions pro-Moscow countries Syria, Libya, PLO, and South Yemen had vehemently opposed condemnation of the USSR, and, but for the tactful diplomacy by some Muslim states, the conferences were nearly wrecked. A mitigating feature for the pro-Moscow lobby was the equally stern tone of the Conferences towards the United States (for the Camp David accord, Iran-hostage crisis, and support to Israel, etc.) and other Western 'imperialist' powers. Even the Soviet Union itself, which was annoyed at the harsh resolutions against her, hailed the ICFM resolutions against the United States. Thus not only did Muslim unity on Afghanistan, as on the Palestine issue, remain unscathed, but also, the OIC came out as a radical, non-aligned, and anti-imperialist organization.

And two, all the OIC resolutions on the Afghan crises were implemented. Nearly all Muslim states, even Indonesia, broke diplomatic relations with Kabul, substantial funds were raised for the support of the Afghan resistance groups, the boycott of Moscow Olympics as far as the OIC states were concerned was almost universal, and in November 1980, the UN General Assembly adopted a resolution condemning the Soviet armed intervention by a massive majority of 111 votes. It can be argued here that this could have been accomplished because of Washington's crusade against the Soviet invasion. But observing that the OIC offensives against Israel and the USSR were equally successful in those years, the contribution of the OIC, in its own right, cannot be under-estimated.

The 3rd Islamic Summit (Taif; 1981), ignored Kabul's warnings and, debated the Afghanistan situation thoroughly, re-affirmed that complete Soviet pull-out was the only answer to the problem, and asked the OIC Committee on Afghanistan to step up its efforts for the resolution of the conflict.[62] Consequently, the three-member Committee met Prof. Abdul Rab Rasul Siyaf, a prominent resistance leader, at Mont Pelerin in Switzerland but the mission was a failure as the *Mujahideen* leadership refused to negotiate with the puppet Kabul regime. The Committee nonetheless reaffirmed the OIC support to *Mujahideen.*[63] The Afghanistan Committee was later enlarged to five with the induction of Tunisia and Guinea. It launched another diplomatic offensive in August 1982 asking Moscow to initiate a dialogue but the latter turned down this request.[64]

On the battlefields in Afghanistan, the *Mujahideen* became overly confident with the passage of time. Outside the big cities their writ was obeyed. And their military vehicles no longer moved in the night only. As the fighting intensified during much of 1981, on 10 November of the year Iran floated a new peace plan, which inter alia, called for an unconditional withdrawal of Soviet troops from Afghanistan, deployment of the OIC peace-keeping troops therein, creation of conditions conducive for the immediate return of the refugees, and finally, the constitution of a thirty-eight-member interim Higher Islamic Council, consisting of leading *ulema*, entrusted with the task of carrying out the executive and legislative functions pending the nation-wide elections. Striking are the similarities between what the OIC was offering to Iran to end the Gulf War and the plan that Iran was propounding for the Afghanistan imbroglio.

Pakistan always looked towards the Islamic Conference not only for financial support to feed 3.5 million Afghan refugees but also for political one as by 1984, Soviet Air Force had begun regular bombardment of Pakistani territory. The 15th ICFM (Sana'a; 1984) 'deeply deplored the violation of Pakistani airspace and bombardment of its territory...resulting in loss of life and property' and expressed 'appreciation for the restraint shown by Pakistan'.[65] In return for the OIC support, Pakistan had limited its own options by involving the whole Muslim world in the Afghan crisis and by vowing to go by the OIC decisions on Afghanistan.

The Afghanistan issue figured in every OIC conference during this period. The OIC's consistent position was that the Soviet occupation as well as its installed Kabul regime were illegal, and have been imposed against the will of the people of Afghanistan, and that nothing short of restoration of sovereignty and restoration of the Islamic identity of Afghanistan would be acceptable. To this end, the OIC continued its unabated struggle on political and diplomatic fronts, besides providing material help to the Afghan *Mujahideen.* The OIC factor had become so important that when in August 1984 a US Senate staff study asked the government to recognize a *Mujahideen* government-in-exile, it recommended that the aid to such government be channelled through the OIC.[66]

In 1986, Soviet leader Mikhael Gorbachev sent feelers about his inclination to get out of the Afghan quagmire. His famous 6 August message to the OIC Secretary General was obviously welcomed by the OIC. In a message to the leaders of the 5th Islamic Summit (Kuwait; 1987), Moscow gave the assurance that it would withdraw her troops as a part of a general agreement to stop 'outside meddling in the affairs of *sovereign, Muslim and non-aligned* Afghanistan' (emphasis added). As a token of sincerity, Moscow withdrew 8000 troops from Afghanistan on the eve of the Summit.[67]

The OIC closely monitored the Geneva negotiations, welcomed the UN-brokered Geneva agreement (14 April 1988) between Pakistan and Afghanistan, with the USA and the USSR as guarantors, and finally expressed satisfaction when the last Soviet contingent left Afghanistan on 15 February, the following year, in accordance with the time-table.

In this phase, the OIC has been criticized for treating the Palestine and Afghanistan issues differently; it has been accused of giving preference to the former both on paper and in practice. This may be so because of two reasons, first, as Abdullah Ahsan points out, the reverence Muslims always showed to the holy city of Jerusalem engendered an emotional attachment to its cause; and secondly, unlike Afghanistan where a government of Afghan nationals was nominally ruling the country, with the Soviets in the advisory

capacity at least theoretically, Palestine was occupied and being ruled by Israel.[68] Had Israel been a European country which had sent forces to install and sustain a Palestinian figurehead in the Arab lands, the situation might have been different there as well. It was for this reason that the Afghan *Mujahideen* attended the Islamic Conferences as observers and were not given Afghanistan's vacant seat, despite their consistent pleadings, until much later. Similarly, before the 16th ICFM (Fez; 1986), neither the *Mujahideen* were referred to as such, nor was their struggle called *jihad* in the OIC resolutions.[69] Till then, the ambiguous references to the struggle of the 'Afghan People' did not explain whether by Afghan people was meant the *Mujahideen* or the Kabul regime.

Second Phase (1989–92): For years, the OIC had not recognized the Kabul regime as it was being propped up by the troops of a foreign country. But after February 1989, when the Soviet troops had left, President Dr Najibullah's government was a government in its own right, much like the other non-representative totalitarian regimes in many other parts of the Muslim world. That the OIC still did not recognize the Kabul regime was rather unprecedented. On 23 February 1989, seven major Afghan *Mujahideen* groups formed an interim government with Prof. Sibghatullah Mojaddedi, as President and Rasul Siyaf as Prime Minister. The first cabinet meeting took place in an Afghan hamlet in the *Mujahideen*-controlled area of the country. The 18th ICFM (Riyadh; 1989) hailed the heroic struggle of the Afghan people, the Soviet withdrawal, and the formation of the interim government, to which recognition was given by a majority of thirty-five votes against ten. Much to the chagrin of the Kabul regime, and despite its protests, Prof. Mojaddedi represented Afghanistan at the 6th Islamic Summit (Dakar; 1991) also.[70] A review of the OIC resolutions during these three years, shows that the Organization saw the overthrow of Dr Najibullah's government as a consummation of the Afghan *jihad.* For this purpose, the OIC continued to give all political, diplomatic, moral, and material help to the interim *Mujahideen*-led government. And most important of all, it continued to broker agreements among the *Mujahideen* factions, lest they started fighting amongst themselves, thereby giving Dr Najib a respite. The OIC repeatedly offered all the warring factions, its good offices for a smooth transfer of power. But, unfortunately, blood and iron, to quote Bismarck, were to decide the fate of Kabul.

Third Phase (1992–onward): If nothing else, a common enemy, first the Soviet Union and then Dr Najib's PDPA regime, had kept the *Mujahideen* factions united. The tenacity evinced by the Kabul regime in clinging to power, astonished its friends and foes alike. Only the demise of its mentor, the USSR, in December 1991 cast the first spells of doom on the regime's fate. Troops loyal to Dr Najib fought to the end till Kabul fell to the *Mujahideen* in April 1992 and a *Mujahideen* coalition government took over. With the help of Pakistan, Saudi Arabia, and the OIC, the Afghan factions agreed on a six-month interim arrangement during which Prof. Mojaddedi and later Prof. Rabbani were to hold power. The six months passed quickly without any signs of the return to normalcy. Mutual rivalries and jealousies surfaced as the *Mujahideen* factions started fighting one another. Again the OIC brokered the power-sharing Islamabad Accord (6 March 1993), the third in a series. The earlier Jalalabad Accord and Peshawar Accords had already broken down.[71] Article 10 of the Islamabad Accord gave OIC the mandate to monitor cease-fire.

The following month, the 21st ICFM (Karachi; 1993) took place, that noted the 'successful outcome of the Afghan *jihad* and the establishment of an Islamic government' with satisfaction and asked the member states to help in the reconstruction of the war-torn country. The Conference deplored the continued violence in Afghanistan and approved the Secretary General's recommendation to send military observers from OIC states to monitor the cease-fire. Peace, however, remained elusive and fragile and the cease-fire soon broke down, each side accusing the other of treachery. So much so that a few months later President Burhanuddin Rabbani and Prime Minister Gulbadin Hikmatyar's forces found themselves locked in pitched battles with each other, in and around the capital, Kabul. There was no cease-fire for the OIC to monitor.

The OIC chief's special emissary on Afghanistan arrived in Islamabad on 9 January 1994 and started fresh talks with the Afghan leaders.[72] A special OIC Permanent Mission on Afghanistan was established in Islamabad on 3 April.[73] Meanwhile, the final two-year extension to the tenure of Prof. Rabbani's presidency given by the Islamabad Accord elapsed on 30 June. No solution of the crisis was yet in sight. The situation was not conducive for 'free and fair' elections either. Rabbani, instead of stepping down, unilaterally extended his tenure by another six months. This became the last straw; many warlords who had a marriage of convenience with Rabbani's government, questioned his legitimacy after 30 June. Afghanistan was then plunged into the abyss of civil war for years to come.

Meanwhile, Pakistan and the United Nations requested the OIC to play its role as it was the only forum that enjoyed the respect of all Afghan sides.[74] The OIC Secretary General Dr Hamid al-Gabid arrived in Islamabad on 30 June 1994, the last day of the mandate given to the Rabbani regime by OIC, and started consultations anew. He met President Rabbani, at the latter's invitation, in Kabul and presented his proposals. During the meeting a rocket fired by Hikmatyar's troops hit the Presidential Palace. The OIC Secretary General was furious. The next day, he invited Hikmatyar to hold talks with him at Jalalabad. Hikmatyar insisted on Cherhasiab, his headquarters in the vicinity of Kabul, but Dr Gabid refused to go there, which was viewed as a polite protest by the latter over the previous day's incident.[75] The OIC announced its own peace plan a few days later and claimed the backing of all significant Afghan groups. The plan envisaged an interim government, a consultative assembly, free and fair elections, and the reconstruction and rehabilitation work to begin in earnest. A preparatory meeting of leading politicians and warlords, and representatives of the *ulema*, High Court judges, university professors, doctors, and eminent persons representing all the geographical and ethnic divisions of Afghanistan, was proposed in the plan. After hectic negotiations, President Rabbani rejected the plan in early September.

Another major initiative by the OIC later in 1994, led to the Tehran talks (28 Nov.–7 Dec.

1994) which nonetheless failed. In July 1995, the OIC tried to hammer out the differences by floating a plan for talks in Jeddah. The Rabbani faction rejected it while a number of other factions, including that of the Uzbek warlord Rashid Dostum, had accepted it. So the OIC mission led by Ambassador Ahmet Ansay had to return after an unsuccessful assignment. In October 1995, October 1996, and November 1997, the OIC Assistant Secretary General, Ibrahim Bakr, came with three fresh attempts to mediate cease-fire but to no avail.[76]

Meanwhile, in September 1996, a new radical faction called *Taliban* (literally: the students), made up of tens of thousands of former Afghan students of religious schools in Pakistan, captured Kabul and ousted the Iran-backed Rabbani. Three months later, the 24th ICFM (Jakarta;1996) decided to declare the Afghan seat at the OIC vacant once again. The *Taliban* government had been recognized by only a few Muslim countries; Pakistan, Saudi Arabia, and UAE. The *Taliban* claimed that when Rabbani was clinging to his seat after the lapse of the OIC-given mandate, and was rejecting the OIC peace initiatives one after the other, recognition to his government was not withdrawn by the OIC. And in the teeth of opposition by all Afghan factions, except Rabbani's himself, his nominees continued attending the OIC conferences. But now even though the *Taliban* had emerged as the victors, the OIC did not invite President Mullah Mohammad Omar, the *Taliban*'s supreme leader, to the Islamic Summits. It is interesting to note that Pakistan gave full protocol to the *Taliban* Prime Minister at his arrival in Islamabad at the Islamic Summit (March 1997) though he attended the conference as an observer. On the other hand, Iran gave full protocol to the ousted President Rabbani at the Tehran Islamic Summit (Dec. 1997), though there too the Afghan seat remained vacant as per the OIC decision.[77]

Presently, the OIC position is that it had given unflinching support to the *Mujahideen* to throw out the intruder but after the successful conclusion of the *jihad*, the system generated into anarchy and chaos. The escalating hostilities are causing untold hardship to the common man. The OIC is continuing relentless efforts for the formation of a multi-party broadband government. It has called upon all Muslim states to provide economic assistance, especially to the famine-hit areas of war-shattered Afghanistan. Lately, the OIC has been expressing serious concern over the production and smuggling of drugs from Afghanistan besides deploring the immense loss of life in the conflict and calling for an early repatriation of refugees from Pakistan and Iran.[78]

In the autumn of 1997, the new OIC Secretary General Izzeddienne Laraki claimed that the OIC was the only organization that enjoyed the confidence of all the factions in Afghanistan. He announced that the OIC was shortly going to float a fresh peace initiative, jointly with the United Nations. After hectic diplomatic efforts, the representatives of the *Taliban*-led government and the opposition Northern Alliance, led by the ousted president Burhanuddin Rabbani, were brought to the negotiating table in March 1998 at Islamabad, Pakistan. The first-ever face-to-face parleys between the too sides since the rise of the *Taliban*, were co-chaired by the representatives of the OIC and the UN. The talks made significant headway in the first four sessions but eventually broke down on the insistence of the Opposition that the *Taliban* government sould first lift the siege of the Opposition-held Bamiyan province, for the talks to proceed. The OIC expressed deep regret at the stalling of talks and vowed to launch more peace bids in the near future.

Lately, the OIC and the Afghan government developed friction over a host of issues. The murder of nine Iranian diplomats in Afghanistan (Sept. 1998), led to a near war situation between Iran (the incumbent OIC Chairman) and Afghanistan. The previous month, the Kabul administration was furious when the OIC condemnation of the US air and missile strikes against Afghanistan had been mild. Another source of rancour is the harsh legislation by the *Taliban* government regarding women's rights, educational institutions, and the control over electronic media. The OIC believes that the ultra-conservative and medieval laws of the *Taliban* are bringing a bad name to Muslims all over the world.

Ethnic Crises: It is pertinent to note that unlike the problems of Palestine and Afghanistan, which faced physical occupation, hostilities in Cyprus, Azerbaijan, and Bosnia have three prominent characteristics. Firstly, in these regions conflicts have their roots in ethnic rivalries. Secondly, systematic genocide, arson, rape, and torture, were rampantly employed as instruments of war. What transpired under the label of ethnic cleansing, evinced the worst bestial instincts of man and will remain a slur on humanity. Since we are studying the problems from the OIC perspective, we have taken the Muslims as victims. But in these conflicts, even the victims cannot be totally absolved from war crimes. Rape, torture, and mutilation of dead bodies, even as isolated incidents of reprisal against systematic persecution, can be justified neither from a legalistic nor from a moralistic point of view. And thirdly, all these three disputes also fall under the purview of the Organization for Security and Cooperation in Europe (OSCE). Since the OSCE, from the OIC's line of thinking, was supporting the aggressor in the Cyprus conflict (i.e., Southern Cyprus), siding with the victim in the Karabagh conflict (i.e., Azerbaijan) and was neutral in the Bosnian conflict (i.e., treating Serbia and Bosnia on equal terms), the OIC had to adapt its own responses accordingly.

(iii) The Cyprus Conflict: The tiny Mediterranean island of Cyprus was annexed by the Muslim empire, and the establishment of the first Muslim settlement immediately followed, back in the year AD 654, in the early years of Islam. It became part of Turkey's Ottaman empire in AD 1571. By the year 1790, over 75 per cent of the island's total population of 80,000 professed the Muslim faith.[79] In 1878, the island was leased to Britain on the condition that it was eventually to be returned to Turkey. However, Britain unilaterally abrogated the treaty, annexed Cyprus and declared it a crown colony in May 1925. A defeated and weak post-First World War Turkey acquiesced to this as a *fait accompli*. During the next quarter of a century, the ethnic Turkish community remained quiescent and did not demand reunification with Turkey but the Greek Cypriots kept harping about uniting Cyprus to 'mother Greece', which was the last thing Turkish Cypriots would have agreed to. It should be noted that by this time, because of

massive immigration by Greeks and emigration by the Turks, the demographic balance in Cyprus had been heavily tilted in favour of the former community.[80]

The long and arduous negotiations preceding independence resulted in a compromise Zurich Agreement (19 Feb. 1959); that *inter alia* provided for a bi-communal state with a Greek Cypriot President and a Turk Cypriot Vice-President and a legislature with 70–30 representation for the two communities. Important executive action required the concurrence of the President and the Vice-President, and important legislative actions needed separate majorities of both the communities. The Guarantor powers, Greece and Turkey, had the right to station a limited number of troops on the island and either could come to the aid of her allied community. Eisenhower, the US President, endorsed the agreement as 'a victory for common sense' and an 'imaginative act of statesmanship'.[81]

In 1963, three years after independence, the Greek Cypriot side unilaterally repealed a few important provisions of the Agreement, upon which the Turk Cypriots took recourse to the Supreme Constitutional Court. Greek Cypriot President Makarios said that if the Court ruled against them they would ignore its ruling. The Court did rule against them and they did ignore the ruling. As for the consent of Guarantor powers for any change in the constitutional arrangement, another requirement under the agreement, it was neither sought, nor given. Consequently, large scale riots broke out and the rule of law collapsed. Daily 'Express' of London described the slaughter of Turks as a 'horror so extreme that the people seemed stunned beyond tears'. The situation came to a head when ethnic leader Nicos Sampson replaced Makarios after a bloody coup by the Greek Cypriot National Guard in July 1974. A large-scale massacre of ethnic Turks and incidents of gang-rape of Muslim women followed, prompting Turkey to send troops under Article IV of the Treaty of Guarantee. Since then, the island is divided into the Muslim/Turk North, and Christian/Greek South.[82]

It was at this juncture that Turkey sought the political backing of the OIC, which was duly given. Being the host of the 7th ICFM (Istanbul; 1976), Turkey pleaded for grant of observer status to the Turk Cypriots. After listening to Rauf Denktash, a London-trained barrister and leader of the Turkish Cypriot community, the Conference gave full support to 'the right of the Turkish Cypriot community to be heard, on the basis of equality with the Greek Cypriot side, on all international fora' and agreed to invite them at all future meetings of the Islamic Conference'.[83] An observer status was, however, denied to them at that time.

The OIC remained seized with the Cyprus question for the next seven years. In September 1978, the Secretary General, Dr Amadou Gaye, undertook a visit to North Cyprus to assess the situation and to hold talks with its leadership.[84] Though the OIC did not play direct role in the negotiations between the two sides held under the aegis of the UN, but a review of its resolutions during those years shows, that it remained 'mindful of the necessity of a just and durable settlement' of the Cyprus question, and continued to 'invite both sides to a truce conducive to peaceful settlement'. The OIC particularly welcomed and appreciated the 4-point agreement of February 1977, 10-point agreement of May 1979, the Opening Statement of 1980, and the UN evaluation document of 1981.[85] No matter what the OIC urged both sides to do, the talks broke down each time since the Greek Cypriot side insisted on treating the 1960 Constitution as the basis for negotiations while the Turkish Cypriot side argued that a Constitution which had been unilaterally repudiated by the other side in 1963 could not be binding on it. Another major point of discord is the Greek insistence that any future arrangement should deny either of the Guarantors the power to launch unilateral military action. In response, Turkey says that it can neither watch silently another massacre of Turkish Cypriots in the future, nor can it 'leave their security to the Greeks who cannot even rule themselves'.[86] Then there are other disputed issues including those concerning missing persons, POWs, property claims, and re-settlement rights of the displaced persons from both sides, arising out of, what Greece calls, 'Turkey's aggression of 1974', but what Turkey deems as compliance of its treaty obligations.

Meanwhile there was another important factor in the dispute, that was the UN resolution 353

(1974) which recognized the government of Southern Cyprus as the government of the whole Cyprus on the basis of the defunct 1960 Constitution.[87] It was, the Turkish side argued, putting expediency behind principle, since (a) no settlement could be arrived at without treating both the sides equally, (b) the 1960 arrangement that was repudiated by the Greek side, could not be a basis for according legitimacy to the Greek Cypriot government to the exclusion of the Turkish side; and (c) even going by the 1960 agreement, the Greek Cypriot government was illegal since the concurrence of Turkish Cypriots for all executive actions was not being realized. But following the UN position, the whole world recognized the Nicosia government as the government for the whole of Cyprus. This resulted in the economic blockade of North Cyprus, since all trade and aid was channelized through the government of South Cyprus. In those years, the OIC was the only forum that continued to give full moral support to the Cypriot Muslims. All the Muslim states were urged by the Islamic Conference 'to use their good offices' and 'to do everything in their power' so as to enable North Cyprus also to benefit from international assistance.[88]

On 15 November 1983, the Turkish Cypriots declared the establishment of the Turkish Republic of Northern Cyprus (TRNC) after the re-unification negotiations were deadlocked. This decision was endorsed by the 14th ICFM (Dhaka; 1983) held the following month. Though, the meeting stopped short of giving recognition to the new Republic, it did confer the long-sought observer status on the Cypriot Muslim community.[89]

Since then, the OIC has become more active in support of North Cyprus. The Conference has started expressing 'solidarity' with the Cypriot Muslims, instead of expressing 'sympathy', as it earlier used to do. The Cypriot Muslims are increasingly being referred to as 'an integral part of the Islamic world'. The OIC has continued to support Turkey's military actions of 1974 as legal, and to call for 'meaningful and constructive dialogue' for a 'negotiated and mutually acceptable' solution to the problem. The OIC believes that sovereignty was jointly vested in the two communities in 1960, so while giving tacit support to the establishment of a separate republic by North Cyprus, it considers a bi-zonal, bi-communal united Cyprus as the ultimate goal. It asks both sides to 'refrain from actions that may increase tension'. However, it believes that 'provocative actions' and 'fatal blows to the peace process' have been committed by the Greek side. It has repeatedly expressed concern over the 'excessive armament by the Republic of (South) Cyprus' which amounted to $365 million yearly arms purchases by mid-1990s.[90] The OIC also considers most of the UN resolutions on the issue as inadequate, and the European Court of Justice ruling barring European states from importing goods from North Cyprus as unjust. It also deplores the destruction of the tourists industry of North Cyprus resulting from the requirement that airlines seek the permission of the government of South Cyprus (as the government of the whole of Cyprus) for landing and operating rights. The South has thus blockaded the North.

The UN Security Council resolution 649 (March 1990) was the first UN resolution which called for a 'mutually acceptable' solution and did not refer to the government of South Cyprus as the government of Cyprus. The OIC coordination meetings at the UN, had always reaffirmed North Cyprus' right to be heard at all international fora on the basis of equality, and the Muslim states had pursued the cause of Cypriot Muslims at the UN, accordingly. This might have been a contributing factor for the change of heart at the Manhattan.

The 6th Islamic Summit (Dakar; 1991) directed the Islamic Development Bank (IDB) to prepare a study on the economic situation and needs of the Cypriot Muslims. The study was duly prepared and presented to the 7th Islamic Summit (Casablanca; 1994) which requested the Secretary General to take action on the recommendations of the report. Both the Summits also asked all the Muslim states to establish trade and cultural relations with North Cyprus to counter its economic blockade. The OIC Secretary General was also asked to prepare a comprehensive report on the Cyprus situation, which was prepared and presented to the 23rd ICFM (Conakry; 1995). The report merely summarized and reiterated all the OIC declarations on the Cyprus question.[91]

In November 1996, the OIC strongly protested against, what it called, the intransigence of the Greek Cypriot side. The latter's Foreign Minister, Mihaididis, had earlier called upon the OIC not to take a stand 'contrary to that of the UN'.[92] The following year, in December 1997, another round of UN-sponsored peace talks on the future of Cyprus again broke down when President Rauf Denktash accused the UN of not treating his republic on an equal footing with South Cyprus. Around the same time, he also turned down the invitation of the European Union to enter its enlargement talks since North Cyprus was asked to be a part of the delegation of the Republic of Cyprus (i.e. South Cyprus) and not the other way round. Denktash insisted that his government had as much claim to be called the government of (all of) Cyprus.[93]

Coming back to the OIC, the Republic of North Cyprus (TRNC) applied for full membership of the Islamic Conference at the 20th ICFM (Istanbul; 1991). Since then, it has repeated this request at every OIC conference but the latter has not so far obliged. However the OIC has pledged each time to strengthen the participation of Cypriot Muslims at all levels in the Organization. Apparently the OIC does not want to polarize the conflict and tends to avoid open confrontation with the UN and the OSCE by recognizing the TRNC as the Republic of (all of) Cyprus. Furthermore, the OIC does not want to depart from its stand that the future of the island lies in a single bi-communal republic, not two antagonistic republics. And lastly, the OIC does not want to open up a Pandora's box, after earlier recognizing the PLO and the *Mujahideen* as legitimate governments of Palestine and Afghanistan, respectively, by recognizing TRNC also. What will then stop the government of Azad (Free) Kashmir, Muslim South Philippines, and possibly separatist movements within Muslim states as well, to demand similar privilege?

(iv) The Nagorno–Karabagh dispute: Most of the territories of the present day Azerbaijan and Armenia were conquered by the Muslims in the late 7th century AD. After facing many vicissitudes, the region was annexed by the Russian empire at the outset of the 19th century.[94] It was during the Russian rule that the first Armenian settlements appeared in Azerbaijan, mostly established by the Armenian refugees from Turkey and Iran. Still, by the end of The First World War, the Armenians were a bare majority in Armenia itself (53 per cent Armenians, 39 per cent Azeri Muslims, and 8 per cent other nationalities); but they formed a substantial majority within the Nagorno–Karabagh region. The USSR declared the region as an autonomous region within the Azerbaijan Republic in 1921, rejecting the Armenian claims over it. This set-up continued up till the final days of the Soviet Union.

Under the USSR Constitution, alteration in the territories of the Union Republics was permissible, subject to the concurrence of both the states concerned as well as the USSR. On 20 February 1988, the Supreme Soviet of Nagorno–Karabagh adopted a resolution appealing to the Supreme Soviets of Azerbaijan, Armenia, and the USSR, to allow it to be joined to the Armenian Republic. The demand was immediately rejected by Azerbaijan, and later a special session of the Presidium of the Supreme Soviet of the USSR, on 18 July 1988, discussed and rejected the demand of secession by the Nagorno–Karabagh region. Both the above decisions were welcomed by mass protests and strikes in Nagorno–Karabagh. The third concerned party, Armenia, remained quiet for some time but on 1 December 1989, its Supreme Soviet adopted a resolution on the unification of Nagorno–Karabagh with Armenia.[95]

In 1990–91, sporadic incidents of racist violence against Azeris turned into full-fledged ethnic cleansing operations. The militiamen of the Armenian National Movement, started attacking Azeri villages in Nagorno–Karabagh to harass them. The Azeri population started fleeing to 'safe areas' of the Azerbaijan. In the first two months of 1990 alone, the Armenian militants made 311 attacks on Soviet Union's internal security troops' arms depots, looting heavy quantities of arms. By the spring of 1991, anti-Muslim riots had become a routine occurrence within Armenia itself, and Muslims of Azeri and Kurd origin alike were targets of violence; 200,000 of them abandoned their homes and moved to Azerbaijan. Impunity encouraged the militants and they started shelling and conducting cross border raids into the bordering villages of Azerbaijan. In December

1991, both Azerbaijan and Armenia became sovereign states and it was then, that the crisis took on international dimensions.

Azerbaijan requested and was granted OIC membership within days of its independence. By the beginning of 1992, Armenia's regular forces crossed international borders and captured a significant part of Azeri territory. On 3 March 1992, the OIC, Turkey, and Britain launched the first serious peace bids for amicable resolution of the conflict but nothing came out of it. Azerbaijan accused Armenia of committing aggression with the help of Russia, although forcible annexation of territory, it argued, was a blatant violation of the Charter of the Russia-sponsored Commonwealth of Independent States (CIS) also. In return, Armenia accused the regional Muslim states of arming Azerbaijan. Meanwhile, the OIC held two extraordinary sessions of ICFMs on Bosnia (June 1992 and Dec. 1992); Azerbaijan raised the issue of 'Armenian aggression' which was taken up on the sideline. Azerbaijani Foreign Minister, Tofik Kasimov, gave a moving account of the ethnic violence against Azeri Muslims at the ICFM (Istanbul; 1992). The ICFM adopted very favourable resolutions from the Azerbaijan point of view.

The war went on for the most part of 1992 and 1993 and Armenian troops captured around 20 per cent of Azerbaijan territory that included 4388 sq. km. of the disputed Nagorno–Karabagh region (which was, for all practical purposes, annexed to Armenia) and 4741 sq. km. in the Shusha and Lachin region which Armenia wants to retain on the pretext of providing a land corridor to the Karabagh region. Another 5038 sq. km. of Azeri territory, including Agdam and Fizuli areas, had also been occupied forcibly but Armenia was willing to evacuate it if it was given the status of an international legal party in the Karabagh region. This total area had an Azeri population of 837,000 that was totally displaced; another 200,000 had fled from Armenia proper.[96]

Nobody forsakes his home happily; the same was true of these refugees. Out of the 700 settled areas destroyed and plundered, only 170 were in Nagorno–Karabagh while the rest were in Armenia itself or the occupied Azerbaijani territories. Around 80,000 houses, 800 schools, and 250 medical institutions were destroyed in these years. In addition, over 208 historical monuments declared by the Azerbaijan governments as Azeri-Islamic heritage, were also torn down. In the war, 18,000 people lost their lives while 4000 are still missing. The ethnic conflict took a religious colour since the whole Azeri community is Muslim and the Armenian population is Christian. Incidents of torture, mutilation of bodies, rape of Muslim women, charging ransom for hostages (15 million roubles for a living person and 1 million roubles for a corpse) and placing of scorching metal cross on the chests of Muslim males, were frequently reported.[97] No doubt the figures are highly debatable but the occurrence of atrocities by the Armenians on an alarming scale is taken as an established fact by the UN, the OSCE, and the OIC alike.

The 21st ICFM (Karachi; 1993) again deliberated on the Azerbaijan war and listened to the Foreign Minister of Azerbaijan. The conference expressed its 'full solidarity with the *Muslim Republic*'. The OIC Secretary General, Dr Hamid al Gabid, also denounced the killing of Muslims, charging that it was being 'encouraged and backed from abroad'. A few days earlier, Turkish President Suleiman Demiral had also warned Armenia to halt its offensive against Kelbadzhar as his patience was 'running thin'.[98]

Earlier, Armenia had sent Dr Edward as its representative at the 21st ICFM (Karachi; 1993) who met the OIC Secretary General and repeated the Armenian claims that there was not one Armenian soldier on the Azeri soil and it was the local Armenian self-defence forces that were protecting the civilian population. Armenia had consistently denied the use of its regular troops in Azerbaijani territory and had much later hinted that some of them might have been there for protection of local Armenians. In early 1993, under international pressure, Armenia renounced its territorial claims on Azerbaijan, saying Nagorno–Karabagh was an internal affair of Azerbaijan, as the local Armenians wanted to establish an 'independent' republic. However, Armenia never formally rescinded its resolution of December 1989, calling for incorporation of Nagorno–Karabagh into Armenia. All these views were conveyed to Dr Gabid by the Armenian envoy who

insisted that Armenia shares the same principles which guide the OIC and lauds the OIC role in conflict resolution. He formally requested the OIC to mediate in the dispute and extended an invitation to the Secretary General to visit Armenia to be explained the Armenian position in detail. He asked Dr Gabid to visit Nagorno–Karabagh himself to assess the real situation and the fallacy of Azerbaijan accusations.[99] All this had apparently no effect on the OIC, as the very next day the Conference passed a very harsh resolution 'condemning the aggression of Armenia' against a Muslim state.

A fragile cease-fire took effect in May 1994 under the aegis of the Organization for Security and Cooperation in Europe (OSCE) after six years of conflict that had left 30,000 people dead and close to a million displaced, though one-fifth of Azerbaijan territory remains in Armenian hands. Since then, all the OIC conferences, especially the 7th Islamic Summit (Casablanca; 1994), 24th ICFM (Jakarta; 1996) and 8th Islamic Summit (Tehran; 1997) have adopted very strong resolutions in favour of Azerbaijan. Though the UN and the OSCE resolutions also betray a clear tilt towards the Azerbaijan position by reaffirming the inviolability of international frontiers and the inadmissibility of forceful acquisition of territory, and by expressing alarm over the humanitarian problems of Azeri displaced persons; the OIC resolutions go far beyond that. The OIC unequivocally condemns Armenian 'aggression', holds Armenia responsible for any escalation or resumption in hostilities, condemns the atrocities on the Azeri people and the destruction of archaeological sites, supports Azerbaijan's claims for reparations, besides calling for withdrawal of Armenian troops from Azerbaijan and early repatriation of refugees. The OIC has always supported the peace efforts of the OSCE and has meanwhile barred its member states from supplying or allowing transit to supplies of military equipment to Armenia and has asked the Muslim states to provide political and economic support to Azerbaijan.[100]

Taking note of the decisions of the 20th ICFM and the recommendations of the 20th session of the Islamic Commission for Economic, Cultural and Social Affairs (ICECS), the Tehran Summit requested the Secretary General to prepare a report on the conflict, requested the Islamic Development Bank (IDB) to assist in the economic development of Azerbaijan, and welcomed the decision of the Research Centre on Islamic History (IRCICA) to organize the international symposium on Islamic Civilization in the Caucus, under the patronage of President Haider Aliyev of Azerbaijan, at the capital, Baku, in October 1998.

Meanwhile, the peace process received a jolt when the Armenian President Levon Ter-Petrossian announced his resignation on 3 February 1998. Re-elected for a second five-year term in September 1996, he soon fell out with his cabinet colleagues over the proposed peace deal on the Nagorno–Karabagh problem. There naturally arose serious apprehensions in Baku on how the new Armenian administration would tackle the issue.

It may be asked: why did the OIC let go an opportunity to mediate in the dispute, when for the first time the non-Muslim party to the conflict had expressed confidence in the good judgement of the OIC to do so? And secondly: why did the OIC pursue the Bosnian dispute more seriously than the Nagorno–Karabagh one? (The OIC had adopted ten resolutions on Azerbaijan, sent nine special missions to Baku and had discussed it in fourteen of its coordination meetings at the UN, by 1996. The corresponding figures for the Bosnian war were 35, 30 and 45, respectively.) Actually it is an unwritten practice of the OIC, not to interfere in a conflict which falls under the domain of another regional organization, be it OAU, OSCE, or the Arab League. Since both the concerned states in this case are OSCE members, and the latter is actively pursuing the matter, the OIC is content with welcoming the OSCE initiatives, asking both parties to cooperate with the OSCE and, at the same time, conveying its own resolutions to the OSCE Chairman-in-office. It is of significance that fifty-three of the fifty-four OSCE member-states (minus only Armenia) are supportive of Azerbaijan's position. Hence, the OIC does not see any threat to the existence of Azerbaijan, unlike in the case of Bosnia, as we shall see below, where the OIC felt that the onus of protecting an isolated Muslim state in Europe, fell on itself.

(v) Bosnia Crisis: The OIC role has been very noticeable and effective in the recent Balkan crisis that followed the disintegration of Yugoslavia. The secession of Muslim-dominated Bosnia was the result of a referendum on 29 February 1992 wherein 75 per cent people had voted for independence. The Serb minority in Bosnia revolted and the country had plunged into a full-fledged war by early April. The OIC moved in with a well drafted Action Plan, which does not have a precedence in its previous activities, to save Bosnia from extinction. Thus the OIC showed practical commitment to the security of all Muslim states, not necessarily member states alone, as Bosnia is still not an OIC member. The crisis in Bosnia, as we shall see, put a question mark on the notions of international morality and resulted in the first departure from the framework of international legality, by the OIC.

Support to the Muslim Cause: The OIC showed an early awareness of the problem when the 20th ICFM (Istanbul; 1991) allowed the representatives of the Muslim communities of Yugoslavia to explain their situation. The 6th Islamic Summit (Dakar; 1991) took place at a time when hostilities had already broken out in the Croatian and Slovenian republics of the defunct Yugoslavia. The Conference expressed concern over the exploding situation that could spread to Bosnia and expressed support for the territorial integrity of Bosnia.[101] As soon as the OIC warnings came true, it provided $200,000 to the Bosnian government as assistance and called for sanctions against Serbia. This resulted in the UN Security Council resolution 757 (May 1992) that imposed economic sanctions, oil embargo, and air embargo against the rump Yugoslavia (i.e., Serbia and Montenegro). On 19 May, the OIC asked its members to withdraw their ambassadors from Belgrade as a mark of protest; the decision was promptly complied with.

As the situation deteriorated, the OIC held an emergency session on Bosnia (Istanbul; June 1992) which expressed full solidarity with the Bosnian government, emphasizing the 'common goals and destinies of the Islamic *ummah*'. The meeting condemned the 'senseless slaughter' of Muslims, declared Bosnia to be 'a test case embodying the manifold problems surfacing in the post-cold war era' and emphasized 'the need for it to be solved through international measures'.[102] It thus demanded that the UN Security Council take enforcement measures to force Serbia to renounce aggression, since economic sanctions had failed to work. This was the first OIC call for military intervention in Bosnia and it is more than clear that the Conference envisaged collective security measures under a multinational UN force to liberate Bosnia, just as had been done to liberate Kuwait, the preceding year. The OIC assured full financial and material support for such a UN venture. Turkey and Iran pledged troops also. The OIC asked all member states and agencies to raise funds and donate generously to a fund for Bosnia.[103] The Islamic Development Bank (IDB) and the Islamic Solidarity Fund (ISF), responding to a similar request, allocated $21 million and $650,000, respectively, for Bosnia.[104]

It may be recalled that an OIC contact group comprising the permanent representative to the UN of Egypt, Iran, Pakistan, Senegal, and Turkey the previous month, was already active at the United Nations and remained instrumental in the passage of several favourable resolutions on Bosnia in later years also. This Conference raised the OIC Contact Group on Bosnia to ministerial level and added Malaysia, Saudi Arabia, and the OIC Secretary General to the enlarged group. Through hectic lobbying by this OIC Contact Group, on 25 August, a resolution co-sponsored by forty-seven Muslim states calling for the territorial integrity of Bosnia was carried in the UN General Assembly by a wide margin.[105] Meanwhile, the Secretary General lashed out at the Serbian atrocities in very harsh terms.

On 23 September, the OIC Foreign Ministers met for a coordination meeting in New York and called for the lifting of the arms embargo on the victims (i.e. Bosnia), enforcement of no-fly zone and closing of concentration camps against Muslims. In November 1992, the OIC again urged the Steering Committee to lift the arms embargo but the request was rejected again. Consequently, the OIC met in another emergency ICFM session (Jeddah; Dec. 1992) which reiterated the request to the UN to enforce all its resolutions regarding territorial integrity of Bosnia, no-fly zones, control of heavy weapons etc., and also asked the big

powers to respect their commitments made at the International Conference on Former Yugoslavia (known as London Conference of Aug. 1992).[106] The Conference supported the passionate appeal by Alija Izzetbegovich, President of Bosnia, for provision of defensive weapons and virtually gave an ultimatum to the UN Security Council to review the arms embargo or face (unspecified) consequences. This strong support led Izzetbegovich to reject the Vance-Owen peace plan, floated by the European negotiators some time earlier. Both Cyrus Vance and Lord Owen attended the Jeddah meeting on invitation. Reacting to the OIC demand for use of force against the Serb rebels, they categorically ruled out any such option.

As the deadline was fast approaching, the OIC held a mini-Summit at Dakar on 11 January 1993, which *inter alia* considered the assassination of Bosnian Deputy Premier Hakija Turajlic, mass rapes of Muslim girls, and the destruction of the Islamic heritage of Bosnia, by the Serbian National Army and the marauding Serb irregulars. The moot called for military intervention, (but) 'under the framework of internal law and the United Nations', as this was the only language the Serb aggressors could understand. The moot promised financial and military support of the OIC for the purpose and threatened to break UN arms embargo after 15 January.[107]

The date came and went by peacefully, as the Serbs made some compromises on the conference table at Geneva, meanwhile renewed US military manoeuvres against Iraq stole all the world attention. As the said OIC resolutions were silent on what the OIC would do if all its demands were ignored, President Izzetbegovich was upset when he received the mere reiteration of expressions of solidarity after 15 January. He then accepted the Vance-Owen plan but, unfortunately for him, the Serb side had withdrawn its acceptance by then.[108]

The 21st ICFM (Karachi; 1993), received a request from Amnesty International urging the OIC to use its influence to end the war. The moot also listened to the OIC Secretary General's report on Bosnia that expounded fiery criticism of the international bodies' paralysis in the crisis. It accused them of acting too little too late. The report stressed the need for a re-evaluation of the situation and lifting of embargo on Bosnia for its legitimate self-defence.[109] The ICFM also considered an OIC Rapid Reaction Force (OICRRF) for Bosnia. The Conference sent an urgent message to the session of UN Security Council, on the instigation of Pakistan which was holding the Council's rotating presidency, asking it to act decisively to halt the Serbian aggression against Bosnia. The Conference called upon the world body to freeze all Serbian assets and withdraw recognition to it unless it complied with the UN resolutions. The OIC decided to formally launch an offensive to expel Serbia from the United Nations. The conference asked Muslim states that were already not recognizing Serbia to sever all economic ties with it and to take measures against any state that supported Serbian aggression. The Muslim states pledged $210 million for aid to Bosnia at the Conference. Though a substantial amount was subsequently transferred to Bosnia, it is difficult to verify precisely how much of the pledge was honoured.[110]

The following month, the OIC once again rejected the now dead Vance-Owen peace plan as 'legitimizing and rewarding aggression', in its meeting in Vienna. The Organization also rejected the concept of 'safe havens' for Bosnian Muslims saying that the solution lay in thwarting aggression as a whole.[111] It also warned against any attempts by the European Community Contact Group on Bosnia to endorse the partition of Bosnia on ethnic lines. This emergency meeting also decided to negotiate with all other international groups working for a settlement in the Balkans, and to coordinate its efforts with them. On 25 May, the OIC announced its rejection of the Joint Action Plan of the United States and her allies for Bosnia. The Organization described the said plan as having 'disappointed the Muslim States' by 'legitimizing aggression'. Two days later, the OIC group raised the issue of the 22 May Plan at the UN Security Council also. The three Muslim member states of the Council, Djibouti, Morocco, and Pakistan (supported by the NAM colleagues Cape Verde and Venezuela) jointly asked the UN Security Council to explain how the concept of 'UN-Declared Safe Havens' was going to work.

In June, the OIC Group threatened to wreck the UN Human Rights Conference at Geneva by refusing to sign the final declaration unless the OIC-sponsored resolution on Bosnia was included in the main text.[112] The Chairman of the OIC-group, Pakistan's Agha Shahi, categorically stated that there was no question of further discussion and bargaining on the OIC draft with the Europeans and that the OIC would not accept it to be a part of the annexure, rather than the main text, of the Geneva declaration. 'For the OIC, there is an irreducible bottom line on Bosnia', he added. The Vice-President Ejup Ganic of Bosnia thanked the OIC for this and declared that OIC was the only hope they had.

A day earlier, the OIC-group had held its coordination meeting that had bluntly called the 'ethnic cleansing of Bosnians' as actually being 'Islamic cleansing' to efface an Islamic nation from Christian Europe. The OIC-group managed to get passed the resolution by eighty-eight votes to one (the only opposing vote was that of Russia) calling for an end to Serb aggression. All the European states and India (which feared Pakistan may use it as a precedent for getting India condemned on Kashmir) abstained. Later, the Geneva Conference also unanimously sent a message to the UN Security Council urging it to 'take necessary measures' to 'stop massacre of Bosnians'. The Security Council considered the matter of lifting the arms embargo on Bosnia under pressure, but then the European states threatened to withdraw their troops from the United Nations Protection Force in Bosnia (UNPROFOR) if the embargo was lifted. The Security Council thus turned down the request.

The OIC ministerial contact group met at Islamabad on 12–13 July 1993 and adopted its 20-point 'Action Plan' on Bosnia. As against 7500 troops requested by the UN Secretary General, he was conveyed the OIC desire to contribute 17,000 troops, pledged by seven Muslim states to protect the beleaguered Bosnians. The meeting reiterated the 'inevitability' of military action and decided to prepare a report analysing the role of different countries, especially the Security Council members, regarding the conflict.[113] In this meeting, the Bosnian Prime Minister Haris Siladjic, apprised the OIC members of the lack of water supply in Sarajevo and drew parallels with the 'Karbala' tragedy.

Initially, the UN Secretary General Boutrous Ghali was inclined to accept the OIC offer and formally offered his 'grateful thanks' to the Muslim countries. But the European Union gave a very cool and cautious response, expressing its fears that the OIC troops would be partial towards the Muslims in Bosnia (The OIC had been likewise accusing the NATO/European troops of being partial to the Bosnian Christian forces.) The Iranian offer was thus outrightly termed unacceptable while offer of troops from the 'moderate Muslim' countries was deemed as 'likely to be considered'. Iran had offered a full army division, Turkey a brigade, and Tunisia had decided to spare a battalion for Bosnia.

In pursuance of the Islamabad decision, the OIC compiled the report on the Bosnian situation. The report, released in August 1993, fiercely attacked the UN and shed doubts on its credibility. It accused the new world order of duplicity and double standards and for the first time referred to the 'angry public opinion in the Muslim states' and their 'frustration with the new world order'. The report, nevertheless, stressed that the Muslim states would fight for Bosnia only under international legality. [114]

For the latter part of the year, the OIC continued reiterating its demands of lifting the arms embargo on Bosnia, formation of war crimes tribunals to try Serb crimes, war reparations by Serbia to the Bosnian government, enforcement of no-fly zones and so on. On 27 December 1993, the OIC observed a 'Day of Solidarity with Bosnia', all over the Muslim world.

The OIC contact group meeting (Geneva; Jan. 1994) supported the principled position of Bosnia and flexibility shown by it in peace negotiations, called for an end to the siege of Sarajevo and noted the NATO Summit decision authorizing air strikes against Serb rebels. Another meeting (New York; Apr. 1994) held the Belgrade regime, and its surrogate Bosnian Serb rebels, responsible for the cold-blooded massacre of Muslims in the UN 'safe haven' of Gorazde. The next meeting (Geneva; Aug. 1994) declared the Western Contact Group's new peace plan as unjust, and as legitimizing aggression. It noted that Bosnia had accepted the plan in the interest of peace while the Serb rebels had rejected it. Noting that no action was taken

against the Serb rebels, as the Western group had warned, the OIC meeting called Bosnia 'a victim of double standards and cynical manipulation'. [115]

On 21 September 1994, the OIC expressed shock at the statement of UNPROFOR Chief Micheal Rose who had threatened the use of force against the Muslim-led Bosnian government (and not the Serb rebels). The following week, the OIC rejected, what it called, 'blackmailing tactics' by the UK and France and reiterated that OIC would replace every soldier, if the afore-mentioned states withdrew their peacekeepers. The OIC group announced that 5000 UNPROFOR peacekeepers belonging to Muslim states, viz. Egypt, Jordan, and Malaysia would stay in Bosnia, even if other states withdrew their troops. In a letter to the UN Security Council President, the OIC group expressed anguish over resolution 943, that envisaged the easing of sanctions against Serbia and demanded an effective border monitoring regimen on the Serbia-Bosnia border. [116] In November 1994, the OIC decided to increase diplomatic efforts to save the city of Bihac from falling into rebel hands. In December, the 7th Islamic Summit (Casablanca; 1994), *inter alia*, rejected confederation or partition of Bosnia, pledged handsome financial support, and endorsed the OIC contact group's decision to cooperate with the European group to find a just and acceptable solution to the conflict. [117]

By the end of 1994, around 200,000 people including 34,000 children had already been butchered, 60,000 crippled for life, and another 1.8 million displaced. Several hundred mosques had been torched and over 60,000 Muslim girls reportedly sexually assaulted (a particularly sensitive issue for the Muslims). It was with the beginning of 1995 that the OIC decided to try a different approach. [118]

The question of morality: The Bosnian crisis, if nothing else, had opened a debate on international morality, regardless of whether the whole rhetoric around morality was merely hollow polemic, or whether its selective use was a justifiable instrument to further one's national interests in realpolitic terms. We shall explain the dilemma here in order to explain the later policies of the

OIC. No attempt shall be made to answer the conundrums; this task is best left to history.

There were many mind-boggling aspects of the Western response to the Bosnian conflict; (a) All the Western-sponsored peace plans from Vance-Owen to Dayton, had legitimized aggression and annexation by force, this was a unique and unprecedented phenomenon in contemporary international politics; (b) The UN treated aggressor and victim on, at best, equal terms. But the arms embargo, it was no secret, hurt Bosnia only. Croatia's long Adriatic coastline and Serbia's unmonitored borders with friendly states, guaranteed uninterrupted access to weapons; (c) No-Fly Zones and Safe Havens were honoured more in the breach than in observance, but at no time did the UN contemplate effective action to counter its shrinking credibility. All the Safe Havens, where Muslims from hard-hit areas took refuge for safety were busted one after another, proving that they were 'traps'. The Muslims thus became soft targets for rebel forces who found it easy to carry out genocide there; (d) For the first time in history, the UN forces deployed in a crisis area served as an excuse for obviating military action and some times the logic was extended to justify the suspension of the provision of humanitarian assistance to the victims, on the pretext that the peacekeepers' lives might be endangered; (e) Even if the allegations of UN troops illegally selling weapons and fuel to rebel forces are discounted, several factors indicated a collusion between the two. Sarajevo airport was closed on the flimsiest of excuses and the UN used to plead with Serb rebels to permit the passage of relief goods to troubled areas, and at least in one case, the UN promised surrender of all arms of the Muslim defenders of Srebrenica in return for allowing access; (f) The US Presidency and the Congress alternately pledged to lift the embargo on Bosnia, i.e., when the Clinton administration promised, the Congress dithered and when the US Congress demanded it, President Clinton faltered and vetoed the move.[119]

On the other hand the Iraqi occupation of Kuwait provides a glaring contrast. In the case of Iraq, the sanctions were not allowed to have effect and military action which included massive bombing of Iraqi civilian population was resorted to immediately. Moreover, Iraq continued to be punished even after nine years of her misadventure, through various enforcement measures. Whereas, neither the rendering of economic sanctions ineffective, nor the colossal human rights tragedy could ever impel the West to take on the Bosnian Serb rebel forces militarily, let alone, carry out a bombardment of Serbia itself. Was it that the allied troops were ready to sacrifice lives to face the 1.8 million strong well-equipped defiant Iraqi army in order to restore a dictatorship in Kuwait but were afraid of 40,000 Serb irregulars for fear of loss of life of UNPROFOR troopers?

Neil Ascherson, writing in the daily *Independent*, called the West's behaviour 'mere pretence', 'shameful' and 'dangerous', and termed the 'failure of the guardians of Europe' in deterring manslaughter in a European country; 'Europe's most humiliating defeat since Munich in 1938'.[120] G.H. Anderson, in his lucid article in the daily *Khaleej Times*, accuses the US and some Western powers of reaching a decision not to allow the emergence of a Muslim state in Europe which would, he goes on to say, disrupt the homogeneity of a Christian continent.[121] The press and media in the Muslim countries were even more prolific about such conspiracy theories. The media in both the Western and Muslim countries was thus chiding the Muslim leadership for not doing enough to protect the hapless Bosnian Muslims, as if no responsibility for the same rested with the European states. The pressure of public opinion led the OIC to finally bid farewell to its commitment to international legality.

Military option and international legality: The mandate given by the 7th Islamic Summit to the OIC Contact Group to coordinate with the Western Contact Group, comprising the US, Russia, UK, France, Spain, and Germany, did not prove to be of much avail, as the two groups differed in their basic approaches. Meanwhile, the OIC decided to observe its year-long silver jubilee celebrations in 1995 with 'due solemnity', to express solidarity with the Muslims of Bosnia. In response to the directives of the General Secretariat, all the OIC organs followed suit. The Islamic Chamber of Commerce and Industry started regular contacts with the Bosnian Chamber and sent an experts' team to Bosnia to prepare a study identifying the areas in which the Muslim countries could expand trade with Bosnia; Islamic Sports Federation held friendly sports tournaments in Muslim States involving the Bosnian teams and proceeds from the matches were transferred to Bosnia; Istanbul Centre conducted research, held symposia, and published books on different aspects of the history and cultural heritage of Bosnia; and so on.

It may be recalled that the OIC was the first international forum to demand military intervention against the Serbs, as early as within a month of the start of hostilities. As the situation deteriorated, public pressure for concrete action mounted in the Muslim countries, so a military solution to the crisis under the OIC umbrella became a serious possibility. An Egyptian official said aptly that whatever happened in Bosnia or Chechenya affected the mindframe of all Muslim peoples. 'It is in our national interest, not to let our people feel that the West is against them', he added. Even Saudi Arabia favoured defying the UN embargo while Iran believed that the Muslim states should pull out from the UN.[122] The Turkish Foreign Minister, Hikmet Citen, had stated at the emergency ICFM (Istanbul; 1992) that his country was ready to spill blood, if necessary, to save Bosnia. Early the following year, at the Dakar mini-Summit on Bosnia (Jan. 1993), he proposed an oil embargo by the Muslim states to force international intervention in Bosnia. In spring 1995, Turkey's parliament formally adopted a resolution calling for 'Desert Storm'-like operation against Serbia. Behind this chorus, the arms embargo had already been *de facto* broken as Iran, Malaysia, Pakistan, and Turkey were discreetly supplying weapons to the Muslim authorities in Bosnia. A story to this effect in the *Washington Post* was denied by the concerned Muslim States, but after all, the Bosnian army could not have fought bare-handed. After the Dayton Accord, Bosnia was to publicly thank the OIC states for assisting it 'despite the UN embargo'.[123] On 4 June 1995, the OIC expressed shock at the murder of the Bosnian Foreign Minister Dr Irfan Ljubljankic and dismay over the silence of the world community.

The breaking point came when in the first half of July 1995, two UN-declared 'safe-havens' fell

to the Serbs and a gruesome carnage followed. The West continued to fudge on the issue of distinguishing between the aggressor and the victim. The London Conference, convened to discuss the latest Serb challenge to the UN prestige, proved to be 'a big joke' as its policy was 'morally untenable and legally indefensible'. The choices of Bosnia were stark as it felt boxed in by the presence of UN troopers, the major pretext for inaction against the Serbs. The enlarged OIC contact group on Bosnia comprising Bosnia, Egypt, Iran, Malaysia, Morocco, Pakistan, Saudi Arabia, Senegal, and Turkey, met in an emergency session at Geneva on 22 July 1995, and decided that 'enough was enough' as they did not have 'the luxury of time'. The OIC bade *adieu* to international legality and threw the gauntlet by declaring the arms embargo on Bosnia as 'invalid'.[124] The meeting announced that the troops belonging to Muslim countries in UNPROFOR would not be withdrawn and would instead be given enhanced fire-power to defend the Muslims. With the induction of contingents from the armed forces of Bangladesh, Pakistan, and Turkey earlier, there were now six Muslim states represented in the UNPROFOR. Pakistan's Foreign Minister, S.A. Ahmad Ali called the OIC decision 'the greatest and the most serious challenge ever thrown to the UN during its fifty years of history'.[125] As Mohammad Sacirbey, the Bosnian Foreign Minister, noted, the UN arms embargo had thus become rightfully invalid.

Egyptian diplomats at Geneva said that another OIC meeting would be held as soon as the formal request for weapons from the government of Bosnia was received. President Hosni Mubarak called for an emergency Islamic Summit 'to take firm decisions and measures' on Bosnia. Turkey's semi-official Anatolian news agency reported that Turkey had planned to train the Bosnian army and to assist its defence industry as a first step to breaking the embargo. Iran was more direct by saying that its forces were ready to fight along with other Muslim states to defend Bosnia. Malaysia went as far as saying that it would provide military help to Bosnia even if it had to go it alone and was willing to face international economic sanctions for the cause. Prime Minister Dr Mahatir Mohammad said bitterly '[West] talks about human rights. And their rights are just to help the Serbs kill the Muslims'.[126]

Iran offered to host the first meeting of OIC military experts in late August, but later the venue was shifted to Yemen. The Yemen meeting could not take place for want of quorum, so it was re-scheduled for the end of September at Kuala Lumpur, Malaysia, wherein military officers of the Muslim states were to finalize the strategy on Bosnia. Meanwhile, the United Nations offered the OIC to send semi-armed personnel to monitor UN posts in Gorazde; the offer was bluntly turned down.[127] On 11–12 September, the chiefs and deputy chiefs of the armed forces of thirteen OIC member states met at Kuala Lumpur and finalized the modalities for military action in Bosnia. This was followed by the meeting of the OIC countries' Foreign and Defence Ministers on 13-14 September, at the same venue, to consider the strategy for meeting the political implications of the OIC military action.

Even the United States was alarmed at the OIC's tone and came up with its new peace plan on 17 August, which the OIC again rejected in its entirety.[128] The OIC meant business this time, and this laid the foundations of the Dayton Peace Accord. The US told Serb rebels to make peace, otherwise the use of Muslim States' ground forces would become unavoidable; this was obviously the last thing the Serbs could have relished.[129]

Peace implementation and reconstruction: The peace negotiations outpaced progress towards the military option. The leaders of Bosnia, Serbia, and Croatia initialled a peace accord on 20 November 1996 at the city of Dayton, Ohio, USA. And the formal signing ceremony took place in Paris on 13 December, in the presence of the representatives of the OIC and the European Union. The OIC Group held its meetings at Paris to deliberate what it could contribute in the new scenario. In the Royaumont Abbey in Paris, the OIC contact group held meetings with European counterparts. In their joint declaration, the two groups pledged to cooperate with each other in post-war arrangements, called upon all groups within Bosnia to respect its territorial unity and ethnic diversity and urged the world community to donate

generously for the reconstruction of the war-ravaged country.[130]

Meanwhile, the OIC had established an Assistance Mobilization Group (AMG) for Bosnia which held eight meetings at Istanbul (Aug. 1995), Tehran (Nov. 1995), Islamabad (March 1996), and Sarajevo (Jul. 1996), again in Sarajevo (Nov. 1996), Doha (Mar. 1997), Sarajevo (June 1997), and Cairo (March 1998). The meetings decided to bolster the defence capabilities of Bosnia, as a strong army could be a formidable deterrent against aggression in the future. The meetings approved a number of measures for development of both public and private sector partnerships with Bosnia in the economic, commercial, technical, and cultural areas. On the bilateral level, Malaysia and later Iran formed consortiums with Bosnia. Pakistan presented donation cheques to Bosnia for preparation of war-crimes cases and establishment of office at the International War Crimes Tribunal at Hague.[131] In mid 1996, the OIC had organized a donors' conference at Sarajevo, which pledged $241 million to Bosnia.

In June 1997, it was noted by the 7th AMG meeting at Sarajevo, that the Bosnian government had received $100 million only, by then. The OIC decided to convene a bigger donors' conference which would generate $1.4 billion for Bosnia by early 1998.[132] In July 1997, training for Bosnian army officers also started in Bangladesh, under the AMG programme. Meanwhile, in an important meeting of the OIC Contact Group on Bosnia, at New York on 28 September 1997, the OIC decided to coordinate the policies of the Member States at the UN debates on Bosnia and reiterated that it would monitor the full implementation of the Dayton peace accord.[133]

The high profile shown by the Islamic Conference on Bosnia with one permanent working group, three emergency ICFMs, thirty coordination meetings, thirty-five resolutions, forty-five visits by OIC Secretary General's special envoys and ten special delegations to Bosnia, in a span of four years, proved to be quite successful. Almost all the OIC resolutions, regarding non-recognition of Serbia, freezing of its international assets, constitution of war crimes tribunals, NATO airstrikes against rebel positions, UN control of Serb heavy weaponry and the ultimate prize of territorial integrity of Bosnia, got translated into reality, sooner or later, one way or the other. However, the final settlement had the flaw that, to borrow from the OIC lexicon, it 'legitimized aggression' by granting 29 per cent Serbs, 49 per cent of the territory of Bosnia and Herzegovina. There is no doubt that, the plight of a Muslim community and the threat to the very existence of a Muslim state, brought about an uncharacteristic unity in the Muslim world that prompted all Muslim states, conservative and radical alike, to action. The OIC thus vindicated the rationale for its existence.

A postscript on Kosovo: Encouraged by the freedom of Bosnia from the Serb rule, the Muslim majority province of Kosovo in the rump Yugoslavia, launched a freedom movement under their moderate leader, President Ibrahim Rugova. The Serb authorities employed the same brutal ethnic cleansing tactics on the Muslim population of the province till it became a full-fledged war between the Serb forces and the Kosovo Liberation Army (KLA) guerrillas in 1998–99. The OIC entrusted its Contact Group on Bosnia to include the Kosovo situation in its mandate. The Group condemned the Serb policies in Kosovo, urged the international community to teach the Serbs a lesson and gave unqualified support to Albania, an OIC member, in case its tensions with Yugoslavia over the mass exodus of ethnic Albanian Muslim refugees from their homes in Kosovo into Albania, were to result in a war.

This time around, the world community reacted a bit differently. When all diplomatic initiatives to persuade the Serb leadership to talk sense failed, the NATO forces led a 79-day punitive bombing campaign against Serbia (24 March–10 June, 1999) involving 1200 jets and 30,000 air sorties. The war broke the nerve of Belgrade which suffered an estimated 16,000 casualties (including 4000 troops and 1200 civilians dead) and incurred losses worth $40 billion. The final agreement concluded, however, was not very unfavourable for the Serbs. Not the least because no penalties were imposed, the Russian role in peacekeeping was assured and finally the right of Kosovo to independence was not recognized. It was given an internal autonomy only.

The OIC remained fully supportive of the NATO-led camapign. The 26th ICFM (Ougadougou; July 1999) welcomed the outcome and reaffirmed its commitment to peacekeeping and humanitarian support for the Kosovar people and for the arrest and bringing to justice of all the war criminals, guilty of genocide of the Muslims. In his message to the same conference, the UN Secretary General Kofi Annan sought the support of the Muslim world for the reconstruction of and peace consolidation in Kosovo. The OIC, in its response, expressed its keen desire to work with the UN for the establishment of a democratic and multi-ethnic Kosovo.

Conflict Resolution

Noted Egyptian scholar, Dr Muhammad el Selim, observes that the ratio of the wars and civil wars that have taken place in the Muslim world since the the Second World War, perfectly corresponds with the proportion of the Muslim states as a fraction of the total number of states in the world.[134] This places a heavy responsibility on the OIC, the largest political institution of the Muslim world, to resolve such conflicts. But the OIC role in this field has remained, to say the least, dismal. In the conflicts between a Muslim and a non-Muslim party, the OIC is known to side with the former. The cases of Palestine, Bosnia, North Cyprus, Comoros, and Somalia are some obvious examples. This creates a paradox. For instance, if the OIC claims to be on the fair side of morality in supporting the Comoros dispute on Mayotte islands with France, the same cannot be true for OIC's support to Somalia's use of force against Ethiopian territory in 1977 (Somalia was an OIC member state while Ethiopia was not), since inadmissibility of annexation of land through military means is one of the cardinal principles governing the OIC. So the question of mediation by the OIC in such disputes does not arise as its posture becomes clearly biased in favour of one (Muslim) side.

As far as the conflict resolution within the Muslim states is concerned, here too, the OIC does not have anything substantial to its credit. One reason for this, Selim points out, is that the OIC has an unwritten convention of not interfering in disputes between Muslim states that fall under the jurisdiction of other regional organizations, particularly the Arab League, the Organization of African Unity, and the Organization for Security and Cooperation in Europe.[135] Thus the OIC kept, at best, a marginal profile in the solution of the conflict between North and South Yemen, and the civil wars in Somalia and in Tajikstan, which fell under the purview of these three organizations respectively. However, the OIC role in mediation during the civil war in East Pakistan (now Bangladesh) and the Iran–Iraq war was quite visible.

We can discern three major obstacles that come in the way of effective handling of an intra-Muslim conflict by the OIC. First of all, we note that there is no provision in the OIC Charter that specifically requires it to resolve the conflicts among Muslim states. The article that comes closest to this subject is Article II-A (1) which describes the 'promotion of Islamic solidarity among the member states' as the first objective of this Organization. Needless to say, there can hardly be an iota of solidarity between states that are, at any given time, engaged in an armed conflict with each other. Other than this, there is Article II-B(4) that invites the members towards 'settlement of any conflict that may arise, by peaceful means, such as negotiation, mediation, reconciliation or arbitration'. At no point does this article ascribe any role to the OIC. Least of all, does this article require the member states to follow a certain order of the given four options for peaceful settlement of disputes i.e. negotiation first, if this fails, mediation, then reconciliation and, as a last resort, arbitration. That is to say that the OIC Charter is very ambiguous about conflict resolution, member-states can sit on the negotiating table but if it does not work, they are not obliged to exhaust the mediation option, and even if they do, they may not necessarily approach the OIC for mediation, nor is the latter obliged to offer its services for the purpose.

The 2nd Islamic Summit (Lahore; 1974) added a new dimension to the OIC's concept of conflict resolution by emphasizing that this has to take place in the 'fraternal spirit' of Islamic solidarity, thereby excluding the framework of the Charter and principles of the UN from the concept of conflict resolution in Muslim states. The

Conference alluded to the need of utilizing the 'good offices' (a fifth option) of Muslim states for such resolution, in its final declaration.[136] The 3rd Islamic Summit (Taif; 1981) and the 4th Islamic Summit (Casablanca; 1984) decided to establish an Islamic International Court of Justice (IICJ) and Regional Reconciliation Committees on geographical bases, respectively. Thus the two Summits added judicial and political options to the gamut of possibilities for conflict resolution among member states, thus raising the total number of available options to seven. Since the IICJ or the Reconciliation Committees have not come into existence so far, technically speaking, the member states are left with five options, namely, negotiation, mediation, reconciliation, arbitration, and good offices, not necessarily under the OIC auspices. So there is no provision, a member state may invoke, to prompt the OIC into action for conflict resolution.

Secondly, there is a convention in the OIC, not to interfere in a dispute unless both the parties welcome its efforts for the settlement. As we shall see below, the OIC had offered its services to solve the Iran–Iraq dispute as early as in 1974 but Iran had declined the offer on the grounds that the matter had already been placed before the UN Security Council. The OIC backed out. At that time, the Libyan leader Moammar Qaddafi was critical of OIC's pusillanimity, as well as Iran's reluctance to involve the OIC. Years later, when the 5th Islamic Summit (Kuwait; 1987) was going to deliberate on the Libya–Chad conflict, it was Libya which blocked the move saying the matter was already under the consideration of the OAU. More recent examples are Algeria's obduracy not to allow an OIC discussion on its civil war (1992–98) and Saudi Arabia's lack of sympathy for any positive initiatives by the OIC towards the Kuwait crisis (1990–92). If the OIC envisages any effective role regarding dispute settlements in future, this tradition of seeking approval from all parties to a dispute, prior to any initiative or even discussion, will have to be done away with. It would be instructive to note that had the UN sought the joint permission of Iraq and Kuwait before undertaking collective security measures against the latter, inaction would have been the only outcome.

Last, but not the least, the absence of any implementation machinery is a big practical hurdle with the OIC. The problem was most accentuated during the two Gulf wars as any party could flout the OIC decisions and get away with it. The OIC would argue and argue with the belligerents but the internecine conflicts took their course. This lacuna in the OIC structure has been felt time and again and several resolutions have been adopted by the Islamic conferences calling for a permanent apparatus in the Organization's framework dealing with conflict resolution between member states. So far, all efforts in this direction have been prematurely undermined.

Given the situation, it is hardly surprising that there were a number of conflicts in the Muslim world that never received even a passing reference in the OIC resolutions. We will look at the few disputes, where the OIC did get involved. One such conflict was between the PLO and Jordan (1970–74) in the early years of the OIC's existence. The Arab League took the lead to broker a truce. The 2nd ICFM (Karachi; 1970) viewed with satisfaction the Amman and Cairo agreements and asked the two sides to adhere to them in letter and spirit. The OIC called for 'fraternity and coordination' for combating the 'Zionist enemy'.[137] Likewise, the 3rd ICFM (Jeddah; 1972) reiterated the same resolutions and commended the efforts of Saudi Arabia and Egypt for bringing about a rapprochement between Jordan and the PLO. Likewise, the OIC did not make any offer to mediate the dispute between Sudan and the Uganda (1979) that was sparked by the overthrow of Ugandan President Idi Amin, a Muslim, by a Christian General. It, however, expressed concern over the humanitarian dimension of the conflict arising from the mass exodus of refugees from Uganda. The 11th ICFM (Islamabad; 1980) expressed satisfaction over the agreement between Sudan and Uganda concerning the repatriation of refugees. It also 'decided to give assistance to Sudan as a contribution towards sustaining these refugees'.[138]

As regards the civil war in Chad in the late seventies, the 9th ICFM (Dakar; 1978) adopted a resolution entitled 'Solidarity with the People of Chad' which called upon the warring factions to respect the cease-fire agreement and requested Libya, Niger, and Sudan to accelerate their efforts for an early solution. The 11th ICFM (Islamabad; 1980) deliberated upon the condition of Chadian refugees and appealed to the main factions 'to put an end to their dispute so that Chad may enjoy peace and security...[that is] indispensable for the re-settlement of refugees'.[139]

At the 5th Islamic Summit (Kuwait; 1987), Chad brought up a complaint against Libya for occupying its northern territory. Libya insisted that the matter was already under the consideration of the OAU, so the OIC should avoid taking it up. The OIC, nonetheless, discussed the Libya-Chad dispute and in its resolution 28/5-P(IS) expressed the apprehension that the heavy military activity in Northern Chad could endanger the peace and security of the whole region and demanded that no action that could increase tensions in the region should be taken by either side. It invited Libya and Chad to 'resolve the dispute peacefully' in the 'spirit of the OIC Charter'.[140] The OIC asked the OAU to solve the conflict and requested the OIC Secretary General to cooperate with the OAU Secretary General for the follow-up of this resolution. We find that on the one hand, the OIC shifted the responsibility of resolving the conflict between two member states to a regional organization and on the other hand stressed that the settlement should be reached in the spirit of OIC Charter principles. How is it possible for the OAU to solve a problem with the objectives and principles of another organization (i.e., OIC) in mind? The 18th ICFM (Riyadh; 1989) commended the OAU for successfully bringing about a settlement of the Libya–Chad dispute, and encouraged both the countries to restore their erstwhile fraternal relations.[141]

The dispute between Mali and Burkina Faso (1985) is another case in point. Though there is no reference to this conflict in the OIC resolutions, but we find mentioned in some speeches of the then OIC Secretary General Sharifuddin Pirzada, who contacted the leadership of both the states to offer his good offices. Pirzada later noted with satisfaction the amicable resolution of the dispute. In the civil war in Somalia (1992–96), the OIC coordinated its efforts with those of the UN and OAU for a cease-fire. Later, the OIC was one of the witnesses and guarantors of the Moscow cease-fire pact ending the civil war in Tajikstan (1994–97), along with the OSCE and the CIS. As for the civil war in Afghanistan (1989–98), the OIC's mediatory role was a bit more proactive, but that has already been noted in the previous section.

In all the aforementioned cases the OIC shrugged off its responsibility to resolve conflicts between two Muslim states and was content with playing second fiddle to the United Nations or to some regional organization. The OIC, in most of the cases, shied away from offering its services for mediation or good offices, to the belligerents. In four cases only, namely, should be taken by either side Pakistan–Bangladesh dispute, should be taken by either side Iran–Iraq war, should be taken by either side Mauritania–Senegal conflict, and the Iraq–Kuwait crisis, the OIC role was a departure from its usual passivity. We shall discuss all the four in detail.

(i) The Pakistan–Bangladesh dispute: Pakistan consisted of two parts, geographically separated by a distance of over 2000 km; the territory of a hostile state, India, lay in between. Islam was the only bond that was keeping the two wings together. For several reasons, the common man in East Pakistan gradually started harbouring the feeling that he was being exploited by the West Pakistani elite. In 1967, a conspiracy was unearthed, divulging that some East Pakistani nationalist leaders, belonging to the Awami League, had plotted the dismemberment of Pakistan with the active connivance of India.[142] In the general elections of December 1970, the Awami League and Pakistan People's Party, romped home with thumping majorities in East and West Pakistan, respectively. The fact that neither of the parties could secure even one seat from the other wing showed up the cleavage that had developed between the two peoples. Much to the chagrin of Pakistan's military and the Establishment, the Awami League had got an absolute majority in Pakistan's united parliament, securing 160 of the 313 seats, since East Pakistan had, on the basis of its numerical majority, more seats in the parliament than West Pakistan.

The government dilly-dallied over the transfer of power and the Awami League became impatient and started defying State authority. President Yahya Khan, a West Pakistani, hit back by clamping a ban on the Awami League, calling its leadership traitors and Indian agents. The Awami League lost no time in proclaiming an independent Bangladesh, forming a government-in-exile in India and sending armed infiltrators from across the Indian border. Horrendous atrocities were carried out by the infiltrators on the, what the government called, 'loyal Pakistani' civilian population (the term included all the West Pakistanis settled in East Pakistan, all bonafide East Pakistanis, other than the ethnic Bengalis and all the Bengalis loyal to the State). In the wake of the situation, President Yahya's above decision along with the military crackdown on the rebels came on 25 March 1971. To this day, Dhaka accuses Islamabad of genocide of ordinary East Pakistanis in the garb of neutralising the action of the rebels, New Delhi accuses Islamabad of carrying out systematic victimization of the non-Muslims, especially the Bengali Hindus, in the erstwhile East Pakistan, and Islamabad accuses both of butchering ordinary civilians, women, and children, in hit-and run terrorist attacks.

East Pakistan had plunged into a civil war that culminated in a full-scale India–Pakistan war on 22 November 1971. To reduce the pressure on its beleaguered troops on the Eastern front, Pakistan attacked India from the West on 3 December 1971.[143] The hotly contested fight raged on with fury for another fortnight. On 16 December, finding his forces in a no-win situation, the Pakistan army commander in East Pakistan accepted cease-fire on India's highly unflattering terms, to avoid further bloodshed. East Pakistan seceded to become Bangladesh and Pakistan accepted a cease-fire on the Western front also, a couple of days later, as continuation of war was an exercise in futility, once its dismemberment had been effected.

At the height of the civil war, in June 1971, the OIC experts' committee meeting to draft the Charter, was in session at Jeddah. The meeting went out of the way to condemn external interference in East Pakistan, without naming India.[144] A three-member OIC delegation comprising the Secretary General, Iran, and Kuwait, visited both parts of Pakistan, to try to mediate between the Pakistan government and the rebels. When the delegation tried to visit India to meet the leaders of the self-proclaimed government of Bangladesh, India declined visas to the members of the OIC mission on the grounds that the first OIC Summit (Rabat; 1969) had expelled the Indian delegation.[145]

At that time, a number of rebel leaders were in jails in Pakistan facing sedition charges, while those who had managed to flee, were virtual prisoners in India, issuing statements against Pakistan on the bidding of their mentors. The so-called Bangladesh leadership was on a very weak wicket at that time and could have been amenable to the OIC's influence to come to an amicable settlement with the Pakistani authorities. In fact, the India-based East Pakistani rebels, approached Pakistan's High Commission at Delhi, with an offer for secret negotiations, but India then imposed an immediate ban on their contacts with the Pakistani government. India had decided not to let go the golden opportunity that had presented itself to bifurcate its arch-rival—Pakistan—and the same thinking led to India's undiplomatic treatment of the OIC mission. Though India later apologized to OIC for the discourtesy shown to its mission, the immediate objective of torpedoing an initiative that could have saved Pakistan's territorial integrity, had been realized.

A couple of months prior to the 3rd ICFM (Jeddah; 1972), Pakistan (i.e., the erstwhile West Pakistan) released the Awami League leader Sheikh Mujib-ur-Rehman, who was undergoing a trial for high treason, and then allowed him to proceed to Indian-occupied East Pakistan, to become the Prime Minister of 'Bangladesh'. The 3rd ICFM refused to recognize Bangladesh and declared its full support for Pakistan's independence, sovereignty, and territorial integrity. Both India and Pakistan were urged to vacate each other's territories captured during the war of 1971, withdraw their troops to positions behind their internationally recognized frontiers, and exchange prisoners of war in accordance with the Geneva conventions. The Conference gave a veiled threat to India to accept the OIC resolutions so that 'the existing relations between India and the Muslim states are not affected'. The Conference decided to establish a committee of reconciliation comprising Algeria, Iran, Malaysia, Morocco, Somalia,

Tunisia, and the OIC Secretary General, that was asked to contact President Zulfikar Ali Bhutto in Islamabad and Mujib-ur-Rehman at Dhaka, 'to bring about reconciliation between estranged brothers'. The Conference expressed deep sorrow over the tragedy that had struck Pakistan and wished that 'future relationship between the population in the East (Pakistan) and West (Pakistan) should be decided upon by their elected leaders through a meeting between them in the atmosphere of freedom and dignity'.[146]

The OIC Secretary General contacted both sides and as soon as the replies were received, he sent a letter to Bangladeshi leader Rehman through the Indian embassy at Cairo, since Bangladesh had not been recognized and did not have any diplomatic missions in Muslim states. It is not known whether the letter reached Dhaka or not, since the OIC Secretary General received a reply from the Indian Prime Minister Indira Gandhi that said that the Bangladeshi authorities were not in a position to receive the 7-member delegation of Muslim states, since the OIC had not cared about the sufferings of Bangladeshi people earlier. So this second mission failed.[147]

To increase international pressure on India, Pakistan unilaterally released all the Indian POWs, and thus managed to get a resolution approved by the 4th ICFM (Benghazi; 1973), censuring India for continued detention of the Pakistani POWs. Following this conference, the OIC made the third major attempt to bring about a reconciliation between Pakistan and Bangladesh but, Mujib-ur-Rehman demanded equal status as the head of a sovereign state, along with the Pakistani Prime Minister Zulfikar Ali Bhutto. The attempt failed.[148]

Premier Bhutto was on a weak wicket after the Pakistani forces' debacle in the 1971 war against India. He was under strong pressure by the emotionally charged Pakistani public not to recognize Bangladesh, while India was holding thousands of Pakistani POWs as a trump card to gain credit for eventual Pakistani recognition of Bangladesh. Due to the efforts of the new OIC Secretary General, Hassan Tohami, Bhutto announced Pakistan's recognition of Bangladesh, one day prior to the 2nd Islamic Summit (Lahore; 1974) in 'the spirit of Islamic solidarity'. The OIC then persuaded Mujib-ur-Rehman to come to Pakistan to attend the Islamic Summit, which he did. The OIC as a collective body, and several Muslim states like Iran and Turkey individually, recognized Bangladesh on the same day.[149] Bhutto thus pulled the rug from under India's feet, which had to release Pakistani POWs soon without a quid pro quo, as he never forgot to insist that it was the OIC and the Islamic spirit, that made Pakistan recognize Bangladesh, not any external pressure. It was one of the finest hours in the history of the OIC and that of Pakistan.

A new stage: Fourteen years later, the OIC services were once again requested on the issue of the repatriation of 'stranded Pakistanis' in Bangladesh. It is well-known that a large number of East Pakistanis refused to accept Bangladeshi nationality. In fact the first Vice President, the Chief Justice of Supreme Court, and Secretary General of the ruling People's Party in the truncated Pakistan (former West Pakistan), namely, Dr Nur-ul Amin, Justice Hamood-ur-Rahman, and J.A. Rahim, respectively, to name a few, belonged to the erstwhile East Pakistan. The ethnic Bihari community in East Pakistan was worst affected by the riots between pro-Pakistan and pro-Bangladesh activists, after the creation of Bangladesh, since the Biharis always called themselves Pakistanis. Bangladesh asked Pakistan to take them back. During Zulfikar Ali Bhutto's tenure, Pakistan accepted hundreds of thousands of Biharis who could trace any linkage with (West) Pakistan like kinship, employment etc. Pakistan refused to absorb all Biharis on the plea that till 1971, every person living in Bangladesh was a Pakistani and Pakistan could not now accept every citizen of Bangladesh if he insists on still being a Pakistani. The 'Stranded Pakistanis' issue took emotional undertones in Pakistan since Biharis had made a lot of sacrifices, when fighting for a united Pakistan.

In July 1988, Pakistan and the OIC established a trust for raising funds for undertaking the gigantic task of repatriation and rehabilitation of 238,000 stranded Pakistanis.[150] Later in 1991, the then Pakistani Prime Minister Nawaz Sharif chaired another meeting of the OIC Fund which decided to go ahead with the repatriation. Only a few hundred people had been repatriated when the government dithered and the process dried up. In early 1998, the government of Pakistan decided to prepare an action plan for a prompt repatriation of stranded Pakistanis, after a meeting of the Prime Ministers of Pakistan and Bangladesh at Dhaka in January.[151] The progress still remains very slow.

(ii) The Iran–Iraq War: When the dispute between Iran and Iraq over the *Shatt-al-Arab* (Arab Waterway) resurfaced in 1973, the then OIC Secretary General Hassan Tohami tried to involve the then OIC Chairman, King Hassan of Morocco, in order to make use of his personal good offices for its amicable resolution, but the matter got placed before the UN Security Council.[152] At the 2nd Islamic Summit (Lahore; 1974), President Idi Amin of Uganda suggested, and the OIC Secretary General supported him, that the OIC should constitute a committee for the settlement of the Iran–Iraq dispute. Amin also read out a message from the Iraqi President Hassan al Bakr at the conference welcoming the OIC initiative. Iranian Foreign Minister Abbas Khlatebry objected to the proposal saying that the UN Security Council should first be given a chance to solve this problem. The presidents of Algeria, Libya, Palestine, and Uganda insisted that the OIC should become involved in the affair even if Iran did not like it but the chairman of the conference Zulfikar Ali Bhutto winded up the debate with the statement that the OIC would be ready to offer its good offices in this dispute whenever both the parties so required.[153]

In 1979, the relations between Iran and Iraq sharply deteriorated following the change of government in both the countries.[154] Border clashes became a routine and the climax came when Iraq unilaterally abrogated the 1975 Algiers Treaty, that had divided the waterway between Iran and Iraq at the median line, and crossed the international frontiers at three points on 22 September 1980.

The OIC responds: The OIC met in an emergency session of the ICFM at New York on 26 September 1980 to consider the outbreak of hostilities. It formed a goodwill mission comprising the OIC Secretary General and the Pakistani President Ziaul Haq to proceed to Iran and Iraq, and request the parties on the Muslim world's behalf, to halt the war.[155] The mission met President Saddam Hussein at Baghdad on 28 September and President Abul Hassan Bani Sadr at Tehran on 30 September. Iran is reported to have refused to accept cease-fire unless Iraq was declared aggressor, while Iraq showed willingness to halt fire by 5 October, provided Iran agreed to renegotiate the Arab waterway dispute as, according to it, the Algiers agreement was a dead letter. The mission reported back to the OIC ministers at New York who asked the mission to continue its efforts.[156]

At the end of October, the OIC Secretary General offered to send a high-level delegation, comprising the Kings and Heads of State of Islamic states, to Tehran and Baghdad. Iran rejected the offer, since it believed that the aggressor and aggrieved were being treated at par. Iran's paramount leader Imam Khomeini said that the 'Muslim brothers were welcome in Tehran, [but only] to investigate the Iraqi aggression against Iran'.[157]

On 17 January 1981, the OIC Secretary General stated that the forthcoming 3rd Islamic Summit would end the Gulf war. Meanwhile, the Islamic Solidarity Fund decided to send a 100 respected *ulema* of the Muslim world to the Gulf, to try to stop the war.[158] Iran announced its boycott of the Taif Summit since it could not sit on the same table with the aggressor Iraq. On 23 January, a four-member OIC mission led by the Secretary General, Habib Chatti, arrived at Tehran to persuade Iran to attend the Summit. It received a firm 'No' from the Iranian Prime Minister Mohammad Ali Rajai. Two days later Rajai said that Iran could have attended the OIC Summit to discuss Muslim issues in general, but the Gulf war was to be decided on the battlefields.[159] The 3rd Islamic Summit (Taif; 1981) expressed concern over the internecine conflict, asked both sides to accept immediate cease-fire and called upon them to accept the mediation offer of the OIC. The Conference approved in principle, the establishment of an Islamic military force to monitor the cease-fire. The OIC goodwill mission was renamed Islamic Peace Committee and its membership was enlarged to include Bangladesh, Gambia, Guinea, Malaysia, Pakistan, Palestine, Senegal, Turkey, and the OIC Secretary General.[160] Meanwhile, the Islamic Summit conference

received tens of thousands of telegrams from Muslims all over the world to try to bring about an end to the fratricidal war.[161]

The new peace committee, headed by the Guinean President Ahmad Sekou Toure, started functioning as soon as the Summit concluded. Iran welcomed the OIC initiative and Iraq too showed its inclination to withdraw from Iranian territory if an acceptable compromise was arrived at. Toure held talks with Iran and Iraq. He agreed with the former on three points that could be a basis for a meaningful solution; one, establishment of a committee to apportion the blame for starting the war; two, adherence to the Algiers agreement, and three, complete Iraqi withdrawal. It was stressed that aggression, unilateral abrogation of a treaty, and annexation of land by force were inadmissible under international law.[162] On 3 March, the Committee hinted that a cease-fire agreement was in the offing.[163] The OIC compromise formula was announced on 6 March, which envisaged:

1. Five cardinal principles for peaceful co-existence between Iran and Iraq, namely, to respect each other's sovereignty, non-use of force for annexation of land, non-interference in each other's domestic affairs, obligatory acceptance of peaceful means for dispute settlement, and freedom of navigation on the Arab waterway.
2. Cease-fire on 13 March at midnight, Iraqi withdrawal to commence from 20 March and to be completed in four weeks under OIC military observers' supervision, direct negotiations to follow immediately thereafter and the OIC to be guarantor that both sides would adhere to the agreement.
3. An OIC committee with the acceptance of Iran and Iraq for determining the future status of the Arab waterway, the waterway to remain open for free navigation under the full control of the OIC, pending the agreement, and the OIC to be the arbiter if any party were to have a complaint regarding the freedom of navigation.
4. A committee comprising the incumbent Presidents of Guinea, Pakistan, and Bangladesh, the PLO Chairman, the Prime Minister of Turkey, the Foreign Ministers of Senegal and Malaysia, and the OIC Secretary General, to place its good offices at the disposal of Iran and Iraq, for smooth implementation of the agreement.

Iran immediately rejected the plan since respect to the Algiers Agreement was not declared as a basis for negotiations. Three days later, Iraq also turned down the formula since it was not willing to withdraw forces from Iranian territory unless Iran accepted full Iraqi sovereignty over the Arab waterway. Iran, on its part, did not want to negotiate from a position of weakness. On 10 March, President Sekou Toure announced the failure of his mission.[164] The fighting intensified and the demands of the two sides radicalized. Iraq started harping on the right of self-rule for the Arabic speaking Iranian province of Khuzistan while hard-liners in Iran declared the overthrow of Saddam Hussein's regime in Iraq as a pre-condition for cease-fire.

It appeared that neither side had a genuine desire to end the bloodshed. This was the view of the OIC, and even the UN corroborated this understanding as the UN Secretary General's special emissary on the Gulf war, Olaf Palme, a former prime minister of Sweden, remarked, 'There appears to be no political will on the part of the parties concerned to resolve the problems and in the absence of that will, even small problems look bigger.'

Meanwhile, President Bani Sadr showed flexibility in negotiations and the Peace Committee was able to float a new plan in the first weak of April that accommodated the two basic demands of Iran that, the Algiers agreement was to be a basis of future negotiations and, a committee or an Islamic Court was to determine who the aggressor was. Its binding decision would have made the aggressor liable for payment of damages to the aggrieved party. The plan also called for immediate cease-fire, unconditional troops withdrawal to the international border, OIC military observers to monitor cease-fire, and an Islamic Fund for the reconstruction of Iran and Iraq.[165] This plan also failed. Meanwhile, the Foreign Ministry spokesman in Tehran, on 23 April, accused the OIC Secretary General Habib Chatti of being pro-Iraq. President Bani Sadr promptly denied that it was Iran's official view and censured the Ministry for issuing irresponsible statements without his permission.[166] The frictions between radicals and moderates in Iran's political hierarchy soon became apparent. They were to cause President

Bani Sadr's exit very soon, for he was criticized for being 'soft' on Iraq. With him was gone the loudest voice of moderation on the Iranian side.

The OIC caused a severe blow to its own credibility by holding the 12th ICFM (Baghdad; Jan. 1981) in one of the belligerent countries, Iraq. Iran's pleadings to shift the venue to a neutral place were rejected on a 'flimsy, untenable and irrelevant' ground that since Iran had boycotted the 3rd Islamic Summit, its request could not be acceded to. In the absence of Iran, Iraq used the forum for Iran-bashing. President Saddam Hussein, in his inaugural speech, absolved his country of 'all moral and legal responsibility for initiating the war' and put all the blame 'fairly and squarely on Iran'.[167] As if this was not enough of an insult for Iran, the Conference committed another blunder by deciding to make the Iraqi President's speech an official document of the conference because it contained 'useful guidance for the Organization'. Thus the credibility of OIC was rendered suspect in the eyes of one of the parties to the dispute, the OIC never recovered from this crisis of confidence as long as the war lasted.[168]

In 1982, the OIC made three serious efforts to halt the war. The Peace Committee headed by President Sekou Toure visited the two capitals in March, June, and October. Finally, on 24 October, Toure admitted the failure of all the peace bids.[169] Earlier, the 13th ICFM (Niamey; Aug. 1982) adopted a resolution requesting both sides to stop the bloodshed and renewed the offer of deployment of OIC military observers at the Iran–Iraq border. The Muslim states were asked to refrain from any measures that might lead to the continuation of the conflict. It also appealed to all states to exert their good offices to facilitate the implementation of the resolution. In this conference, Iraqi Foreign Minister stated that his country was ready to face an international OIC tribunal to apportion the blame as to who was the aggressor. He asked President Sekon Toure to proceed with the establishment.[170] Another significant event of 1982 warrants a mention. The OIC Chairman, King Khalid of Saudi Arabia, called for a general strike on 14 April, to protest against the alleged Zionist attack on the Dome of the Rock in Jerusalem. Most Muslim countries including Pakistan, Bangladesh, Malaysia, Iran, Iraq and others reported complete strike. So there was at least one focal point, i.e., Al-Quds, on which the OIC had united Iran and Iraq.[171]

The end of 1982 is a cut-off date in the Gulf war because the time was marked by the Iranian forces redeeming their honour by liberating their territory. The foreboding that the Iranians would take the war into the Iraqi territory made the Iraqis, the Arabs and the world at large panic. President Hussein tried to play on the Arab fears by declaring that his forces were battling to stop Iranian invasion of his country. The Arab states like Egypt and Oman warned Iran against any such misadventure. The United States and the Soviet Union plus their European partners threw their full weight behind Iraq. Iran now started exploiting the handiest linkage, that of the termination of war with the Israeli withdrawal from the Arab lands.

From now on, the ground realities had altered considerably. Iraq therefore welcomed virtually every peace bid, regardless of where it came from. Iran was unfortunately carried away by the illusion that its ultimate victory was only a matter of time, as its Foreign Minister said that his forces were poised to invade Iraq and besiege its capital Baghdad. It was this illusion that sealed the fate of all the subsequent peace initiatives and the war continued unabated with a virtual stalemate on the battlefront for years to come.

A new approach (1983–88): As the year 1982 drew to a close, the OIC Secretary General Habib Chatti announced that very soon the OIC would resume its peace bids that would definitely end the war. But events were to disprove his optimism. By 1982, the Iranian forces had retrieved all their occupied territory and had pushed the war, in some cases, into Iraqi territory. At that time, a moderate section in the Iranian decision making circles had favoured an end to the war as Iran had vindicated its honour. But the radicals believed that Iran could gain more on the battlefront, and their view prevailed. Consequently Iran's price for a settlement sky-rocketed; which included, *inter alia*, unconditional acceptance of the Algiers Agreement by Iraq, payment of war reparations, and overthrow of the Baath Party regime in Baghdad. The OIC had earlier exhausted all its options when the two states were willing to listen to it, but both had

been shunning all the OIC formulas in search of a face-saving device. By 1983, the OIC had nothing to offer. One finds an increasing reference to the UN resolutions on Iran–Iraq dispute, in the OIC literature during the period 1983–88. It appears that the OIC had by then opted for a secondary role for itself over the Gulf crisis. Meanwhile, Iraq unconditionally accepted all the OIC resolutions on cease-fire but it was too late. Iran was in no mood for compromise.

Serious differences erupted over the final text of the resolution on the Gulf war at the 14th ICFM (Dhaka; 1983) but the Conference was unanimous in asking both the states to treat the POWs well and appealed to them to accept an OIC fact-finding mission that would investigate the condition of POWs in both countries. The Committee was to consist of the OIC Secretary General and the Foreign Ministers of some Muslim states, with the concurrence of Iran and Iraq.[172] The OIC Peace Committee continued its efforts and presented its report to the 4th Islamic Summit (Casablanca; Jan. 1984). The report stated that the standpoints of the two sides were widely divergent and there had not been any change of thinking from either side. The Conference commended the Islamic Peace Committee for doing *whatever could possibly have been done* to end the conflict (emphasis added). The Summit resolution 8/4-P(I.S) expressed satisfaction over Iraq's willingness for an unconditional cease-fire and appealed to Iran to respond positively to the Iraqi gesture. The resolution reiterated all the OIC resolutions calling for the cessation of hostilities, to be immediately followed by direct negotiations and ultimately a peaceful settlement of the Gulf conflict. The Conference gave its support to the UN Security Council resolution 540 (dated 31 Oct. 1983), in this context.[173]

In March 1984, Guinean leader Sekou Toure died. Daud Jawwara, the President of Gambia, replaced him as the Chairman of the Islamic Peace Committee on 18 July. The Committee became active once again. It propounded a new peace plan that envisaged a cease-fire monitoring committee under the Palestinian leader Yasser Arafat. Iran rejected the formula.[174] The 15th ICFM (Sana'a; Dec. 1984) praised Iraq for cooperating with the Peace Committee. It asked both sides to respect the injunctions of Islamic *Shari'ah* [on the conduct of war], the Geneva Protocol on Chemical Weapons, and the Geneva Convention on Prisoners of War. The Iranian Foreign Minister repeated his country's position that war itself was the only way to end the conflict.[175] But at the end of the moot, the OIC Secretary General announced a breakthrough, as according to him, both sides had agreed to cooperate with the Islamic Committee. The euphoria over this announcement turned out to be short-lived. A seemingly endless war continued to be fought with relentless determination during 1985–86 by both the sides.

In March 1985, the OIC expressed profound shock at the bombing of civilian targets in the war and urged both sides to refrain from continuing to do so. The OIC made an abortive peace bid again in May 1985. The 16th ICFM (Fez; Jan. 1986) debated the Iran–Iraq issue for three hours but every solution offered was rejected by one side or the other. As it was the only issue of the ninety-one-item conference agenda, where no consensus had been arrived at, so the final communiqué of the 16th ICFM made no mention of the protracted war. Malaysia then suggested that the Ummah Peace Committee, of which she was a member, should dissolve itself, in protest against the non-cooperation by Iran and Iraq.

As the war escalated during 1986, the OIC described it as 'most unfortunate' and President Daud Jawwara, Chairman of the Peace Committee, put forward another four-point formula to end the war. President Yasser Arafat of Palestine, suggested the addition of a new provision in the formula whereunder, in the event of the rejection of the new formula by either or both sides, the OIC countries would use military force to exact compliance from the belligerents. The OIC, the President said, should send peacekeeping troops that will first forcibly separate the warring sides The proposal was dismissed by the majority as being unrealistic.

Iran stayed away from the 5th Islamic Summit (Kuwait; Jan. 1987) which became its third consecutive boycott of an Islamic Summit. Tehran was willing to attend if the venue were shifted to a neutral country, especially Pakistan, since Kuwait was known to be supplying Iraq with money. A change of venue at the last hour was found to be

unfeasible, and the OIC Secretary General Sharifuddin Pirzada's efforts to persuade Tehran to change its mind and drop its demand did not fructify.[176] The Islamic Summit reiterated the cardinal principles for permanent peace in the Gulf that had been expounded in earlier OIC peace formulas (see above). The Conference called for an end to hostilities, immediate release of all POWs and direct negotiations for a peaceful solution. The Islamic Peace Committee was told to make attempts to prevent the sale of military equipment to the parties to the conflict. Iran was requested to accept the UN Security Council resolutions 582 and 588 that Iraq had already accepted. Iran again rejected all the OIC resolutions.[177]

The 7th ICFM (Amman; March 1988) came out with nothing new, except requesting both sides to respect the new Security Council resolution 598 on the Iran–Iraq war. On 18 July 1988, came the surprise announcement by Imam Khomeini, the supreme Iranian leader, that he had decided to accept UN resolution 598 on cease-fire, in the best interest of Iran, though 'it was more difficult than drinking a cupful of poison'. The cease-fire agreement was reached on 9 August and the guns fell silent on the Iran-Iraq border on 20 August.

After the war: The 19th ICFM (Riyadh; 1989) hailed the end of the war and felicitated and commended Iran and Iraq for accepting the cease-fire agreement. It appealed to both countries to respect the truce and release the POWs.[178] In the following years, the OIC was indirectly the most significant single contributor to the normalization process between Iran and Iraq. We will see later that Iran, along with Turkey and Pakistan, tried its best to bring about a negotiated end to the Kuwait imbroglio under the OIC auspices. So much so, that Iraq found Iran to be the only neighbour it could trust during the Kuwait war. It sent hundreds of its Air Force planes to Iran to save them from destruction by the allied bombing. The latter, however, confiscated all the Iraqi jets as a contribution towards war damages, which it believed, Iraq owed it.

The Iran–Iraq diplomatic breakthrough was achieved during the first ever direct meeting between the officials of the two countries on the sidelines of the extraordinary OIC Summit (Islamabad; March 1997). The ice was broken and Iran formally invited Iraq to attend the Tehran Islamic Summit, which the latter accepted. Iraqi Vice President Taha Yaseen Ramadhan was accorded full protocol on his arrival at the Iranian capital for attending the 8th Islamic Summit (Tehran; Dec. 1997). As a gesture of goodwill to each other, Iran released 500 Iraqi POWs while Iraq released two Iranians (Iraq had already released all Iranian POWs at the outset of Kuwait crisis in 1990, unilaterally). Ramadhan, who became the first Iraqi leader to set foot in Tehran in two decades, used the OIC-created opportunity to mend fences with the erstwhile foe. His meetings with the Iranian President Dr Mohammad Khatami were held in a warm and cordial atmosphere. Khatami said that both Iran and Iraq were victims of imperialist conspiracies. In a veiled reference to the US, Khatami said to his Iraqi guest that if they looked back to the past twenty years, they would realize who their common enemy was. Both sides, for the first time, agreed to start negotiations for peaceful settlement of all outstanding issues between them. At long last, harmony was in sight.[179]

By early February 1998, the countries had come so close that a leading paper of Britain, *Times* was able to carry a story alleging that Iranian and Iraqi senior officials had met in the Iraqi border town of al-Shalamja on 5 February to hold preliminary talks for forging an anti-West alliance. Both the countries decried the report as baseless. The reports about military cooperation between the erstwhile foes might have been purely speculative, but economic coordination between the two was definitely in the offing. The First Vice President of Iran, Dr Hassan Habibie, accepted an invitation to undertake a state visit to Iraq in the autumn of 1998 for the purpose.

The above views of President Khatami are reflective of Iran's bitterness over its own follies and reminds one of a statement by a western leader during the conflict that the only bad thing about the Iran–Iraq war was that it would some day come to an end.[180] Apart from pumping the bulk of petro-dollars into the coffers of the flourishing global arms producing and trading cartels, the war served apparently no other purpose. The final count

showed 1 million dead, 1.7 million displaced, and a loss of $300 billion from both sides. And finally, what the UN resolution 598 offered was the same, if not much less than what all the OIC resolutions had been offering since 1980. Certainly, neither Iran nor Iraq had gained anything or got any better terms, by spurning all the OIC mediation efforts during the eight-year-long war.

(iii) The Mauritania–Senegal dispute: A scuffle took place between the Mauritanian shepherds and Senegalese peasants in the village named Jawwara, situated on the Senegal–Mauritania border, on 9 April 1989. The situation took an ugly turn when ethnic riots engulfed both the countries. The life and property of Senegalese expatriates were attacked in Mauritania while the Mauritanian nationals residing in Senegal also became victims of wanton killings and arson. On 26 April, no less than 740 casualties were reported from both sides. Two days later, Senegal's President Abdou Diouf lodged a strong protest with Mauritania for, what he called, inhuman atrocities on Senegalese nationals in Mauritania. He accused the Mauritanian law-enforcing agencies of complicity, and threatened reprisals if this involvement was conclusively proved. In his rejoinder, the Mauritanian leader Muawiya Taeh described the violence as the result of a conspiracy, accused Senegal of masterminding the plot and demanded compensation for the loss of Mauritanian lives. Tensions heightened and hostilities broke out as each of the two countries started the evacuation of their citizens from the other country with the help of Morocco, France, and Spain.[181]

The OIC decided to intervene in the dispute, as was evident from the statement of the OIC Secretary General Dr Hamid al Gabid which he issued on the OIC's behalf. He said that the OIC would play its role to resolve the conflict and restore normalcy. He wrote letters to the two heads of state requesting them to put an end to the conflict. The OIC appealed to the two states to enter into negotiations with the objective of arriving at an amicable settlement.

In addition, the OIC Chairman, Sheikh Jabber al Sabah, Amir of Kuwait, sent his Foreign Minister as his special envoy to Dakar and Nuakchatt. He met the two Presidents separately and conveyed the messages of the OIC Chairman asking them to reduce tensions. He later disclosed that both the leaders had expressed their willingness to bury past bitterness and open a new page in their relationship.

On 12 May, Musa Tarawari, President of Mali, visited Senegal and Mauritania and succeeded in persuading both states to avoid hostile accusatory statements, to withdraw their troops 10 km behind the border, and to initiate direct negotiations. The interior ministers of the two countries duly met in Bamako, capital of Mali, to start direct talks. Thereupon, the OIC left the entire theatre to the Organization of African Unity.

Though, the OIC rarely intervenes in regional conflicts that fall under the purview of other organizations, its interest in the conflict might have been the outcome of the personality factor. Dr Gabid, an ex-Prime Minister of Niger, who had taken over as the OIC Secretary General a few months earlier had rich experience in dealing with the African affairs. He was instrumental in involving the good offices of the Islamic Conference to end 'all forms of hostilities' between two Muslim-majority African states. In any case, the OIC role was limited as it did not offer mediation or give specific proposals for a lasting settlement when a truce had been effected. This was left for the OAU to accomplish.

(iv) The Iraq–Kuwait Crisis: The Iraqi economy had never recovered from the ravages of the Iran-Iraq war. The Iraqi regime was looking for scapegoats as the economic hardships of the common man increased when the oil prices continued to decline. From May 1990, Iraq started accusing Kuwait of exceeding her oil production quotas as determined by the OPEC. Dumping the oil market with extra quantities means a fall in oil prices, and even a small fluctuation, Iraq claimed, affected its revenues terribly. In July, relations seriously deteriorated when Iraq publicly accused Kuwait of 'stealing' its oil, by pumping oil from the southern part of Iraq's Al-Rumeila oil fields. Kuwait responded by saying that the decline in oil prices was not solely its responsibility, and as for exceeding OPEC ceiling quotas, nine states were doing so and it was improper, on the part of Iraq, to single out one state for criticism. Till then, the

Iraq–Kuwait border had not been demarcated and Kuwait was of the view that the geological layers of Rumeila field extended into Kuwaiti territory and Kuwait was producing oil from well inside its border with Iraq. The Amir of Kuwait charged that it was not Kuwait but Iraq which had made territorial encroachment by trying to dig wells inside Kuwait.[182]

Both the countries had agreed not to approach the UN for solving the dispute since they were two 'brotherly' states. The medium chosen so far for the exchange of memoranda and counter-memoranda, accusations and counter-accusations was the Arab League and not the OIC. With the mediation of some Muslim countries, notably Egypt and Saudi Arabia, talks were held in Jeddah where Kuwait agreed to reduce its oil production and write off the $15 billion war debt that Iraq owed it. But the latter then increased its price and demanded a virtual re-negotiation of land and maritime boundaries.[183] Though, there was some haggling over peripheral issues like Iraq's proposed water supply to Kuwait and Kuwait–Basra air passage etc; the primary deadlock was over Iraq's 'request' to Kuwait to grant it another $10 billion as loan immediately, as well as to cede part of its maritime borders including Bubian islands to Baghdad. On Kuwait's refusal the talks collapsed on 31 July 1990, and within 48 hours, the Iraqi forces had overrun Kuwait.[184] Apparently, Iraq had already made up its mind to solve its economic problems by seizing the Kuwaiti wealth. There can hardly be another explanation for Iraq's uncompromising, if not absolutely domineering, attitude at the 'negotiations'.

The period of occupation: The 19th ICFM (Cairo; 1990) was in session when the Iraqi invasion took place. The Conference set aside the remaining agenda and discussed the grave situation. The sessions of the conference were then frequently adjourned as the Arab Foreign Ministers held their separate meetings and finally the Conference was extended by one day. In its final declaration, the conference strongly condemned the Iraqi occupation of Kuwait and called for immediate, unconditional, and complete withdrawal of all Iraqi forces and the restoration of the legitimate government of Kuwait (headed by the incumbent OIC Chairman) before 12 August, at the latest.[185] The Conference also took note of the Iraqi announcement of its intention to withdraw soon. Jordan, Mauritania, Palestine, Sudan, and Iraq itself, did not support the resolution of condemnation, while Djibouti, Libya, and Pakistan called for caution in totally antagonizing one of the parties to the conflict that could, and eventually did, compromise the Organization's neutral role in conflict resolution.[186]

If the Iraqi version is to be believed, Iraq had sent troops ostensibly in response to the request of the Revolutionary Government of Free Kuwait, that had overthrown Sheikh Jabber al Sabah's rule a few hours earlier (notice the similarity with Moscow's official position regarding its military invasion of Afghanistan). Iraq also pledged to withdraw its forces as soon as the conditions allowed.[187] But, ignoring the ICFM resolutions, and contrary to its own undertakings, Baghdad annexed Kuwait a few days later, again using the pretext that the free government had requested the merger. The so-called free government, if it did exist at all, was said to be headed by a son-in-law of the Iraqi President Saddam Hussein. The OIC coordination meeting at New York on 3 October 1990, rejected the annexation as inadmissible under Islamic as well as international laws and declared it null and void. The OIC had earlier hinted that the timetable of the 6th Islamic Summit scheduled for January 1991 would remain unaffected, but when the UN 'resolution 678 (29 Nov. 1990) authorized the use of force to vacate Kuwait after 15 January 1991, a date coinciding with the Islamic Summit schedule, the OIC announced postponement of the Summit *sine die*.

As the deadline approached, there was hectic activity by several Muslim states to seek OIC's intervention in averting bloodshed. In the first week of January, Iran, Pakistan, and Turkey formally called for an urgent Islamic conference to consider the escalation of the crisis in the Gulf.[188] The anti-Iraq group of nations, with Egypt and Saudi Arabia in the forefront, thwarted all moves to convene an extraordinary Islamic Summit or ICFM. Their money and American manpower (Iraq always termed the US troops as 'mercenaries' and 'paid murderers'), was to solve the problem on their terms. The BBC also reported that

Pakistan, Iran, and Malaysia would fail to muster the required two-third majority to hold an OIC moot. The OIC Secretary General met with several OIC Foreign Ministers to fathom the level of interest for an emergency meeting. On 8 January 1991, he chaired an OIC meeting in Jeddah that considered the feasibility of an extraordinary ICFM session at that point in time. However, nothing came out of it.

Just one day before the war, the OIC Secretary General made a fervent call to Iraqi President Saddam Hussein to comply with the UN/OIC resolutions and vacate Kuwait. He assured the President that the OIC would then be willing to use its influence to help solve all outstanding disputes between Iraq and Kuwait, in 'the spirit of cooperation and brotherhood'. In his historic letter, Dr Hamid al Gabid drew the attention of President Hussein to 'the time of bitterness and anguish for the Muslims', and reminded him of 'the brotherhood of Islam' and the 'exigencies of Justice'. Gabid beseeched the Iraqi High Command to respond to 'the requests of millions of [Muslim] men and women...to avert bloodshed between two Muslim countries'. 'For the sake of the lofty values of Islam and for the sake of the highest interests of the Muslim nations', the OIC chief urged 'His Excellency to prevent war, which would lead to incalculable consequences towards our people and our future generations'. Baghdad ignored the OIC pleadings, all the same.[189]

The second Gulf war began on 16 January and it was unique in the sense that the war was not fought on the front. The US Air Force was busy in relentless bombardment of Iraqi territory while Iraq was responding by launching Scud missile attacks on Israel. The direct engagement of ground forces of the two sides in the legitimate theatre of war, the territory of Kuwait, did not take place until the final ninety-six hours of the war.

The first week of the war was characterized by hectic diplomatic activity by several Muslim leaders. The then Speaker of the Iranian Parliament, Mehdi Karoubi, presented his 5-point formula that envisaged simultaneous withdrawal by 'all aggressors' in the Middle East.[190] Pakistani Prime Minister Nawaz Sharif propounded his proposals for a resolution of the crisis under the OIC framework and visited several Middle Eastern countries to hold talks with the Muslim leaders.[191] The Iranian and Pakistani proposals did figure in the consultations among various Muslim leaders but the OIC Secretary General was not encouraged to launch a meaningful initiative, or perhaps he too felt helpless. Iran's President Rafsanjani expressed regret that the OIC had failed the Islamic nation on the occasion. Iraq remained sceptical of any meaningful role on the part of the OIC.[192] The OIC never opposed the UN enforcement measures but was sympathetic to Baghdad's protestations that respect to territorial integrity of member-states could not be applied selectively. The OIC urged the UN to implement its resolutions on Palestine as well.[193]

As the pressure on the OIC built up to break its silence on the ongoing war, a bureau meeting of the Islamic Conference was convened reluctantly at Cairo on 21 February 1991. It was attended by Egypt, Gabon, Maldives, Pakistan, Palestine, Saudi Arabia, Senegal, Turkey, and Kuwait's government-in-exile. Nothing productive came out of it. The OIC Foreign Ministers reiterated that Palestine was the primary Islamic cause but rejected Iraq's linkage of the occupation of Kuwait with Palestine. The meeting expressed solidarity with the (Jeddah-based) exiled government and the people of Kuwait, and simply reiterated all its previous demands—for Iraq to respect all the OIC and the UN resolutions and vacate Kuwait unconditionally.[194] Within days, Iraq shed its defiance and for inexplicable reasons suddenly ordered its forces to withdraw. The hundreds of thousands of Iraqi troops ran back in chaos. The US Air Force started unabated carpet bombing of the fleeing troops on the Kuwait–Basra Road and all but 12,000 Iraqis perished *en route*. On 27 February 1991, Kuwait was liberated.

OIC and the UN sanctions on Iraq: It could hardly have been anybody's guess that the UN sanctions on Iraq would remain in force till the turn of the decade. The OIC on its part kept playing the UN's tune in demanding Iraq's full compliance with all the relevant UN resolutions. Just a few months after the war, Iraq failed to raise the issue of UN sanctions at the 20th ICFM (Istanbul; 1991) which was marred with differences over whether or not to condemn Iraq. The Iraqi delegation listened in

dead silence when the Turkish President Turgat Ozal blasted Iraq for its adventurism. The Conference condemned Iraqi 'aggression' and demanded its full compliance with the UN resolutions. Though it expressed 'sympathy with the genuine sufferings of Iraqi people' resulting from the UN embargo, it held the 'Iraqi government fully responsible for their plight'. The Iraqi press called it a 'calamitous and scandalous event'.

Iraq then boycotted the forthcoming 6th Islamic Summit (Dakar; Dec. 1991) dubbing it a 'theatre to peddle suspect US policies against Iraq'.[195] The memories of war were still afresh when the Dakar Summit met. Twelve key Arab leaders, belonging to pro-Kuwait alliance stayed away from the Summit, apparently to protest the presence of Palestinian President Yasser Arafat and Jordan's King Hussein who had supported Iraq during the war. The Secretary General of the Islamic Council of Europe, Saleh Azzam, related harrowing details about the miseries of Iraqi children due to the shortage of food and medicine but the Conference could not be moved in favour of Iraq.[196]

Nothing new came out of this Summit regarding Iraq except a proposal by the OIC Secretary General for creating a conflict resolution set-up within the OIC so that occupation by one Muslim state of another would not be repeated. Needless to say, Kuwait was the first to endorse this call.[197]

Just before the 21st ICFM (Karachi; 1993), Baghdad sent a special envoy to Islamabad to win its support for the lifting of the UN sanctions against Iraq. Pakistan, deemed to be a neutral country in all intra-Islamic disputes, was the Chairman of the UN Security Council and that of the ICFM, at that time. Whatever sympathy Pakistan might have had for the Iraqi sufferings, it was overwhelmed by the anti-Iraq faction at the ICFM. Speaking at the plenary session, Iraqi Foreign Minister Saeed al Sahaf, criticized the OIC for its 'words without meaning and resolutions we know will not be implemented'. He insisted that Iraq had implemented all the UN resolutions and requested the support of the Conference for lifting of sanctions. He demanded that the Islamic Conference should concern itself with the plight of Muslim people and suggested that it was due to the policies of external powers that the OIC had failed.[198]

The next year at the 7th Islamic Summit (Casablanca; 1994), Iraq launched another abortive bid for the OIC to review its stance on Iraq. The Conference did not adopt a resolution 'commending Iraq for its full compliance with the UN resolutions', as Iraq had been requesting.[199] The next three years saw several UN–Iraq crises. Every other week, the two sides differed over the interpretation of UN Arms Inspectors' mandate and Iraq's responsibility to cooperate. There was one stand-off after the other. Sometimes Iraq and the US came to the brink of another war. The Americans kept accusing Iraq of hiding its chemical and biological weapons from UN arms destruction teams while Iraqis kept complaining that tens of thousands of infants were dying each year due to malnutrition and disease caused by the sanctions. For the most part, OIC behaved like an indifferent observer. Finally, it was at the end of 1997, that the OIC called for an end to the economic embargo on Iraq as 'it had lasted long enough'. The public call, made by the OIC Secretary General Izzeddienne Laraki at Riyadh, also stressed the need to 're-examine all the causes of the suffering of Iraqi people.'[200]

The extraordinary session of the Islamic Summit (Islamabad; March 1997) was widely flayed by public opinion in the Muslim states for ignoring the crisis in Iraq. So the 8th Islamic Summit (Tehran; Dec. 1997) showed concern with the problem and adopted two resolutions on Iraq. One affirmed that Iraq should fulfil its obligations towards the United Nations while the other reaffirmed the OIC's commitment to Iraq's security and integrity, and rejected any foreign intervention in Iraq that infringed on the inviolability of Iraqi borders.

In February 1998, Iraq and the United States again found each other on a collision course when Baghdad refused cooperation with the UN weapons inspectors (mostly Americans) to inspect its presidential palaces, on the grounds that it was a violation of her sovereignty. Tension gripped the region as the American forces flexed their muscles in preparation for major air raids on Iraq. The OIC opposed the imminent US attacks or any other

'efforts aimed at violating the territorial sovereignty of Iraq'. The Secretary General, Laraki, believed that recourse to force would 'complicate the crisis and expose the region to serious dangers'. On the directives of the OIC Chairman, President Khatami of Iran, he started mediation efforts between Iraq and the UN. The OIC Chairman himself also made contacts with the Muslim leaders to seek their cooperation in diffusing the crisis. However, the 23 February Iraq–UN accord at Baghdad averted the threat of an imminent war, at least temporarily.

In the Iraq–Kuwait conflict, there was no possibility of a positive contribution from the OIC as it was *ab initio* siding with one of the parties. It never tried to employ any of the means like mediation, good offices etc., given in the OIC Charter and declarations, to resolve the conflict. Instead, it become a mouthpiece for the Saudi–Kuwaiti position and kept arguing with Iraq on their behalf. The OIC's lopsided demands alienated Iraq. A point can be made here that this failing was not a fault of the Organization itself. Actually it was never allowed to work. The exigency of the grave circumstances called for an extraordinary Islamic Summit or an ICFM; but since a good number of member states were party to the conflict, they torpedoed the Pakistan–Iran efforts to garner a two-thirds support, required for the convening of such a conference. Even the scheduled regular Islamic Summit was postponed. The rivalries among the Middle East leaders were so strong that no one was willing to let go an opportunity to settle scores with others. The OIC homilies on Muslim brotherhood could have been heard at a later date; so it was marginalized for the given time.

Its role in the Iraq–Kuwait dispute, was the weakest ever played by the Islamic Conference. Neither a semblance of neutrality, nor pretence of concern for the suffering of a Muslim (Iraqi) people, was discernible. It was one of the greatest crises that the Muslim world faced in the latter half of the 20th century and the OIC could not be found centre-stage. The OIC became one of the casualties of the second Gulf war.

Muslim Minorities

In its nascent years, the OIC was careful not to consider the problem of Muslim minorities for fear of annoying the states concerned. The first time that the plight of a Muslim minority came up for consideration was at the 3rd ICFM (Jeddah; 1972) when a report on the condition of Muslims of Southern Philippines was presented. At the same conference, the OIC decided to prepare a statistical index on Muslims living in non-member states.[201] Through another resolution, the Conference noted that 'Muslim minorities in some countries do not enjoy the political and religious rights guaranteed by international law and norms'. The Conference appealed to the countries with Muslim minorities 'to respect those minorities and their culture and beliefs and grant them their rights in accordance with the UN Charter and the Universal Declaration of Human Rights'.[202]

The following year, at the 4th ICFM (Benghazi; 1973), on the instigation of the host state, Libya, the Conference deliberated on ways and means of ameliorating the sufferings of the Muslims of South Philippines and of Burma. Besides a request made by the Moro National Liberation Front of Philippines at this conference for grant of an observer status, Mohammad Jaffar Habib, Chairman of the Rohingya Patriotic Front, also mooted such a request on behalf of the Burmese Muslims. There ensued a vigorous argument as some countries asked the Conference to desist from taking up any issue which constituted an internal affair of a sovereign nation state.[203] Though the two requests were declined at the time, but the determination of the ICFM to go ahead with the task of finding amicable solutions to the crises, opened up a new chapter in the legal and political history of the OIC.

Though the Muslim minorities have no status in the OIC Charter, neither are they represented in the OIC structure, the OIC could not resist coming to the help of persecuted Muslim communities, particularly when the latter had no other recourse. This placed the OIC in a unique position, impelled to defend the rights of co-religionist ethnic communities in non-member states—a thing not expected of other regional organizations like the NAM or the OAU. Even the European Union started taking serious interest in the protection of ethnic minorities in non-member sovereign states, a couple of decades later. As for the OIC, without deviating from its principle of respect to state sovereignty, it fully exploited the Universal Declaration of Human Rights to the advantage of those it supported. Since 1973, the issue of Muslim minorities has appeared on the agenda of each and every OIC conference in one form or the other. But whether it be the issue of the Muslims of Philippines, Thailand, Cambodia, or those of Kashmir, all the OIC resolutions start by accusing the concerned state of violating the universal human rights declaration. In dealing directly with the central government of a non-Muslim State, the OIC acknowledges its sovereignty and argues on the behalf of the Muslim community, to demand their basic rights or, (if the case calls for it), autonomy for them. The OIC has never, except for Kashmir, argued for the right of secession.

The 6th ICFM (Jeddah; 1975) entrusted the General Secretariat 'with the task of preparing a comprehensive study of the conditions of Muslim minorities and communities throughout the world'. The study found the conditions of Muslims, in some cases, 'unacceptable'.[204] While at the 7th ICFM (Istanbul; 1976), the then WMC Secretary General Dr Inamullah Khan also presented a report on the subject.[205] The 8th ICFM (Tripoli; 1977) likewise expressed 'concern at the inhuman treatment meted out to Muslim minorities in some countries' and asked the Secretary General to carry out a new and extended survey of the matter. It also called on the governments concerned to 'ensure full respect for the legitimate...rights of Muslim minorities' while asking the Muslim states to 'manifest support...to the people under the yoke of colonialism and racism.'

The 9th ICFM (Dakar; 1978) decided to establish within the General Secretariat a Department of Muslim Minorities, to be headed by an ASG (Legal and Minorities Affairs), and approved the $0.5 million for the first year of its activities.[206] The 11th ICFM (Islamabad; 1980), while recognizing that one-third of the Muslim *ummah* lived in non-member states, formed a ministerial committee, comprising Tunisia, Senegal, and the OIC Secretary General, mandated to prepare recommendations for the well-being of

Muslim minorities. The next two ICFMs requested the Secretary General to report on the implementation of the recommendations of the committee and entrusted him with the responsibility of holding seminars and symposia on the subject of Muslim minorities to inform the world opinion about their miserable conditions.[207]

The 5th Islamic Summit (Kuwait; 1987) approved a draft resolution on Muslim minorities whereby the Islamic Conference decided to shoulder the responsibility for the protection of the Muslim communities' rights. The resolution went on to ask the concerned governments to 'ensure the full enjoyment of all legitimate rights' by the Muslim minorities in their respective countries, so that their bilateral and multilateral relations 'with the Muslim states are not jeopardized'. Three years later, the then OIC Secretary General, Dr Hamid al Gabid, stated that he would use his influence on the following Islamic Summit to make allowance for the OIC to regularly invite the representative delegations of the largest Muslim minority communities, notably from India and China, to attend the OIC conferences. Gabid eventually failed to carry through his ideas.

As in the case of crisis management in other areas, the role of the Islamic Conference with regard to the plight of Muslim minorities has been selective and tentative. Before moving to our case studies, let us define the term 'Muslim Minority'. For our purpose, we borrow Kettani's definition of Muslim minority as being 'the Muslim community of a state that is not a member of the OIC [irrespective of the share of Muslims in the total population]'.[208] Human history is replete with instances of persecution of ethnic and religious minorities; the Muslim minorities are no exception. Broadly speaking, the Muslim minorities can be categorized as follows:

a. Muslims in Philippines, Kashmir, Eritrea etc., minority in the broader context but a majority in a particular part of a non-Muslim country, who are waging a secessionist struggle.
b. Muslims in Bulgaria, India, and Burma (now Myanmar) etc., where they are allegedly persecuted as a result of an unconscious (as in the case of India)

or a conscious (as in the case of Bulgaria) state policy.
c. Muslims in the liberal developed world like the US, UK, France etc., mostly consisting of Third World immigrants and recent converts, where they claim to be discriminated against.
d. Muslims in Cambodia, Liberia, and Sri Lanka etc. where they are politically marginal and are perforce victims of civil wars. Accused of siding with the rival side, the Muslims at times bore the brunt of the fury of Sinhalese troops and Tamil rebels in Sri Lanka; the forces of the warlords, Charles Taylor and Dr Samuel Doe, in the Liberian civil war in the early 1990s; and of the Pol Pot's guerrillas in Cambodia in the late 1970s.
e. Muslims in Korea, South Africa, and most of Latin America where they constitute a very small percentage of the population. The problems of Muslims there, are cultural and educational and not political. Cut off from the mainstream Muslims, these minorities are facing cultural assimilation with the respective majorities for want of Islamic schools, qualified clerics, religious literature, and proper organization.

The OIC played an active role in the Philippines and Kashmir problems (our case studies in category A) but left the Eritrean struggle to the purview of the Organization of African Unity, save for occasional resolutions expressing support to the right of self-determination of the Muslim people of Eritrea. In category B, the OIC role was truly selective. Though, it took interest in the plight of Muslims in Bulgaria and India (our case studies), but the plight of Muslims in stronger countries like China (Eastern Turkistan region) and the ex-USSR was never taken up for discussion.

For reasons, better known to itself, the OIC has been pusillanimous in dealing with the persecution of Muslims in the Indo–China region, particularly the Arakan region in Myanmar. The support has mostly been confined to verbal expressions of concern and solidarity. For instance, when the OIC Fact-Finding Mission on the Burmese Muslims presented its report to the OIC Secretary General in March 1992, he publicly condemned Rangoon for, what he called, the 'campaign of repression and persecution of Muslims, launched by the Burmese authorities', and urged the OIC states to help the victims. It is not known which of the Muslim states and to what extent had responded to this call. In any case, the matter was not pursued properly. As for category C, the OIC has limited itself to criticizing, what it calls, the discrimination against Muslim immigrants in Europe.[209] The activity of the Conference, regarding the last two categories is conspicuous by its absence. We shall discuss the OIC role with respect to Filipino, Kashmiri, Bulgarian, and Indian Muslims.

A (i) Philippines: Muslims constitute around 12 per cent of the total population of the Philippines but most of them are concentrated in the Southern thirteen provinces spread over the Mindanao island and the four archipelagos of Basilan, Palawan, Sulu, and Tawitawi. The Moro Muslims, as they are called, have long been complaining of being treated as second class citizens. To please the Catholic majority, they allege, the doors of senior positions in the country's political, judicial, military, and civil hierarchy have been closed to them. The statistics regarding Muslim representation in the state structure do not belie these accusations. A firebrand speaker since his student days in early 1970s, Nouri Misauri, founded the Moro National Liberation Front (MNLF) and launched an armed insurgency. He was, or so it was believed, being financed by at least one Muslim state and some Islamic philanthropist organizations.

The case of Filipino Muslims was the first problem regarding the Muslim minorities that came up before the OIC. The 3rd ICFM (Jeddah; 1972) expressed concern over the 'plight of Muslims living in Philippines' and felt the need to 'seek [the] good offices of the government of Philippines to guarantee the safety and prosperity of Muslims there as citizens of that country'.[210] The following year, at the 4th ICFM (Benghazi; 1973), the OIC expressed deep concern over the continuation of what it now referred to as a genocidal campaign by the Filipino government against the Muslims in the Southern Philippines. It decided to send a delegation composed of the foreign ministers of Libya, Saudi Arabia, Senegal, and Somalia to Manila to discuss the problem. It also appealed to

peace-loving states and religious and international authorities to use their good offices with the Philippines government in order to halt the campaign

of violence against the Muslim community in the Philippines and ensure its safety and the basic liberties guaranteed by the Universal Declaration of Human Rights...

In addition, the Conference requested the member states, Indonesia and Malaysia, to use their good offices for the same purpose in the Association of South East Asian Nations (ASEAN).[211] The ICFM also established a Philippines Fund to support the Filipino Muslims.

The OIC resolution went even deeper into the problem at the next ICFM (Kuala Lumpur; 1974). In addition to expressing 'deep anxiety over the situation prevailing among the Filipino Muslims', it urged 'the Philippine government to find a political and peaceful solution through negotiations with the Muslim leaders, particularly with the representatives of the Moro National Liberation Front (MNLF), in order to arrive at a just solution to the plight of the Filipino Muslims'. It also called upon the government to 'halt organized Christian immigration from the North, intended to change the demographic structure of the South of the country'.[212]

The four-member OIC ministerial mission, which later became the OIC Permanent Committee on the Philippines, undertook a trip to Manila and succeeded in convincing President Marcos' regime to sit on the negotiating table with the MNLF. On 28 January 1975, President Marcos sent a delegation to Jeddah to apprise the OIC Secretary General of his government's position. Manila also accepted the good offices of the OIC on an issue that it had theretofore considered an internal matter. In return, the OIC elicited a pledge from the MNLF leadership, at the 5th ICFM, to drop the call for total independence and settle for regional autonomy. (Till then, the MNLF had been saying that the union of the Muslim areas with the Philippines had been artificially brought about during the American colonial rule over the country, and hence should be nullified).[213]

The 6th and 7th ICFMs noted with satisfaction the pace of negotiations that culminated in the Tripoli Accord on 23 December 1976, whereby autonomy was promised for the thirteen Muslim-majority provinces in *accordance with the Philippines constitution* (emphasis added). Libya, as the head of the OIC mission on the Philippines, signed as witness. The details of the autonomy plans were to be worked out later by the two sides themselves, once the cease-fire took effect.[214]

But soon, the Manila government had second thoughts and it partially reneged from the pact, which was then implemented unilaterally according to its own interpretation. The government refused to grant autonomy to the three mineral-rich Muslim provinces. About the remaining ten, it was of the view that it had to consider the wishes of the Christian minority as well and, in any case, the Constitution demanded a referendum to be held to grant autonomy to any of the regions. Despite the protestations of the MNLF, the government went ahead with its plans to divide the ten provinces into two groups of five each and conducted a referendum to judge the public response to a certain set of proposals, which the MNLF believed were preposterous, about the future of the regions concerned.

There were a host of other serious disagreements. For instance, the Muslim population of the region was five million out of a total of 6.5 million according to the MNLF estimates while the government maintained that it was only three million.[215] Moreover, there was a deadlock over the power of taxation and levying royalties on mining firms.[216] The MNLF announced a boycott of the referendum. The Commander of Philippines Constabulary, Maj. Gen. Fidel Ramos (later President), visited Tripoli on 10 March 1977 to prevail upon Libya to use its influence on the MNLF not to boycott the referendum. Anyway, the referendum on 17 April 1977 was duly held, and according to official figures, 97.93 per cent of the voters rejected the MNLF demand for autonomy. The government reported a 75 per cent turnout, a figure disputed by the Muslims as well as by the foreign correspondents covering the ballot.[217] The MNLF cried foul, accusing the government of treachery with the Moro Muslims and the OIC. The latter was equally furious with Manila and assured MNLF of full backing.

In may, the 8th ICFM took place, coincidentally in Tripoli, which granted observer status to Filipino Muslims 'as an exception', and called for a fund to assist the Moro Muslims. Misauri reverted to his demand for complete independence.[218] Just three days after this conference, Marcos offered to negotiate again and offered some autonomy to thirteen provinces and eleven regions but the offer was turned down by the MNLF High Command. From July 1978, the MNLF resumed military operations. At this time, infighting broke out in the MNLF itself with the Abul Khair Alonto faction accusing the OIC of backing the Misauri faction.[219] The 10th ICFM (Feb; 1979) recognized the MNLF as the sole representative body of Filipino Muslims and declared that all aid to Filipino Muslims would be channelled through the MNLF.[220]

While the war continued, the OIC continued to express solidarity with the Filipino Muslims, giving them economic and humanitarian aid and providing them the opportunity to present their case on all international fora with the unqualified support of the Muslim bloc. The 16th ICFM (Fez; 1986) met in the wake of worsening political turmoil in the Philippines, as the mass agitation to topple President Marcos was gaining momentum. The meeting expressed 'indignation over the non-implementation of the Tripoli accord', pledged to continue the support to the Filipino Muslims, and expressed hope of getting a better deal for them, with any future political arrangement in Manila. In February 1986, a new government under President Corazon Aquino took office in Philippines. It showed keen interest in solving the Muslim problem, and sought the OIC's mediation in August 1986.

A summit was held between Aquino and Misauri in the Jolo island on 5 September 1986 and the talks which began resulted in the Jeddah Pact of 3 January 1987.[221] The Manila government repealed the earlier provision of Mindanao autonomy and promised greater liberty to all the twenty-three areas of the Bangsamoro region. The government pledged to work for the social uplift of the region. But the Manila talks, set to work out the details of the Jeddah Pact, broke down on 23 May.[222] The MNLF reverted to armed militancy. Just before the 18th ICFM (Amman; March 1987), the MNLF tried to gain advantage from Manila's snub to the OIC, and applied for full membership at the OIC. The MNLF delegations visited many Muslim states to garner support for their demand, and later claimed the backing of thirty-five of the then forty-eight member states of the OIC. To defuse the tension, the Aquino government offered renewed talks with the MNLF, which the latter's representative at the OIC, Dato Ibrahim Uy, rejected.

At this, the Filipino government hurriedly sent a delegation to Jeddah, led by a Muslim member of the Philippine's Congress (Parliament), Michael Mastura, to hold parleys with the officials at the OIC Secretariat. The delegation made its counter-claim that the OIC officials had given an assurance that the OIC wanted autonomy, not independence, for the Moro Muslims, and that the OIC would not accord full member status to the MNLF, at least at that point in time. Just two days prior to the ICFM, President Aquino signed into the law a Congressional Act, ushering in an autonomous Muslim region unilaterally. She also announced a fifty-five-member Regional Consultative Commission, which was to define and demarcate the structure and powers of the autonomous region. Though the MNLF rejected the plan, the gamble paid off for Manila, as the OIC deferred the decision on granting full membership to the MNLF, reciprocating the apparent sincerity shown by the Manila government. In August 1989, President Corazon Aquino once again unilaterally signed a law allowing plebiscite in the thirteen southern provinces in the following November. The MNLF rejected this as a bluff while the OIC declared the new move as being tantamount to a declaration of war. The Aquino administration rejected the OIC protest.[223]

Finally on 15 November 1991, the OIC Assistant Secretary General (Political Affairs) Ibrahim Bakr announced the resumption of the stalled peace talks.[224] This time again, the change of government in Manila, gave a new impetus to the peace process. In early 1992, the new government of President Ramos initiated the dialogue, with the good offices of the now-enlarged OIC Committee on the Philippines, comprising Bangladesh, Indonesia, Libya, Saudi Arabia, Senegal, and Somalia. The preliminary talks were held at Tripoli, Libya (Oct. 1992), and Cipanas in West Jawa, Indonesia (April 1993). Two interim agreements were reached in 1994 and 1995. By virtue of the latter, a general amnesty was granted to all the Muslim insurgents.[225] The Manila pact was signed on 2 September 1996 and autonomy was granted to the Muslim majority region immediately. An Autonomous Region of Muslim Mindanao (ARMM) was established in the South, and with the help of the OIC, a South Philippines Council for Peace and Development (SPCPD) was also set up. Gubernatorial elections followed soon, resulting in the victory of Nur Misauri. In a letter to the OIC Secretary General, Hamid al Gabid, President Ramos assured him that Manila would implement the agreement in good faith.[226] He publicly thanked the OIC for its good offices.[227]

Though some extremist factions of the local Christians as well as a splinter radical Islamist group (the MILF) rejected the accord, and the former carried out bomb explosions and street demonstrations against it, the implementation went on smoothly. The 24th ICFM (Jakarta; 1996) and the 8th Islamic Summit (Tehran; 1997) noted with satisfaction the successful outcome of OIC's twenty-four-year association with this problem. While felicitating the Filipino Muslims, the OIC accepted Misauri's request to help in re-construction and called upon the member states to extend all material help to the ARMM.

A (ii) Jammu and Kashmir: When the British quit the subcontinent in August 1947, after eighty-eight years of direct colonial rule, two sovereign states viz. India and Pakistan emerged. Under the agreed partition formula, all Muslim majority provinces were to go to Pakistan while the non-Muslim majority ones went to India. This formula was universally applied to all provinces of the undivided subcontinent, except for the state of Jammu and Kashmir, where India maintained that even the Muslim population wanted to accede to India. The two countries agreed to maintain a status quo pending a plebiscite to ascertain the wishes of the Kashmiri people. However, mutual mistrust soon resulted in the outbreak of hostilities in which India captured a substantial part of Kashmir. As the first Pakistan–India war of 1948 raged on, Pakistani forces recaptured several districts of the disputed region before the UN Security Council brokered a cease-fire. Its two famous resolutions of 13 August 1948 and 5 January 1949 provided for an immediate cease-fire, demilitarization of the

Kashmir State, and a UN-sponsored plebiscite in the region to ascertain the wishes of the Kashmiri Muslims about acceding to India or to Pakistan.

The UN appointed several plebiscite commissioners, but India and Pakistan kept bickering on the details. In 1963, India annexed the part of Kashmir under its occupation on a very untenable ground. While reneging from its pledge to the UN, to Pakistan, and to Kashmiri Muslims, about holding the plebiscite, India based its claim on the instrument of accession of a former Hindu prince of Kashmir who had been ousted in the Muslim insurgency in 1947. Pakistan responded sharply to the annexation and the indecisive war of 1965 erupted. Again in the Simla agreement of 1972, both countries agreed to resolve the Kashmir dispute amicably. Both countries continue to be locked in a bitter war of attrition over Kashmir for the last half a century.[228]

Pakistan has almost always referred to the Kashmir problem in all the OIC conferences. At the 2nd Islamic Summit (Lahore; 1974) held on its soil, Pakistan was not confident of mustering enough support to get a resolution on Kashmir adopted. So the Pakistani leader Z.A. Bhutto made only veiled references to the problem. The President of Azad Jammu and Kashmir (formed on the portion of the state 'liberated' by Pakistani forces in 1948 war that has its own government purporting to represent the whole Jammu and Kashmir state) was invited to the Lahore Summit. In his meetings with several Muslim leaders he explained the genesis of the problem.[229]

In January 1989, a mass uprising broke out in the Indian-held Kashmir which soon took alarming proportions. India claimed that Kashmir was now an integral part of India and that it would not accept third party mediation nor agree to a recourse to the International Court of Justice. It dubbed the insurgency as Pakistani-inspired terrorism. As the Indian forces' brutalities to suppress the movement started making headlines, and the Muslim countries became increasingly concerned, Pakistan felt that it was time to bring in the OIC. Pakistani Prime Minister Benazir Bhutto flew into a whirlwind tour of sixteen Muslim states to personally request the Muslim heads of state to support Pakistan on Kashmir at the OIC. The August of 1990 was one of the finest hours in Pakistan's diplomatic history

when the 20th ICFM (Cairo; 1990) adopted a resolution calling upon Pakistan and India to resolve the Kashmir problem in accordance with the relevant UN resolutions. It expressed concern over human rights violations of the Kashmiri Muslims and offered to send a good offices mission to South Asia.[230] The Prime Minister of Azad Kashmir, Mumtaz Rathore, welcomed the OIC's interest in the Kashmir dispute whereas India turned down the OIC mediation offer, saying Kashmir was a settled issue.

On 22 May 1991, Pakistan wrote to the OIC Secretary General drawing his attention to the escalation repressive activities of the Indian forces.[231] Consequently, the 20th ICFM (Istanbul; 1991) reiterated the previous OIC resolutions while calling upon the Secretary General to send a fact finding mission to Kashmir and report the findings to the next ICFM.[232] India refused visas to the members of the OIC fact finding mission on the grounds that OIC had no *locus standi* on Kashmir.[233] The mission, however, visited the pro-Pakistan state of Azad Kashmir in February 1993. It interviewed a large number of displaced persons and victims of Indian atrocities, now living in makeshift refugee camps in Pakistani-controlled territories. Mostly, it had to rely on secondary sources including despatches from foreign journalists and Amnesty International reports. The Mission's thirteen-page report was presented at the 21st ICFM (Karachi; 1993) which cited strong evidence to the effect that state terror, including custodial killings, unprovoked firing on unarmed protestors, molesting of Muslim girls before their male relatives, and inhuman torture and body mutilation, was rampant in the Indian-held parts of Kashmir and was being used as a consistent policy instrument.[234] The Secretary General's report at the ICFM recommended that Muslim states should review trade ties with India, impose a ban on the Indian labour force working in the Gulf Muslim states, support the Kashmiris' rights on all international fora, and use their influence over India to stop her from committing genocide.[235]

The Indian ambassador to Saudi Arabia, Ishrat Aziz, a Muslim, met the OIC Secretary General on 11 February, to convince him of his country's justification for not allowing the OIC Mission to occupied Kashmir, and reiterated that India had great respect for the OIC and that India cherished her relations with the Muslim states. The OIC then started toying with the idea of sending a mission to India, comprising 'friendly Muslim states' to prevail upon her to change her mind. A few months later, the OIC Secretary General while welcoming the scheduled India–Pakistan talks, reiterated that the OIC would continue to explore all possible avenues to support the Kashmiris.[236]

In the OIC annual coordination meeting at New York in October 1993, it decided to table a resolution on Kashmir at the 48th session of the UN General Assembly but later dropped the idea for want of the requisite support.[237] During the same year, a UN Human Rights Conference was held at Geneva. In her address there, the then Pakistani Prime Minister Benazir Bhutto accused India of murdering 60,000 innocent Kashmiri civilians in the previous four years and of destroying the economy of the state. She proposed that a UN fact-finding mission go to Kashmir to ascertain these allegations and sought OIC support in tabling such a resolution. India requested the OIC not to press for a UN Mission to occupied Kashmir. As a *quid pro quo*, it suggested that the OIC ambassadors in New Delhi were welcome to visit Indian-held Kashmir (India had earlier been rejecting permission to the OIC fact-finding mission to visit Kashmir) to ascertain the facts about the Kashmir situation. The compromise was accepted and announced by Iran as such. An Indian delegation visited the OIC Secretariat at Jeddah to work out the details.[238] Pakistan announced that the OIC, and not India, was to decide the composition of the mission. India started having second thoughts, and in April 1994, Assistant Secretary General Ibrahim Bakr publicly asked India not to renege from her promise.[239]

As the controversy had not died down, the OIC for the first time invited Kashmiri leaders from both sides of the cease-fire line to the 22nd ICFM. Before it could be held, Pakistan convened an extraordinary session of the ICFM at Islamabad in September 1994 to consider, *inter alia*, the deteriorating situation in occupied Kashmir. The Conference unanimously demanded a halt to massacres and state repression and constituted an OIC Contact Group on Kashmir.[240] The Secretary

General, several Muslim countries and the leaders of Pakistani Kashmir and those from the Indian-held Kashmir lambasted India in their addresses to the meeting. The 7th EICFM decided to constitute an OIC contact group on Jammu and Kashmir in order to stay informed on the crisis.

The following month, Pakistan again tried to table, from the OIC platform, a resolution on Kashmir in the first committee of the UN General Assembly. India took a 'calculated risk' by summoning twenty-six OIC ambassadors at the Foreign Ministry in New Delhi to warn them against supporting the Pakistani move.[241] Pakistan wanted twenty co-sponsors but soon the idea had to be abandoned as Pakistan was not sure of getting the requisite support.[242]

Meanwhile in India, there were apprehensions that the All Parties Huriyyat (Liberation) Conference, commonly known as the APHC, might form a government-in-exile, and on receiving a green signal from Pakistan, may apply for full membership in the OIC.[243] To pre-empt it, India has banned the participation of APHC delegations in OIC moots since early 1995. In retaliation, the 23rd ICFM (Conakry;1995) termed occupied Kashmir as a land under 'colonial occupation'.[244]

Since 1990, all the four Islamic Summits and all the ICFM/EICFMs have reiterated full support for Kashmiris' rights of self-determination, asked India to desist from human rights violations and to withdraw its troops from Kashmir, and called for a solution in accordance with the UN resolutions— the very reference which is anathema to India. The OIC and even its subsidiary cultural institutions especially the Islamic Commission for Economic, Cultural and Social Affairs (ICECS) have made it a point not to miss an opportunity to castigate India for particular incidents in Kashmir; like the burning of a Muslim shrine at Charar Sharif (May 1995), murder of human rights activist Jalil Adrabi (April 1996), reported incidents of gang rape (June 1997), and so on. The OIC Contact Group has so far held over a dozen meetings, which have helped in internationalizing the issue. The typical response of India on each of the plethora of OIC resolutions is that the OIC views are 'highly objectionable', 'aimed at prolonging Pakistani-sponsored terrorism', 'interference in domestic affairs', and 'touching an already settled issue'. India has always been regretting the 'vulnerability of the OIC to be misled by the vicious Pakistani propaganda and falsehood'.[245]

The Islamabad and Tehran Islamic Summits (March and Dec. 1997) reiterated all the previous OIC resolutions on the Kashmir question. The latter Conference asked India to accept the OIC good offices for the resolution of the problem, and urged the member states to influence India into allowing an OIC fact-finding mission to held Kashmir. The 25th ICFM (Doha; March 1998) also condemned India for the human rights violations of the Kashmiri Muslims and asked her to stop this 'state terrorism'.

The Kargil War: In the spring of 1999, the *Mujahideen*, as Pakistan calls the pro-independence fighters of the occupied Kashmir, belonging to various guerrilla outfits including the much-dreaded *Lashkar-e-Tayyabah* (literally: the holy army) captured several strategic heights in the North of held Kashmir, in the vicinity of a town called Kargil. India made it a point of prestige to recover the peaks wherefrom the Kashmiri irregulars were playing havoc with the Indian army units. Since the guerrillas were well-entrenched and well-positioned, all the Indian attempts to retake the peaks were resulting in heavy casualties for them.

Those were election times in India and the opposition parties took full political advantage of the fighting by embarrassing the ruling Hindu nationalists by accusing them of ineptitude and cowardice. The New Delhi government decided to employ the full might of their military and the Air Force to 'redeem the national honour' in the wake of the heavy reverses suffered by the regular army brigades at the hands of a few hundred irregulars. However, India maintained that the occupiers of the Kargil heights were regular Pakistani troopers, rather than Pakistani-backed Muslim fighters, a charge that Pakistan vehemently denied. As the pressure for the *Mujahideen* on the Kargil front increased to breaking point, Pakistan felt obliged to give artillery support to the fighters from well within its side of the cease-fire line. Thus, both countries inadvertently found themselves involved in the fourth war of the past fifty-two years. The war remained essentially a limited war as both the

sides made attempts at de-escalation at every juncture. The fruitless eleven-week conflict (6 May –18 July 1999) ended when Pakistan agreed to 'use its influence' over the *Mujahideen* to vacate the Kargil heights in order to avoid a full-fledged war between the two nuclear powers, which could have been catastrophic. The war ended in a status quo with both the sides claiming victory, but not before thousands of soldiers and hundreds of civilians had died in the conflagration.

The 26th ICFM (Ougadougou; 26 July 1999) took place while the war was raging with full fury. The host President, Blaise Compaore of Burkina Faso, expressed sympathy with Pakistan, as its Foreign Minister told him that Pakistan was a victim of Indian aggression. Most of the delegates who took the floor supported Pakistan's initiative in seeking a negotiated settlement of the Kashmir dispute. The ICFM was the only international forum which supported the Pakistani position, expressed concern over the escalation caused by the heavy Indian shelling and air strikes, lauded Pakistan's initiatives for defusing tension, urged India to respect the UN resolutions on Kashmir since Kargil hostilities had to be seen in the broader context of the Kashmir conflict, and finally affirmed 'complete solidarity with Pakistan in its efforts to safegaurd its sovereignty, political independence and territorial integrity' in the war.

The OIC also asked the Secretary General to appoint a Special OIC Representative on Kashmir. And lastly, the OIC call for the Nuclear Weapon Free Zones excluded reference to South Asia as Pakistan warned that it may consider using all options (i.e., its nuclear arsenal as well) for its security, were the war with India to escalate. Various other OIC organs also expressed sympathy with Pakistan over the loss of lives. The IULA, for instance, condemned India for shooting down a Pakistan Navy reconnaissance aircraft, killing all the sixteen Naval officers and sailors on board, many days after the cease-fire had already come into effect.

As an endnote, it may be added that unlike the case of Philippines, the OIC does not recognize India's 1963 annexation of Kashmir and wants both countries to withdraw their troops from the state and agree to a UN-sponsored plebiscites so that the people of Kashmir, and not guns and bayonets, can decide the fate of Kashmir. The OIC also terms the inhuman treatment of Kashmiri Muslims by the Indian army as simply unacceptable. It also appreciates Pakistan's willingness to accept any kind of mediation, good offices, arbitration, adjudication or fact finding, by UN, OIC, or the ICJ, and to abide by the decision. The OIC deplores India's spurious intransigence at refusing every overture on the grounds that, for India, Kashmir was a settled issue and it would not even abide by the UN resolutions on Kashmir which it had earlier accepted. The OIC is also critical of the fact that India is bent upon holding on to a region whose predominantly Muslim population is hostile to the Indian rule, and that India is defying the UN resolutions since a plebiscite may, in all likelihood, give the whole of Kashmir to Pakistan.

B (i) Bulgarian Muslims: Muslims constitute 19.3 per cent of the population of Bulgaria. A substantial portion is of Turkish or Albanian origin. They have been living there for centuries, as their forefathers converted to Islam or settled there during the centuries of Ottoman rule in Europe. Like in other Communist states, religion was suppressed in Bulgaria too. As the organization and culture of Muslims was systematically destroyed, and religious rites prohibited, Turkey raised the issue of persecution of ethnic Muslims in Bulgaria at various international fora.

In 1985–86, a series of Muslim-specific discriminatory laws evoked a strong reaction from the OIC. On 14 March 1985, the then OIC Secretary General, Sharifuddin Pirzada, sent a message to the Bulgarian leadership, demanding a safeguard for the rights of the Muslim community in the country. He also called on the Muslim states, to exert their influence on Sofia, to protect the Muslim community there. On Turkey's request, the 16th ICFM (Fez; Jan. 1986) approved a resolution calling upon Bulgaria to halt the 'forced Bulgarization of its Muslim minority'.

As a follow-up to the 16th ICFM decision, in March 1986, the OIC Secretary General constituted a three-member committee, comprising Ambassador Umar Jha (Gambia), Dr Abdullah Omer Naseef (Muslim World League), and Justice Usman Ali Shah (Pakistan), entrusting it with the task of investigating the conditions of the Bulgarian Muslims. Ambassador Ahmet Ansay, the OIC representative to the United Nations, called upon Sofia to cooperate with the Committee. The report released a few months later was very unflattering towards the Bulgarian authorities.

As the OIC lodged a strong protest with Bulgaria over the Draconian law forcing Muslims to change their surnames (Bulgarianization of names), and asked Sofia to rescind the law, the Foreign Minister of Bulgaria, Peter Mladenov, wrote to his Pakistani counterpart Yaqub Khan on 27 January 1987, inviting an OIC mission to visit Bulgaria and see for themselves the falsehood of accusations regarding persecution of Bulgarian Muslims. 'Turkey is interfering in our domestic affairs and distorting the reality...[she] will try again to seek a condemnation of Bulgaria by the OIC at the 5th Islamic Summit', the letter added. Mladenov informed Khan that Islam was a respected religion in his country, all the mosques were open, and that the OIC leaders were particularly welcome to meet the Muslim representatives and their high clergymen, during their visit to Bulgaria.

The OIC formed a Contact Group on Bulgaria and sent a fact-finding mission to that country. The mission released its report to the 17th ICFM (Amman; 1988) which was convinced of the justification of all Turkish complaints about the persecution of Muslims.[246] The report recommended that the OIC express its concern over the plight of Muslims in Bulgaria; the OIC ambassadors in Sofia visit Muslim populated areas of Bulgaria; it raise the issue on all international fora, and threaten the Bulgarian authorities with the cessation of economic ties with Muslim states in case the condition of Muslim minority remained the same.[247] The Deputy Foreign Minister and Chairman of Committee of the Affairs of Orthodox Church of Bulgaria, Lyubomir Popov, said that this was an 'attempt to mislead the OIC and to place its prestige at the service of pan-Turk objectives'.[248] All these recommendations were more or less implemented.

The following year, the 18th ICFM (Riyadh; 1989) also blasted Bulgaria for its treatment of Muslims and asked her to fulfil her international obligations in this regard. Turkey's

Foreign Minister Mesut Yilmaz (later Prime Minister), unsatisfied by the language of the resolutions, lashed out at the OIC's reluctance to condemn Bulgaria and called for an attack on Sofia.[249] Prior to the ICFM, Secretary General Dr Gabid had met Popov in Jeddah wherein the latter had claimed that Muslims in Bulgaria were not ethnic Turk but rather Bulgarian citizens converted to Islam. He thus maintained that there was no question of discrimination.[250] But when the OIC went ahead with its resolutions, Bulgaria rejected them as interference in her domestic affairs.

On 26 June 1989, the OIC Secretariat issued a statement saying that the 'condition of Muslims in Bulgaria spotlights the international inability to take action against human rights violations by a state.' The Bulgarian policy, it added, was a 'medieval answer to the contemporary ethnic questions that continue to plague the modern nation-states'. Bulgaria lodged a protest over the 'harsh and unwarranted' tone of the OIC, but in the meantime many more Muslim states joined the chorus of rebuke. Kuwait, Tunisia, and especially Saudi Arabia criticized, what they called, Bulgaria's 'humiliating racist manner that contravenes the most basic humane norms and international charters'. On 24 July, the OIC endorsed Turkey's offer for a treaty that would 'organize voluntary emigration of the Muslims, being forcefully assimilated by the East European state', and called upon the world community to play its role in solving the crisis.

A few months later, Turkey reported that the condition of Bulgarian Muslims had not improved and requested a special ICFM session on this issue.[251] Though a special session could not take place, but the issue remained on the agenda of 20th and 21st ICFMs. The latter requested the Secretary General to undertake a visit to Bulgaria and report to the next ICFM.[252] Earlier in July 1990, the OIC expressed concern over the sharp deterioration of relations between Turkey and Bulgaria, and through its then Chairman, Jabber al Sabah, the Emir of Kuwait, offered to mediate between the two countries to avert a war. The matter, which was related to the oil exploration activities in the Adriatic sea got resolved amicably without international intervention as both the sides

showed maturity. In the meantime, Communism had fallen apart in the region and the post-communist regimes were not anti-religion. The condition of Bulgarian Muslims consequently registered improvement. The OIC's concern also diminished correspondingly.

B (ii) Indian Muslims: The statistics about the Muslims' share in India's 960 million population are highly controversial; different estimates put their figure anywhere between 12.5 to 20 per cent of the total.[253] This makes them the second largest Muslim community, of the world, after Indonesia. The primary Muslim grievances against the State are: one, discrimination in education, jobs etc; two, anti-Muslim riots resulting in colossal loss of life and property; and three, threat to their religious places and their culture. An analysis of any ten or so randomly taken variables such as literacy rate, poverty level, number of Muslims in higher income bracket, their proportion among civil or military officers, bankers, doctor, engineers, lawyers, or members of Parliament, in India, shows that the allegations about gross under-representation of Muslims are not totally unfounded.[245] Moreover, according to a modest estimate, around 20,000 incidents of anti-Muslim rioting have taken place in India since 1947, in a substantial number of which, the police force had remained a silent spectator.

The OIC concern with the Indian Muslims, excluding the Muslims of Kashmir (since the OIC does not recognize Indian annexation of the state), started as early as the 1st Islamic Summit (Rabat; 1969) where the Indian delegation was unceremoniously expelled when Pakistan cited the killing of 1000 Muslims in the ongoing anti-Muslim riots in the Indian city of Ahmadabad.[255] Since then, Pakistan has consistently raised the issue of Indian Muslims in the OIC, which has sometimes mildly rebuked India about the treatment of Muslims. The Islamic Development Bank (IDB) and the Islamic Solidarity Fund (ISF) have, on many occasions, provided assistance for a school, a hospital, or a social welfare set-up for the Indian Muslim community; the former has been generously providing scholarships to a number of Indian Muslim students for higher studies each year. The OIC organs in the cultural sphere, especially the ICECS have always raised their voice against the threats to Muslim historic monuments, forts, and mosques, by several fanatic Hindu outfits.

In 1989, several major bouts of anti-Muslim riots were reported and the OIC expressed grief over the loss of [Muslim] lives. On 11 November 1989, the Secretary General accused India of discrimination, saying that the 'religious and cultural rights of the Muslims are being trampled and non-cooperation is being exercised against the Indian Muslims'.

As with the other Muslim minority problems, the OIC came out boldly in favour of the Indian Muslims when the latter found themselves in a very grave situation. On 6 December 1992, a mob of Hindu fanatics razed to the ground the 462-year-old, historic Babri Mosque in the northern city of Ayodhya. In late 1940s, the Hindus had started claiming that emperor Babar, the founder of the famous Mogul dynasty, had built this mosque after demolishing a temple. Successive secular governments of India had guaranteed protection of this mosque to the Muslims. As the mosque fell, furious Hindu-Muslim riots engulfed virtually the whole of India resulting in 2000 deaths and loss of millions of dollars worth of property. As the Muslims all over India came out on the streets for demonstrations, they were mercilessly fired upon by the police. The former Indian Prime Minister, V.P. Singh acknowledged that 90 per cent victims of police firing were unarmed Muslims. India imposed a state of emergency in the whole country and promised to re-build the mosque soon. Pakistan rejected Indian promises and announced days of mourning. Violence soon spread to Pakistan, Bangladesh, Iran, UAE etc. where police found it difficult to control angry Muslim mobs attacking minority Hindu temples and trying to set ablaze Indian diplomatic missions. In Pakistan alone, forty persons lost their lives on the first day of violent and bloody protests.[256]

The OIC had been warning India since 1990 to protect the mosque, any damage to which was to be an act of provocation against the Muslims. On 7 December 1992 the very next day of the tragedy, the OIC Secretariat General issued a strongly-worded statement condemning the incident, accusing the Indian government of complicity by failing to take adequate security measures, and demanding the safety of lives and property of the Muslims.[257] On 8 December, the OIC group held an emergency session at New York which expressing its outrage over the Mosque demolition, demanded the punishment of those guilty, protection of Muslim lives, and immediate reconstruction of the mosque. The group decided to formally raise the issue at the United Nations.[258]

In January 1993, the 17th ICECS session at Jeddah, adopted condemnation resolutions with the same tone and tenor and asked India to combat the threat to Islamic heritage and ensure the protection of 3000 other mosques targeted by the Hindu extremists.[259] A couple of days later, the enlarged OIC Summit Bureau meeting (Dakar; 11 Jan.), also condemned the destruction of the mosque and denounced the massacre of Muslims and arson of their shops and houses. It asked the Muslim states to make effective and coordinated efforts to safeguard the Muslim holy places in the world. India, which had earlier asked the Dakar Bureau not to comment on her internal affairs, expressed regret over these pronouncements.[260]

The matter figured up again at the 21st ICFM (Karachi; April 1993) which reviewed the latest developments and considered imposing a ban on trade with India and on its manpower working in the oil-rich Muslim states. The Istanbul Centre of the OIC, called IRCICA, also expressed its 'outrage and profound anguish' over the 'martyrdom'(destruction) of the Mosque and warned about the security of 3000 other historical mosques in India, under threat from the followers of the idol-worshipping majority religion of India.

Since then, the OIC has closely monitored the plight of Indian Muslims. Though India has taken measures to obviate recurrence of anti-Muslim violence on such scale, but she has not honoured the promise to rebuild the mosque, nor does she seem to be inclined to do so. Every year, Muslims celebrate Babri Mosque Day on 6 December by street demonstrations all over India, and the OIC continues to remind India not to renege from her promises to and responsibilities towards the Muslim minority.

New Delhi is always irked by the OIC's concern over the Indian Muslims. Reacting to the resolutions of the 23rd ICFM (Conakry; 1995), a spokesman of the Ministry of External Affairs hoped that the OIC would in future refrain from, what he alleged, were 'unwarranted and unacceptable' references to India. According to him, India was 'proud of its Muslim population of over 130 million and its rich heritage of Islamic culture which was an integral part of the secular society of the country'.[261]

Domestic Political Problems

The OIC has faithfully adhered to the Westphalian concepts of state sovereignty and domestic jurisdiction, and has carefully avoided dabbling in the internal affairs of any member state.[262] But this has not deterred individual member states from raising issues regarding domestic political turmoils at home to defend their state policy on some controversial issue, or bringing up political crises in other countries, to score political gains by embarrassing a rival. In the former case, the OIC adopts a resolution expressing solidarity with (the government of) the affected country while in the latter case, the matter is ignored—not even included in the formal agenda.

The first time the OIC intervened in a domestic political crisis was in 1971 when Pakistan requested the OIC to use its influence to convince the opposition Awami League and its armed wing *Mukti Bahini*, to come to the negotiating table with the government. A delegation comprising the OIC Secretary General, Iran, and Kuwait visited East and West Pakistan and met the pro-government and anti-government politicians of both sides in 1971.

In 1979, the US cut off aid to Pakistan to punish her for pursuing a nuclear programme. The 10th ICFM (Fez;1979) immediately decided to consider sending aid to Pakistan, if the US decision resulted in serious economic problems for her.[263] The following year, Iran informed the 11th EICFM (Islamabad; 1980) about the conspiracies hatched by a super power against the Islamic revolution. The Conference passed a resolution expressing its respect for the right of the Iranian people to 'choose whatever system they prefer...(for) their social and political life'.[264] In 1996-97, the

Albanian government beset by opposition-led agitation, invoked moral support from the OIC; it was readily granted.

But on the other hand, when Libya tried to involve the OIC in the labour riots in Tunisia and the induction of French troops there, or when Iran tried to bring the issue of the ex-monarch's extradition on the ICFM agenda, the OIC showed no enthusiasm for it.[265] Similarly, the OIC has never offered to mediate between the ruling juntas of Algeria and Egypt and the opposition Islamist parties, locked in gory civil wars, for the simple reason that the *de facto* governments of these two states, the question of their legitimacy to rule notwithstanding, do not relish the idea of their domestic problems being discussed on OIC fora.[266]

The case of Sierra Leone was handled a bit differently. A *coup d'etat* against the elected civilian president, Ahmad Tejan Kabbah, a Muslim, brought a coterie of military officers led by Maj. Johnny Paul, a Christian, to power. This replacement was obviously not to the OIC's liking. The Organization refused to extend recognition to the new regime and called for President Kabbah's restoration.

The 8th Islamic Summit (Tehran; 1997) invited the ousted President Kabbah to represent his country. The Conference resolution no. 43/8-P (I.S) condemned the military takeover in Sierra Leone, called on the 'junta' to restore the government of Ahmad Kabbah, supported the ECOWAS' efforts including the mobilization of the forces to pressurize the military rulers to give in, and appealed to all Muslim states to make efforts for the 'restoration of normalcy' and that of the 'legitimate elected government of President Ahmad Kabbah' in Sierra Leone. (The Maj. Paul clique was overthrown within a year by the Nigeria-led ECOWAS troops and President Kabbah was restored.)

In this section, we have selected the OIC's concern with the Bhutto case in Pakistan (1977–79) as our case study, to illustrate the dilemmas and constraints faced by the Islamic Conference in dealing with the issues, that fall within the domestic domain of a member state against the will of the incumbent government. It was indeed one of the rare occasions when the OIC was tempted to over step a member state's sovereignty to save the life of its (i.e., the OIC's) Chairman.

The Bhutto Case: The behaviour of the OIC in the Pakistani crisis of 1977, which led to the overthrow and later execution of the then Prime Minister Zulfikar Ali Bhutto, though not of active participation, was not of complete indifference either. There were quite a few reasons for adopting this demeanour. For one thing, Zulfikar Ali Bhutto was a leader of international stature in the true sense of the word. He was the Chairman of the OIC at that time and had personal rapport with a number of Muslim heads of state and governments. Bhutto was the first ever directly elected leader of Pakistan whose charisma and oratory had swayed the masses in his country. His overt ambitions for acquiring nuclear weapons for Pakistan, his zeal for Islamic causes, his eloquence, and not the least, his bravado like tearing apart resolutions calling for Indo–Pak cease-fire, etc. were well-known.

The roots of the Pakistani crisis can be traced to the decision of the Prime Minister to dissolve the National Assembly twenty months ahead of the schedule and call for mid-term elections on 7 March 1977. Though it was a demonstration of self-confidence on his part, but the opposition parties were not going to let the opportunity go, and contested elections from a common platform named Pakistan National Alliance (PNA).[267] The final tally turned out to be a 137–36 lead, out of the 182 seats of the lower house of the Pakistani parliament contested, in favour of the ruling Pakistan People's Party. Thus, the main opposition alliance bagged only three dozen seats, while the rest went to independents and a smaller party.[268] The opposition cried foul and launched a street agitation, calling for fresh elections. The movement soon turned into a movement for strict enforcement of Islamic laws.

On 28 April, speaking on the floor of the parliament, Bhutto openly blasted the US for masterminding and financing the international conspiracy to penalize him, for his relentless pursuit of the nuclear option for Pakistan, a Muslim country.[269] His government's claims about the existence of an American conspiracy to topple it, enjoyed wide credence at that time. In these circumstances, Bhutto's decision to seek mediation

from the Muslim states in his stand-off with the opposition leadership, was widely hailed. In response, Kuwait, Libya, and the UAE called on the opposition parties to come to the negotiating table with the Prime Minister. Palestine's special representative Hani al-Hassan and Saudi ambassador Riadh al Khatib met the opposition leadership. And the latter remained a bridge between the government and the opposition till the end. Bhutto had thus involved the stakes of Muslim states in seeing an early resolution.[270]

In the meantime, the 8th ICFM (Tripoli; 1977) took place. It took note of the prevailing political crisis in Pakistan and addressed a message of solidarity to the Prime Minister of Pakistan, Zulfikar Ali Bhutto. It also adopted a resolution recalling the important decisions of the second Islamic Summit and the 'great contribution of the Government of Pakistan and the preponderant role of Prime Minister Bhutto, the current Chairman of the Islamic Summit, in this context'.

The Conference also expressed its 'profound concern' over the 'external manoeuvres directed against the Islamic Republic of Pakistan' and affirmed its solidarity with the Government and people of Pakistan in their efforts to 'thwart all foreign interference and to maintain and consolidate their national unity in their consistent attachment to the cause of Islam'.[271] Anyway, the mediation proved successful as Mr Bhutto virtually enforced all the Islamic laws being demanded, including prohibition of liquor and gambling, and accepted all but one of the thirty-two points in the Charter of demands of the opposition parties including fresh elections under an impartial administration. He then left for a tour of several Muslim countries to personally thank them for their support. But as fate would have it, the military struck and imposed martial law, on the promise of holding free and transparent elections within ninety days. The elections were never held, Bhutto was thrown into a death cell in an ordinary prison and, during the military rule, punishments reminiscent of those of the medieval ages were wrought on his supporters.

The OIC found itself in a big dilemma during the ongoing trial of Mr Bhutto, when neither the regard for his person by a number of Muslim leaders could be brushed aside, nor could the legality of the Pakistan's incumbent ruling military junta's representation at the Conference, challenged. A bigger irony was that it was not clear whether the 2nd Islamic Summit (Lahore; 1974) had elected Mr Bhutto or Pakistan, as the Chairman of the OIC. The Charter was silent on the matter. Mr Bhutto had maintained till the last that he was still the OIC Chairman (since the Lahore Islamic Summit had elected his person, not his country, as the OIC Chairman, or so he believed), and, in fact, many of the Muslim leaders referred to him as such, in their personal clemency appeals to the military ruler, Gen. Zia.[272]

At the 9th ICFM (Dakar; 1978), the intense lobbying by Gen. Zia's Foreign Affairs Advisor Agha Shahi succeeded in obviating the passage of a resolution expressing concern about Mr Bhutto's life.[273] Shah's was but part of a broader mission by the military junta, to prevent intercessions by friendly states on Mr Bhutto's behalf. The non-adoption of a resolution was because of subtle political considerations and expediency, but the Foreign Minister of Kuwait, Sabah al Ahmad, and many others remonstrated vigorously against the death sentence on Bhutto.[274] When Agha Shahi started expounding the Anglo–Saxon legal traditions of Pakistan and affirmed that the military government had a policy of non-interference with the judicial system, he was bluntly told by the Palestinian representative Abu Muzeir that the realities of courts and laws in dictatorial regimes of the Third World were well-known and Bhutto's trial was 'political and nothing else'. He went on to add that the American conspiracy to eliminate Bhutto had been designed to foil his efforts at making a nuclear bomb.[275] In his formal speech at the ICFM, the Palestinian Foreign Affairs Advisor Farook Kadoumy formally appealed for protecting 'the life and dignity of Zulfikar Ali Bhutto, *the present Chairman of the Conference*' (emphasis added).[276]

However, on 4 April 1979, Bhutto was executed unceremoniously after a highly dubious and controversial trial, on a minority judgement.[277] Mr Bhutto spurned the option of filing his clemency appeal to the military junta and preferred to go to the gallows. Meanwhile Gen. Zia remained adamant in signing the death warrant for Mr Bhutto, ignoring the 400 clemency pleas from virtually all over the world. The UN, the European Union, and scores of Muslim and non-Muslim heads of state had asked the General to show restraint.

Soon thereafter, the 10th ICFM (Fez; 1979) was to be held where again it fell upon Agha Shahi to lobby against the passing of a condolence or sympathy message on Mr Bhutto's tragic death, which Islamabad construed would be a criticism of the execution and thus a diplomatic setback.[278] The Conference in a marked departure from an established tradition of offering prayers on the demise of a Muslim statesman, let alone the Chairman of the OIC, did not send a condolence message to the Pakistani people. The OIC had succumbed to the pressure by the new regime. The OIC stood quiet at this final hour but French President Giscard d'Estaing publicly expressed 'deep emotion' over the death of Mr Bhutto, on behalf of the European Union.[279] However, some Muslim leaders sent individual condolences to the widow of the late statesman. In conclusion, it is notable that after Mr Bhutto's death, the OIC never again discussed Pakistan's domestic politics during the Zia era, though the military tribunals continued to award death penalties, public flogging and rigorous imprisonment sentences to the PPP supporters and the human rights and pro-democracy activists.

Contemporary Issues

Much has already been written on the OIC's policies on non-alignment, colonialism, racism, and similar issues during the past few decades. It cannot be gainsaid that the Organization has always stood for the principles of justice and freedom. It has struggled against racism and colonialism actively when the oppressed community were the Muslims, and passively otherwise. It is also fairly obvious that during the cold war, the Islamic Conference retained a posture of strict non-alignment towards the two super powers, nay, of antagonism, as one scholar puts it.[280] In fact, it was this very radical rhetoric in the OIC resolutions that distinguished it from other non-aligned organizations, particularly the NAM. In the early years, the unnamed super powers were indirectly condemned, but after the Camp David Accord (1978), both the United States and the USSR used to be referred to by name in the resolutions of condemnation. The presence of foreign forces in the Gulf and their eye on setting up of military bases in the Muslim countries, particularly irked the OIC, which warned the super powers to abstain from setting up such bases in Islamic territories 'under any form, pretext, cover or for any reason whatsoever'.[281]

In the new political landscape of the globe, since the end of the cold war, many of these issues have lost relevance, or at least, have receded from the limelight.[282] An attempt will be made here to explain the OIC's position on contemporary issues like human rights, terrorism, and nuclear non-proliferation and disarmament.

Human Rights: In its preamble, the OIC Charter mentions that its member-states are: *resolved* to preserve Islamic spiritual and ethical values, *committed* to the fundamental human rights, *determined* to protect the freedom of their people, and *endeavouring* to increase human well-being, security, justice and freedom. If read together, these articles mean that the OIC wants to promote human rights consonant with the ideals espoused by Islam; the OIC's commitment to the UN Charter, notwithstanding.

It cannot be over-emphasized that the UN Declaration on Human Rights and the Islamic value system are not fully congruent. By definition, a Muslim is one who surrenders to the will of Allah. For a Muslim, the will of Allah is expressed in the form of the Quran. So, ideally speaking, a Muslim's freedom of action is limited by the lines drawn by the holy book. While the West advocates absolute freedom of belief, speech, action, and movement; the Islamic countries cannot allow heresy, blasphemy, or for that matter, the right to have sexual relationship outside marriage. Thus in an Islamic polity, any law repugnant to the Quranic injunctions even if legislated by parliament, becomes automatically invalid to the extent of repugnancy; hence the limitation on individual freedom. Saudi Arabia has not ratified the UN Declaration on Human Rights arguing that Islamic values are enough to ensure human rights.[283] Consequently, the OIC did a fine job by coming

out with an Islamic Declaration of Human Rights, adopted by the 19th ICFM (Cairo; 1990) the sole source of which is the Islamic *Shari'ah*.[284]

In fact, the OIC has been mildly advocating the implementation of *Shari'ah* in the member states, while obviating the risk of annoying the twelve or so member states who have secular constitutions.[285] So, at least theoretically, the OIC believes in promoting the fundamental rights and individual freedoms *enshrined in Islam* (emphasis added), for the peoples of the member states. So that, no one in the Muslim world shall have the right to criticize the person of Prophet Mohammad (PBUH), to incite a Muslim to change his religion, to partake of drugs or liquor, or to indulge in sexual promiscuity; but on the other hand, a woman will have the right to retain her name and lineage after marriage, a child will have the right to inherit his share in his father's property come what may, and a man will be entitled to unquestioning obedience and care from his children, even in old age.

The OIC's concern over human rights also incorporates the humanitarian issues of refugees, war crimes, and of rape of women and girls in conflict situations. The 8th Islamic Summit (Tehran; 1997) expressed solidarity with the states hosting the Muslim refugees, condemned repression against the latter, expressed concern over the fall in amounts of donations for them, and asked the member states to help each other in solving the problem. Another resolution called for the adoption of the Cairo Declaration of Human Rights by all the member states, while praising the 'formulation and codification of Islamic norms and values into a set of universally recognized Islamic instruments of human rights.' Yet another resolution of the same conference expressed awareness of 'the attempts to exploit human rights to discredit the Islamic values'' and emphasized the need for coordination on the issue of human rights among the Muslim states.

In a similar vein, the OIC Secretary General, Dr Izzeddienne Laraki, while speaking at the UN Human Rights Commission at Geneva on 17 March 1997, explained the OIC viewpoint on human rights by recalling that the OIC had been the only international organization to raise its voice on a number of human rights problems such as those in Palestine, Kashmir, and South Philippines.

He urged the world community to join the OIC efforts to protect the human rights of the Palestinian and the Kashmiri people. He also demanded the doubling of efforts to ensure prosecution of the Serb war criminals.

'Human rights and universal freedoms are integral parts of the Islamic faith...[We] have passed the Islamic Declaration of Human Rights, which sets forth the highest standards of conduct, morality, tolerance, freedom, and the right to a dignified life'. Laraki averred. He insinuated that the West had double standards on human rights, therefore, it was the OIC that internationalized even such humanitarian crises that the West had opted to abet.

In Practice, the OIC has done very little to enforce its lofty harangue about human rights. Most of the OIC member states are under the worst kind of totalitarianism, and very few have ratified the Islamic Declaration. The OIC has never even considered launching collective action to restore democracy in Algeria, Nigeria, Sierra Leone, or Turkey, as the United States did in Haiti.[286] Tangible OIC activities in the field of human rights are limited to declaring a particular year as the year of handicaps or a year of human rights, following the UN decision to the same effect, holding seminars, preparing and presenting working papers on the rights and condition of women and children, adopting resolutions on family values and respect to women, and calling upon member states to actively participate in UN conferences on population, environment, and human rights, etc.[287] The OIC has been instrumental in the Muslim countries adopting a coordinated stand on human rights issues at the UN conferences. It has also tried to coordinate member states' activities in the fields of eliminating crimes like drug trafficking, illegal trafficking of women, and terrorism. The OIC has also concerned itself with the plight of Muslim immigrant workers in Europe. Any mention of the condition of immigrant labour force working in oil-rich Gulf states has evaded the OIC resolutions, for obvious reasons.

Terrorism: The OIC has lately started taking up the issue of terrorism because: one, many Muslim countries are facing an armed uprising from Islamist opposition parties who often resort to terrorist attacks against 'soft targets'; and two, some Muslim states like Iran, Iraq, and Libya are accused of sponsoring terrorist activities against Western countries and citizens. This has resulted in very unflattering portrayal of Islam in the world media. The OIC has consistently and strongly condemned all manifestations of terrorism and violence, perpetrated in the name of Islam or otherwise. The Organization has tacitly supported the Muslim government efforts to ruthlessly crush armed Islamic militancy at home, and has encouraged member states to cooperate with each other, especially by sharing intelligence, to root out crime and terrorism.

At the same time, the Islamic Conference is highly reactive to the negative image of Islam portrayed in the Western media, which it believes, is a calculated campaign to malign the Muslims by playing up isolated terrorist incidents carried out by some fanatic Muslim group, while ignoring large-scale state terror employed against the Muslims under their control by Israel, India, etc. The OIC has repeatedly called for a distinction between legitimate struggles for self-determination and terrorism.[288] The 21st ICFM (Karachi; 1993) has even called for a UN-sponsored conference to define terrorism, in order to be able to distinguish it from the just liberation struggles. The meeting decided to constitute an OIC Working Group to combat terrorism. On 26 June 1993, the OIC released a statement, deploring the fact that the eight terrorists arrested in New York, for an alleged plot to blow up the United Nations secretariat building, happened to be Muslims. This, the OIC believed, was not the way to vent the pent-up Muslim feelings on the UN actions or inaction in Bosnia, Iraq, Kashmir, and Palestine—the crises that had resulted in colossal loss of Muslim lives.

The 7th Islamic Summit (Casablanca; 1994) adopted a Code of Conduct for Combating International Terrorism, and declared Islam 'innocent of all acts of terrorism'. The special Islamic Summit (Islamabad; March 1997) made a scathing attack on the Western media for levelling accusations against Islam, its civilization, and its followers. The OIC accused the Western media of turning a blind eye to the acts of Christian, Jew, and Hindu extremists against the Muslims all over the world. It urged the world community 'not to judge Islam on the basis of the conduct of a few of, its followers, rather, in the light of the text of the Quran and the Prophetic tradition'.

The 8th Islamic Summit (Tehran; Dec. 1997) reiterated all the previous OIC resolutions on terrorism and added a new dimension by deciding to 'strengthen the solidarity of Islamic states in combating hijacking' in the light of the Tokyo Convention (1963), the Hague Convention (1970), and the Montreal Convention (1971). The 25th ICFM (Doha; 1998) introduced another definition of terrorism to the international legal lexicon by condemning 'state terrorism' and expressing the determination to 'concert efforts to combat it', an obvious reference to the excesses of the Indian and Serb regular troops against the Muslims in Kashmir and Bosnia, respectively.

Non-Proliferation and Disarmament: There was no disagreement over the fourth objective of the OIC regarding taking necessary measures to support international peace and security, but whether that could be achieved by armament and nuclearization of the Muslim world or working for just the opposite, has been the unresolved conundrum *ab initio*. Hawks like Libya argued for forming a defence pact among the Muslim states[289] while doves like Saudi Arabia emphasized that the Muslims would never form a NATO-type defence arrangement as they (the Muslims) were inherently against the arms race.[290] These differences were accentuated in the backdrop of the international campaign against nuclear weapons and weapons of mass destruction that gained momentum in the decade of the seventies.

By that time, several Muslim states were actively pursuing the nuclear option while others were showing willingness to adhere to the objectives of the Non-Proliferation Treaty.[291] Pakistan and Egypt entered the nuclear race in 1955, Turkey and Indonesia in 1956, Iraq and Algeria in 1958, Iran in 1974, and Libya in 1975; all had embarked on nuclear research projects ostensibly for peaceful purposes.[292] As fate would have it, the 'peaceful' nuclear programmes of India and Israel made headway relatively early, a fact that the Muslim states could hardly relish. This

was the beginning of the OIC's concern for disarmament and non-proliferation.

India conducted its first successful nuclear test on 18 May 1974, which caused security concerns for the Muslim countries in South Asia. Pakistan was quick to draw the attention of the 5th ICFM (Kuala Lumpur; 1974) to the Peaceful Nuclear Explosion (PNE), as the Indians called it, conducted by India. The Conference adopted a resolution expressing 'serious concern over the nuclear test by India' and expressed the apprehension that 'Israel might follow suit'.[293] Since then it has been the OIC's consistent policy to oppose nuclear weapon proliferation all over the world and it has repeatedly called for establishment of Nuclear Weapons Free Zones (NWFZs) in South Asia, Africa, and the Middle East.[294]

The OIC has also struggled for the elimination of landmines and other destructive left-over war materials. In this regard, the 8th ICFM (Tripoli; 1977), adopted three specific resolutions: (1) reiterating the danger posed by the proliferation of nuclear weapons to the security of Islamic States in Africa, the Middle East, and South Asia, and the implementation of the relevant resolutions adopted by the UN General Assembly; the Conference called upon the nuclear powers to accept their obligation with regards to the denuclearization of these regions and declaring the Indian Ocean a Zone of Peace; (2) calling upon Islamic countries to seek credible assurances from nuclear weapon states not to use or threaten to use nuclear weapons against non-nuclear weapon states; the Conference specifically pointed out that the nuclear powers have not affirmatively responded to the recommendations adopted by the United Nations and other international organizations in this regard; and (3) reiterating that most developing countries which were subjected to foreign occupation and their lands used as war theatres were now faced with the problem of leftover war materials causing grave losses to those countries; the Conference called upon the colonial states to provide compensation for those losses and bear the responsibility of providing technical and informational assistance for clearing of the mines and minefields and removing those destructive leftovers.[295]

Since then the issues of nuclear non-proliferation and NWFZs has sprung up in virtually every Islamic Summit and ICFM, and the policy of the Organization has remained unaltered. In fact, the resolutions adopted are usually the verbatim replicas of the ones cited above. Two recent Islamic Summits at Casablanca (1994) and Tehran (1997) have simply reiterated the OIC's resolve to work against nuclear proliferation, asking the nuclear weapon states to sit down for sincere and meaningful negotiations aimed at total elimination of nuclear weapons. As for the Chemical Weapons Convention, Biological Weapons Convention and the Landmines Treaty, the Islamic Conference has not been so prolific in adopting resolutions. It has, however, welcomed these conventions, and some Muslim states had coordinated their policies in the negotiations leading to these conventions.

The importance that the OIC is giving to the issues is evident from the fact that the 8th Islamic Summit (Tehran; 1997) adopted eight resolutions on the topic. The resolution 21/8-P (I.S) dealt with the steps taken in the world for complete disarmament and their implications for the Muslim world. This resolution acknowledged that the security and sovereignty of the NNWS should be ensured through credible guarantees; expressed concern at the dangers to the world peace; called for the total elimination of the weapons of mass destruction; reaffirmed the Muslim states' inalienable right to acquire nuclear energy for peaceful ends; and called upon the nuclear weapon states (NWS) to 'commit to total nuclear disarmament' in a universally acceptable time-frame'.

Resolutions 22 to 27 dealt with the NWFZs in Africa, Central Asia, South Asia, and South East Asia; strengthening security of the NNWS against nuclear threats through binding and non-discriminatory treaties; encouraging regional arms controls and confidence-building measures; enhancing regional military balances to enhance stability; dumping of nuclear and toxic wastes in Muslim countries; and the elimination of land mines. Finally, Resolution 31/8-P(I.S) demanded reparations for the effects of the Second World War, from the developed world.

Given the OIC's past anti-nuclear rhetoric, the five nuclear tests conducted by India in May 1998, evoked a strong response from the OIC. The Organization expressed solidarity with Pakistan and showed empathy towards her legitimate security concerns. The OIC Secretary General described the Indian tests as constituting 'a dangerous threat to the South Asian security' that have 'undermined the efforts to establish a NWFZ in that region'. India's nemesis and arch-rival, Pakistan, was dismayed at the tentative and half-hearted condemnation of the Indian tests by the world community at large. When India told Pakistan that she would now settle the Kashmir issue by force, Pakistan called that a day and gave a tit-for-tat by carrying out six powerful nuclear tests of its own a fortnight later, thereby restoring the strategic balance in the region. This time the OIC took a somersault and defended Pakistan for going nuclear, owing to her 'legitimate security concerns'.

Conclusion

In the final analysis, we find the OIC to be an active and dynamic organization. If its achievements are rarely acknowledged and failures seldom mourned, it is because of what has come to be known as the CNN factor. If the world media network cameras do not cover an event, a place, or an institution, this does not mean that it is not there. This applies in the case of the OIC. A former Secretary General, Tunku Abdul Rahman, had said, 'There was very little coverage of the OIC. We thought it was because of lack of information available, so we started feeding information to the world news agencies; the situation remained the same'. We have seen above, the OIC role in Bosnia, for instance; the number of times that the BBC news network in its news coverage of Bosnia during the four-year civil war, referred to the OIC, can be counted on finger tips.

It is true that the OIC has not been directly responsible for the final settlement of many of the disputes, it has been involved with. But the same holds good for most of the other regional organizations. If two countries are adamant on not coming to terms with each other, there is little an organization can do. The OIC has been more successful in cases falling under sections A and C, above, and less successful in those falling under sections B and D. It is because in the former, there is almost a complete consensus within the OIC membership, while in the latter, the Muslim states have their own stakes directly involved. Hence, the OIC's intervention in the latter has substantially high political costs involved as far as its own existence and viability are concerned. In any case, the OIC has managed to coordinate the foreign policies of Muslim states in three ways; (i) by harmonizing their foreign policies; (ii) by formulating an Islamic vision on international affairs of its own; and (iii) by becoming the spokesman of the Muslim world on issues of Islamic concern.

It goes without saying that there is still much to be desired. To become an effective organization, the OIC should assume a more pivotal role in Muslim world politics. The Organization should not shy away from intervening in a bilateral conflict between the member states, or a civil war or political turmoil within a member state, no matter if one or both the parties object to its unsolicited intervention. Even the Arab League member states are bound to accept the League's mediation, though they have a right to refuse the solution being offered. An amendment to this effect can be made in the OIC Charter also. Moreover, the OIC should rethink its policy of blindly supporting a Muslim country or a community against a non-Muslim party. This causes a blow to the OIC's credibility. The idea of religion, as a factor in international politics, does not appeal to the OIC's interlocutors in the West. The OIC should, nevertheless, concentrate more on the international issues of population, environment, drug trafficking, landmine elimination and the like, and formulate its own vision on them.

NOTES and REFERENCES

1. Keesing's Contemporary Archives, 1980, p. 30242.
2. Noor Ahmad Baba, *OIC: Theory and Practice of Pan-Islamic Cooperation*, (Karachi: Oxford University Press, 1994), p. 121.
3. Keesing, 1986, p. 34260.
4. Ibid., 1980, p. 30241.
5. See, *The Muslim*, Islamabad, 14 December 1994.
6. There was one significant interregnum when the Crusaders captured Jerusalem in AD 1099 but Saladin retook it in AD 1186. The author is grateful for the material provided by the Embassy of Palestine, Islamabad, on the history and background of the Palestine problem.
7. The fourth Arab Summit at Khartoum, Sudan (August, 1967), shortly after the 1967 war, declared these three No's as the corner stone of the Arab policy.
8. Mohammad el Syed Selim, 'OIC and the Palestine problem' (in Arabic), *Shau'un Arabiyyah*, no. 56, 1989, pp. 203–204. Also see the text of Rabat declaration in the Annexure.
9. Haider Mehdi, *OIC: A review of its political and educational policies*, (Lahore: Progressive Publishers, 1988), p. 42.
10. Ibid., p. 43.
11. Ibid., p. 44.
12. Ibid., p. 45.
13. Abdullah Ahsan, *OIC: Introduction to an Islamic political institution*, (Herndon: IIIT, 1987), p. 61. Also see Mehdi, ref. 9, pp. 48–49, and Selim, ref. 8, p. 205.
14. Quoted by Ahsan, ref. 13, p. 60.
15. Selim, ref. 8, p. 206. Also see the final communiqué of the 6th ICFM.
16. Ahsan, ref. 13, p. 61.
17. Inamullah Khan (ed.), 'World Muslim Gazetteer: 1985', (Karachi: WMC, 1987), p. 621.
18. Iqbal Akhund, *Memoirs of a Bystander*, (Karachi: Oxford University Press, 1997), pp. 249–250, where Akhund gives a frank assessment of the UN resolution no. 3379.
19. Ibid.
20. Facts on File, 1975, p. 177, see the entry under the date of 30 September.
21. Keesing, 1976, p. 27900B.
22. Facts on File, 1980, p. 736 and 775.
23. See, *Pakistan Times*, Islamabad, 13 May 1979 and 28 January 1981. Also see 'Declarations and Resolutions of the Islamic Conference on Political Issues: 1969-81', (Jeddah, n.d), p. 329.
24. Ola A. Abou Zeid, 'OIC policies towards international issues', in Mohammad el Selim (ed.), *The OIC in a changing world*, (Cairo: Cairo University, 1994), p. 71.
25. Mehdi, ref. 9, pp. 54–55.
26. Ibid., p. 69.
27. Ibid., pp. 54–55.
28. On this assurance by President Hosni Mubarak, the 4th Islamic Summit restored Egypt's membership in 1984 while maintaining that the OIC's principled opposition to Camp David remained unaffected.

29. Mehdi, ref. 9, p. 66.
30. Facts on File, 1980, p. 491.
31. Mehdi, ref. 9, pp. 67–68.
32. Baba, ref. 2, p. 138.
33. Mehdi, ref. 9, p. 70.
34. Ibid.
35. Keesing, 1984, p. 32824.
36. Zeid, ref. 24, p. 68.
37. Ahsan, ref.13, pp. 60–61.
38. Ibid., p. 61.
39. Ibid., p. 59.
40. Zeid, ref. 24, p. 67.
41. 'Intifada' is the name given to Palestinian uprising that started on 9 December 1987 and continued for the next seven years.
42. This is one incident, which the detractors of the OIC never fail to mention. I have not found any plausible explanation of the OIC's inaction on the 1982 events in Lebanon. Palestinian President Arafat bitterly complained in 1984 that the PLO 'was besieged for 88 days in Beirut while no one extended any help...It was then besieged in Tripoli while...no Muslim moved a finger'.
43. Passionate speeches suggesting that the 'silent stones of al-Quds' and the 'innocent tears of Palestinian children' were calling for unity dominated the 10th ICFM proceedings. It was soon realized that the foot march was not a feasible option and so it was dropped.
44. See Zeid, ref. 24, p. 69, and Mehdi, ref. 9, p. 66.
45. Ahsan, ref.13, p. 60.
46. Ibid., p. 62.
47. Zeid, ref. 24, p. 71. It was the same Summit that for the first time endorsed the call for an international conference on the Middle East, to be participated by all big powers also.
48. Besides the PLO and Iraq itself, Yemen, Sudan and Libya, and to some extent Algeria and Jordan also, were critical of the US policy of wanton bombardment and destruction of Iraq, instead of a direct attack on Kuwait.
49. See, *Kuwait Times*, Kuwait, 8 and 9 December 1991, and *Tehran Times*, Tehran, 19 December 1991.
50. See, *The Muslim*, 7 September 1994, and also *The News*, Islamabad, 8 September 1994.
51. See, *The News*, 15 December 1994.
52. See for instance, *The Muslim World*, (Karachi: WMC), vol. 34, no. 49, 28 June 1997, p. 2. Also see Keesing, 1993, p. 39299; *Pakistan Times*, 9 March 1994; *Dawn*, Karachi, 18 August 1991 and 28 February 1994.
53. Selim, ref. 8, p. 202.
54. Ibid.
55. For years, the Soviets continued to insist that Babrak Karmal had taken power a few hours before the invasion. And the Soviet troops came to the aid of friendly government of Babrak Karmal on his request.

Karmal was replaced by Dr Najibullah in February 1986.
56. Resolution 1/EOS/1980, quoted by Mehdi, ref. 9, p. 59. Also see Keesing, 1980, pp. 30241–42.
57. Ibid., p. 59.
58. Resolution 2/EOS/1980, quoted in ibid., p. 120.
59. Facts on File, 1980, p. 362. Also see, *Pakistan Times*, 9 April 1980.
60. For details about the 11th ICFM proceedings, see, Keesing, 1980, p. 30385. Also see *Pakistan Times*, 23 May 1980.
61. Saudi Arabia announced $25 million, Malaysia $117,000 and Indonesia $20,000 for the Afghanistan Fund. See, *Morning News*, Karachi, 20 May 1980.
62. Keesing, 1981, pp. 30881–82. The Summit expressed surprise at the French President Giscard d'Estaing's announcement calling for an eight-country international conference on Afghanistan. It was a diplomatic discourtesy on his part not to inform the leaders of Muslim states, who were discussing Afghanistan at the Summit.
63. Ibid.
64. See the statement of Secretary General Habib Chatti in *Pakistan Times*, 23 August 1982.
65. See bimonthly *Foreign Affairs Pakistan*, (Islamabad: Ministry of Foreign Affairs), vol. 11, November–December 1984.
66. Facts on File, 1984, p. 53, see the entry under 8 April.
67. *Dawn*, 8 February 1987. Earlier, the OIC Secretary General Sharifuddin Pirzada undertook a trip to Moscow in November 1986 and said that the USSR and OIC had started seeing eye to eye on Afghanistan. Also see, *Frontier Post*, Peshawar, 31 January 1987.
68. Ahsan, ref. 13, p. 64.
69. Zeid, ref. 24, p. 80.
70. Keesing, 1989, p. 36449 and 36537. Also see Keesing, 1991, p. 37668.
71. Facts on File, 1993, p. 214. It may be noted that the agreements came to be named after the city in which they were signed. Islamabad Accord is also called Mecca Accord, since the Afghan leaders ratified the accord in the city of Mecca on 11 March 1993.
72. *The Muslim*, 10 January 1994.
73. Ibid., 4 April 1994.
74. *The News*, 30 June 1994. The UN's special envoy on Afghanistan Mehmud Mestiri hoped that OIC Secretary General Hamid al Gabid will hold talks with him also. The OIC later assured him that it also wanted coordination with the UN on Afghanistan crisis, not a competition.
75. *The Muslim*, 15 July 1994.
76. See Keesing 1994, p. 40103, 40208, and Keesing, 1995, p. 40642. Also see, *Dawn*, 6 April 1993, 31 July 1995, 9 September 1995, 10 January 1996 and 15 October 1996, and *The News*, 11 November 1997.

77. Pakistan and Iran accuse each other of meddling in Afghanistan's internal affairs by backing *Taliban* and Rabbani, respectively. One major reason why *Taliban* government was not recognized by the OIC, is the poor human rights record of the fundamentalist *Taliban* who have closed down theatres and cinemas and banned girls from education and employment.

78. See Resolution 9/8-P(IS) of the 8th Islamic Summit. The author is grateful to Dr Khalil Saeed, head of the OIC Mission on Afghanistan (Islamabad) for providing him valuable material on the OIC role in Afghanistan, including copies of resolutions.

79. M. Ali Kettani, *Muslim Minorities in the World*, (Lahore: Services Book Club, 1990), p. 33.

80. By 1990, the Greek Cypriots outnumbered Turk Cypriots by five to two in total 700,000 population of Cyprus island. However, over 600,000 Turk Cypriot diaspora lived in Turkey, 60,000 in UK and 40,000 in Australia. See ibid., pp. 34–35.

81. See 'Cyprus Question: Concise Briefing Note', (London, 1992) published by the British Parliamentary Group of Friends of North Cyprus, pp. 6–33, for history and background of the Cyprus conflict. The author is grateful to the TRNC embassy in Islamabad, for providing this book, texts of all OIC resolutions on Cyprus and other related material.

82. Ibid.

83. Resolution 16-7/P of the 7th ICFM. Also see Keesing 1976, p. 27900B.

84. *Pakistan Times*, 10 September 1978.

85. For instance, see Resolution 14/14-P of the 14th ICFM.

86. Cyprus Question, ref. 80, p. 26.

87. Ibid., p. 30.

88. Resolution 11/10-P.

89. Keesing, 1984, p. 32823.

90. 'OIC resolutions on Cyprus', (Lefkosha, 1996), published by TRNC President's office, p. 37.

91. OIC Secretary General's Report contained in ibid., pp. 32–41.

92. *The Nation*, Lahore, 29 November 1996.

93. *The Muslim World*, (Karachi: WMC), vol. 35, no. 23, 27 December 1997, p. 2. Also see, *The News*, 15 December 1997.

94. See 'The Armenian Aggression against Azerbaijan', (Baku, 1994) pp. 30–53, for background of the conflict. The author acknowledges the help of Azerbaijan embassy, in Islamabad, providing the book and other valuable material on OIC role.

95. Ibid., pp. 54–55.

96. Ibid., pp. 6–9.

97. Ibid., pp. 47–52.

98. *The News*, 30 April 1993.

99. Ibid., 28 April 1993.

100. See, for instance, Resolutions 97/8-P(IS) and 18/8-E(IS) of the 8th Islamic Summit, Resolution 18/

24-E of the 24th ICFM, and para 8 of the Tehran Declaration.

101. Zeid, ref. 24, p. 82.

102. Ibid.

103. Keesing, 1992, p. 39970. Also see, *Pakistan Times* and *The Muslim* of 19 June 1992.

104. Dr Mohammad el Selim, 'An evaluation of OIC performance,' in Selim (ed.), ref. 24, p. 122.

105. Keesing, 1992, p. 39987.

106. *Pakistan Times*, 3 December 1992. It is worth noting that it was the 1st ICFM where presidents of two European countries (Alija Izzetbegovich of Bosnia and Sali Berisha of Albania) had turned up. European negotiators Cyrus Vance and Lord Owen also attended.

107. See 'Introduction to the OIC', (Islamabad, 1993), published by Directorate of Films and Publications, Pakistan's Ministry of Information, p. 12. Also see 'Facts on File', 1993, p. 35; *The News*, 12 January 1993; and *Dawn*, 13 January 1993.

108. Selim, ref. 104, p. 123.

109. Zeid, ref. 24, pp. 87–88.

110. Keesing, 1993, p. 39442. Also see, *The Muslim*, 26–30 April 1993. Also see *Dawn* of the same dates. In addition to this amount, later another $58 million were promised (Saudi Arabia, $20 million; Kuwait, $10 million; Pakistan, $5 million; Turkey and UAE, $3 million each).

111. Keesing, 1993, p. 39469.

112. Most of the story about OIC group's activities at UN Human Rights Conference at Geneva has been taken from Nasim Zehra, 'For Bosnian Muslims, OIC finally digs-in', *The Nation*, 20 June 1993. Also see, *Dawn*, 23 June 1993.

113. Keesing, 1993, p. 39564. Also see, *The Muslim*, 14 July 1993, and editorial of *Dawn*, 15 July 1993. When the UN Secretary General's request for 7600 troops was discussed in the meeting, the members states offered 20,720 men; Iran (10,000), Pakistan (3000), Turkey (3000), Malaysia (1500), Bangladesh (1220), Palestine (1000), and Tunisia (1000). But the OIC decided that it would at the moment pledge 17,000 troops, a figure more than twice what the UN had requested. See, *The Muslim*, 16 July 1993.

114. Zeid, ref. 24, pp. 88–89.

115. The account of the three OIC Contact Group meetings in 1994 is largely based upon Aslam Sheikh, 'OIC and the Bosnian tragedy', *The News*, 31 August 1994.

116. *Dawn*, 1 October 1994. Also see, *Frontier Post*, 22 September 1994 and 3 October 1994.

117. 'Facts on File', 1994, p. 971.

118. Aslam, ref. 115.

119. For a thorough understanding of Western responses to the Bosnian conflict, Thomas Cushmon and Stjepan G. Mestrovic (eds.), *This Time We Knew: Western responses to genocide in Bosnia*, (New York: New York University Press, 1996) is highly recommended.

120. Quoted in Dr Inayatullah, 'Bosnia, West and OIC', *Pakistan Times,* 26 March 1995.

121. Quoted in Dr Inayatullah, 'OIC's role in Bosnia', *The Nation,* 14 August 1995.

122. See the editorials of *The Muslim,* 27 July 1995, *The News,* 24 July 1995, and *Pakistan Times,* 24 July 1995.

123. *Pakistan Times,* 30 November 1995. The *Washington Post* report about arms supplies to Bosnia was quoted by *Frontier Post,* 29 July 1995.

124. *The News,* 23 July 1995. The UN had declared the cities of Sarajevo, Bihac, Gorazde Tuzla, Zepa, and Srebrenica as safe havens. When the latter two were overrun by Serb rebel forces, the London Conference confined itself to warning the Serbs of a stern response if Gorazde was taken; as if massacre in Zepa and Srebrenica was a non-event and the fate of remaining three cities did not matter.

125. See Ghani Jafar, 'Blinkered OIC', *The News,* 30 July 1995.

126. Most of the quotes mentioned here have been taken from a story of *Gulf News,* entitled 'OIC states challenge unjustified arms ban', carried by *Pakistan Times,* 14 August 1995.

127. *The News,* 28 August 1995. Also see, *Dawn,* 11 September 1995.

128. *Dawn,* 17 August 1995.

129. *Le Monde* story carried by *Pakistan Times,* 13 August 1995.

130. *The News,* 14 December 1995.

131. See, *The Muslim,* 12 March 1996, and *Frontier Post,* 14 March 1996.

132. *The News,* 29 June 1997.

133. Ibid., 29 September 1997.

134. Dr Mohammad el Syed Selim, 'The OIC and Conflict Resolution' (in Arabic), *Siyasiyah al Dawliya,* Cairo, July 1991, p. 46.

135. Ibid., p. 47.

136. See 'Declarations of the OIC conferences held in Pakistan', published by Directorate of Films and Publications, Ministry of Information, (Islamabad, 1993). See para 4 of the Lahore Declaration on p. 14.

137. Ibid., see para 10–12 of the 2nd ICFM declaration on p. 9.

138. Ibid., see para 89 of the 11th ICFM declaration on p. 45.

139. Ibid., see para 86 also.

140. Selim, ref. 134, p. 48.

141. Ibid., p. 49.

142. For an objective analysis of the reasons and background of the secession, two books by a leading East Pakistani intellectual Muti-ur-Rahman *Bangladesh Today,* (London: News & Media Ltd., 1977), and *Second Thoughts on Bangladesh* (London: News & Media Ltd., 1979) are highly recommended.

143. A discussion on the chronology of events leading to Pakistan's break-up is beyond our scope here. Interested readers may see G.W. Choudhry, *The last days of united Pakistan,* (London: C. Hurst & Co., 1974). Mr Choudhry was a noted scholar and politician of East Pakistan (now Bangladesh) and was a member of the last cabinet of united Pakistan.

144. *Pakistan Times,* 23 June 1971.

145. Ahsan, ref. 13, p. 77.

146. 'OIC Declarations', ref. 23, p. 179 for the full text of the 3rd ICFM resolution on Indo-Pakistan situation. Also see, *New Times,* Rawalpindi, 10 March 1972. Also see Qadeeruddin Ahmad, 'East Pakistan Crisis and the Islamic Conference', *Pakistan Horizon,* (Karachi: PIIA), vol. 25, no. 1, January–March 1972. The Conference also gave its support to UN General Assembly resolution 2793 (dated 7 December 1971) and Security Council resolution 307 (dated 21 December 1971).

147. Ahsan, ref. 13, p. 78.

148. Ibid. Also see, *Morning News,* Karachi, 25 March 1973.

149. Ibid., p.78. Also see Keesing, 1974, p. 26689.

150. *The News,* 5 January 1998.

151. Ibid.

152. Selim, ref. 134, pp. 47–48.

153. Ibid.

154. On 11 February 1979, Shah's monarchy was overthrown by an Islamic revolution led by Imam Khomeini in Iran. A few months later, Saddam Hussein replaced Hassan al Bakr as President of Iraq in a bloodless palace coup.

155. Ahsan, ref. 13, p. 79.

156. 'Facts on File', 1980, p. 734.

157. Ibid, p. 794.

158. See, *The Muslim,* 17 December 1980; and 19 January 1981.

159. *Pakistan Times,* 25 January 1981.

160. 'Facts on File', 1981, p. 63 and p. 83.

161. *Pakistan Times,* 25 January 1981, reported that 35,000 telegrams had already reached the Taif Summit and that the number was expected to rise to 100,000 in the following three days.

162. See, *Pakistan Times,* 12 February 1981, and 3 March 1981; *The Muslim,* 7 March 1981, and Selim, ref. 14, pp. 52–53.

163. The text of proposals of the OIC peace plan appears in Selim, ref. 134, p. 53.

164. See 'Facts on File', 1981, pp.152 and 171.

165. Ibid., p.171 and 230. Also see Selim, ref. 134, p. 54.

166. Ibid. p. 314.

167. Ahsan, ref. 13, p.79. Also see Keesing, 1981, p. 31014.

168. Ibid., p. 80.

169. Keesing, 1982, p. 30524. Also see, *The Muslim,* 26 August 1982.

170. Ibid., p. 30848.

171. 'Facts on File', 1982, p. 263.
172. Selim, ref. 134, p. 54. Also see Keesing, 1984, p. 32824. Also see, *Pakistan Times*, 27 December 1982; and *Dawn*, 10 December 1983.
173. Selim, ref. 134, p. 54.
174. Ibid., p. 55.
175. Ibid.
176. See, *Dawn*, 8 January 1987, *Pakistan Times*, 16 January 1987 and *The Muslim*, 17 January 1981.
177. Selim, ref. 134, p. 55. Also see *Frontier Post*, 30 January 1987.
178. Ibid. Also see Keesing, 1989, p. 36537.
179. See, *The News*, 10–12 December 1997.
180. Ali Nawaz Memon, *The Islamic Nation*, (Lahore: Vanguard Publishers, 1997), p. 192.
181. See Selim, ref. 134, pp. 56–57, for the full story of this conflict and the OIC intervention. Also see, *Al-Ahram* (Arabic), Cairo, 29 April, 2 May, 9 May and 3 June 1989.
182. The author wishes to acknowledge the receipt of nine books and booklets, from the Kuwait's diplomatic mission in Islamabad. This material about Kuwait and Kuwait crisis was very helpful in writing this section. See 'Iraqi Invasion of Kuwait: Truth and Tragedy', published by the Centre for Research and Studies on Kuwait, (Kuwait, 1994), pp. 53–62, for the text of Iraqi and Kuwaiti memoranda and letters to the Arab League Secretary General during July 1990.
183. Ibid., pp. 60–62.
184. Ibid. p. 62. Also see *Al-Ahram,* 1 August 1990 and 3 August 1990.
185. Selim, ref. 134, p. 57; Keesing, 1990, p. 37668; *Pakistan Times*, 6 August 1990.
186. Ibid.
187. 'Truth and Tragedy', ref. 182, p. 63.
188. *Pakistan Times*, 8 January 1991.
189. Selim, ref. 134, p. 58; Selim, ref. 104, p. 128; *The Muslim*, 16 January 1991.
190. Keesing, 1991, p. 37943.
191. Ibid.
192. *Dawn*, 8 February 1991.
193. Ibid.
194. Selim, ref. 134, p. 58; *The News*, 22 February 1991.
195. Keesing, 1991, p. 38699; *The News*, 5 August 1991; *The Muslim*, 6 August 1991; Also see Shamim Akhtar, 'Wither Muslim Unity', *Dawn*, 18 August 1991.
196. *Pakistan Times*, 12 December 1991.
197. *The News*, 10 December 1991.
198. Ibid., 28 April 1993.
199. *Dawn*, 13 December 1994.
200. *The News*, Lahore, 16 November 1997.
201. Ahsan, ref. 13, p. 66.
202. Ibid.
203. Ibid., p. 68.
204. Ibid., p. 66.
205. Gazetteer, ref. 17, p. 63.
206. Ahsan, ref. 13, p. 67.
207. Ibid.
208. Kettani, ref. 79, p. 161.
209. Keesing, 1995, p. 40211, reports that OIC Foreign Ministers coordination meeting on 3 October 1994 made unprecedented reference to discrimination against Muslim immigrants in Europe.
210. Resolution 12/3-P.
211. Resolution 4/4-P.
212. Resolution 8/5-P.
213. Ahsan, ref. 13, p. 69.
214. Ibid.
215. Keesing, 1977, p. 28440.
216. 'Facts on File', 1977, p. 241.
217. Ahsan, ref. 13, p. 69.
218. Keesing, 1977, p. 28440.
219. 'Facts on File', 1978, p. 650.
220. *Pakistan Times*, Islamabad, 13 May 1979.
221. Ibrahim Qureshi, 'World Muslim Minorities', (Karachi: WMC, 1993), p. 152.
222. *The News*, 24 May 1987. The OIC Secretary General Sharifuddin Pirzada met Habib Hashim to reiterate the OIC support to MNLF.
223. *Pakistan Times*, Islamabad, 9 August 1989.
224. *The News*, 16 November 1991.
225. Ibid., 1 September 1996.
226. *Pakistan Times*, 24 July 1996.
227. *The News*, 1 September 1996.
228. Though a large number of books have been written on the genesis and history of Kashmir dispute, Alastair Lamb's *Kashmir: A disputed legacy*, (Islamabad, 1994) is highly recommended.
229. See Mehrunnisa Ali, 'The Lahore Islamic Summit', *Pakistan Horizon,* Vol. 27, no.1, January–March 1974, p. 34.
230. Abouzeid, ref. 24, p. 76.
231. *The News*, 23 May 1991.
232. Resolution 11/20-P.
233. 'Introduction to OIC', ref. 107, p. 8.
234. The full text of this report appeared in two parts in *Dawn*, 28 and 29 April 1993.
235. *The Muslim,* 27 April 1993.
236. *Frontier Post*, Lahore, 29 November 1993.
237. *The Muslim*, 2 October 1993.
238. Ibid., 19 April 1994.
239. *The News*, 4 April 1994.
240. *Pakistan Times*, 9 September 1994. Pakistan had earlier claimed that Indian Foreign Secretary and senior officials had visited several Islamic capitals with a request to boycott the conference but, to quote the Pakistani spokesman, 'Indian bid to sabotage the ICFM' failed. On the sidelines of this conference, Secretary General met an APHC delegation and assured financial and moral support. The OIC Contact

Group on Kashmir, formed at this ICFM, comprises Guinea, Morocco, Niger, Pakistan, Saudi Arabia, Turkey, and the OIC Secretary General. It started functioning on 3 October 1994.

241. See *Times of India*, New Delhi, 31 October 1994.

242. *Pakistan Times*, 11 November 1994. Pakistan had by that time already got six co-sponsors viz. Albania, Bosnia, Gambia, Niger, Saudi Arabia, and Turkey. Pakistan announced that although she had withdrawn the resolution from the First Committee, however, she reserved the right to raise it at the Third Committee. India thanked the OIC for, what she called, not supporting Pakistan. On 16 November, the OIC Secretary General asked the UN Security Council to take up the Kashmir dispute.

243. *The News*, 23 March 1994, quoted the *Times of India* story.

244. *Frontier Post*, Lahore, 19 December 1995. Not surprisingly, Indian media reacts sharply at such OIC pronouncements calling it as a surrogate of Pakistan. When the 7th Islamic Summit (Casablanca; 1994) adopted a resolution on Kashmir the Indian press castigated Secretary General Hamid al Gabid for being behind this resolution, who, it was claimed was displeased at not being well treated when he had earlier visited India as the OIC Assistant Secretary General.

245. See, for instance, Indian external affairs ministry's statement carried by *The News*, 16 December 1995. It may be mentioned that a few months earlier Salman Haider, a Muslim, had taken over as the Foreign Secretary of India. He had said that India would enlarge dialogue with the OIC and counter the diplomatic challenge posed by Pakistan on Kashmir. (*The News*, 1 March 1995.)

246. *Jordan Times*, Amman, 22 March 1988.

247. Ibid.

248. Keesing.

249. *The Nation*, Lahore, 19 March 1989.

250. Keesing, 1989, p. 36771.

251. *Frontier Post*, 24 September 1989.

252. *Dawn*, 18 August 1991.

253. The problem of statistics is compounded by the fact that two sects, *Qadianis and Bahais*, have been excommunicated as heretics but they still claim to be Muslims. Moreover, some groups and communities pay nominal allegiance to Islam so they can be counted either way.

254. To quote some examples, literacy rate among urban Muslims is 57 per cent as against 75 per cent for other communities. The ratio of Muslim officers in civil service is 1 to 70. There are only 27 Muslims in the 545-member lower house of parliament. Giving all the details would take us too far; interested readers may consult the available literature on Indian Muslims.

255. See Chapter 1.

256. *The News*, 9 December 1992.

257. 'Introduction to OIC', ref. 107, pp. 8–9.

258. Ibid.

259. Ibid.

260. *The News*, 14 January 1993.

261. Ibid., 16 December 1995.

262. As for non-member states, OIC's position on the definition of domestic jurisdiction is rather vague and shaky. For instance, the OIC has continuously spurned the protests of India and Philippines over her right to discuss the liberation (secessionist) struggles of the Muslims of Kashmir and Mindanao, respectively.

263. *Jang*, 6 May 1979.

264. Baba, ref. 2, p. 121.

265. *The Muslim*, 26 January 1980.

266. Pakistan Television's evening English News bulletin (11 January 1998) reported that the OIC has issued a statement condemning the massacres in Algeria as un-Islamic. The OIC did not directly apportion the blame on Algeria's state security forces for the murders but called upon the government to allow the European Mission to investigate the situation.

267. The Pakistan National Alliance consisted of nine major opposition (mostly extreme right wing) parties of Pakistan, including the *Jamaat-e-Islami*, which was on the forefront of the anti-Bhutto agitation later.

268. Out of the 200 general constituencies for the lower house of Pakistani parliament, eighteen members had already returned unopposed.

269. Bhutto claimed that the US Secretary of State Henry Kissinger had warned him of being made a 'horrible example', in case he did not roll back the country's nuclear programme. It was also claimed later that his government had provided conclusive proofs of US involvement in the conspiracy to the then US ambassador to Islamabad, Henry Byroade.

270. Rafi Raza, *The Bhutto Years 1967–77*, (Karachi: Oxford University Press, 1997), pp. 354-382. Also see Kausar Niazi, *The last days of Prime Minister Bhutto*, (Lahore, Jang Publishers, 1988), pp. 110–140.

271. See 'OIC Declarations', ref. 23, p. 198.

272. See Chapter 3 for discussion on the legal position of the OIC Chairman.

273. Akhund, ref. 18, p. 168.

274. Ibid., pp. 349–350.

275. Ibid. In fact the Palestinians reminded Agha Shahi, a career diplomat, that till a few months ago, he had himself been lobbying at the ICFM for resolution condemning foreign conspiracies against the Bhutto government. Shahi was one of the many close aides of Bhutto, who had switched over to the military after the *coup d'état*.

276. Ibid.

277. So much has already been written on the trial of Bhutto and the inhuman treatment meted out on him in jail and, in any case, the conduct of trial is outside the

scope of this book. He had been arraigned for ordering an abortive assassination attempt on a renegade party member during his rule. It is, however, pertinent to note that only four of the 9-member bench of the Supreme Court found Bhutto guilty while three judges called the charges against Bhutto as '*mala fide*, calumnious, ridiculous and without any basis'. Two judges were summarily removed on technical grounds before the verdict was announced.

278. Akhund, ref. 18, pp. 341, 344.

279. Ibid. pp. 345, 358.

280. Ahsan, ref. 13, p. 71.

281. Ibid.

282. See Mehdi, ref. 9, pp. 85–129, for a thorough discussion on the OIC policies towards racism, imperialism, colonialism, etc.

283. Abdullah Ahsan, *Ummah or a Nation: Identity crisis in the modern Muslim World*, (Leicester: Islamic Foundation, 1992) p. 110, and its footnote 10 on p. 140.

284. See the full text of the Islamic Declaration (especially Articles 24 and 25) in the Annexure.

285. In its efforts to enforce *Shari'ah* in all member states, the OIC has discussed *Shari'ah* implementation at the highest level including the Islamic Summit (see the statement of Saudi Foreign Minister Saud al Faisal carried by *Pakistan Times*, 24 January 1981). In addition, all the OIC conferences of the Ministers of Religious Affairs have, in their final declarations, called for enforcement of *Shari'ah* in the member states. The OIC takes the lead in welcoming the enforcement of *Shari'ah* laws by an individual member state (see *The News*, 23 August 1992). The OIC also coordinates Islamic states' policies in the propagation of Islam. The latest meeting on Joint Islamic Action for such purpose took place at Kuala Lumpur in January 1996 (see *Dawn*, 13 January 1996).

286. Even in the Muslim countries, it was the United States that showed concern over curbs on democracy. On 24 November 1997, it showed concern over the trial of pro-Islamist Welfare Party of Turkey in the country's powerful Constitutional Court that could lead to the banning of the party. (Head of the Court, Yekta Gungor Ozden, criticized the US for, what he called, interfering in Turkey's internal affairs, see *The News*, Lahore, 27 November 1997.) Similarly, the US was worried over escalation of violence in late 1997 in Algerian civil war and considered sending a fact finding mission, whereas the OIC was content with a single statement condemning the massacres in Algeria as un-Islamic without naming any party as being culpable.

287. The OIC has shown concern for humanitarian issues like the rights of the handicapped, women, children, and ethnic and religious minorities, and problems related to population and environment. For instance, 1981 was declared as a year of the handicapped by the 11th ICFM (see, *Pakistan Times*, 22 May 1980). The 6th Islamic Summit Dakar, thoroughly discussed problems faced by women and children in the Muslim countries, on the basis of the working papers on their rights in the Muslim world that were prepared by Iran and Senegal (Ibid., 3 December 1991); the OIC decided to hold its first symposium on rights of child in Jeddah in 1994 (see ibid., 21 March 1994). The Islamic Conference asked the member states to attend the UN Conference on Human Rights (Geneva; 1991) and adopt a common stand on the basis of Islamic Human Rights Declaration (see, *Dawn*, 18 August 1991). The OIC urged the member states to attend UN population moot (Cairo; 1994), which was, nevertheless, boycotted by Iraq, Sudan, Saudi Arabia (see Keesing, 1994, p. 40208).

288. See the statement of OIC Secretary General Pirzada on the eve of 5th Islamic Summit (*Pakistan Times*, 21 January 1987). Also see the relevant paras of the final communiqués of 21st ICFM and of the 7th and 8th Islamic Summits.

289. Libyan Foreign Minister Dr Ali Abdul Salam Treiki's speech at the 10th ICFM, in which he also said that Libya had 217 agreements with Muslim states. See, *Pakistan Times*, 18 May 1979.

290. Saudi Foreign Minister's statement. See, *The Muslim*, 27 January 1981.

291. See Saad S. Khan, 'Defence Capabilities of the Muslim World', *National Development & Security*, (FRIENDS: Rawalpindi), vol. 6, no. 4, May 1998, pp. 81–123, for details about the nuclear weapon programmes of Pakistan, Iran, Libya etc.

292. S. Irfan Yousaf Ali, 'Nuclear Energy in the Muslim World', *Pakistan Horizon,* (Karachi: PIIA), vol. 34, no.1 January–March 1981, pp. 59–74.

293. See, *Star*, Dhaka, 25 June 1974.

294. This again shows the OIC's apprehensions about India, South Africa, and Israel (rogue states, according to OIC definition) respectively. Otherwise. It has never criticized the nuclear weaponization programmes of Pakistan, Libya, or Iraq. In fact in 1993, Secretary General Hamid al Gabid gave a clean bill to these states stating that Muslim countries are pursuing the nuclear option for peaceful purposes. He went on to advise Pakistan to share its nuclear know-how 'with brotherly Muslim states'.

295. Resolutions 12, 13 and 14/8-P. See Mehdi, ref. 9, pp. 112–113.

7 Political History III: OIC and Other Organizations

The basic objectives of most of the international organizations are the same; political and economic cooperation, promotion of peace and harmony, and support to justice, human rights, etc. Except that it has an Islamic tinge in its list of objectives, the OIC likewise stands for peace, cooperation, and development, and is against all kinds of colonialism, exploitation, religious intolerance, and racism. In many of these areas, it finds a lot of common ground with other regional organizations, besides the UN and its bodies. The OIC has repeatedly affirmed that it wants to work hand in hand with other organizations for achieving the common goal of a free, peaceful, and prosperous world. The 6th ICFM (Jeddah; 1975) passed a resolution expressing the OIC's desire to enhance cooperation with the Arab League, the Organization of African Unity (OAU), the Non-Aligned Movement (NAM), and the UN.[1] Through a separate resolution, approving the suggestion of Pakistan, it also decided to seek observer status for the OIC at the UN, which it did acquire just a few months after the conference.[2] The 12th ICFM (Baghdad; 1981) adopted a resolution deciding that the OIC should have a distinct representation at all the international organizations and conferences.[3] The aim of this chapter is to provide a brief description of the nature of the relationships that the OIC has with other international organizations.

The OIC member states form a significant proportion of a large number of inter-state organizations, since the membership of more than one inter-governmental organization is not mutually exclusive. The OIC constitutes about one-third of the total membership of the UN. Most of the regional organizations in Asia, Africa and Europe are either exclusively composed of, or have shared membership with, the OIC. In the former case, the OIC acts as a guide for those regional organizations, and in the latter, the OIC bloc behaves as a pressure group. Hence we can now analyse the relationship of the OIC with other international organizations in four categories:

Category A: Universal organization; the UN and its affiliated organs.

Category B: Organizations having shared membership with the OIC, like OAU, NAM, and the NATO, etc.

Category C: Organizations exclusively composed of the OIC membership, like the Arab League, ECO, etc.

Category D: Regional organizations having no common membership with the OIC, like the European Union, OAS, etc.

Chart 7.1
Muslim States' Proportionate Membership in International Organizations

Category	Name of the Organization	Total Membership	Membership shared with the OIC	Proportion of the OIC Members in total membership
A	United Nations	186	55	29.6%
B	ASEAN	7	3	42.8%
	British Commonwealth	50	10	20.0%
	Commonwealth of Independent States (CIS)	11	6	54.5%
	ECOWAS	16	11	68.8%
	NAM	103	43	41.7%
	NATO	14	1	7.1%
	OAU	51	26	51.0%
	OECD	26	1	4.0%
	OPEC	12	11	91.7%
	OSCE	47	8	17.0%
	SAARC	7	3	42.8%
C	Al-Maghrib Union	5	5	100.0%
	Arab League	21	21	100.0%
	ECO	10	10	100.0%
	GCC	6	6	100.0%
D	EU	12	0	0.0%
	G-7	7	0	0.0%
	NAFTA	3	0	0.0%
	OAS	35	0	0.0%

Note: *Full names of several organizations appear in the text of this chapter. For the unknown acronyms, consult the List of Abbreviations.*

Relationship of Subordination

The OIC has arrogated for itself a subordinate role *vis-à-vis* the UN. The preamble of the OIC Charter, *inter alia*, affirms its commitment to the UN Charter, since its 'purposes and principles... provide the basis for fruitful cooperation amongst all people'. This places a limitation on any independent initiative by the OIC in the political sphere, since the OIC wants to take each step under the framework of international legality, i.e., under the authority of the UN Security Council. The Charter of the Islamic Conference was registered with the UN Secretariat on 1 February 1974. As noted above, the 6th ICFM (Jeddah; 1975) through its resolution no. 14/6-P decided to enhance its cooperation with the world body.[4] In pursuance of a separate decision made at the same meeting, the OIC applied for observer status at the UN, which was granted on 10 October 1975, with a near universal support from the General Assembly. The lone voice in dissent was that of Israel which blasted the very notion of granting observer status to a religious organization. 'This will open up a pandora's box. What if the NATO starts claiming a separate status as a Christian organization?' the Israeli ambassador had asked.[5]

The OIC bloc soon became very active at the UN and the latter recognized the potential for partnership that the Islamic Conference had. On 26 October 1985, the 159-member General Assembly adopted the resolution calling for cooperation with the OIC unanimously, without vote. Even Israel had preferred to stay quiet. A similar resolution moved by Turkey and others in October 1991, calling for strengthening of cooperation between the UN and the OIC was carried by the UN General Assembly, but this time the Indian ambassador Abrar Ahmad raised the sole voice in dissent, by criticizing the OIC position on Kashmir.

Ever since, the cooperation between the two organizations is growing. The OIC has a Permanent Observer Mission at New York and another one at Geneva, for better coordination with the UN system. In 1994, the third external office, directly under the OIC Secretary General, was opened up in Islamabad, Pakistan, to coordinate the OIC efforts to bring about an end to the civil war in Afghanistan, with those of the UN. In turn, the UN Secretariat General also takes its own initiatives to enhance cooperation with the OIC. Besides the coordination meetings between the two organizations, a regular feature since 1983, the Secretary Generals of the two organizations invite each other to their conferences. The UN Secretary General, or his representation, has participated in and addressed all the Islamic Summit conferences, held so far.

Political and technical affairs: The OIC has mostly supported all the UN activities in the political field. The UN initiatives to resolve the Cyprus question, the Kuwait crisis, the Nogorno–Karabagh dispute, and a host of other crises have met with unqualified and unequivocal support from the Islamic Conference. The OIC does take its own course for crisis management and conflict resolution, but has never failed to emphasize that it does not want a competition with the world body. Most of the times, and civil wars in Somalia, Tajikistan, and Lebanon are prominent examples, the OIC has just followed the UN line by supporting the latter's peace endeavours. On rare occasions, the reverse has happened. Afghanistan's civil war is a case in point, when the OIC kept a high profile in trying to bring about an end to the war and the UN kept supporting the OIC's efforts and seeking its cooperation. In a significant meeting between the OIC Secretary General Izzuddiene Laraki and UN General Assembly President Hennady Udovenko in New York on 25 September 1997, both sides once again agreed that coordination between the polices of the two organizations was necessary for solving political problems.

On the issues of Palestine, Bosnia, and Kashmir, however, the OIC and the UN do not see eye to eye. That is why, the OIC resolutions and decisions on these problems, are not reflective of the UN viewpoint. The OIC believes that the UN has, at times, employed double standards. The OIC supports the territorial integrity of Iraq and believes that Israel should be punished for aggression and illegal occupation of other countries' territories in the same forceful manner as was Iraq. At the height of the war in Bosnia, the OIC had decided to openly defy the UN decision to continue an arms embargo on Bosnia. A similar case of disagreement pertains to the UN approach towards Kashmir. Though the UN has adopted several resolutions on Kashmir, it no longer reiterates them and is least inclined to take any assertive action to implement its resolutions. On its part, the OIC is insisting that the solution to the civil war in Kashmir lies in the 'full implementation of the relevant UN resolutions'.

Their interaction is not limited to the political field. Today several agreements between the UN and the OIC bodies exist in five principle areas; food and agriculture, peace and security, development of science and technology, investment mechanism and joint ventures, and lastly, the eradication of illiteracy and assistance to refugees. Lately, the development of trade and technical cooperation in Islamic countries was added as another priority area of cooperation.[6] The subsidiary and affiliated organs of the two organizations working in educational, economic, social, and cultural fields remain in close touch with each other to harmonize their activities, and to avoid their overlapping or duplication. The UN agencies not only assist the individual member states in various projects but also provide advice and expert opinion to the OIC organs in their activities. Since the recipient states seek all avenues for assistance for gigantic economic projects, it is not unusual for a big dam or some such large project in a Muslim country to be partially financed by the IDB and partially by a UN donor agency. In the words of an OIC Secretary General:

> The OIC has accelerated contacts and cooperation with the UN system in the past years. A number of cooperation agreements have been concluded with the Agencies of the UN system which provide for frequent contacts and exchange of information and technical assistance for the mutual benefit of the organizations....At the same time, it attends all the conferences and meetings organized by the UN, on reciprocal basis. The cooperation arrangement was finalized following the adoption of a resolution by the General Assembly...Coordination meetings between the two organizations at Geneva have enabled the pursuit of more meaningful cooperation.[7]

The OIC's desire for cooperation has won plaudits from the UN also. The UN Secretary General Kofi Annan, in his message to the OIC Foreign Ministers' coordination meeting at New York on 2 October 1997, described the OIC as 'a bridge to the world community...a bastion of principle and an advocate on behalf of Islam and its peoples...'. Citing the OIC–UN cooperation in Afghanistan, Somalia, and Tajikistan in his encomium, Annan declared the two organizations to be 'natural partners for Peace'.

The OIC has designated the IRCICA, commonly known as the Istanbul Centre, as its focal point for cooperation in the field of research on history, art, and culture with the UN system.[8] The latter's focal point is the UNESCO, and several Memoranda of Understanding (MoUs) have been signed between the two agencies. In the field of technical cooperation, the OIC has designated the Ankara Centre, or SESRTCIC, as its focal point. Its counterpart in the UN system is the UNDP.[9] Both the organs are collaborating with each other in a number of areas. Lately, the Food and Agriculture Organization (FAO) of the UN, has given a grant to the SESRTCIC to set up a parallel institution within the OIC structure.[10]

The OIC role within the UN: The OIC has acted as a more or less coherent pressure group at the UN. Starting from 1980, the OIC has regularly held the annual coordination meetings of the Islamic Foreign Ministers, at the beginning of the UN General Assembly session, in New York every year. One can discern the OIC activity at the UN in four areas.

The first thing that the OIC has largely been successful in accomplishing is the development of an Islamic vision of foreign policy. On the issues of fundamental concern to the Muslim world, the OIC states have almost always voted *en bloc*. We have seen in the preceding chapter that the OIC tried to expel Israel from the United Nations several times. Though the OIC fell short of the requisite two-thirds majority at the General Assembly, it did expel Israel from a principal UN organ, the UNESCO. The OIC succeeded in getting a UN resolution equating Zionism with racism adopted with a comfortable majority. Years later, the OIC lobby blocked Serbia's bid to retain the

UN seat rejecting its claim of being the successor state of the former Yugoslavia. On a number of other issues like population, environment, and disarmament, the OIC has developed a distinct 'Muslim world view' at the UN debates.

The second area of coordination is in the selection of Muslim states to various positions at the UN. Many a time a Muslim country aspiring to contest the UN Security Council seat, the post of President/Vice President of the UN General Assembly or the post of Director General of a UN specialized agency, places its case before the preceding ICFM. The ICFM considers the request so as to make certain that the Muslim votes in the UN will not be divided to the benefit of a non-member country. Usually, the OIC bloc supports the country whose candidature has been endorsed by the Islamic Conference earlier. The OIC's concerted efforts at the UN also resulted in the approval of the General Assembly to declaring the two Muslim festivals of *Eid-ul-Fitr* and *Eid-ul-Adha* as official holidays at the United Nations.[11]

The third area where the OIC has maintained a high profile is the debates on colonialism, imperialism, and neo-exploitation. The OIC group at the UN has always strived for the implementation of a just and humane New International Economic Order. The group has been most vocal in support of all the UN decisions regarding the apartheid in South Africa, the liberation of Namibia, issues of racism and colonialism in a number of countries, and so on.

And lastly, the OIC has been working for a restructuring of the UN system to make it democratic and non-discriminatory. As early as in 1977, when the OIC's association with the UN was only two years old, the 8th ICFM (Tripoli; 1977) discussed the 'unjust and undemocratic system' of the UN Security Council. Addressing the Conference, Libyan President Moammar Qaddafi had called for the abolishment of the right of veto and the realization of equality among nations. 'How can a single country have the right to oppose the will of the whole world?' Qaddafi had asked.[12] Since then, the OIC has been struggling for an egalitarian UN system.

Lately, the OIC has changed its policy of criticizing the veto power and has started thinking of getting the right for itself. The idea of the 6th

veto right being given to the OIC, was first mooted in the final declaration of an international conference of the World Muslim Congress (WMC). At the 8th Islamic Summit (Tehran; 1997), the host Iran's paramount leader Ali Khaminei, demanded veto power for the Muslim world in the UN Security Council. The text of the OIC resolution no. 40/8-P(IS) on UN reforms, however, stopped short of demanding the veto right. It reiterated 'the need for reform and democratization of the Security Council' and called for its expansion on the basis of 'equitable geographical distribution and sovereign equality of member-states'. The Conference reaffirmed the readiness of the Muslim states to help in the restructuring.[13]

Relationship of Coordination

The OIC has a relationship of coordination with the organizations having a shared membership with it. The NAM, OAU, and CIS are some of the prominent organizations falling in this category. The OIC supports these organizations for the solution of different problems, on reciprocal basis. On issues like Somalia, Eritrea etc., the OIC has repeatedly asserted that it will work together with like-minded organizations to achieve the common goals of peace and stability. It can hardly be overemphasized that it is in the best common interests of these organizations, and their memberships, to pool their efforts to achieve the common objectives against imperialism, poverty, and disease, especially in the face of increased coherence in posture being shown by the developed states.

Being as non-aligned and anti-racist in orientation as the NAM, and as cooperation-oriented as the OAU, it is but natural that the OIC cooperated with these organizations on issues such as Apartheid, Portugal's colonial possessions in Africa, and the question of Namibia, where all of them saw eye to eye with each other. In fact, on a problem where Muslims are not the direct victims, the OIC seldom has a separate policy at all. It just harmonizes its resolutions with the tunes played by the like-minded regional organizations. One such example is that of South West Africa where the OIC resolutions used to be a verbatim replica of the NAM resolutions. Speaking at the NAM meeting on Namibia at New Delhi in April 1985, the then OIC Secretary General Sharifuddin Pirzada assured the assembly that the 'decisions adopted and the declarations made by the Non-Aligned Movement on the question of Namibia will enjoy the full and unstinted support of the OIC'.[14]

In such regional organizations, the OIC also plays the role of a pressure group. For instance, in May 1994, the OIC members did not allow Serbia to attend the NAM Summit at Cairo, Egypt, though Yugoslavia was one of the founder members of the NAM, because Serbia had not recognized Bosnia as a sovereign state. Similarly, within the OAU, the OIC group has given that organization, an anti-racist and anti-Zionist tinge, though some of the African countries had had diplomatic relations with Israel. One area in which the OIC is content with playing second fiddle to these organizations is that of conflict resolution. If a conflict erupts between two of the OIC members, which are concurrently the members of, say, the OAU, the OIC usually leaves the responsibility of dispute settlement with the latter, conforming its own role to expressing support for the peace initiatives being undertaken by the regional organization concerned.

In the CIS and the OSCE, the OIC members have substantial representations, but most of these states are new-entrants in the OIC and hence do not necessarily share the convictions of the OIC on the issues of Al-Quds, North Cyprus, etc. Still, these member states have got additional leverage, simply by virtue of holding the concurrent membership of the OIC. As for ASEAN, ECOWAS, and the SAARC, they are primarily economic, not political organizations. The fact that around half of their memberships are composed of the OIC member-states is reflected in their policies, inasmuch as they are not likely to take a position in open conflict with that of the OIC on a given issue. They may not think about trade partnership or any kind of economic cooperation with, say, Israel, as long as the OIC does not soften its stance towards it. The commitment of Malaysia, Senegal, and Pakistan alone, for instance, to the causes espoused by the OIC, are too strong to be

sacrificed in the interests of these three organizations, respectively. Though the OPEC is also placed in this category but, except Venezuela, all its members are Muslim states, hence members of the OIC also. The OPEC arrangement has the potential to influence global economic stability through adjustments in oil prices and quotas. Thus the overwhelming Muslim majority in OPEC also gives the Muslim world, a tool to re-employ the 'oil weapon'. At the other extreme, within this category come the NATO and the OECD, which have too small a representation of Muslim states, to influence any decision in a meaningful way. (See Chart 7.1)

Relationship of Compatibility

The organizations that are exclusively composed of the OIC member states (our category C), usually have objectives, compatible with those of the OIC. The Charter of the OIC allows for cooperation with the international Muslim organizations which, by definition, include inter-governmental as well as non-governmental organizations. The role of selected Islamic NGOs is discussed in Chapter 14, so here we are concerned with the Muslim Inter-Governmental Organizations like the Arab League and the Economic Cooperation Organization (ECO), both of which enjoy observer status at the OIC.

The Arab League is working for the economic uplift of the Arab region and the ECO is striving for the development of the Muslim states in Central and South Asia. The OIC, which aims at the prosperity of the whole Muslim world, these two regions not excepted, can only be happy to provide maximum financial, moral, and political support to these organizations. Likewise, on political issues including Palestine, Bosnia, and Kashmir, etc., where a near consensus exists among the individual Muslim countries, the policies of regional economic arrangements of the Muslim countries do not find them at variance with those of the OIC. So, both, in the economic and the political frays, the OIC and the Muslim States' regional arrangements find their objectives and policies in complete harmony with each other. Despite this mutual positive input between the OIC and the smaller regional Muslim organizations, some problems do occur due to *en bloc* voting patterns of different regional groups in the Islamic Conference which does not augur well for the Organization.

Relationship of Competition

It is indeed difficult for the OIC to influence the decisions of organizations such as the European Union (EU) or the Organization of American States (OAS) which have an exclusive non-Muslim composition (our category D). Here the OIC tries to influence them from outside. The relationship between the OIC and a category D organization may be of competition or cooperation depending on whether the objectives of the two sides on a given problem are conflicting or compatible. The war in Bosnia (1992–96) is a case in point where the relations between the Islamic Conference and the European Union saw several ups and downs. The former was concerned about the war since the country had a Muslim government while the latter was interested in the problem as the country lay in Europe; as for the Republic of Bosnia, it was not, and still is not, the member of either. Since the OIC and the EU do not share any common membership, neither of them had a lobby within the other.

In the early years of war, it appears that both the organizations were competing with each other to take the credit for the final solution to the crisis. The OIC contact group and the EU contact group on Bosnia were working independently and, sometimes, at cross-purpose. Both groups vied with each other to float their own peace plans alternatively and by the end of 1993, it appeared that a mutual rivalry had erupted. It was a time when the EU had come very near to accepting a permanent division of Bosnia on ethnic lines while the OIC would not agree to anything short of an unqualified guarantee for the territorial integrity of Bosnia. The OIC was instrumental in pre-empting any move by the EU that could legitimize the gains made by the Serb rebel forces. As the fighting lingered on, all parties directly or indirectly associated with the crisis, came to be taken over by war fatigue. By mid-1995, the Muslim and the European teams started cooperating with each other.

It is well-known that the European Union was reluctant to engage in a direct military showdown with the Serb rebel forces while the Islamic Conference was losing patience when arial bombardment to wipe out the rebel Serb war machine was not taking place. Still, the European negotiators employed the threat of replacing their peace-keeping troops with those from the OIC states, in the final stages of negotiations with the Serb leadership.[15] This was the last thing the Serbs would have wanted, so they gave in. Finally, when the Dayton peace accord was reached, both the EU and the OIC representatives attended the final signing ceremony at Paris as witnesses. Ever since, both sides are cooperating with each other in the world efforts aimed at assisting in the reconstruction of war-ravaged Bosnia. This single episode is enough to demonstrate the nature of the OIC relationship with an organization, which does not have an OIC state in its fold.

Conclusion

The OIC's relationship with other international organizations, is a major facet of its political history. One may not fail to notice that whereas the OIC is on good terms with other regional organizations and enjoys a mutually beneficial relationship of harmony with most of them; its attitude towards the UN, however, gives a whiff of an inferiority complex. It may indeed be imprudent to flout international legality or to challenge the authority of the UN, which may nudge the world into a state of anarchy; still the OIC would be well-advised to show a bold face, where it feels the UN is employing double standards. The OIC can extend the hand of benign cooperation with the world body for the solution of all the issues concerning the Muslim world. Moreover, it can share the burden of the UN by playing a pivotal role in conflict resolution among the Muslim states. This it can do by making it mandatory for its member states to exhaust the OIC option for a dispute settlement, before approaching the UN or any regional organization, for the purpose.

Conflict and rivalry among the regional organizations of the world would only help the present faultlines to become the battlelines of the future. This may not turn the world into a wonderful place to live in. It is in the common interest of all international organizations, as well as of all mankind, that international interaction is based upon good faith, a spirit of cooperation, and division of responsibilities. This is precisely what the OIC purports to be doing in its relationship with other international organizations.

NOTES and REFERENCES

1. See resolutions no. 11/6-P, 12/6-P, 13/6-P and 14/6-P of the 6th ICFM in 'Declaration and Resolutions of the Islamic Heads of State and Foreign Ministers' Conferences: 1969-81', (Jeddah: OIC, n. d.), p. 41.

2. Ibid., pp. 97–116.

3. Ibid.

4. It is notable that a similar resolution was adopted by the UN General Assembly in mid-November 1984, that called upon the world body to increase cooperation with the Organization of the Islamic Conference. See Inamullah Khan (ed.), 'World Muslim Gazetteer: 1985', (Karachi: WMC, 1987), p. 104.

5. 'Facts on File', 1975, p. 775.

6. See the OIC Secretary General's report A/41/532, presented at the coordination meeting of the heads of the OIC organs held at Geneva, 28–30 July 1986.

7. Extract from Sharifuddin Pirzada's speech on 'The role of the OIC as an international organization' at the Institute of Strategic and International Studies, Kuala Lumpur, Malaysia (May 1985), quoted in *Speeches and Statements of H. E. Sharifuddin Pirzada*, (Karachi: n. p., 1989), p. 67.

8. See IRCICA Quarterly Newsletter, Istanbul, August 1996, No. 40, pp. 4-6.

9. See 'Ankara Center: Functions, Facilities, Activities', (Ankara, SESRTCIC, 1995), pp. 10–11.

10. *The Muslim*, Islamabad, 9 May 1988.

11. The decision to the effect was taken at the end of 1996. So, 10 February 1997 and 17 April 1997, were for the first time observed as holidays on account of the two Muslim festivals respectively. See, *The Muslim World*, (Karachi: WMC), vol. 34, vol. 29, 11 January 1997, p. 8.

12. 'OIC Declarations', ref. 1, p. 165.

13. The text of the Iranian leader's speech was provided to the author by the Iran's diplomatic mission at Islamabad, while the copies of the resolutions adopted by the 8th Islamic Summit were provided by the OIC Permanent Mission at Islamabad.

14. See *Speeches and Statements*, ref. 7, p. 40.

15. *Le Monde*, story was quoted by *Pakistan Times*, Islamabad, 13 August 1995.

⑧ Problems and Weaknesses

The OIC was never taken very seriously even by its sympathizers, let alone by its detractors. Wherever the Organization did something positive, like in Afghanistan, Bosnia, and Philippines, etc., it largely went unnoticed but whenever it failed, everyone joined the chorus of criticism. The press and the media in the OIC member states taunt it as 'Oh, I see!' and as the 'Organization of Impotent Countries'. Others suggest the name to be changed to NIDC (No, I don't see!) or DIC (Disorganization of the Islamic Countries).[1] As for the media in the non-OIC countries, it is simply indifferent. This amply demonstrates that a principal shortcoming of the Organization is its utter failure to construct a favourable image of itself in the media. Today, what is aptly described as the 'CNN factor', has become a very important phenomenon. If a thing is not reported by the CNN or, for that matter, by other international electronic or print news networks, it does not mean that that particular occurence had not taken place at all. It is no mean failure on the part of the OIC and other Islamic institutions of international character that they have not recognized the self-evident realities of this age of information revolution and have been unable to make their presence or importance felt by employing information technology.

There is no dearth of conspiracy theorists among the Muslims, and even some of the OIC Secretary Generals, including Tunku Abdul Rahman, the first OIC Secretary General, were open and vocal critics of what they called, the deliberate apathy of the Western media towards news relating to the Islamic Conference.[2] It is definitely not fair to find a scapegoat and impute to it one's own shortcomings. It can hardly be gainsaid that the OIC has achieved much less in the first three decades of its existence than what its potential warranted.

The diffidence and irresolution that characterize the OIC, more often than not, stem from a number of innate implicit and explicit weaknesses that the

Organization is afflicted with. Though this topic has been the subject of serious debates in the past few years, but the lack of transparency, virtual absence of accountability, and unavailability of information has made it well nigh impossible to assess reliably the exact nature and extent of these maladies. Consequently, no independent scientific study to delve into the etiology of the malaise has ever been carried out. On several occasions, the Secretary Generals have formed committees to investigate the causes of, and suggest solutions for, the inefficiency of the OIC. Each time the latent pressures and inertia outweighed the genuine desire for change; many a time the reports failed to address the real issues and prevaricated into non-issues. After a half-hearted attempt at the implementation of selected recommendations, the reports invariably found their way into cold storage.

Before plunging into the thicket of a detailed discussion on the factors that militate against a strong and confident OIC, a few reflections may not be amiss.

After the UN, it is the OIC alone that has so much of diversity within its fold. The single common denominator among the OIC member states is Islam, otherwise there is not one thing, geography, language, culture, national priorities etc., that is common among, say, Bosnia, Senegal, Libya, Qatar, Tajikistan, and Maldives. The Organization has miserably failed to transform the diversity from a liability into an asset. One can identify most of its problems as those any inter-governmental organization is bound to face in the present modern nation-state system, where the 'sovereign' state is the unit actor, jealously protecting its own national interests. In an organization whose member-states are geographically contiguous, there is much more likelihood of finding a lot of common ground in the pantheons of national interests. This is not the case with the OIC. In the European Union, for example, Germany is as likely to feel threatened by an imperialist Russia as, say, Spain or Belgium are, but within the Islamic Conference, Suriname, Brunei, or Guinea simply cannot take Israel as a security risk as much as Lebanon or Syria do.

Consequently, the conflicting and occasionally diametrically opposite national priorities of the member states encumber the OIC's capacity to act decisively. More so, the spectacular increase in the OIC membership has made it a large, unwieldy organization which, in turn, has accentuated the phenomenon of regionalism. These two factors translate into a very strong reaction on the part of the OIC on one particular issue and a very timid one, lacking initiative, on the other. This is tantamount to having double standards. The organizational weakness is another facade of the same malaise, which merits consideration in its own right. These problems are compounded further by the ambiguities in the OIC Charter. And last, but not the least, the core problem with the OIC, all its affiliated organs, and coincidentally, with most of the Islamic institutions worldwide, is the perennial financial stringency. We should look into these problems one by one.

The Problem of Conflicting National Interests

It is hardly debatable that Islam had never tried to destroy the social and political identities of the believers. All it purported to do, was to change the hierarchy of their personal loyalties where the *ummah* (trans-national Muslim community) identity came at the top. This is precisely where the OIC has failed, that is, to change the hierarchy of each member state's priorities. Hardly any Muslim country has made its interests subservient to the demands of the Muslim world solidarity. Just a few facts are enough to demonstrate this contention.

It is indeed bizarre that an Organization whose membership includes some of the world's richest states becomes so cash-strapped at times that it fails to pay salaries to its staff for months in a row. The member states are particularly frugal in defraying the basic annual contributions to the OIC budget. While most member states are oblivious

of their obligations towards the Islamic Conference, none ever refrains from clamouring for its due from the Organization. Pakistan has never faltered in soliciting, as a matter of right, unequivocal support from the OIC on the Kashmir problem; Indonesia, Morocco, and Turkey have the same kind of expectations from it on the questions of East Timor, Western Sahara, and North Cyprus, respectively. This is the point where the national interests of individual states justify their making a beeline to affirm their commitment to 'the ideals espoused by the OIC'.

The OIC provides the member states with a vibrant political forum. That the OIC is seldom miserly in offering unqualified support to the cause of any Muslim state or community, the merits of the case notwithstanding, has been a self-standing incentive to all Muslim states for joining it. The diplomatic support for a certain cause, from a solid bloc of fifty-five states on all international fora is a piece of pie that every state would relish. It would be in the fitness of things to add that a given Muslim state cannot reasonably be expected to be inextricably committed to an amicable resolution of a territorial dispute involving another Muslim state on the other side of the globe. So even if the OIC membership is not supporting a member-state, on a particular issue in the way it should, the latter still finds the platform useful for explaining the country's policies or to defend its position for which it may be under flak by the world community.

In order to further their national interests the member countries (mis)use this forum in many ways. It has become customary to criticize their rival states from the OIC floor; Pakistan castigates India, Turkey takes on Bulgaria, and so on. But the matter does not stop here. The Muslim countries feel no qualms in using this forum to attack each other. This creates an ill will in the target state. Iraq, since its 1990 invasion of Kuwait, is an obvious example as almost fifteen Arab states, most of whom were part of the US-led alliance during the Gulf war, invariably use all the OIC fora for Iraq-bashing.

Thus it is not unusual for many of the OIC meetings to be marred by squabbles and nibbling. During the 1980s, verbal duels between Iran and Iraq, Iran and Saudi Arabia, Mauritania and

Morocco were a common feature; in the following decade repartees exchanged between Sudan and Uganda, Iraq and Kuwait, and others, started overshadowing the proceedings. One example might suffice to show how deep the cleavages are. In the 5th meeting of the OIC standing Committee on Science and Technology (COMSTECH) in 1991 at Islamabad, Muslim countries were being represented by delegations of scientists and experts, to discuss ways and means for scientific and technological advancement in the Muslim world. During the second session, the leader of the Iraqi delegation saw that a Kuwaiti delegate had a pistol in his belt. The Iraqi minister demanded that the Kuwaitis leave the meeting or remove the gun. Since the Kuwaiti delegation did neither, the Iraqi minister announced that he was going to fetch his gun. Pakistan's Minister of Science and Technology, Illahi Bux Soomro (now Speaker of the parliament), who was chairing the session, intervened to pacify the two delegates but neither side budged, so the session had to be adjourned. A sorry ending to the discussion on Science and Technology![3]

In addition, the domestic priorities of the member states that are reflected in the OIC moots, create problems for effective action. Many Muslim countries with autocratic regimes in power, do not take any interest in the discussion on environment, wildlife, and population explosion but are very enthusiastic about the passage of resolutions condemning terrorism, by which they mean, their Islamist oppositions. But if the issue of state terrorism against their domestic political opponents is raised, they dismiss it as an interference in their internal affairs. In a similar vein, the member states feel free to hinder any OIC initiative that they perceive to be against their national interests. For example, during the 7th ICFM (Istanbul; 1976), Mauritania, Algeria, and Morocco requested the OIC not to discuss the civil war in Sahara on the plea that they were already holding parleys on the issue amongst themselves. It was up to the OIC to question how the blocking of discussion on the subject at the said ministerial meeting would complement their trilateral talks, or in other words, how any initiative by the Conference could have hampered the early solution of the crisis. Another illustration of the same trend is that of the Gulf

War, where it was in the national interests of the Arab states not to have peace with Iraq without having its war machines destroyed. So these states, Saudi Arabia being prominent, thwarted all efforts by Iran, Malaysia, and Pakistan, etc., to call an ICFM to debate the problem.

The OIC organs also suffer for this 'selective morality' of the member states whose commitment to one particular organ is usually more than that towards other organs. For instance, there are more than forty-five OIC member states who are also members of the Islamic Development Bank (IDB) but still have not ratified the Islamic Court's Statute. This is because the former organ provides loans and financial assistance in the development projects while the latter will only clip the wings of their sovereignties.

These are the grim realities that dictate the current politics of the OIC. It is up to the states to decide where to draw the line between the demands of national interest and the advantages of having a strong and confident Organization. The necessity for the member states to evince some degree of altruism can scarcely be overstated.

Bloc Politics

It is but natural that individual member states feel greater affinity with the states belonging to their own respective regions, both in the political and the cultural contexts, than with those from other geographical zones. The problem of regionalism thus creeps into the large trans-continental organizations which sometimes hampers their capacity to act or to react. This is particularly true of the OIC where internal frictions between collectivities is an acute problem. It is not rare that the Arab and African member states would prevail upon the OIC, not to consider a particular problem since they wish to put it before the Arab League or the Organization of African Unity (OAU), as the case may be, and only after exhausting the option, they might consider approaching the OIC.

Divisions do not exist on the basis of geography and culture alone, political leanings and ideologies are also potent factors on the stage. Thus within the OIC there are a number of blocs or factions that often act at cross purposes to each other. One is the Arab versus non-Arab factionalism, another is the divide between the radical and the conservative countries, yet another between the rich and the poor Muslim states, and finally, between the aligned countries, allied to rival centres of power. With the demise of the Soviet Union in 1991, this last distinction has lost meaning.

The *en bloc* voting pattern on regional basis has been used at least by three regional blocs, namely, Arab, West African, and the Central Asian blocs. This problem of regionalism dates back to the sixties and the seventies when Nasser's ideas about pan-Arabism were popular in the Middle East. Even those Arab states that were opposed to Nasser, practiced the 'Arab first' policy. Today the idea of Jerusalem being an Arab issue seems ridiculous, but three decades back, the reference to Al-Quds as an Islamic problem was frowned upon. Precisely for that reason, many Arab states led by Jordan and the PLO, were insisting on calling an Arab summit to discuss the Al-Aqsa mosque arson in August 1969.[4] Even when their objections were overruled and the 1st Islamic Summit (Rabat; Sept. 1969) took place, these countries continued opposing the establishment of a permanent secretariat, which Egypt described as 'futile and irrelevant to the *Arab struggle*' (emphasis added).[5] As late as in May 1979, the Arab bloc insisted on Egypt's expulsion from the OIC following a similar decision taken by the Arab League earlier. This tacitly implied that the Arab countries were more hurt by Egypt's betrayal of the Palestine cause, than was the rest of the Muslim world. Again in January 1984, the Arab bloc attempted to make Egypt's re-entry to the OIC, conditional on a similar decision by the Arab League. However, this time the non-Arab States took a firm stand on not holding the OIC hostage to the Arab League decisions.[6]

In a similar vein, the West African States also have a tendency of *en bloc* voting. They act in unison in making demands for economic assistance for their poverty-stricken region. On the political side, they do not see eye to eye with the Arab States. This is shown by their voting against the expulsion of Egypt as well as the breaking off of diplomatic relations with Israel.

Among the Asian members, Pakistan has normally favoured the Arab bloc while Iran and Turkey have usually not. Iran, for example, made impossible the participation of Abu Dhabi in the 2nd ICFM (Karachi; 1970) on the plea that Abu Dhabi was not a sovereign state. It may be mentioned that the Amir of this oil rich emirate, Sheikh Zaid Bin Sultan (now President of the UAE) was desirous of attending this moot.[7] Since 1991, the former Communist Muslim republics of Central Asia have also been voting *en bloc* in the OIC, as they face common problems and share more or less a common destiny as well. A prominent example is the firm opposition of all the six ex-Soviet Muslim states to the recognition of Taliban-led government of Afghanistan, by the OIC.

Then comes the sharp division between the radical states like Iran, Iraq, Syria, Libya, and Yemen etc., who always take a hard-line stand on all political issues, as against the moderate stance taken by conservative states like Saudi Arabia, Morocco, Bahrain etc. Speaking at the 4th Islamic Summit (Casablanca; 1984), the Libyan Prime Minister had stated that only one division existed between the Muslims countries, and that was between the *progressive revolutionary* and the *conservative reactionary* states (emphasis added). Though his contentions were strongly refuted by other Muslim states in their rejoinders but the voting patterns in the OIC fora suggest that the deviation in the angles was so wide between the radical and the conservative states that a consensus in the OIC, except on issues like Palestine, Kashmir, and Bosnia, was virtually impossible.[8]

Till 1991, the cold war too had cast its shadow on the OIC, where the radical-conservative divide was sharpened by pro-Soviet and pro-American stances of the two sides. The states depending on Moscow for the arms purchases had no choice but to support Moscow as the 'friend of Muslims'.[9] When the 1st EICFM (Islamabad; 1980) condemned the Soviet invasion of Afghanistan, four members, namely, Syria, South Yemen, Algeria, and the PLO had strongly opposed the resolution. As President Hafiz-al-Asad later explained to the Pakistani Foreign Minister Agha Shahi, he understood the position of the general Muslim *ummah* on Soviet aggression against

Muslim Afghanistan, but since Syria was at daggers drawn with Tel Aviv and Washington, and wholly dependent upon Moscow for its defence procurements, she could not afford to give the slightest offence to Moscow. 'If I give the smallest pretext to Soviet Union to stop arms sales, I would be at the knees of Israel', the Syrian leader had remarked.[10]

It is interesting to note that at the same conference, a separate resolution on the Iran-hostage crisis was also adopted that condemned the United States, holding it responsible for escalating the crisis and warning against any misadventure to release its hostages. It was now the turn of Saudi Arabia and eight African states to oppose the reference to the US by name in the said resolution.[11] The latter were receiving food aid from the United States at that time. Thereafter, the OIC became more prolific in condemning either or both the super powers throughout the following decade. In its extremely radical and non-aligned rhetoric, the OIC never lost an opportunity to castigate, what it called, the forces of exploitation; and this term, of course, took care of everyone amongst the developed states. Such controversial resolutions obviously led to clashes between the two camps in the Islamic Conference. As it turned out, it was easier to pass harsh resolutions, but their implementation, which required unqualified commitment from the members, was far more difficult. With the disintegration of the former Soviet Union, the divide between the pro-US and pro-Soviet states has naturally disappeared and a fortiori, the OIC has been able to meaningfully assert itself in the conflicts in Bosnia and Kosovo, to name just two instances.

Similarly, the tensions between the poor African countries and the oil-rich gulf sheikhdoms have also been blurred in recent years. The former had high expectations from the OIC, through which they believed, their oil-rich 'brotherly' states would channel aid to them. However, the unified demands by African states like, to have a three-tier oil-price structure, one per cent of the GNP of rich Muslim states to be given to the poor ones, and such others, have not fructified, so this *modus operandi* has been abandoned.[12] Now the African countries

secure financial help through bilateral relationship with individual rich states.

The primary objective of the Organization, that is, Islamic solidarity, has been the casualty of this wide variety of factionalisms. The Organization tends to be coherent in such emotive issues such as saving a particular Muslim community from ethnic cleansing as in Bosnia, Kashmir, and Philippines, that is to say when one of the parties to the conflict is non-Muslim. In a conflict between two Muslim parties, the sympathies and prejudices of individual member states come to the fore, ripping apart the chances of a common stand. The two Gulf wars are cases in point. During the 1980–88 period, it was in the perceived security interests of the Arab bloc, not to allow the emergence of a strong military or economic power on the eastern coast of the Gulf. So not only was Iraq supported against Iran, by most of the Arab states in their individual and collective capacities, the OIC also was used for their parochial objectives. In this regard, the decision to hold the 12th ICFM in Baghdad (June 1981), despite strong protests from Tehran, left the latter disillusioned with the OIC. It believed that the organization, was being used as a tool by a certain bloc within it. Moreover, this move destroyed even a semblance of the OIC's neutrality in the Iran–Iraq war.

Just two years after the end of this war, it was Iraq's turn to be feared by the same Arab states which earlier were afraid of Iran's growing power. Extra-regional powers were called in and paid to crush Iraq. Not only was Iraq badly mauled, fifteen of the twenty-member Arab club scuttled the move to convene an OIC conference to mediate the issue.[13] This *en bloc* resistance to the idea, foiled the attempt to bring in the OIC because the required two-third majority to convene an ICFM could not be mustered up. The bloc politics and factionalism has eroded the ideals the OIC espouses, from within. All its rhetoric comes to naught if any one bloc within the Islamic Conference, refuses to compromise.

Legally Deficient Framework

The problems of the Islamic Conference are further compounded by its deficient legal framework. The Charter of the Organization very loosely defines the broader contours of the objectives and principles. It is vague in explaining how they are to be attained, what are the responsibilities of the Muslim states and what is the mandate of the Organization in this respect. It is probably taken for granted that the member states would have altruistic motives and everything would be worked out through consultations. Such idyllic assumptions can hardly withstand the stark truths of the world of realpolitik. Taking the example of the Iraqi invasion of Kuwait cited above, it can safely be assumed that had the OIC Charter had a well-defined course of action for such eventualities, such as binding recourse to the OIC for mediation or reconciliation (like there is in the Arab League Charter) or an automatic convening of an emergency ICFM; this could have mitigated the negative impact of non-cooperation by a certain section of the OIC membership.

The ambiguities and deficiencies in the legal documents of the Islamic Conference have hit the very foundations of its prestige and credibility. Much has already been said about the problems emanating from the absence of a well-defined membership criterion. Since a few countries where the Muslims do not constitute a simple numerical majority, have also now found their way into the Organization, it has become all the more difficult for the views of all the individual members states to coalesce into a coherent policy of the OIC. Similarly, the purposeless magnanimity with which scores of states and organizations are granted observer or guest status at the Islamic Conference, serves to gain no palpable advantage.

Another legal deficiency that compromises the effectiveness of the OIC is the impotency of the office of the Secretary General. Except in matters of appointment, promotion, and dismissal of the secretariat staff, his hands are tied. This makes him more of a chief administrative officer of a government bureau than the chief executive of a large inter-governmental organization. Empowerment of the office of the Secretary General is a *sine qua non* for making the Organization truly responsive at the moment of decision.

And then, the quintessential problem revolves round the absence of any statutory role for the Organization in case of a crisis situation. First of all, there is no provision for an automatic convening of an Islamic Foreign Minister's Conference when hostilities or a natural calamity involving one or more member states, break out. Neither has any precise course of action for the state(s) so affected, like a binding recourse to the OIC, been stipulated, nor a code of conduct for the remaining Muslim states, known. Everything being left to the individual decisions of each member state, the final outcome may or may not be to the ultimate advantage of the OIC group as a collectivity.

Secondly, even if the majority of the OIC membership is seriously concerned about an issue, there is no monitoring mechanism such as the Security Council at the UN that can meet even at a few hours' notice, any time during the year, depending upon the gravity of the situation to be considered. The OIC reaction has to wait for the holding of an emergency ICFM that meets, if at all, when much water might already have flowed under the bridges.

Thirdly, even if the OIC manages to meet and arrive at a few decisions, there is no implementation machinery as such. For instance, the 3rd Islamic Summit (Taif; 1981) had decided to establish an Islamic Court of Justice but even after about two decades, not much progress has been made. Worse still was the fate of the famous decision of the 4th Islamic Summit (Casablanca; 1984) of forming regional mediation committees to solve the localized disputes between Muslim states, judiciously and expeditiously. The Charter is silent as to what the responsibilities of the Organization and of the member states are, if the decisions of the Islamic Summits go unheeded. Going back to our example of the Islamic Court, there is no allowance for, say, the Secretary General to take remedial steps such as forming an experts' committee comprising the OIC officials or three or more Islamic countries' foreign ministers to negotiate with the member states to ratify the Court's Statute and, in case of failure, recommend the following Islamic Summit to rescind the decision. The very business of making loud decisions and then becoming slack on the follow-up is tantamount to making a mockery of the prestige of the Islamic Conference.

Fourthly, there is no enforcement mechanism in the OIC system. Whatever the political theorists may say about the international organizations being one of the three actors that have become more important than the state-actors in the international system, the same does not hold true as far as the OIC is concerned.[14] Its directives may be, and are, flouted with impunity, like Serbia ignoring the OIC calls to recognize Bosnia, India refusing to allow the OIC fact-finding mission to visit occupied Kashmir and so on. There is no coercive machinery, military, economic, or otherwise that can be applied by the OIC. It has no control even over its own member states that are sometimes selective in enforcing the OIC decisions.

The Organization itself is much more selective in taking punitive action. Egypt was expelled from the OIC for signing a peace treaty with Israel but when Palestine itself struck a peace deal fourteen years later, the matter of Palestine's expulsion never even came up for consideration. By analogy, Pakistan can also be expelled from the OIC if it makes peace with India overlooking the interests of the Muslim people of Kashmir, but it is highly unlikely that the OIC would do so. The suspension of the membership of the Soviet-backed Kabul regime of Dr Najibullah in 1980s and then that of Major Johnny Paul in Sierra Leone in 1997, for being unrepresentative of their peoples, are also cases in point. The yardstick was never applied against the Ziaul Haq regime of Pakistan or the Ahmad Zereoul-led junta in Algeria, which were equally undemocratic and non-representative.

To sum up, the OIC Charter is a deficient document with many loopholes. Broader principles are defined, details are left to be worked out, on the assumption that the membership would be able to chart a course of action, as and when the situation warrants. Sometimes this works, at other times, it does not. In the latter case, a lack of initiative characterizes the OIC's response.

Lack of initiative: Whenever the Islamic Conference finds itself divided, it hides behind two

relatively misused legal concepts of *international legality* and *state sovereignty*. In showing deference to these theories, the Islamic Conference excels all the Western Organizations, though it was from the West that these concepts about modern nation-state had emanated in the first place.

A litmus test for the OIC was countering the threat of extinction looming large over a Muslim state, Bosnia and Herzegovina. Here, the OIC was reluctant to commit itself any further than offering political, diplomatic and financial support, at least, in the initial years. Since this was the maximum, the member states were willing to contribute at that time. The OIC started drawing its justification for inaction from international legality, confusing legality with UN resolutions. The inconsistency in the UN decisions, marked by the sanctioning of ruthless use of force against the Iraqi invasion of Kuwait in 1991 and remaining a silent spectator of Serbian aggression against Bosnia during 1992–95, limiting itself to humanitarian assistance and dispatch of unarmed monitors for the UN-declared safe-havens in Bosnia, speaks volumes about the dubious credibility of that world body as a pontiff on international legality. There is hardly any instance when, say, the security of any one American national was endangered abroad and the US, or for that matter any Western state, shirked its responsibility to physically rescue him by waiting for the UN Security Council to sanction the operation. It may be added that even the OIC never made any attempt to behave as 'more Catholic than the Pope' for the concept of international legality, in the South Philippines affair. Since there existed a consensus within the Conference, the OIC did not feel the need to refer it to the UN or to seek refuge under international legality before giving open support to the Muslim guerilla groups fighting for autonomy. In its negotiations with the Manila regime, the OIC made it bluntly clear that it wanted absolute guarantees for the security of the Muslim community of Philippines.

If the OIC is indecisive on an issue where inaction cannot be justified by invoking the doctrine of international legality, the doctrine of state sovereignty is taken out of the shelf. Such was the case in Algeria's civil war where the OIC did not take up the case declaring the problem to be a domestic affair of a sovereign state. The only statement that the OIC could issue was condemning the massacres in Algeria as 'un-Islamic'. Obviously this had no significance as no one required a sermon from the OIC to know whether murdering people was Islamic or not. Nobody took the trouble to mention that the political unrest had arisen as a fallout of the stepping in of the military to deny power to the Islamic Salvation Front (FIS) which had romped home with a thumping majority in the first-ever free and fair multi-party elections in Algeria since its independence in 1962. In the first six years of the civil war that ensued, beginning in 1992, around 80,000 people lost their lives.

An interesting contrast can be made with the local bodies elections in Serbia in the winter of 1997 which were annulled by the government since an opposition alliance had bagged a plurality of seats in the municipal councils of some key cities. The resulting mass protests by the opposition supporters against the decision continued for over eight weeks in the chilling cold of Eastern Europe's winter. Occasional encounters with riot police had left at least one person dead. It was the Organization for Security and Cooperation in Europe (OSCE) that took the matter seriously and its emissaries continued to shuttle to Belgrade to defuse the crisis. Dismissing the Serbian government's protests of it being a domestic issue, the OSCE kept applying pressure until the government conceded defeat.

Comparing the magnitudes of the electoral crises in Algeria and Serbia, and the respective responses by the OIC and the OSCE, no further comment is necessary. A similar situation had emerged in Nigeria where President Ibrahim Babangida announced presidential elections for 1991, as part of the democratization process. Against the wishes of the incumbent military rulers, Masood Abiola won hands down. The government annulled the elections and Babangida quit the office. He was replaced by his military chief Gen. Sani Abacha whose government proved to be vindictive in dealing with the pro-democracy activists. Though the crisis did not aggravate to Algerian proportions, nevertheless, the OIC never raised a finger. It was the (British) Commonwealth organization that suspended Nigeria's membership over its human rights record. To add a postscript, Gen. Sani Abacha, 54, died of a heart attack in June 1998. A few days later, the imprisoned Abiola was reported dead in mysterious circumstances in his prison cell.

No doubt, the OIC does not cling to the state sovereignty doctrine as gospel truth. In the crises in Philippines, Kashmir, and Bulgaria, the OIC simply scoffs at the notion that the condition of Muslim communities falls under the domestic jurisdiction of the states concerned and that the OIC has no business involving itself in it. In the formative years, the OIC was unsure whether it should take a stand on such issues or not. Minority view being overruled, the OIC concluded that no state could eschew accountability for its human rights violations against its Muslims by invoking sovereignty doctrines. As it came out, however, the OIC never ventured to take on China for its treatment of Ulghur Muslims, nor was Russia taken to task for wanton killings in Chechenya following the latter's abortive secessionist bid.

To conclude, the OIC Charter has left many things to chance. The Organization has two ready-made doctrines that are exploited whenever it is reluctant to take a resolute step. Apparently, the OIC cannot tolerate a non-Muslim state mistreating its Muslim community. It becomes a different matter, however, when a Muslim state itself is persecuting its population or when the non-Muslim state concerned is extra-ordinarily powerful. Such are the vagaries of international politics.

Organizational Weaknesses

Organizational weakness is generally understood in terms of non-implementation of the OIC decisions and its lack of consistency. But these are only two facets of a wider syndrome. For instance, the identity crisis within the OIC is a big problem. Then there are problems related to the administrative structure of the Organization. And finally, lack of discipline and the lack of direction are also serious organizational challenges.

Identity crisis: The crisis of identity within the OIC is no mean failure. For instance, the OIC has failed to determine its own acronym, the date of foundation, and the number of founder members, not to mention its general direction.

First of all, the OIC has failed to give currency to any one of its acronyms. It is called the Organization of the Islamic Conference (OIC), Islamic Conference Organization (ICO), *Organization de la Conference Islamique* (OCI), and Islamic Organization for Conferences (IOC), in addition to its Arabic acronym, *Munazzamah Al-Mutamar Al-Islami* (MMI), in different texts. Similarly, one of its principal organs, the Islamic Conference of Foreign Ministers (ICFM) is erroneously referred to as the Islamic Foreign Ministers' Conference (IFMC) also. Due to these wild variations, it becomes quite a job to locate the entry on OIC in a catalogue, encyclopedia, or a reference book. Furthermore, the acronym's phonetic proximity with International Olympic Committee (IOC) or the Conference on Indian Ocean (CIO) creates further confusion. No wonder, most of the people thus fail to guess what the OIC stands for.

Secondly, though the historians have recorded exact dates of events occurring centuries ago, the OIC is not sure when it was born. The OIC's official publications give different dates, and various other reference books have their own 'opinion' about the date and year of the emergence of the OIC. The year of the OIC's inception is given variously as 1969 (when the 1st Islamic Summit took place); 1970 (when the decision to establish a permanent Secretariat in the 1st ICFM was arrived at); 1971 (when the first Secretary General assumed office); or 1972 (when the Charter was ratified). More stupefying is the OIC's track record of observing its anniversaries. The 1st Islamic Summit at Rabat had concluded on 25 September 1969 with a vague decision to establish a permanent secretariat. The OIC purports to calculate its birth from that date. The OIC observed its 7th foundation day on 12 July 1976, 16th foundation day on 3 April 1985, 20th anniversary on 9 February 1990, and silver jubilee on 11 September 1995.

Apparently, this maze has something to do with the OIC's practice of following the Islamic (lunar) calendar, which has a 355-day year. Since there is a lag of ten days between the Islamic and the Christian calendars, any given date on the former would fall on a different date of the latter in the following year, and vice versa. The date of the conclusion of the 1st Islamic Summit (Rabat; 1969) corresponds with 12 Rajab 1389 AH on the Islamic calendar. Till 1985, the OIC foundation days were observed on 12 Rajab every year, no matter what the date on the Christian calendar was. The OIC had its 16th anniversary in 1985 and strangely enough, five years later, on 9 February 1990 (12 Rajab 1410 AH), the OIC marked its 20th, and not 21st, anniversary. Exactly five years, seven months and two days after celebrating the 20th anniversary, the OIC marked its 25th foundation day on 11 September 1995, which did not even coincide with the 12 Rajab on the *Hijrah* calender.[15]

And this is not all, the OIC has yet to determine the number of its founder members; is it twenty-five (the states that attended the Rabat Summit) or thirty (i.e. the states attending the 3rd ICFM at Jeddah where the Charter was finalized). Finding out such basic data about the OIC like the name and date of emergence, is like solving a jigsaw puzzle. The information Section of the OIC Secretariat cannot be deemed competent unless it makes sure that the ambiguities about its date and year of foundation, acronym, and the number of founder members are conclusively removed. These facts are indeed a sad comment on the efficacy of the Organization.

Administrative Weaknesses: Unlike the juggernaut of a bloated bureaucracy at the UN, the OIC bureaucracy is innately small, weak and chaotic, and appears not to have undergone any cognitive development since its inception. The minuscule size of the OIC bureaucracy is hardly reflective of the size and scope of the Organization. All its organs are grossly under-staffed. Outside its Secretariat, the OIC does not have any resident mission in any member state's capital, except in Islamabad. Its subsidiary organs and affiliated institutions are also mostly concentrated in four member countries (Morocco, Pakistan, Saudi Arabia, and Turkey). Thus the OIC fails to make its presence felt in most of the world.

Next comes the lack of transparency and competition in the recruitment of the OIC staff. The posts are rarely advertised and are usually filled by government officers on deputation against the seats reserved for their respective countries. More often than not, it is the political connections of the candidate in his home country rather than merit, which determines whether or not he will be nominated for lucrative posts at the OIC Secretariat. A former ASG, Fouad A.H. al-Khateeb had once publicly acknowledged that the OIC performance could be drastically enhanced if only it adopts a rational policy for recruitment on merit, instead of accepting the services of mediocre officials from the member states.[16]

The quality of the official publication of the General Secretariat brought out on the eve of its silver jubilee celebrations, entitled 'Guide to the OIC', exposing the poor printing, spelling and grammatical mistakes, factual errors, lack of continuity, scanty information as well as its poor over all impact on the readers, bespeaks the sorry state of affairs at the OIC bureaucracy.

Indiscipline: The Islamic Conference has failed to maintain discipline among its member states. Most of the member states do not even respond to the OIC's correspondence or that from its subsidiary organs, even on substantive matters. (It is another issue that the General Secretariat itself is slack in acknowledging or responding to official and private correspondence addressed to it.) The crisis of financial indiscipline would be dealt with in the next section; but non-seriousness in all kinds of dealings with the Islamic Conference is somewhat an unhealthy attitude. For instance, the decision of the 6th Islamic Summit (Dakar; 1991) to oppose the US move at the United Nations, aimed at rescinding the 1975 General Assembly resolution equating Zionism with racism, was flouted by many member states. The resolution got rescinded in 1993. Another demonstration of carelessness was the twice postponement of the OIC military experts meeting to discuss the defence needs of Bosnia in 1995, due to lack of quorum.

Yet another form of indiscipline is rooted in the member states' diminished interest in the OIC conferences. Most of the international organizations today have summit meetings as a regular feature. Given that the states take the hosting of a summit conference as an honour, last minute regrets are simply inconceivable in other

organizations. The OIC has a different story because of the uncertainty about the date and venue of an OIC gathering till the last moment. As early as 1971, Afghanistan first postponed and then cancelled the ICFM scheduled for September of that year in Kabul, on very flimsy and dubious grounds. Since then a large number of ICFMs and Islamic Summits have been postponed. At least three of the Islamic Summits were held far behind the schedule dates, namely, the 2nd (Lahore; 1974), the 3rd (Taif; 1981) and the 6th (Dakar; 1991) Islamic Summits. In the 7th Summit (Casablanca; 1994) the would-be-host state, Saudi Arabia, had rescinded from its commitment to host the Summit at the last moment. The Summit did not have to be postponed since Morocco with a double experience to conduct Islamic Summit conferences, had offered to host it.

The trend is even more lax in the case of the ICFMs. A few recent examples will suffice. In spring 1990, there were speculations about the postponement of the 19th ICFM, scheduled for May at Cairo, in the Indian Press. When the attention of Pakistan's Foreign Ministry spokesman was drawn to it in the weekly press briefing, he reacted by dubbing the reports as a figment of imagination of the Indian Press. The very next day, the OIC Secretariat formally announced the postponement of the ICFM by two months and it was eventually held during 30 July–5 August 1990.

In October 1992, without prior consultation with, let alone approval of, the government of Sudan, the OIC Secretariat made the surprise announcement that the venue of the 21st ICFM scheduled for the year's end was being changed from Khartoum, Sudan, to the city of Karachi, Pakistan. Sudan resigned from the OIC immediately as a protest, though it later rejoined and did attend the 21st ICFM held belatedly at Karachi in April 1993.[17]

In May 1994, Tunisia announced that it had deferred the 22nd ICFM, scheduled for Tunis, till after the *Hajj*, for unspecified reasons. Two months later, the government conveyed its inability to hold the ICFM in Tunis altogether. So a whole lot of decisions including the approval of the OIC budget, awaiting the Foreign Ministers moot, were delayed till December when an alternative venue and date for the 22nd ICFM was found.[18]

If the OIC wants itself to be taken seriously, it should make the voluntary offer to host a conference binding upon the member states and the tradition of refusal to honour the commitment should not be taken as an innocuous faux pas. The schedule of conference for a three-year period should be finalized well in advance and, in each case, the alternative venue should be designated, so that the conference is held on time, even if the original host state is hit by a war or calamity.

Inflated workload: The OIC has taken so much upon itself by extending its area, scope, and subjects of interest that it can scarcely handle the ensuing workload. Thus it is stymied by its sheer inability to disentangle itself from the problems in which it has unnecessarily involved itself. For one thing, the heavy agenda before the OIC moots, can only be taken as an outward sign of intrinsic weakness. The Organization has failed to set its priorities, whereby a five-day conference of foreign ministers, meeting only once a year has an agenda of almost 60–90 items before it. It is simply impossible for the participants to seriously consider even a fraction of the agenda in such a short space of time. Compare the ninety or so resolutions in each single OIC meeting with the ninety-three resolutions adopted in 171 meetings of the UN Security Council. The OIC may well confine its agenda to manageable limits in any given conference, discuss it threadbare and act decisively on it. The piling up of scores of resolutions, donned in the OIC's rhetorical jargon, serves no purpose other than an unnecessary wastage of paper.

Budgetary Quagmire

The perennial budgetary deficit is the most serious challenge to the very existence of the Islamic Conference. The topic had been reserved for the end since it merits a detailed analysis and provides food for thought for the well-wishers of this international organization. It cannot be gainsaid that if only the OIC manages to rid itself of the ever-deepening financial crisis, its effectiveness would increase manifold, all the other handicaps discussed above, notwithstanding.

The OIC budget compared to the other international organizations is ridiculously small. The OAU, which is smaller in size and scope, and comprises states with lower average incomes than the OIC states' gross average, had a budget of US$26.7 million in 1992 while the OIC had a meager $8.6 million for the same year. The budgets of the Arab League and the GCC, which are exclusively composed of the OIC membership, were to the tune of $50 million and $40 million, respectively.[19] Former Secretary General Sharifuddin Pirzada once said that economic difficulty was the major reason advanced by the member states for non-payment of mandatory dues. He aptly questioned why the same had not led to the stoppage of their contributions to the UN and the various regional organizations. He underlined that the OIC, with the smallest budget and yet the second-largest membership in the world, requires the smallest financial obligation on the part of the member states, but they pay relatively higher amounts to other organizations, withholding the same from the OIC.[20]

The stark truth is that only eleven of the fifty-five member states pay their contribution regularly, but not necessarily fully. They are Bangladesh, Egypt, Indonesia, Jordan, Kuwait, Libya, Malaysia, Pakistan, Saudi Arabia, Senegal, and Yemen. On the other end of the spectrum, a number of countries including Afghanistan, Burkina Faso, Chad, Comoros, Gambia, Guinea-Bissau, Maldives, Mali, Sudan, and Syria have never even once paid their contribution completely.[21] So not only at the Secretariat General, but in almost all the organs, the financial picture is very bleak. The ISESCO, the ICDT, and the COMSTECH, etc. hardly realize one out of seven dollars committed, barely enough to pay salaries and to meet the running expenses. The IINA, for instance, has consistently defaulted in rents, electricity and telephone bills, and other financial liabilities since 1983–84. It usually does not have enough money to pay salaries to its meager staff of twenty-six members.[22]

In this section, we will confine our discussion to the scale of assessment of the member countries' contributions, their breach of obligations and the consequent financial woes of the OIC General Secretariat. Otherwise, the picture in most of the

OIC organs is much more gloomy and depressing than that of the General Secretariat, and their tales alone may claim a separate volume.

Like all inter-governmental organizations, the OIC depends upon the contributions of the members. The contribution of an OIC member state is assessed on the basis of its ability to pay i.e. its population, resources, and financial circumstances. The mandatory contributions are so insignificant that the OIC budget is much less than that of Maldives or Burkina Faso. The basic contribution is US$94,000 per annum or multiples thereof. Saudi Arabia and Kuwait are assessed to pay twenty times and eighteen times the basic scale, making their contribution 10 per cent and 9 per cent of the total OIC budget respectively. Pakistan, Morocco, and Oman are assessed to pay four times the basic scale. While thirteen countries (all African except Maldives) like Mali, Niger, Gambia, Djibouti, etc. are required to pay the minimum basic contribution of $94,000 (i.e., just 0.5 per cent of the OIC budget) only.

As per Article VII of the Charter, a Permanent Finance Committee that meets once a year, debates, formulates, and adopts a budget which is finally approved by the annual session of the ICFM. There is also a Financial Control Organ (FCO) which audits the OIC accounts in income and expenditure. Usually out of each $94,000, a sum of $43,000 goes to the budget of the OIC Secretariat while the rest is diverted, varying from $3,200 to $10,000 each, to seven OIC organs: Islamic Institute of Technology, Islamic Fiqh Academy, Islamic Centre for Trade and Development, Research Centre for History, Art and Culture, Ankara Centre (SESRTCIC), Islamic Commission for Preservation of Heritage, and the IFSTAD. The fact that the last mentioned organ was dissolved in December 1997, for reason no other than financial bankruptcy, puts a big question mark on the viability of other OIC organs, not to speak of the OIC itself, if the precarious financial state of affairs does not show signs of improvement.

The problem of default in payments is as old as the OIC itself. The first OIC Secretary General Tunku Abdul Rahman, one of the first protagonists of the idea of an Islamic commonwealth, had very bitterly complained, '(the members) are not at all serious...They don't take the business of Muslim unity seriously. They just join because they happen to be Muslims. They do not respond to such vital correspondence as holding of ICFMs. They promise to share expenses but never pay the committed amount.'[23] This has remained the common grievance of all his successors. Hassan Tohami described the default in payments as problem no. 1 of the OIC. Dr Gaye and later Habib Chatti always complained of financial crisis.

Sharifuddin Pirzada was more vocal and blunt in criticizing the defaulter member states. In 1985, the arrears amounted to US$1,707,243 of the total estimated budget of $6,207,243. To counter this problem, the OIC introduced a system of voluntary, besides the mandatory, contributions that year. The Secretary General later lamented that of the expected $2.0 million from this source, only $58,000 have been realized as a voluntary contribution that too from one country—Pakistan. 'When the members do not pay their mandatory contributions, it is unrealistic to expect voluntary contribution from them,' Mr Pirzada had remarked.[24] Addressing the coordination meeting of the OIC organ heads, he described the financial position of the OIC as 'desperate', saying that the state of affairs 'obviously impedes our work programme, limits our effectiveness, and is detrimental to the role of the General Secretariat for coordinating and supervising the vast network of OIC activities.' He speculated that there were doubts and misgivings in the minds of Muslim states' leaders about the Organization, which he claimed were created by 'vested interests located outside the Muslim world which view the OIC system as a direct threat to their objectives...that are opposed to Islamic unity and solidarity.'[25]

The OIC budget fell from $9.88 million in 1982–83 to $8.52 million in 1986-87 due to a downward revision each successive year. Pirzada's successor Dr Gabid was an equally vocal critic of the member states' pusillanimity in their financial obligations but was less fulsome in dubbing it as a foreign conspiracy against the OIC. Gabid termed as 'embarrassing for an organization of such size, scope, and potential, to suffer such a critical situation'. It was also during the tenure of Dr Hamid Al-Gabid, that the financial crisis resulted in a head-on collision between him and the Permanent Finance Committee (PFC). The PFC meeting on 5 March 1993, rejected the Secretary General's modest request to increase the OIC budget to $22 million and $28 million for fiscal years 1992–93 and 1993–94 respectively. The Committee nevertheless, decided to freeze the budget at 1991–92 level of $8.6 million because of what it described as mismanagement, overstaffing, corruption, and shortage of funds. The Secretary General became so angry that he suspended the meeting and withdrew the facilities including the electricity and air conditioning from the conference room. The PFC members, offended by this, declared the actions of the Secretary General as 'illegal'.[26]

It may be mentioned that in the year 1993–94, the UN Secretariat budget was $2.3 billion and its peace keeping operations were costing another $3.0 billion. Thus the total UN expenditure, if the costs of the projects run by UN organs and agencies are included, was $10.5 billion. Now to contrast it with the PFC's refusal to increase the OIC budget from $8.6 million appears incomprehensible. The ratio of about 1 to 1250 in the financial resources of the two Organizations, makes it very, evident why the OIC's scope of activities is much less than that of the UN. (As for the defaults in payments to the UN budget, the US alone owed it roughly $1.8 billion in arrears, as of Oct. 1999.)

The problem is made all the more acute by the member states' consistent unwillingness to pay this small amount. Ten big defaulters in the terms of arrears ($2.5 million and above) are Iran, Qatar, Iraq, Algeria, Libya, UAE, Brunei, Lebanon, Syria, and Yemen in this order, who owe a total of $42.7 million, i.e., 56 per cent of the total arrears. In terms of over all default (current dues plus arrears, exceeding $3.0 million and above in 1992) the top ten defaulters are Iran, Qatar, Iraq, Algeria, UAE, Libya, Brunei, Kuwait, Saudi Arabia, and Lebanon owing a total of $50.5 million (54 per cent of the amount owed to the Organization). Only two member states, Pakistan and Egypt, had no arrears against them but were rather five and two months ahead in the payment plan by the end of that year. The lists show the biggest defaulters to be the oil rich states, not because the poor states are regular in payments but because the African states'

assessments are so small that they owe relatively less amount in absolute terms.

On the average the members have not paid 6.7 years equivalent of contribution. Saudi Arabia was 1.5 year behind the schedule in 1992. At that time. Kuwait, Turkey, Indonesia, Malaysia, Bangladesh, and Tunisia were 2–3 years each; Qatar, seven years; Iran, eight years; Iraq and Djibouti, ten years each; Afghanistan, Comoro, Guinea-Bissau, Lebanon, and Syria, twelve years each; Maldives, thirteen years and Chad was fourteen years behind schedule, in their payments to the OIC budget. Thus the total default in 1992 had reached $93.9 million, including $76.7 million in arrears. The OIC asked its members to pay the arrears before 1 December, but only four members, Pakistan, Egypt, Kuwait, and Bahrain responded by paying that year's contribution only.[27] There appears no hope of a bright future for the OIC as long as the member states fail to fulfil their financial obligations. And it is very unfair to hold the OIC culpable for not coming up to the expectations of the Muslim states when the financial state of affairs is as described.

The 1995–96 budget of $10.6 million suggested a little upward revision over the past few years' budgets but taking into account the annual inflation of the preceding years, it was still less in absolute terms. In the year 1997, the OIC got a new chairman and a new Secretary General. In their joint call on the eve of the 8th Islamic Summit (Tehran; 1997); Dr Khatami and Dr Laraki, asked the Muslim countries to help the OIC, as 'only a financially independent OIC will do all in its power to work in the best interests of the Muslim world'.[28] In response, seven Muslim countries including Saudi Arabia, announced donations totalling $22 million, to rescue the OIC from financial collapse.[29] The 8th Islamic Summit was thus able to approve the slightly revised budgets of $2.2, $2.0, $1.91, $1.65, $1.17, and $0.64 million for the IIT, Ankara Centre, Istanbul Centre, Fiqh Academy, ICDT, and the ICPICH, respectively. Even these budgets are far from being commensurate with the mandate given and expectations pinned to these subsidiary organs.[30] In any case, such piece-meal and *ad hoc* measures do not offer a lasting solution to the OIC's critical monetary woes.

Conclusion: The Road Ahead

We have seen that the member states have been selective in their loyalty to the Islamic Conference, which is confined to the area and to that extent where a cash return is assured. The same is not true of their observance of membership discipline at the UN, so to speak. The latter has clout enough to offer a carrot, like an IMF bail-out loan, or to apply the stick, that is, to employ punitive measures against a member state, if need be. Whereas the OIC usually finds itself pitted against heavy odds on account of the member states' individual political agendas. This has, however, not deterred the OIC from involving itself in many more cases than it can possibly handle. For instance, the draft communiqué of the four-day 24th ICFM (Jakarta; 1996) had 172 resolutions (though the number was scaled down to 130 when the final communiqué was released to the press). The Organization does not have the moral courage to disentangle itself from the mesh.

We have also noted that with hundreds of problems to work on and over four dozen institutions to run, the Organization remains virtually penniless. It is an established fact that one can talk and talk all day, but if he has no money, he has no way. It is confounding that the Organization which has the world's richest states in its fold, often defaults in paying salaries to its staff. The UN can find a person, Bill Gates, generous enough to donate one billion dollars to it, while no country or legal or physical entity in the Muslim world ever showed such magnanimity to the Islamic Conference. For instance, Saudi Kingdom's earnings from petroleum exports in a single year, 1983, amounted to $95 billion. The OIC budget for the same year was $6.3 million. Had the Kingdom just enough commitment to spare one per cent of its oil proceeds for the OIC, the annual interest from this $1 billion would have been twenty times the OIC budget. Saudi Arabia is sometimes slack in paying its meager mandatory contribution to the OIC budget, an amount far less than a single shopping spree of the scions of its royal family in Europe.

As a corollary to the host of problems is that it becomes highly unpredictable what the OIC response to a particular problem will be. On one issue, the OIC may fight with determination (Palestine, Bosnia, etc.), on another it may show tentativeness (civil wars in Kashmir, Tajikistan) and on yet others remain indifferent (independence bids of Chechenya, Xinjiang, etc.) It may condemn India for massacre of the Muslim community during riots but remain tight-lipped at the ruthlessness of the ruling juntas in Algeria and Egypt against their oppositions. The Organization accords full member status to the Palestinian liberation movement, but an observer status to South Philippine's Muslim group, (that too as an exception) and only a guest status to the government of Azad Kashmir. One can cite more examples like these.

Needless to say, that double standards on the part of the OIC, or for that matter, any international organization, are indefensible under any pretext whatsoever. If exceptions are to be made in such dealings, at least all those exceptions should be non-discriminatory amongst themselves. Selective morality creates ill will in the state that is negatively affected, and undermines the confidence reposed in the Organization concerned.

The assertion that the roots of the problems lie outside the OIC might be correct, but to suggest that they lie outside the Muslim world, as many Secretary Generals have implied harping on 'hidden hands' and 'vested interests', is rather a self-defeating exposition. Such a prognosis betrays an inherent vulnerability of the OIC and the Muslim world to outside manipulation by the so-called 'forces inimical to Islam'. It would be more realistic to find the clues from within the Muslim world. The very absence of democracy, civil liberties, and rule of law from most of the OIC member states, is a potent factor working against the empowerment of the OIC. Any dictatorial regime would be the last one to voluntarily accept a supra-national organization dictating to it what to do and how to behave. There appears to be a symbiotic relationship between the non-representativeness of Muslim regimes and the weakness of the Islamic Conference. The European Union might have been a mere rubber-stamp if the European states had still been under the clutches of totalitarian regimes. For the OIC, the ray of hope lies in the present growing global trend towards democratization and liberalism, provided that it manages to survive till the rule of law dawns in the whole of the Middle East and Africa.

The need to evolve a *modus vivendi* to enhance the OIC's effectiveness, has resonated many a times in the Islamic conferences. The 8th Islamic Summit (Tehran; Dec. 1997) constituted a new eleven-member experts' committee comprising Brunei, Egypt, Guinea, Indonesia, Kuwait, Pakistan, Saudi Arabia, Senegal, Turkey, and the UAE, to look into the matter. Through the same resolution, no. 2/8-97/AF(IS), a four-member supervisory body, headed by the incumbent OIC Chairman and comprising the outgoing Chairman, the would-be next Chairman, and the OIC Secretary General was also set up.[31] It still remains to be seen, however, if this new establishment will deliver any tangible goods to Organization for its future.

NOTES and REFERENCES

1. See Saad S. Khan, 'OIC: A White Elephant', *The Muslim*, Islamabad, 9 January 1992. Also see Mushtaq Madni, *OIC: An analysis*, in ibid., 16 December 1994.
2. Abdullah Ahsan, *OIC: An Introduction to an Islamic Political Institution*, (Herndon: IIIT, 1988), p. 109.
3. *The News*, Islamabad, 13 November 1991. Iraq's reactionism and sensitivity is understandable, since Iraq-bashing had become more like an 'opening ritual' in various OIC conferences, so much so that the President of Palestine and King Hussein of Jordan, had to plead with the Arab countries at the 6th Islamic Summit to 'overcome' the Gulf war.
4. Keesing's Contemporary Archives, 1969–70, p. 23689.
5. Noor Ahmad Baba, *OIC: Theory and Practice of Pan-Islamic Cooperation*, (Karachi: Oxford University Press, 1994), p. 71. Also see its Chapter 3 for an account of the opposition by several Arab states to the idea of an Islamic Secretariat.
6. Sabiha Hassan, 'Casablanca Islamic Summit', *Pakistan Horizon*, Karachi, PIIA, vol. 37, no. 1, January–March 1984, pp. 74–88.
7. Keesings, 1971–72, p. 24482.
8. See Hassan, ref. 6, pp. 74–88.
9. Baba, ref. 5, pp. 119–120.
10. This was stated by Agha Shahi, Pakistan's ex-Foreign Minister, while giving a lecture on Pakistan's foreign policy at the Department of International Relations, Quaid-i-Azam University, Islamabad, in September 1995.
11. Baba, ref. 5, p. 121.
12. In fact, this idea to have a higher petroleum price for the developed states, a modest one for the developing states, and much lower for the Muslim states was propounded by an oil-rich Arab state, Libya, and not by an impoverished African state. See the text of Colonel Qaddafi's speech in *Second Islamic Summit: 1974*, (Islamabad: Directorate of Films and Publications, Ministry of Information, 1974), pp. 81–88.
13. Since Kuwait was annexed by Iraq just a few days after its invasion of 2 August 1990, there were twenty Arab states left. Except Algeria, Libya, Palestine, South Yemen, and Iraq itself, all the remaining fifteen Arab states had put up a united front against Iraq. It was principally these states that did not want the OIC to intervene in the conflict.
14. Three international actors, namely, prominent inter-governmental organizations (IGOs), large multi-national corporations (MNCs) and the global media channels are, in some respects, more powerful than the nation-states. Moreover, the bigger non-governmental organizations (NGOs) and the Currency phenomenon are two more entities trying to gatecrash into the club of powerful international actors.
15. Different encyclopedias, yearbooks, and reference books give different dates of the OIC's establishment which correspond with the days when the 1st Islamic Summit was opened, when the Secretariat was established, when the first Secretary General assumed office, or when the necessary number of ratifications of the OIC Charter got deposited with the Secretariat. Likewise, the OIC's year of birth is quoted differently in different texts. The General Secretariat's official publication of 1995, 'Guide to the OIC', shows the year of foundations as 1969. But since it was published in September 1995 on the eve of 25th anniversary of the OIC, it implies that OIC was formed in 1970. Keesing's Contemporary Archives, 1995, shows the OIC to be established in 1971. But technically speaking the OIC came into being when the simple majority of the states having participated in the 3rd ICFM, Jeddah, had ratified the Charter (i.e., in 1972). See Article 14 of the OIC Charter.
16. Baba, ref. 5, p. 213.
17. *The Nation*, Lahore, 2 October 1992.
18. The Islamic Foreign Ministers' preparatory meeting for the 7th Islamic Summit (Casablanca; 1994) also served as the 22nd regular ICFM.
19. See *Speeches and Statements of H. E. Sharifuddin Pirzada as OIC Secretary General*, (Karachi: n. p., 1989), pp. 190–192, for the text of Mr Pirzada's annual report to the 16th ICFM (Fez; 1986), from which the quotes have been taken.
20. Ibid. Iran is an obvious example of this trend whose annual contribution to the UN budget is around $25 million but the same to the OIC budget is less than $1

million. Iran is more or less regular in paying its dues to the UN budget, but has fourteen years equivalent of arrears with the OIC.

21. The discussion that follows, except where otherwise indicated, has been taken from M. A. Niazi, 'OIC reaches close to point of insolvency', *The Nation*, 15 January 1992, and Syed Rashid Hussain, 'OIC facing acute financial crisis', *Dawn*, Karachi, 14 February 1994.

22. *Speeches*, ref. 19, pp. 190–192.

23. Ahsan, ref. 2, p. 20.

24. Secretary General's speech at the sixteenth session of the Permanent Finance Committee (PFC) of the OIC on 27 November 1985. See *Speeches*, ref. 19, pp. 152–155.

25. Ibid., pp. 82–83.

26. *The News*, 5 March 1993.

27. See Niazi, ref. 21, and Hussain, ref. 21.

28. *The News*, 10 December 1997.

29. Pakistan Television (PTV), Islamabad Centre's daily news bulletin of 9 p. m. on 21 December 1997.

30. See resolution 3/8-97/AF(I.S) of the 8th Islamic Summit. The copy of this and all other resolutions of the 8th Summit were provided to the author by Ambassador Dr Khalil Saeed, Head of the OIC Mission in Islamabad.

31. 8th Summit resolutions. (Source: Same as above.)

PART–2

PART-2

⑨ Specialized Committees

The specialized committees are set up, either by the Islamic Summit or the ICFM, to coordinate the OIC policies on issues of vital interest to the Muslim World.[1] Some of them like the OIC standing Committee on Science and Technology (COMSTECH) or the Permanent Finance Committee (PFC), are created on a permanent basis; while others are set up on *ad hoc* basis. The examples for the latter category include the Ad hoc Committee on Afghanistan and the OIC contact groups on Bosnia and Kashmir. In all, the OIC had established fifteen specialized committees and contact groups. The Committee on South Africa and Namibia was dissolved in October 1994, following the demise of Apartheid and the independence of South West Africa; nevertheless many other *ad hoc* committees are continuing, at least on paper, though they have outlived their utility. The aim of this chapter is to give a brief sketch of the functions, composition, and modus operandi of the committees, hence, account or analysis of the role of each committee, which would have been an unnecessary repetition, has been avoided. The readers may revert to Chapter 6 to study the role of various OIC Committees/contact groups on crisis areas (Kashmir, Bosnia, etc.), where the same has been covered in the relevant sections.

In addition to the above the Organization has had many more committees, such as the six-member committee (comprising Algeria, Morocco, Tunisia, Saudi Arabia, and the OIC Secretary General) to bring reconciliation between Pakistan and Bangladesh in the early1970s; the three-member committee (comprising Saudi Arabia, Pakistan, and the OIC Secretary General) to channelize aid to Afghan *Mujahideen* in the early 1980s; the Committee to Examine Ways of Confronting Zionism established in the mid 1980s, and the like. Besides, there are experts committees to consider the performance of OIC Organs, preparatory committees for finalizing the agenda of an ICFM, and sub-committees within the committees. Taking them all into account, the total number may run well into hundreds. However, we will confine ourselves to the fourteen specialized committees that are in operation at the General Secretariat.[2]

I. Al-Quds Committee

The Al-Quds (Jerusalem) Committee was established to assist in the implementation of Resolution No.1 of the 6th ICFM (Jeddah; July 1975).

Objectives: The Islamic Conference of Ministers of Foreign Affairs entrusted the Al-Quds Committee with the following:

- to study the evolution of the situation in Jerusalem.
- to follow the implementation of resolutions adopted by the Islamic Conferences in this regard.
- to follow the implementation of resolutions adopted by various international bodies on Jerusalem.
- to make contacts with other international institutions that could play a role in safeguarding Jerusalem.
- to put forward proposals to the member states, as well as all bodies concerned on measures to be taken to ensure the implementation of these resolutions and to face new situations.
- to submit an annual report to the Islamic Conference of Ministers of Foreign Affairs.

Composition and Meetings: The Al-Quds Committee is chaired by the King of Morocco (King Mohammad VI, at present). It comprises fifteen member states elected by the ICFM. The present members are Bangladesh, Egypt, Guinea, Indonesia, Iran, Iraq, Jordan, Lebanon, Mauritania, Morocco (Chairman), Niger, Pakistan, Palestine, Saudi Arabia, Senegal, and Syria. The Al-Quds Committee meets on the request of its Chairman or that of the Secretary General of the OIC. It has met eight times since it was established.

II. Committee for Information Affairs and Culture (COMIAC)

This ministerial-level Committee is the first of the three permanent standing committees that were established in implementation of resolution No.13/3-P (IS), adopted to that end, by the 3rd Islamic Summit (Taif; January 1981).

Functions: The Committee is entrusted with following up the implementation of resolutions adopted by the Islamic Conference on information and cultural affairs; examining all possible means of strengthening cooperation in those fields among the Muslim States and putting forth programmes and proposals likely to improve the capabilities of Islamic States in these sectors.

Composition and Meetings: The Committee is open to all member states. The President of the Republic of Senegal is the *ex-officio* Chairman of the Committee. The Committee first met on 18–19 January 1983 at Dakar (Senegal). Since then, five meetings have been held, all in the same city. The meetings are inaugurated by President Abdou Diouf, Chairman of the COMIAC, and are attended by the Ministers of Culture and Information of the Muslim States or their authorized representatives.

III. Committee on Commercial and Economic Cooperation (COMCEC)

This second permanent standing Committee of the OIC, was also established in January 1981 in implementation of resolution No.13/3-P(IS) adopted to this end by the 3rd Islamic Summit Conference held in Taif, Saudi Arabia.

Functions: This Committee is entrusted with following up the implementation of resolutions adopted by the Islamic Conference in the economic and commercial fields; examining all possible means of strengthening cooperation among Islamic States and putting forward programmes and

proposals likely to improve the capabilities of Islamic states in those sectors.

Composition and Meetings: The membership of COMCEC is open to all member states. The President of Turkey is the *ex-officio* Chairman of this Committee. Hence, at present, President Sulayman Demirel, heads the COMCEC. To date, fourteen meetings of COMCEC have been held in Istanbul, Turkey; the first being on 14-16 November 1984. These meetings have held discussions, added recommendations, and sometimes taken decisions to implement the OIC Plan of Action on Economic Cooperation finalized by the 3rd Islamic Summit.

IV. Committee on Scientific and Technology (COMSTECH)

The COMSTECH is the third committee established in implementation of resolution No.13/3-P(IS) adopted in this regard by the 3rd Islamic Summit (Taif; January 1981).

Functions: The Committee is entrusted with following up the implementation of resolutions adopted by the Islamic Conference in the scientific and technological fields, examining all possible means of strengthening cooperation among Muslim States in those areas and putting forward programmes and proposals likely to improve the capabilities of Islamic States in these fields.

Composition and Meetings: The membership of this Committee is open to all the OIC members. President Mohammad Rafiq Tarar of Pakistan, who is the *ex-officio* Chairman of COMSTECH, heads this Committee. In addition, the Prime Minister of Pakistan enjoys the status of its *ex-officio* co-chairman. The Committee first met in Islamabad on 10–13 May 1983 and has held eight meetings so far. It supervizes the activities of the OIC organs in the field of science, technology, and technical education and coordinates their policies. The Committee has a large number of publications and conferences to its credit.

v. Islamic (*Ummah*) Peace Committee (IPC)

This Committee was established in implementation of resolution No. 6/3-P(IS) adopted by the 3rd Islamic Summit in response to the Gulf war between Iran and Iraq.

Functions: It was instructed to undertake exploratory missions and hold talks with Iranian and Iraqi leaders with a view to seeking ways and means of bringing about a peaceful, just, and lasting solution to the conflict opposing the two sisterly countries. It should be noted that the Chairmen of the 3rd, 4th and 5th Islamic Summits and the successive OIC Secretary Generals directed this Committee to do everything in its power to follow up the implementation of all the OIC resolutions adopted on the Iraq–Iran dispute.

Composition and Meetings: Initially, the 3rd Islamic Summit appointed Ahmad Sekou Toure, President of Guinea, as the Chairman of this Committee. He was succeeded by the President of Gambia, Daud Jawwara, in 1984. The Committee comprises nine members including the OIC Secretary General and the Heads of State and Government of Bangladesh, Gambia (Chairman), Guinea, Malaysia, Pakistan, Palestine, Senegal, and Turkey. The Committee met eight times during the eight-year war.

In August 1988, the cessation of hostilities on the Iran–Iraq border took place, outside its ambit. The *Ummah* Peace Committee, has been dormant since then, though its mandate includes the amicable resolution of the points of discord between the two brotherly Muslim States, including the disputes over POWs and war reparations.[3]

VI. Islamic Commission for Economic, Cultural and Social Affairs (ICECS)

This Commission with its present name and form came into being as a result of a resolution adopted by the 7th ICFM (Istanbul; 1976). Earlier, for the purpose of proper planning and coordination in socio-economic fields in order to attain the goals set by the OIC, the 2nd Islamic Summit (Lahore; 1974) had established an eight-member expert committee. The Committee was assigned the work of preparing recommendations for evolving a framework for cooperation in economic and cultural fields.[4] The 7th ICFM decided to expand the membership of the Committee from eight to eighteen and named it the 'Islamic Commission for Economic, Cultural and Social Affairs'. It was decided that the Commission should meet twice a year and present a comprehensive report and recommendations to the ICFM regularly. Many of the proposals of the OIC for cooperation in socio-economic fields were originally mooted by this Commission.

Objectives: The objectives of the Commission were[5]:

- to formulate, implement and follow up progress of economic, cultural and social cooperation among the member-states;
- to review and follow up implementation of decisions and resolutions adopted by the ICFM in the economic, cultural, or social fields;
- to examine and study economic, social, and cultural issues submitted by the member-states to the Foreign Ministers Conference.

Functions: The Commission plays the role of a unique assembly responsible for examining all activity programmes in the economic, cultural, and social fields at the level of the General Secretariat, Islamic Summits, and Conferences of Ministers of Foreign Affairs. Furthermore, the Committee studies and ensures the follow-up of the implementation of resolutions adopted by the ICFM in the economic, cultural, and social sectors. It also draws up, implements, and follows up the programme of economic, cultural, and social cooperation among member states. It studies and analyses the economic, cultural, and social issues that the member states intend to submit to the ICFM.

Composition and Meetings: The Committee comprises representatives from all member states of the Organization. It meets once a year on the request of the Secretary General of the OIC. So far, it has held eighteen sessions: First (Jan. 1977) in Karachi; second (Dec. 1977) in Mecca; third (Apr. 1978) and fourth (Dec. 1978) in Jeddah; fifth (Jan. 1980) in Conakry; sixth (Nov. 1980) in Jeddah; seventh (Mar. 1981) in Jakarta; eighth (Jan. 1982) in Tripoli; ninth (Apr. 1982), tenth (Oct. 1983), eleventh (Sept. 1984), twelfth (Nov. 1985), thirteenth (Jan. 1988), fourteenth (Feb. 1989) and fifteenth (Feb. 1990), all in Jeddah; sixteenth (Jan. 1991) in Tehran, and seventeenth (Jan. 1993) and eighteenth (Jan. 1994), again in Jeddah. The agendas covered in the meetings range from economic integration and the Muslim World's response to World Trade Organization (WTO) regulations, to the condemnation of mosque destruction by Hindu fanatics in India and recommendations on improving the standard of universities, etc.[6] One of the most important functions of the Commission is that it acts as the joint General Assembly of all the subsidiary organs of the OIC (see Chapter 3) except for the Islamic Solidarity Fund and the Islamic Fiqh Academy, which do not have a General Assembly within their administrative structure.

VII. Permanent Finance Committee (PFC)

It was established in implementation of Para 3 of Article VII of the Charter of the OIC.

Functions: It assists the General Secretariat in drafting and controlling its budget in compliance with the regulations approved by the ICFM.

Composition and Meetings: The Committee consists of the accredited representatives of all member states of the OIC. It meets once a year at the request of the OIC Secretary General.

VIII. Financial Control Organ (FCO)

The Financial Control Organ was established in implementation of Article VIII (a) of the Financial Regulations of the OIC.

Functions: The functions of the FCO are:

- to audit the accounts in income and expenditure, making sure that financial operations and books are in conformity with financial regulations.
- to audit accounts, deposits, loans, end-of-service, and social security allowances, making sure, that such accounts and operations are in conformity with established regulations.
- to study entries in stock and ledgers, deposit, disbursement and income documents, to try to spot cases of negligence or financial irregularities, to find the reason behind weaknesses and suggest solutions.
- to check administrative practices concerning the personnel and the execution of the budget to ensure that they are in line with established administrative and financial procedures.
- to examine the closing accounts and make sure that they are genuine; to indicate the true financial situation while noting errors, breaches, and shortfalls observed in the implementation of existing regulations.

Composition and Meetings: The eight members of the Organ are elected by secret ballot for a two-year term. They can be re-elected. The following eight members were elected by the 17th ICFM: Iran, Jordan, Libya, Morocco, Pakistan, Saudi Arabia, Tunisia, and Turkey. The Secretary General of the OIC calls a meeting of the Organ at least once a year, after the closing accounts.

IX. Ad Hoc Committee on Afghanistan

It was established by the 11th ICFM (Islamabad; May 1980), in implementation of resolution No.19/11-P.

Functions: The Committee is responsible for coordinating the aid and assistance designed to alleviate the sufferings of the Afghan people fighting to defend their inalienable rights. The Committee shall cooperate with the UN Secretary General or his personal representative with a view to finding a peaceful, just, and lasting solution to the Afghan problem.

Composition and Meetings: The Committee comprises five members, namely Guinea, Iran, Pakistan, Tunisia, and Secretary General of the OIC (Chairman). During the Soviet occupation of

Afghanistan, the Committee met several times at the UN General Assembly, but since the Soviet withdrawal from Afghanistan was completed in February 1989, this *ad hoc* committee has become dormant. The OIC initiatives to stop the post-Soviet-withdrawal civil war in Afghanistan do not necessarily involve this Committee.

x. Committee of Islamic Solidarity with the Peoples of the Sahel

This Committee was established in implementation of resolution No.7/3-P (IS) by the 3rd Islamic Summit (Taif; January 1981).

Functions: It ensures the follow up of the implementation of measures taken within the framework of assistance programmes to the peoples of the Sahel in the form of emergency food aid as well as priority development projects. The Committee is also expected to explore all means likely to strengthen drought control and desertification, to take any initiative in this regard and apprise the ICFM.

Composition and Meetings: The Committee consists of Iraq, Kuwait (Chairman), Malaysia, Morocco, Palestine, Saudi Arabia, UAE, the Secretary General of the OIC, and the representative of the current Chairman of the Inter-state Committee for Drought Control in the Sahel.

It is pertinent to note that the Vice-President of the Republic of Iraq used to be the *ex-officio* Chairman of this Committee. But the 6th Islamic Summit (Dakar; December 1991) appointed the Foreign Minister of the State of Kuwait, as head of the Committee. Iraq was removed from the chair, apparently as a reprisal for its occupation of Kuwait. The Committee meets once a year during the ICFM annual meeting.

xi. Six-Member Ministerial Committee on the Situation of Muslims in the Southern Philippines

The Committee was established in implementation of resolution 4/4-P of the 4th ICFM (Benghazi; March 1973).

Functions: The Ministerial Committee discusses with the Government of the Philippines the condition of Muslims in the Southern Philippines.

Composition and Meetings: Bangladesh, Indonesia, Libya, Saudi Arabia, Senegal, Somalia, and the OIC Secretary General are its members. The OIC chief chairs this Committee. It has held several meetings to deliberate upon the condition of Muslims in South Philippines. Since the crisis between the Muslims and the Manila government was amicably resolved in September 1996, under the auspices of the OIC, this Committee has ceased to function but has not been officially dissolved.

xii. The Six-Member Committee on Palestine

It was established by the 12fth ICFM (Baghdad; January 1981), by virtue of resolution No. 1/12-P.

Functions: To follow up and implement sanctions envisaged by the Islamic Conference as well as under Chapter VIII of the UN Charter against the Zionist entity for having scoffed at international law, refused to implement UN resolutions, and violated UN Charter principles and those of the Universal Declaration on Human Rights.

Composition and Meetings: Members of the Committee are Guinea, Malaysia, Pakistan, Palestine, Senegal, and the Secretary General of the OIC (Chairman). The Committee meets each year at the UN Headquarters in New York, alongside the annual session of the UN General Assembly.

XIII. Contact Group on Bosnia-Herzegovina

This Contact Group was established on 24 May 1993, by a declaration of the OIC member states at the United Nations regarding the situation in Bosnia-Herzegovina.

Functions: To coordinate the activities of the member states in connection with Bosnia-Herzegovina.

Composition and Meetings: The members of the Contact Group include Egypt, Iran, Malaysia, Pakistan, Saudi Arabia, Senegal, Tunisia, Turkey, and the Secretary General of the OIC. The Chairmanship is held through rotation. The Group meets at the request of the OIC Secretary General or that of any of the members. It has met frequently at New York, Geneva, Sarajevo, and elsewhere. It has been the most active group in the OIC framework in the 1990s. Though the Group's role in brokering the Bosnian peace accord has been marginal, it has successfully acted as a pressure group, so that the interests of the Muslim-dominated Republic of Bosnia-Herzegovina are not compromised on the NATO-sponsored conference tables.

XIV. Contact Group on Jammu and Kashmir

This Group was set up on 3 October 1994, in pursuance of resolution No.3/7-EX adopted by the 7th Extraordinary Session of the ICFM (Islamabad; September 1994). It is the latest addition in OIC's specialized committees.

Mandate: To coordinate the efforts of member states for promoting the right of self-determination of the Kashmiri people in accordance with the UN resolutions and safeguarding their fundamental human rights.

Composition and Meetings: The five-member Group includes Niger, Pakistan, Saudi Arabia, Turkey, and the OIC Secretary General. It meets periodically at the UN headquarters in New York.

The establishment of this group is a milestone in internationalizing the problem of Kashmir as well as the blatant abuse of human rights by the Indian occupation forces therein.

XV. Committee on Southern Africa and Namibia (Dissolved)

This Committee was established by the 5th Islamic Summit (Kuwait; January 1987) in implementation of resolution No.12/5-P(IS).

Functions: The Committee was entrusted with coordinating all forms of aid and assistance of member states to the oppressed people of Southern Africa and Namibia as well as to the recognized Liberation Movements of these countries.

Composition and Meetings: The Committee consisted of Algeria, Cameroon, Indonesia, Mali, Pakistan, Yemen, and the Secretary General of the OIC as the Chairman. The Committee used to meet once a year in New York during the UN General Assembly.

Dissolution: Since the liberation of South Africa and Namibia, the Committee, having fulfilled its mission, has been dissolved, on 3 October 1994, by the Annual Coordination Meeting of Islamic Foreign Ministers held at New York.

NOTES and REFERENCES

1. The OIC General Secretariat Publication, 'Guide to the OIC' (Jeddah: OIC Secretariat, 1995), p. 36.
2. The information about the composition and functions of the fifteen committees has been taken from OIC Guide, ref.1, pp. 35–48.
3. Iraq claims that it had released all the Iranian POWs at the outset of Kuwait crisis in 1990. Iran has refused to reciprocate by releasing all of the 19,000 Iraqi POWs, since Iran believes that Iraq is still holding 5000 Iranian POWs, whom the Iranian military declares as Missing in Action. Iran has, however, released all the very old, sick, and disabled, of the Iraqi prisoners.
4. Noor Ahmad Baba, *OIC: Theory and Practice of Pan-Islamic Cooperation*, (Karachi: Oxford University Press, 1994). p. 216.
5. Ibid. See, *The Nation*, Lahore, 21 September 1996.

🔟 Specialized Institutions

The specialized institutions work in a particular specialized field like economics, education, law, etc. So far, the OIC has established five such organs within its framework. Their budgets are independent of the Secretariat General budget, so they do not receive any subsidies from the latter as do the OIC subsidiary organs. These institutions are required to generate their own resources, whenever applicable, on commercial basis. The legislative bodies, as stipulated in their statutes, are responsible for the approval of budgets as well as for making provisions for income generation, that usually includes mandatory annual contributions from the member states of the respective organs. At present, the Islamic Development Bank, Islamic International News Agency, Islamic States Broadcasting Organization, and Islamic Education Scientific and Cultural Organization are operational, while Islamic Law Commission is in the process of being set up.

i. Islamic Development Bank (IDB)

The Islamic Development Bank, commonly known as IDB, is the principal organ of the OIC in the economic field.[1] Not only is it the largest OIC organ, in terms of manpower employed, financial resources, and scope of activities, etc., but is also the most active institution under the OIC umbrella. The IDB is basically an international financial institution but its scope of activities is limited to the Muslim World, i.e., OIC member states and the Muslim communities in the non-Muslim states. Consequently, the primary condition of the membership of IDB is, that the applicant state should be a member of the OIC.[2] The prospective member-state is also required to be willing to accept such terms and conditions as may be decided upon by the board of governors of the Bank.[3] Almost all the OIC members also hold IDB membership. In fact, the Bank follows the

OIC decisions in suspension/expulsion of the members as well.[4] The Bank has a staff of 685, fifty of whom are Muslims from non-Muslim states.

General Information: The headquarters of the Bank are located in Jeddah, Saudi Arabia. Considering the increasing volume and diversity of the Bank's operations and the need to improve its operations, expedite disbursements, ensure better project follow-up and implementation, and strengthen mutual contacts with the private sector, it was decided in 1993 to establish two regional offices: one in Kuala Lumpur, Malaysia, for member countries and Muslim communities in South East Asia; and the other in Rabat, Morocco, for member countries South of the Sahara and the Arab Maghreb Union. Both of these offices started functioning in 1994.[5]

The official language of the Islamic Bank is Arabic, though English and French are additionally used as working languages.[6] The financial year of the Bank is the lunar *(Hijrah)* year of the Islamic Calendar.[7] Up to mid-1992, the authorized capital of the Bank stood at two billion Islamic Dinars, which become ID 6 billion in July of that year by virtue of the decision of the Board of Governors, divided into 600, 000 shares having a par value of ID 10,000 each.[8] The Islamic Dinar (ID) is the accounting unit of the Bank, whose value is equal to one SDR (Special Drawing Right) of the International Monitory Fund. In 1999, ID 1 was roughly equivalent to US$1.4.

Establishment: The idea of the establishment of the IDB is as old as that of the OIC itself. As the distinction between the high politics and low politics was increasingly becoming blurred in the post-Second World War era, the protagonists of a pan-Islamic arrangement had envisaged economic cooperation in the Muslim world, as a primary objective for such a venture. That is why, the proposal for the establishment of an Islamic Bank was first discussed as early as in the 2nd ICFM (Karachi; December 1970), when the OIC had not been formally established.[9] The following year, one of the four expert committees that the OIC formed for study of specific proposals, dealt with the proposed Bank.[10] This committee met in February 1972 at Cairo, Egypt, and recommended the convening of an Islamic Finance Ministers' Conference, that was duly held on 18 December 1973 at Jeddah, Saudi Arabia.[11]

The 1st Islamic Conference of Finance Ministers issued a declaration of intent to establish the Islamic Development Bank. It also decided to establish a preparatory committee with Tunku Abdul Rahman, the former Secretary General of the Islamic Conference; Anwar Ali, Governor of the Saudi Arabia Monetary Agency (SAMA); and Dr Saeed Ahmad Meenai, Deputy Governor of the State Bank of Pakistan, as Chairman, Vice-Chairman, and Secretary, respectively. It examined the draft of agreement articles in Jeddah in May 1974, and presented them before the 2nd Conference of Finance Ministers held in Jeddah in August 1974, which adopted them.[12]

After completion of the interim arrangements, preparation of basic documents, their ratification by the member governments and payment of the initial instalment of subscription, the inaugural meeting of the Board of Governors of the Bank took place in July 1975 under the Chairmanship of Sheikh Muhammad Abul Khail, the then Minister of State for Finance and National Economy of the Kingdom of Saudi Arabia. The meeting examined and approved the by-laws, rules of procedures of the Board of Governors, and rules for the election of the Executive Directors. It elected a president and executive directors and decided that the Bank should formally open on 20 October 1975.[13] This date coincided with 15 Shawwal 1415 AH of the Islamic Calendar. Tunku Abdul Rahman took over as the first President of the IDB.[14]

Purpose and Functions: The purpose of the Bank is to foster the economic development and social progress of member states and muslim communities, individually as well as collectively, in accordance with the principles of the *Shariah*.[15] For the purpose, it provides equity participation

and grants loans for productive projects and enterprises. It also gives financial assistance to member states in other forms for their economic and social development and to foster foreign trade among member countries. The functions of the Bank, as stated in Article 2 of the Articles of agreement, are as follows[16]:

- to participate in equity capital of projects and enterprises in member countries;
- to invest in economic and social infrastructure projects in member countries by way of participation or other financial arrangements;
- to make loans to the private and public sectors for the financing of productive projects, enterprises and programmes in member countries;
- to establish and operate special funds for special purposes including a fund for assistance to muslim communities in non-member countries;
- to operate Trust Funds;
- to accept deposits and to raise funds, in any other manner;
- to assist in the promotion of foreign trade, especially in capital goods, among member countries;
- to invest suitably, funds not needed in its operations;
- to provide technical assistance to member countries;
- to extend training facilities for personnel engaged in development activities in member countries;
- to undertake research for enabling the economic, financial and Banking activities in Muslim countries to conform to the *Shari'ah*;
- to cooperate, subject to this Agreement, in such a manner as the Bank may deem appropriate, with all bodies, institutions and organizations having similar purposes, in pursuance of international economic cooperation;
- to undertake any other activities which may advance its purpose.

Structure: The IDB has over fifty member states. Each member has to subscribe to a minimum of 250 IDB shares, each with a value of ID 25,000. The three-tier administrative structure of the Bank consists of the Board of Governors, the Board of Executive Directors, and the President.[17]

Board of Governors:[18] The Board of Governors is the supreme authority of the Bank. Each member-state is represented by a Governor, usually its finance minister or representative and an alternate Governor. The Board meets once a year.

All powers of the Bank are vested in the Board of Governors who may delegate to the Board of Executive Directors any or all its powers except the power to admit new members and determine the conditions of their admission, increase or decrease the authorized capital stock of the Bank, suspend a member, authorize the conclusion of agreements for cooperation with other international organizations, elect the president and the executive directors of the Bank, approve, after reviewing the auditor's report, the general balance-sheet and the statement of profit and loss of the Bank, determine the reserves and distribution of the net income and surplus of the Bank, exercise such other special powers as are expressly assigned to the Board of Governors in the Agreement. In its annual meeting the Board reviews the Bank's activities of the previous year and approves the future policies. The Board also elects a procedural committee, consisting of the Governors of any five of its members, every year.[19] The committee is responsible for making recommendations about the schedule, conduct, and agenda of the meetings of the Board of Governors.[20]

Board of Executive Directors: The Board of Executive Directors is composed of eleven members, of whom five are appointed by each of the five member countries having the largest number of shares, and the remaining six are elected by the Governors of all other member countries with the exception of the Governors representing the five big shareholders. The five states, (the percentage of their subscribed shares is given in brackets) are:

- Saudi Arabia (26.6 per cent)
- Kuwait (13.2 per cent)
- Libya (10.7 per cent)
- Turkey (8.4 per cent)
- UAE (7.5 per cent).[21]

These five states above account for around two-thirds (66.4 per cent) of the subscribed capital of the IDB. All the members of the Board of Executive Directors, are required to be persons of high competence in economic and financial matters. Executive Directors hold office for a term of three years and may be re-elected. The Board of

Executive Directors is responsible for the direction of the general operations of the Bank and approves all financing operations. It also exercises the powers delegated by the Board of Governors. It has three standing committees, one each on Operations, Administration and Finance, and Longer Term Trade Financing.

President:[22] The President is the chief executive of the Bank, its legal representative as well as the chairman of the Board of Executive Directors. He is elected by the Board of Governors for a renewable term of five years. The President conducts the business of the Bank under the direction of the Board of Executive Directors. He is assisted by three Vice Presidents, and an Adviser to the Bank. A Vice President holds office for such term, exercises such authority, and performs such functions in the administration of the Bank, as may be determined by the Board of Executive Directors. Currently, the term of a Vice President is three years and is renewable.

Financial Resources:[23] At the end of 1416 AH (17 May 1996), the authorized and subscribed capital of the Bank stood at ID 6 billion and ID 4 billion (US $9 billion and US $6 billion) respectively. The paid-up capital amounted to about ID 2 billion (US $3 billion).

The ordinary capital resources of the Bank consist of the members' funds (i.e., the paid-up capital, reserves, and retained earnings) and receipts from its Investment Deposit Scheme. As of 30 Dhul Hijja 1416 AH (17 May 1996), the members' funds of the Bank amounted to ID 2.75 billion (US $3.97 billion) while the funds raised through the Investment Deposit Scheme amounted to ID 51 million (US $74 million). Thus, the total resources for financing the ordinary operations of the Bank, derived from these two main sources, amounted to ID 2.80 billion (US $4.04 billion). This represents 70 per cent of the Bank's total resources of ID 3.97 billion (US $5.73 billion).

The Bank is successfully pursuing the policy of placing the liquid funds of ordinary resources with financial institutions operating in conformity with *Shari'ah*. Now, the entire liquid funds from the ordinary resources of the Bank are invested in *Shari'ah*-compatible placements. As of 30 Dhul

Hijja 1416 AH (17 May 1996), the aggregate placements in such investments amounted to ID 1,292 million.

Proceeds from liquid funds, conventional deposits and other placements are allocated to the Special Reserve and the Special Assistance Account. In 1412 AH (1992), the proceeds provided the initial amount of US$100 million for a Special account for the Least Developed Member Countries (LDMCs). At the end of 1416 AH (17 May 1996), the total resources in the Special Account stood at ID 859 million (US$1,240 million).

Resource Mobilization:[24] Unlike other financial institutions, the Bank does not augment its financial resources by borrowing funds from conventional world financial markets because this would involve payment of interest which is not compatible with *Shari'ah*. The Bank therefore has developed new schemes and financial instruments which are in conformity with the principles of *Shari'ah*, with a view to supplementing its ordinary financial resources. These include Investment Deposit Scheme, IDB Unit Investment Fund, Longer-Term Trade Financing Scheme, and Islamic Banks' Portfolio for Investment and Development. The investment development scheme provides investors (both individual and institutional) with an Islamic alternative to making short-term investment through participation in the financing activities of the Bank for use in the Import Trade Financing Operations (ITFO). While the purpose of IDB Unit Investment Fund, which is a trust fund, is to contribute to the economic development of member countries by pooling the savings of institutional investors in the initial phase and then investing these savings in productive projects. The size of the Fund stands at US $275 million. The twenty-nine unit holders of the Fund are mainly Islamic financial and charitable institutions. By the end of 1416 AH, the Fund mobilized for the Bank US$447 million worth of resources, mainly through disinvestment of IDB's matured projects. The latter two schemes will be discussed in the following section.

Chart 10.1

Subscription to IDB share capital (in million ID) as on 30th Dhul Hijah 1415H (29 May 1995)

S. No.	Country	Initial	Total Subscribed	Percent-age
01	Afghanistan	2.50	5.00	0.13
02	Albania	2.50	2.50	0.07
03	Alberia	25.00	124.26	3.31
04	Azerbaijan	2.50	4.92	0.13
05	Bahrain	5.00	7.00	0.19
06	Bangladesh	10.00	49.29	1.31
07	Benin	2.50	4.92	0.13
08	Brunei	6.30	12.41	0.33
09	Burkina Fasso	2.50	12.41	0.33
10	Cameroon	2.50	12.41	0.33
11	Chad	2.50	4.92	0.13
12	Comoros	2.50	2.50	0.07
13	Djibouti	2.50	2.50	0.07
14	Egypt	25.00	49.23	1.31
15	Gabon	3.00	14.77	0.39
16	Gambia	2.50	2.50	0.07
17	Guinea	2.50	12.41	0.33
18	Guinea-Bissau	2.50	2.50	0.07
19	Indonesia	25.00	124.26	3.31
20	Iran	2.50	349.97	9.33
21	Iraq	10.00	13.05	0.35
22	Jordan	4.00	19.89	0.53
23	Kuwait	100.00	496.64	13.24
24	Kyrghyz	2.50	2.50	0.07
25	Lebanon	2.50	4.92	0.13
26	Libya	125.00	400.00	10.66
27	Malaysia	16.00	9.56	2.12
28	Maldives	2.50	2.50	0.07
29	Mali	2.50	4.92	0.13
30	Mauritania	2.50	4.92	0.13
31	Morocco	5.00	24.81	0.66
32	Niger	2.50	12.41	0.33
33	Oman	5.00	13.78	0.37
34	Pakistan	25.00	124.26	3.31
35	Palestine	2.50	9.85	0.26
36	Qatar	25.00	49.23	1.31
37	Saudi Arabia	200.00	997.17	26.58
38	Senegal	12.50	12.42	0.33
39	Sierra Leone	2.50	2.50	0.07
40	Somalia	2.50	2.50	0.07
41	Sudan	10.00	19.69	0.52
42	Syria	2.50	5.00	0.13
43	Tunisia	2.50	9.85	0.26
44	Turkey	10.00	315.47	8.41
45	Turkmenistan	2.50	2.50	0.07
46	Uganda	2.50	12.41	0.33
47	U.A.E	110.00	383.03	7.54
48	Yemen Republic	5.00	24.81	0.66
	Total	826.80	3781.27	99.98

Financial Operations

Now we come to the quintessence of our discussion on the IDB, i.e., its financial operations. The Bank extends financial support to its member countries for their development project. It also helps the Muslim minority communities, mainly for social, educational, and humanitarian programmes. Being an Islamic financial institution, its activities should not only be financially and socially rewarding but also compatible with the dictates of *Shari'ah*. Herein lie the three daunting challenges under which the IDB is operating that are not shared by other international development institutions.[25] In the first instance, it has to conduct its operations according to the principles of the *Shari'ah* which, among others, prohibit the charging of interest which is the very basis of the international banking system. Simultaneously, it has to generate and rely on its capital subscriptions and attract deposits mainly from Muslim communities, in conformity with the *Shari'ah*. Meanwhile, as the current world recessionary economic conditions exacerbate the already serious and rapidly mounting socio-economic problems of the developing countries, the challenges facing the IDB increase correspondingly.

Furthermore, it is the only regional development bank whose membership is composed entirely of developing countries, attempting to foster cooperation among themselves for their socio-economic development, within a spirit of collective self-reliance. The Bank's membership has a high proportion of the Least Developed Countries. Out of the thirty-seven countries designated as Least Developed Countries (LDCs) under the UN criteria, twenty-one are members of the IDB. These countries need special attention, in terms of investments in physical and social infrastructure.

Last, but not the least, the Bank became operational, as the first of its type in Islamic international development financing, with no precedents from which to derive any lessons. Therefore, it has had to develop its own experience, simultaneously as its activities increase in volume. It goes to the credit of IDB that it has overcome the challenges and made tremendous strides in making innovations for conducting its financial operations.

The ten financing operations of the Bank can be broadly divided in three principal categories, namely, Ordinary Operations, Trade Financing Operations, and Special Assistance Operations.[26] Up to the end of 1416 AH (17 May 1996), financing approved by the Bank amounted to ID 11,950 million (US$15,112 million) excluding cancellations. The total amount approved by the Bank for each form of financing was as follows:

I. ORDINARY OPERATIONS:
1. Project Financing: ID 2,954 million (US $3,745 million);
2. Technical Assistance: ID 71 million (US$88 million);

II. TRADE FINANCING OPERATIONS:
1. Import Trade Financing Operations: ID 7, 526 million (US$9,361 million);
2. Longer-Term Trade Financing Scheme: ID 253 million (US$355 million);
3. Islamic Banks' Portfolio: ID 781 million (US$1,129 million):

III. SPECIAL ASSISTANCE OPERATIONS: ID 365 million (US$434 million).

A description of the working of all these modes of financing is in order.

I. Ordinary Operations: Ordinary operations is the collective name given to Project Financing and Technical Assistance schemes. The purpose of these operations is the development of basic infrastructure of the member countries. Agriculture, industry, transport, and social sector projects receive assistance under these operations.[27]

Out of the ID 3.025 billion spent during the first twenty years in this category, 23 per cent each has gone to the Industry and Mining sector, and the public utility projects. Lately, the emphasis in the public utilities sector has shifted to the power generation projects. The Transport and Communication sector, has received 18 per cent allocation during the period under review. It is followed by Agriculture and Agro-industry, which also received 18 per cent of the total approvals, primarily for projects aimed at integrated rural development. In recent years, the share of this last sector, in total IDB allocations, is on the decline while that of the social sector, which aims at human resource development through financing of health and education operations, is on the rise. The social sector accounts for 16 per cent of the financing; the remaining 2 per cent has largely been given to Islamic financial institutions. The IDB financing, needless to say, has been playing a significant role in development in Muslim countries. This is shown by the number of projects financed by IDB as well as the ever-increasing spate of requests for assistance, so much so, that the Board of Executive Directors had to approve a 16 per cent rate of growth for the ordinary operations in 1994.[28] In the beginning, loan and equity were the only modes of financing to which leasing was added in 1977. With the passage of time, the Bank has introduced a number of other modes.[29]

i. Loan financing: Projects, that are expected to have a significant socio-economic impact on the intending beneficiaries, have a long term implementation phase and are unlikely to be revenue generating, like construction of roads, airports, rural water-supply, schools and hospitals etc., are financed through loans. This is similar to interest free loans given by the World Bank's IDA (International Development Assistance) window.

Among the fifty member countries of the Bank, twenty-one are least developed. These countries are given priority in respect of concessionary financing of the Bank. Loans are provided free of interest and the Bank charges a modest service fee to recover only the administrative costs incurred in its financing. In addition, loans provided by the Bank include a grace period of three to seven years and the repayment is spread over a period of fifteen to twenty-five years. The least developed member countries (LDMCs) are usually given maximum grace and repayment periods. Loan is provided for projects with a significant socio-economic developmental impact. The share of the LDMCs in the total amount of Loan approved up to the end of 1416 AH (17 May 1996) stood at 58 per cent. During 1976–95, loans worth ID 975 million were provided for 216 projects. [30]

ii. Equity participation: Investments in share capital of new or existing enterprises is made through equity participation.[31] The Bank acquires equity mainly in industrial and agro-industrial projects. As a policy, the Bank restricts its participation to not more than one-third of the total share capital of the project, partly because of its policy not to acquire a majority or controlling share. However, here, its role is mainly catalytic, so as to attract other institutions which may then participate in the venture, through loans or the acquisition of equity. Equity obviously includes a risk of loss and the Bank's accounts show write-offs due to losses in equity. In 1995, thirty-eight companies representing 70.2 per cent of the Bank's total investment in equity portfolio, were profitable. During 1976–95, the Bank invested ID 213 million in seventy-two ventures.

iii. Leasing: This is a popular mode because of its flexibility. Through this strategy, the Bank is able to fill critical gaps in the foreign exchange requirements of member countries, by making it possible for them to acquire ships, railway wagons, tractors assembly plants, machinery and equipment, etc. The leasing fee is based on the profitability and cash flow of the operation. In other words, leasing involves the purchase and subsequent transfer to the beneficiary of the right of usage of equipment for a specific time, during which the IDB retains the ownership of the asset. Funds are made available for seven to fifteen years including a two to four year gestation period, depending upon the particular project.[32]

After the stipulated time the goods become the property of the lessee, without being subject to loss or price fluctuations, provided the last lease payment has been made. In this way, leasing is *Shari'ah* compatible and financially remunerative. During 1976–95, IDB spent ID 689 million on seventy-one leasing projects.

iv. Instalment sale: As the name indicates, the mode operates through sale of capital goods on instalment basis. The Bank purchases machinery on behalf of the beneficiary and sells at a higher price in easy instalments, normally ranging from six to ten years. This mode was introduced in 1985, in order to eliminate some problems encountered in Leasing, especially those resulting from continued ownership of the relevant assets by the IDB. This mode is similar to Leasing, but entails the immediate transfer of ownership of the relevant assets to the buyer. The buyer can pledge these assets as collateral, in order to secure relevant payment guarantee from private Banks. During 1976–95, the IDB spent ID 592 million on seventy-three instalment sale cases.

v. Profit sharing: This medium term form of financing was introduced in 1978 but it could not, however, gain much importance as a mode of financing. During 1976–95, IDB participated in four projects, investing ID 19 million on profit sharing basis. Modifications are being made in this mode to increase financing in it.

vi. Istisna'a: This mode has been developed recently by the Bank. The objectives of *Istisna'a* are promotion of trade in capital goods among member countries and enhancement of their production capacity. It is a contract for manufacturing (or construction) of goods or other assets where the manufacturer (seller) agrees to provide the buyer with goods specified after they have been manufactured/constructed within a certain time and for an agreed price.

vii. Lines of Finance Extended to NDFIs: The primary objective of extending lines of finance to National Development Financing Institutions (NDFIs) is to assist small and medium size enterprises. It is also the main method of providing funds to the private sector. Lines are utilized through Equity participation, Leasing and Instalment Sale operations. During the 1976–95 period, thirty-two project financing lines, amounting to ID 198 million were extended to NDFIs of the member countries. The five lines of Equity, three lines of Leasing, four lines of Instalment Sale, and twenty combined lines, accounted for 1.0, 1.0, 1.2 and 4.0 per cent of total ordinary operations, respectively. In order to improve the disbursement and utilization of these lines, the IDB is continuously taking actions to encourage their usage.

It may be noted that between 1976 and 1995, Loans, Equity, Leasing, Instalment Sale, and Profit Sharing, accounted for 35.4, 7.7, 25.0, 21.5 and 0.7 per cent respectively, of the ordinary operations while the sum of Lines of Financing had 7.2 per cent share. Thus, 97.5 per cent of money for ordinary operations, went to project financing

while the remaining 2.5 per cent was utilized for Technical Assistance.

2. Technical Assistance: The Bank also supports the development efforts of its member countries by providing technical assistance (TA). Technical assistance is also provided under the Technical Cooperation Programme (TCP) and through various activities of the Islamic Research and Training Institute (IRTI). TA is funded from both ordinary resources and the Special Assistance Account and is provided in the form of loan and/ or grant. TA is provided to prepare feasibility studies, detailed designs, or institution building. The Bank finances consultancy services to assist its own staff in project preparation and follow-up. The selection of consultants is made through competition. Pilot projects are also financed through TA.

The Bank pays special attention to the needs of LDMCs in implementing its TA programme. Technical assistance given by the Bank is in the form of either grants or loans, or a combination of both. TA is also provided to member countries with high per capita income and relatively greater need for technical support. Various initiatives are underway within the Bank to enhance the scope, size, and quality of TA. Till the end of 1416 AH (17 May 1996), the Bank approved 207 Technical Assistance operations in forty-two countries involving an amount of ID 72 million (US $88 million). 70 per cent of this amount went to the LDMCs.

II. Trade Financing Operations: Trade is an indispensable element in the development process. The IDB, as an international development financing institution, has established various modes of financing to foster cooperation and trade among its member countries and as world trade expands under the Uruguay Round umbrella, trade will become even more important in the development process. The Articles of Agreement of the Bank have laid a special emphasis on the promotion of trade among member countries. The trade financing operations in IDB in 1977 were short term in nature and introduced mainly as a placements operation in order to provide a means of investing surplus funds of the Bank not immediately needed for project financing. Trade financing has proved an important part of the overall financing activities as well as one of the most effective ways in which the Bank has been able to promote cooperation among member countries.

The Import Trade Financing Operations (ITFO) was the first facility in this direction. The ITFO facility soon became an important operational activity of the Bank, enabling a number of member countries to use it to finance the import of developmental raw materials. The facility is a source for generating a substantial portion of the Bank's income, which supplements its resource base for the implementation of its other concessionary and non-concessionary activities. To further expand efforts towards promoting intra-trade amongst its member countries, two new trade-related programmes were introduced in 1987, namely, the Longer Term Trade Financing Scheme (LTTFS) and the Islamic Banks' Portfolio for Investment and Development (IBD).

In addition to the above financing schemes introduced with a view to promoting trade amongst its member countries, the IDB has also initiated a trade cooperation programme within the Trade Promotion Department (TPD). This programme primarily aims at informing member countries about intra-trade opportunities by holding workshops and seminars and arranging and facilitating participation of Least Developed Member Countries in trade exhibitions of member countries. Countries unable to exhibit their export goods are helped by IDB to exhibit at trade fairs in other member countries. Most of the cost of shipping the articles and the expenses of officials accompanying the articles are borne by the IDB.

With a view to promoting intra-trade, the IDB has identified a number of products, which could be exported by member countries but with are imported by other member countries from non-member countries. The export products from member countries specially promoted, include:

(a) capital goods
(b) intermediate industrial goods
(c) fertilizers
(d) industrial chemicals
(e) cotton

(f) palm oil
(g) copper and aluminium rods
(h) jute
(i) timber products.[33]

Even though the intra-trade generated through IDB financing has not been very significant in relation to the total size of the intra-trade of the IDB member countries, the IDB has often played a catalytic role in initiating and promoting trade contacts in specific commodities which have subsequently contributed towards substantial growth in trade amongst the member countries of IDB. One early instance of this type of initiative was the Bank's efforts to encourage member countries to purchase jute directly from Bangladesh with ITFO financing. This initiative contributed to a substantial increase in exports of jute from Bangladesh to several IDB member countries. In the early 1980s, several member countries began importing palm oil from Malaysia with ITFO financing. One of the countries from amongst these countries has since emerged as one of the largest importers of Malaysian palm oil. More recently, the IDB has had similar successes in arranging the promotion of exports of power and tele-communication cables, fertilizers and fertilizer raw materials, industrial chemicals, and wheat through its LTTFS. In most cases member countries were importing these commodities with ITFO and LTTFS financing from other IDB member countries for the first time. It is expected that with these new trading links established, the trade in these commodities between member countries will continue to grow.

In recent years, the Board of Executive Directors and IDB Management have actively focused on enhancing efforts to promote IDB trade financing schemes. More attention has been paid to improving customer services, with particular attention to regular meetings with customers to elicit their views on the efficacy of IDB systems and procedures and how the Bank could serve their needs more efficiently.

It is interesting to note that so far the IDB has approved, respectively, 62 per cent, 2.5 per cent, and 7.5 per cent of its allocations for ITFO, LTTFS, and IBP schemes. This implies that the combined trade financing operations have accounted for 72 per cent of all financial operations of the Bank since its inception.

1. Import Trade Financing Operations (ITFO): This is the oldest and the largest of the trade financing operations of the IDB. It accounts for 62 per cent of the total financial operations of the Bank. Also, over 86 per cent of all trade financial operations is done through this scheme. It was introduced in 1977 with the following three objectives:

i. To assist the member countries in their developmental efforts by enabling them to import goods which have a developmental impact.
ii. To promote trade among the member countries by ensuring as far as possible, that operations are conducted between them.
iii. To serve as a mode of placement for the liquid funds of the Bank in accordance with the requirements of *Shari'ah* and, thereby, to generate legitimate income for the Bank.

This scheme enables the Bank to utilize its surplus funds, not immediately needed for its ordinary operations, in short-term financing, thus enabling its member countries to meet their import requirements of developmental nature. In doing so, the Bank also provides temporary relief for the balance of payments problems encountered by member countries. The *modus operandi* involves the purchase of goods and their re-sale to recipient member countries against a reasonable mark-up with deferred-payment arrangement. The total amount of financing approved under the ITFO up to the end of 1416 AH (17 May 1996) stood at ID 7,526 million (US $9,361 million) for thirty-seven countries. The trade among the member countries accounted for 78 per cent of the total amount approved under the ITFO.

2. Longer-Term Trade Financing Scheme (LTTFS): The Longer-Term Trade Financing Scheme, is a supplement to the ITFO. The purpose of this Scheme is to promote export of non-traditional goods among OIC member countries through the provision of necessary funds to participating member countries for periods ranging between six and sixty months.[34] The scheme has its own independent budget and resources and is managed and operated under IDB supervision. Till the end of 1416 AH (17 May 1996), ID 253 million (US$355 million) was approved under the Scheme. The subscribed capital stood at ID 314 million, including the IDB subscription and that of the twenty-two member countries at that time. In each participating country of LTTFS, there are one or more national agencies for the scheme.

3. Islamic Banks' Portfolio (IBP) for Investment and Development: The Islamic Bank's Portfolio, launched in 1987, is an independent fund subscribed to by the IDB and a number of Islamic commercial Banks and financial institutions (the number, including IDB, was twenty in 1996), which administers the IBP as *Modarib*.[35] The Portfolio aims at providing trade financing both for imports and exports and financing for the industrial sector through Equity, Leasing, and Instalment Sale operations. It is also active in syndicated financing for both trade and project investments through Leasing and Instalment Sale Operations. The Portfolio is designed to be composed of assets other than cash and debts in order to conform to the provisions of *Shari'ah* regarding the trading and negotiability of certificates. It is also active in syndicated financing for both trade and project investments through Leasing and Instalment Sale Operations. Share certificates of the initial capital are negotiable and tradable only among Islamic Banks.

The IBP aims specifically to cater to the needs of the private sector. The IBP in recent years has been playing a vitally important role in resource mobilization through managing trade and leasing syndicated financing arrangements. The trade and leasing syndications arranged by the IBP also provide high credit quality investment opportunities, not only for itself, but also for the Unit Investment Fund, for IDB Liquid funds, for the IDB pension fund, and for Islamic commercial Banks and institutions and conventional Banks in the member countries. Total financing approved by the Portfolio till the end of 1416 AH (17 May 1996) amounted to ID 781 million (US $1,129 million).

III. Special Assistance Operations: The Bank maintains a Special Assistance Account, which was established in 1979. The Account is kept separate from its ordinary resources and is used, among others, for the following purposes:

- Training and research aimed at helping and guiding member countries to re-orient their economies, financial, and banking activities in conformity with *Shari'ah*.
- Provision of relief in the form of appropriate goods and services to member countries and Islamic communities afflicted by natural disasters and calamities.
- Provision of financial assistance to member countries for the promotion and furtherance of Islamic causes.
- Provision of financial assistance to Muslim communities in non-member countries to improve their socio-economic conditions.

The Bank finances various special projects in member countries as well as Muslim communities in non-member countries. The operations in member countries are mainly for meeting situations arising out of natural calamities, refugee problems and any other unforeseen events. The operations for Muslim communities, on the other hand, mainly relate to upgrading their economic and social status.

The total amount approved by the Bank out of the Special Assistance Account up to the end of 1416 AH (17 May 1996) stood at ID 365 million (US $434 million). Out of this amount, ID 248 million (US $297 million) was approved for 160 operations in member countries and ID 116 million (US $137 million) for 218 operations for Muslim communities in non-member countries. The amounts approved include, among others, funds for Special Programme of Emergency Aid to Sahelian member countries; assistance to member countries affected by locusts, floods, and earthquake; assistance to mitigate refugee problem; and several educational, health, and social projects for Muslim communities in non-member countries. Among the other prominent schemes launched under Special Assistance Operations, are the scholarship programme for Muslim minority communities, the merit scholarship programme for high technology, and the sacrificial meat utilization project.[36]

Affiliated Bodies

The IDB has three affiliated bodies:

(a) Islamic Research and Training Institute (IRTI): Article 2 of the IDB's Agreement stipulates, that one of the Bank's functions is 'to undertake research for enabling the economic, financial, and banking activities in Muslim countries to conform to the *Shari'ah*, and to extend training facilities for personnel engaged in development activities in member countries'. In order to realize the objective, the third annual meeting of the Board of Governors (March 1979) adopted a resolution, establishing the Islamic Research and Training Institute. On 27 April 1981, the Board of Executive Directors approved the statute of IRTI and it became operational in 1983.[37] The objectives of the IRTI are to undertake basic and applied research in order to enable the economic, financial, and banking activities in Muslim countries to conform to *Shari'ah*, enhance professional capabilities in research in Islamic economics and banking, and to extend training facilities for personnel engaged in development activities in the IDB member countries.

Research Activities: The research activities of the IRTI consist of reference (preparation of bibliographies, indexes etc.),[38] basic research (development of concepts), and applied research (seeking solutions of specific economic problems). The IRTI undertakes studies on various subjects. The research projects are implemented through its own staff as well as eminent external researchers. The research studies so far undertaken, related mainly to subjects like *Zakat*, social welfare, Islamic financial instruments, public debt, fiscal reform capital market, privatization, etc. Up to the end of 1996, the total number of IRTI publications stood at 182.

Some of the latest in-house researches include 'Model for Islamic Companies Law', 'House Building Finance in Islamic Perspective', 'Impact of ECO Enlargement', 'The Evolution of Islamic Capital Market', 'Islamisation of Insurance Sector', and 'Various Aspects of Privatization in Islamic Perspective'. The IRTI seminars are held in different countries, employing any of the international languages understood in host countries like Arabic, Russian, English etc. Some recent examples include the seminars on Islamic economics (Turkey), on *Awqaf* (Sudan) and on *Zakat* Management (Chad).

The IRTI also arranges lectures by distinguished scholars as part of its Distinguished Lectures Series. Under the Visiting Scholar Series, the IRTI invites scholars to undertake research for six to twelve months using the Institute's facilities. Then comes the Encouragement and Programme Series, under which the IRTI finances private research initiatives on Islamic economics in the scholars' home countries. The IDB awards on Islamic Banking and Islamic Finance are also managed by this institute. It also brings out a bi-annual journal under the name of *Islamic Economic Studies*.

Training Activities: The IRTI also holds seminars, conferences, and workshops. These usually dwell upon different subjects from the Islamic perspective. The training programme of the IRTI includes offering courses in various subjects and organizing workshops and seminars with the purpose of imparting training to the staff of the National Development Financing Institutions (NDFIs) and other development agencies in member countries. By the end of 1996, the IRTI had arranged a total of sixty-three seminars/ conferences and seventy-five training programmes. The eleven courses conducted in the financial year 1415 AH included courses on Sustainable Development (Pakistan), Project Identification and Appraisal (Uganda), Debt Management (Guinea), Management Development (Kazakhstan), and others.

Information Activities: The IRTI has an Information Centre that collects, systematizes, and disseminates information relating to socio-economic variables of member countries. It also collects information and develops databases relating to the areas of Islamic economics, banking, and finance. The database on expertise available in Muslim countries is in the process of development. Data collection activities are carried out through contacts with 164 OIC national organizations to collect information related to trade, industrial, agricultural, and social sectors. Databases on country profiles, fair and exhibitions and trade promotion organizations are also maintained.

(b) Islamic Corporation for the Insurance of Investment and Export Credit (ICIIEC): The Bank, on the initiative of the COMCEC, established the Islamic Corporation for the Insurance of Investment and Export Credit (ICIEC) in 1994 as an autonomous subsidiary, based in Jeddah, Saudi Arabia, with an authorized capital of ID 100 million (about US$150 million).[39] The Bank subscribed to and fully paid 50 per cent of the capital. Fifteen OIC member countries subscribed to the remaining 50 per cent.

The ICIEC, which commenced business in July 1995 provides, in accordance with the principles of *Shari'ah*, export credit insurance to cover the non-payment of export receivables, resulting from commercial (buyer) or non-commercial (country) risks. At a later stage, ICIEC will offer investment insurance against country risks, mainly the risks of exchange transfer restrictions, expropriation, war and civil disturbance, and breach of contract by the host government.

(c) International Islamic Lease Financing Company (IILFC): The decision to create an International Islamic Leasing Company is the product of IDB's cooperation with various Islamic financial institutions.[40] The IDB has been leading a group of Muslim investors from Kuwait and other Gulf States for the purpose. The IILFC is located at Kuwait where a special law for the purpose is being framed. The company will start functioning by the end of the current year, with an initial capital of $50 million.[41] The IILFC is a holding company that will, in turn, establish specialized national leasing companies. The first two national leasing companies are to be created in Malaysia and Turkey. The IDB has the largest stake of 33 per cent. The other non-Kuwait investors include Saudi Arabia's National Commercial Bank and Qatar International Islamic Bank.

An Appraisal

The IDB has been a success story since the beginning. It goes to its credit that if there is one organ the OIC can be proud of, it is certainly the IDB. For one thing, it is an organ that strictly follows merit in all recruitments—a rare distinction within the OIC infrastructure. The IDB has financed, wholly or partially, around two thousand projects, besides providing technical assistance in hundreds of others in the member states. No need to emphasize how significant such aid is, for the developing states. Besides the financial operations that the Bank is supposed to perform anyway, it has excelled as a role model for the other OIC organs, as well as the various humanitarian relief organizations, in the true sense of the word. Be it the reconstruction of the war-torn Bosnia,[42] the succour to flood victims in Bangladesh, emergency aid to the oppressed Arakanese Muslims in Burma, the IDB is there wherever a Muslim state or a Muslim community needs it.[43]

The IDB has taken the leading role in the research on Islamic economics and Islamic Banking. Along with its subsidiary, the Islamic Research Training Institute (IRTI), the Bank has to its credit a large number of studies, training courses, and seminars and symposia on Islamic Banking and Finance. It has published many papers and reports on the subject and has indeed revolutionized Islamic economics as an academic discipline. It is, in itself, the testing ground for the theories propounded on Islamic economics. To promote research in the field, IDB initiated two prizes worth ID 30,000 (US $43,000) each in 1988 for outstanding work in the disciplines of Islamic Banking and Islamic finance. Since 1992, one prize is awarded annually alternating between the two disciplines.

The Bank is contributing to the cause of education in the Muslim world in other ways as well. It awards merit scholarships for advance studies in sixteen fields (mostly related to science and technology) to promising Muslim students, in order to help develop qualified human resources in the member states.[44] The IDB also runs another scholarship programme for deserving Muslim students of non-Muslim states, to pursue higher studies in their home countries or elsewhere.[45]

Several OIC member states like Palestine, Afghanistan, and ex-Communist Muslim Republics have been included in the latter programme on exceptional basis. Thousands of students have benefited from these two programmes all over the Muslim world. The IDB has also established a Technical Cooperation Programme (TCP) to mobilize technical capabilities and promote exchange of expertise in the member countries.

The Islamic Bank is also engaged in activities related to information and cultural affairs. It has undertaken implementation of the OIC Information Systems Network (OICIS-NET) project, which aims at improving the flow, exchange, and sharing of information resources among the member countries to support their development activities. In the cultural field, the Bank has been involved in the execution of the Sacrificial Meat Utilization Project of the Kingdom of Saudi Arabia since its launching in 1403 AH (1983). The purpose of the Project is to assist the pilgrims in performing the ritual of Sacrifice related to *hajj* as well as to ensure proper utilization of the meat of the animals sacrificed on the occasion of *hajj*.

Cooperation with different Institutions: The IDB holds cordial relations with over fifty Islamic Banks. It has equity participation in twenty of them. The IDB has achieved cooperation with these Banks in the fields of Islamic Banking, project co-financing, research, training, and exchange of information. The Bank has special cooperation links with a number of Arab national and regional development financing institutions and the OPEC Fund for International Development. These institutions and the IDB, commonly known as the Coordination Group, include the following:

- Abu Dhabi Fund for Development
- Arab Bank for Economic Development in Africa
- Arab Fund for Economic and Social development
- Arab Monetary Fund
- Iraqi Fund for External Development
- Kuwait Fund for Arab Economic Development
- OPEC Fund for International Development
- Saudi Fund for Development
- Islamic Development Bank.[46]

The Bank is working to promote economic cooperation at the sub-regional level through signing memoranda of understanding (MOUs) with several sub-regional economic cooperation organizations, which have members from the IDB constituency. These include Arab Maghreb Union (AMU), Economic Cooperation Organization (ECO), Gulf Cooperation Council (GCC), and the ECOWAS Fund.

And finally, the Bank holds regular consultations with other leading financial institutions of the world, especially the World Bank. It also maintains special ties with ten major UN agencies like UNICEF, FAO, UNESCO and the WHO.

II. Islamic Educational, Scientific, and Cultural Organization (ISESCO)

The ISESCO is a specialized institution of the OIC in the field of education, science, and culture. The idea of setting up an Islamic Educational, Scientific, and Cultural Organization (ISESCO) was conceived at the first International conference on Islamic Education which was held at Mecca, in 1977, under the sponsorship of King Abdul Aziz University.[47] The idea materialized when the 10th ICFM (Fez; 1979) decided to establish it and designated Rabat, Morocco, as the permanent venue of the proposed Islamic cultural organization. The following year, the 11th ICFM (Islamabad; 1980), through its resolution no.2/11-C adopted its Statute. Eventually, the 3rd Islamic Summit (Taif; 1981), while noting the diversity of educational systems and of cultural and scientific policies in Islamic countries, as well as the need to reconsider and reactivate them, decided to endorse the decision of setting up the ISESCO in an attempt to remedy that situation.[48]

The first General Conference took place in June 1983 at Casablanca that adopted a plan of action for the future. The second General Conference was held in September 1985 at Islamabad wherein King Hassan of Morocco pledged to bear all the expenses for the construction of ISESCO headquarters at Rabat.[49]

Objectives: The objectives of the ISESCO, as laid down in its statute, are as follows:[50]

- To strengthen cooperation among the member-states in the field of education, scientific and cultural research, and to make Islamic culture the axis of educational curricula at all levels.
- To support the real Islamic culture and to project independence of Islamic thought against the elements of cultural invasion, distortion, and debasements.
- To encourage cooperation among the member-states in the field of scientific research to develop applied science and the use of advanced technology within the framework of permanent Islamic values and ideals, and to preserve features of the Islamic civilization.
- To find ways and means of protecting the Islamic identity of the Muslims in non-Muslim countries.
- To promote understanding between the peoples and to help maintain peace and security in the world by all means, especially through education, science, and culture; and
- To coordinate among the specialized institutions of the OIC in the fields of education, science and culture and all the member-states of the Islamic Conference with a view to consolidating Islamic solidarity and cultural complementarity in the Muslim world.

Membership and Structure: Any state that is a member of the OIC and agrees, in principle, with the aims and objectives of the ISESCO, can become its member. In the beginning, only twenty-two states joined the ISESCO but soon the numbers swelled. All, but a few, OIC states are today members of the ISESCO.[51] Any Muslim country that does not join ISESCO, automatically becomes an associate member. Associate members attend the meetings but do not have the right to vote.[52] Moreover, all observers at the OIC *ipso facto* enjoy observer status at the ISESCO also. The ISESCO has a three-tier structure.[53]

General Conference: It is composed of representatives of the member states of ISESCO. The OIC Secretary General or his representative is entitled to attend the General Conference. The Conference elects a President and three Vice-Presidents.

Executive Council:[54] The Executive Council is composed of fifteen members, nine of whom are elected by the General Conference. Three members are nominated by the Secretary General of the OIC, while the remaining three are *ex-officio* members representing the other OIC agencies. (All OIC organs have observer status at the ISESCO.) No state can have more than one member in the Council. All members are elected for three-year terms, one-third of the membership retires each year.

Director General: He is elected by the General Conference for a renewable mandate of three years. He is assisted by three Deputy Directors General.[55] The Secretariat is further divided into the departments of Education, Science, Culture, and Information etc.

Finances: The resources of the organization consist of the contributions of the member states; subsidies and donations offered by member or non-member states; and the subsidies and donations provided by bodies or individuals.[56]

Activities: The first General Conference took place in Casablanca from the 7th to 9th of June 1983. The Executive Council met, for its part, in the preceding three-day period. The Conference laid down a two-year plan of action (1983–85), that focuses mainly on the following projects:[57]

(a) Setting up an Islamic information and data bank.
(b) Eradication of illiteracy in Islamic countries, with particular emphasis on rural areas.
(c) In-service training of teachers of Islamic culture and the Arabic language.
(d) Investigating the situation prevailing in schools of religious education, and improving their working procedures on the basis of scientific principles.
(e) Supporting Islamic Studies departments in member state universities, by supplying them with books on Islamic culture and civilization.
(f) Consolidating scientific cooperation, as well as renovating scientific syllabus in member-countries, by reviewing scientific textbooks, modernizing school laboratories and improving teacher training courses in the scientific fields.
(g) Protection of Islamic civilization features and safeguard of the Islamic heritage.
(h) Enhancing Islamic cultural and educational institutions in host countries of Muslim minorities.

(i) Exchange of students, teachers and lecturers, as well as scientific experiences.
(j) To set right allegations and published material in the West, which are aimed at debasing the lofty values of Islam.

In order to implement the programme, ISESCO established a computer section for data storage, processing and dissemination. It entered into 'eradication of illiteracy' projects in Niger and Bangladesh. It conducted teacher-training programmes in Malaysia and Sierra Leone. A project to introduce teaching based on scientific principles at Quranic schools was carried out in Senegal. A project on the review of textbooks of Molecular Biology and Microbiology was carried out with the cooperation of the Pakistan's Ministry of Education. The scientists of Pakistani universities under the leadership of scientists of the Punjab University and the National Academy of Higher Education were entrusted with the task. In addition, technical aid was provided to schools in certain Islamic countries, for example, Guinea and Yemen, to improve their facilities for science education.[58]

The second General Conference of ISESCO was held during 1–5 September 1985 at Islamabad. It noted with concern that out of $11 million estimated earnings for the first three years, an amount of $1.5 million only, that is about 1/7, could be realized.[59] This not only resulted in some of the ISESCO projects being abandoned but also required other trimming measures including the reduction of annual increment to the employees from 10 to 5 per cent.[60] The Conference adopted a new three-year Plan of Action and approved $4.5 million for the budget as against $33.8 million requested. The plan envisaged a spending of 17.5 million for forty-eight projects (of which eighteen were educational, eight scientific, ten cultural, and twelve were of general nature), in addition to five extra-budgetary projects.[61] The third General Conference of ISESCO was held during 12–15 November 1988 at Amman, Jordan, while the fourth General Conference was inaugurated on 28 November 1991 at Rabat, Morocco.[62] It was here that Director General Dr Abdul Hadi Boutalib retired. Both these Conferences also reviewed the activities of ISESCO and approved new projects in the scientific, cultural, and educational fields.

New Direction of Activities:[63] Since the third General Conference (1988), the programmes of the Education Sector of ISESCO are mainly concerned with the promotion of Arabic language and its teaching to non-Arabic speakers, adult education and the struggle against illiteracy, development of an educational strategy for the Islamic countries, preparation of a model programme for teaching of computer science, and promotion of educational research. The ISESCO is also implementing its programme on 'Basic education and training in the perspective of human resource development in the Islamic countries', within the framework of cooperation between OIC and the UN.[64]

Cultural programmes of the Organization, are lately directed towards the elaboration of an Islamic cultural strategy, correction of erroneous information published on Islam and Muslims, preservation of Islamic cultural heritage, providing support to cultural institutions and centres and protecting Islamic society against the harmful influence of cultural invasion.

The ISESCO believes that the 'improvement of science education at all levels and promotion of scientific research are of fundamental importance for the success of the efforts aimed at the achievement of excellence in the modern fields of science and technology for the socio-economic well being of the Muslim World'. The emphasis on science programmes is in the following areas: (a) improvement of science teaching; (b) strengthening of scientific research and promotion of mutual contacts and cooperation between Muslim scientists; (c) development of trained scientific manpower; (d) support of Muslims in non-member states; (e) popularization of science.

Activities in the fields of Education and Culture: The second meeting of the COMSTECH had entrusted to ISESCO the task of establishment of the Federation of Universities of the Islamic World. The Founding Conference of the Federation was held in Rabat during 30 November–1 December 1987, and was attended by representatives of a large number of universities in the Islamic countries. This Conference laid down the Statute of the Federation and, appointed, *ex officio*, the Director General of ISESCO as the Secretary General of the Federation.

For the promotion of effective linkages among universities, research organizations and production sectors, ISESCO programmes provide for the organization of seminars on university-industry interaction, staging of exhibitions/open houses in universities and other research organizations for highlighting their research findings and work in progress, and holding of industrial forums for researchers from universities/research organizations and representatives of Chambers of Commerce and Industry.

With a view to help in the improvement of the standards of teaching of science, the ISESCO completed an exercise in the modernization of curricula in Biology, Chemistry, Mathematics, and later Physics, for secondary and higher secondary levels. The draft model curricula, prepared by experts committees appointed by ISESCO, were distributed among the member states for comments. The curricula were revised in the light of member states' observations and have been published in Arabic, English, and French. As a next step, the ISESCO prepared teachers' annotated guidebooks and circulated the same among the members. The ISESCO then conducted a survey of the use by member states of these curricula. The Organization expressed concern that most of the member states had not formally adopted them.

In 1992, the ISESCO embarked upon the next leg of the project, i.e., preparation of the unified undergraduate syllabi for the Muslim states' universities in the same four subjects. The project was almost complete by the end of 1995, when the curricula of these subjects, except that of Physics, were circulated in the Muslim states for comments and opinions. In early 1996, the final stage of the project, preparation of the graduate science curricula in all the three OIC official languages, was inaugurated. The model syllabi for Environmental Chemistry and for Water Resource Management, is nearing completion while the work on many other subjects is well in progress. These modernized curricula in applied sciences for various academic levels, incorporating recent advances and developments in the subjects with emphasis on the teaching of science from an Islamic perspective, have been distributed among the member states for consideration and adoption as minimal standards for the teaching of these subjects at the relevant levels.

To improve laboratory facilities for the effective teaching of science in schools, model laboratory equipment and materials have been provided to some schools in Bangladesh, Gambia, Guinea, and Yemen Arab Republic. Recently, a training course for thirty Guinean school teachers was organized at Conakry to familiarize them with the use of the model scientific equipment supplied by ISESCO. Schools in Burkina Faso, Chad, Mali, and Niger, have also been beneficiaries of this programme.[65]

For the training of technical personnel for the repair and maintenance of electronic and other laboratory equipment in educational institutions, ISESCO organized several regional training courses in Egypt, Malaysia, and Morocco, a few of which were co-sponsored by UNESCO, for the benefit of regional Muslim states. Recognizing the need for personnel trained in handling high speed machines for data processing, the ISESCO has conducted several training courses on methods of storage collection and retrieval of data. A couple of them were held at Islamic Information and Data Bank (BIDI) at the ISESCO Directorate General in Rabat, while the rest were conducted in Tunisia, Malaysia etc.[65]

In the cultural field, the ISESCO, in association with the 'Islam and the West' a French organization, held a regional conference entitled 'Islam, France and Europe' at Paris in January 1997. Some delegates from the OIC member states also attended.[67] During 27 May–5 June 1997, it organized a training course for teachers of Islamic education and Arabic language in Europe. It was attended by thirty teachers, working in Islamic cultural centres and Muslim schools in Britain.[68] Similarly, a well-attended workshop on the University-Industry Interaction was held in Karachi, Pakistan, during September 1997.

Activities in the field of Science: In the area of science and technology, the ISESCO has sponsored or co-sponsored with local universities or regional research centres, a large number of conferences and symposia in the Muslim countries. In addition,

it financed the participation or contributed towards the travel expenses of Muslim scientists in various international seminars. Some of such conferences are:[69]

- International Training Workshop on 'Advanced Research Techniques in Spectroscopy' at Karachi, Pakistan;
- Training Course on 'Genetic Engineering Technology' at Rajshahi, Bangladesh;
- Regional Seminar on 'Horticultural Techniques' at Tunis, Tunisia;
- Training course on 'Microbial Technologies' at the Punjab University, Lahore; and a similar course at Cairo University, Egypt;
- First Asian Science and Technology Conference 'Science Asia' at Kuala Lumpur, Malaysia.

In addition, the provision of technical assistance to active research centres in the member states, by way of research grants and organization of research seminars and courses in advanced research techniques, is a major ongoing programme in this field. The ISESCO is also engaged in different scientific research programmes on topics like earthquake monitoring, management of national parks, remote sensing for environmental purposes, etc., in collaboration with a number of universities and research establishments of the Muslim world. The ISESCO has provided grants for the purchase of urgently needed equipment·and chemicals to scientists in Bangladesh, Egypt, Jordan, Morocco, Pakistan, Yemen, and some other states.

Help to students, youth, and Muslim minorities:[70] The provision of career development grants to promising young scientists to encourage them to start and develop their research careers in their own countries is another activity ISESCO is trying to support.

To identify and nurture talent and to encourage talented Muslim youth to pursue careers in basic sciences, ISESCO invited member states to send their nominations for the award of ISESCO Merit Scholarships. The scholarships were awarded beginning from January 1988 for studies in basic sciences in the scholars' own countries. Beneficiaries are from Bangladesh, Egypt, Guinea, Mali, Morocco, Pakistan, Senegal, and Yemen. Beginning from 1992, the ISESCO expanded its scholarship programme and now it is divided into three heads: (i) postgraduate scholarship programme; (ii) undergraduate scholarship programme; and the (iii) Muslim minorities support scholarships. The selectees are provided funding for pursuing their studies in their home country, in another Muslim country, or a renowned university in a Western country, depending on the decisions of the selection committee on a case-to-case basis. The number of beneficiaries varies every year, depending upon the availability of funds. The composition of scholars, in terms of nationalities, is also different each year. As part of its endeavour to increase the Muslim scientific manpower, the ISESCO also gives career development grants to promising youth of the Muslim states.

In addition to providing travel grants to some Muslim scientists from non-Islamic countries to enable them to participate in international scientific meetings, representative of Muslim communities in non-member states have been contacted to send nominations for the award of scholarships to deserving Muslim youth for specialization in scientific and technological fields.

ISESCO Publications:[71] In order that a wider section of the scientific community may benefit from the proceedings of a scientific event, the ISESCO encourages the publication of proceedings of meetings sponsored or co-sponsored by it. For instance, two books based on the proceedings of the ISESCO-sponsored Symposia on Chemistry of Natural Products have been published in Europe and Pakistan to international acclaim.

To create awareness of the important advances made in the fields of science and technology and to generate popular interest in science, some books on selected topics have been published under an agreement with the Royal Scientific Society (RSS), Amman, Jordan. Three books in Arabic, on 'The Computer', 'Space Travel', and 'The Process of Unification in Field Physics' have been produced. The ISESCO has also published a 360-page documentary book 'One Decade in the Service of the Islamic World' about its own activities.

The ISESCO is securing the particulars of eminent Muslim scientists and technologists from its member states and of eminent Muslim scientists

and technologists working in the non-Islamic developed countries, in order to prepare briefs on Muslim scientists and technologists who have achieved eminence and are presently active in their fields of research.

The ISESCO also brings out several periodicals including the *ISESCO Bulletin* and *Islam Today* on a quarterly and six-monthly basis, respectively. It also publishes the ISESCO triennial.[72]

Future Outlook: The ultimate goal of the ISESCO is the cultural unity of the Muslim nation. It wants to develop a Muslim identity among the Muslims and aims at promoting Arabic language for the purpose. It wants to make the Islamic culture 'as the axis' of school curricula. It wants to defend the Muslims against, what it calls, the 'cultural invasion of the west'. It aims at promoting Islamic ideals and values. It wants all the schools in the Muslim world to have unified syllabi and the universities to have an integrated super-structure for close coordination in educational and research activities. And finally, the ISESCO seeks to encourage cooperation in the Muslim world in scientific research, and to develop the applied sciences and advanced technology among the Muslims 'within the framework of Islamic values'.[73]

These are, no doubt, no easy goals to achieve. But the ISESCO is forging ahead and only time will tell whether such a cultural unity, as the Organization envisages, is achievable within the parameters of reality. We have noted above that the main impediment with ISESCO as is the case with the majority of other OIC Organs, is the paucity of resources. A strong will on the part of member states' leadership, to respect their financial obligations towards this biggest cultural forum of the Muslim world is absolutely essential.

III. International Islamic News Agency(IINA)

The International Islamic News Agency (IINA) is one of the oldest and one of the most important of the OIC organs. The idea of setting up of a news agency came up in the 2nd ICFM (Karachi; 1970), which constituted an expert committee to consider its establishment. The experts met in Tehran, Iran, during 20–22 April 1971 and finalized the recommendations. The 3rd ICFM (Jeddah; 1972) formally established IINA as a specialized organ of the OIC through its resolution No.6/3-C which envisaged it as a federation of the Muslim states news agancies.[74]

The establishment of a Pan-Islamic news agency was a tacit realization of the information and communication challenges and the result of frustration over Muslim peoples' dependence on Western media where the portrayal of the image of Islam was, to say the least, not very flattering. After a long delay IINA started operation in May 1979.[75] The headquarters of IINA are located in Jeddah.

Objectives: The basic objectives of the IINA are:[76]

- To develop close and better relations between member states in the Information field, to safeguard and consolidate the rich cultural heritage of Islam.
- To promote professional contacts and technical cooperation between the news agencies of member states.
- To work for better understanding of Islamic peoples and their political, economic, and social problems.
- To enhance and preserve the huge Islamic cultural heritage.
- To work for the unification of the objectives of the Muslim world.

The OIC resolutions establishing the IINA also indicated that it would work to facilitate the exchange of information articles and photographs, and also that of reporters and journalists in the Muslim world.

Structure: The organizational structure of the IINA is as follows:[77]

General Assembly: Under the statute, the General Assembly stands at the apex of the IINA's structure. It is composed of representatives of the national news agencies of the member-states. It meets once every two years.

Executive Board: It is composed of eleven members, of whom nine are elected by the OIC General Assembly. The host country and the

Secretary General are permanent members of the Board. It follows up the activities of the Agency and controls its technical, administrative, and financial affairs.

Director General: The Director General is appointed by the General Assembly for a four-year renewable mandate.

Finance:[78] We have seen earlier that the OIC specialized organs are supposed to have independent budgets. Consequently, the IINA is financed through:

- the contributions of its members, fixed by the General Assembly;
- voluntary donations and subsides from Member states;
- resources generated by the IINA on commercial basis.

The IINA is the worst-hit victim of the OIC member's pusillanimity towards their financial obligations. The initial project of $35 million had soon to be shelved as the member-states reneged on their financial commitments, hence the IINA started without any semblance of the infrastructure that an international news agency ought to have. It has a meagre $2 million annual budget and a regular staff of 26 only at its headquarters.[79] Save in Bangladesh, Morocco, and Tanzania, the IINA does not have full-time correspondents outside Saudi Arabia. All it can barely afford to have is part-time or per-piece journalists, mainly in the capitals of OIC member-states.

Only ten member states, namely, Egypt, Indonesia, Kuwait, Libya, Morocco, Pakistan, Qatar, Saudi Arabia, Tunisia, and the UAE pay their contributions. At any given time, the IINA is facing a default by 75 per cent of the member states.[80] Consequently, there were times, when the IINA failed to pay salaries to its staff, once for a long stretch of ten months. The IINA has also defaulted on the payment of electricity and telephone bills. It has been surviving on donations by some member-states, particularly Saudi Arabia.[81] The example of IINA is often cited whenever a criticism of the OIC is made, because one of the most vital organs of the Organization, fell victim to gross neglect. In the given circumstances, the IINA can hardly be deemed culpable for its inefficiency.

Activities: The Islamic News Agency is an epitome of apathy and neglect on the part of the Muslim world. It is there to tell the sorry tale of how an institution should not be run.

Early history: Though IINA was established in 1972, it did not start operating then. In November 1973 the representatives of monthly *Muslim News International* met the then OIC Secretary General and offered to bring Arabic and English editions of the magazine under the OIC auspices. Tunku Abdul Rahman thanked them and appreciated their commitment but regretted his inability to accept the offer.[82]

The IINA affairs kept pending for seven years and it started working in May 1979. In the last week of October that year, the first conference of Muslim states' news agencies was held in Istanbul, Turkey, that discussed a joint news strategy. In the beginning, IINA used to telecast around 2000 words daily for each of its English and Arabic files.[83] Since it was unable even to have its own telecommunication network, it had to sign a contract with a Rome-based company to broadcast its news through a high frequency radio transmitter. This transmitter is connected with twenty-member news agencies via three channel satellites.[84]

Activities in the 1980s: In December 1982, it established a twenty-four hour duplex satellite line with Indonesian news agency ANTARA and the Malaysia-based BERNAMA, thus replacing the daily three hour news cast via radio transmitters.[85] By 1986, according to the official claims, the IINA was transmitting news in Arabic and English for seven hours each day. Although French is one of its official languages, the IINA had failed in transmitting news in this language. The daily average of news casts came to about 15,000 words, roughly 7500 in each of the two languages, consisting of thirty-five to forty-five news items. News in English was transmitted from 0800 to 1500 hours GMT. In Arabic, the transmission is conducted between 1200 and 1900 GMT. In

addition, it used to transmit daily about 700 words in Spanish for use in thirteen Latin American Countries.[86] It may be noted that this news was not available to the public directly. It is not accessible to a number of member states' news agencies either.[87]

The shortcomings: Whatever may be the opinion of the IINA about its own achievements, trumpeted through its official brochures, the fact of the matter is that it is a failed Agency. As seen earlier, the IINA could not maintain regular full-time correspondents of its own, Consequently, hardly any news coverage is conducted by the IINA itself, not even that of the OIC and its subsidiary organs' activities. The IINA remains absent from the Islamic Summits and Foreign Ministers Conferences and the newspapers in the Muslim world have to rely on West-based news agencies like Reuters, AFP, and AP, for reports about the decisions taken. The IINA covers only those meetings and activities of the OIC, that take place in Saudi Arabia, the host country.

Since the IINA monitors the news agencies of Muslim countries, its newscasts are mostly based on this source. Thus IINA acts as a source to transmit the news of one Muslim country to the others.[88] It is obvious that these national news agencies mostly prefer local news or international news with local relevance. Thus, the IINA newscasts reflect this fact, for instance, on a single day (18 July 1984), only one of the thirty-four news items released by IINA, related to Islam in the broad cultural sense. Another three news items were on related topics like Morocco sends 150 Arabic teachers to Europe or King Fahd donates $1 million to Australian Islamic Council, etc. The remaining thirty news items had no direct or indirect relation with Islam as such.[89] Another problem with the IINA is that its stories have no depth. It has to care for the sensitivities of all Muslim countries. It cannot take sides with either party in a fratricidal conflict within the Muslim world, though, its news items sometimes show some bias in favour of the position of Saudi Arabia, its main donor. The Agency has so far not managed to start a feature service or a photo service.[90] The following is an excerpt from an editorial comment about IINA, carried by a leading daily of Islamabad: 'The International Islamic News Agency is neither international, nor Islamic, and has nothing to do with news. An agency it is, but moribund, inoperative...'.[91]

Activities in the 1990s: In the last decade of the nineties, the IINA expanded its scope of activities. It started its news service in the French language and made arrangements for the wider circulation of its news. First of all, it entered into an agreement with the Qatar News Agency (QNA) to disseminate its news reports to 700 points in the Arab world, Europe, and America; in Arabic, English, and Portuguese. Under separate agreements, the Associated Press of Pakistan (APP), and the Pan-African News Agency (PANA) distribute its news in Asia and Africa, respectively. The ANTARA and BERNAMA continue to circulate the IINA news in East Asia and Oceana.[92]

The IINA has recently been equipped with the latest computers. It has also become able to exchange news with the Muslim states' news agencies through its Email address iina@mail.gcc.com.bh. It receives on the average, fifty articles a day from this source and redistributes them. The IINA launched its home page on the web with the address www.islamicnews.org to provide the millions of Internet users with its daily news bulletin. Thus the IINA news are now accessible to over eighty countries at very cheap rates.[93] The IINA has now started sending printed news bulletins to media and news agencies and to Islamic centres and organizations world-wide. Lately, the IINA appointed correspondents in some new countries and has started sending them to other countries on reporting assignments.

News emphasis: The IINA news coverage has a special emphasis on the Islamic causes (Palestine, Bosnia, etc.), condition of Muslim minorities, religious and humanitarian activities, development projects in the Muslim countries, and the opinions of Islamic leaders about the problems being faced by the Muslim states.

The IINA claims that it has brought closer the Muslim communities living in the four corners of the globe through listening to and reading news about each other. The Agency also claims to have become a pressure group by denouncing oppression and publicising aggression and persecution against Muslim communities. The IINA takes credit for creating awareness about the Islamic news in the media, since the news agencies and TV channels have started appointing special editors in charge of preparation of Islamic news. Finally, the IINA purports to have countered, what it calls, the anti-Islam propaganda campaigns, through disseminating the replies and responses of the leading Muslim intellectuals.[94]

Publications: Since 1991, the IINA has regularly published an *Annual Book of Events in the Muslim World*. Six volumes have been brought out thus far, containing selected news items from the IINA's daily news bulletins. Each volume thus gives a bird's eye view of the preceding year's events in the Muslim world. All copies of the book are distributed free of charge to the Islamic centres, universities, and organizations worldwide.

The IINA published a book *Bosnia and Herzegovina*, detailing the history, culture and politics of the country as well as the events of the war, drawn from the reports and articles circulated by the IINA. The book was very well received and was reproduced in several Muslim countries. Another book of the type entitled *Somalia* was produced during the civil war in Somalia.[95]

Future Outlook

The IINA has a number of plans for the future; first and foremost is to set up its own receiving and transmission station that is indispensable for its growth into an independent international news service. It also plans to start a photo service and to introduce a newscast in French language, particularly for the Francophone African member states. All these programmes are awaiting financial aid.

We know that IINA is one of the three pillars of the OIC Information Plan, the other two being the ISBO and the Information Section in the General Secretariat. The chief executives of IINA and ISBO, and the OIC Assistant Secretary General (Information) hold regular coordination meetings to discuss the implementation of the Plan.

The failure of the OIC to achieve its objectives in the field of information is no mean failure. It would not be an exaggeration to suggest that the poor showing of IINA/ISBO is the failure of OIC itself because wherever the OIC or its organs do something tangible, their achievements go unreported. So if the people at large in the Muslim world believe that the OIC is a failed organization, they are correct in so far as they never came to know what the OIC, the IDB, or the Islamic Solidarity Fund, for instance, did accomplish. The sense of solidarity in the peoples of the OIC member states, which the IINA and the ISBO could have fostered in two and a half decades, is another casualty of this state of affairs. On the other hand, the flood of news from the Western sources, that has a different perspective, has plunged the Muslim countries into a crisis of information. The Muslims feel at a loss not to find their point of view in the ocean of information.

Out of the four big international news agencies, United Press (UP), Associated Press (AP), Reuters, and the AFP, the latter two have regular Arabic service while the AP has a feature service in Arabic language. The AFP alone has 8500 client agencies in almost 200 countries. But this does not show the exact influence of AFP because, for instance the Russian ITAR–TASS news agency, a client of AFP, has 6000 subsidiary beneficiaries within the country.

Coming back to IINA, we find that it has a staff of twenty-six, no full time correspondents, and a meagre budget of $2 million. There is no reason why a potential subscriber would opt for it. Compare it with the AP, which has 132 bureaux with a $50 million budget within the USA and seventy-six bureaux budget of $40 million abroad. It has 400 full-time correspondents, 315 of whom are international correspondents stationed at destinations outside the home country. Depending upon the speed of printers at the subscriber point, one can get 250 to 600 news items consisting of 51,000 to 112,000 words on the average, every day. The AP did not grow into such a gigantic outfit overnight. It is the quantity and quality of news that a news agency offers, that can expand its business.

The IINA can follow in the footsteps of these news agencies and work on a commercial basis.

Donations are not a panacea for a sick agency; actually they have the opposite effect. Such parasitic tendency only enhances lethargy. To resuscitate the IINA, an unqualified commitment of the Muslim states is required.

IV. Islamic States Broadcasting Organization (ISBO)

Originally proposed by Saudi Arabia, the Islamic States Broadcasting Organization (ISBO) was established by the 6th ICFM (Jeddah; 1975) as the fourth specialized organ of the OIC. The same Conference decided to make Jeddah its permanent venue.[96] The ISBO is a pan-Islamic institution with dual, political and cultural, roles. It is meant to work for the projection of the Muslim world's viewpoint on international issues and of the image of Islam on the electronic media. It is basically a federation of the broadcasting corporations of the Muslim states. Its objectives, and to a large extent its constraints, are similar to those of the IINA. Likewise, the structure and financial arrangements are almost identical.

Objectives: The ISBO stands for:

- Spreading *da'wa* and promoting awareness of the heritage of Islam.
- Promoting Islamic causes and deepening the spirit of Islamic fraternity.
- Identifying the political, social, economic, and educational bases of Islamic solidarity.
- Improving valuations among member states on those bases.
- Planning to coordinate radio transmissions, broadcasting programmes, and technological information among member countries in the spirit of Islamic fraternity.
- Developing cooperation between the Islamic technical organizms and broadcasting institutions of member states.
- Producing and exchanging radio and television programmes in order to further the objectives of the OIC.
- Promoting awareness of the Islamic heritage in the world.
- Solving broadcasting problems that may arise among the member states.

- Ensuring a unified stand and coordinating actions of the Muslim states on issues such as allocation of wavelengths etc.

Membership and Structure: The membership of the ISBO is open to all national broadcasting corporations of the Muslim states. Any broadcasting agency, public or private, owned by a Muslim country is eligible to apply for membership, but one country can have only one full member. Hence, except the one nominated by the government of a state, all the other broadcasting organizations are given Associate Memberships. In all, forty-five countries have membership at the ISBO. The ISBO has a four-tier structure: [98]

General Assembly: It is the supreme organ of the organization. It is composed of representatives of the member broadcasting agencies. It meets once every two years. The General Assembly supervises the activities of the standing committees for programmes, engineering affairs, and financial and administrative affairs.

Executive Council: It is composed of fifteen members, of whom twelve are elected by the General Assembly for a period of two years. The host country, Palestine and the OIC Secretary General or his representative, are the three *ex-officio* permanent members of the Council. It is chaired by the representative of the host country and meets once a year, at least. The Secretary General of the ISBO is also Secretary of the Council.

Secretary General: The General Assembly appoints the Secretary General of ISBO from amongst the candidates of member states for a four-year renewable mandate.

Permanent Committees: There are three permanent committees in the ISBO, namely.:
 (i) Programme and News Committee;
 (ii) Administration and Finance Committee;
(iii) Engineering Affairs Committee.

Finance: Its activities are financed through (a) mandatory contributions of member states; (b) donations and voluntary grants; and (c) resources from services rendered by the ISBO. Like the IINA, the ISBO finds itself in a perennial financial crisis. Due to the income shortfall from source (a) the ISBO has failed to develop an infrastructure. Consequently, its output in terms of production of programmes is poor. So the question of revenue generation of its own, through the sale of its commercial productions, does not arise. The ISBO has thus to rely on donations from member states, that are not very generous.

Of the forty-five member states, the three countries of Egypt, Kuwait, and Saudi Arabia alone have paid their contributions regularly. Iraq, Libya, Pakistan, Qatar, Tunisia, and the UAE defray the dues less consistently. The rest have huge arrears against them. The annual ISBO budget roughly equals $2.5 million and the scale of assessment for each member agency's contribution varies from $2,500 to $10,000 usually. The average default is 80 per cent to 90 per cent of the budget in a given year.

The highest contribution was realized in 1982 and 1983, at 45.4 per cent and 43.6 per cent of the allocation respectively. In these two years, the ISBO showed the highest output. Subsequently, the budget required downward revision each year. By 1987, the arrears had crossed the $8.9 million and the fortunes of the ISBO dwindled further for want of money.

Activities: After being set up in 1975, it held its first three meetings in Riyadh, Istanbul, and Abu Dhabi, respectively, to formulate the policies to be followed by the ISBO and to decide upon the future plan of action. These meetings were participated in by twenty-three countries in all.[99] But today, the radio and television corporations of almost all the fifty-five member states are considered its members. It began its operations, practically in 1979, on an optimistic note. The ISBO Secretary General Ahmad Farooq declared that the Organization would produce 14 centuries of the history of Islam, in the form of TV/radio programmes.[100] The ISBO also planned to become the primary agent for audio-visual exchange programme in the Muslim countries. A review of the ISBO activities of the last two decades is in order.

Programme exchange: Given the inadequate resources of the ISBO, the programme exchange was the cheapest activity and the easiest one for it to implement. Such a flow of programmes promotes closer intellectual and cultural links among the participating states. Naturally, the area received the ISBO attention since the very beginning. The ISBO asked the member broadcasting agencies to supply it with religious programmes, talk shows, discussion programmes, and interviews (both TV and radio) for the ISBO Audio-Visual Exchange Facility.

Algeria, Bahrain, Egypt, Iraq, Jordan, Kuwait, Libya, Malaysia, Morocco, Oman, Pakistan, Qatar, Saudi Arabia, Syria, Tunisia, and the UAE donated programmes. Kuwait, for instance, was more enthusiastic and supplied the ISBO with a list of 100 television programmes, expressing readiness to make copies of any of those for transmission to member states upon request. The ISBO was thus able to establish a recording library and prepared a 135-page catalogue of programmes available for exchange.

During 1979–80, six countries exchanged forty-five programmes (250-hour duration); in 1981–82, the volume rose to 600 programmes (364-hours); in 1983, twenty-one countries benefited from 1802 programmes (810-hours); and in 1984, forty-eight countries received 6090 programmes (covering 1423 hours) which was a record. A new catalogue of 174 pages was then prepared and circulated. The interest later dwindled and in 1994, for instance, thirty-four countries and centres benefited from 363 materials provided in 8423 episodes totalling 1702 hours.[101]

Initially, the slogan was 'present one hour of programme and get forty hours in return'. Many African member states like Gambia, Guinea, Mali, Niger, and Senegal received programmes free of charge (Djibouti once got 100 ISBO programmes as donation) while the wealthier Muslim states used to purchase the ISBO programmes. The total volume provided by the ISBO under the exchange programme was 35,564 episodes of 1037 programmes, and there were sixty-seven beneficiary states and centres by 1994.

Radio programmes: The ISBO has produced 1200 radio programmes, some of them jointly with

the radio centres of Egypt, Jordan, and Kuwait, etc. The ISBO headquarter had got a radio transmission unit fairly early. The ISBO produced programmes on the Prophet's life, Islamic teachings, Palestine cause, History of Islam, intellectual invasion by the West, and Arabic teaching.[102] The most prominent serials are as follows:

i) **Jerusalem—the city of heaven:** A thirty-part serial jointly produced by authors, producers, actors, and artists from six countries, on the religious, political, and legal aspects of the history of Jerusalem.

ii) **Basic obligations of Islam:** A thirty-part serial, in which Muslim youth from fifty nationalities participated, to present and explain the fundamental tenets of Islam. The Islamic Solidarity Fund (ISF) had funded the production.

iii) **Glimpses from the Prophet's life:** This thirty-part serial dilates upon the life history and the legacy of the Prophet Mohammad (PBUH).

iv) **The Raid:** The thirty-part serial traces the history of selected Muslim minorities, their struggles against oppression and the stories on the fall of Muslim empires in Asia.

v) **The Muslim Family:** The twenty-five-episode programme describes the Muslim style of life, social values, and the family structure.

vi) **Heart's inner voice:** A twenty-five-part programme on Imam Shafei's poetry.

vii) **The interpretation of the Quran:** A complete explanation of the Holy Quran in 179 parts.

In addition, there are hundreds of productions on the Prophet's life and childhood, documentaries on Islamic historical cities, commentaries on Muslim minorities, history of wars, and interviews etc. Most of the programmes are available in Arabic but, for many, English and French versions have also been prepared. Many of these ISBO programmes have been bought by as many as twenty countries.

Television programmes: The ISBO has only seventy-five television programmes to its credit. The Organization did not have its own TV recording and transmission facilities. So till 1979, it could produce only ninety hours of TV programmes using the facilities of the Saudi Television Centre at Jeddah. In 1980, the ISBO entered into agreement with the French and

German television networks for jointly producing a six-part series on the History of Islam, but apparently, the plan did not go through, as the ISBO failed to fulfil its part of the financial obligations.[103] The ISBO, however, has been able to produce a few very popular serials, such as:

i) **The jewel in the palace:** A thirteen-episode colour serial, dealing with the life of the famous pious Caliph, Omer bin Abdul Aziz.

ii) **The martyr's mission:** A nineteen-part colour serial on the heroism and sacrifice of the six Rajei companions of the Prophet Mohammad against the conspiracies of the infidels. A galaxy of leading artists from Egypt, Iraq, Jordan, Libya, Pakistan, Palestine, and Syria participated in the serial. Some Muslim states bought this programme at very high donative prices.

iii) **The Islamic justice:** A thirteen-part programme on the lives of eminent Muslim judges, co-produced with the Iraqi television.

A popular sixty-minute documentary on the 1400-year history of Islam; one-hour dialogue programmes on Islamic solidarity, Muslim character and contemporary challenges; interviews with leading personalities like the Shiekh Gad-ul-Haq and Hassan Turabi; and debates on Islamic teachings, are some of the ISBO productions that have been telecast repeatedly by television centres in Muslim countries.

The script of the serial 'The City of Jerusalem' has been approved. The work on the joint production of the ISBO and Palestine could not take off since the funding to cover the $675,000 estimated cost, could not be arranged. Meanwhile, the ISBO has also got its TV reproduction and dubbing equipment which will facilitate the exchange of TV programmes by the ISBO in future.

Arabic teaching: With the cooperation from the Egypt Broadcasting Authority, two radio serials teaching the Arabic language in English and in French, with 153 episodes each, have been prepared. Many countries have bought these serials. Now the ISBO is preparing the same programme for the television audience (the costs are being borne by the Saudi and Egyptian governments) in the same two languages. Because

of the different nature of the TV medium, only sixty-three episodes of half an hour each, will cover the Arabic language course. The project is expected to be completed soon. The TV students of the Arabic language will be able to learn without necessarily having to buy the syllabus of ten books, costing $50 a set.

Research and Training: The ISBO has produced nine research works in the form of studies/reports. They deal with the conditions of Muslim communities in America, Bulgaria, Bosnia, Central Asia, and Philippines and on the city of Jerusalem, Islamic ethics and the concept of human rights.

The ISBO has so far conducted only one training course in the field of information and media at Cairo in 1993. Participants from the broadcasting networks of Jordan, Morocco, Oman, Saudi Arabia, Syria, Tunisia, and the UAE, attended the course. The ISBO now plans to start regular training courses in cooperation with the Arab Centre for Broadcasting and Television Training at Damascus, Syria.[104] The Organization extends positive assistance to Ph.D. and post-graduate students from the Islamic countries doing research works on Islamic media and the information challenge etc.

Cooperation with other organizations: The ISBO represents its parent body, the OIC, in conferences and meetings of international and regional media and communication agencies. It has cooperation agreements with the educational and cultural wings of the OIC, the Arab League and the UN, namely, ISESCO, ALESCO, and the UNESCO, respectively.

Under a protocol signed between the ISBO and the UNESCO, the two organizations are considering holding a joint seminar on the 'Problems of Communication' at Jeddah and to issue a joint bibliography of movies and TV documentaries produced so far on issues related to Islam and the Muslims.[105]

Future Outlook

The ISBO wants to get rid of its acute financial crisis and to have its own production and broadcasting facilities. ISBO wants to produce a series on the history of Islam, its cultural heritage, the crises of contemporary Muslim world and the status and condition of Islam today, for consumption within the Muslim world as well as outside it. It also wants to complete the ongoing projects, stymied for want of money.

The ISBO is preparing a Declaration on the Islamic Broadcasting Code of Ethics. It has also worked on the Strategy of Islamic Information Activities. It has contacted some news agencies of Muslim countries to assign a special news service to be broadcast through the ISBO channels. In 1994, the ISBO floated an Islamic Vision Project and circulated questionnaires on the topic to its sister broadcasting networks. On the basis of the responses received, it is giving final shape to its recommendations to be presented to the next Islamic Summit.

v. International Islamic Law Commission (IILC)

The IILC, an Islamic version of the International Law Commission (ILC) is the fifth specialized organ of the OIC. Right at the time of the inception of the OIC, the ideas of four specialized organs concerning economics, culture, and information were conceived, but surprisingly, no consideration was given to the need of having a specialized law organ. In fact, the charter of the OIC is the first major document of modem international Islamic law in the post-Second World War era. Thereafter, with the passage of time, the OIC extended its scope and ambit, with the setting up of a plethora of affiliated institutions, and concomitantly the global trends towards regional integration had had their impact on the Muslim countries, goading their entry into a number of mutual cooperation agreements on bilateral and multilateral levels. The obvious result was the appearance of a large number of legal papers in the shape of statutes of OIC organs and texts of agreements. Prominent among them are the Agreement on Promotion, Protection and Guarantee of Investments in Muslim States, the Statute of Islamic Court of Justice and the Islamic Declaration on Human Rights.

It was in this backdrop that the decision to establish an Islamic Court of Justice was taken, that was to be, *inter alia*, the final arbiter in the interpretation of Islamic laws. But the codification of the law was a task in its own right. It may not be out of place to mention here that Islam, unlike some other religions, was never a set of dogmas and rituals alone. It was a complete code of life for its followers in their individual and collective relationships. As an eminent lawyer of his time, and the founder and first head of state of Pakistan, Mohammad Ali Jinnah, had aptly pointed out that Islam governed not so much 'man's relation with God, as man's relation with his neighbour. It governs the social life, culture and law of the believers'.[106] Hence Islamic law, known as *Shari'ah* is one of the oldest laws retained more or less in the original form for centuries, though interpretations have varied with time. The branch of *Shari'ah* which dealt with international law, mainly the conduct of war, peace, treatment of prisoners, and non-Muslim minorities *(Ahl-ul-Dhimma)*, was called *Ilm-e-Sear*.[107] The Islamic international law is quite distinguishable from the Westphalia-based concepts on the subject, though, there are points of concurrence. *Pacta sunt servanda,* for instance, is an inalienable part of Islamic international law.[108]

The need for codification of modern Islamic law, has been translated into the decisions to establish two institutions; the IILC and the Islamic Jurisprudence Academy (to be discussed in the next chapter). The formation of Islamic Jurists Committee in 1979 was a milestone in the direction of Islamic Law Commission.[109] The 11th ICFM (Islamabad; 1980) formally decided to establish the IILC while the 12th ICFM (Baghdad; 1981) decided to make Baghdad, its headquarters.

Objectives: Its functions were:[110]

- To conduct research in various fields related to the *Shari'ah*;
- To examine laws or draft laws referred to it by the member states or sub-committees in the light of injunctions of Islamic *Shari'ah* and to pronounce whether these are or not in accordance with it; and
- To devise ways and means of securing representation for putting forward the Islamic point of view before

the International Court of Justice and such other institutions, of the UN whenever, a question requiring projection of Islamic view arises.

Structure: The Commission is composed of Islamic legal experts nominated by the member states. Each member state may nominate one expert. The Commission comprises three organs:

- *Chairman*: The Commission is to have one chairman and two vice-chairmen to be elected by a majority of the members present for a non-renewable period of two years.
- *Rapporteur*: The Commission shall elect a rapporteur for each series of its meetings.
- *Secretary General*: The Secretary General of the OIC shall appoint the Secretary General of the Islamic Law Commission from amongst the nominees of the member-states.

It appears that the Commission has not started functioning, primarily because its proposed venue, Iraq, after its occupation of Kuwait and subsequent defeat, became a pariah state within the OIC.

NOTES and REFERENCES

1. See 'Guide to the Organization of the Islamic Conference', (Jeddah: OIC Secretariat, 1995), pp. 83–85, for a general introduction of the Bank.
2. Ibid., p. 84.
3. Noor Ahmad Baba, *OIC: Theory and Practice of Pan-Islamic Cooperation*, (Karachi: Oxford University Press, 1994), p. 218.
4. For instance, in the meeting of the Board of Governors on 28–29 May 1991, Iraq was not invited since it was being treated as a pariah in the OIC for its invasion of Kuwait the preceding year. Similarly, IDB has followed OIC decisions regarding the expulsions of Egypt and Afghanistan; see Keesing's Contemporary Archives, 1991, p. 38313.
5. IDB publication, 'Twenty-two years in the service of development', (Jeddah, 1996), p. 2.
6. Twentieth Annual Report of IDB, (Jeddah, 1995), p. 5.
7. Ibid.
8. Ibid., pp. 4–5.
9. Baba, ref. 3, p. 218.
10. The other three committees concentrated upon the drafting of Charter, the establishment of an Islamic news agency, and setting up of Islamic cultural centres. See chapter 1 for details.
11. World Muslim Congress publication, 'World Muslim Gazetteer 1985', (Karachi: WMC, 1987), p. 720.
12. Baba, ref. 3, p. 218.
13. Ibid.
14. Gazetteer, ref. 11, p. 55.
15. Guide to OIC, ref. 1, p. 83.
16. Gazetteer, ref. 11, p. 723.
17. Guide to OIC, ref. 1, p. 84.
18. Baba, ref. 3, p. 219.
19. For example, the nineteenth annual meeting appointed the Governors for Indonesia (Chairman), Albania and Kirghizia (Vice Chairman), and Jordan and Afghanistan (members) as members of the committee for the Twentieth meeting. See Report, ref. 6, p. 154.
20. IDB brochure, ref. 5, p. 2.
21. At the time of writing, the remaining six executive directors belonged to Algeria, Burkina Faso, Djibouti, Malaysia, Morocco, and Qatar. The complete list of names and votes obtained by each director can be seen in Twentieth IDB Reports ref. 6, p. 270.
22. IDB brochure, ref. 5, p. 2.
23. The discussion on financial resources is based upon the information given in IDB brochure, ref. 5, p. 3.
24. Ibid., p. 4.
25. Gazetteer, ref. 11, p. 722.
26. IDB brochure, ref. 5, p. 5.
27. Ibid., see chart-3 on p. 8. Also see the Twentieth Report, ref. 6, pp. 75–78.
28. Ibid., p. 72.
29. See V.A. Jaffery, 'A Review of Monitory System in Muslim, Countries', *The Muslim,* 27 December 1991, for explanation of different modes of financing. The information given here about the modes of financing has been compiled from IDB brochure, ref. 5, p. 511; Twentieth Annual Report of IDB, ref. 6, pp. 78–102, 111–029 and 135–49; Gazetteer, ref. 11, pp. 719–23; Jaffery, op. cit.; and several press reports.
30. The figures given about the number of projects do not include cancellations, unless otherwise indicated.
31. Investments are made in such enterprises only which do not run their business on interest basis.
32. Mark-up rate for member states is 6.5 per cent p.a. while that for non-member states is 7.5 per cent p. a. A rebate of 15 per cent is given for regular and timely payment. See, *The News,* Islamabad, 9 May 1995.
33. Capital Goods mean railway engines, tractors, ships, cement plants, power transformers, and industrial machinery, etc; Intermediate Industrial Goods include steel sheets and steel products, power cables, wire products, etc. While the Industrial Chemicals refer to ammonia, sulphur, soda ash, glycol, and the like.
34. Financing is provided for six to twenty-four months for consumer goods, for up to thirty-six months for intermediate goods, and for up to sixty months for

capital goods. See, *The News*, Islamabad, 9 May 1995. Also see ref. 33 above for definitions.

35. *Mudarabah* is a form of partnership where one party provides the funds while the other provides expertise and management. The latter is referred to as the *Mudarib*. Any profit occurred are shared between the two parties on a pre-arranged basis, while capital loss is borne by the partner providing the capital.

36. The Muslim communities residing in countries that are not IDB members, are usually treated as Muslim minorities, irrespective of their number. Exceptions are made as in the case of Bosnia, Albania, Kirghizia, etc, where generous aid is given to Muslim population on a priority basis from Muslim minority funds, due to special circumstances.

37. See IDB brochure, ref. 5, pp. 14–16 and Twentieth Report, ref. 6, pp. 105–8, for details about IRTI structure and activities.

38. IRTI has published a comprehensive bibliography on Islamic Economics comprising 600 entries. See Gazetteer, ref. 11, p. 103.

39. IDB brochure, ref. 5, p. 17.

40. Ibid., p. 20.

41. *The Muslim World,* Karachi, vol. 35, no. 3, 9 August 1997, p. 3.

42. The war in Bosnia started in April 1992. By November that year, the IDB had approved $6 million as aid and $15 million for the reconstruction of the war-ravaged country. Thus IDB became the pioneering international financial institution to support Bosnia's reconstruction. See Keesing's Contemporary Archives, 1992, p. 39031.

43. See Twentieth Report, Ref. 6, p. 94–95 for a list of IDB special assistance operation in different parts of the world.

44. Ninety-three scholars from thirty-five member states had benefited from this programme by the end of 1996.

45. There were 3476 students from forty-nine states who benefited from this scheme till 1996.

46. Though all these institutions assist the members for economic development, the chunk of financial support for LDMCs comes from the IDB alone which, sometimes, is more than the total aid given by all other Muslim development funds combined. (See Gazetteer, ref. 11, p. 98). It is for this reason that when in November 1994, the United States proposed a multi-billion dollar Donor Bank for development projects in the region, Saudi Commerce Minister Soleiman Selim reacted by saying that the existing institutions like IDB and Arab Fund were enough and the future aid could be channelled through them. See 'Facts on File', 1994, p. 841.

47. See the special feature 'ISESCO Forges Ahead', *The Muslim*, Islamabad, 3 September 1985, on the eve of second General Conference of ISESCO at Islamabad.

48. Ibid.

49. *Pakistan Times*, Islamabad, 6 September 1985. The author is indebted to the National Archives of Pakistan, Islamabad, where access to file No. C-181/66-10 (ISESCO file), containing valuable press clippings about ISESCO, was provided to him.

50. Baba, ref. 3, p. 240.

51. By the time of the second General Conference of ISESCO, there were forty-five members of the OIC, forty of whom had joined the ISESCO.

52. *Pakistan Times*, Islamabad, 6 September 1985.

53. 'Guide to OIC', ref. 1, p. 86.

54. *Pakistan Times*, 6 September 1985.

55. 'Guide to OIC', ref. 1, p. 87.

56. Ibid.

57. 'ISESCO Forges Ahead', ref. 47.

58. Ibid.

59. *Pakistan Times*, 6 September 1985.

60. Ibid., 8 September 1985.

61. Ibid., 4 September 1985.

62. *The Nation*, Lahore, 29 November 1991.

63. For most of the information on ISESCO that follows, I have relied on the ISESCO Activity Report, presented at the Fourth meeting of the COMSTECH, by Dr Khairat Ibne Rasa, DDG, on behalf of the Director General Dr A. Hadi Boutalib. See ISESCO Report in *Proceedings of the Fourth meeting of COMSTECH*, (Islamabad: PASTIC, 1991), pp. 127–35. Also see the ISESCO Report presented to the Seventh COMSTECH meeting contained in *Proceedings of the Seventh COMSTECH Meeting*, (Islamabad: PASTIC, December 1995), pp. 205–18, as well as the unpublished ISESCO Report presented to the eighth COMSTECH meeting (Islamabad, December 1997), available from the COMSTECH office on request.

64. Twentieth Report, ref. 6, p. 57.

65. ISESCO Report, ref. 63.

66. Ibid.

67. *The Muslim World,* Karachi, vol. 34, no. 43, 17 May 1997, p. 1.

68. Ibid., vol. 35, no. 1, 26 July 1997, p. 3.

69. ISESCO Report, ref. 63.

70. Ibid.

71. Ibid.

72. Europpa Year Book, 1995, p. 210.

73. Abdullah Ahsan, *Ummah or a Nation: Identity crisis in the Muslim World*, (Leicester: Islamic Foundation, 1992), pp. 122–26.

74. 'Guide to OIC', ref. 1, p. 88.

75. Abdullah Schleifer, 'Islam and Information: Need and Limitations of an independent Islamic news agency', *American Journal of Islamic Social Sciences,* (Washington: IIIT), vol. 3, no. 1, September 1986, pp. 109–25.

76. The author wishes to register his thanks to the Permanent Representative of the OIC in Islamabad,

Dr Khalil Saeed, for arranging the required material on the IINA and the ISBO for him, by using his personal influence in the OIC circles in Jeddah. See the IINA publication *Background of the Islamic News Agency*, (Jeddah: IINA, 1995), p. 2.

77. Ibid.
78. Ibid., p. 3.
79. Scheleifer, ref. 75.
80. Baba, ref.3. p. 236.
81. Ibid., p. 237.
82. *Jang*, Rawalpindi, 8 November 1973.
83. Scheleifer, ref. 75.
84. Baba, ref. 3, p. 236.
85. Scheleifer, ref. 75.
86. Baba, ref. 3, p. 236.
87. Abdullah Ahsan, *OIC: An Introduction to Islamic Political Institution*, (Herndon: IIIT, 1988), p. 39.
88. Ibid.
89. Scheleifer, ref. 75.
90. Baba, ref. 3, p. 237.
91. Editorial of *The Muslim*, 18 January 1991.
92. IINA Background, ref. 76, p. 3.
93. Ibid., p. 1-A.
94. Ibid., p. 2-A, 3-A.
95. Ibid., p. 4.

96. The source of the ISBO brochures and the activity reports is the same as in ref. 76 above, for which the author again expresses gratitude to the Ambassador Saeed. See the ISBO official publication, *The Islamic States Broadcasting Organization*, (Jeddah: ISBO, 1981), pp. 1–5.
97. Ibid., p. 29.
98. Ibid., pp. 30–33.
99. Gazetteer, ref. 11, p. 77.
100. Ibid.
101. Third ISBO Activity Report, (Jeddah, 1994), p. 2.
102. See the Second ISBO Activity Report (Jeddah, 1987), pp. 7–11, for an account of the audio production activities of the Organization.
103. Ibid., pp. 11–15.
104. Third ISBO Report, ref. 101, p. 5.
105. Ibid.
106. Hector Bolitho, *Jinnah: The Creator of Pakistan*, (Peshawar: n.p., 1991), p. 127.
107. Dr Mehmud A. Ghazi, *Islam's international law* (Urdu), (Islamabad: Shari'ah Academy, 1995), pp. 2–5
108. The second chapter of Hassan Moinuddin's book *The Charter of the Islamic Conference*, (Oxford: Clarendon Press, 1987), gives an excellent description of Islamic codes of international relations.
109. *Pakistan Times*, 13 May 1979.
110. Baba, ref. 3, p. 239.

11 Subsidiary Organs

The organs established by the OIC within its framework, through a resolution of the Islamic Summit Conference or that of the Islamic Conference of Foreign Ministers, are known as the subsidiary organs of the OIC.[1] They are set up for the purpose of fostering political, economic, and cultural cooperation in the Muslim world. They are run under the direct supervision of the OIC General Secretariat and are dependent on it for financial support. The Directors/Director Generals of these bodies are nominated by the OIC Secretary General and their budgets are approved by the annual ICFM sessions. The Islamic Commission for Economic, Cultural, and Social Affairs (ICECS) acts as a joint General Assembly for most of these organs. The heads of the OIC subsidiary organs hold regular coordination meetings. At present there are ten subsidiary organs of the OIC:

I.   Statistical, Economic, and Social Research and Training Centre for Islamic Countries, at Ankara, Turkey.
II. Research Centre for Islamic History, Art and Culture at Istanbul, Turkey.
III. International Commission for the Preservation of the Islamic Heritage, at Istanbul Turkey.
IV. Islamic Solidarity Fund and its *Waqf*, at Jeddah, Saudi Arabia.
V.   Al-Quds (Jerusalem) Fund and its *Waqf*, at Jeddah, Saudi Arabia.
VI. Islamic *Fiqh* Academy, at Jeddah, Saudi Arabia.
VII. Islamic Centre for Development of Trade, at Casablanca, Morocco.
VIII. Islamic Institute of Technology, at Dhaka, Bangladesh.
IX. Islamic Foundation for Science, Technology and Development, at Jeddah, Saudi Arabia.
X.   Islamic Civil Aviation Council at Tunis, Tunisia.

I. Statistical, Economic, and Social Research and Training Centre for Islamic Countries (SESRTCIC)

During the 2nd Islamic Summit Conference, (Lahore; 1974), it was felt that sound political cooperation required the extension of joint action in specific economic fields of interest to the member countries. At this stage, the need to establish specialized institutions to provide technical support to the Organization was found to be pressing. The creation of a specialized technical organ to operate in the fields of statistics, socio-economic research and training was proposed and adopted in this spirit. The Statistical, Economic, and Social Research and Training Centre for Islamic Countries (SESRTCIC) was, consequently, founded in Ankara, Turkey, in pursuance of Resolution No. 2/8-E adopted by the 8th ICFM (Tripoli; 1977) on a proposal by Turkey. The Centre, more commonly known as the Ankara Centre, started operations on 1 June 1978 as a subsidiary organ of the OIC.[2]

Objectives: The Centre aims particularly,[3] at:

• Evaluating, studying, and collecting basic data on the economic and social structure of member states, doing so on a permanent basis while trying to improve on erroneous data.
• Carrying out research on the means for developing trade relations among member states and providing basic data, necessary for marketing goods and services.
• Studying industrial structures in member states and examining complementaries and possibilities of establishing cooperation.
• Determining the possibilities, and development to the maximum level of the available resources of member states.
• Studying agreements in the social field concluded among member states, and determining the framework of agreements in the field of Manpower and Social Security.

- Conducting regular training courses in the field of Statistics for the benefit of member states.

Administration and Finance: Though the Centre is doing a lot of work in the fields of statistical and social research, as we shall see below, but not quite surprisingly the total number of staff at the Centre has always been limited due mainly to the dearth of funds and their irregular flow to the Centre. For the last decade the total number of technical staff at the Centre, including translators and research assistants, remained around twenty, with less than ten of them being professionals with at least a Masters degree.[4] The Centre has a three-tier structure:[5]

- *General Assembly*: The SESRTCIC Assembly, as is the case with other subsidiary organs, is composed of the members of Islamic Commission for Economic, Social, and Cultural Affairs (ICESC). It meets annually.
- *Board of Directors*: The eleven-member Board sets the policies of the Centre. It is composed of nine members elected by the General Assembly for a period of three years, the Director General of the Centre, and a representative of the OIC General Secretariat.
- *Director General*: The Director General is appointed by the Secretary General of the Organization of the Islamic Conference, in consultation with the Board of Directors, for a four-year term, renewable once. He is the chief executive of the Centre.

The activities of the Centre, as delineated in the annual work programmes, are financed by the mandatory contributions of the member states of the OIC within the framework of annual budgets as well as the revenues from the services rendered. Both of the annual programmes and the annual budgets, through which these programmes are financed, are officially approved through the resolutions of the ICFM. Furthermore, the Centre is bound to carry out its mandate and activities in all spheres under full scrutiny, in keeping with the OIC Charter and Rules and Regulations.

Activities: The SESRTCIC has been very active in the implementation of many of the provisions of the OIC Plan of Action to Strengthen Economic Cooperation among member states, adopted by the

3rd Islamic Summit (Taif; 1981). The Centre was again the main OIC institution to be involved in the technical work relating to implementation of the 6th Summit (Dakar; 1991) resolution on the formulation of the new Strategy for Strengthening Economic Cooperation. In the same vein it also undertook the preparation of the new OIC Plan of Action on Economic Cooperation, which was based on the New Strategy and was to replace the 1981 Plan. Both of these documents were approved by the COMCEC and adopted eventually by the 7th Islamic Summit (Casablanca; 1994).[6]

In addition to the regular implementation of its mandated activities, the Centre also undertakes extensive assignments to prepare and present background documents and reports to the OIC meetings in the areas of economic and technical cooperation. In this context, the Centre not only contributes studies and reports regularly to the relevant agenda items of the Islamic Summits, ICFMs, and COMCEC sessions, but is also called upon to participate in the technical preparations for OIC expert group, task force, follow-up and Ministerial meetings in specific areas of economic and technical cooperation. In most cases, the Centre was the OIC organ to prepare the main background documents for these meetings as well. The Centre, now, primarily has three areas of activity;

(i) Statistics and Information: The collection, collation and dissemination of socio-economic information, in general, and statistics, in particular, constitute major aspects of the mandate that was drawn up for the Ankara Centre. This was based on the realization that such information and data about the member countries were largely missing or were not readily available to the OIC community, especially at a time when there was rising interest among the member countries to enhance and develop cooperation amongst themselves within the OIC framework. Consequently, the Centre had to put in a lot of effort to fulfil this major task.[7]

The Centre, within just over five years after its inception, managed to become a major socio-economic databank on and for the OIC community. The initial step was the establishment of a specialized library, continuously enriched by official publications, sent directly from member state institutions, as well as by accessions made directly from international institutions and organizations. Through relatively fast computerisation of the technical, as well as the administrative, functions at the Centre, it has been able to develop and maintain a wide range of databases. Furthermore, the Centre took special care to enter into direct contacts with the National Statistical Organizations by organizing, three general meetings of the heads of these institutions. The theme of the first meeting was strengthening the capacities of the Centre in the field of statistics, while the second one debated upon the issues and potential of cooperation among the national statistical institutions. The subjects decided to be taken up by the third meeting were environmental statistics and natural resources accounting.

(ii) Socio-Economic Research: One principal assignment of the Ankara Centre is to undertake indigenous research on the socio-economic situation, potentials, and developments in the OIC member countries, with a view to bringing forth the existing possibilities of cooperation, as well as generating proposals for new ones. For this purpose, the Centre has been engaged in extensive research in a number of fields and at two complementary levels; country level and sectoral level.[8] These activities had been undertaken in line with the ten-sector OIC Plan of Action on Economic Cooperation adopted by the 3rd Islamic Summit (Taif; 1981) and with the decisions of the 4th Islamic Summit (Casablanca; 1984), which accorded a higher priority to six of the original ten sectors. Since 1994, the SESRTCIC has been working according to the revised Plan of Action adopted by the 7th Islamic Summit (Casablanca; 1994).

By mid-1995, the SESRTCIC had put out around 246 substantial papers, reports, and other technical documents in eleven different general subject areas, namely, General Cooperation (26), Statistics and Information (22), Economic Development (36), Least Developed Countries (31), Food and Agriculture (21), Industry (27), Trade (26), Money and Finance (19), Transport (4), Technical Cooperation (22), and Social Issues (12).[9] This makes on the average about fourteen documents per year and, excluding the area of Transportation, just over twenty-four papers per subject field.[10] Moreover, there were no less than forty ongoing projects in the same year. Some prominent recent research publications of the Centre include 'Problems of Research in Islamic Economic Cooperation', 'The Information Age and the Islamic World', Annual World Economy Reports, 'Problems of Land-Locked member states', 'Food and Agricultural Strategy', 'Fertilizer Industry in OIC States', 'Impact of Single European Market on OIC Countries', 'Stock Markets in OIC Countries', 'Developments in Telecommunications', 'OIC-UN Cooperation', 'Human Resources Development in Muslim States', 'The OIC Strategy and Plan of Action', 'Training opportunities in the OIC states', and many others.[11]

Finally, as the principal research arm of the OIC, the Centre has regularly been asked to participate actively in and contribute to the deliberations of its meetings. For instance, at the 25th ICFM (Doha; March 1998), the Centre came up with four reports. One was the Director General's annual report while the other three pertained respectively, to the world economy, problems of the least developed land-locked Muslim states, and the trade regulations in the OIC states. In this connection, since shortly after becoming operational, the Centre has participated in all the Islamic Summit Conferences, ICFMs, and COMCEC sessions and its follow-up meetings and 95 per cent of the expert group, task force, and other technical meetings, to almost all of them with at least one paper or report.

(iii) Technical Cooperation and Training: It is the third major area, in which the Centre operates. All of its activities undertaken in this field, constitute a direct response to the expressed needs of the member countries to upgrade and build up the specialized skills essential for their development. Various publications issued by the Centre in this field also make available in readily compiled form certain basic information on availability of skills, facilities, and potentials for ready reference and immediate use.[12] The training programmes of the Centre were initiated in 1981. Ever since, the Centre has been organizing short-term courses in

selected fields of interest to the OIC member countries, in collaboration with national and regional training institutions. Towards this end, the Centre also collaborated with the UN Specialized Agencies, particularly the FAO, which has extended technical and material support to the Centre for the realization of its training courses.

All in all, the Centre has so far conducted nineteen training programmes and seminars, and placed participants in ten such programmes held in the member countries. As a result of this activity, 469 trainees from forty-one member countries, have been trained in fourteen different subjects in twenty-four courses.[13] One important and differentiating feature of the Centre's training activities was the substantially lower costs at which these programmes on average were realized, as compared to similar activities organized under the UN and other international organizations. Some of the recent seminars and training workshops organized by SESRTCIC were on Planning Techniques, Education and Development, and Population Planning Assistance while some on Investment, Privatization, and Environmental issues were scheduled for the near future at the time of this writing. In the area of technical cooperation, the Centre is primarily engaged in activities related to the compilation of specific and specialized indigenous information on the skills and institutional facilities existing in the OIC member countries. Most of this information is published in the form of directories and disseminated for the ready reference of the concerned parties in the OIC community.[15]

The Centre has spent a lot of effort in associating itself with the field activities related to technical cooperation in the member countries and has tried to establish direct contacts and dialogue among the actual operators. As one such 'field activity' aimed at bringing directly into contact the real experts working on specific subjects and helping them cooperate extensively, the Centre has been assigned, by the Agriculture Ministers of the OIC member countries, the task of establishing a network of agricultural research centres and of helping in the development of coordinating centres in the network.

In a similar vein, and more importantly, in May 1990, 1991, 1992, 1993, and 1994, five meetings of the Technical Cooperation Focal Points in the OIC member countries were organized.[16] The annual meetings enabled the country representatives to enter into direct bilateral and/or multilateral consultations amongst themselves and/ or with the representatives of the OIC institutions and international organizations on specific issues, problems and even projects. Many bilateral agreements among the participating parties were signed on specific cooperation projects during these direct consultations. Parties from the private sectors have also recently started to associate with these annual gatherings.

Finally, in recognition of the Ankara Centre's activities and experience in the area of technical cooperation, the General Secretariat of the OIC designated the Centre as the focal point for the whole of the OIC in the area of technical cooperation in relation to its collaboration with the UN system. In this capacity, the Centre represents the OIC and its institutions in making arrangements for undertaking joint projects and programmes with the UN and its specialized agencies.

OIC Website: Though a project of the Centre within the area of statistical research, the significance of this endeavour has made its description a separate topic in its own right. The website address of the Ankara Centre is <http// :www.sesrtcic.org>. The site contains basic information on the OIC and its structure and history. It contains statistics regarding area, population, literacy rate, life expectancy, GDP and forty other denominators on all the OIC member states. By the end of 1997, the site had over 1080 pages. The site is continuously updated and is being enriched by more information. Readers interested in the country profiles of Muslim states may access this site on the internet.[17]

In the first quarter of 1998 alone, 30,464 people had used the website, only five per cent of them were from the Muslim states. The highest number of users was from the United States, followed by Canada. Among the Muslim countries, the maximum users were from Malaysia, Turkey, and the UAE in that order.

Publications: The publication activities of the Centre reflect two major concerns. The first and the more prominent one is to increase the volume and quality of the documented information on the various aspects of the socio-economic institutions, facilities, potentials, and developments in the member countries. The second is to ensure that the end-results of the multifarious research activities of the Centre are disseminated as widely as possible.[18] Out of the periodical publications, the *Yearbook of Socio-Economic Indicators of OIC member countries* and the *Bulletin on Training Opportunities in OIC Countries* are annuals while the *Journal of Economic Cooperation Among Islamic Countries* and the *Information Report* are quarterlies. The tri-lingual Journal, which contains articles written by the Centre staff members or by researchers in the member countries, is the more scholarly of the two Centre magazines, while the *Information Report*, is more news-oriented.[19]

Besides a host of other reports and documents, the Ankara Centre issues three-publication series.[20] The *Directory Series* contains institutional information. 'Research Institutions' 'Training Institutions', and 'Mass Media in OIC Countries' are some prominent titles published in this series. The second, *Legislation Series*, assembles texts of selected laws of Muslim countries. Volumes on 'Free Zones Regulations' and 'Banking Laws' are prominent. The *Information Series*, as the name indicates, provides information on Muslim countries, and reference books on Agriculture, Telecommunication and Infrastructure of the Muslim countries have been brought out.

Library: The Library of the Centre functions as a specialized library covering material limited mainly to socio-economic issues involving the Islamic countries. The Library boasts a multilingual (English, French, Arabic) collection of around 1800 titles in books, almost 1000 titles in reference material, 667 periodical titles of statistics from the member countries, and more than 6400 documents and reports, including those from the member countries, the OIC and its subsidiary and affiliated bodies, and relevant regional and international institutions and organizations. Moreover, it subscribes to 200-plus periodical publications and regularly receives 300 more, free of charge.[21]

The databases maintained by the Library include bibliographic databases (LIBRARY, PERIOD-ICALS), a database that stores the abstracts of material covering the Islamic countries (ABSTRACTS) and a database that stores the full reports and documents of a wide range of OIC-related meetings (*ISDOC*) relevant to the Centre's mandate and areas of specialization. The activities of the library are fully computerized. All facilities including private study space and photocopying services are provided to outside users and researchers.[22]

Future Plans: Planned research projects of the SESRTCIC include research and publications on Financial Structure of OIC countries, Foreign Investment Laws, Training opportunities in OIC states, and an Economic almanac of the OIC. Besides, as we have mentioned earlier, seminars and workshops on investment, privatization, economic management and environmental issues are also on the cards.[23]

II. Research Centre for Islamic History, Art and Culture (IRCICA)

The decision to establish a centre for Islamic History, Art, and Culture (IRCICA) as a subsidiary organ of the OIC, was taken by the 7th ICFM (Istanbul; 1976) through its resolution No.3/7-ECS.[24] The 9th ICFM (Dakar; 1978) adopted the Statute of the Centre by virtue of resolution 1/9-C. It may, however, be added that a revised statute was approved by the 12th ICFM (Baghdad; 1981) which was again revised by the 6th Islamic Summit (Dakar; 1991).[25] Following the approval of its work plan and first budget by the 10th ICFM (Islamabad; 1980), the Centre started functioning in the Yildiz Palace, Istanbul, in 1980. The three historic buildings within the Yildiz Palace complex were donated by the Turkish government to this Centre.

Commonly known as the Istanbul Centre in the OIC circles, it is the first OIC organ to work in the field of culture. Now the IRCICA undertakes research, publishing, documentation, and information activities to better make known the Islamic culture and civilization and promote mutual understanding between Muslims and other communities of the world. The Centre's work covers various subject areas in Islamic history, history of science, history of arts, arts, culture and the cultural heritage.[26]

Objectives: The main functions of IRCICA as determined by the revised statute (1991), are the following:[27]

- To act as a focal point and meeting place for scholars, researchers, historians, intellectuals, and artists from the member countries and the best of the world in the field of research on the Islamic legacy towards a better understanding of Islam and its civilization.
- To create objective conditions for a close cooperation among researchers and research institutions of the member countries in order to eliminate prejudices regarding the history, art, and culture of the Muslim world.
- To publish studies in the form of books and monographs in order to better make known and disseminate information on Islamic culture and civilization throughout the world.
- To publish periodicals of a scholarly and informational nature concerning Islamic cultural activities, and to organize conferences, symposia, exhibitions, and other activities in subject areas.
- To establish and promote linkages, cooperation and exchange of knowledge and reference material on Islamic culture and civilization, with the concerned institutions in the world.
- To establish a reference library specialized in Islamic culture and civilization to serve researchers working in these fields; comprising audio-visual material as well as published material.
- To establish a database related to studies and expertise in various areas of Islamic culture.
- To organize training courses and to establish incentive programmes in order to promote excellence in research in the fields of Islamic culture and civilization.
- To render advice to member states and to the Secretary General on all matters connected with Islamic civilization and carry out special studies required by the Islamic Conference.

Structure and Finance: The Centre functions through the following organs:[28]

General Assembly: The Islamic Commission for Economic, Cultural, and Social Affairs (ICECS)

acts as the General Assembly. So far the IRCICA General Assembly has held three meetings; the third and last one was held during the 19th session of the Islamic Commission in June 1995. The Commission, when acting as the IRCICA General Assembly, examines and submits to the approval of the ICFM the annual activity programmes, budget proposals, and final accounts of the Centre.

Governing Board: The activity reports, annual work programmes, and annual budget proposals of the Centre are examined and approved by its 12-member Governing Board which is composed of ten scholars and specialists elected from the member states, the Secretary General of the OIC or his representative, and the Director General of the Centre, in accordance with the Statute of the Centre.

The reports and programmes are then submitted to the Foreign Ministers Conference, through the IRCICA General Assembly. It may be added that the members of the Board, usually professors, historians, and directors of museums or archaeological institutes, etc., are nominated for a four-year term, based on equitable geographical distribution. By the end of 1997, the Board had held thirteen meetings in all, at different venues including Damascus, Kuwait, Tripoli, and Istanbul etc. The incumbent Board (1994–98 mandate) is the fourth Governing Board of the IRCICA.

Executive Committee: The Executive Committee of the Centre is composed of the heads and senior members of the Centre's Departments. The Committee meets weekly to report to the Director General on the progress and implementation of the activities and at the same time, to act as a consultative board for the planning of activities, the implementation of work programmes and the distribution of tasks among the Departments and the staff of the Centre.

Director General: The Chief Executive of the IRCICA is appointed by the OIC Secretary General in consultation with the Governing Board, for a four-year renewable term. The Directorate General.[29] is subdivided into four departments:

- The *Corporate Research and Publications Department* undertakes research, disseminates research results, organizes seminars and symposia, provides advisory services, administers data banks, and prepares the activity reports for IRCICA.
- The *Department of Bibliographies and Manuscripts* collects and studies manuscripts and documents and prepares bibliographies and catalogues on relevant themes.
- The *Library and Archives Department* identifies and acquires relevant material, provides library services, undertakes cooperation for exchange of information, and participates in book fairs etc.
- The *Administration and Finance Department* manages IRCICA's administrative and financial matters. The financial resources of IRCICA consist of contributions and donations by member states and revenues from the services rendered.[30]

Activities: The IRCICA is one of the very active organs in the OIC framework as the long list of achievements shows. From 1980 to 1995, IRCICA published 55 books resulting from its research projects. It organized and actively participated in 29 international symposia and seminars. The Centre also organized 120 exhibitions of art works, documents books, and illustrations.[31] We shall see the various aspects of the IRCICA activities.

Research Projects: The themes and modalities of the research projects are determined in accordance with the Centre's objectives and taking into consideration needs felt in research on Islamic culture and civilization. The majority of the research projects are planned on a long-term basis, with several stages and aspects, to give frequent products on a variety of topics. The results of research are disseminated in the world by means of publications, presentations at scholarly meetings, exhibitions of documents and illustrations, and by other means.[32]

Some of the prominent research works of the IRCICA include Islamic Civilization in South Asia, Islam in South East Asia, Islam in West Africa, History of Turks, Islam in Korea, and the like. All these are sub-projects of a mega research project on the History of Muslim Nations. The output of these projects has been in the form of authentic reference books. The Centre embarked upon a project on History of Science in the Muslim World.

The project successfully produced many books dealing with scientific activities, scientific institutions, and scientists, in different eras of the Islamic history. Several international symposia on related subjects were held and proceedings published.[33]

In response to the directives of the Islamic Conference for all-out help to Bosnia-Herzegovina, the IRCICA launched an ambitious research project on History and Culture of Bosnia. Five monumental volumes on related topics were produced, one of which dealt solely with the historic bridge of the Bosnian Muslim city of Mostar.[34] Architectural workshops on the preservation of Bosnian heritage wore conducted and were well-attended from a large number of countries. As a part of this project numerous audio-visual and photographic exhibitions depicting cities, monuments, and people of Bosnia, as well as scenes of wars were held in different parts of the world, as well as in various universities of the United States.

Besides a project on Directory of Islamic Cultural Institutions, the Centre has another large-scale research project aiming to survey and record translations of the Holy Quran in different languages of the world which are produced in printed or manuscript form or recited orally. World Bibliography of (printed) Translations of the Holy Quran (1515–1980) has been published while one of the manuscript translations of the Quran is under preparation. Oral translations of the holy book in different languages, as recited in mosques during the month of Ramadhan, are being recorded on cassettes and thus an audio reference would soon be available. Though the list is very long, the project on Islamic Arts still needs special mention. Two of the many books appearing as a result of this project are *Islamic swords and swordsmiths* and *Holy Ka'aba: Collection of locks and keys.*

Crafts Development Programme: Under this comprehensive programme, the Centre wants to promote the handicrafts of the Muslim world and encourage their revival, preservation, and development through international cooperation.[35] The Centre works in close collaboration with UNESCO in this respect. It has held several international seminars on the subject. The first

Islamic Artisans-at-work festival was held at Islamabad in October 1994. The Centre wants to hold such festivals every three years. The second and third in the series are to be held at Cairo and Kuala Lumpur, respectively.[36]

Publications: We have already seen that the IRCICA has dozens of important publications in its field. Some titles include 'The Muslim Pious Foundations in Palestine', 'Ottoman Postal Stamps', 'Arabo-Turkish Relations', 'Islamic Art Terms' and 'Turkish Architecture'. New titles including 'Astronomy in Islam', 'Curtains of Holy Ka'aba' and some others are forthcoming in the near future. Besides, the IRCICA gets the credit for making audio-visual documentaries on Islamic Art.[37] The quarterly IRCICA newsletter is published in all three official languages of the OIC and is distributed to nearly 10,000 institutions and personalities in sixty-five countries.[38] It contains news on cultural, artistic, and academic activities taking place in the Muslim world.

Seminars and Exhibitions: The topics covered in the international symposia and seminars organized by the IRCICA range from traditional Islamic crafts, Islamic architecture, and manuscripts in Islamic languages, to topics as diverse as computer applications in the library and the role of woman and the family in Islam.[39] Likewise, the IRCICA has held a large number of exhibitions, presenting works from many categories of art including calligraphy, miniatures, paintings, ceramics, engravings, prayer beads, and book binding, etc. Furthermore, photographic exhibitions of Islamic cities, peoples, war scenes, and other themes have taken place under the Centre's auspices.[40] Though a significant proportion of these activities was concentrated in Istanbul city, many seminars or exhibitions have been held in different countries including, in rare cases, non-Muslim states as well. The complete list of seminars or exhibitions is available from the IRCICA Directorate on request.

Other Activities: There are several other activities of the Centre, like making of documentaries, invitation of artists and researchers to work at the IRCICA office and use its facilities, and conducting of training courses on restoration of

manuscripts, to name a few. The Centre also arranges a fortnightly lecture from a distinguished scholar on Islamic art or history, at its premises.[41]

IRCICA Library: IRCICA established a reference library on Islamic culture and civilization. The Centre's library presently meets the modern research requirements in its fields of specialization. More than 1500 researchers use this library annually.[42] The library collection covers various subject areas in the fields of Islamic culture, history, arts, history of arts, history of science, literature, cultural and intellectual history, with an emphasis on the Muslim world. A number of incunabula and rare books further increase the value of the library collection. The library collection comprises 40,000 volumes of books and research works, nearly 7000 grey literature containing off-prints, reports, and seminar papers, 300 microfilms and unpublished dissertations, 971 atlases, maps, and plans; and 1291 periodical titles; 400 of them scholarly journals in complete sets. The holdings are in fifty-four languages primarily the OIC official languages, and in Urdu, Persian, and Turkish. The library exchanges material with 350 institutions worldwide and several catalogues and accession lists have been prepared for the purpose.[43]

Archives of historical photographs: The Centre set up an archive of historical photographs consisting of various collections some of which were put together and reproduced by the Centre and others donated by institutions and personalities.[49] An important collection kept in the archives is the Yildiz Photograph Albums which is composed of 35.000 photographs showing cities, monuments, transport equipment, scenes of social life, etc. from various parts of the Muslim world. The Centre has prepared a catalogue of these Albums to facilitate the task of researchers. The Centre also publishes, on different occasions, albums comprising photographs selected from this collection. Historical photographs of Istanbul were published in an album titled 'Istanbul: A Glimpse into the Past'. In addition, the archives comprise 62,417 historical photographs, donated by different personalities. It may be added that both the library and the Archives welcome donations of rare books, manuscripts, and photographs.

Cooperation with other institutions: The IRCICA maintains liaison with a number of institutions in this field. The coordination meeting of the heads of lead agencies of the OIC and the UN, held at Geneva during June, 1996 asked IRCICA and UNESCO from the respective sides, to coordinate the activities in social and cultural fields.[45] Consequently, a Memorandum of Understanding between the two Director Generals was signed on 8 January 1996. The eighteenth Mediterranean conference (Istanbul; July 1996), jointly organized with Dowling College, New York; the Symposium on Islamic Civilization (Dakar; Dec. 1996) co-sponsored by Islamic Call Society; and an international seminar on Traditional Crafts of OIC Countries (Damascus; Jan. 1997) co-sponsored by UNESCO, clearly speak of the determination of the IRCICA to join hands with other institutions in the fields of history, art, and culture.[46]

The IRCICA Vision: The Centre as the cultural arm of the OIC has assumed a dynamic role in a changing international environment. In the implementation of its activities most of which come under long-term projects, the Centre closely observes the developments taking place in the OIC member countries on a global scale. In the light of the resolutions of the Islamic Summit Conference and the Islamic Conference of Foreign Ministers and the recommendations of its Governing Board, the Centre revises its work programmes whenever needed, making adjustments to accomodate fresh needs.[47]

The Centre's activities cover a wide geographical area from South East Asia to West Africa. The 1990s, the second decade of the Centre's activities, started concurrently with the advent of major transformations on the world political scene. These changes had important consequences in international relations, particularly in the cultural realm. The membership in the OIC of the newly independent states in Central Asia, Caucus, the Balkans, and Africa enlarged the scope of the Centre's studies. These developments are reflected in the Centre's work programmes as required by its mandate. Since its establishment,

the Centre has cooperated with various cultural institutions in the member countries and around the world, and with international and regional organizations working in related fields. A great number of activities were realized in cooperation with other institutions, which has made it possible for the Centre to accomplish more than what its own means would allow.

On the basis of the experience it has acquired as an institution of research and learning, specialized in Islamic culture and civilization, the Centre hopes to respond in an increasingly better way to the needs of the member states in the fields of its mandate. The IRCICA is now preparing to celebrate the 700th anniversary of the foundation of the Ottaman empire in 1999, throughout the Muslim world.

III. International Commission for the Preservation of the Islamic Cultural Heritage (ICPICH)

Originally, the idea for the Commission was mooted during the 6th ICFM (Jeddah; 1975), but it was the 9th ICFM (Dakar; 1978) that finally adopted resolution no.7/9-C calling for the establishment of the International Commission for the Preservation of the Islamic Cultural Heritage (ICPICH). The Statute of the Commission was approved by the 13th ICFM (Niamey; 1982), by virtue of which, the IRCICA acts as the Executive Secretariat of the Commission and carries out a number of activities in this capacity.[48] The head office of the Commission is located in Istanbul, Turkey, at the IRCICA premises while the Chairmanship is in Riyadh, Saudi Arabia. The Bureau of Liaison and Coordination in Riyadh acts as a link between the Chairmanship, Executive Secretariat, and the OIC General Secretariat.

Objectives: The Commission for Islamic Heritage has been entrusted with:[49]

- Providing a wide, comprehensive, and unified view of cultural heritage, covering monuments, historical cities and places, in addition to the manuscripts, libraries, and arts.

- Developing activities aimed at collecting and preserving Islam's cultural heritage.
- Promoting cooperation, coordination, and exchange of ideas and information, on cultural heritage in the Muslim world.
- Classifying and publishing books, manuscripts, and other sources of information the Islamic heritage.
- Establishing funds and providing financial assistance to member states in this field with special emphasis on the heritage of Holy Jerusalem.
- Giving priority and due attention to the relics in the holy city of Jerusalem.
- Maintaining a pool of Muslim expertise and know-how in the field of religious and cultural heritage.
- Methodically cataloguing and publicizing works, manuscripts, and other items of the Islamic heritage and to negotiating their retrieval to their countries of origin.

Composition and Structure: The International Commission for the Preservation of Islamic Cultural Heritage is composed of seventeen members and is chaired by HRH Prince Faisal bin Fahd of Saudi Arabia.[50] The twelve members of the Governing Board of IRCICA are *ex-officio* members of this Commission, the remaining five are nominated by the OIC Secretary General. Among these five is the Chairman Prince Faisal himself, a representative of Palestine, and three other members. As noted above, the IRCICA acts as the Executive Secretariat of this Commission and its Director General also acts as the Secretary of the latter.[51] The resources of the International Commission for the Islamic Heritage come from the contributions of member states, donations by individuals, and income from the services rendered by it.[52]

Activities: The ICPICH holds exhibitions, conducts training courses, arranges competitions, and carries out publications to fulfil the tasks entrusted to it.

Competitions: The Commission has organized competitions in three areas, namely architecture, calligraphy, and photography:[53]

i. The King Fahd Awards Competition for Design and Research in Islamic Architecture was organized in 1986. Awards totalling US$100,000 were distributed to forty-two winners who had submitted thirty-one projects, from among 270 entries in the design category and ninety entries in the research category from forty countries.

ii. The Commission organizes international calligraphy competitions once every three years. Each calligraphy competition is dedicated to the memory of a famous calligrapher of the Muslim world to encourage young calligraphers to follow the example of the masters of classical calligraphy.[54] During the first calligraphy competition (1986), 352 participants representing thirty-two countries submitted 1272 entries to the jury. A sum of US $3500 was distributed as prizes for sixty-two winning calligraphies of forty-three participants. In the second such competition (1989), twelve awards and thirty-eight mentions totalling US$24,500 were conferred on winning entries out of a total of 1780 entries. In the third calligraphy competition (1992), the jury selected ninety-five calligraphers for honours. Almost 1200 pieces by 550 participants from thirty-five countries, were in the contest. The first three competitions were, respectively, named after the three big names in the history of calligraphy, Hamid al-Amidi, Yaqut al Mustasimi, and Ali bin Hilal.

iii. The first-ever photography competition on Islamic heritage attracted 1500 photographs from 229 participants. Thirty-two photographers were lucky to receive cash prizes worth $9600. The Commission Secretariat published a catalogue of the winners' works.

The Commission is now making preparations to organize the Second King Fahd Awards Competition in Islamic Architecture, the Second International Photography Competition, and the Fourth International Calligraphy Competition in the near future.[55] The purpose of these competitions is to encourage scholarly research on specific topics of the history and theories of architecture and calligraphy; pursuit of compatibility and continuity between the historic traditions and the futuristic visions of contemporary Muslim societies; initiation of new debates on the Islamic heritage; and the discovery of creative capacities of Muslim artists.

Consequently, efforts are always made for the widest participation in the ICPICH competitions. For instance, the first architecture competition was advertised in no less than 116 international magazines, and over 2600 brochures announcements were sent to universities, architectural colleges, and departments of research on archaeology and antiquity studies. The entries were judged by a committee of seven eminent Muslim experts on the subject.

Publications: Besides bringing out one comprehensive special issue on 'Arts and Islamic World', the ICPICH has also published catalogues of winning entries of architecture, photography, and calligraphy competitions.[56] For the near future, the Commission has planned to publish a book on Islamic architecture in Palestine and an exercise book for the teaching of calligraphy.

Exhibitions: The Commission organized a number of exhibitions in some member states and at its Secretariat in Istanbul to introduce its activities and to present the results of the calligraphy competitions, the photography competition, and the King Fahd Awards competition. Eleven exhibitions have been organized until now on different occasions, during conferences of the OIC and award ceremonies of competitions, or as joint projects with the member states. Travelling exhibitions of winners' works in the calligraphy competitions were held in Malaysia, Oman, United Arab Emirates, Qatar, and Kuwait etc. Winners' works were also exhibited at the eleventh session of the Tunis International Book Fair in 1992.[57]

Training Courses: To date, the Commission has held two courses, both at Suleymaniye Library in Istanbul. The first one on the restoration of archive materials (Oct. 1990) mainly for African member states, and the second one on the same subject (Oct. 1993) mainly for Asian member states.[58]

Miscellaneous Activities: The 14th ICFM (Dhaka; 1983) proclaimed 1410 AH/AD 1989–90 as the 'International Islamic Heritage Year' upon the recommendation of the Commission at its first meeting (November 1983). On the occasion of the International Islamic Heritage Year, the Commission published and distributed a brochure to promote awareness around the world on the concept of Islamic cultural heritage. Furthermore, the First International Photography Competition and the Third International Calligraphy Competition were held in the framework of the

International Islamic Heritage Year. Some member states organized cultural activities to celebrate the event.[59]

The Commission endeavours to preserve Islamic heritage. For the purpose, it cooperates with IRCICA in carrying out various activities related to the restoration and preservation of the cultural heritage of Bosnia and Herzegovina, which has largely been destroyed and damaged during the war.

It cooperates with other institutions for the restoration of Islamic monuments. One example is that the Commission Secretariat participated in technical studies related to the restoration of the historical Damak Mosque in Indonesia and the mosque of Rhodes Island. Another major activity of the Commission Secretariat is to provide guidance and assistance to visiting artists, in particular calligraphers, who wish to upgrade their skills.[60]

Future Plans: The Commission wants to revivify its activities of holding competitions, suspended for want of funds. It is also contemplating the launching of children's competitions in drawing and calligraphy. The ICPICH has plans to launch a research periodical on Islamic heritage to be distributed in the Muslim world. It is also drawing up a permanent mechanism for vigilance and observation for the protection of Islamic heritage in the non-Muslim countries. It is exploring the possibility of coordination with the ISESCO, to avoid duplication of efforts in the field of restoration of manuscripts.

The Islamic Heritage Commission is always willing to render advice to the Muslim countries for the preservation of Islamic heritage and is always available to assist them in carrying out specific functions. It is now considering the preparation of legal documents to ensure protection of craftsmen, and of the cultural heritage itself. Article IV (4) of the Statute pinpoints Jerusalem (Palestine), Quairawan (Tunisia), Fez (Morocco), Timbuktu (Mali), Hirat (Afghanistan), Sana'a (Yemen), and some cities in Niger and other parts of West Africa, to institute experimental projects on the preservation of Islamic cultural sites. The Commission has decided to ensure its participation in all the international projects concerned with the preservation of the architectural monuments of the holy city of Jerusalem.

IV. Islamic Solidarity Fund (ISF)

The Islamic Solidarity Fund is the most important of the OIC subsidiary organs. The 2nd Islamic Summit (Lahore; 1974) decided to set up a Solidarity Fund to meet the needs of the Muslim communities (both in the Muslim majority and minority states).[61] In fact, it is an endowment fund which is supposed to provide emergency aid and the wherewithal for building mosques, hospitals, universities etc. There is no mandatory contribution to this Fund, instead, the member states as well as individuals are welcome to contribute to it in the form of movable or immovable assets as donations. The Fund started functioning in 1976 on a very optimistic note. During the 8th ICFM (Istanbul; 1976), Saudi Arabia, Libya, and UAE announced donations of $15 millions, $6 million, and $3 million respectively.[62] The then OIC Secretary General Dr Amadou Gaye expressed the hope that the Fund would go a long way in solving the problems of the Muslim world. 'The ISF will build mosques, help Muslim minorities and educate our youth', he remarked.[63] The office of the Fund is located within the OIC General Secretariat at Jeddah.

Objectives: According to the Statute, the Islamic Solidarity Fund was established for the following purposes:[64]

- to take all possible steps to raise the intellectual and moral levels of Muslims worldwide;
- to provide the required material relief in case of emergencies such as natural catastrophes and man-made disasters, that may befall the Islamic states;
- to grant assistance to Muslim minorities and communities in order to improve their religious, social, and cultural standards.

Administration and Finance: The Fund has a two-tier administrative structure:[65]

Permanent Council: The Permanent Council of the ISF is responsible for the activities of the Fund

before the ICFM. Its task consists of achieving the Fund's objectives by planning, drawing up, and implementing the assistance programmes, through the Executive Bureau established for this purpose. Moreover, the Council is empowered to consider the amount of each assistance and determine who the beneficiaries will be. It examines and adopts the budget of the Fund. The ISF Permanent Council is composed of the OIC Secretary General as permanent member and thirteen members elected for a mandate of two years by the Islamic Conference of Foreign Ministers. The Council elects, from among its members, a Chairman and a Vice-Chairman. It periodically meets in ordinary sessions and, should the need arise, in extraordinary session as well, on the request of the Secretary General, or of the Chairman, or two-thirds of the members.

The Chairman of the Council submits an annual report on the activities of the Fund to the ICFM. To supervise the work of the Executive Bureau, a five-member *follow-up committee* comprising the Chairman/Vice-Chairman of the Council, Secretary General of the OIC or his representative, and three members elected by the Permanent Council, is also set up.

Executive Bureau: The Fund is administered by an executive organ headed by a Director General who is appointed by the OIC Secretary General in consultation with the Permanent Council, for a four-year term, renewable once.

Under Article 6 of the ISF Statute,[66] its sources of finance are: (a) contributions by member states, donations and grants given by public or private institutions and individuals, as well as revenues of the Fund's *Waqf*; and (b) experts and technical assistance provided by member states.

The *Waqf* of the Islamic Solidarity Fund: The 11th ICFM (Islamabad; 1980), through resolution no.23/11-C, adopted the Statute of the *Waqf* under which, the *Waqf* aims at strengthening the financial position of the Islamic Solidarity Fund, to secure an annual income so as to boost its budget and to enable it to carry out its mission without major hurdles.[67]

Defining of the general policy and orientation of the *Waqf*, supervision of its activities and adoption of its budgets and programmes is done by the Permanent Council of the ISF. The job of implementation of the programmes of the *Waqf* rests with the Executive Bureau that is the same as that of the Islamic Solidarity Fund. However, as in the case of other endowments (*Waqf*s), the ISF *Waqf* is also administered and supervised by a Board of Trustees. The status of permanent member of the *Waqf*'s Board of Trustees shall be granted to member states and personalities that contribute more than two million dollars to the *Waqf*'s capital.[68]

Presently, the *Board of Trustees* is composed of eight members. The OIC Secretary General and the Chairman of ISF's Permanent Council are *ex-officio* members, the former is Chairman of this Board. In addition, the three states of Kuwait, Iraq, and UAE are represented by one member each. Three individuals, Sheikh Saleh Abdullah Kamel (Vice-Chairman), Sheikh Hussein Mohsin Al-Harithy, and Sheikh Ubaid Rashid Al-Aqrobi, are the also members of the Board of Trustees.[69]

The initial capital of the *Waqf*, fixed at $100 million,[70] was to be funded by: (a) liquid assets donated by the Governments of OIC member states and by natural or legal entities from the Muslim world; and (b) immovable property and other fixed assets donated by Governments, natural and corporate persons from the Muslim world.

Activities: The paucity of funds has been responsible for hampering the activities of the Solidarity Fund. Even the donations pledged to the Fund at the ICFMs or other fora could not be realized as some of the donors later reneged on their promises. To bail out the Solidarity Fund and the Al-Quds Fund from financial crises, the 11th ICFM (Islamabad; 1980) decided to establish a *Waqf* (endowment) for each of the two Funds. An initial capital of $100 million each was set for the two *Waqf*s. The Foreign Ministers of fifteen member states pledged donations there and then.[71]

Bangladesh announced that it would continue its present contribution to the two Funds. Three oil-rich states of Libya, Iran, and Kuwait promised to donate generously but said that they would announce the exact amount of the donations later. Thus over $12 million and $8 million were pledged

Chart 11.1

Contributions of the Muslim States to the ISF Budget

Amount in US$

		Islamic Solidarity Fund	Al-Quds Fund
1.	Qatar	1 million	1 million
2.	Turkey	20,000	20,000
3.	Iraq	1 million	2 million
4.	Saudi Arabia	10 million	5 million
5.	Pakistan	40,000	50,000
6.	Morocco	–	200,000
7.	Niger	75,000	20,000
8.	Senegal	40,000	–
9.	Cyprus*	2,000	2,500
10.	Oman	50,000	–
11.	Tunisia	200,000	–

* Refers to the Muslim-majority Republic of Northern Cyprus

for the ISF and Al-Quds Fund respectively when several of the key states were still to announce substantial donations.[72] At that moment the $100 million targets set for the *Waqf*s of the two Funds did not seem too difficult to achieve. But six years down the road, on 7 April 1986, the OIC Secretary General had to tell the 26th session of the ISF Council that till then only $2.8 million out of $100 million capital for the ISF *Waqf* had been realized.[73]

The ISF has, however, made optimum use of all the resourses at its disposal to achieve its objectives. For instance, during the first five years of its operations (1976–80), it allocated $11.5 million to people affected by crises, catastrophes, and natural disasters.[74] Another $12.8 million were diverted to build or support mosques, schools, hospitals, and Islamic centres. During the period under review, $2.7 million were spent on *Da'wa* (i.e., spreading the message of Islam) through the publication of translation of the Quran and *Sunnah* (traditions of the Holy Prophet [PBUH], distribution of Islamic literature, sending missionaries and organizing lectures etc. A sum of $1.5 million was provided for Muslim Youth Care. It may be noted that the Muslim communities in non-member states have varyingly received thirty-five to ninety per cent of the total allocations under different heads.[75]

One of the major roles of the Fund is to provide assistance for resisting Judaisation of Jerusalem and to support Palestinian refugees in distress. It carries out this function in coordination with the Jerusalem Committee and the Jerusalem Fund.[76]

Moreover, the Fund has performed a variety of subsidiary functions such as organizing the 15th Hijra century reception programmes. It has been making steady progress in the expansion of its area of operations in terms of the growing number of governments, associations, universities, and institutions receiving assistance from it. The following table gives an indication of its activities:

Chart 11.2
Beneficiaries of the ISF Activities

Amount in US$

No. of beneficiaries	1978/79	No. of beneficiaries	1988/89
Africa and the Middle East (23)	1,205,000	49	2,435,000
Asia and Australia (20)	1,165,500	57	1,431,000
Europe and America (24)	1,187,000	38	7,533,000
Universities, Institutions and Research Centres (15)	2,075,000	31	3,975,000

Source: Organization of Islamic Conference, Islamic Solidarity Fund (Jeddah, n.d.), p. 3.

The latest activity reports of the ISF are not available, but it is clear that the ISF is pursuing its diverse range of activities. It contributed substantially to the establishment of the Islamic universities in Niger and Uganda.[77] It also undertook a project to set up an Islamic teachers training college in Chicago, USA. The ISF has continued to assist the OIC organs with fragile financial position, including the Islamic Solidarity Sports Federation, Al-Quds Funds, Islamic Capitals Organization, and so on.

The Fund has a large number of seminars and symposia to its credit. Notable among them are 'Human and material resources in the Muslim World' (Dhaka), 'Human rights and liberties in Islam' (Niamey), 'Islamic Banking Systems' (Benghazi), 'Muslim minorities in non-Muslim states' (London), 'Application of *Shari'ah* in contemporary situation' and 'Contribution of Islam in human civilization' (Islamabad), etc.[78] The Islamic Solidarity Fund has contributed to a large number of assistance programmes for the Muslims

of Bosnia, Kashmir, and Philippines. In 1995, the Fund donated $200,000 each for Bosnian and Kashmiri refugees and $100,000 for the Somali refugees.[79]

As was noted at the beginning, the ISF is the most important of the OIC subsidiary organs. If only it had money, there are a lot more things it could have done. Today not only many communities but virtually all the OIC organs look towards the Fund for support. In the face of the spate of demands and requests, the Fund looks towards donors in the hope that money would be poured into the Fund at a greater pace.

v. Al-Quds Fund

The Al-Quds (Jerusalem) Fund was established by the 7th ICFM (Istanbul; 1976) to support the struggle of the Palestinian people in the city of Jerusalem. As the name suggests, the Fund is specifically meant for the cause of Al-Quds Al-Sharif (Holy Jerusalem), the third-holiest shrine for the Muslims. The Fund supports the Palestinian liberation struggle against Zionism, in the city of Jerusalem in particular and in all Palestinian lands (i.e. the present day Israel) in general, in the context of its commitment to the Jerusalem cause. The Fund is administered by the Al-Quds Committee and its office is located within the OIC General Secretariat in Jeddah.[80]

Objectives: The objectives of the Al-Quds Fund are:

- To prevent and resist the judaisation policy, pursued by the Israeli occupation authorities.
- To preserve and maintain the Arab character of the City of Jerusalem.
- To support the struggle of the Palestinian people in Jerusalem and in the rest of the occupied territories.

Administration and Finance: The Fund is administered through two organs:

General Assembly: The Islamic Commission for Economic, Cultural, and Social Affairs (ICECS), also acts as the General Assembly of the Al-Quds Fund and normally meets once a year.[82]

Council: This Fund is administered by an autonomous council comprising five members drawn from and elected by the Jerusalem Committee for a two-year renewable term which prepares the work programmes in the light of the objectives, set for the Fund. These programmes cannot be implemented unless approved by the Jerusalem Committee. The Council normally meets annually in an ordinary session before the meetings of the Jerusalem Committee and at its venue. The Fund is financed by voluntary contributions of the member states as well as contributions from the Islamic Solidarity Fund and public and private grants.

The *Waqf* of the Al-Quds Fund: Through resolution no. 1/11-P, the 11th ICFM (Islamabad; 1980) adopted the Statute establishing the *Waqf* of Al-Quds Fund.[83] Also located within the OIC General Secretariat building, the *Waqf* aims at strengthening the financial position of the Al-Quds Fund, securing it an annual income which guarantees its financial resources thus enabling it to carry out its mission, i.e. to support the struggle of the Palestinian people.

The Statute declared that the initial authorized capital of the *Waqf* would be $100 million and would consist of:

- Cash and movable assets in the form of *Waqf* of the member states and physical and moral persons of the Muslim world.
- Immovable assets and all possessions held by the member states and physical and legal entities in the form of *Waqf*.

To administer this money and to channelize it for the cause of Jerusalem, the Statute envisaged a Board of Trustees and an Executive Board.[84]

Board of Trustees: The *Waqf* of the Al-Quds Fund is run by a Board of Trustees which defines its general policy, guides and supervises its activities, approves its annual budgets and programmes as well as its periodical reports. The Administrative Board responds to the Jerusalem Committee and to the Islamic Conference of Foreign Ministers.

Executive Board: It administers the *Waqf* under the Board of Trustees of the Al-Quds Fund and comprises seven members, namely, the State of Palestine; the Chairman of the Board of Trustees of the Al-Quds Fund, or any other member elected by the Board from amongst its members; the Chairman of the Jerusalem Committee or any other member appointed by the Committee; the OIC Secretary General or in his place, the Assistant Secretary General (Al-Quds Al-Sharif); and three experts appointed by the Jerusalem Committee on the proposal of the Board of Trustees of the Al-Quds Fund. We have seen in the previous section that the suggested initial capital of $100 million for the *Waqf* of the ISF could not be realized and very little of the money pledged by the states at the ICFMs was actually paid. The same was the fate of the elusive target of $100 million set for the *Waqf* of Al-Quds Fund. The financial stringency compelled the Al-Quds Fund to abandon many of its planned activities. The limited finances at the Fund's disposal are diverted towards propaganda activities against the Judaisation of the holy city of Jerusalem.

vi. Islamic Fiqh Academy (IFA)

We have seen in the last chapter that the need to revise the Islamic laws was increasingly being felt since the time of the establishment of the OIC. There was no single supreme authority for the whole Muslim world, which could consider, and give authoritative opinions on, the contemporary problems of Islamic jurisprudence. There are a large number of sects and schools of thought among the Muslims, hardly any of whom can be deemed as homogeneous within itself, and all but two of them do not have a semblance of a central religious authority. The calls for a review of the interpretations of Islamic law, were being made by various quarters; that of the King Fahd of Saudi Arabia was one such voice.

As the Muslim clergy could not, by itself, unanimously agree upon a supreme council for *Ijtihad* whose decisions could enjoy enough moral sanctity and authority, to become *Ijma'a*, the OIC took it upon itself to constitute a Fiqh Academy to achieve the 'theoretical and practical unity of the *ummah*'.

The decision to the effect was taken through resolution no. 8/3-C(IS) at the 3rd Islamic Summit which requested the General Secretariat to take necessary steps to prepare a draft statute for this purpose.[85] An experts' committee was formed, which held its first meeting in May 1981 and prepared the draft statute of the academy. The statute was presented to the 12th ICFM (Baghdad; 1981) which recommended that it be circulated among the member states for their comments. The General Secretariat was asked to expand the experts' committee to study the draft statute afresh along with the recommendations of the members. The expanded committee drafted a fresh statute in the light of the comments of the member states.[86] The seat of the Academy is located in Jeddah, Saudi Arabia.

Objectives: The Academy has these basic objectives[87]:

- To achieve the theoretical and practical unity of the Islamic *ummah* by persuading Muslims to adhere, in practice, to the principles of the Islamic *Shari'ah* at the individual, social, as well as international levels;
- To strengthen the link of the Muslim community with the Islamic faith and to draw inspiration from the Islamic *Shari'ah;*
- To study contemporary problems from the *Shari'ah* point of view and to make fresh efforts to find solutions in conformity with the *Shari'ah*, through an authentic interpretation of its content.

Membership, Structure, and Finance: Each member state of the OIC is represented by an active member, who is supposed to be an expert on Islamic law.[88] The Academy is empowered to coopt as a member, any Muslim scholar or jurisconsult who fulfils all the required conditions. All the eight major schools of thought of the Islamic jurisprudence are represented in the Academy. The Academy has the following organs:

- *The Council*: The Council comprises all the active members of the Academy.
- *The Bureau*: It is composed of the Secretary General of the OIC, six members elected by the Council, and the Secretary General of the Academy.

- *The General Secretariat*: The IFA General Secretariat is headed by a Secretary General appointed from amongst the members of the Academy by the OIC Secretary General. In addition, there are specialized sections, which work for the realization of the duties assigned to the Council. The Academy is one of the subsidiary organs, financed by the OIC General Secretariat budget. It also accepts voluntary donations.

Activities: The Islamic Fiqh Academy started functioning quite late because of the differences on the draft statute which had to be drafted again, and later due to the pusillanimity shown by member states in nominating the scholars against the seats reserved for them in the Council of IFA. Till the end of 1995, the Academy had held only a few meetings. The Council of the Fiqh Academy considers a problem of Islamic jurisprudence when:

a) The OIC requests its opinion. For instance, the cultural committee of the 21st ICFM (Karachi; 1993) called for the universal observation of Friday as the weekly holiday, all over the Muslim world, and for a unified *Hijra* Calendar, and asked the Islamic Fiqh Academy to issue an edict on whether it was allowed under the Islamic law for the Muslim world to have a unified *Hijra* calendar, in order to be able to observe Islamic religious festivals on the same day all over the world.[89]
b) An organ of the OIC seeks its legal opinion. A prominent example is the ruling given by the Islamic Fiqh Academy, in response to a request made by the Islamic Development Bank (IDB), declaring the equity participation to companies which carry interest-based finance, as un-Islamic. Consequently, the IDB, a specialized organ of the OIC, has restricted its equity participation to those companies only which have no interest-based finances on their books.[90]

The Academy has given its opinion on scores of topics. They include the legality or otherwise of certain marriage customs, birth control, human organs transplant, test-tube babies, and the like. It has given *Fatwas* on the excommunication of the Qadiani and the Bahai sects, responsibilities of a Muslim doctor, and the Muslim teacher, and the limits on the techniques to counter anti-Islam propaganda in the present world. The IFA has also given its recommendations on a wide range of economic problems including usury and interest, status of the Islamic banks, hoarding, loans, and national budgetary deficits, etc. The Academy also adopted resolutions on various aspects of the Islamic rituals including prayers, alms, and *Hajj* (pilgrimage) rites.[91]

The Academy arranges seminars and discussions on the problems of the Muslim world. It publishes updated versions of its book *Resolutions and Recommendations of the Islamic Fiqh Academy*, every two years. The scholars at the Academy are working to produce three major volumes:

• Glossary of Islamic *Fiqh* Terms
• Revival of Islamic *Fiqh* Heritage
• Collection and Simplification of Islamic *Fiqh* rules

The IFA has planned to bring out an encyclopaedia of Islamic jurisprudence. This last monumental research endeavour will take several years to complete.

VII. Islamic Centre for Development of Trade (ICDT)

In order to encourage regular commercial contacts, harmonize policies, and promote investments among the OIC member states, the 3rd Islamic Summit (Taif; 1981) decided to establish the Islamic Centre for Development of Trade (ICDT) and approved its Statute. The Centre is located in Casablanca, Morocco.[92] It started operating in 1983.

Objectives: The ICDT wants to promote trade exchange among OIC member states by[93]:

• Undertaking studies and researches in the subject;
• Helping disseminate trade information and data among member states; organizing fairs, exhibitions, and other trade activities to contribute to the promotion of member states' product;
• Encouraging contacts among businessmen of member states and bringing them together;
• Organizing symposia and training seminars for participants from member states; and

• Helping member states create national organizations or associations for the promotion of trade, or reinforcing existing ones.

Structure and Finance: The ICDT has a three-tier structure:[94]

• *General Assembly:* The General Assembly, consisting of one representative each from the member states, the OIC Secretary General or his representative, Director of the Centre, and one representative each of the Islamic Chamber of Commerce and the Ankara Centre, supervises the activities of the ICDT. It meets once every two years.
• *Board of Administration:* It is made up of nine members, six of whom are elected by the General Assembly for a three-year term. A nominee of the host state, the ICDT Director and the OIC Secretary General or his representative, are the *ex-officio* members. It meets at least once a year.
• *Director:* The Director is the chief administrative officer of the Centre. He is appointed by the OIC Secretary General, in consultation with the Board of Directors for a four-year mandate, renewable once.

The Centre's budget is financed through annual contributions from member states, income from the services rendered by the Centre, and donations and other resources.[95]

Activities: The activities of the ICDT span four principal areas.[96]

Information and Documentation: A documentation department has been set up which is busy establishing a trade information network. Seven databanks with information on trade regulations, trade agreements between the OIC states, foreign trade statistics, trade opportunities, and trade events in the Muslim countries and other related subjects are under preparation.

The Information Unit of the ICDT has established contacts with the national focal points in the OIC countries to collect information. It also maintains a web page of the ICDT to disseminate the information. The interested businessmen or entrepreneurs can also contact the Centre by the email for free information: icdt@icdt.org. The said information unit of the ICDT also brings out a trilingual magazine called *Tijaris* as part of its information-disseminating activities.

Research: The Centre has a Research and Study Wing that undertakes regular studies on market trends and product surveys. It also produces an annual report on the mutual trade of the Muslim countries and gives recommendations for enhancing the same. The Wing monitors the implementation and follow-up to the draft agreement on Trade Preferential System in the OIC States.

Training: The ICDT arranges training programmes, workshops, seminars, and symposia on the subjects of trade promotion, business opportunities, hurdles in the way of the Islamic Common Market, tariff laws, effects of the WTO on the Muslim states, and other topics. Economic advisers and experts, commercial attaches, and persons of the private sector in the Muslim countries benefit from these training activities.

Trade promotion: Finally, the ICDT organizes trade fairs of the Islamic countries once every two years, which it considers the most effective way of trade promotion. The first Islamic International Trade Fair was held in November 1979 at Istanbul before the establishment of the ICDT. In 1986, the Centre decided to organize biannual fairs. The second Islamic Trade Fair at Casablanca (April 1986), the third at Cairo (October 1988), and the fourth at Tunis (October 1990) were successfully held, while the one scheduled for 1992 could not take place for certain reasons. Then the fifth and the sixth trade fairs, held at Tehran (July 1994) and Jakarta (October 1996) respectively, attracted a lot of businessmen who exhibited their products. At the latter fair, the ICDT decided to hold the seventh Islamic Trade Fair at Tripoli, Lebanon, jointly with the Lebanese Ministry of Trade and Commerce and the International Trade Promotion (IFP) Company, in October 1998.

VIII. Islamic Institute of Technology (IIT)

Recognizing that the Islamic states had vast resources of manpower and know-how but inadequate facilities for training, to meet the specific requirements of these states, the 9th ICFM (Dakar; 1978) decided to establish an Islamic Institute of Technology (IIT) at Dhaka, Bangladesh, through its resolution No. 5/9-E.[97] Earlier known as the Islamic Institute of Technical and Vocational Training and Research (ICTVTR), this Institute is meant to provide skilled technicians and instructors in mechanical, electrical, electronic, and chemical technologies, and to conduct research in these fields. The first meeting of the IIT Board of Directors took place in June 1979. The 11th ICFM (Islamabad; 1980) approved its statute. The foundation stone of the thirty-acre campus was laid by President Zia-ur-Rahman of Bangladesh, in the presence of the then OIC Secretary General Habib Chatti, on 27 March 1981. The academic activities of IIT started in October 1985.

The change of name to IIT was effected following a decision by the 22nd ICFM (Casablanca; December 1994). The Institute Board had long been clamouring for this new name, as it believed that the renaming would help graduates in getting their degrees and diplomas recognized abroad. In February 1995, the newly christened IIT entered into a Headquarter Agreement with the OIC Secretary General, which solved the problem of taxation and guaranteed duty-free import of books and equipment. On the occasion of the 9th convocation ceremony on 21 September 1995, the IIT was jointly inaugurated by the OIC Secretary General and the Prime Minister of Bangladesh.

Objectives: The Statute mandates the IIT to:[98]

- Train instructors, technicians, and tradesmen in technologies and trades needed in the member states and to upgrade the mid level and lower level manpower to international standards;
- Conduct and guide research in industrial and technological fields and in technical and vocational education to benefit the member states of the OIC;
- Confer certificates, degrees, and diplomas on persons who have pursued courses of study provided by the Institute and have passed the examinations under such conditions as may be prescribed by the academic rules and regulations of the IIT;
- May confer other academic distinctions on persons of high eminence from the member states, with the approval of the Joint General Assembly;

- Promote technical cooperation, exchange technical know-how, and disseminate basic information in the field of human resource development;
- Ensure coordination between the objectives of the Institute and those of other national and regional institutions of the Islamic countries;
- Undertake advisory and consultancy services for Governments, International foundations, or allied organizations;
- Participate in the meetings of OIC commissions and committees with appropriate background and technical papers.

Structure and Finance: The structure of the IIT particularly resembles that of the Ankara Centre (SESRTCIC):

- *General Assembly*: The ICECS acts as the General Assembly of the IIT and meets once a year in an ordinary session.
- *Governing Board*: It is made up of nine members, elected by the General Assembly for a period of three years. The representative of the OIC Secretary General as well as the Director General of the Institute are *ex-officio* members of the Board. The Board has an *Executive Committee* consisting of five members. Secretary, Ministry of Labour and Manpower, Government of Bangladesh, is its *ex-officio* Chairman. Three Heads of Missions of OIC member states stationed at Dhaka, nominated by the Governing Board, and the Director General of the Institute, are the remaining four members.
- *Academic Committee*: It comprises ten members, that are, the IIT Director General as *ex-officio* Chairman, five members nominated from the Embassies/High Commissions of the OIC member states stationed at Dhaka by the Governing Board and four other members (three nominated by the Government of Bangladesh and one nominated by the Vice Chancellor, Bangladesh University of Engineering and Technology).
- *Director General*: The Director General of the Centre is appointed by the Secretary General of the Organization of the Islamic Conference in consultation with the Governing Board for a four-year term, renewable once.

The budget of the Institute is financed through mandatory contributions and donations by the member states of the OIC.[100] Some funds are generated by the Institute itself through fees, charged from the students.

Activities: Initially the IIT (called ICTVTR at that time) had a capacity of sixty-five staff and 650 trainees.[101] The Institute had twenty-six workshops and laboratories where equipment worth $2.4 million was installed and commissioned. A computer centre was also set up and a library with a capacity of 52,000 volumes was established. It has specialized reading rooms for scholars and research fellows, separate sections for rare books, microfilms and video-cassettes etc.[102]

By mid-1984, most of the physical infrastructure was completed and the academic activity started with the first short course in Instructor Training in October 1985. In February 1986, the academic regulations were finalized by the Governing Board in its eleventh meeting, though they were amended more than once in the following years. In the Fall of 1986, the Institute launched regular long courses of Higher Diplomas in Engineering etc., so the first convocation was held on 21 October 1987.[103]

Academic Activities: By 1998, the twelfth batch of the IIT trainees was expected to complete the studies and receive their degrees and diplomas. The Institute offers four academic programmes:[104]

I. *One-year Instructor Training Programmes*: It has six categories of courses;

- Master in Technical Education (MTE) and Post Graduate Diploma in Technical Education (PGDTE) with specializations in five Engineering fields, namely, Thermofluid, Chemical, Production, Electrical, and Electronic.
- Bachelor of Science and Technical Education (BSTE) and Diploma in Technical Education (DTE) with specializations in Automotive Technology, Refrigeration and Air-conditioning, Electrical Machines, Power System Technology, and Instrument Control Technology.
- Diploma in Vocational Education(DVE) and Certificate in Vocational Education (CVE) with specializations in Automotive Metal Machining, Electronic Instrumentation, and Control Trades etc.

II. *Four-year Bachelor of Science in Engineering Programme*: It offers B.Sc. (Engg.) degrees in Mechanical, Electrical, and Electronics disciplines in four-year integrated programmes.

III. *Three-year Higher Diploma in Engineering Programme*: It offers higher diplomas in the fields of Mechanical, Electrical, and Electronic Engineering. In all the three disciplines, there are further specializations in various sub-disciplines. The Institute may approve promoting student to an Engineering degree programme provided he scores very high grades in the higher diploma examination. So by studying for another year, a student may be awarded the B.Sc. (Engg.) degree in his field.

IV. *Two-year Engineering Trade Certificate Programmes (ETCP)*: The Department of Chemical and Mechanical Engineering offers the ETCPs in the fields of Automotives, Metal Machining, Refrigeration, and Welding and Fabrication. The department of Electrical and Electronic Engineering offers this programme with specializations in the fields of Radio and Television Servicing and Instrument Mechanics.

It may not be out of place to mention here that the Institute offers a wide range of co-curricular and extra-curricular activities, Regular visits to industrial units and, in some cases, mandatory internships in the field are features of the IIT academic life. Moreover, special activities on the occasions of the Muslim festivals of Eids and the Prophet's (PBUH) birth anniversary, and the OIC foundation day, regular lectures by Islamic scholars, besides sports events and debate and quiz competitions add colour to campus life.

Research Activities: Research activities of the IIT had been seriously hampered by the resource crunch. Since many countries did not contribute towards the IIT establishment fund, many of the laboratories and other facilities envisaged in the Master Plan are yet to be provided. The existing laboratories have failed to update themselves with modern research accessories, This is the prime reason why the IIT has not been able to offer research degrees such as the Ph.D. and the M.Phil. The Institute, however, has to its credit some. fifteen international workshops/short courses and three international symposia. The topics covered a wide range such as 'Micro-computer applications', 'Modern practices in designs of tools', 'Operation

of fertilizer projects', 'Management of technical training in the OIC Countries', and others. From different Muslim countries, 423 participants attended the IIT seminars.

A few technological research projects like the ones on solar resource assessment and the development of a compatible micro-computer were accomplished jointly by the students and the research faculty. A few teachers published their own books. The IIT also published proceedings of at least five of its seminars, concerning topics like manpower and educational research. Among other IIT publications are its annual News Bulletins, annual issues of the Prospectus and souvenirs on the occasions of its 10th anniversary or that of the silver jubilee of the OIC, etc.

And finally, the IIT has entered into different agreements for joint research and training with the OIC, its specialized organs, and UN agencies like the UNESCO, UNDP, FAO, and the UNIDO.

Student Information: The Institute provides exemption from tuition fees, medi-care and sports charges to all regular students and trainees. In addition, it disburses a handsome monthly allowance to the students to cover the cost of transport, laundry, and stationery etc. Three meals a day at the main cafeteria, within a certain limit, are provided to all the students free of charge.

Only the final year students of the BSc (Engg.) programmes are expected to pay a final year fee, equivalent to $4500. The IIT does not contribute to the round trip airfare for the students, which has to be borne by the students themselves or the nominating country.

The IIT has a diverse composition of students. Less than half come from the host state while the remaining belong to Bahrain, Gambia, Indonesia, Iraq, Pakistan, Palestine, Saudi Arabia, Sudan, and other Muslim states. The governments of the Muslim countries send nominations to the admissions committee while a large number of students prefer to apply directly. The closing date of applications/nominations is usually 30 June for the class commencing from the Fall of that year.[105] The prospective students and research fellows may contact the concerned department at home or approach:

Director (Academics)
Islamic Institute of Technology,
P.O. Box No. 3003, Ramna,
P.O. KB Bazar, Distt. Ghazi Pur
Dhaka-Bangladesh.

The Future: The incomplete infrastructure and the average yearly default of 60–90 per cent of the mandatory contributions, has impeded the healthy growth of the Islamic Institute of Technology, The 7th Islamic Summit (Casablanca; 1994) offered a 50 per cent discount to the member states, as an incentive for them to clear their dues by paying half the amount in arrears against them. Only three countries, Brunei, Iran and the UAE, availed the concession. So even after writing off half the amount, the Muslim states had $15.48 million outstanding mandatory contributions, as of early 1996.

The IIT degrees are getting wider recognition day by day. Even in the UK, the IIT Higher Diploma graduates are allowed to complete Bachelor of Engineering (Honours) degree in one year and Masters degree in one year. The number of nominations received by the IIT for admission by the Muslim countries is increasing each year. But the incomplete infrastructure and the bloated budgetary deficits, lead the IIT to dismiss over three-fourth of the nominations. Thus the annual intake does not usually exceed 300 students,

The IIT has repeatedly made fervent calls to the Muslim countries to defray their contributions but to no avail. Hence a plethora of projects approved by the Academic Council could not take off. Finally, unless the Institute gets rid of its financial problems, there is no way it can expand its activities.

IX. Islamic Foundation for Science, Technology, and Development (IFSTAD)

The 6th ICFM (Jeddah; 1975) decided to create a subsidiary organ named Islamic Foundation for Science, Technology, and Development (IFSTAD) to promote cooperation in the field of science and technology within the Muslim world.[106]

Objective The objectives of the Foundation are as follows:[107]

- To promote and encourage research activities in the fields of science and technology, within an Islamic framework, to help solve some of the problems of the Muslim world, and of mankind, in general.
- To promote cooperation and coordination in the field of science and technology within the Muslim world and to strengthen the bonds of Islamic solidarity.
- To ensure that all Muslim states, both individually and collectively, optimise the use of science and technology (including social sciences), in the formulation of their socio-economic plans keeping in view the need to consolidate the unique Islamic personality and character.
- To provide advice and carry out scientific studies for the OIC, whenever necessary.

Structure and Finance: The structure of IFSTAD is described below:[108]

- *General Assembly*: The ICECS acts as the General Assembly of the IFSTAD and meets once a year.
- *Scientific Council*: It is composed of fifteen members appointed by the Foreign Ministers Conference for a period of three years on the recommendation of the OIC Secretary General. The Council supervises the activities of the Foundation.
- *Executive Committee*: It is composed of five members elected from amongst its members by the Scientific Council for a period of three years.
- *Director General*: He is appointed by the OIC Secretary General for a period of four years from amongst the leading scientists of the member states. He can be re-appointed only once. He is responsible for running the affairs of IFSTAD.

The finances of the Foundation were to come from mandatory contributions from the OIC member states, donations, as well as revenues from the services rendered. We have already seen in the previous sections that the financial crunch is seriously and adversely affecting the efficiencies of the OIC organs. Likewise, the IFSTAD had to carry on its activities under acute financial constraints which ultimately led to the collapse of this Foundation. At the 8th General Assembly meeting of the COMSTECH held at Islamabad in December 1997, it was announced with regret that the IFSTAD had been dissolved.

Activities during 1983–97: The IFSTAD started functioning in mid-1983. It used to work out five-year plans of action to set its objectives and then operate accordingly.[109] The plans were prepared along the following lines:

- Information collection
- Programme coordination
- Advice and consultancy
- Strengthening scientific and technological capabilities of member states.
- Creation and/or coordination of institutions in technologies of interest.
- Creation of International Muslim Centres of Excellence in the field of science and technology.
- Building the scientific capability of the *ummah*.

The 4th Islamic Summit (Casablanca; 1984) entrusted the IFSTAD with the mission of implementing the programmes of COMSTECH as well. Therefore, it had to carry out activities within the frameworks of both, the COMSTECH's and its own plans. of action.[110] But as with the other OIC organs, the IFSTAD had to face, what Dr M. Ali Kettani, the then Director General, described in an interview, 'Much optimism but little money.'[111] Through the 3rd Islamic Summit (Taif; 1981), the member states pledged $50 million for the Foundation but by June 1983, when it started functioning, only $5.17 million could be realized, out of which $5 million had been contributed by Saudi Arabia alone, and the remaining $171,000 by four other states.[112] This gloomy state of affairs did not change for the better during the nearly fifteen years of the IFSTAD's active life. The Foundation failed to generate 'revenues from the services rendered', since most of the time, the beneficiary states expected the IFSTAD itself to bear the costs of service provided.[113] In this situation, the member states could scarcely be expected to pay the mandatory contributions, let alone donations, when they sought donations from the Foundation. A brief review of the IFSTAD activities follows.

Research, Training, and Publication: The IFSTAD organized a large number of seminars, symposia, and training workshops on topics related to science and technology. Some of the events sponsored or co-sponsored by the IFSTAD include, the Conference on Semi-conductors and Physics of Materials, and the Regional Physics Education Symposium, in Malaysia; Seminar on the Role of Universities in the National Development of Islamic Countries, in Senegal; and the Training Course on Recombinant DNA Techniques, the International Workshop on Protein Structure, Function Relationship and the Islamic Countries Conference on Statistical Sciences, in Pakistan, etc.[114]

The IFSTAD launched a scholarship programme for Muslim students for higher studies in science and technology. For the first academic year, i.e., 1983–84, IFSTAD granted 160 scholarships, out of which ninety-nine went to Muslim students belonging to non-Muslim countries.[115] Besides such schemes, the IFSTAD has been instrumental in the exchange of scholars within the Muslim states. For example, Pakistan accepted scholars from Muslim states for M.Sc. in Nuclear Engineering while Malaysia took the same for training in Tropical Medicine, through the IFSTAD. The Foundation has also frequently financed, wholly or partially, the participation of scientists from Muslim states to conferences, symposia, and workshops in other states.[116]

Publications constitute a significant part of the IFSTAD research activities. Besides the Annual Reports of IFSTAD, it also publishes proceedings of conferences and symposia held under its auspices.[117]

Activities in the field of Information: The computer section of the IFSTAD maintained data bases on Consultants, Manpower, Universities, and Research Institutes of the Muslim states as well as on the Islamic Foundation of Research Institutes (IFRI) and on Meetings and Documentation.

The IFSTAD completed the two first phases of its four-phase Information Network Programme aiming at interlinking S&T and Education data bases of OIC member states. At that stage, activities relating to the programme were transferred to the Islamic Countries Information Network (ICINET). Feasibility study to consider the establishment of an Islamic Information Network was carried out by the IFSTAD along with the Islamic Development Bank (IDB) and the Islamic Centre for Development of Trade (ICDT).[118]

The Foundation has attended all the Islamic Summits and ICFMs during its existence, as observer. Besides, it has actively participated in the sessions of the COMCEC, the COMSTECH and the Islamic Academy of Sciences, meetings of most of the OIC organs like IDB, ICECS etc; and the conferences organized by the Arab Thought Forum, Jordanian Royal Academy of Research, the ISESCO, and the like.[119] Further, the publications of IFSTAD (noted above) and preparation of directory of Muslim consultants etc. (discussed later), also fall in information related activities of this Foundation.

Consultancy and Promotion of Science Culture: The IFSTAD had always tried to develop scientific and technical facilities in OIC member-countries. For example, it was on its initiative and advocacy, that the Islamic Development Bank agreed to finance a project for solar coolers. The Foundation exhibited greater interest in arranging consultancies for the Muslim community in scientific and technical matters from among Muslim experts. It gained importance because of the fact that 93 per cent of the consultancies in the Muslim world are done by experts from industrially developed non-Muslim nations, although well-qualified Muslim consultants are available in many of these specialized areas. Many of these work in the developed countries. The IFSTAD compiled a comprehensive list of such Muslim consultants with their addresses and fields of specialization and has made it available to the OIC member countries. This was reported to have had a positive response from the member-states.[120]

Likewise, about 800 consultants and experts were recorded in a specialized data base, and a directory was published in 1989. They included nationals of OIC member states, as well as Muslim expatriates all over the world. Three specific directions were approved in developing IFSTAD consultancy services: (1) to offer consultancy services to organizations in the member states; (2) to develop consulting projects proposed by other organizations, and (3) to develop projects initiated by IFSTAD employees. The terms and conditions

of this service were decided by IFSTAD Scientific Council. Several institutions in the member states expressed their interest. IFSTAD received several requests and projects submitted by individuals and organizations. But most governmental agencies requesting technical assistance and consultancy services expected IFSTAD to meet the cost, which was possible neither from the statutory nor the financial points of view. An approach involving 'packages' where consultancy could be integrated within a development project was also considered, but all such schemes called for greater cooperation from the member states.[121]

For the promotion of a science culture, the IFSTAD had a programme for developing Muslim manpower also, whereby it proposed to (1) encourage qualified students to pursue advanced studies; (2) develop highly skilled manpower; (3) develop independent research capabilities; (4) reduce the brain drain (to industrialized countries); (5) increase the transfer of technology to Muslim countries/ communities, and (6) help Muslims retain and develop an Islamic identity.[122]

The IFSTAD was particularly concerned about the Muslim brain-drain, referred to in point (4) above, which it believed happened because their native countries were neither sufficiently developed to provide them with proper jobs, nor in a position to offer adequate financial rewards. The IFSTAD was striving to halt all three types of brain-drain; namely, migration of skilled or unskilled labour to the developed West, migration of highly qualified persons to industrialized countries, and unemployment of talented youth within a Muslim country. The migration to non-Muslim countries alone, IFSTAD believed, constituted the Muslim brain-drain whereas migration from one Muslim state to another was encouraged by it as being a conducive to inter-dependence in the field of science and technology, within the Muslim *ummah*.[123]

Coordination in Science and Technology: As requested by the third COMSTECH meeting, the IFSTAD implemented six inter-Islamic S&T networks and their foundations meetings were held during 1987.[124] The networks were autonomous, self-financing bodies linked to the OIC system through IFSTAD which was a member of their respective General Assemblies and Executive Committees; they are as follows (names of headquarter cities in brackets):

i)   Water Resources Development and Management network (Amman)
ii)   Renewable Energy Sources Network (Islamabad)
iii) Space Sciences and Technology Network (Karachi)
iv)   Tropical Medicine Network (Kuala Lumpur)
v)   Genetic Engineering and Biotechnology Network (Cairo)
vi)   Oceanography Network (Izmir)

A total of eighteen member states joined officially in one network or more. Of these some joined all six networks. They are: Algeria, Bangladesh, Egypt, Indonesia, Iran, Iraq, Jordan, Malaysia, Mali, Morocco, Niger, Pakistan, Qatar, Saudi Arabia, Senegal, Syria, Tunisia, and Turkey.

Other coordination activities of the IFSTAD included its designations as the Secretariat of the Islamic Federation of Research Institutes (IFRI), its joint activities with the SESRTCIC (Ankara Centre), and cooperation with the UN agencies as the focal point of the OIC in the area of science and technology.[125]

Future: The demise of the focal point of science and technology of the Muslim world, for no other reason than financial stringency, appends a sorry note to the level of commitment of the Muslim leadership to this vital area. The dissolution of the Islamic Foundation for Science, Technology, and Development was announced at the 8th Ministerial Meeting of COMSTECH on 15 December 1997 at Islamabad. Noor Ahmad Baba aptly notes:

> The mere creation of institutions with laudable objectives does not serve any purpose. What is more important is the will to make them work for the attainment of the desired objectives.[126]

It appears that the very absence of IFSTAD will once again make the necessity of its existence felt. Thus the Foundation, though possibly with some modifications in mandate and structure, might be revived in the near future. In the meantime, a special responsibility falls on other inter-Islamic institutions in the field of science, like the Islamic

Academy of Sciences (IAS), to enhance the scope of their activities and fill the vacuum created by the disappearance of IFSTAD.[127]

x. Islamic Civil Aviation Council (ICAC)

The idea of establishing some Islamic organs in the field of aviation first came up during an international seminar in February 1980, at Jeddah.[128] The moot proposed the establishment of the Islamic version of the International Civil Aviation Organization (ICAO) as well as a Pan-Islamic airline or, at least, a federation of Muslim countries airlines. The proposed Aviation Council was supposed to coordinate the policies of member states in the field of aviation and to confront common problems. Likewise, a number of roles were being envisaged for the proposed Pan-Islamic Airlines. Several LDMCs who do not own any air travel company could jointly own it, under the auspices of the OIC. Their reliance on Western airlines could then be reduced, thus effecting the saving of substantial capital flow towards outside air travel companies. Whereas the creation of a Federation of Muslim States Airlines would have accrued a different set of advantages such as the coordination of flights for the transport of millions of pilgrims to Saudi Arabia during *Hajj* each year, an understanding on provision of *halaal* food to all passengers, and the like.

The 3rd Islamic Summit (Taif; 1981) decided to set up a civil aviation council for Muslim countries as a subsidiary organ of the OIC. No decision, however, was taken on the proposed Pan-Islamic Airlines. Taking cognisance of this decision the 12th ICFM (Baghdad; 1981) named the new organ, the Islamic Civil Aviation Council. Saudi Airlines drafted the Charter of the Council that was sent to the member states for consideration.[129]

Objectives: The objectives of ICAC are:[130]

• to provide coordination among member states in the field of civil aviation
• to consider any special problem that could arise in the field of civil aviation

- to study the possibility of using effectively the air transport capacities of the member states.
- to coordinate and harmonize policies relating to fares and transit of member states' airlines.

Composition: The Civil Aviation Council is composed of member states of the OIC. Its administration has been proposed to be run by a general secretariat headed by a secretary general, who is to be appointed by the Secretary General of the OIC. Its headquarter is located at Tunis, Tunisia.[131]

Even after the passage of one and a half decade, the ICAC has not started operations. At the time of its inception, it was being speculated that the Council would be a milestone in the history of cooperation among Muslim states. At least, ten ratifications of the ICAC Charter were required for the Council to start functioning. Apparently, the magic number has not been attained in this case, so to date the ICAC is still on paper.

Conclusion

In sum, it is clear that the OIC has been able to lay down an elaborate organizational structure comprising various subsidiary organs and institutions that have come up within its framework. Most of the OIC organs are doing commendable jobs within the constraints imposed by the limited resources. Needless to emphasize that the performance of all these organs can be improved without much effort. One should not overlook the necessity of addressing many other shortcomings of the OIC mega structure, such as the excessive influence of the host state on the activities of the OIC organ located on its soil; lack of transparency in their conduct of affairs; dependence of the organ heads on the pleasure of one person, i.e. the OIC Secretary General, for the renewal of tenures; and an unnecessary concentration of most of the OIC bodies in a few member states.

To improve efficiency, the first step is a strict adherence to the policy of recruitment on merit only. The composition of their staffs should reflect the diversity within the Muslim world. The ratio of the local staff in an OIC organ should be no more and no less than the quota assigned to the host state on the basis of its contribution to the OIC General Secretariat budget. Under no circumstances, should the chief executive of an OIC organ belong to the host state. There should be greater transparency involved in the conduct of business in such bodies and the Directors General should be personally available before the Islamic Foreign Ministers' Conferences and later the media, to defend the performance of their respective organs and to answer the queries. The renewal of their terms of office should be made by the ICFMs/Islamic Summits, subject to satisfactory performance of the institutions concerned. The de-concentration of these institutions is also advisable so that no single state can have more than two OIC organs on its soil. This may help develop concern among the member governments for the success of the OIC organs located on their territory.

Last but not the least, it is imperative to adopt all conceivable measures to rescue the OIC institutions from the quagmire of perennial financial crises. Default in contributions to the OIC budget, should entail immediate suspension of voting rights in the legislative wings of all OIC subsidiary organs for the defaulting state, pending the clearance of all outstanding dues. Money is the fuel for proper functioning of such institutions. Hence bold steps have to be taken if tangible results are to be realized from the institutions. The recent collapse of the IFSTAD has put a big question mark before the financial viability of some other OIC organs as well. This incident should ring alarm bells and should spur a re-thinking of the whole strategy of management of various organs. Noor Ahmad Baba rightly comments:

> The OIC seems to have been over ambitious in the creation of these bodies, which has led to duplication or overlapping of activities. Emphasis has been laid on diversification of these bodies rather than on their consolidation. The objectives of these institutions are very well in tune with the problems and requirements of Muslim society in present times. But...[they] are handicapped on more than one account and therefore incapable of realizing their objective. The member-states that have voted to create them do not seem to be serious about their actual working. That is why there is a long time lag between the time the decision

for their establishment is made and the time they actually begin their operations. Even when they start operating they are concerned more with their survival than delivering the goods for which they were created. This is mainly because of the financial constraints with which most of them are confronted.[132]

NOTES and REFERENCES

1. General Secretariat Publication, 'Guide to the OIC', (Jeddah, OIC, 1995), p. 50.
2. Most of the information that follows is based on *Ankara Centre: Functions, Facilities, Activities*, (Ankara: SESRTCIC, 1995), which the Centre sent to the author in response to his request. Also see the Inamullah Khan (Ed), *World Muslim Gazetteer*, (Karachi: WMC, 1987), pp. 730–32.
3. OIC Guide, ref. 1, p. 51.
4. *Ankara Centre*, ref. 2, p. 3.
5. Noor Ahmad Baba, *OIC: Theory and Practice of Pan-Islamic Cooperation*, (Karachi: Oxford University Press 1994), p. 228.
6. *Ankara Centre*, ref. 2, p. 2.
7. Ibid., p. 3.
8. Ibid., p. 5.
9. Ibid., see the table on p. 6 for year-wise progress.
10. These are substantial numbers given the fact that they reflect strictly the technical output, excluding administrative documents like the budget proposals, work programmes, activity reports, and the like.
11. *Ankara Centre*, ref. 2, Annexure A of the booklet, pp. 21–40, gives a complete list of the papers and documents prepared by the Centre in its first seventeen years (1978–95) of activity.
12. Ibid., p. 7.
13. Ibid., see the chart on p. 9 for country-wise distribution of participants in these training programmes.
14. Ibid., Annexure B, pp. 41–44, gives a complete list of the technical cooperation and training activities, including workshops and seminars, conducted by the SESRTCIC since 1981.
15. Ibid., see p. 10–11 for detail.
16. These meetings have been made possible by the generous assistance of the Government of Turkey and the United Nations Development Fund (UNDP).
17. Details such as map, national flag, and tourist information is also available.
18. *Ankara Centre*, ref. 2, p. 12.
19. The *Journal of Economic Cooperation* was launched in 1979 while the *Information Report* started getting published in 1985. Both the periodicals are brought out in January, April, July, and October, every year.
20. *Ankara Centre*, ref. 2, Annexure C, pp. 45–53, lists the annotated publications of the SESRTCIC.
21. Ibid., p. 13.
22. Ibid., p. 14.
23. Ibid., Annexure D, pp. 54–57.
24. The IRCICA acknowledged the request of this author for information vide letter no.IRC/96-611, dated 16 December 1996 and sent some information in response; especially the issue No. 37 of the IRCICA newsletter (Istanbul: 1995) brought out on the occasion of the fifteenth anniversary of the Centre as a special issue. Better part of the information about this Centre as well as the Islamic Heritage Commission (next section) is based upon the material provided by the IRCICA. For instance, see p. 11 of special issue, op. cit., for initial developments regarding the establishment of IRCICA.
25. To date, one ICFM and one Islamic Summit Conference have taken place in the city of Dakar, Senegal. The IRCICA statute was adopted by the Dakar ICFM and revised by the Dakar Summit. Coincidentally, Dakar is also the seat of the OIC Standing Committee on Information and Culture (COMIAC).
26. Special Issue, ref. 24, p. 11.
27. OIC Guide, ref. 1, pp. 53–54.
28. Ibid., pp. 54–55. Also see Special Issue, ref. 24, pp. 15–20. The lists of names and designations of the members of the successive Governing Boards are also given therein.
29. Ibid., pp. 19–20 for more details on its working.
30. OIC Guide, ref. 1, p. 55.
31. Special Issue, ref. 2, p. 25.
32. Ibid.
33. See ibid., pp. 25–39, for descriptions of important research projects.
34. One book entitled *The Old Bridge in Mostar* from this project is exclusively devoted to the historic bridge of Mostar, destroyed by Serb shelling during the war.
35. Special Issue, ref. 24, p. 38.
36. Ibid.
37. See ibid., pp. 40–42, for complete list of publications.
38. Ibid., p. 43.
39. See ibid., pp. 44–45, for complete list of symposia held.
40. See ibid., pp. 45–47, for complete list of exhibitions arranged.
41. See ibid., pp. 48–49, for details about public lectures held.
42. Ibid., p. 51.
43. Ibid., p. 52.
44. Ibid., p. 53.
45. IRCICA Newsletter, Istanbul, August 1996, p. 6.
46. Ibid., pp. 8–9.
47. Special Issue, ref. 24, p. 14.
48. *Dawn*, Karachi, 28 August 1982.

49. OIC Guide, ref. 1, p. 72.

50. Prince Faisal is the son of the incumbent Saudi monarch, King Fahd bin Abdul Aziz.

51. OIC Guide, ref. 1, p. 73.

52. Ibid., p. 72.

53. For details about the competitions see Special Issue, ref. 24, pp. 63–64.

54. Ibid.

55. Ibid.

56. See ibid., pp. 64–65, for complete list of ICPICH publications.

57. See ibid., p. 65, for complete list of exhibitions held by ICPICH.

58. Ibid., p. 66.

59. Ibid.

60. Ibid.

61. OIC Guide, ref. 1, p. 65.

62. Keesing's Contemporary Archives, 1977, p. 28556.

63. *Pakistan Times*, Islamabad, 27 August 1978.

64. OIC Guide, ref. 1, p. 65.

65. Ibid., pp. 65–66.

66. Ibid., p. 66.

67. Ibid., p. 67.

68. Ibid., p. 68.

69. Ibid.

70. Ibid.

71. See 'OIC, Declarations and Resolutions of Islamic Summit and ICFMs Held in Pakistan' (Islamabad: Directorate of Films and Publications, 1993), pp. 36–37. The given chart is also taken from the same source.

72. Ibid.

73. See the text of Secretary General Pirzada's address to the twenty-sixth session of the ISF in *Speeches and Statements of H.E. Sharifuddin Pirzada: Secretary General of OIC*, (Karachi: n.p., 1989).

74. Baba, ref. 5, pp. 232–33.

75. Ibid.

76. Ibid.

77. Keesing, ref. 62, p. 28556.

78. *Dawn*, 31 May 1979.

79. *Pakistan Times*, 27 April 1995.

80. OIC Guide, ref. 1, p. 69.

81. Ibid.

82. Ibid.

83. Ibid.p. 70.

84. Ibid.

85. Ibid., p. 63.

86. Baba, ref. 5, p. 238.

87. OIC Guide, ref. 1, p. 63.

88. Ibid.

89. *Dawn*, 30 April 1993.

90. See the twentieth Annual Report of the Islamic Development Bank (Jeddah, 1996), p. 83.

91. Most of this discussion on the IFA activities, except where otherwise indicated, is based upon *The Declarations and Resolutions of the Islamic Fiqh Academy*, (Jeddah: IFA, n.d.). The Academy itself did not entertain the request of this author for information.

92. OIC Guide, ref. 1, p. 59.

93. Ibid.

94. Ibid.

95. Ibid.

96. The information about the activities has been taken from the Internet website of the SESRTCIC and other secondary sources. No response was received from the ICDT, despite repeated requests by this author for supply of information.

97. Most of the information about the establishment, development and early years of the Institute, is based upon the Activity Report presented by Dr A.M. Patwari, Director, ICTVTR, at the fourth COMSTECH meeting held at Islamabad in 1989. The report is a part of *Proceedings of Fourth COMSTECH Meeting*, (Islamabad: PASTIC, 1990), pp. 150–75.

98. OIC Guide, ref. 1, pp. 56–57.

99. Ibid., p. 57.

100. Ibid., p. 58.

101. They consist of 250 Trainees for Instructor Training Courses (one-year duration), 200 for Technology Courses (three years), 100 for Trade Courses (two years), and 100 Trainees for Skill Knowledge Updating short courses (maximum three months duration).

102. Report, ref. 97, pp. 152–53.

103. See the Annual Report of the Director, IIT, at the seventh meeting of the COMSTECH held in Islamabad in December 1995. Its text is part of the *Proceedings of the Seventh COMSTECH Meeting*, (Islamabad, 1996), pp. 243–75.

104. Ibid. The Report dilates at length on the academic programmes being offered by the IIT.

105. Ibid. Also see the unpublished IIT Report presented to the eighth COMSTECH meeting (Islamabad, December 1997), available from the COMSTECH Secretariat in Islamabad on request.

106. OIC Guide, ref. 1, p. 61.

107. Baba, ref. 5, p. 226.

108. Ibid.

109. It was not unexpected, taking into account the financial position of IFSTAD, that no response was received by the author for his requests for information even before December 1997. The author had therefore to, rely largely on secondary sources. The description of the IFSTAD activities for the first six years of activity has been taken from the Activity Report of IFSTAD, presented by its then Acting Director Ahmad Saleh Taib, carried in the *Proceedings of the Fourth COMSTECH Meeting*, (Islamabad, 1990), pp. 137–49.

110. Ibid., p. 138.

111. See interview of the IFSTAD Director General in the journal called *Arabia* (April 1984), p. 56, as quoted by Abdullah Ahsan, *OIC: Introduction to an Islamic Political Institution*, (Herndon: IIIT, 1987), p. 99.

112. Baba, ref. 5, p. 228.
113. IFSTAD Report, ref. 109, p. 143.
114. Ibid., pp. 146–47.
115. Ahsan, ref. 111, p. 100.
116. IFSTAD Report, ref. 109, p. 146.
117. Ibid., p. 140.
118. Ibid.
119. Ibid., pp. 140–42.
120. Baba, ref. 5, p. 229.
121. IFSTAD Report, ref. 109, p. 143.
122. Abdullah Ahsan, *Ummah or a Nation Identity Crisis in the Muslim World*, (Leicester, Islamic Foundation, 1992), pp. 137–38.
123. Ibid.
124. IFSTAD Report, ref. 109, p. 143.
125. Ibid., pp. 144–45.
126. Baba, ref. 5, p. 228.
127. It may be noted that the Islamic Academy of Sciences (IAS), Islamic Federation of Research Institutions (IFRI) and some others, have been established by the COMSTECH, which is a specialized committee of the OIC. Since we are here concerned with the subsidiary organs of the OIC itself, hence any discussion on the institutions created under the auspices of OIC organs, is outside the scope of this book.
128. *Pakistan Times*, 19 February 1980.
129. Ahsan, ref. 111, p. 36.
130. Baba, ref. 5, p. 230.
131. Ahsan, ref. 111, p. 37.
132. Baba, ref. 5, p. 241.

12 Islamic Universities

The development of human resources in the Muslim world and the provision of quality education of the Muslim youth for the purpose, has remained one of the top priorities of the leading international Islamic organizations, primarily the OIC. The OIC has, at different times, decided to establish educational institutions for higher learning where modern education can be imparted to the young generation in an atmosphere imbued with the Islamic spirit. The setting up of four Islamic universities in Bangladesh, Malaysia, Niger, and Uganda, and the extension of a university in Tunisia are prominent examples of this trend.[1]

Other notable endeavours in this direction include the Regional Institute for Complementary Education (Islamabad), Centre for Research on Islam (Timbuktu)[2], World Centre for Islamic Education (Mecca), Centres for Arabic Language Teaching (Sudan and Pakistan), Islamic Translation Institute (Sudan)[3], and the Islamic Centres at Guinea Bissau, Comoros Republic and New York, USA.[4] It may be emphasized that this is not the complete list of educational institutions of the OIC as a number of institutions and colleges, both with and outside the member states, receive full or partial financial assistance from the OIC Secretariat or the Islamic Solidarity Fund.[5]

The purpose of this chapter is to introduce the structures and activities of Islamic Universities being run by the OIC; the discussion on the structure and activities of the other OIC-sponsored Islamic educational bodies is beyond its scope. Anyway, very little information was available about the latter.[6] There are four universities, set up on the initiative of the OIC, namely, Islamic University of Bangladesh, Islamic University of Malaysia, Oum al Qura University of Niger, and the Islamic University in Uganda.[7] It may be added here that all these universities are non-sectarian, non-racial, and co-educational academic bodies. None of these universities is confined to the teaching of Islamic jurisprudence and Quranic studies alone. Engineering, medicine, law, economics, literature, history, and other human sciences are taught in the OIC-sponsored universities. Non-Muslim students are welcome to apply to all of them. Nevertheless, the Islamic way of life remains the dominant social value in the campus life and so an alcohol-free environment is maintained there. These universities have proved to be centres of excellence; International Islamic University of Malaysia (IIUM) above, for instance, produces 3000 graduates annually. And based on their performance, Malaysia Business Week has categorized it as the number one university in the country.[8]

i. International Islamic University of Bangladesh

The establishment of the Islamic University in Bangladesh was first considered during an Islamic Conference of Foreign Ministers in the late 1970s. The University was to be set up as a distinctive institution of higher education and research in Islamic Studies and other modern disciplines. The Government of Bangladesh offered to merge the existing Institute of Islamic Education and Research with the proposed University. The date of establishment of the University is 27 December 1980.[9]

The OIC Standing Committee for Information and Cultural Affairs (COMIAC) at its second session in 1985, expressed its 'appreciation for the steps taken by the Government of the People's Republic of Bangladesh to establish the University and hoped for more cooperation between the University and the specialized institutions emanating from the OIC in the implementation of this Islamic project'.[10]

Objectives: The Islamic University has been established with the following objectives:[11]

- To provide instruction in Islamic Studies and such other branches of learning at graduate and post-graduate level as the University may think fit, and to make provision for research and for the advancement and dissemination of knowledge;
- to prescribe courses of studies;
- to hold examinations and grant and confer certificates, diplomas, degrees, and other academic distinctions on persons who: (i) have pursued a course of study provided for or prescribed by the University, or (ii) have carried on research or private study under conditions laid down in the Statute;
- to confer honorary degrees or other distinctions in the manner laid down in the Statute;
- to provide lectures and instructions for, and to grant, under conditions laid down in the Statute, diplomas or certificates to persons deemed suitable by the university;
- to institute Professorships, Associate Professorships, Lecturerships, and any other teaching posts required by the University, and to appoint persons thereto in accordance with the Statute;
- to institute and award fellowships, scholarships, prizes, and medals in accordance with the prescribed conditions;
- to demand and receive such fees as may be prescribed by the ordinances;
- to establish and maintain Halls;
- to supervise and control the residence and discipline of the students of the University; to promote their extra-curricular activities and to make arrangements for promoting their health and moral character;
- to do such other acts and things as may be necessary, incidental, or conducive to the performance of its functions or otherwise to carry out the purposes of the Act.

Administrative Structure: The University is headed by a Rector who is assisted by two Deputy Rectors. The Board of Governors lays down the policy guidelines for the institution while the University Senate is the final authority for running the day-to-day affairs of the University. The Senate finalizes the rules and regulations for exams, code of conduct for students, and admission requirements etc. The Islamic University has five Faculties.

Faculties, Departments, and Degrees: The University offers fourteen degree programmes including Doctorate and Master of Philosophy and Master and Bachelor (with Honours) degrees, in a variety of disciplines.[12] The Faculty-wise break-up of courses follows:

i) *Faculty of Theology and Islamic Studies*: It offers Master (MTIS) and Bachelor (BTIS-Hons.) degrees in the above subject.

ii) *Faculty of Humanities and Social Sciences*: Master of Arts (MA), Master of Social Sciences (MSS) and the corresponding Bachelor degrees, BA-Hons. and BSS-Hons., are awarded by this Faculty.

iii) *Faculty of Applied Science and Technology*: The faculty has courses leading to M.Sc. and B.Sc-Hons. degrees.

iv) *Faculty of Business Administration*: Master (MBA) and Bachelors (BBA-Hons.) courses in the subject are taught here.

v) *Faculty of Law and Shari'ah*: The students of this Faculty learn the Islamic jurisprudence and law, and obtain LLM and LLB-Hons. degrees.

The University has over four and a half thousand strong multi-national student community. The department-wise enrolment of the students, as of 1997 was:[13]

- Al-Quran and Islamic Studies (384)
- *Da'wa* and Islamic Studies (331)
- *Al-Hadith* and Islamic Studies (299)
- Law and Muslim Jurisprudence (395)
- Economics (366)
- Bengali Language and Literature (348)
- English Language and Literature (445)
- Arabic Language and Literature (274)
- Islamic History and Culture (420)
- Politics and Public Administration (405)
- Accounting (377)
- Management (382)
- Electronics & Applied Physics (29)
- Applied Mathematics and Computer Science (34)
- Applied Chemistry and Chemical Technology (27).

In addition, fifty-one students were working for M.Phil. degrees while another twenty-one were pursuing for Doctorate in various disciplines.

Funding: Besides the limited finances generated by the University itself, it is supported by the government of Bangladesh from revenue and development budget without direct financial support from OIC. From time to time the vice-chancellors of this university have been invited to attend the OIC conferences.[14]

The 4th and 5th Islamic Summit Conferences commended the efforts of Bangladesh for the establishment of the University, and requested the member states, the ISF, and all specialized institutions of the OIC to extend material and moral assistance to this project. Since the occasional assistance from the IDB and the ISF has not been sufficient; the onus has remained on the host government.

Research and other facilities: The University has a big Library and many well-equipped science laboratories. Each department has got the facility for conducting research pertaining to the subject, by the teachers as well as the students registered for Ph.D. and M.Phil. degrees. The Islamic University's Faculty of *Shari'ah* comprising the departments of

- *Al-Quran wa Ulum al Quran* (Quran and Quranic Studies)
- *Ulum al Tawheed wa al Da'wa* (Studies of Oneness of God and of Preaching) is very active in research of Islamic law.[15]

The University is taking pains to inculcate the Islamic spirit in the students of other disciplines, as well. The curricula of the Faculty of Humanities and Social Sciences, which is the largest Faculty, comprising the departments of Accounting, Management, Economics, Public Administration, and Islamic History and Culture, have been Islamized. Furthermore, a subject on the Fundamentals of Islam and functional Arabic language, has been made compulsory for the students of this Faculty.[16] In the near future, the University wants to raise the number of Faculties to eight. Hence, it has made plans to open three new Faculties in near future, namely, the Faculty of Islam & Comparative Religion, the Faculty of Medical Science, and the Faculty of Agriculture.[17] The following address may be contacted for information regarding admissions etc:

Deputy Registrar (Academics)
Islamic University of Bangladesh
Kushtia
Bangladesh.

II. International Islamic University of Malaysia

The First World Conference on Muslim Education, held at the holy city of Mecca in 1977, was a landmark in many ways.[18] The Islamic University of Malaysia is also a brainchild of that conference. It was established in 1983 and was co-sponsored by the OIC. Besides the host state, which bore the bulk of the expenditure of the $330 million project[19], seven other Muslim states financed the establishment of this university and are represented on the Board of Governors (see below). Initially, the Malaysian government offered the old complex of Muslim College of Malaya, at Petaling Jaya, a satellite town to the south-west of capital Kuala Lumpur, to the IIUM, which still houses the main campus of the University.[20] The permanent campuses are under development at Combak, near Kuala Lumpur, and Kuantan, on the east coast of peninsular Malaysia.[21] The first batch of 153 students graduated in 1987. Now the University produces 3000 graduates annually.

Objectives: The University regards knowledge as 'a trust from Allah to be utilized in accordance with His guidance to serve for the welfare of the universe'. The quest for knowledge, therefore, is regarded as 'an act of worship' by the IIUM. The University strives to 'combine the ideas of material progress with the spiritual needs of the individual and society'.[22]

As is well-known that South East Asia is one of the three regions with the heaviest Muslim concentration in the world (the other two are the Middle East and South Asia); the University aims at becoming the principal institution of Islamic learning for the South East Asian region, and wants to impart education in various disciplines, in an Islamic ambience.

Administrative Structure: The constitutional head of the University is HRH Sultan Haji Ahmad

Shah al-Musta'in Billah, ruler of the state of Pahang. The Right Honourable Anwar bin Ibrahim, the Deputy Prime Minister and Finance Minister of Malaysia, is the President of the University. Below him is the Rector of IIUM, two Deputy Rectors (one each for Academic and Student Affairs), and two Directors for Finance and Management Services Divisions, respectively.[23]

- *Board of Governors*: The fifteen-member Board decides the general policies of the University and is chaired by the President of the University.[24] Its Vice-Chairman also comes from Malaysia. The seven sponsoring states of Bangladesh, Egypt, Libya, Maldives, Pakistan, Saudi Arabia and Turkey, and the host state Malaysia, are represented by one member each. The Secretary General of the OIC, a representative of the Board of Trustees, and the Rector, and two Directors of the University are *ex-officio* members.
- *University Majlis (Council)*: It consists of the IIUM President, the Rector, two members representing the host state, one member each representing Egypt, Libya, Saudi Arabia, and Turkey, and two representatives of the University Senate, as well as a Secretary.[25]
- *University Senate*: The University Senate consists of twelve members.[26] The Rector and two Deputy Rectors are *ex-officio* members while the remaining nine are nominated from amongst eminent academicians, educationists, and professors.

Faculties, Departments, and Degrees: The Malaysian Islamic University has five Faculties that offer thirty-eight Masters and Bachelor degrees and graduate diplomas in all. In addition, some departments also offer research degrees such as Doctorate of Philosophy and Master of Philosophy.[27]

i) *Faculty of Law*: The Faculty offers Doctor of Philosophy in Law; Master of Comparative Law; Bachelor degrees in Law, and in Law and *Shari'ah*; Diploma in Law and Administration of Islamic Judiciary; and Diploma in *Shari'ah* Law and Practice.
ii) *Faculty of Economics and Management*: Master of Economics and Bachelor degrees in Accounting (B.Acc.), Business Administration (B.B.A.), and Economics (B. Econs.) are offered by this Faculty.
iii) *Faculty of Islamic Revealed Knowledge and Human Sciences*: This is the largest Faculty of the

University, offering the widest range of degrees. Its Masters Programmes include those in Arabic Language, English Language, Education, Islamic Revealed Knowledge and Heritage, and Library and Information Science. It offers Diplomas in English, Islamic Studies, and Education. Bachelor of Human Science degree is awarded in nine disciplines, namely, Islamic Revealed Knowledge and Heritage, Arabic Language and Literature, English Language and Literature, Communication, History and Civilization, Political Science, Psychology, Sociology and Anthropology, and Philosophy.

iv) *Faculty of Engineering*: At the moment, there is no Masters programme in this Faculty. Computer and Information, Manufacturing Systems, and Mechatronics are the three disciplines, in which Bachelor of Engineering degrees are conferred.
v) *Faculty of Medicine*: This is a recent addition in the IIUM's profile. The Board of Governors and the University Senate approved the intake of the first batch for undergraduate degree in Medicine, in the academic year 1997–98.

Currently there is a student body of about 7000 undergraduates and 600 postgraduates, which include around 1000 international students representing 173 countries.[28] The Faculty of 500 or so, is a distinguished group of scholars from different Muslim countries.

Funding: At the time the University does not receive direct assistance from the OIC. The University partially generates its funds through course fees. Each student to about US $2000 for an academic year excluding living expenses. The operating budget is, therefore, provided by Malaysia.[29] The University also receives some assistance from the seven sponsoring states. The 21st ICFM (Karachi; 1993) requested the IDB, ISF, and the member states to extend all financial, material, and other relevant assistance such as providing teachers, scholarships, etc., to the University, to contribute to its development and progress, and to enable more students to pursue their studies at the IIUM.[30]

Research and Other Facilities at the University: The Research Centre conducts and manages the research activities of the University. The Main Library, and two smaller ones (Matriculation and

Education Libraries) have a combined dealing capacity of 1475 users at a time and have a collection of hundreds of thousands of books and CD-ROMs, and on-line databases.[31] The University has a Language and Academic Development Centre, Information Technology Services Centre, and several Computer Centres. In addition to health, financial, and student affairs services, the University's Students Representative Council (SRC) runs more than fifty clubs and societies under its umbrella. For enquiries and information about admission, the following address can be contacted:

Admission and Records Division
International Islamic University Malaysia
P. O. Box 70, Jalan Sultan
46700 Petaling Jaya
Selangor Darul Ehsan, Malaysia.

III. Oum Al-Qura University of Niger

The 2nd Islamic Summit (Lahore; 1974), proposed the creation of the Islamic University of Niger, with a view to responding to the needs of the Muslim populations in West Africa. The 8th ICFM (Tripoli; 1977) allocated $10 million for the construction of the two Islamic Universities, the other one in Uganda.[32] The work on the project started soon thereafter. The 13th ICFM (Niamey; 1982) was held in the capital of Niger. The ICFM appealed for financial assistance for the under-construction university and many countries pledged donations for the same.[33] The ICFM was told that the university would cost around $60 million, but it appears that the full amount could not be realized. Hence not all the proposed departments and facilities could be built.[34] The one-third of the $31.2 million actually spent on the University was paid by the government of Niger while the rest was contributed by the ISF and several OIC member states.[35] The Statute of the University was approved by the 15th ICFM (Sana'a; 1984). The Oum al-Qura University of Niger was inaugurated in November 1986.

Administrative Structure: Under the Statute, the University administrative structure is composed of two organs:[36]

- *Administrative Board*: The Administrative Board lays down the general policy of the University and takes all decisions necessary for the implementation of its objectives. It also deals with the academic, administrative, and financial matters and appoints the Rector of the University. The Administrative Board meets once a year and comprises fifteen members including four members appointed by the Government of Niger; the Chairman of the Permanent Council of the Islamic Solidarity Fund; the Secretary General of the OIC; four members appointed by the OIC Secretary General from among men of letters and scientists of the Islamic world, regardless of their nationalities; three members appointed by the Administrative Board from among Muslim candidates proposed by French-speaking African States; the Rector of the University, and one representative of the Faculty proposed by the Executive Board.

- *Executive Board*: Under the Statute, the Executive Board which is responsible for the day-to-day business of the University, is composed of the Rector of the University (Chairman), two Vice-Rectors, all the Deans of Faculties and the Treasurer of the University. At present, the provisional Executive Board, in place, is comprised of the Rector of the Islamic University, the Rector of the University of Niamey, and the OIC Secretary General.

Academic Activity: No information from any source was available on the number of Faculties and departments, degrees offered, current enrolment, or the research activities being undertaken by the Islamic University of Niger. It is, however, clear that since the University was established for the francophone Muslim countries of West Africa, the bulk of its enrolment comes from those countries, and that several departments should deal with the teaching of Islamic history, culture and law.[37] Prospective students may, however, correspond with the following address for prospectus /admission form etc:

Rector,
Islamic University, SAY,
P.O. BOX 11507
Niamey, Niger.

IV. **Islamic University in Uganda**

The 2nd Islamic Summit Conference (Lahore; 1974) decided to establish this University to cater for the needs of the Muslim populations of Central and East Africa.[38] The decision was inspired by the realization that the Muslim minorities in Africa had limited educational opportunities and were therefore lacking in professional and academic preparation. Out of the two proposed Islamic universities, the Islamic University in Niger was mainly for the French-speaking countries of Africa, while the Islamic University in Uganda was meant mainly for the English-speaking countries in the continent.

Following the decision of the 8th ICFM (Tripoli; 1977), construction work started as late as in the early eighties.[39] The 13th ICFM (Niamey; 1982) called for financial support for the ongoing construction of the two universities.[40] The Islamic University in Uganda was inaugurated in February 1988. It is located in the Mbale Municipality in Mbale District. The town is about 250 kms from the capital Kampala, to the eastern part of the country.

Objectives: The Islamic University in Uganda was established with the following mission as stipulated in the University Statute:[41]

* To function as an academic and cultural institution within the OIC in accordance with its Statute;
* to promote and enhance the civilization and scientific influence of Islam, to promote culture and science among African peoples, and to contribute to rapport and solidarity between such peoples;
* to give special care to Islamic studies and research, teach Arabic, spread Islamic culture in African countries;
* to enable African countries to assimilate science and technology to acquire scientific and technological know-how and to use it in the best interests of African countries and their peoples;
* to train adequate manpower and secure the necessary methods for higher education, scientific research, and advanced studies in the various fields of knowledge;
* to promote cultural, sports, social, and scientific activities within the University; and;
* to award its own degrees, diplomas, certificates and other academic awards.

Administrative Structure: The University is made up of the following organs that initiate, formulate, and implement University policies and resolutions:[42]

* *University Council*: The University Council, the institution's supreme authority, is composed of sixteen members, five of whom are nominated by the Ugandan Government. Another five are appointed by the OIC Secretary General from amongst the academic and scientific personalities of the Muslim world, regardless of their nationalities. The remaining six are *ex-officio* members including the OIC Secretary General or his representative, the Chairman of the ISF Permanent Council or his representative, the Chairman of the Supreme Council of Uganda Muslims or his Assistant, the Rector, Registrar, and the Secretary of the University. Also known as the Board of Trustees, this Council elects its Chairman and meets once a year. The current Chairman of the Council is Sheikh Jassim al Hijji of Kuwait. The Council lays down the policy of the University and takes all decisions necessary for the implementation of the said objectives. It deals with academic, administrative and financial matters of the University and appoints the Rector for a five-year, renewable term.
* *Executive Board*: The Executive Board is responsible for conducting the day-to-day administration of the University, particularly the academic activities. It is chaired by the University Rector. Its other members are the two Vice Rectors, the Academic Registrar, the Deans of Faculties, Heads of Departments, Faculty representatives, the Bursar, the Coordinator, the University Engineer, the University Librarian, Directors of Institutes, the University Medical Officer and the University Secretary. The Executive Board may, from time to time, initiate policies and submit to the Council proposals for the budget of the University.
* *Rectorship*: The Rectorship is made up of the University Rector, the Vice-Rector for Academic Affairs, and the Vice-Rector for Finance and Administration. The Rector is the chief executive of the University.
* *Council Committees*: The University Council has established three committees for the smooth operation of the University. These are: the Finance and Tender Committee; Estates, Planning, and Development Committee; and the Appointments and Disciplinary Committee.
* *Academic Staff*: The academic members of the University are Professors, Associate Professors,

Senior Lecturers, Lecturers, Assistant Lecturers, Teaching Assistants, and their various equivalents in the research area.

Faculties, Departments, and Degrees: The University admits both male and female students from English-speaking African countries. Under special circumstance, the University may enrol a few students from other OIC countries or French-speaking African countries.[43] The following are the Faculties, Departments, and Courses of Study at the Islamic University in Uganda:

i) *Faculty of Islamic Heritage*: The Faculty has four departments including the Department of Arabic Studies, the Department of Islamic Studies, the Department of *Shari'ah*, and the Department of Sociology and *Da'wa*. The former three offer B.A. Hons. degrees in the respective subjects while the last one has B.Sc. Hons. in Sociology.

ii) *Faculty of Education*: It consists of the Department of Curriculum and Instructions, the Department of Educational Planning and Administration, the Department of Educational Psychology, and the Department of Foundations of Education. The Faculty awards B.A. and B.Sc. Honours in Education. The students may select any two subjects from the other Faculties as their teaching subjects. The Faculty of Education conducts and awards a Post-Graduate Diploma in Education for individuals holding a B.A. or B.Sc. degree. The Faculty also conducts a concurrent Diploma in Education, for University Students enrolled in the B.A./B.Sc. undergraduate programmes at IUIU.

iii) *Faculty of Science*: It is composed of the Department of Mathematics and Statistics, Department of Physics, Department of Biological Sciences (Botany, Zoology, and Microbiology), Department of Chemistry and Biochemistry, and the Department of Computer Science. In all, the Faculty offers B.Sc. (Hons.) degrees in the following fields: Mathematics, Statistics, Physics, Botany, Zoology, Microbiology, Chemistry, Computer Science, and Biochemistry.

iv) *Faculty of Arts and Social Sciences*: The Faculty has six departments, namely, Department of History; Department of Geography and Environmental Studies; Department of Languages, Literature, and Linguistics; Department of Political Science; Department of Mass Communication; and the Department of Economics. The Degree programmes offered in this Faculty include B.A.

Hons. in History and Languages (English/French/Swahili/Luganda/Hausa/English Literature); and B.Sc. Hons. in Geography, Political Science, Environmental Studies, and Economics.

v) *Faculty of Management Studies*: The two departments of this Faculty, Department of Business Studies and the Department of Public Administration, respectively, offer Bachelor of Business Studies (B.B.S. Hons.) and Bachelor of Public Administration (B.P.A. Hons.) degree.

All the Bachelors degree programmes in the University last for a period of three years. Each Faculty is administered by a Dean and the Heads of the Departments. All students enrolled in the Faculty of Education undergo a programme of School Practice in the second and third year. Those enrolled in Public Administration, Business Studies, and Mass Communication have to undertake an Internship programme.

Funding: Islamic University in Uganda is a cost-sharing University. All students are required to pay US$900 per annum for Bachelors degree and diploma courses and US$1500 per annum for Remedial courses and Masters and Doctorate degree courses.[44] Students also meet all personal expenses for their studies. The University is unable to provide any allowances for students. The funds generated by the University are insufficient. Hence the Islamic University in Uganda is being run mainly on funds obtained through grants from the OIC sources and through donations from individuals and organizations. The University requests donations from the states and individuals.[45] The contributions can be sent to the Rector, Islamic University, P. O. Box 2555, Mbale, Uganda.

Research, Training, and Other Activities: The University conducts a one-year Remedial Programme for students whose primary and secondary school education is based on the twelve-year system. At the end of the year, the students take an examination that is equivalent to the 'A' level. Those who pass, enrol for degree programmes in different Faculties.[46] The University Council decided that the vocational training courses in Carpentry at the Institute of Vocational

Training of the University would start from 1997. Admission is open to all members of the public. Plans were made to start vocational courses in Metal work, Tailoring, and Typing in the course of the same year. The University is also making arrangements to start short-term courses in Computer Science and Applications.[47]

Since, like its sister Islamic universities, the Islamic University in Uganda also wants to become a seat of higher learning, it is working to launch postgraduate taught and research degrees. As a first step, the University decided to start Masters degree programmes from October 1996, in Arabic and Islamic Studies only. However, now other Departments are also being encouraged to start postgraduate programmes in the near future.[48] The groundwork for initiation of Doctorate degree programmes based on research and thesis, though only in Arabic Studies and Islamic Studies for the time being, has been completed and the first intake would be in 1998. Other departments will follow suit in due course. The University Council has also approved the horizontal expansion of IUIU's academic activities. Four new Faculties are to be established in the near future under the plan. They are the Faculties of Agriculture, Law, Medicine, and Engineering and Technology.[49]

The observance of ethics and moral values has always been the cornerstone of IUIU's academic milieu. Alcohol is forbidden. Similarly, smoking in public is also prohibited. For all enquiries on admission, contact:

The Academic Registrar,
Islamic University in Uganda,
P.O. Box 2555, Mbale, Uganda.
Tel: (045) 33502.

NOTES and REFERENCES

1. It has to be clarified here that two most prestigious Islamic universities, namely, Al-Azhar University at Cairo, Egypt, and International Islamic University at Islamabad, Pakistan, are not affiliated with the OIC, as is sometimes erroneously believed. Nevertheless, the successful experience of running universities under the OIC framework has led to the proposals for setting up of more universities and for bringing all the existing Islamic Universities of international character,

including these two, under the OIC umbrella. A serious effort towards the implementation of such ideas is yet to take place.

2. Noor Ahmad Baba, *OIC: Theory and Practice of Pan-Islamic Cooperation*, (Karachi: Oxford University Press, 1994), p. 144.

3. See paragraph 107 of the final declaration of the 11th ICFM (Islamabad; 1980) in 'OIC: Declarations of Islamic Summits and ICFMs held in Pakistan', (Islamabad: Directorate of Films & Publications, Government of Pakistan, 1993). p. 49.

4. Abdullah Ahsan, *OIC: Introduction to an Islamic Political Institution*, (Herndon: IIIT, 1988),p. 105.

5. A prominent example of OIC-sponsored colleges is the American Islamic College, Chicago, USA. The Secretary General of the OIC holds *ex-officio* chairmanship of the Board of Trustees of the College. See *Speeches and Statements of Sharifuddin Pirzada*, (Karachi: OIC, 1989), p. 52.

6. Quite a few of the projects failed to take off in the first place. For instance, when this author visited the Allama Iqbal Open University, Islamabad, where the proposed Regional Institute for Complementary Education (RICE) was supposed to be located, he found out that as of early 1998 it had not been established. Likewise the fate of some other similar bodies is not known.

7. Though we have incorporated all the four universities in one chapter, but actually the former two are independent universities under the sponsorship of the OIC, while the latter two are considered subsidiary organs of the Organization. The difference lies in the mode of funding as the former are independently financed while the latter receive direct subsidies from the OIC budget.

8. See the undergraduate prospectus (1996) of the University, p. 3.

9. The author wants to acknowledge with gratitude the information provided by the University. In fact, it was the only institution within the OIC framework that took the trouble of providing para-wise response to the author's questionnaire, instead of sending printed brochures of general nature. Deputy Registrar's letter (vide no. 59/Aca/IU-97/484, dated 15 January 1997) enclosed a fact-sheet about the University. All information given in this section, unless mentioned otherwise, is based on that fact sheet.

10. The OIC Secretariat Publication, 'Guide to the OIC', (Jeddah: OIC, 1995), p. 79.

11. Fact-sheet, ref. 9, p. 1.

12. Ibid., p. 2.

13. Ibid.

14. Ibid., p. 3.

15. OIC Guide, ref. 10, p. 79.

16. Ibid., p. 80.

17. Fact-sheet, ref. 9, p. 3.

18. The Public Relations Office of the University (vide letter No. IIU.1.1/PRO/33, dated 20 January 1997) accepted the request of the author and despatched the IIUM Undergraduate prospectus (1996). The information given in this section, unless otherwise stated, is based on the prospectus.

19. OIC Guide, ref. 10, p. 80.

20. Prospectus, ref. 18, p. 3.

21. The two sites are spread over 288 and 400 hectares respectively. See ibid., p. 3.

22. Ibid., p. 1.

23. Ibid., p. 231.

24. Ibid., p. 232.

25. Ibid., p. 233.

26. Ibid., p. 234.

27. For details about course requirements for each degree, see ibid., pp. 55–209.

28. Ibid., p. 3.

29. Ibid., pp. 53–54.

30. OIC Guide, ref. 10, p. 81.

31. Prospectus, ref. 18, pp. 7–19.

32. Keesing's Contemporary Archives, 1977, p. 28556.

33. *The Muslim*, Islamabad, 25 August 1982.

34. *Dawn*, Karachi, 28 August 1982.

35. OIC Guide, ref. 10, p. 74.

36. Ibid.

37. The University did not respond to the repeated requests by this author for information. No related information from any secondary source was available either.

38. The author wants to acknowledge the University Secretary's letter No. IU/OIC/18/1, dated 13 January 1997, along which the brochure *Islamic University in Uganda; Basic Information 1996–97* was sent. The information in this section, unless mentioned otherwise, is based on the said brochure.

39. Keesing, ref. 32, p. 28556.

40. *The Muslim*, 25 August 1982.

41. *Basic Information on IUIU*, ref. 38, pp. 2–3.

42. Ibid., pp. 4-6. Also see 'OIC Guide', ref. 10, pp. 76–77.

43. Details taken from *Basic Information on IUIU*, ref. 38, pp. 7–11.

44. Ibid., p. 7.

45. Ibid., pp. 12–13.

46. Ibid., p. 11.

47. Ibid., p. 12.

48. Ibid., p. 11.

49. Ibid.

⒀ Affiliated Institutions

To date, there are eight, relatively autonomous pan-Islamic institutions that are affiliated to the OIC. They cannot be called the subsidiary organs of the OIC, in the strict sense of the word, since these bodies are basically the groupings of entities, national institutions, or legal persons belonging to the Muslim countries. For instance, the Islamic Chamber of Commerce and Industry is a union of the Muslim countries' respective chambers of commerce, the Islamic Solidarity Sports Federation is a federation of National Olympic Committees of the member states, and so on. They are established through the resolutions of, either or both, the Islamic Summit Conference and the ICFM, and usually enjoy observer status at the OIC and some of its organs. Their budgets are independent of the budgets of the OIC General Secretariat or its specialized or subsidiary organs, though, they may receive subsidies from the OIC or the Islamic Solidarity Fund.[1] These institutions aim at forging cooperation among the institutions of the Muslim countries working in a related field. They are:[2]

I. Islamic Chamber of Commerce and Industry at Karachi, Pakistan.
II. Islamic Solidarity Sports Federation at Riyadh, Saudi Arabia.
III. Organization of Islamic Capitals and Cities at Mecca/Jeddah, Saudi Arabia.
IV. Islamic Committee of the International Crescent at Benghazi, Libya.
V. Organization of the Islamic Shipowners Association at Jeddah, Saudi Arabia.
VI. World Federation of International Arabo–Islamic Schools at Jeddah, Saudi Arabia.
VII. International Association of Islamic Banks at Jeddah, Saudi Arabia (also at Cairo, Egypt).
VIII. Islamic Cement Association at Ankara, Turkey.
IX. Islamic Women's Association.
X. Islamic Union of Legislative Assemblies.

Besides the eight institutions already established, the formation of two more affiliated institutions, namely, the Islamic Women Association and the Islamic Union of Legislative Assemblies, is in the offing. Considerable homework has already been done, but since both were the initiatives of a former government of Pakistan, they received a setback on the dismissal of the PPP regime in Pakistan.

I. Islamic Chamber of Commerce and Industry (ICCI)

To promote trade and industry among the Muslim states, the 7th ICFM (Istanbul; 1976) put forward the idea of creating an Islamic Chamber of Commerce and Industry. It was approved by the first meeting of the Chambers of Commerce and Industries of the member-states of the OIC held in Istanbul in October 1977, on the initiative of the Turkish Union of Chambers of Commerce and Commodity Exchange. It was during the second such meeting of Chambers of Commerce of Islamic states held in Karachi in December 1978 that the Constitution of the proposed Chamber was approved. Consequently, the 10th ICFM (Fez; 1979) endorsed the establishment of the Islamic Chamber of Commerce, Industry, and Commodity Exchange (ICCI and CE) as an affiliated body within the OIC framework. Its headquarter is located at Karachi, Pakistan.[3]

Objectives
The Islamic Chamber was created to work for the following objects:[4]

- To develop cooperation among its members and other similar institutions in the Islamic World.
- To encourage trade, industry, agriculture, and handicrafts.
- To propose economic policies advantageous to its members and create avenues for the collaboration amongst its members and similar organizations throughout the Islamic World in their efforts for economic development.

- To make recommendations to safeguard economic and business interests of the Islamic World, and adopt collective measures which may include economic boycott against any party that commits aggression against any of the Islamic countries.
- To promote cooperation between the Islamic Chamber on the one hand and other international, commercial, industrial, and agricultural organizations on the other.
- To encourage member countries to give preferential terms of trade to each other.
- To promote investment opportunities and joint ventures among the member countries.
- To further develop cooperation in the fields of banking, insurance, re-insurance, shipping, and other means of transportation within the Islamic World.
- To provide for arbitration in the settlement of disputes arising out of commercial and industrial transactions between parties who are willing to abide by the judgment of the Islamic Chamber.
- To organize trade fairs, joint showrooms, exhibitions, seminars, lectures, and publicity campaigns as and where may be thought advisable.
- To promote the exchange of commercial, technical, industrial management, and scientific information, education, and know-how amongst its members.
- To undertake all other efforts that are likely to promote the aims and objectives of the Islamic Chamber.
- Finally, to strive towards the gradual realization of the Islamic Economic Community.

Membership and Organizational Structure: The Islamic Chamber is composed of national chambers or federations of chambers of Commerce and Industry, or similar institutions existing in the member countries of the OIC. A state is entitled to only one institution as member of the Islamic Chamber. Currently all the OIC members are represented at the ICCI. The Chamber of Economy of Bosnia and Herzegovina enjoys an observer status since the Bosnian State is an observer at the OIC.[5] Its structure is composed of three bodies:

General Assembly: It is composed of delegates duly appointed by the Chambers of Commerce of the member states. It meets once a year in an ordinary session and elects the Chairman/Vice-chairman at the beginning of each session.[6] It is the supreme authority of the Chamber. Its functions include determining the general policy and work

programme of ICCI, approval of new admissions or the termination of membership, adoption of budget, and election of the nineteen members of the Executive Committee.

Executive Committee: The nineteen members elected by the Assembly, for a three-year tenure, elect from amongst themselves a President and six zonal vice-presidents.[7] The ICCI Secretary General and a representative of the OIC Secretary General are *ex-officio* members of the Executive Committee. It is responsible for implementation of the decisions of the General Assembly. The President is authorized to sign all documents on behalf of the Islamic Chamber and to take decisions in matters of urgency, with the concurrence of at least three vice-presidents. In addition, the Executive Committee also comprises of the following committees:

i. Financial Control Committee
ii. Financial Committee
iii. Islamic Chamber's Council for Textile (ICCT)
iv. Council for Islamic Chamber Arbitration Rules

As stipulated in its Statute, the Textile Council of Islamic Countries (TCIC) shall endeavour to contribute and coordinate the efforts of the member states in attaining close cooperation in the field of textile industry and work for maximum utilization of their resources and potential in this sector, with the ultimate objective of attaining their collective self-reliance in the textile industry. The Council shall work for the development of the textile industry in the member states by providing sound counsel for the development of their textile industry and shall protect the collective interests of the member-states in International fora, dealing with textiles, by negotiating with regional and international trade organizations, on behalf of its members.

General Secretariat: The General Secretariat at the Islamic Chamber is headed by a Secretary General appointed by the General Assembly, in accordance with the recommendations of the executive Committee for a term of four years which may be renewed once only.[8] The Secretary General is responsible for the working of the

General Secretariat. It is financed through the contributions of commercial chambers that are ICCI members.

Functions of the Islamic Chamber:[9] The ICCI Statute delineates the following functions for it:

- Providing guidance to businessmen and industrialists in identifying joint venture projects within the framework of priority areas defined by OIC Industrial Ministerial Consultations and Summit Conferences.
- Sending of Economic Delegations to member countries, with the object of helping businessmen bridge their information and communication gap and to have a first hand knowledge about the socio-economic potential of such countries.
- To organize private sector meetings, aimed at bringing the representatives from the private sector in the forefront for strengthening economic cooperation among member countries.
- To organize training programmes for the staff of member chambers and business organizations, in order to enhance their skills and expertise, to better perform their tasks and functions.
- Working towards the expansion of intra-Islamic trade by disseminating information on trade opportunities and by providing the members a Wide Area Computer Network with all trade and industry related information.
- Helping project sponsors from member countries in identifying cooperation partners from other member countries and in the preparation of feasibility reports.
- Coordinating with Islamic and other international financial institutions for the technical and financial assistance to be provided to feasible and agreed joint venture projects.
- Providing arbitration and reconciliation facilities for satisfactory settlement of trade misunderstanding and disputes.
- Encouraging the exchange of expertise and the transfer of technology among Islamic countries.

Activities and Future Outlook: The ICCI has the honour of being one of the very few institutions, under the OIC framework, to have an impressive performance to its credit. Though, the major constraint of the Chamber has remained the paucity of funds at its disposal, primarily due to the non-payment of member chambers' annual subscriptions; it has, nevertheless, emerged as a potent institution.[10] The Chamber has been doing

useful work by gathering and disseminating information about various aspects of the working of the economies of Islamic states as well as the products, marketing techniques, and transport facilities in these countries with a view to seeking ways and means of more effective and useful cooperation among them. For instance, it regularly publicizes the names of trading companies engaged in the import and export business within the member states, gathers statistics about the nature of the import and export trade of the Islamic states and the companies involved in it, and organizes trade fairs and exhibitions. In order to encourage joint ventures it makes feasibility studies and identifies projects that may be undertaken.[11]

The Islamic Chamber recognizes that the Muslim world accounts for 40 per cent of world export of raw materials but the volume of trade in the member states is around 13 per cent only. The Chamber aims at rectifying the situation by undertaking trade promotion activities. For the dissemination of trade information, there is a publications unit. Within this context, the Islamic Chamber publishes a quarterly magazine titled, *Perspectives on the Islamic Economy*, which covers information on the investment climate, potential markets, and trade inquiries. In addition, the Islamic Chamber has also set up its own data base, consisting of information on trade in general, exports/imports statistics, country profiles, information on industry, agriculture, textile technology and other related data, for the benefit of the business community. As part of its future plan of action, the Islamic Chamber is also working to link its computer network with other Islamic countries and international institutions and thereby establish a Wide Area Network for quick and timely exchange of information.[12] In addition, training programmes are being held according to the Plan of Action for the Islamic Chamber, approved by the twelfth ICCI General Assembly meeting, held in Tunisia in 1994. The Islamic Chamber has started holding private sector meetings following a mandate given by the ninth session of the Standing Committee for Economic and Commercial Cooperation of OIC Countries (COMCEC) in 1993. The first such meeting was held at Istanbul (October 1994). The 2nd, 3rd, 4th, and 5th private sector moots were organized at

Cairo (October 1995), Jakarta (October 1996), Karachi (October 1997) and Beirut (October 1998), respectively. Concurrently, the Islamic Chamber has been successfully holding Islamic trade fairs. By the end of 1998, six such fairs had been held; the last one at Jakarta during 22–27 October 1996.

Each of these moots and fairs is showing better and more positive results, which is manifested by the number of countries participating and the business transactions that have been conducted. The 3rd Private Sector Meeting, for instance, was attended by 400 delegates from thirty-one member countries, the OIC, and its institutions. There was also a strong participation from the ex-Communist Muslim Republics, namely, Azerbaijan, Kazakhstan, Kyrghyzstan, Turkmenistans and Uzbekistan. In addition, representatives from Albania, Bosnia-Herzegovina, and some Muslim Associations from non-Islamic countries, such as Muslim communities in the Philippines and the USA also participated.[13]

Business contacts were made between entrepreneurs from thirty-one Islamic countries and financial institutions. Within the context of trade, business transactions to the tune of approximately US$200 million were discussed in the areas of textile, foodstuffs, ready-made garments, polypropylene bags, chemicals, and leather. In addition, the Islamic Development Bank also agreed in principle, to provide training, financing and technical assistance for the preparation of feasibility studies for about twenty-five projects from Chad, Mali, Niger, Pakistan, Senegal, Sierra Leone, and Turkey.

The preliminary estimates have shown that a total of seventy-five projects were identified by the Islamic Chamber from thirteen OIC member countries, totalling an investment cost of approximately US$554 million, of which forty projects amounting to US$238 million had had initial agreements. In addition, twenty-eight Memorandums of Understanding (MOUs) were also signed between the Project Sponsors and Cooperating partners. Projects mentioned above covered the areas of food processing leather and leather products, textiles; chemical industries, such as cement, petro-chemicals, fertilizers, pharmaceuticals; engineering and metal working.[14] The extent of cooperation is not only limited to equity

participation but also includes supply of equipment, technical know-how, marketing, joint venture, constancy, training, and the preparation of feasibility studies as the case might be. At the end of the meeting, the Bandung Economic Declaration was issued containing eighteen recommendations which were then submitted to the 12th session of the COMCEC for consideration.

On the sidelines of the 3rd Private Sector Meeting, the Islamic Chamber also organized an Investors Services Workshop in coordination with the World Bank Group of Multilateral Investment Guarantee Agency (MIGA) and a presentation by the Islamic Corporation for Investment and Export Credits. The Corporation's objectives are to enlarge the scope of trade transaction and the flow of investments among member countries of the OIC, by providing export credit and foreign investment insurance, in accordance with the principles of *Shari'ah*.

Likewise, the 4th ICCI Private Sector Meeting (Oct.1997), attended by 500 delegates from forty Muslim countries, proved to be equally successful. The moot approved 154 projects worth $16.013 billion and the ICCI took it upon itself to make efforts for the implementation of all the joint venture partnerships. The IDB agreed to finance seventeen of the projects, needing $3.025 billion to kick-start. The beneficiaries for the seventeen projects were Bangladesh, Iran, Kazakhstan, Pakistan, Suriname, Tajikstan, and Turkey.

The twenty-one-point Declaration released at the conclusion of the private sector moot called for the establishment of an Islamic Common Market and Free Trade Zones, conclusion of bilateral agreements, and for minimizing the adverse effects of the WTO-proposed Customs Union. The Declaration exhorted the Muslim-owned multi-national corporations to raise investments for partnership ventures.

As a result of the Plan of Action for the Islamic Chamber approved by the 12th meeting of its General Assembly held in Tunisia in 1994, the Islamic Chamber has also undertaken various practical activities designed to generate more interaction and understanding among businessmen and industrialists from Islamic countries. In this connection, the First Islamic Chamber Economic

Delegation visited the West African region namely Niger, Burkina Faso, and Mali in December 1994. The Second Islamic Chamber Economic Delegation visited Gambia, Guinea, Senegal, and Sierra Leone in December 1995. The third Economic Delegation was scheduled to visit some of the Central Asian Republics in 1997. The objective of these Economic Delegations is to hold bilateral and multilateral contacts with the businessmen of these countries and to discuss avenues and areas of cooperation.[15]

Like the other organs of the OIC, the Islamic Chamber comes to the rescue of needy Muslim countries. In pursuance of the directives of the Assistance Mobilization Group (AMG) for Bosnia, the Islamic Chamber held a meeting with the Bosnian Chamber of Commerce and Industry in May 1996.

The report prepared thereafter underlines the need of a private sector in Bosnia-Herzegovina for rehabilitation of their industries. Accordingly, the Islamic Chamber, at the initial stage, noted that the Bosnia-Herzegovina Chamber requested assistance for rehabilitation of four industries; textile and garments, footgear, building materials, and furniture making. The details about the specific nature of assistance required a simplified Feasibility Report of these projects that has been requested from them. In the light of their response, further progress in providing assistance will be taken.[16]

Another achievement of the Chamber is the establishment of its Arbitration Council. Realizing the fact that arbitration of trade and industry-related disputes lends more confidence and stability to international trade, the Islamic Chamber has formulated its rules and regulations for Arbitration.[17]

The ICCI cooperates with a number of international institutions like UNIDO and the Islamic Development Bank. The IDB approves financing a large number of joint venture projects, that are initiated by the Chamber.[18] A recent example of cooperation between the IDB and ICCI is the joint seminar held in December 1996 at Karachi on 'Support Services for Small and Medium Enterprises (SMEs)'. The seminar was attended by many experts from ICCI/IDB member countries who highlighted their views on the role

of small and medium enterprises in OIC member states and the need of support services for these enterprises in the areas of management, marketing, technology adaptation, and financing.

The seminar concluded that such enterprises were proving highly effective in generating income and employment for their managers and owners. Moreover, as SMEs operate through labour intensive technologies, substantial opportunities for labour absorption are created for semi-skilled and unskilled manpower. The chief representative of Kazakhstan, an ex-Soviet Muslim state, informed the delegates that her country had a huge and fully developed infrastructure but in the absence of expertise in open market economy and lack of knowledge about modern banking, Kazakhstan was facing a lot of hardship in developing trade relations with Pakistan and other Muslim countries.

A number of innovative ideas have emanated from such ICCI seminars and meetings. The Islamic Chamber floated the plan for an Islamic Free Trade Area (IFTA) in 1993.[19] The following year it proposed a reduced tariff schedule recommending an upper limit of 20 per cent for the duties levied on imports and exports from the Muslim countries.[20] The ICCI is steadily marching towards its ultimate goal of an Islamic Common Market in an Islamic Economic Union.[21]

II. Islamic Solidarity Sports Federation (ISSF)

The 11th ICFM (Islamabad; 1980) first discussed the holding of mini-Olympics for the Muslim countries and decided to constitute an institution for the purpose.[22] The ISSF came into existence by virtue of resolution No.17/11-C of the 11th ICFM. This resolution was endorsed by the 3rd Islamic Summit (Taif; 1981) through its resolution No.7/3-C, which called for the organization of sports tournaments among the OIC member countries, and for the formation of a body responsible, for the management of such tournaments.[23] It was later decided that the Muslim countries' Olympics would be called Islamic Solidarity Games, and will be held every four years on the pattern of the international Olympic games. In pursuance of the directives of the Islamic Summit, the OIC General

Secretariat in collaboration with the Saudi Arabia's General Presidency of Youth Welfare, made preparations for the constituent meeting of the Federation.[24]

The constituent conference of the Islamic Solidarity Sports Federation was held during 6–8 May 1985 at Riyadh. Representing thirty-four of the forty-four member states of the OIC at that time, eighty-one delegates participated in the conference, that adopted the Statute and elected Prince Faisal bin Fahd of Saudi Arabia, as the first chairman of the ISSF Executive Council. The meeting decided to make Riyadh the ISSF headquarter, though, the seat may be transferred to any other member state, provided that the ISSF General Assembly makes the decision with a majority.[25]

Objectives: Article 4 of the ISSF Statute declares that the objectives of the Federation are[26]:

- To strengthen Islamic solidarity among youth in member states and promote Islamic identity in the fields of sports.
- To inculcate the principles of non-discrimination as to religion, race, or class, in conformity with the precepts of Islam.
- To reinforce the bonds of unity, amity, and brotherhood among youth in member states.
- To make youth in member states aware of the objectives of the OIC.
- To unify positions in Olympic International and continental conferences and meetings and to cooperate with all the international and continental sports bodies and organizations.
- To promote cooperation among member states on matters of common interest in all fields of sports activities.
- To preserve sports principles and to promote the Olympic sports movement in the Muslim world.

The 5th Article of the Statute goes further to elucidate the means to be adopted for achieving the above objectives.[27] These are: (a) to supervise the Islamic solidarity games to be held once every four years; (b) to frame rules and regulations for such games; (c) to facilitate the exchange of bilateral visits between sports teams in member states; (d) to train and develop sports cadres in member states; (e) to provide the member states with all possible facilities and technical assistance in order to develop their establishment with a view to raising the standard of sports, and (f) to convene conferences and symposia in furtherance of the Federation's objectives.

Membership and Structure: The National Olympic Committees or the official sports authorities in the member states of the OIC, which attended the Constituent Conference (Riyadh; 1985) are the founder members of the Federation and the National Olympic Committees or other competent authorities in the OIC member states have the right to be affiliated to the Federation.[28] The Federation comprises of a General Assembly, an Executive Committee and a General Secretariat.

General Assembly: It is composed of the representatives of the National Olympic Committees of member states of the Federation as well as the members of the Executive Committee of the Federation.[29] Each state has one vote though it can send as many as three representatives to the General Assembly meeting. Ordinarily, the General Assembly meets once every two years, and requires the presence of a simple majority of the members for the meeting to be valid. Before concluding, the General Assembly is also supposed to finalize the date and venue of its next regular session.

There exists a provision for convening an extraordinary session of the ISSF General Assembly, on the request of the Executive Committee, or that of one member supported by one-third of total membership. The ISSF Assembly may in its discretion, invite some national and international sports institutions of Muslim youth organizations to attend a session as observers. The General Assembly is authorized to approve the general policy and plans of the ISSF, endorse the work and approve the budget, evaluate the performance of the Federation, select the venue for the Islamic Solidarity Games each time, and to amend the Statute.

Executive Committee: The fourteen-member ISSF Executive Committee, elected by the General Assembly through secret ballot for a four-year tenure, is composed of a chairman, three vice-chairmen (one each from Asia and Africa and the third from the country hosting the next Islamic Solidarity Games) and seven members, in addition to the Secretary General and Treasurer of the ISSF, who are *ex-officio* members, and a representative of the OIC General Secretary (without the right to vote).[30] No single state may be represented on the Committee by two members. The Committee meets annually in a regular session and is chaired by the Chairman who represents the Federations before the official and non-official quarters. The Executive Committee conducts the administrative and financial affairs of the ISSF, implements the General Assembly decisions, supervises the games and competitions conducted by the ISSF, prepares the annual activity reports and budget estimates, and appoints the Secretary General and his staff.

Secretary General: As the head of the ISSF Secretariat, the Secretary General is supposed to conduct all Federation activities and affairs to ensure their sound functioning in all respects, to keep files and records of the meetings, supervise the implementation for Executive Committee decisions, and to keep the liaison with the OIC General Secretariat.[31]

Finances: The fiscal year of the ISSF is the Islamic (lunar) year. Its activities are financed by:[32] (a) Admission and annual subscription fees; (b) a certain percentage of the revenues of sports competitions and games, organized and supervised by the Federation among member states, to be fixed by the Executive Committee; (c) revenues from TV broadcasting, sponsorships, and commercial advertising; (d) donations and grants from governments of OIC member states; (e) annual subsidies by the OIC and the Islamic Solidarity Fund, and (f) any other revenues, donations, or grants from individuals or institutions, subject to approval by the Executive Committee. The Statute stipulates that any state that does not pay the subscription for two consecutive years, will lose its voting rights at the General Assembly till the clearance of the outstanding dues.

Activities and Future Outlook: The very absence of any dynamic role by the ISSF is a textbook case of the problems being faced by other bodies and institutions affiliated with the OIC. The financial crisis and the lack of interest by the member states are the two major hurdles towards progress. In the first ten years since its inception, the ISSF received US$187,820 out of the expected $500,500 from annual subscriptions, i.e. just over one-third of the amount due.[33] The total subsidy received from the OIC Secretariat and the Islamic Solidarity Fund during the same period was just $30,000. Since the other sources of revenue envisaged by Article 40 of the Statute remained dry, the ISSF could manage an income of just around $20,000 per annum. This money was far from being sufficient for the payment of salaries to the Secretariat staff, let alone organizing a mini-Olympic for fifty-five countries every fourth year. It has barely survived through some donations by scions of the Saudi royal family. The second hurdle, no less significant, is the lack of interest by the members. Many states do not turn up in General Assembly meetings, fail to send nominations for the ISSF training courses and do not respond to the ISSF correspondence. In these circumstances, the ISSF performance is understandably poor.

Taking note of the difficulties being faced by the Federation, resolution No.5/6 of the 6th Islamic Summit (Dakar; 1991) called for the setting up of an experts committee to make recommendations on the matter. The Committee, comprising Sports experts from thirteen member states, which was formed shortly thereafter, met in January 1993 at the ISSF headquarters.[34] It came to the conclusion that the Federation could not fulfil the huge responsibilities entrusted to it, unless the member states respected their obligations towards it. The 7th Islamic Summit (Casablanca; 1994) adopted the recommendations of the experts' committee. While requesting the members to honour their commitments, the Summit asked the ISSF to organize regular quadrennial tournaments, even for one or two sports.[35] Resolution No.34/23-C of the 23rd ICFM (Conakry; 1995) made similar recommendations.[36]

A brief resumé of the ISSF activities in 1995–96 includes the hosting of Bosnia's football team in September 1995. The team played four matches with Saudi Arabia in different cities of the kingdom and the entire proceeds of the matches were donated to the government of Bosnia.[37] The same year, the ISSF secretariat, in coordination with bodies concerned, finalized the regulations of the proposed Islamic Solidarity Games and also the administrative and financial regulations of the ISSF.[38] In March 1996 and September 1996, the ISSF participated in the 5th session of COMIAC and the twentieth session of the Islamic Commission for Economic, Social, and Cultural Affairs, respectively. On the directive of Prince Faisal, the Federation is providing assistance to Bosnian sports and sportsmen. The ISSF has also prepared the draft agenda for the First Islamic Conference of Ministers of Youth Affairs of the OIC member states, to be organized by the OIC General Secretariat. The ISSF also decided to hold three training courses in administration of sports events. For the first course (Jan. 1997), only eighteen countries sent nominations, so the number of participants was twenty-seven.[39]

For the future, the ISSF has a very ambitious plan. Subject to the availability of resources, it wants to hold a number of courses on sports medicine, athlete performance, and the like, arrange international Muslim youth camps and youth festivals in member states, organize seminars and symposia for greater bilateral and multilateral cooperation in the field of sports, and last but not the least, to organize Islamic Solidarity Games every four years.[40] In this respect, it would be advisable that the ISSF does not restrict the participation in its Solidarity Games to OIC member states only. It would be better, to allow every country of the world to send teams, provided a simple majority of the athletes belongs to the Muslim faith. Such a step will truly internationalize the sports gala, increase revenues for the Federation and encourage the Muslim minority communities to excel in sports, and at the same time, be party to an event for Islamic solidarity. With the initiative of Pakistan and later Iran, the first and second Islamic Solidarity Women Games have been held at Islamabad (1996) and Tehran (1997) respectively. It appears that they were held outside the ISSF framework. If the OIC succeeds in devising a mechanism for generating sufficient funds for the Federation, it can still play a role to keep the ball rolling by conducting the Women Games as well as larger events, regularly.

III. Organization of Islamic Capitals and Cities (OICC)

The idea of establishing an Organization of Islamic Capitals and Cities (OICC) was first floated at the fourth meeting of the Arab Towns Organization (Baghdad; April 1974), which decided to constitute delegations of Arab Mayors to visit the Islamic capitals for the purpose. The delegations met with encouraging response from Ankara, Istanbul, Jakarta, Kabul, Kuala Lumpur, and the other Islamic capitals they visited. So the fifth meeting of the ATO (Rabat; June 1977) finalized a summary of proposals and sent it to the Secretary Generals of the OIC and the Muslim World League.

On the recommendation of the OIC Secretariat General, the establishment of the Organization was approved by resolution No. 9/9-C adopted by the 9th ICFM (Dakar; 1978). A meeting of the representatives of the Islamic capitals (Mecca: April 1979) approved the draft of the Statute of the Organization that was then endorsed by the 10th ICFM (Fez; 1979).[41] The first Constituent Conference at the holy city of Mecca, attended by the Mayors of the Islamic capitals, formally established the OICC on 30 January 1980. The conference elected the first Secretary General and the Administrative Council. Egypt, Libya, Oman, and Saudi Arabia announced donations for the formative expenses of the new Organization.

The holy city of Mecca was declared as the permanent seat of the OICC, while the Secretariat was to be located at Jeddah. In 1990, an architectural competition for the designing of the new Secretariat building was held and architect Ja'afar Toquan of Jordan was declared the winner. Through the contributions of the Muslim states, the building was constructed. The OICC has now shifted to its new premises; the impressive edifice is a masterpiece of Oriental Islamic architecture.

Objectives: The aims of the Organization are:[42]

- To strengthen the bonds of friendship, brotherhood, and solidarity among Islamic capitals and cities;
- To develop cooperation among the Islamic capitals and cities, and to preserve their character and the Islamic heritage;

- To promote public service through the exchange of visits, research studies and expertise, among the Islamic capitals and to achieve a wide scope for interaction in the cultural, social and construction planning fields;
- To organize conferences, to discuss projects of interest to the capitals in the Islamic world, and to propose suitable solutions in the form of recommendations; and
- To seek to implement comprehensive urban, architectural plans which may guide the growth of Islamic capitals and cities in accordance with their actual economic, social, cultural, and environmental characteristics.
- To upgrade the public services and utilities in the Islamic capitals and cities.

Membership: Membership is open to all capitals of the member states of the OIC. The cities of Mecca, Medina, and Jerusalem are permanent members due to their holy status. Membership in the Organization of Islamic Capitals and Cities is open to a maximum number of eight cities from every Islamic country in addition to the member Capital City.[43]

Membership is open to Islamic capitals and cities situated in the non-OIC Muslim countries and even to the non-Muslim countries, provided that Article 1 and 3 of the Statute of the Organization of Islamic Capitals should apply. In all, 130 cities from fifty-eight countries are members of the OICC. Egypt, Morocco, Tunisia, and Turkey are represented by the maximum-allowed eight cities each, Saudi Arabia by six, Jordan by five, Palestine and the UAE by four each, Syria by three, Iraq, Libya, Niger, North Cyprus, Senegal, Uzbekstan, and Yemen by two each, and Lebanon, Mali, Nigeria, and Oman by one city each, besides obviously their capital cities. The remaining thirty-four states are represented by their capital cities only.

Togo is the only OIC member state, whose capital is not a member of the OICC. Two observer states at the OIC, Bosnia and North Cyprus, have their cities on the OICC rolls. The capitals, Grozni and Kazan, of the breakaway Russian Muslim Republics of Chechenya and Tartaristan have also joined this Organization. In addition, several Islamic historical cities in the non-Muslim states such as Granada in Spain and Silves in Portugal enjoy an observer status.

Structure and Finance: The Organization of the Islamic Capitals has five organs:[44]

- *General Conference*: The General Conference is the supreme authority of the Organization. It defines the goals and draws up plans and policies of the Organization. It consists of governors and mayors of the member capitals and cities. It meets once every three years. A simple majority of the members constitutes the quorum and the mayor of the host capital presides over its sessions.
- *Administrative Board*: It is also known as the Board of Directors. The Administrative Board is responsible for following-up and implementing the decisions and recommendations of the General Conference. It is composed of the representatives of Mecca, Medina, and Al-Quds al-Sharif as permanent members, and eighteen members to be elected by the General Conference every four years in addition to the Secretary General of the Organization and the member capital or city which hosts the session if it is not a member of the Administrative Board. It used to meet once every six months but now with an amendment in the rules, it is to meet once a year.
- *General Secretariat*: It is the executive organ of the Organization. It is headed by a Secretary General who is elected by the General Conference for a renewable period of four years. The General Secretariat staff carries out all technical, administrative, and financial work of the Organization, and reports it to the Administrative Board and the General Conference. The Secretary General represents the Organization in the international meetings, conferences, symposiums, and seminars. He is assisted by the ASG (Technical Affairs), the ASG (Members and Organizational Affairs), the Director General (Administration), and a few Directors, heading the respective departments. The staff at the Secretariat has a multi-national composition.
- *Cooperation Fund of the Islamic Capitals and Cities*: The Centre which is located in Cairo, Egypt, is designed to assist the municipalities in the Islamic capitals and cities, in development schemes. It provides financing for maintenance and preservation of the Islamic architectural heritage, and for research and training of the municipal officials.
- *Training and Development Centre for Islamic Capitals and Cities*: This Centre, also located at Cairo, Egypt, aims at providing training and development to the municipalities of Islamic capitals

and cities. It provides opportunities to the city administrators and officials to improve their skills and to keep abreast of the latest developments in the local government systems.

The Organization is financed through contributions by the member states' capital cities as well as through donations.

Activities: The major problem with the OICC, as with all the other OIC institutions, is the penurious condition of its kitty. However, the OICC has employed its limited resources to the best of its capacity.[45]

The Organization holds various exhibitions that demonstrate its achievements or the successful works of the competitions organized by it. It participates in different exhibitions and book fairs held in the Muslim capitals and cities to introduce itself and to promote Islamic publications.

Another major activity is the organization of conferences of Mayors and Governors of the Islamic capitals and cities. Over fifteen such moots have been held so far, which have helped the Islamic cities' administrators to benefit from each others' experiences. These meetings result in joint declarations, signing of protocols for cooperation between the capitals, and the symbolic gestures of declaring two Islamic capitals as twin cities. Other heads of the OICC activities warrant separate treatment.

Information and Training: The OICC has maintained a well-stocked Information Centre, a library, and a databank. All these sources are continually updated by information on the history, culture, architecture, and the statistics of the Islamic capitals and cities. The OICC library has a valuable collection of books, atlases, maps, charts, brochures, photographs, and microfilms on the Islamic capitals and cities. There is also sufficient material available there on urban and town planning in general, sustainable development, and road traffic management, etc.

The OICC supplies the member cities with the required information. It has also launched a web page on the Internet <www.oicc.org> to facilitate easy access of the information to the people. The Organization encourages exchange of bilateral visits of the Mayors of the Islamic cities to each other's places. It also arranges the exchange of research material on urban affairs, produced by one city or the other. The Cairo Centre conducts training programmes for urban administrators.

Analytical Studies: The Organization of Islamic Capitals undertakes analytical studies of historical cities, jointly with the local governments of the cities concerned. Three major research projects on the urban architectural designs and city expansion through the ages on Cairo (1994), Baghdad (1996), and Damascus (1997) were successfully completed. Now the OICC has targeted six more cities known for their Islamic architectural grandeur. They are: Bukhara (Uzbekistan), Fez (Morocco), Isfahan (Iran), Lahore (Pakistan), and Tunis (Tunisia). Preliminary negotiations for the purpose are underway with the Governorates and the concerned departments of the cities.

A parallel exercise of the OICC towards studies on the cities is through conferences and symposia. The first seminar was on housing in an Islamic city (Ankara; 1984), the second on Urban Cleanliness and Environmental Protection (Cairo; 1986), the third on Fundamentals of Numbering and Naming Streets (Amman; 1989), the fourth on Islamic Methodology on Urban Design (Rabat; 1991) and the fifth one was on Road Safety and Accident Reduction (Ankara; 1993). Then there were a large number of seminars on the history and problems of specific cities, so the list is quite long.

Publications: The OICC has a long list of publications to its credit. It brings out a periodical named *Islamic Capitals and Cities*, around thirty volumes of which have been produced so far. The magazine contains reports about the OICC activities, tour of an Islamic historic city, articles on town planning, and separate sections on environmental and developmental studies.

The OICC has produced many books. First of all, the proceedings of all the symposia and seminars, mentioned in the last section have been published in book form with the same titles. Likewise, the reports of analytical studies on Islamic cities have also been published. In addition, many other research volumes like *Principles of*

Architecture Design and Urban planning, *Local Administration and Municipal System*, *The City of Bukhara,* and *The City of Khawarzim* are the notable OICC volumes. Work is in progress on some other books as well.

The OICC Awards: Since 1988, the OICC has announced awards for writings in four disciplines; (a) Islamic Architecture; (b) Urban, City, and Service Planning; (c) Municipal Services; and (d) Municipal Management, Organization, and Legislatures.

The first winner in each category receives a Shield of the first rank, a certificate of honour, and $6600 as cash prize. The runners up receive the Shield of second rank and a certificate. These awards are meant to encourage and reward quality research on urban affairs. The nineteenth OICC Administrative Council meeting (Casablanca; August 1996) approved four new awards of the same denominations on carrying out practical improvements in the cities. The new awards on (e) Architectural Establishments; (f) Beautification of the Cities; (g) Urban Development and Renewal; and (h) Protection of Environment, are shared by the owners, contractors, or the artists, as the case may be.[46]

Important Projects of the Cooperation Fund: The OICC has financed the restoration of historical buildings in its member cities, through its Cairo-based Cooperation Fund. Ashrafiya school building in Jerusalem (Palestine), Beer ul Ahjar school building in Tunis (Tunisia), and the Ahmad historical monument in Lefkosa (North Cyprus) are some buildings, whose restoration work was conducted by the OICC. Construction of an OICC monument at the Alexandria International Park (Egypt) and supply of maintenance equipment of the historical quarters in Damascus City (Syria) are the other notable activities of the OICC Fund. As a matter of policy, 25 per cent of the Fund's annual revenues are allocated to supporting the cultural, educational, and health services in the holy city of Jerusalem.

Cooperation with other Institutions: The OICC maintains a close liaison with the subsidiary organs of the OIC and the Arab League. It has signed

agreements with the Arab Towns Organization (ATO), Union Towns Organization (UTO), International Union of Local Authorities (IULA), Association of Major Metropolis (METROPOLIS), and many other organizations. The list of joint programmes, exchange of information and participation in each other's conferences on reciprocal basis, is very long and such events run into hundreds.

IV. Islamic Committee for the International Crescent (ICIC)

The Islamic Committee for the International Crescent is a specialized institution of the OIC. It helps to alleviate the sufferings caused by natural disaster and war. The 10th ICFM (Fez; 1979) approved the creation of this commission as an Islamic alternative for the International Committee of the Red Cross (ICRC). Its headquarter is to be located in Benghazi, Libya.[47]

Objectives: This organ is designed to:[48]

- Provide medical assistance and alleviate the sufferings caused by natural catastrophes and man-made disasters.
- Offer all necessary assistance within its power, to international and local organizations, serving humanity.

Administration and Finance: The Committee is administered by an Executive Committee headed by its Chairman.[49] The funds of the Committee consist of contributions and donations from member states of the OIC as well as donations and income from its own resources.

Activities: The Charter of ICIC required ratification by at least ten member states of the OIC, for it to come into operation.[50] Till December 1998, the ICIC Executive Committee had held ten sessions in the cities of Benghazi, Jeddah, Ankara, Bamako, Amman, Riyadh, Istanbul, Casablanca, and Tehran. The meetings chalked out the plans of activities. The ICIC kept a high profile in relief operations in the famine-stricken countries of Djibouti, Mali, and Sudan in Africa. The ICIC, in cooperation with the Red Crescent Society of Turkey, sent relief aid to the Bulgarian Muslims. In a joint operation with the Iranian Red Crescent Society, the Commission sent succour to the earthquake victims in North West Iran.

During the initial years, the operating budget of the Commission was being provided by Libya. Now, the host state itself is beset with serious problems owing to the international sanctions, and other countries are lax in paying their contributions, so the ICIC appears to be in hibernation and its activities have been substantially reduced.[51] That is why, the OIC has been obliged to invite the International Committee of the Red Cross (ICRC) to act as its surrogate in taking care of the prisoners of war (POWs) in the Iran-Iraq war.[52] The OIC had also considered the establishment of an Islamic Relief Organization but that idea too has not materialized yet.[53] The Red Crescent Societies of Muslim States like Pakistan, Oman, etc. are national institutions and have no association with the ICIC. It may be noted that the symbol of Red Crescent signifies the same things in Muslim states as does the Red Cross sign in the rest of the world.

v. Organization of the Islamic Shipowners Association (OISA)

At the beginning of the1980s, the negotiations at the Law of the Sea Convention had entered the final stages. The Muslim leadership felt the need for an Islamic body for maritime cooperation. Strictly speaking, the factors that prompted them to study the feasibility of OISA included the making of such an Association as a factor of economic linkages and cooperation among the Muslim countries, breaking the monopoly of foreign shipping companies, consolidating the rights of sea transport for the Muslim countries; coordinating the efforts of members in realizing cooperation among the shipping companies; and finally, employing as many Islamic ships as possible in international sea trade, thus employing Islamic labour and utilizing its maximum potential.[54]

Resolution 5/10-E of the 10th ICFM (Fez; 1979) and resolution 5/11-E of the 11th ICFM

(Islamabad; 1980) emphasized the need for establishment of OISA for the foregoing reasons. The 3rd Islamic Summit (Taif; 1981), by virtue of resolution 4/3-E(IS) approved the Statute of the Association and called upon the member states to cooperate with the Association to enable it to achieve its objectives.[55] The head office of the Association was decided to be in Jeddah, Saudi Arabia. Through the Royal Decree No.M/50, King Khalid of Saudi Arabia approved the Statute in May 1982, and the Association was formally set up.[56]

Objectives: Article V of Section II of the OISA Statute has defined its objectives as the following:[57]

- To coordinate and unify the efforts of the members in realizing cooperation among the maritime companies in member states, to maximize profit.
- To encourage members to set up joint maritime companies and shipping lines between member states.
- To establish contact between the Islamic world and other countries within an integrated maritime network.
- To develop periodical and regular freight and passenger voyages between Islamic and other countries.
- To assist in drawing up a unified policy for the Islamic maritime transporters; and
- To conduct studies and research in the various disciplines of maritime transport.

Membership: The membership of the Association is open to:[58]

- Maritime transport companies engaged in the field of international trade, or similar associations registered in one of the OIC member states.
- Every company enjoying the nationality of one of the Muslim states and owning no less than 70 per cent of the total shares.
- All nationals of the OIC member states, having a stake of no less than 51 per cent in the capital of a maritime company, on condition that the representative of the company is a Muslim.

As of late 1997, twenty Muslim states were members of the Association. In all, forty-three shipping companies belonging to these states, had joined the OISA. Eight companies each were registered in Saudi Arabia and Egypt, while four were based in Kuwait. Bangladesh, Pakistan, and Turkey were represented by three shipping companies each. The remaining fourteen companies belonged to the other Muslim states.[59]

Structure and Finance: The Association has three organs:[60]

- *General Assembly*: It is composed of all the active members of the Association. It meets once a year.
- *Executive Committee*: The Executive Committee consists of fifteen members. The General Assembly elects twelve members on the basis of geographical distribution, for a three-year mandate. The OISA Secretary General and one representative each of the General Secretariats of the OIC and the Islamic Chamber of Commerce, Industry, and Commodity Exchange (ICCI&CE) are *ex-officio* members of the Executive Committee, without voting rights.
- *Secretary General*: The Islamic Shipowners Association is headed by a Secretary General, elected by the General Assembly for a three-year period.

The Association is funded by fixed admission fees, annual subscriptions and subsidies, grants and donations, and income from service rendered.

Activities: The Association claims[61] that it shall:

(a) organize maritime conferences for member states
(b) develop periodical and regular feight and passenger voyages between parts of Islamic states
(c) assist in drawing a unified policy for Islamic maritime transporters
(d) make suggestions to and advise member states on management and development of maritime codes
(e) conduct studies and research in relevant disciplines, and
(f) provide technical and other assistance to Muslim states in the area of maritime safety, marine pollution and laws of the sea.

In 1994, the OISA decided to establish an Islamic Shipping Company with a capital of $100 million. It was initially to have a fleet of four cargo ships or tankers (costing $8–12 million each) and was to be registered in Liberia or Cyprus or any other free-flag country. The Naval Research Centre of the Naval Academy at Alexandria, Egypt, was entrusted with the task of preparing a study on the project. The OISA is still short of the required money.

The second major project, also costing an estimated $100 million, was the setting up of an information Centre at Jeddah. Two Iranian shipping companies volunteered to provide the finances for the proposed Centre. The project of collection of data on the fleet, like their tonnage and capacities, owned by the Muslim states or persons, and the compilation of information on the trade and shipping rules and prices and brokerage systems in the OISA member states is nearing completion. A third major project of the Association, that of setting up an Islamic Insurance Company, is currently in the final stages of planning.[62]

It may be noted that no less than forty of the fifty-five Muslim states are littoral states. Ninety per cent of their international trade is maritime and foreign/non-OIC ships conduct a further 90 per cent of it. The only body in the field of marine navigation needs to be fully activated, as it will boost the trade between the OIC member states. A recently floated proposal is to convert OISA into a Federation of Islamic Ship Owner companies (FISO).[63]

VI. World Federation of International Arabo–Islamic Schools (WFIAIS)

The Federation's constituent conference was held in March 1976 at Riyadh. The project had been approved a little earlier by the 7th ICFM (Istanbul; 1976).[64] The Federation represents the Arab–Islamic Schools all over the world and seeks to support and assist them. The headquarter of the Federation is situated in Riyadh, while its central administration is in Jeddah near the OIC General Secretariat. The Federation also maintains an efficient Research and Studies Centre.

Objectives:
The Federation of Arabo–Islamic Schools seeks to:[65]

- Act as an umbrella for the vast network of Islamic Schools.

- Support and assist, financially and otherwise, the Islamic schools particularly those in non-Muslim countries.
- Work for the dissemination of Islamic culture and the teaching of Arabic language, by supporting the Islamic schools and cultural centres, and training personnel therein.
- Develop cooperation among the institutions endeavouring to spread Arabic language and Islamic culture.
- Create a supervisory body for Arab and Islamic schools.

Lately, the Federation has also considered the implementation of uniform syllabi and a joint examination system for the Muslim schools.

Membership: The membership of the Federation consists of the Arab Islamic schools spread throughout the world; the private institutions which establish, run and supervise these schools and cultural facilities; and the representatives of the states who offer technical, financial, and material support to these schools.[66]

Structure and Finance: The Federation has a three-tier structure:[67]

- *Federation's Board*: The Board is made up of representatives of national and regional federations representing the schools, and the Directors of member institutions or their accredited representatives. It is convened once every two year.
- *Federation's Bureau*: It consists of five members, elected by the Board of the Federation.
- *Chairman*: The chief executive of the Board is the Chairman, who is assisted by a Vice-chairman. Both are elected for a three-year renewable term. A Secretary is also appointed, on the Chairman's recommendation.

The Federation is financed through members' subscriptions, donations, and the assistance offered by official institutions, non-governmental organizations, and individuals.

Activities: No information is available about the activities of the Federation; nor did the Federation respond to this author's request for activity reports.

VII. International Association of Islamic Banks (IAIB)

The International Association of Islamic Banks was founded under the auspices of the OIC on 21 August 1977. Its General Secretariat is located at Cairo, Egypt.[68] The fundamental objective of the Association is to augment and enforce the ties and links amongst Islamic financial institutions and promote intra-cooperation and coordination. It is also designed to ascertain the institutions' Islamic observance and character in order to achieve their common and mutual goals. At present, twenty-eight financial institutions from eleven countries are its members.

Objectives
The IAIB has the following aims:[69]

- Promoting the concept and ideas of Islamic banking.
- Coordinating with Islamic banks to resolve common conceptual and operational problems including standardization of operations and application of Islamic *Shari'ah*.
- Undertaking/facilitating research and development in Islamic economics.
- Providing assistance in manpower development.
- Maintaining databank of all Islamic financial institutions.
- Providing technical assistance in Islamic banking.
- Representing, mediating, and acting as arbitrator for and between Islamic banks.
- Representing the common interests of the Islamic banks at the national and international levels.

Organization and Finance: The IAIB pursues its objectives through four main organs, namely, General Assembly, Board of Directors, General Secretariat, and the Supreme *Shari'ah* Board.[70]

- *General Assembly*: The General Assembly of IAIB is composed of representatives, one each from every member bank. It sets the general direction of the IAIB policies.
- *Board of Directors*: The Board is elected by the General Assembly and is responsible for the operations of the Association.
- *General Secretariat*: The Cairo-based General Secretariat represents the executive branch of IAIB and is headed by a Secretary General.

Supreme Shari'ah Board: It consists of the Heads of *Shari'ah* Boards of Islamic financial institutions. The Association is entitled to invite other prominent Islamic *Shari'ah* scholars to be members of this Board if deemed necessary.

The primary sources of financial support for the Association are the membership fees from the respective institutions. The Association encourages donations from parties that support its cause and objectives.

Activities: The meetings of the IAIB General Assembly provide opportunities to the representatives of different Islamic Banks to interact with each other. This promotes cooperation in the Islamic financial institutions.[71] The Association also gives technical assistance to member banks. Its research activities include maintaining a database of Islamic financial institutions as well as holding seminars on Islamic banking. An IAIB seminar in April 1997 at Karachi deliberated upon the feasibility of setting up a model Islamic bank, strictly operating on profit-loss sharing basis, under the Islamic laws.[72] The speakers pointed out that such a bank could not operate in an alien environment. So the reformation of society for correct ethics and morals, restructuring of economic system, and re-framing of laws according to the dictates of Islam were prerequisites for successful implementation of an Islamic banking system.

VIII. Islamic Cement Association (ICA)

The Islamic Cement Association was founded in 1984. Its major objective is to encourage cooperation among the Muslim countries in the production of cement.[73] Its headquarter is located within the head office building of the Turkish Cement Manufacturer's Association (TCMA) at Ankara, Turkey. Established in 1957, the TCMA is basically a private umbrella organization for the Turkish cement industry.

Functions and Activities: Besides administering the cement fund and controlling the selling price of cement, the Association carries out the following functions:[74]

- Maintains international ties with the world's cement manufacturers' union.
- Trains personnel of Turkish and developing countries' cement sectors.
- Carries out basic and applied research for the cement sector.
- Acts as information centre for technical data and information.

It appears that the Islamic Cement Association is not very active and most of the activities referred to above, are carried out under the framework of TCMA, rather than the ICA, as the Ankara office acts as the head office of both.[75] The OIC Secretary General has not appointed the Director General of the ICA. No specific administrative structure exists for the Association.

ix. Islamic Women's Association (IWA)

The suggestion to establish an Islamic Women's Association first came up during the 14th ICFM (Dhaka; 1983) on Pakistan's proposal.[76] The Pakistani representative alluded to the need to dispel misconceived notions propagated 'by the forces inimical to Islam' about the 'place and status of women in an Islamic society'.[77] The conference constituted a thirteen-member expert committee to consider the establishment of an international forum for Muslim women. The Association was to serve as a nucleus for interaction between Muslim women belonging to different cultures and backgrounds. It was to conduct research on the condition of women in Muslim societies and to focus on remedial measures by fighting for the rights that Islam gives to women. But no practical steps were taken for the next few years.

The experts' committee took a long time to meet and then consumed some more years to agree on a draft Charter for the Islamic Women Association. The same was reviewed by the OIC Legal Affairs Department and ultimately the Secretariat General put its stamp of approval on it. The draft was presented before the 21st ICFM (Karachi; 1993) for adoption. The ICFM accepted all the recommendations and formed another committee to oversee the implementation.

By the end of the 1980s, the Soviet empire was crumbling and a wave of democratization swept over the world. The Muslim states could not remain aloof, and political liberalization started in a number of them. Women won the right to contest the elections in many Arab countries around that time. In recent years, a number of women candidates have run for parliamentary seats in Jordan, Morocco, Oman, Syria, etc. Though few have been returned but the trend has been set. In 1988, Benazir Bhutto, the daughter of the slain Prime Minister Zulfikar Ali Bhutto, romped home in multi-party elections in Pakistan, becoming the first ever woman to democratically rule a Muslim country. Turkey and Bangladesh followed suit when Mrs Tansu Ciller and Mrs Khalida Zia took over as Prime Ministers.

Several events took place during 1995–97, which are important steps towards the establishment of IWA. During her second term in office, Prime Minister Benazir Bhutto took the initiative of convening the first-ever Muslim Women Parliamentarians Conference.[78] The Conference took place in the first week of August 1995 and was attended by 118 women parliamentarians from thirty countries, though Mrs Zia and Mrs Ciller remained conspicuous by their absence.[79] The Conference established the Islamic Women Parliamentarian Association (IWPA) and elected an Executive Committee for the nucleus secretariat of IPWA.[80] Later, Ms Fizza Jonejo, a member of the upper house of the Pakistani parliament, was elected the President of the Follow-up Committee. Accepting the offer of the representative of Malaysia, the Committee decided to hold the second moot of IWPA in Malaysia.[81]

The following year, that is, in 1996, the Benazir government took another major initiative to hold the first-ever Muslim Women Sports Festival in Islamabad. It was attended by women athletes from nine Muslim countries including Bosnia, Bangladesh, some ex-Soviet Muslim republics, and the host state, Pakistan. The Pakistan government had decided to host a bigger event in 1997, to coincide with the golden jubilee celebrations of the establishment of Pakistan. The 1996 sports event was actually the rehearsal for a bigger event next year. By the time twenty-eight Muslim countries had confirmed participation in the proposed Muslim women sports gala (1997), the Benazir Bhutto government had already been dismissed in November 1996 by the then President of Pakistan for domestic political reasons. With the fall of the government, the plan to hold the event in Pakistan was also shelved.[82] The second Islamic Women Games were duly held on schedule when Iran offered to host them. Just one day after the 8th Islamic Summit concluded, the Games were inaugurated in Tehran on 12 December 1997, where Pakistan was represented by a strong contingent of eighty-three women athletes.

The third milestone on the road towards the establishment of IWA was the holding of the first Islamic Women Gathering in early 1997 at Nias City, Senegal.[83] The agenda was Muslim Woman's Role in Reviving and Supporting Sufi Centres. The conference was organized by the Call of Islam Society and the Muslim Women Society of Senegal. Though the conference was outside the ambit of the OIC and did not address the broader issues concerning the Muslim woman, the very holding of the first international conference of Muslim women is a step in the right direction.

In autumn 1997, the International Union of Muslim Women Non-Governmental Organizations (NGOs), concluded its meeting in Tehran, and recommended the formation of an Islamic women's organization within the framework of the OIC. The Union also sought permanent observer status at the OIC meeting.[84] At the 8th Islamic Summit (Tehran; 1997), the host state Iran put forward a proposal to establish an OIC Women Wing and the Conference adopted a draft resolution to that effect. Addressing a press conference in Tehran, on the eve of the Summit, the Iranian woman representative at the OIC experts committee preparatory meeting, Fatima Hashemi said that the formation of an international Muslim Women Organization would be an effective measure to present the Islamic view of women and their rights, to the world.[85] A number of Muslim states supported Iranian proposals. At the time of writing, the IWA is yet to be set up, though paper work for the purpose is being done.

x. Islamic Union of Legislative Assemblies (IULA)

We noted in the last section that Pakistan took the initiative to hold the first Muslim Women Parliamentarians' Conference that was held in August 1995 at Islamabad. The Conference had faced some problems since it failed to adopt a common agenda for the UN-sponsored International Conference on Women that was to take place in Beijing, China, a few months later.[86] It was also criticized by the Revolutionary Association of the Women of Afghanistan (RAWA) for ignoring the plight of Afghan women, who were being denied basic rights under the rules of fundamentalist Islamic parties.[87] Nevertheless, the Conference was a good start, so far as it had led to the establishment of IWPA and had deliberated not only upon the role of Muslim Woman but also on the broader issues concerning the Muslim world. In its final declaration, it had called for immediate lifting of 'unjust' sanctions against the 'Muslim States of Iraq and Libya'.[88]

Establishment: The idea of this Union had first been floated at the 83rd conference of the International Parliamentary Union (IPU), held at Nicosia (South Cyprus) in 1990. Encouraged by the good response that the Islamic women's parliamentary initiative had received, the then Speaker of the National Assembly of Pakistan, Yousaf Raza Gillani decided to actively pursue the idea of an Islamic Union of Legislative Assemblies (IULA). The Muslim states used to have an Islamic parliamentary group, comprising twenty-one of the IPU's membership of 112 states, in the six-monthly IPU conferences. The Group had its own chairman and it used to coordinate the policies of the Muslim states at the Union. But Gillani proposed that the Muslim states ought to have a separate parliamentary union.

He sent summaries of the proposal for the establishment of the Union to the Speakers and Chairmen of the legislative bodies of OIC member states.[89] Many countries supported the idea and a thirteen-member organizing committee consisting of, Bangladesh, Indonesia, Iran, Libya, Malaysia, Morocco, Palestine, Saudi Arabia, Sudan, Syria, and Turkey, besides Pakistan, was formed. The second meeting of the Committee held at Tehran, Iran, on 22–23 October 1996, found that there was a unanimity of views on the necessity of having an Islamic Parliamentary Union, among the participating states. Iran proposed that the Statute of the Union should be adopted by the beginning of 1997.[90] Pakistan's offer to host the first-ever Islamic Countries Speakers' Conference in Islamabad between 25 February and 5 March 1997, to coincide with its golden jubilee celebrations, was endorsed by the Committee. Pakistan's Minister of State for Works, Afaq Shahid, who had led the country's delegation at the Tehran meetings said that Speaker Yousaf Raza Gillani had been striving for the establishment of this union for the previous three years and had contacted all the Muslim countries in this regard, and gained success. He said the services being rendered by OIC for the Muslim *ummah* were laudable and now establishment of this Union would prove to be a great help in understanding and solving the problems of the *ummah*.[91]

Expressing appreciation and gratitude to the parliamentary delegations attending the meeting, he hoped the Islamabad Speaker's Conference would adopt the Statute of the Union and the hosting of the Conference would be an honour for Pakistan. The Minister further observed that various proposals from different Islamic countries aimed at promoting meaningful cooperation among parliaments of Islamic countries, would also be considered in detail. The occasion would also provide a timely opportunity for coordination among the parliaments of Islamic countries on issues to be taken up at the forthcoming IPU meeting in Seoul. A call was made at the 8th Islamic Summit (Tehran; December 1997) for proceeding ahead with the establishment of the IULA. Tehran then hosted a three-day founding conference of IULA in Tehran from 15 June 1999, attended by forty-nine of the fifty-five OIC member states. This meeting marked the founding of the Union by adopting the Statute of the Union.[92]

Objectives: According to the Statute, the Union shall:

- Encourage and enhance the existing cooperation between the parliaments of the Muslim states.
- Help the member states confront the challenges of cultural, political, and economic domination.
- Create solid foundations for establishing prosperous coordination and solidarity among the member states.

Structure and Finance: It has been decided that the Union will consist of a three-tier structure. Its *General Assembly* will consist of the Parliaments of all the OIC member states, as represented by the Speakers or Chairmen of the Legislatures. The *Executive Committee* will consist of nine members and will be the decision-making body of the Union. And lastly, there will be a *Secretary General,* who will head the Secretariat. Dr Galal Mohammad Ahmad, Secretary of the Election Commission of Sudan, and Ahmad Goraya, Secretary of the National Assembly of Pakistan, are in the field for the election of the post of IULA Secretary General. Provisionally, the Secretariat at Tehran is being headed by Ambassador Mohammad Peyrovi.

The Union will be run by mandatory contributions by the Muslim states, equivalent to one fourth of their respective contributions to the OIC budget.

Activities: So far only the first meeting of the IULA Executive Committee has been held in Islamabad, Pakistan, on 11–12 August 1999, which determined the rules of business of the Union. It has also received nominations for the election for the Secretary General. Pakistan was elected the Chairman of the Executive Committee, while Mali and Morocco became the two Vice-Chairmen. Bangladesh, Kuwait, Malaysia, Saudi Arabia, and Turkey also attended the meeting.

Conclusion

In recent years, proposals have surfaced regarding the establishment of an Islamic States Tele-communication Union, Islamic Postal Authority, Inter-Islamic Police and Crimes Investigation Bureau, and an Islamic Writers Forum. Since, we have seen above that, with rare exceptions, the affiliated institutions of the OIC have been a miserable failure so far, it can be questioned what purpose the mushroom proliferation of such unions would serve. It is high time that the leadership and the intelligentsia of the Muslim world think about what went wrong, and how, where, and why it went wrong. The institutions which were established with so many expectations, present a sorry tale of apathy by the Muslim countries.

NOTES and REFERENCES

1. The OIC General Secretariat Publication, 'Guide to the OIC', (Jeddah: OIC, 1995), p. 93.
2. Ibid.
3. In response to the questionnaire sent by the author, the Manager Trade Promotion of the ICCI and CE, vide letter No. 50/MISC/768, dated 4 November 1996, sent two short monographs entitled *The Islamic Chamber in Brief* and *Report on the Activities of the Islamic Chamber.* Information in this section is largely based on this material.
4. *Chamber in Brief,* ref. 3, pp. 1–2/6.
5. *Activity Report,* ref. 3, p. 4–5.
6. *Chamber in Brief,* ref. 3, pp. 2–3/6.
7. Ibid.
8. Ibid.
9. Ibid., pp. 4, 5/6.
10. As with the Secretariat of the OIC and other organizations within the OIC framework, the majority of the member organizations of the Islamic Chamber have not been paying their due contributions to it regularly. For example, in 1983, out the forty-two member-states of the OIC only eighteen paid their dues and in 1984 only six members did so. In 1985 contributions had come from only twelve countries. See Noor Ahmad Baba, *OIC: Theory and Practice of Pan-Islamic Cooperation,* (Karachi: Oxford University Press, 1994), p. 225.
11. Ibid.
12. *Activity Report,* ref. 3, pp. 1–2/5.
13. Ibid., p. 2/5. Also see, *The Nation,* Lahore, 21 September 1996.
14. Ibid., p. 3/5.
15. Ibid., p. 4/5.
16. Ibid.
17. Ibid., p. 5/5.
18. *The Muslim World,* (Karachi: WMC), vol. 34, no. 29, 11 January 1997, p. 7.
19. *The News,* Islamabad, 28 April 1994.
20. Ibid., 12 December 1993.

21. Also see Salahuddin Kasim 'Towards an Islamic Common Market', *The News*, 7 January 1991.

22. *Pakistan Times*, Islamabad, 22 May 1980.

23. The Secretary General of ISSF, Dr Mohammad S. Gazdar showed keen interest in this research project through his letters No. 207 (8 Sha'ban 1417 AH), and No. 227 (17 Sha'ban 1417 AH). He sent to this author the *Statute of the Sports Federation of Islamic Solidarity* and *The ISSF Activity Report*.

24. *Activity Report*, ref. 23, p. 1.

25. Ibid.

26. *Statute*, ref. 23, p. 4.

27. Ibid.

28. OIC Guide ref. 1, p. 99.

29. Chapter two of the *Statute* (Articles 7–16) deals with the General Assembly. See *Statute*, ref. 23, pp. 5–7.

30. Chapter three of the *Statute* (Articles 17–33) deals with the composition and functions of the Executive Committee. See *Statute*, ref. 23, pp. 8–12.

31. Article 34 of the *Statute*, ibid., pp. 12–13.

32. Chapter four of the *Statute* (Articles 36–46) discusses the financial and budgetary matters of the Federation. See Article 40, ibid., p. 15.

33. *Activity Report*, ref. 23, p. 1.

34. Ibid., p. 2.

35. Ibid.

36. Ibid.

37. Ibid., p. 3.

38. Ibid., p. 4.

39. Ibid., p. 6.

40. Ibid., p. 7.

41. The author wishes to register his thanks to the Secretary General of the OICC for sending the Organization's official publication *OICC: A March of Achievement and Progress*, (Jeddah: n.d.), and some other material, in response to his request. The section on the OICC is primarily based on this source.

42. *March of Achievement*, ref. 41, p. 169.

43. Ibid., pp. 39–41.

44. Ibid., pp. 14–16. Also see OIC Guide, ref. 1, pp. 97–98.

45. Ibid., pp. 16–36 and 52–129.

46. Ibid. Also see OIC Guide, ref. 1, p. 97.

47. Ibid., p. 101.

48. Ibid.

49. Ibid.

50. Abdullah Ahsan, *OIC: Introduction to an Islamic Political Institution*, (Herndon: IIIT, 1988), p. 35.

51. At the time of writing, Libya was facing a UN embargo, making even postal correspondence very difficult. No response was received from ICIC on the author's questionnaire. The preceding information about the activities is based on secondary sources.

52. Ahsan, ref. 50, p. 112.

53. Ibid.

54. Vide letter No. 466/GEN/97, dated 16 December 1997, the Organization sent a 251-page book entitled *Organization of Islamic Shipowners Association*, (Jeddah: n.d.). The information that follows is largely based on this publication. For example, see p.12, for reasons of establishing the Organization.

55. Ibid., p. 13.

56. Ibid., p. 14.

57. Ibid., pp. 15–16.

58. OIC Guide, ref. 1, p. 102.

59. See OISA, ref. 54, p. 18, for the list of member states. Pp. 19–20 carry the list of companies.

60. OIC Guide, ref. 28, pp. 102–103.

61. OISA, ref. 54, pp. 15–16.

62. The OISA publication, ref. 54, carries the names, addresses, authorized agents, the number of vessels owned, and the activities of each of the forty-three member shipping corporations, but gives no information about the activities of the Association. So the given information is based on various secondary sources.

63. See Muchrim Hakim, 'Possibility to increase OIC cooperation in shipping', *Frontier Post*, Peshawar, 24 September 1996. Also see Mehdi Masud, 'OIC & Maritime Cooperation', *Dawn*, Karachi, 6 October 1996.

64. OIC Guide, ref. 1, p. 104.

65. Ibid.

66. Ibid.

67. Ibid.

68. Ibid., p. 106.

69. Ibid.

70. Ibid.

71. Information from secondary sources was limited while the IAIB did not send any material.

72. *The Muslim World*, ref. 18, vol. 34, no. 42, 10 May 1997, p. 3.

73. Europpa Year Book, 1995, p. 210.

74. Based on the booklet 'General Information' and several other brochures sent by the Cement Association.

75. OIC Guide, ref. 1, does not mention it in the list of affiliated institutions of the OIC. The information provided by the TCMA does not speak of any activity, specifically carried out by the ICA.

76. *The Muslim*, Islamabad, 11 December 1983.

77. Ahsan, ref. 50, p. 114.

78. The author is indebted to the reference library of *The News*, Rawalpindi, for providing the author the file on Muslim Women Parliamentarian Conference, containing press clippings. The information given about the conference is based on the clippings file.

79. *The News*, 1 August 1995.

80. Ibid., 28 December 1995.

81. Ibid., 8 April 1996.

82. The Benazir government had planned to hold an OIC Summit Conference, Islamic Speaker's Conference and Islamic Women Solidarity Games to mark Pakistan's golden jubilee. The successor Nawaz government showed no interest in the latter two events. Nevertheless, the OIC Summit was duly held on schedule.

83. *The Muslim World,* Karachi, vol. 34, no. 45, 31 May 1997, p. 4.

84. *The News,* 5 December 1997.

85. Ibid.

86. *The Muslim,* 6 August 1995.

87. Ibid.

88. *The Nation,* Lahore, 4 August 1995.

89. *Jang,* Rawalpindi, 13 July 1995.

90. *The News,* 27 October 1996. It appears from the news item that Iran had made this suggestion on 31 July 1996, at the first meeting of IULA coordinating committee.

91. Ibid., 22 October 1996.

92. Ibid., 13 August 1999 and 18 June 1999. Also see, *The Muslim World,* ref. 18, vol. 36, no. 49, 26 June 1999, p. 3.

14 Islamic Non-Governmental Organizations

The total number of Islamic non-governmental organizations (NGOs) in the world, to give a modest estimate, should be in tens of thousands. These include Islamist political parties in a number of countries, Muslim military outfits in several conflict areas like Palestine, Kashmir etc., Muslim students' associations in thousands of universities, the governing Trusts of Islamic mission schools and hospitals, and large and small Islamic cultural, educational, missionary, and philanthropist organizations worldwide. To give a small example, France, which has a four million strong Muslim community has as many as 600 notable Islamic organizations. For our purpose, only the international Islamic organizations, the ones whose scope of activities extends beyond and across the national frontiers, are relevant. Five major international Islamic organizations shall be discussed in this chapter.[1]

I. World Muslim Congress (WMC)
II. Muslim World League (MWL)
III. World Society of Islamic Call (WSIC)
IV. World Assembly of Muslim Youth (WAMY)
V. Islamic Council of Europe (ICE)

After reviewing the activities of the five organizations, a brief analysis of the role and scope of the non-governmental Islamic organizations will follow.

i. World Muslim Congress (WMC)
(Mu'tamar al-Alam al-Islami)

The World Muslim Congress, popularly known as *Mu'tamar*, is a leading Islamic organization, that aims at fostering unity in the Muslim world. It came into being at the famous Mecca Convention in 1926. It held its second General Conference in 1931 at Jerusalem which for the first time organized its administrative structure by electing a President, a Secretary General, and a twenty-five-member Executive Council. The Grand *Mufti* of Palestine, Amin al-Hussaini became its President and Ziauddin Tabatabai, former Prime Minister of Iran, took over as the Secretary. During and immediately after the Second World War, the Congress remained dormant. In 1949 and 1951, the third and fourth General Conferences were held and the *Mu'tamar* became active once again. We have already discussed in Chapter 1 the early developments leading to the establishment of the WMC in 1926, as well as its activities till the 6th General Conference in Mogadishu, Somalia, in 1964.[2] The 7th General Conference was held at Amman, Jordan (1970) while the 8th one took place in Lefkosa, capital of the Republic of North Cyprus (1980).

Objectives: Since its inception, the *Mu'tamar* is striving to:

- Bring unity in the ranks of the Islamic *ummah*.
- Act as a think-tank for the Muslim *ummah*.
- Introduce Islam to non-Muslims through its publications and literature.
- Encourage research on the political, economic, and social conditions of the Muslim world.
- Support the liberation movements conducted by Muslims.
- Lead a Christian–Muslim dialogue for better understanding and harmony.
- Perform welfare activities for the Muslims.

Structure: The *Mu'tamar* has a three-tier structure:

- *General Conference*: The General Conference of the WMC is convened periodically to determine the general direction of the *Mu'tamar's* activities. It also elects the office-bearers of the *Mu'tamar*. It is usually attended by over 400 delegates representing Muslim and non-Muslim states. There is no regular pattern in the interval between the two consecutive General Conferences.

- *Executive Council*: It consists of twenty-five members and is the main decision-making body of the WMC.
- *Presidency and Head Office*: The WMC is headed by a President and two Vice-Presidents; while the head office, located at Karachi, is looked after by the Secretary General. Conventionally, these four office-bearers belong to different states. Usually, Muslims representing non-Muslim countries are given representation in the top echelons of the WMC system. The WMC conference held at Islamabad (Sept. 1997) unanimously re-elected Dr Abdullah Omer Naseef (Deputy Chairman of Saudi Arabia's Consultative Assembly) as President, M. Hanifa Mohammad (ex-Speaker of Sri Lanka's parliament) and Abdul Rahman Sawar al Dahab (ex-President of Sudan) as Vice-Presidents, and Zafar-ul-Haq (the then Minister for Islamic Affairs of Pakistan) as Secretary General for another five years.

Activities: The activities of the WMC range from the organization of Islamic conferences and publication of religious literature to political activities such as providing input to the OIC, bringing about truce between Muslim factions fighting for the independence of Southern Philippine, and the like.

Conferences: The *Mu'tamar* has so far organized more than a dozen international conferences in Mecca, Jerusalem, Baghdad, Mogadishu, Karachi, Amman, Kibris, and Islamabad etc. In 1955, *Mu'tamar* organized the first-ever Muslim Youth conference at Karachi. In 1963 the first-ever Muslim regional moot for Asia and the Pacific regions was held in Kuala Lumpur. Since 1981, *Mu'tamar* has started organizing a series of seminars. The first one was held in Tokyo in 1981. Since then, the resource constraint has compelled the *Mu'tamar* to hold most of its conferences in Pakistan. The topics have ranged from different themes of spiritual and political Islam and contemporary Muslim world to those of non-proliferation and world peace.

Though the list is very long, the latest international event conducted by the *Mu'tamar* is the Islamabad Conference held on the theme of 'Muslim *ummah* in the next century—Challenges and opportunities' during 23–25 September 1997. The Conference was attended by over 400 scholars, *ulema,* writers, and political figures from thirty-four countries. In the final declaration, the WMC called for a solution to the Muslim world's problems; pledged to support the 'liberation' of Palestine, Kashmir, and Chechenya, etc.; and stressed the need for effective measures to 'counter the distortion of the image of Islam and the Muslims created by the Western media'. In a formal resolution, it demanded permanent Veto power for the Muslim bloc at the UN Security Council.[3] In November 1997, the *Mu'tamar* held another seminar on 'Solidarity with Palestine' where numerous scholars presented papers highlighting different aspects of the struggle of the people of Palestine.[4]

Political Activities: The *Mu'tamar* has consistently supported the struggles of the Muslim peoples of the world. Since 1931, the *Mu'tamar* was issuing warning about the Zionist conspiracies to establish a state. It has always opposed the creation of Israel and has supported Palestine. Likewise, in November 1950, the *Mu'tamar* presented a scroll with one million signatures from all over the world to the then UN Secretary General, Trigve Lie, on the issue of right of self-determination for the people of occupied Kashmir. In 1991, it presented a 160 page report of human rights abuses in occupied Kashmir to the United Nations. The *Mu'tamar* has also initiated the Christian–Muslim dialogue, which has taken place:

- in Amman, Jordan (1967) with the Catholic and Orthodox Church of the Middle East
- in Colombo, Sri Lanka (1981) with the World Council of Churches
- in Vatican, Italy (1987) with H.H. the Pope.

Since the primary objective of *Mu'tamar* is to bring unity among the Muslims, it has strived for peace in the Muslim world. The first major achievement to its credit in this regard is bringing an end to the war between Saudi Arabia and Yemen as early as in 1934. The *Mu'tamar* has, to date, taken a number of initiatives for peaceful settlement of disputes among the Muslims. During the Iran–Iraq (1980–88) war its delegations visited both the countries and attempted to stop the fratricidal conflict in the Gulf. In 1983, the *Mu'tamar* held a peace conference in Karachi to bring about peace and harmony among the rival Muslim leaders, waging a war of independence in Southern Philippines. This led to better understanding among the fifty participating Filipino Muslim leaders.

Cultural Activities: The *Mu'tamar* has launched a number of programmes for the propagation of Islam and the uplift of Muslims, especially in Muslim minority communities. These include publication of the Quran and Islamic books, and financial support to schools and mosques. Back in 1965, the *Mu'tamar* celebrated the 1400th anniversary of the revelation of the Quran all over the world, and set up Quran Committees. Some countries, including a few non-Muslim ones, issued commemorative stamps on the occasion, through *Mu'tamar's* efforts. In 1981, the *Mu'tamar* was equally active in celebrations for the advent of the 15th century of the Islamic calendar.

Publications: The *Mu'tamar* has a large number of important publications to its credit. Its research wing, which is very active, has produced monumental volumes like *Economic Resources of the Muslim world, Islamic Economic System, Islamic Culture—A few angles, Islamic Common Market, Muslim Countries Socio-Economic Profile, West and the Ummah, and History of Muslim Spain*, to name a few. *Mu'tamar* was the first organization to publish an authentic Islamic map (1962) and a country-by-country profile of Muslim minorities (1976). Its star publication is the *World Muslim Gazetteer*, published every ten years, starting form 1965. This one-volume encyclopaedia gives most up to date information on Muslim countries, communities, and organizations. The revised edition, due in 1995, has not been published yet. However, in 1993, the *Mu'tamar* brought out a reference book *World Muslim Minorities*, which is an excellent research work on the subject. In addition, a large number of books and booklets about Islamic teachings and

the life of the Holy Prophet (PBUH) are also regularly published. The WMC takes pride in two more of its publications; the *Report on the Condition of Muslim Minorities*, prepared in response to the request by the OIC, and another historical and well-documented volume, *Slave Trade in Africa*.

Since 1963, a tabloid news-cum-views weekly, *The Muslim World*, is being regularly brought out. It has an international circulation and is widely reproduced. The regional offices of the *Mu'tamar* also bring out various monthly magazines in the regional languages.

Other Services: The WMC has category 'A' observer status at the United Nations, the first Muslim organization to receive this honour, since 1965. The *Mu'tamar* has its representatives at the UN offices in New York, Geneva, and at various UN organs. In 1986, the UN gave the certificate of 'Messenger of Peace' to this Organization. It was invited in the special sessions on Disarmament (SSOD) twice, in 1982 and 1988, to present the Muslim point of view. It has the unique honour of being the first, among 7000 organizations registered by the UN, to receive the Niwano peace prize in 1984 at Tokyo. In addition, the WMC has represented the Muslims at a number of international conferences and non-governmental fora.

The *Mu'tamar* is also the first organization to be given an observer status at the OIC and is the only Islamic non-governmental organization to attend all the Islamic Summits and ICFMs. It has given a lot of intellectual input to the OIC. In fact, in its sixth world assembly at Mogadishu, Somalia, it gave a call for an Islamic Summit that was taken up by King Faisal and ultimately led to the establishment of the OIC itself. Ideas for an Islamic bank, radio station, and a news agency have also been given to the OIC through WMC reports and proposals. Since July 1987, the *Mu'tamar* headquarters has shifted to its new premises at *Mu'tamar* complex, site 9/A, Block-7, Gulshan-e-Iqbal, Karachi, Pakistan.

II. Muslim World League (MWL) (Rabita al-Alam al-Islami)

The Muslim World League (MWL), popularly called the *Rabita*, was established following a conference of *ulema* in the holy city of Mecca in 1962, with the blessings of the late King Faisal, the then Prime Minister and crown prince of the Saudi Kingdom. In its scope of activities, it vies with the WMC. The *Rabita* also enjoys the category 'A' status with the United Nations and a consultative status with many of its organs including ECOSOC, UNESCO, and the UNICEF.[5]

Objectives: The principal objectives *of Rabita* are as follows:

• To explain and disseminate Islamic culture and teachings.
• Refute false allegations against Islam and repel pernicious trends and concepts.
• Defend Islamic causes in accordance with the interests and aspirations of Muslims and solve their problems.
• Provide assistance in the fields of education, culture, social welfare, health care, etc.

Functions: The covenant of the MWL also defines the following means to be employed:

• Work towards implementation of Islamic *Shari'ah.*
• Disseminate the Holy Quran and the translation of its meanings into various languages.
• Coordinate efforts to promote Islamic *Da'wa.*
• Make as much use as possible of the pilgrimage to promote Islamic consciousness through lectures and symposia etc.
• Extend support to Islamic activists.
• Distribute Islamic literature.
• Encourage publications serving the purpose of Islamic *Da'wa* and expurgate the Islamic media from all non-Islamic contents.
• Examine problems facing Muslim minorities, support their demands and extend necessary assistance to them.
• Extend support to Islamic organizations and institutions connected with *Rabita* and coordinate Islamic endeavours with such institutions.
• Extend relief aid to Muslims affected by disasters, accidents, and calamities.

• Disseminate Islamic education through construction and support of Islamic schools and institutions.

Structure: The basic organizational structure of the *Rabita* consists of the General Islamic Conference, a Constituent Council and the Secretariat-General.

General Islamic Conference: It is the highest authority of the MWL, consisting of Muslim scholars, intellectuals, and preachers drawn from around the world at both the popular and official levels. The Conference adopts resolutions on Islamic causes and nominates members of the Constituent Council. So far the Conference has held three sessions, in 1962, 1967, and 1987.

Constituent Council: The Constituent Council consists of sixty-one members, comprising scholars and intellectuals from Muslim majority and minority communities. The Council chooses the Secretary General, amends the covenant by three-fourths majority, adopts resolutions and recommendations, approves the League's plans, and sets the direction of policy making. The members do not receive any kind of emoluments or allowances.

Secretariat: The Secretariat General is headed by the Secretary General, who is assisted by a Deputy Secretary General and four Assistant Secretary Generals, one each for Finance and Administration, Mosques, Culture and Information, and Organizations and Studies, besides a Director General for Educational and Scholarship Affairs. Each of the four sectors has several departments. Prominent are the Departments of Conferences, Islamic Culture, Publicity and Publications, Muslim Minority Affairs, General Administration, Distribution of Literature, the Department of Islamic Law, and some others.

Prominent Saudi scholar Shiekh Abdul Aziz bin Baz is the President of the MWL. Dr Abdullah bin Saleh al-Obeid (Secretary General), Mohammad Nasir el-Oboudy (Deputy Secretary General), Amin Aqueel el-Attas (ASG-Finance) and Abdullah el-Aqueel (ASG-Mosque Affairs) are the prominent office bearers.

In addition to the three principal bodies mentioned above, the *Rabita* has four subsidiary organs:

1) The *World Supreme Council of Mosques* (Estb. 1975) aims at the revival of the message of the mosque, protection of mosques in non-Muslim states, preservation of endowments, and the defence of freedom of propagation of Islam.
2) The *Fiqh (Islamic jurisprudence) Council* (Estb. 1978) reviews new issues to give legal opinion on the basis of Islamic law, projects the supremacy of *Shari'ah* and publishes *Fiqh* literature.
3) The *International Islamic Relief Organization* (Estb. 1979) tries to alleviate the agony of Muslims afflicted by natural disasters. The IIRO has established a large number of hospitals, schools and orphanages.(See more details below.)
4) The *Commission on Scientific Signs in the Quran and Sunnah* (Estb. 1984) is a research body striving for projecting scientific signs in the Holy Book and *Hadith*.

These four organs publish their periodicals named *Mosque Message, Journal of Islamic Fiqh Council, The Relief Aid*, and the *Journal of the Scientific Signs in the Holy Quran*, respectively.

Activities: Notable achievements of the MWL and its organs include the preparation of cassettes for teaching Arabic, classes for teaching Arabic to non-natives, training to Arabic teachers, a big institute for training of *Imams* and preachers (at Mecca), a charitable fund for mosques, local councils of mosques in a number of countries, and the establishment of an audio-visual centre and a public library at the *Rabita* head offices.

Religious Activities: The *Rabita* has translated the Holy Quran into Chinese, Indonesian, Thai, Bengali, Turkish, Persian, Filipino, Hausa, Japanese, Tamil, Turkistani, and many other languages. It has published a lot of literature to counter the anti-Islam currents. Hundreds of thousands of copies of the Holy Quran and Islamic booklets have been distributed free of charge. A regular feature of the MWL activities is dispatching preachers and Islamic missionaries all over the world, especially to sub-Saharan Africa and Latin America.

Political Activities: The *Rabita* discusses the political problems of the Muslim world in all its conferences. It has played a significant part in internationalizing the Bosnia, Kashmir, Afghanistan, and the Babri Mosque issues. It has a special Islamic Contemporary Issues Committee (ICIC) for the purpose.

Educational Activities: The League has a separate department for the promotion of education. The main beneficiaries of its scholarship programme have been the Muslim minority communities, primarily from Africa, East Europe, and South Asia. It thus encourages higher education in religious and other disciplines. In addition, the *Rabita* has helped organize Islamic Scouting camps and youth meetings, supported a number of schools and mosques, given scholarships to Muslim students, and conducted field research and data collection (especially regarding the condition and needs of the Muslim minorities).

Humanitarian Activities: During the period 1987– 97, the IIRO, an organ of the MWL, had spent over 1 billion Saudi Rials on relief operations. It helped the victims of floods and natural calamities, and established Islamic mission hospitals in many parts of the world. In many cases, health services, vocational training, and refugee relief centres have been established for the Muslim communities.

A notable activity of the MWL in the late nineties is the fund-raising by the *Rabita* Trust. The Trust was set up to assist Pakistan to repatriate around 250,000 'Stranded Pakistanis', left over in Bangladesh since the war of secession in the then East Pakistan in 1971. Pakistan now needs sufficient resources to bring them back to Pakistan, and provide them with housing and employment. The Trust has been successful in providing to Pakistan a contribution towards the sum required.[6]

The total repatriation cost was estimated at around $350 million, out of which $110 million were needed for the provision of housing. By 1992, the *Rabita* completed 3000 residential units for the stranded Pakistanis. In the following years, construction work for another 2000 flats got underway in Mian Channu, near the city of Lahore.

Research and Publications: The gathering of Muslim scholars at Mecca during *Hajj* is a regular MWL-sponsored event. The lectures given are published annually in book form. The MWL has consistently worked to counter the negative image of Islam. Quite at times, it is accused of towing the Saudi government's line in issuing *fatwas* (religious edicts). But usually the scholars pursue independent policies on the MWL platform. The *Rabita* has a long list of conferences and symposia conducted by it in America, Europe, Asia, and Africa. The topics range from Islamic *Da'wa* (propagation) to the prevention of drugs and alcoholism. The *Rabita* publishes a weekly newspaper *Weekly Muslims World* (every Monday), the monthly *MWL Journal* (English and Arabic versions), and a monthly booklet '*Da'watul Haq*' (Call of the Truth).

Rabita enjoys observer status at the OIC and participates in its Summits and ICFMs. The *Rabita* has offices in scores of countries but its permanent Secretariat is situated in Ummal Joud at Mecca, Saudi Arabia. The five-storey office building spread over 50,000 sq.m. has office rooms, conference halls, a library, and a mosque. The address of this organization is, *Rabita al Alam al Islami*, P.O. Box 537 and 538, Mecca al-Mukarramah, Saudi Arabia.

IIRO Activities: Since the IIRO has lately become a separate organization, independent of the MWL, a brief view of its activities is in order. It has now over 120 offices in a hundred countries. Though, the Organization purports to help all humanity but 80 per cent of its beneficiaries have been Muslims. During 1987-97, nearly $500 million have been spent on the refugee relief operations and around three million displaced persons have benefited. The IIRO runs 55 Islamic Mission hospitals providing service to four million patients each year.

The Orphan Trust of the Organization is sponsoring 83,000 Muslim orphan children in fifty-eight countries. The IIRO has many other projects for children like support of thousands of schools, publication and distribution of school books all over the world, and the famous 'Our Children Project', under which audio-visual programmes, children's songs etc., are produced. The same project has produced 150 titles of storybooks. Their contents have morals and they foster Islamic teachings.

Then, there is a women committee of the IIRO, which deals with the problems and welfare of women. The Architectural and Engineering Department supports and promotes Islamic architecture in a variety of ways. The IIRO Agriculture Support Project undertakes research on agriculture, and provides seeds and expert advice to farmers in the Muslim countries to cultivate barren lands and to increase the crop output.

III. World Society of Islamic Call (WSIC)
(Jami'ah al-Da'wa al-Islami)

The WSIC, more commonly known as the Call of Islam Society, is the brainchild of the radical Libyan leadership that came to power following the September 1969 military revolution. The first conference of Islamic Call, held in 1970, decided to form a permanent body for the propagation of Islam. The Society was formally established in 1972. The Libyan government pledged to finance the new institution. Like the Saudi-backed MWL and the Pakistan-backed WMC, this society also is working for the general benefit of the whole Muslim *ummah*. But most of its activities are limited to the African continent.[7]

Objectives: The field of the Society is to 'uncover the great Quranic Cultural Heritage by spreading the Islamic Call into wider and more comprehensive perspectives to include the whole humanity'. The Charter delineates the following objectives:

- Spreading Islamic call and building schools and Islamic centres.
- Staging and holding seminars, lectures, and gatherings aiming at enlightening Islamic awareness.
- Publicizing of Islamic books and researches.
- Conducting charitable and humanitarian work .

Structure: The *General Meeting* of the Islamic Call is the highest decision-making body of the Society. It meets once every few years and approves the general policy of the Society. Then there is the *International Council* which comprises noted Islamic scholars from different countries. And finally, its executive organ is the *Secretariat* located at Tripoli, Libya. Dr Mohammad Ahmad Sharif is the Secretary General. The Society maintains external offices at various African countries. The WSIC finances consist of support from the government of Libya, and public donations.

Activities: The first conference of the Islamic Call, that comprised the elite from among Muslim thinkers and intellectuals interested in the affairs of the Islamic Call, was held in Libya in 1970. Then came the law for establishing the Islamic Call Society in 1972 as an independent committee of public benefit, with its own constitution and its independent financing. After twelve years, the second enlarged conference of the Islamic Call was held in Tripoli, Libya, during August 1982. Delegations from 134 societies, committees, and Islamic unions, besides a number of Muslim scientific personalities from seventy-three countries of the different continents participated in this conference.

The International Committee of the Islamic Call held its second ordinary session in October 1983. This second ordinary session was the beginning of a new way for practising a strategy and work plan, through 'its adopted goals and its initiated ways for spreading the Islamic Call and facing enemies'. The work of the 3rd session of the International Council of the Islamic Call was held in Casablanca, Morocco, in December 1984. It was felt that this Committee was 'becoming deep-rooted in human history, as an Islamic, cultural contemporary movement'. The Committee decided to:

• work for cooperation with International and Islamic organizations, especially those of an international character;
• focus on the youth, the teaching curricula and vocational, technical, and administrative qualifications;
• take care of Muslim refugees and Muslim workers in Europe;
• be concerned with the Arabic language and concentrate its efforts on children and especially on Muslim children in Europe.

Cooperation with other organizations: The Call of Islam Society works in cooperation with other organizations. A work document was established, during the meeting of this session, between the Islamic Call and the Islamic Educational, Scientific, and Cultural Organization (ISESCO) to execute common plans of the Society and the Organization in the field of scientific, compositional, and editorial researches dealing with the Arabic and Islamic culture, and to introduce studies on the different concerns of the Islamic world. There is increasing cooperation between the Society and UNESCO, manifested by the fruitfully executed plans on more than ten humanitarian and cultural projects. There also exists strong cooperation between the Society and the OIC. One outcome of this, was the Conference of the Islamic Minorities in South East Asia, which was held at Perth, Australia, in September 1984. Likewise it has organized several activities jointly with the Islamic Social, Educational, and Cultural Organization (ISESCO) and the Arab League Educational, Social, and Cultural Organizations (ALESCO). In cooperation with the former, it organized a training course for the teachers of Arabic language and Islamic Studies of Europe in May–June 1997. The course was attended by thirty teachers working in Islamic centres and Muslim schools in Britain.[8]

Training and Research: The Society has a college called *Kuliyya al-Da'wa* (College of the Islamic Call) in Tripoli. The College provides training in various disciplines including the Quran, the message of Quran, Islamic history and culture, and other related subjects. The syllabi of the College are patterned on those of the famous Al-Azhar University of Egypt. The College also offers various Western languages, and teaches Libyan President Qaddafi's Green Book. The College boasts of a cosmopolitan faculty. Similarly, it has an enrollment of Muslim students from fifty-two Muslim and non-Muslim countries. The students go on for missionary work all over the world.[9]

As part of the research and training activities, the WSIC undertakes and finances research projects in the field of the Call of Islam and propagation of the Muslim religion. It also imparts training to the *Imams* of mosques, especially those from the non-Muslim countries where training facilities for Muslim jurisprudence are scant. The Society also arranges a large number of workshops and seminars. It has held several international conferences in North Africa. A recent example is the first Islamic Women Gathering in Nias city, Senegal, in early 1997.[10]

Publications: The Society brings out a fortnightly journal, known as *Al-Da'wa Al-Islamia* (The Call of Islam), in three languages; Arabic, English, and French. The number of titles published by the Society runs into hundreds. It has published the books, booklets, pamphlets, and religious literature, not only in its three official languages but also in various regional languages spoken and understood by Muslim and various non-Muslim communities in Africa. The topics of the books include the message of the Quran, the life of the Holy Prophet (PBUH) (*Seerah*), sayings of the Holy Prophet (PBUH) (*Hadith*), the biographies of the Prophet's companions (Caliphs), and heroes of Islamic history, as well as religious issues, performance of Islamic rituals, and problems of jurisprudence. The publications are mostly distributed free of charge for the propagation of Islam.[11] The headquarters of the Call of Islam Society are in the Libyan capital, Tripoli, and the correspondence address is P. O. Box No. 2549, Tripoli, Libya.

iv. **World Assembly of Muslim Youth (WAMY)**

Established in 1972, the WAMY is an independent Islamic Organization serving as a forum for the Islamic youths and modern student organizations throughout the world. Its primary objective is to bring about cooperation and coordination in thought, planning, and implementation of Islamic activities, in accordance with its rules and regulations.[12]

Functions: The WAMY is an organization meant to 'give a helping hand to the youths, to plant pure Islamic ideology in their hearts and minds, and to find solutions to their problems, thus turning them into a force for good in the Islamic society'. Until now it has held several general sessions. In these sessions, the representatives took important decisions and made a number of significant recommendations.

Activities: The WAMY has so far concluded a programme of twelve youth camps that were held in France, Italy, Germany, Spain, the Turkish Republic of Northern Cyprus, Indianapolis (USA), Ottawa (Canada), Sao Paulo (Brazil), Ghana, India, Pakistan, and the disputed territory of Indian-held Kashmir. Thus the camps have been held in the continents of Europe (5), Asia (3), North America (2), South America (1), and Africa (1). Now the WAMY plans to have one or more Muslim youth camps in Australia and Oceana as well. The WAMY is gradually turning into the Islamic version of International Boy Scouts/Girls Guides Associations. The WAMY camps provide an integrated and broad programme of Islamic *tarbiyat* (training) that aim at promoting Islamic awareness and sense of fraternity and solidarity among Muslim youths in various parts of the world.

Funds: The income of the WAMY consists of the annual grant given by the government of Saudi Arabia, and other donations which the President of WAMY, in accordance with its rules and regulations might accept from Islamic institutions whose objectives are in conformity with those of the WAMY.

The WAMY has an observer status at the OIC. Its headquarters are located in Riyadh, Saudi Arabia. Prince Faisal, a son of the ruling King Fahd, is its patron. The WAMY can be contacted at the address of the Ministry of Youth Affairs, P.O. Box 5472, Riyadh, Saudi Arabia.

v. **Islamic Council of Europe (ICE)**

The OIC's first Secretary General, Tunku Abdul Rehman, organized the Islamic Council of Europe in 1972 by holding a founding Conference in London and Mr Salem Azzam became its Secretary General.[13]

Functions: One of the major functions of the Islamic Council of Europe is to project the views and aspirations of the Muslim minority community in Europe. Its second major role is to build the correct impression of Islam in the West, as well as to rid the West of its misconceptions about Muslims. Its functions in this connection are three-fold: Firstly, the Islamic Council of Europe organizes conferences, seminars, and exhibitions; secondly, the Council produces books, pamphlets, and folders explaining Islam; and thirdly, it corrects any wrong and misleading information that may be carried in the press, television and other organs of the media. It is trying to build bridges of understanding between the Muslim world and the West.

Activities: The activities of the Council, as indicated above, are three-fold. At first, it holds conferences and seminars on the problems and crises in the Muslim world, particularly those relating to the Muslim minority communities. These conferences act as a bridge between various Muslim communities in Europe and also between the European Muslims on one hand and the scholars of the Muslim majority countries, on the other. It held conferences, for instance, to condemn the Egypt–Israel peace treaty (1978), to hail the Islamic revolution in Iran (1979), to censure the blasphemous book *Satanic Verses* by Salman Rushdie (1989), and so on. It has also held conferences on 'Problems of Muslim Minorities', 'Future Economic Order of the Muslim World', 'Defence of the Muslim World', and so on. The last mentioned conference was co-sponsored by the London-based Islamic Institute of Defence Technology (IIDT). In addition, it has regularly arranged lectures on topics like 'Quran and Modern Science', 'Islamic Cultural Heritage', 'Advent of Islam in Europe' and others, by noted European Muslim and non-Muslim scholars, thinkers, and authors. Most of these events have been conducted at the headquarter city, London.

The second area of ICE activity falls under its research and publication cell. The cell is engaged in research on topics concerning the Muslims in Europe. It has brought out monumental volumes on different topics. The books include: *Islam and Contemporary Society, Muslim communities in non-Muslim states, Jerusalem: the key to world peace*, and several others.

The third area of activities of the Islamic Council is political. It is struggling to secure the rights of Muslims in Europe, fight the discrimination against them and to counter the hostile propaganda against Islam. It has also set up an International Commission on Muslim Minorities. Its activities in Britain include acting as a forum for discussing Muslim grievances and functioning as a pressure group to convince the government to give financial support to Islamic mission schools, protect mosques from attacks by racist activists, and declare the Muslim festivals (*Eids*) as national holidays for the Muslim minority. The ICE has been successful on a number of points where the government has given in. The headquarters of the Council are located at 16, Grosnover Crescent, London SW1, UK.

Conclusion

All the non-governmental Islamic organizations, working at the international level, are doing valuable work for the betterment of the Muslim peoples, in varying degrees. Given that there is no allowance for any ecclesiastical system in Islam and that the duty to protect, promote, and propagate Islam is vested on each follower of the religion equally, the role of these organizations becomes all the more significant. Most of the activities of these organizations are confined to the fields of culture, education, social welfare, and propagation of religion.[14] These are the very things that most of the states shy away from. For instance, Pakistan might be reluctant to publish literature on Islam and distribute it in, say, Iran, China, and Sri Lanka or to run dispensaries and elementary schools in, say, Niger and Tunisia on its own; but it would be happy to contribute to a non-governmental philanthropist organization like the WMC to perform such tasks. In this way, the Islamic NGOs are indispensable in their own right. Even the Organization of the Islamic Conference may be unable to substitute for the services being rendered by these organizations. A few observations on these organizations are in order.

One, there are several limitations on the resources and scope of the international non-governmental organizations. The donations by the general public and financial support by one or two Muslim states, falls far short of the requirement. Another inhibition that limits their scope is that many governments become suspicious of the activities of these organizations and start discouraging the same on their soil. These Islamic organizations are mostly led by the *ulema* and have a nucleus of committed, motivated workers, so they may be good for adopting strong resolutions on problems confronting the Muslim world at their general conferences but these things do not have any palpable effect on the ground reality. In the international system, only the states and the inter-governmental organizations are the unit actors. A single state may have an annual budget which is more than the budgets of all these NGOs combined; a state has immense resources at its disposal including a state machinery and a say at the world fora. So, effective international (Islamic) NGOs are the ones that are backed by an unequivocal support from at least one sovereign state.

This brings us to, two the dependency dimension of these NGOs. Inter-governmental organizations, like the OIC, are powerful enough to suspend their own members (Egypt, Afghanistan in this case) or to go without some of the members (like Iran, Sudan boycotting the OIC) but consider what would happen, if Libya, due to a change in government, disowns the Islamic Call Society, or for that matter, Saudi Arabia stops all aid to the *Rabita*. This implies that the Islamic NGOs are inherently dependent, and thus, in very precarious position.

And finally, as a corollary, three the activities of these organizations become reflective of the biases and prejudices of the patron government(s). Consequently, the thrust of activities of such organizations becomes unidirectional in one way or the other. The *Rabita* has one purpose, i.e. the propagation of Islam; WAMY focuses on one segment of Muslim society, i.e., the youth; ICE concentrates on one region, i.e., Europe, and so on.

It may be better if these Islamist non-governmental organizations came under a single umbrella organization, to avoid overlapping or duplication of activities and to obviate mutually competitive proclivities. The countries supporting these organizations should do so in a spirit of altruism. Undue interference does not bode well for the future of these NGOs. For instance, there is no point in trying to imbibe the students of WSIC's Islamic colleges with the thoughts and philosophies of the President of Libya. To sum up, these Islamic organizations are playing a dynamic role in strengthening Islam at the national and international levels in spite of the fact that they are beset with many more obstacles than are the inter-governmental Islamic organizations. Though, most of the Islamist international NGOs have no direct political role as such, but they do influence the accentuation of the Islamic factor in international affairs by making the Muslims at the grass-root level more conscious of their Islamic identity.

NOTES and REFERENCES

1. These organizations have been selected because of their significance, in terms of the ambit and scope of activities. For instance, WMC's World Muslim Gazetteer (1985) considers the OIC as the largest Islamic organization. It gives the second, third, fourth, and fifth place to WMC, MWL, Call of Islam Society, and WAMY respectively. The ICE is however, given the nineteenth place.

   The headquarters of none of the five organizations under reviews responded to this author's repeated postal requests for information. The WMC and the MWL have branch offices in Islamabad also, which provided very limited material to the author during his personal visits. Consequently, the author had to rely on secondary sources for most of the information given in the chapter.

2. The information about the *Mu'tamar's* history and activities has been compiled from the three sources, provided to the author by the *Mu'tamar's* Islamabad office:
   1. 'Brief History of Mu'tamar al-Alam al-Islami', (Karachi: WMC, n.d.).
   2. 'WMC: A Bird's Eyeview', (Karachi: WMC, n.d.).
   3. 'List of Office Bearers', (Islamabad: Ref. No. 14/IMC/93, 6 December 1993).

Also see Dr Inamullah Khan (ed.), 'World Muslim Gazetteer: 1985', (Karachi: WMC, 1987), pp. 772–781. Also see Fatima Naeem, 'Islamic Organizations' (Newspost), *The News,* Islamabad, 26 November 1997.

3. *The Muslim World,* (Karachi, WMC), vol. 35, no. 12, 11 Oct. 1997, p. 1.
4. Ibid., vol. 35, no. 20, 6 December 1997, p. 1.
5. Most of the given information has been taken form the MWL official publication, 'Muslim World League: Information Directory', (Mecca: MWL, n.d.). Also see Gazetteer, ref. 2, pp. 781–785.
6. *The News,* 4 February 1998.
7. See Gazetteer, ref. 2, pp. 786–790. Since no response to the questionnaires was received by the author, the given information on WSIC has been derived from secondary sources.
8. *The Muslim World,* vol. 35, no. 1, 26 July 1997, p. 3. Also see Gazetteer, ref. 2, p. 102.

9. Irshad Ahmad Haqqani, *Basti Basti, Nagar Nagar* (Urdu), (Lahore: Jang Publishers, 1989), pp. 24–44.
10. *The Muslim World,* vol. 34, no. 45, 31 May 1997, p. 4. Also see ibid., vol. 35, no. 28, 31 January 1998, p. 2.
11. A number of books and booklets published by the Islamic Call Society were provided to this author by the Libyan diplomatic mission at Islamabad.
12. Gazetteer, ref. 2, pp. 791–792.
13. Ibid., pp. 840–841.
14. Though all these organizations purport to be non-political but following the bomb attacks on the US embassies in Nairobi and Dar es Salam in August 1998, the Government of Kenya banned six leading Islamic welfare NGOs, including the IIRO, Rabital Islam, Help Africa People, Mercy Relief Organization, Al Harmain Foundation, and the Al Ibrahim Foundation, accusing all of them of 'activities inconsistent with their stated objectives.' See, *The News,* Islamabad, 10 September 1998.

Epilogue: Islamic Challenge in the 21st Century

The 20th century was the most eventful epoch in the known history of mankind. It also saw the meteoric rise of several political ideologies; liberal democracy and free market, communism, fascism, and others. Islam, a set of beliefs and a code of life as it may be for over a billion people, gatecrashed into the club of international political ideologies around the 1960s. With the passage of time it consolidated itself by increased intrusion into the domestic and foreign policy agendas of the Muslim states. The rest of the world being preoccupied with the communist 'threat', the presence of political Islam became palpable only after the rise to power of radical Islamists in quite a few Muslim states, Iran and Sudan being the obvious examples. It was only after the end of the cold war, at the turn of the 1990s, that the phenomenon of political Islam drew full-blown attention as a potent factor for global peace and stability, or for insecurity and instability—depending on the bias of the observer.

Before making an attempt to comprehend the phenomenon of international political Islam, one should be cognizant that unlike the various other religions, which are basically sets of dogmas, beliefs, and rituals, Islam has its own theories for national economic systems, work ethics, business and trade regulations, laws of succession and inheritance, a person's attitude towards parents and neighbours, governance, and ruler-subject relations, and finally, the laws regulating inter-state relations in war and peace. This makes Islam the only comprehensive doctrine that influences, and demands unqualified adherence from, the followers in each aspect of their individual and collective lives.

International Islam or *international political Islam* are terms coined to denote the role of Islam in determining the nature of inter-state relations between Muslim states on the one hand and between the Muslim and the non-Muslim states on the other. The very notion of international political Islam brackets in itself the whole gamut of bilateral and multilateral agreements, inter-governmental organizations and other forms of diplomacy in the Muslim world. In this context, the reassertion of international Islam portends a different political landscape for the future than would be there otherwise.

Given that the contemporary international community operates through international organizations and that the latter are effective implements of international diplomacy, the proliferation of Islamic inter-governmental organizations, both in number and in scope, can hardly be brushed aside easily. It would be in the fitness of things to add that policy makers within the Muslim world and outside, had always underestimated the capacity of Islamist forces to seize power through revolution or other violent means; their potential to romp home by ballot victories as in Algeria and Turkey was simply flabbergasting. Much more incredible was political Islam's debut into the realm of international politics.

Taking the known criterion of classifying any state that joins the OIC as member or observer, as a Muslim state; we arrive at the figure of fifty-eight Muslim states; that may collectively be called 'the Muslim world'. These states account for 31.2 per cent of the UN membership, 25.3 per cent of the world's surface area and 22.0 per cent of the global population. This collectivity, if there is one, controls proportionate natural and human resources, strategic locations, and political clout. If the broad spectrum of Muslim states and communities, diverse in culture, geography and political systems, starts orchestrating a distinct

'Islamic worldview' through and from the international organizations, it may be a premonition of a serious challenge to the existing order, though, the phenomenon of divergent perspectives coalescing into a Muslim worldview is yet in an embryonic stage.

Lately, major changes have taken place in the structural as well as behavioural aspects of the international system which today, as far as the OIC and other Islamic organizations are concerned, is characterized by vagueness, uncertainty, and instability. Beset by a multitude of apparently insurmountable problems, these organizations are not found wanting in motivation. Whatever shape international Islam takes in the 21st century, the phenomenon of international Islamic IGOs and NGOs would be counted as the largest single contributing factor. Before even attempting to make value judgements on it, one may well summarize the history of the evolution of these organizations, evaluate their performance, and delve into their future prospects.

Genesis and Growth of Neo-pan-Islamism

The Quran declares all Muslims to be brothers, thereby placing them in a separate closet in relation with all the non-believers. In practice, however, the sense of belonging to the same fraternal community, at least in the ideological plane, alone has rarely ever sufficed to create a political unity among the Muslims. This is not to negate the existence of a unifying thrust in the Islamic religion, but merely to state that such thrusts in history needed being complemented by a host of socio-political factors as well. pan-Islamism found expression in different forms in different eras. The brand of Pan-Islamism presently being professed and propagated is of recent origin.

One can trace the roots of neo-pan-Islamism, as one may call it, in the reaction to colonialism and, what was believed as, the socio-political encroachment on Muslim society by the West. The writings of the prominent Muslim thinkers of the first half of the 20th century, more so after the abolishment of the Caliphate in 1924, evinced

frustration at the state of affairs in the Muslim world and clearly argued for a meaningful unity among Muslims. Even though institutions are quite often products of evolving ideas, the ideas are rarely static and absolute in their manifestations. The same idea can have different practical expressions in different places and at different points in time. The 20th century saw the emergence of Islamic organizations as a manifestation of the need for unity.

This was so principally because of the particular circumstances of the modern times. That is to say that the points made above regarding Islam's ideological ethos notwithstanding, there is no gainsaying that the present international system begot the international organizations, sustained them, and even strengthened them. Their emergence and proliferation in the 20th century, was largely facilitated—rather necessitated—by the rapid industrialization, that revolutionized the transportation and communication systems within and among the states, and thereby reduced the physical world into a smaller unit, creating an unavoidable network of interdependence among them. This system of interdependence stimulated the creation of international organizations that act as channels of cooperation in social, economic, and political fields.

The emergence of Islamic international organizations, dates back to the conferences of Muslim scholars and politicians, that were held in the backdrop of the abolishment of the Caliphate in 1924, after which several non-governmental organizations came into being, among which the WMC (1926), MWL (1962), and the WSIC (1970) are the most notable. The imperative to have a potent inter-governmental organization to articulate the demands of the Muslim world, led Pakistan, Malaysia, and Saudi Arabia successively, into a quest for a pan-Islamic arrangement. The timing was not conducive for such a venture in the fifties and early sixties, as Nasser's secularism and radicalism reigned supreme in the Muslim countries, and few of them were willing to take up the cudgels with Nasser.

The catastrophic defeat of the Arabs in the 1967 war drastically recast Egypt's foreign policy orientation and mollified Nasser's radicalism, who saw the 'reactionary' Muslim states coming out to help him in the hour of grief, rather than his socialist 'friends'. The arson at the holy mosque in Jerusalem became cardinal in the eventual formation of the first inter-governmental arrangement of the Muslim states, namely, the OIC in 1969. The Organization soon made headway in the process of its own consolidation and in a short span of time, a large number of inter-governmental institutions sprang up for cooperation in fields such as trade and economy, air navigation, education and research, and culture and information. Some of these were directly attached to the OIC, others being nominally affiliated. This made the OIC a big umbrella organization.

The nascent Organization was jolted by several inopportune and unwelcome developments in its early years. The assassination of the putative founder of the OIC, King Faisal of Saudi Arabia, in 1975 and the overthrow of Prime Minister Zulfikar Ali Bhutto of Pakistan, the OIC Chairman, in 1977 and his subsequent execution by the military, caused a blow to the OIC, since the stature of the former and charisma of the latter, and the personal identification with, and commitment to, the Muslim cause, of both, was an asset for the new Organization. Then came the shock of Egypt entering a separate treaty with Israel, disengaging itself from the conflict, placing the Palestinians into a more unenviable position and making a mockery of the unity of Muslim states. Next, the Soviet Union threw down the gauntlet by physically occupying a Muslim state, Afghanistan, in 1979. The following year, the effectiveness of the OIC was severely tested and its frailty exposed when hostilities broke out between two member states, Iran and Iraq, and it could not help but let them bleed each other to devastation.

It was not the OIC alone, but all its affiliated institutions, as well as the independent Islamic organizations that were purportedly trying to grapple with the problems. But the decade of the eighties was characterized by inertia, stagnation, and a crisis of legitimacy for the Islamic organizations. Three significant developments of 1988, namely, the Soviet decision to withdraw from Afghanistan, cease-fire on the Iran–Iraq front,

and the decision of the Palestinian leadership to concede the existence of Israel, though consequential to factors outside the purview of the Islamic organizations, at least removed the major irritants undermining their legitimacy.

The OIC and other Islamic institutions got re-invigorated after the end of the cold war around 1989–90, when the shadows of global tensions vanished from the intra-Muslim world relationships. The emergence of eight new Muslim republics in Central Asia, Caucus, and East Europe and their induction into the mainstream Muslim states' club posed one challenge while the sanguinary ethnic conflict in Bosnia posed yet another. International Islam fared comparatively better in the closing decade of the century, in asserting itself.

Overview and Assessment

The post-Second World War Muslim states are not reputed for allowing free debate on political issues. On the other hand the role of Islam in inter-state relations, Islamic instrument of diplomacy, and the rationale of Islamic organizations, are the topics that have been dilated upon, rather extensively, among the intelligentsia of the Muslim states. For our purpose, we cannot critically analyse the balance sheet of each of the numerous Islamic bodies, since they have varying levels of success or failure and, at times, an organization may have had a good record in one facet of its mandate and a poor one at another. For the present we shall thus limit ourselves to a comment on the OIC.

In hindsight, the thirty-year odyssey of the OIC saw many ups and downs. In the area of policy formulation, the OIC needs to be accorded due credit. As Ali Dessouki notes, the OIC's 'Voting behaviour in the UN General Assembly shows a surprisingly high degree of solidarity on a variety of issues, including international security, arms control, nuclear proliferation, human rights and economic question.'[1]

It is in the realm of vital practical denominators such as collective security and conflict resolution that the OIC was found to be wanting, wherein its posture sometimes amounted to sanctimonious hypocrisy. The OIC success stories in this field, such as the Pakistan–Bangladesh dispute and the South Philippines conflict are relatively few.

The performance assessment of an international organization may be approached mainly from two theoretical perspectives; the institution-oriented approach and the function-oriented one.[2] In the former, i.e., Huntingdon's approach, one evaluates the performance by probing the level of institutionalization through four basic indicators, namely (i) Adaptation, which refers to the successful adjustment to a changing environment; (ii) Complexity, by which is meant the multi-functionality of the organization; (iii) Autonomy, the reference here is to the existence of organizational values separate from those of member states; and (iv) Coherence, that stands for the internal coherence in the organization and the loyalty of member states.

As the above approach suffers from basic operational weaknesses since it orients the analyst to the performance processes alone rather than the outcomes, an output-oriented approach is another tool to analyse an organization's performance. Thus the focus would be on (i) the ability of the organization to perform certain functions and to bring about certain outcomes and as a corollary, the degree of success in attaining the declared or latent (those which are not formally stated but performed by similar organizations) goals; (ii) the processes that produced the outcomes, i.e. variables influencing performance; and (iii) the cost of delivery in performing the tasks. In other words, this approach seeks to link the efficiency with the number of decisions of the organization implemented as well as the willingness of the member states to resolve their problems, domestic and foreign, political or technical, under the framework of that organization. Applying the two approaches to the OIC, one may find that the OIC has a better record in institutionalization than in attaining specific goals.

Institutional Approach: The survival of the Islamic Conference against heavy odds, and the more than doubling of its membership since its inception in 1969 are feats in their own right. Since the fall of the Ommayyad Caliphate in AD 750, there never

had been a time when the Muslim world was a political unity. Herein lies the greatest significance of the OIC, that it has provided a setting where the Muslim states' political leaders can assemble and discuss common problems. When the Organization was formed, many had raised questions, some had expressed frustration, but with the passage of time, the staunch opposers of the OIC idea, such as Egypt and Turkey, became the most active members. This alone speaks of the capacity of the OIC to conform to the demands of politics. With the changing times, the OIC continued to evince remarkable *adaptability* to new issues, and its distinct positions on issues such as a new economic order, human rights, non-proliferation etc., made its role transcend from the specific concerns of the Muslim states to broader concerns of the human community as a whole.

There can hardly be two opinions about the OIC's *complexity* in structure and in scope. The OIC has established organs in virtually every field of potential cooperation. It has become rather so profuse in agenda, so expanded in structure, and so varied in membership that its complexity is becoming a liability. But experiences of other organizations suggest that an organization encompassing all issue areas concerning its member states is likely to be more effective in the long run.

The OIC's policies have consistently remained distinguishable from those of its individual member states. Its profusely Islamic, radical, and anti-imperialist jargon hardly matches that of any of its member states, save perhaps for Iran. The *autonomy* of the Organization is also reflected by its policies on contemporary issues and specific problems, which may or may not be congruent with the stance taken by the majority of Muslim states.

And lastly, the OIC has somehow managed to cobble together a *coherent* Islamic viewpoint on all major issues, on which the member states agree. We had noted earlier that an analysis of the voting behaviour of the Muslim states at the UN General Assembly showed a considerable degree of consensus ten years after the establishment of the OIC, as compared to ten years before. Similarly, the intra-Muslim world trade that was only 6.3 per cent of the total trade by Muslim countries in 1970 (when the OIC Secretariat started operating), rose to 10.3 per cent ten years later.

As for the OIC achievements, one can question or defend its utility by analysing whether a particular outcome could have been brought about, had the OIC not been there. Conceding that the OIC did not have the will or the capacity to get its resolutions on Israel and Serbia, implemented by force; more pertinent questions are whether the Palestinian struggle would have been sustained and self-rule attained or, for that matter, could the territorial integrity of Bosnia have been maintained, had the OIC not been there?

The OIC provides such an institutional framework, that even if it has accomplished nothing significant, the promise lies in its latent potential. Perforce, not one voice from amongst the wide spectrum of opinions about the OIC in the Muslim world, has questioned the desirability of its continuance. Both friends and detractors thus take it to be indispensable, its shortcomings in tangible achievements, as we shall discuss below, notwithstanding.

Functional Approach: A study of the OIC performance, using efficiency-related indicators, leads one to a rather different set of conclusions. The pusillanimity of its member states in fulfilling their obligations towards it and resultantly the non-implementation of a significant proportion of the decisions, are glaring lapses in the OIC system. No wonder, armed to the teeth with its Islamic rhetorical homilies, the OIC failed to patch up the differences between the warring parties in Afghanistan, Somalia, and Algeria etc. In the last mentioned case, for reasons better left unsaid, the OIC did not even engage itself in conflict resolution.

Applying the tripartite yardstick of how many goals were achieved, what were the means to achieve ends, and what was the efficiency of the methods, one can discern three principal factors that are responsible for poor efficiency. Firstly, the OIC is a conglomeration of staggering disparities in terms of size, population, wealth, human development, and state of political evolution which makes concerted action extremely difficult. Ironically, the most outspoken member states had limited diplomatic clout and the pro-status quo states were preponderant. Consequently, the resolutions used to be swayed by the hawks while implementation could only be left at the discretion of doves.

Secondly, when the OIC was established, most of the Muslim states were either in the process of consolidating newly-achieved independence or, in some cases, in the more preliminary stage, that of struggling for independence. They had little or no experience in international diplomacy or diplomatic culture. Any international regime that could even remotely infringe on the jealously guarded, hard-won 'sovereignty' was an anathema to the new leaderships. Hence, most of the initiatives fell prey to the divisiveness caused by irreconcilable national interests of the Muslim states. Moreover, the global polarization of the cold war context, from which the Muslim states were not immune, compounded the problems. It took longer for the new states to become politically mature, and in the meantime, the efforts towards political unity continued to evaporate in an atmosphere of mutual suspicions.

Thirdly, there are several constraints, not peculiar to the OIC, under which all the international organizations have to operate. These constraints are dictated by the dynamics of inter-state interaction in the contemporary era of multi-plurality. Take the example of conflict resolution; given the limited resources and ambiguous mandate of most of the international organizations, it is indeed difficult for them to be able to bring the warring sides to the negotiating table unless the stronger side shows magnanimity or the weaker gives in, or until both the sides are exhausted. The Iran–Iraq war (1980–88) is a case in point where the OIC's 'Islamic' arguments could not persuade the antagonists to agree to a cease-fire, but the same was the fate of the non-aligned unity doctrine of the NAM and of the resolutions of the more resourceful United Nations. Thus OIC's utility does not cease because of its failures. It can and does contribute to the achievements of its goals of political, economic, and social cooperation.

The Islamic Role: The OIC and its extended infrastructure is the only inter-governmental framework in the world that overtly draws inspiration from a religion. Therefore, an assessment of the OIC cannot be complete unless we analyse its role in nurturing and preserving 'international Islam', the Organization's isolated successes and failures here and there, notwithstanding. This is particularly important since we have also to establish the relevance of the title of our book.

There is scarcely any OIC declaration or document that does not invoke the 'precepts and principles enshrined in the *Shari'ah* (Islamic law)'. This is so because as the OIC leaders explained:

> Strict adherence to Islam and to Islamic principles and values as a way of life constitutes the highest protection for Muslims against the dangers which confront them. Islam is *the only path* (emphasis added) which can lead them to strength, dignity and prosperity and a better future. It is the powerful stimulant...to regain their rightful place in the world...and strive for equality, peace and prosperity for the whole mankind[3]

This was said in other words by the late President of Turkey, Turgat Ozal, who stated that only pious and devout peoples are capable of building sound societies.

It is explicitly stated in OIC literature that most of the so-called new issues in world politics have been dealt with in Islamic teachings and traditions. In other words, for each new value of the world of today, be it in the area of human and women's rights, environment protection, treatment of POWs, air and sea navigation, or something else, there is an equivalent Islamic value. It is these Islamic values that the OIC and all its subsidiary organs purport to advocate.[4]

For the Muslim world, therefore, the OIC signifies a distinct identity of 'Muslimhood'. The inscription of the Muslim slogan of *Allah-o-Akbar* (God is the greatest) on the emblem and monograms of the OIC and most of its subsidiary organs; the usage the of Islamic *Hijra* calendar in the conduct of business; and the addressing of a Muslim person by adding 'Br.' (abbreviation for *brother* as against 'Mr' for *mister)* before his name

in all official correspondence; all point to a distinct consciousness of identity in the OIC. More than that, the OIC adopts resolutions on a wide range of issues on behalf of the Muslim world. Even if many do not have the desired impact, they at least add legitimacy to the position(s) of a Muslim state or community and invariably result in moral, at times supplemented by material, assistance to the concerned party.

For the 'outside' world, the OIC and its subsidiary organs are trying to project a peace-loving and harmonious image of Islam. Side by side, it is trying to capitalize on the common bonds of Islam to improve the fortunes of its member states and peoples, by championing policies which reflect the need to relocate the Muslim states in the hierarchy of the global system. It is its vision and ideology, that has given the Organization more dynamism than many of its sister regional organizations. It is precisely for this reason that the OIC and its organs are accused of undermining the unity of the developing world, by professing distinct views and values.

Place of the Muslim World in the Emerging Landscape

We had noted earlier that most of the Muslim organizations consider the post-cold-war decade as a period in a state of flux. As the contours of the emerging political landscape gradually become discernible, the protagonists of, what is believed to be the Islamic worldview, are left wondering if the place of the Muslim world could be any other than at the lowest stratum of the emerging hierarchy. The most unwise and naïve thing for them to believe would be that the Muslim states can find a short-cut to the level of economic or political development where the advanced states stand today. The process of evolution, if at all, has to take decades, but there are three principal factors that may catalyse the process.

At first, no nation or group of nations can remain immune from the current trends towards integration that have engulfed the globe. The experience of the European Union has amply demonstrated how the bitter foes of yesteryears can embrace each other on account of commonality of perceived economic and political interests. There is a swiftly dawning realization that in the coming age, where lonely States would be virtual orphans, there would be no bargaining power for the Muslim states unless they are united, in the face of a united Europe, a united America, and a united East Asia, etc.

Secondly, the West's 'over-reaction' at the rise of Islamic fundamentalism is backfiring since there is no dearth of conspiracy theorists in the Muslim world either, who see malice in every Western action or inaction. James Piscatori aptly points out that the problem with the 'presumption of automatic antipathy between Islam and the West is that it overstates the degree of coherence in each. Individuals—let alone governments—rarely speak in civilizational terms, and it is hard to conceive Islam speaking with one voice or the West moving with one purpose'.[5] Apparently, the West has not yet realized the level of frustration among the Muslim peoples after its 'selective morality' regarding democracy in Haiti and in Algeria and about aggression, against Iraq and against the Bosnian Serbs. That is to say it is no longer believed in the Muslim world that if we become good guys in the eyes of the West, it will not squeeze us. That is happening, it is argued, regardless.

And finally, economic crises and burgeoning debt burdens in all the developing states, Muslim countries included, are causing anguish and frustration. With the increase in all sorts of theories about 'neo-exploitation' through the Euro-American Multi-National Corporations (MNCs), International Monetary Fund, and the World Bank etc., it hardly escaped anybody's notice that in 1997, the aid amounting to $2352 million channelled to the developing states was just $42 million more than what the latter had paid to the developed West in debt-servicing etc., the same year. The erstwhile megalomania of the West is bordering on kleptomania against the impoverished South, as by the end of the first quarter of the 21st century, the developing states would be paying much more to the West, than vice versa.

The interplay of these factors limits the choices available to the Muslim states, especially when the developed states are in no mood to let the 'others', like Turkey, jump into their bandwagon. Such brinkmanship was also practised against Bosnia during 1992–96. Left helpless against a Serbia supported by Orthodox Russia and a Croatia that was backed by some Catholic European states, it had only one option, to ask the co-religionist Muslim states for help.

The pace and direction of the consolidation of international Islam, and its generation or degeneration, as one may call it, depending upon which side of the political divide he belongs, into a coherent or semi-coherent Islamic States Union, would be dependent upon the legal framework of the world Islamic bodies (primarily the OIC), the quality of Muslim leadership, and internal and external environments around the Muslim world.[6] Let us discuss all the four elements one by one.

Legal framework: The legal framework refers to the sub-variables like the scope of legal jurisdiction of the Organization, its ability to compel the member states to abide by its decisions, definite membership criterion, and the levels of transparency and democracy in the decision-making process.

No progress can be made if everything is left to the altruistic intentions of the member states. When the mandate of the organization(s) is limited and fewer states are directly involved in decision-making, the performance becomes a bunch of contradictions as credibility gets compromised. For instance, the OIC, with its hands tied at the back due to legal deficiencies, is sometimes obliged to be content with 'noting' an experts' report suggesting an Action Plan 'with appreciation', or 'studying' a working committee's findings about the financial woes of the Organization 'with concern'. In both the cases, it has no mechanism to get its concerns redressed or decisions obeyed. One can deduce therefrom that the existence of a well-defined system of clamping sanctions as punitive measures is a must for a viable organization.

A measure of legal deficiency is the time lag between the decision to establish, and the start of actual performance, of the OIC subsidiary organs. The OIC had been over-ambitious on creating subsidiary institutions that has led to overlapping and duplication of activities, and occasionally, organizational rivalry also. Emphasis was placed on diversification rather than consolidation, with the net result that the institutions so much in tune with the felt needs of the Muslim world, had to be concerned more with the question of survival rather than attaining the declared goals. Without the Muslim states delegating sufficient authority to the OIC and other Islamic institutions to enable them to maintain membership discipline and carry out the function assigned to them, it is well-nigh impossible to expect miracles from these organizations.

Leadership: The role that the political leadership plays in shaping the destiny of nations can hardly be overstated. One may not comment any further except that the quality of leadership, that includes vision, dedication and altruism on the part of the political elite in the Muslim states, would be a principal determining factor in shaping the future of their peoples.

Internal environment: The linkages between the internal political dynamics of the Muslim world with its future place in the world are obvious. At the level of inter-Muslim states politics, it alludes to the non-use of force in bilateral relations, their enthusiasm for entering multi-lateral cooperation agreements, their resolve to strengthen the inter-governmental institutions and finally their willingness to concede some privileges to the larger interests of the Muslim bloc, in return for the anticipated higher collective gains.

At the intra-Muslim state level, the internal environment means the domestic political systems. There are several indicators, like democracy, rule of law, civil liberties and equal opportunities for citizens, which are prerequisites for the development of a nation and a society. The number of representative responsible governments among the Muslim states would be the key to reliably guess the level of coherence in the emerging international scenario.

External environment: The power equations of the 21st century would have influence on the course of events. How the multiple centres of power manage or mismanage their ascendancy, and how the developing world, Muslim bloc included, manipulates the rivalries of economic giants to its advantage or disadvantage, are the most intriguing question marks.

A relationship of 'positive consensus' between the would-be powers about amicably dividing spheres of influence for themselves in the developing world would spell doom for the disadvantaged states. Whereas a relationship of 'negative consensus' among the powers—hands off policy of noninterference in the affairs of the developing bloc—would give the maximum manoeuvrability to the latter. The third probable scenario of a 'confrontation' among the big power centres would expose the weaker states to the same constraints that were operating during the cold war. This will be a middle position for the erstwhile Third World, ensuring limited autonomy.

Which of the scenarios actually transpires, how the economic relations are conducted, and what would be the nature of international diplomacy in the new millennium, all this would collectively determine the external environment of the Muslim world, which in turn would reflect on the future role of international Islam as a unifying force or as a non-factor.

Agenda 21: Future Directions

The answers to the staggering questions about the role of political Islam, its 'hidden' Islamic agendas and its likely directions in the 21st century, are not easy to predict. In any case, the conscious, subconscious and unconscious biases are likely to influence the perceptions of a beholder on the topic. It was never the intention of this book to provide conclusive answers, which should better be left to the final arbiter—History. The underlying purpose of the work was to bring the discussion on the future of international Islam from the realm of rhetoric and prejudice to that of reality.

The academics and policy-makers of the day may get an insight into political Islam through an incisive description of the strengths and weaknesses, as well as past record, present orientation, and the future goals of the international Islamic institutions. These institutions promote the confidence-building process and provide a forum for meaningful cooperation. No group of nations can join together in a Union in a vacuum, without such proper infrastructure and without undergoing the evolutionary process that it entails. Such infrastructure of institutions definitely precedes a meaningful long-term alliance but the latter does not necessarily follow the former.

The argument is that the strength or weakness of international Islam and the Muslim bloc is inextricably intertwined with these organizations. This freemasonry can be the vanguard of an Islamic Union (on the pattern of the European Union), if at all, any progress is ever made in the direction. Arguing on the same line that international organization is the only conceivable framework that can bring together the Muslim states, Noor Ahmad Baba notes:

> The Muslim world, like the rest of the modern world, operates under the dualistic pressures of centripetal and centrifugal forces. This is a phenomenon of the post-industrial revolution world society that has on the one hand, increased interdependence of countries and thereby necessitated cooperation among them and on the other hand proliferated the world into smaller identities and further sharpened and strengthened their consciousness as Nation-States. International governmental organization in this regard has been a product of the human genius to accommodate these conflicting realities and make them converge for positive gains. In this connection, the international governmental organization framework has provided an ideal model for cooperation at different levels while allowing nations to preserve their separatehood.[7]

There is no denying the fact that the OIC and its subsidiary institutions have achieved much less than what the pioneers had envisioned. Most of the lofty goals and ideals are still on paper alone. The Muslim Common Market, the Islamic Free Trade Area, the Islamic Collective Security System and many such things, which the OIC has long been harping about, are yet unrealized dreams. But for our purpose, it is the potential, rather than performance of the Islamic institutions that is

relevant. The atmosphere in the Muslim world at present, owing to separate nationhood of the states, parochial outlook, mutual suspicions, and the often incongruous economic interests may not be very hospitable to a serious effort at evolving a consensus on the future political order. Nevertheless, the decades of experience in diplomacy of the Muslim states and organizations, ramifications of global political trends, fading away of colonial legacies and the existence of a good measure of areas of complementarity, are the counter-factors that cannot be discounted. At best, the Islamic Conference can turn out to be a League of Nations (LoN) of the Muslim states which organization was a failure in its own reference but on its ashes, rose a more assertive and confident organization, the United Nations.

The phenomenon of the OIC and other Islamic organizations should be taken as a process not an event. Based on religious foundations, the Islamic organizations are using the Islamic tradition in convergence with modern organizational framework to serve the community of Muslim states. It is also true that these organizations have challenged the rising role of secular ideas in Muslim societies and have disproved the view that secularism is the order of the day. More than that, the OIC experience has shown that in some respects at least, religious affinity becomes a stronger basis for cooperation than geographical proximity. The Arabs' experience with invoking Arab linguistic nationhood or socialist ideological bonds, to counter Israel failed miserably. It was the OIC, and it alone, that kept the Palestine issue alive on the slogan of a Muslim people (Palestinians) being displaced and oppressed, which the Arab League failed to realize prior to the inception of the OIC.

The role of international Islamic organizations is vital in another respect also. Unlike the hard-line Islamist political parties, with localized influence within the Muslim states, one may agree, the international Islamic organizations are forces of moderation. Their solidification as bridges between Islam and the West, may eventually contain the Islam–West rhetoric. On their part, the Islamic organizations should conduct themselves so as to be seen by the Muslims and other civilizations and societies alike as assets, in order not to fan the atavistic fears about Islamic resurgence in the West.

For the West, any under-estimation or overestimation of the phenomenon would be equally inappropriate. Much more counter-productive would be dubbing Islam in stereotypes of extremism, anti-Westism and as something repugnant to progress and development. Islamic resurgence is a potential agent of change. The West should not take change as anathema, otherwise this may inadvertently precipitate another cycle of uncalled for rivalry and conflict. The best response at present would be cooperation, trust, and mutual respect.

Economic imperatives are rising to the fore and will inevitably overshadow other imperatives such as politics, ethnicity etc. Every actor or group of actors recognizes peace and development for humanity as the ultimate goals, strives for them for its own people but professes them for all mankind. A great challenge awaits the world in the 21st century which will neither be European, American, or an Asian century but will be a world century, not by choice but of necessity. Globalism will force the pace of regionalism and the development of regional economic zones which capitalize on complementarities and synergies with a view to become better competitors in the global market. When that challenge comes, it would require a high degree of sagacity, wisdom, and statesmanship, from the leaders and peoples of all the nations, to work collectively for the common good of the human race and its abode—the earth.

NOTES and REFERENCES

1. As quoted in Haider Mehdi, *OIC: A review of its political and educational policies*, (Lahore: Progressive Publishers, 1988), p. 159.
2. Mohammad el-Selim, 'An evaluation of the OIC Performance', in Mohammad el-Selim (ed), 'The OIC in a Changing World', (Cairo: Cairo University, 1994), pp. 108–113.
3. Abdullah Ahsan, *Ummah or a Nation: Identity Crisis in the Modern Muslim Society*, (Leicester: Islamic Foundation, 1992), p. 109.
4. Abdel Monem al-Mashat, 'The OIC and the post cold war era', in Selim (Ed.), ref. 2, p. 163.
5. James Piscatori, 'International Islam?', *International Affairs*, vol. 66, No. 4, October 1990, pp. 767–789.
6. Selim, in Selim (ed.), ref. 2, pp. 113–115.
7. Noor Ahmad Baba, *OIC: Theory and Practice of Pan-Islamic Cooperation*, (Karachi: Oxford University Press, 1994), pp. 250–251.

Glossary

Ahl-ul-bait	Members of the Holy Prophet's family (or his descendants)
Ahram	Ceremonial white dress worn by Muslims for pilgrimage to *Ka'aba*
Al-Fatah	Literally 'victory'; the Arabic acronym for Palestine Liberation Organization
Allah	God
Allah-o-Akbar	God is the Greatest (i.e. the fundamental Islamic belief as well as a popular Muslim war slogan)
Al-Quds *(al-Sharif)*	(Holy) Jerusalem
Ameer/Amir	Ruler (title used by the rulers of several Gulf emirates as well as the present *Taliban* ruler of Afghanistan)
Andulusia	The Iberian peninsula; especially while referring to Spain and Portugal during the seven centuries of Muslim rule (AD 712–1492)
Ansar	Literally 'Helpers' (people of Medina who helped the Holy Prophet [PBUH])
Ameer-ul- *Mo'mineen*	Leader of the Faithful (title of the Muslim Caliphs)
Arabi/Ajami	The Arabs and the non-Arabs
Asa'biya	Nationalism (especially the one based on primordial tribal or ethnic identities)
Awqaf	Endowments (plural of *Waqf*)
Aya'h/Ayat	Verse of the Holy Quran
Azad	Liberated, free
Ba'ath	Renaissance (Also name of the ruling parties in Iraq and Syria)
Bait Ullah	House of Allah (Shrine of *Ka'aba* at Mecca)
Bait-ul-Maqdis	Holy House (The holy shrine at Jerusalem)
Bay'ah/Bay't	Oath of allegiance
Caliph (ate)	The person holding temporal and spiritual leadership of Muslims. Early Caliphs were known as the Right-Guided Caliphs. But then the institution of Caliphate became a dynastic property that was successively held by the Omayyads, Abbasids, Fatimides, and

	finally the Ottomans. The Caliphate was abolished in 1924.
Da'wa	Islamic Call, Preaching
Du'a	Prayers, supplication
Eid	Either of the two annual Muslim festivals; *Eid-ul-Fitr* and *Eid-ul-Adha*
Emir	See *Ameer* above
Fiqh	Islamic jurisprudence
Fatiha	Opening; name of the first chapter of Holy Quran
Fatwa	Religious edict
Gamiyyah Islamiya	Literally 'the Islamic Group'; the name of an armed Islamist opposition group in Egypt fighting against the autocratic rule of President Hosni Mubarak's party
Hadith	Sayings of the Holy Prophet Muhammad (PBUH)
Hajj/Haj	The annual Muslim pilgrimage to Mecca on the ninth day of the twelfth month of the Islamic calendar. Every Muslim has to perform this ritual at least once in his lifetime.
Halaal	Allowed by religion (the antonym of *Haraam*); also the kind of meat permitted to the Muslims is called *Halaal* food
Haraam	Forbidden, prohibited
Harem	Sanctuary
Hijrah	Migration (refers to the historic migration of the Holy Prophet's followers from Mecca to Medina in AD 622). Islamic calendar is also known as *Hijra* calendar. It starts from AD 622.
Hujjatul Wida	Farewell pilgrimage; the Holy Prophet's last pilgrimage to Mecca in AD 632.
Ijma'a	Consensus; esp. on a religious issue
Ijtihad	Literally 'to exert oneself'; finding the solution of a problem of jurisprudence or *Shari'ah* deducing from the known sources of law, Quran and *Hadith*, or through reasoning
Imam	Leader; esp. one who leads the Muslim prayers

Intifada Name given to the Palestinian struggle in the occupied West Bank and the Gaza strip

Jihad Struggle for a just cause (Not necessarily an armed struggle)

Ka'aba The holy Muslim shrine at Mecca

Karbala The historic plains where Imam Hussain, a grandson of the Holy Prophet, and seventy-two of his friends and family members, were slain in 61 AH (AD 780) by the ruling Governor of what is present-day Iraq

Khalifa Caliph (See above)

Madrassah School; especially Muslim religious school

Mairaj The Prophet's (PBUH) famous journey to the heavens

Majlis Parliament, Council

Mecca Also called Mecca. The holy Muslim city in Saudi Arabia

Masjid Mosque (*Masjid al Haraam*, *Masjid al Nabowi* and *Masjid al Aqsa* respectively, mean the Grand Mosque at Mecca, Prophet's Mosque at Medina and the Holy Mosque at Jerusalem)

Medina The Prophet's city, located in Saudi Arabia

Meesaq Pact

Mir Waiz The supreme preacher; a title used by the supreme religious leader of the Muslims of Kashmir

Mu'akhat Brotherhood, Fraternity (esp. the brotherhood established by the Holy Prophet (PBUH) at Medina)

Mufti Muslim jurist who can issue *fatwa*

Muhajireen People who migrated (esp. those who participated in the *Hijra* in AD 622) The Muslims who migrated to Pakistan from India during 1947 partition riots are also known as such. (Singular: *Muhajir*)

Mujahideen Those who wage *Jihad* (see above). Title popularly used for the Muslim guerrillas of Afghanistan, Kashmir etc. (Singular: *Mujahid*)

Mukti Bahini Literally 'liberation army'. The name of a secessionist rebel outfit in East Pakistan (1971)

Mu'tamar Literally 'congress or conference.' Also used to denote the WMC.

Qawm Nation (see *Ummah* below)

Qarz-e-Hasana Interest free loan. All forms of usury have been declared as absolutely *Haraam* by Islam

Quaid-e-Azam Literally 'great leader'. Title of the founder of Pakistan Mohammad Ali Jinnah

Quran Literally 'the most-read book'

Rabita Literally 'league or liaison'. Also used to refer to the MWL

Ramadhan Ninth month of the Islamic calendar; the month of fasting

Riba Usury, exploitation

Ruet-e-Hilal Sighting of the moon to determine the dates of Islamic lunar calendar (esp. for observing religious rites)

SAW/SAAW See the list of abbreviations

Shaheed A Muslim who lays down his life in the path of truth, for the sake of Islam, for justice, or for any other just cause including the defence of his own life or honour, or for the defence of his motherland. In the present context, the Muslims killed in Afghanistan, Bosnia and Kashmir etc., are also known as such.

Shari'ah Literally 'the path'. It refers to the Islamic Law

Shura Consultation

Sultan Literally 'King'; the titled used by many Muslim monarchs like those of Brunei and Oman

Sunnah The Holy Prophet's way

Sura'h Chapter of the Holy Quran

Taliban Literally 'the students'. Name of the ruling student militia of Afghanistan

Tarbiyat Training

Tawaf Circumbulation of the holy *Ka'aba* as a religious ritual.

Ulema Muslim (religious) scholars

Ummah The Muslim (Fraternal) community

Wahabi Followers of the school of thought of Imam Abdul Wahhab—the 17th century Muslim puritanical reformer of Arabia

Waqf Endowment

Zakat The compulsory alms-giving under Islamic law. This is one of the five basic tenets of Islam. It is ordinarily 2.5 per cent of the net savings of a Muslim during a given year.

Annexures

Annexure I

A. Membership of the OIC

Member States

1.	Afghanistan	1969
2.	Albania	1991
3.	Algeria	1969
4.	Azerbaijan	1991
5.	Bahrain	1970
6.	Bangladesh	1974
7.	Benin	1982
8.	Brunei Darussalam	1984
9.	Burkina Faso	1975
10.	Cameroon	1975
11.	Chad	1969
12.	Comoros	1969
13.	Djibouti	1978
14.	Egypt	1969
15.	Gabon	1974
16.	Gambia	1974
17.	Guinea	1969
18.	Guinea-Bissau	1974
19.	Indonesia	1969
20.	Iran	1969
21.	Iraq	1976
22.	Jordan	1969
23.	Kazakhstan	1995
24.	Kuwait	1969
25.	Kyrghyzistan	1992
26.	Lebanon	1969
27.	Libyan Jamahiriya	1969
28.	Malaysia	1969
29.	Maldives	1976
30.	Mali	1969
31.	Mauritania	1969
32.	Morocco	1969
33.	Mozambique	1994
34.	Niger	1969
35.	Nigeria	1986
36.	Oman	1970
37.	Pakistan	1969
38.	Palestine	1969
39.	Qatar	1970
40.	Saudi Arabia	1969
41.	Senegal	1969
42.	Sierra Leone	1972
43.	Somalia	1969
44.	Sudan	1969
45.	Surinam	1996
46.	Syria	1970
47.	Tajikistan	1992
48.	Togo	1997
49.	Tunisia	1969
50.	Turkey	1969
51.	Turkmenistan	1992
52.	Uganda	1974
53.	United Arab Emirates	1970
54.	Uzbekistan	1995
55.	Yemen, A. R.	1969
56.	Yemen, P. D. R	1969
57.	Zanzibar	1993

Note: Yemen Arab Republic and Popular Democratic Republic of Yemen have united since May 1990, whereas Zanzibar withdrew in August 1993, just a few months after joining.

Observer States

1. Bosnia-Herzegovina
2. Central African Republic
3. Guyana

Observer Communities

1. Turkish Muslim Community of Cyprus
2. Moro Muslim Community of the Philippines

Observer Organizations

a) United Nations and its bodies like, UNIDO, UNDP etc.
b) Affiliated organs of the OIC like IDB, Islamic Fiqh Academy, ISESCO, ICDT etc.
c) Regional organizations like ECO, Arab League, OAU etc.
d) Islamic international organizations like *Mu'tamar, Rabitah* etc.

Note 1: The Charts of the dates and venues of the Islamic conferences and the tenures of the OIC Secretary Generals, contained in the text are not being reproduced here. (See the list of Charts on page V.)

Note 2: For updated country profiles of all the OIC member countries, including information on flag, area, population, currency, and 45 other basic socio-economic indicators, visit the website: http//www.sesrtcic.org

Note 3: For more information on the OIC and its member states, the OIC Mission at the United Nations, Islamic Development Bank, Islamic Chamber of Commerce and Industry, Arab League, and the Muslim World League, access to the following sites might be helpful:

www. sesrtcic.org
www. un.org
www. islamicnews.org
www. idb.org
www. icci.org.pk/islamic/main.html
www. oicc.org
www. arab.net
www. awo.net

B. Charter of the Organization of the Islamic Conference

In the name of God, the Merciful, the Compassionate

The Representatives of:

The Kingdom of Afghanistan, the People's Democratic Republic of Algeria, the State of the United Arab Emirates, the State of Bahrain, the Republic of Chad, the Arab Republic of Egypt, The Republic of Guinea, the Republic of Indonesia, the Islamic Republic of Iran, the Hashemite Kingdom of Jordan, the State of Kuwait, the Republic of Lebanon, the Libyan Arab Republic, Malaysia, the Republic of Mali, the Islamic Republic of Mauritania, the Kingdom of Morocco, the Republic of Niger, the Sultanate of Oman, the Islamic Republic of Pakistan, the State of Qatar, the Kingdom of Saudi Arabia, the Republic of Senegal, the Republic of Sierra Leone, the Somali Republic, the Democratic Republic of Sudan, the Syrian Arab Republic, the Republic of Tunisia, the Republic of Turkey, and the Yemen Arab Republic, meeting in Jeddah from 14 to 18 *Muharram*, 1392H (29 February– 4 March, 1972);

REFERRING to the Conference of the Kings and Heads of State and Government of Islamic countries

held in Rabat, 9–12 *Rajab*, 1389 (22–25 September 1969);

RECALLING the First Islamic Conference of Foreign Ministers held in Jeddah, 15–17 *Muharram* 1390 (23–25 March, 1970), and the Second Islamic Conference of Foreign Ministers held in Karachi, 27–29 *Shawal* 1390 (26–28 December, 1970);

CONVINCED that their common belief constitutes a strong factor for rapprochement and solidarity among Islamic people;

RESOLVED to preserve Islamic spiritual, ethical, social and economic values, which will remain one of the important factors of achieving progress for mankind;

REAFFIRMING their commitment to the UN Charter and fundamental Human Rights the purposes and principles of which provide the basis for fruitful cooperation among all people.

DETERMINED to consolidate the bonds of the prevailing brotherly and spiritual friendship among their people, and to protect their freedom, and the common legacy of their civilization restoring particularly on the principles of justice, tolerance and non-discrimination;

IN THEIR ENDEAVOUR to enhance human well-being, progress and freedom everywhere and resolved to unite their efforts in order to secure universal peace which ensures security, freedom and justice for their people and all people throughout the world.

APPROVE the present Charter of the Islamic Conference:

ARTICLE I

The Islamic Conference:

The member states do hereby establish the Organization of "the Islamic Conference".

ARTICLE II

Objectives and Principles

A) Objectives:

The objectives of the Islamic Conference shall be:

1. to promote Islamic solidarity among member states;
2. to consolidate cooperation among member states in the economic, social, cultural, scientific and other vital fields of activities, and to carry out consultations among member states in international organizations;

3. to endeavour to eliminate racial segregation, discrimination and to eradicate colonialism in all its forms;
4. to take necessary measures to support international peace and security founded on justice;
5. to coordinate efforts for the safeguarding of the Holy Places and support of the struggle of the people of Palestine, to help them regain their rights and liberate their land;
6. to back the struggle of all Muslim people with a view to preserving their dignity, independence and national rights
7. to create a suitable atmosphere for the promotion of cooperation and understanding among member states and other countries.

B) Principles:

The member states decide and undertake that, in order to realize the objectives mentioned in the previous paragraph, they shall be inspired and guided by the following principles:

1. Total equality between member states;
2. Respect of the right of self-determination, and non-interference in the domestic affairs of member states;
3. Respect of the sovereignty, independence and territorial integrity of each member state;
4. Settlement of any conflict that may arise by peaceful means such as negotiation, mediation, reconciliation or arbitration;
5. Abstention from the threat or use of force against the territorial integrity, national unity or political independence of any member states.

ARTICLE III

Conference Bodies

The Islamic Conference is made up of:

1. the Conference of Kings and Heads of State and Government;
2. the Conference of Foreign Ministers, and
3. the General Secretariat and Subsidiary Organs;
4. the Islamic International Court of Justice.

ARTICLE IV

Conference of Kings and Heads of State

The Conference of Kings and Heads of State and Government is the supreme authority in the organization.

The Islamic Summit Conference shall convene periodically, once every three years.

It shall also be held whenever the interest of Muslim Nations warrants it, to consider matters of vital importance to the Muslims and coordinate the policy of the Organization accordingly.

ARTICLE V

Conference of Foreign Ministers

1. Conference sessions:

a) The Islamic Conference shall be convened once a year or whenever the need arises at the level of Ministers of Foreign Affairs or their officially accredited representatives. The sessions shall be held in any one of the member states.
b) An extraordinary session may be convened at the request of any member state or at the request of the Secretary General, if approved by two-thirds of the member states. The request may be circulated to all member states in order to obtain the required approval; and
c) The Conference of Foreign Ministers has the right to recommend the convening of a Conference of Heads of State or Government. The approval can be obtained for such a Conference by circulating the request to all member states.

2. The Islamic Conference of Foreign Ministers shall be held for the following purposes:

a) To consider the means of implementing the general policy of the Conference.
b) To review progress in the implementation of resolutions adopted at previous sessions.
c) To adopt resolutions on matters of common interest in accordance with the aims and objectives of the Conference set forth in this Charter.
d) To discuss the report of the Financial Committee and approve the budget of the Secretariat General.
e) 1. To appoint the Secretary General.
2. The Conference appoints three Assistants to the Secretary General on recommendation of the Secretary General. The post of a fourth Assistant

Secretary General for the cause of Al-Quds Al-Sharif and Palestine shall be created.

3. In recommending his Assistants, the Secretary General shall duly take into consideration their competence, integrity and dedication to the Charter's objectives as well as the principle of equitable geographical distribution.

f) To fix the date and venue of the coming Conference of Foreign Ministers; and

g) To consider any issue affecting one or more of the member states whenever a request to that effect is made with a view to taking appropriate measures in that respect.

3. Resolutions or recommendations of the Conference of Foreign Ministers shall be adopted by a two-third majority.

4. Two-thirds of the member states in any session of the Conference of Foreign Ministers shall constitute the quorum.

5. The Conference of Foreign Ministers decides on the basic procedures which it follows and which could be good for the Conference of Kings and Heads of State and Government. It appoints a Chairman for each session. This procedure is also applied in subsidiary organs set up by the Conference of Kings and Heads of State and Government and also by the Conference of Foreign Ministers.

ARTICLE VI

The General Secretariat

1. The General Secretariat shall be headed by a Secretary General appointed by the Foreign Ministers Conference for a period of four years renewable once only.

2. The Secretary General shall appoint the staff of the General Secretariat from amongst nations of member states, paying due regard to their competence and integrity, and in accordance with the principle of equitable geographical distribution.

3. In the performance of their duties, the Secretary General, his Assistants, and the staff of the General Secretariat, shall not seek or receive instructions from any government or authority other than the Conference. They shall refrain from taking any action that may be detrimental to their position as international officials responding only to the Conference. member states undertake to respect this quality and the nature of their responsibilities, and shall not seek to influence them in any way in the discharge of their duties.

4. The Secretariat General shall work to promote communication among member states and provide facilities for consultations and exchange of views as well as the dissemination of information that may have common significance to these States.

5. The headquarters of the Secretariat General shall be in Jeddah pending the liberation of "*Baitul Maqdis*" (Jerusalem).

6. The General Secretariat shall follow up the implementation of the resolutions and recommendations of the Conference and report back to the Conference. It shall also directly supply the member states with working papers and memoranda through appropriate channels, within the framework of the resolutions and recommendations of the Conference.

7. The General Secretariat shall prepare the meetings of the Conference in close cooperation with the host states in so far as administrative and organizational matters are concerned.

8. In the light of the agreement on immunities and privileges to be approved by the Conference:

a) The Conference shall enjoy, in the member states, such legal capacity, immunities and privileges as may be necessary for the exercise of its functions and the fulfilment of its objectives.

b) Representatives of member states shall enjoy such immunities and privileges as may be necessary for the exercise of their functions related to the Conference; and

c) The Staff of the Conference shall enjoy the immunities and privileges necessary for the performance of their duties as may be decided by the Conference.

ARTICLE VII

Finance

1. All expenses on the administration and activities of the Secretariat shall be borne by member states proportionate to their national incomes.

2. The Secretariat shall administer its financial affairs according to the rules of procedure approved by the Conference of Foreign Ministers.

3. A Standing Financial Committee shall be set up by the Conference from the accredited representatives of the participating States, and shall meet at the Headquarters of the General Secretariat. This Committee shall in conjunction with the Secretary General, prepare and supervise the budget of the

General Secretariat in accordance with the regulations approved by the Conference of Foreign Ministers.

ARTICLE VIII

Membership

The Organization of the Islamic Conference is made up of the States which took part in the Conference of Kings and Heads of State and Government held in Rabat and the two Foreign Ministers' Conferences held in Jeddah and Karachi, and signatory to the present Charter. Every Muslim State is eligible to join the Islamic Conference on submitting an application expressing its desire and preparedness to adopt this Charter. The application shall be deposited with the General Secretariat, to be brought before the Foreign Ministers' Conference at its first meeting after the submission of the application. Membership shall take effect as of the time of approval of the Conference by a two-third majority of the Conference members.

ARTICLE IX

Islamic Organization

The General Secretariat shall act within the framework of the present Charter with the approval of the Conference to consolidate relations between the Islamic Conference and the Islamic Organizations of international character and to bolster cooperation in the service of the Islamic objectives approved by this Charter.

ARTICLE X

Withdrawal

1. Any member state may withdraw from the Islamic Conference by sending a written notification to the Secretariat General, to be communicated to all member states.
2. The State applying for withdrawal shall be bound by its obligations until the end of the fiscal year during which the application of withdrawal is submitted. It shall also settle any other financial dues to the Conference.

ARTICLE XI

Amendment

Amendment to this Charter shall be made, if approved and ratified by a two-third majority of the member states.

ARTICLE XII

Interpretation

Any dispute that may arise in the interpretation, application or implementation of any Article in the present Charter shall be settled peacefully, and in all cases through consultations, negotiations, reconciliation or arbitration.

ARTICLE XIII

Language

Languages of the Conference shall be Arabic, English and French.

ARTICLE XIV

Ratification

This Charter shall be approved and ratified by member states of the Organization of the Islamic Conference in accordance with the procedure prevailing in their respective countries. This Charter goes into effect as of the date of deposition of the instruments of ratification with the General Secretariat by a simple majority of the States having participated in the Third Islamic Conference of Foreign Ministers held in Jeddah from 14 to 18 Muharram 1392 (29 February–4 March, 1972).

This Charter has been registered in conformity with Article 102 of the UN Charter on February 1st, 1974.

C. Islamic Declaration of Human Rights

The member states of the Organization of the Islamic Conference,

Reaffirming the civilizing and historical role of the Islamic Ummah which God made the best nation that has given mankind a universal and well-balanced civilization, in which harmony is established between this life and the hereafter and knowledge is combined with faith; and the role that this Ummah should play to guide a humanity confused by competing trends and ideologies, and to provide solutions to the chronic problems of this materialistic civilization.

Wishing to contribute to the efforts of mankind to assert human rights, to protect man from exploitation and persecution, and to affirm his freedom and right to a dignified life in accordance with the Islamic *Shari'ah*.

Convinced that mankind which has reached an advanced stage in materialistic science is still, and shall remain, in dire need of faith to support its civilization and of a self motivating force to guard its rights;

Believing that fundamental rights and universal freedoms in Islam are an integral part of the Islamic religion and that no one as a matter of principle has the right to suspend them in whole or in part or violate or ignore them, inasmuch as they are binding divine commandments, which are contained in the Revealed Books of God and were sent through the last of His prophets, to complete the preceding divine messages thereby making their observance an act of worship and their neglect or violation an abominable sin, and accordingly every person is individually responsible-and the Ummah collectively responsible-for their safeguard.

Proceeding from the above-mentioned principles,

Declare the following:

Article 1

a) All human beings form one family whose members are united by submission to God and descent from Adam. All men are equal in terms of basic human dignity and basic obligations and responsibilities, without any discrimination on the grounds of race, colour, language, sex, religious belief, political affiliation, social status or other considerations. True faith is the guarantee for enhancing such dignity along the path to human perfection.

b) All human beings are God's subjects, and the most loved by him are those who are most useful to the rest of His subjects, and no one has superiority over another except on the basis of piety and good deeds.

Article 2

a) Life is a God-given gift and the right to life is guaranteed to every human being. It is the duty of individuals, societies and states to protect this right from any violation, and it is prohibited to take away life except for a *Shari'ah*-prescribed reason.

b) It is forbidden to restore to such means as may result in the genocidal annihilation of mankind.

c) The preservation of human life throughout the term of time, willed by God, is a duty prescribed by *Shari'ah*.

d) Safety from bodily harm is a guaranteed right. It is the duty of the state to safeguard it, and it is prohibited to breach it without a *Shari'ah*-prescribed reason.

Article 3

a) In the event of the use of force and in case of armed conflict, it is not permissible to kill non-belligerents such as old men, women and children. The wounded and the sick shall have the right to medical treatment; and prisoners of war shall have the right to be fed, sheltered and clothed. It is prohibited to mutilate dead bodies. It is a duty to exchange prisoners of war and to arrange visits or reunions of the families separated by the circumstances of war.

b) It is prohibited to fell trees, to damage crops or livestock, and to destroy the enemy's civilian buildings and installations by shelling, blasting or any other means.

Article 4

Every human being is entitled to inviolability and the protection of his good name and honour during his life and after his death. The state and society shall protect his remains and burial place.

Article 5

a) The family is the foundation of society and marriage is the basis of its formation. Men and women have the right to marriage, and no restrictions stemming from race, colour or nationality shall prevent them from enjoying this right.

b) Society and the State shall remove all obstacles to marriage and shall facilitate marital procedure. They shall ensure family protection and welfare.

Article 6

a) Woman is equal to man in human dignity, and has rights to enjoy as well as duties to perform; she has her own civil entity and financial independence, and the right to retain her name lineage.
b) The husband is responsible for the support and welfare of the family.

Article 7

a) As of the moment of birth, every child has right due from the parents, society and the state to be accorded proper nursing, education and material, hygienic and moral care. Both the foetus and the mother must be protected and accorded special care.
b) Parents and those in such like capacity have the right to choose the type of education they desire for their children, provided they take into consideration the interest and future of the children in accordance with ethical values and the principles of the *Shari'ah*.
c) Both parents are entitled to certain rights from their children, and relatives are entitled to rights from their kin, in accordance with the tenets of the *Shari'ah*.

Article 8

Every human being has the right to enjoy his legal capacity in terms of both obligation and commitment. Should this capacity be lost or impaired, he shall be represented by his guardian.

Article 9

a) The quest for knowledge is an obligation, and the provision of education is a duty for society and the State. The State shall ensure the availability of ways and means to acquire education, and shall guarantee educational diversity in the interest of society so as to enable man to be acquainted with the religion of Islam and the facts of the universe for the benefit of mankind.
b) Every human being has the right to receive both religious and worldly education from the various institutions of education and guidance, including the family, the school, the university, the media, etc., and in such an integrated and balanced manner as to develop his personality, strengthen his faith in God and promote his respect for and defence of both rights and obligations.

Article 10

Islam is the religion of unspoiled nature. It is prohibited to exercise any form of compulsion on man, or to exploit his poverty or ignorance, in order to convert him to another religion or to atheism.

Article 11

a) Human beings are born free, and no one has the right to enslave, humiliate, oppress or exploit them, and there can be no subjugation but to God the Most High.
b) Colonialism of all types, being one of the most evil forms of enslavement, is totally prohibited. Peoples suffering from colonialism have the full right to freedom and self-determination. It is the duty of all States and peoples to support the struggle of colonized peoples for the liquidation of all forms of colonialism and occupation, and all States and peoples have the right to preserve their independent identity and exercise control over their wealth and natural resources.

Article 12

Every man shall have the right, within the framework of *Shari'ah*, to free movement and to select his place of residence, whether inside or outside his country, and if persecuted, is entitled to seek asylum in another country. The country of refuge shall ensure his protection until he reaches safety, unless asylum is motivated by an act, which the *Shari'ah* regards as a crime.

Article 13

Work is a right guaranteed by the State and Society for each person who is able to work. Everyone shall be free to choose the work that suits him best, and which serves his interests and those of society. The employee shall have the right to safety and security as well as to all other social guarantees. He may neither be assigned work beyond his capacity nor be subjected to compulsion, or exploited or harmed in any way. He shall be entitled—without any discrimination between males and females—to fair wages for his work without delay, as well as to the holidays, allowances and promotions, which he deserves. For his part, he shall be required to be dedicated and meticulous in his work. Should workers and employers disagree on any matter, the State shall intervene to settle the dispute, and have the grievances redressed, the rights confirmed, and justice enforced, without bias.

Article 14

Everyone shall have the right to legitimate gains without monopolization, deceit or harm to oneself or to others. Usury (*riba*) is absolutely prohibited.

Article 15

a) Everyone shall have the right to own property acquired in a legitimate way, and shall be entitled to the rights of ownership, without prejudice to oneself, others or to society in general. Expropriation is not permissible except for the requirements of public interest and upon payment of immediate and fair compensation.
b) Confiscation and seizure of property is prohibited except for a necessity dictated by law.

Article 16

Everyone shall have the right to enjoy the fruits of his scientific, literary, artistic or technical production, and the right to protect the moral and material interests stemming therefrom, provided that such production is not contrary to the principles of *Shari'ah*.

Article 17

a) Everyone shall have the right to live in a clean environment, away from vice and moral corruption, an environment that would foster his self-development and it is incumbent upon the State and society in general to afford that right.
b) Everyone shall have the right to medical and social care, and to all public amenities provided by society and the state, within the limits of their available resources.
c) The Sate shall ensure the right of the individual to a decent living which will enable him to meet all his requirements and those of his dependents, including food, clothing, housing, education, medical care and all other basic needs.

Article 18

a) Everyone shall have the right to live in security for himself, his religion, his dependents, his honour and property.
b) Everyone shall have the right to privacy, in the conduct of his private affairs, in his home, among his family, with regard to his property and his relationships. It is not permitted to spy on him, to place him under surveillance or to besmirch his good name. The State shall protect him from arbitrary interference.
c) A private residence is inviolable in all cases. It will not be entered without permission from its inhabitants or in any unlawful manner, nor shall it be demolished or confiscated and its dwellers evicted.

Article 19

a) All individuals are equal before the law, without distinction between the ruler and the ruled.
b) The right to resort to justice is guaranteed to everyone.
c) Liability is in essence personal.
d) There shall be no crime or punishment except as provided for in the *Shari'ah*.
e) A defendant is innocent, until his guilt is proven in a fair trial, in which he shall be given all the guarantees of defence.

Article 20

It is not permitted without legitimate reason to arrest an individual, or restrict his freedom, to exile or to punish him. It is not permitted to subject him to physical or psychological torture or to any form of humiliation, cruelty or indignity. Nor is it permitted to subject an individual to medical or scientific experimentation without his consent or at the risk of his health or of his life. Nor is it permitted to promulgate emergency laws that would provide executive authority for such actions.

Article 21

Taking hostages under any form or for any purpose is expressly forbidden.

Article 22

a) Everyone shall have the right to express his opinion freely in such manner as would not be contrary to the principles of the *Shari'ah*.

b) Everyone shall have the right to advocate what is right, and propagate what is good, and warn against what is wrong and evil, according to the norms of Islamic *Shari'ah*.

c) Information is a vital necessity to society. It may not be exploited or misused in such a way as may violate sanctities and the dignity of Prophets, undermine moral and ethical values or disintegrate, corrupt or harm society, or weaken its faith.

d) It is not permitted to arouse nationalistic or doctrinal hatred or to do anything that may be an incitement to any form of racial discrimination.

Article 23

a) Authority is trust; and abuse or malicious exploitation thereof, is absolutely prohibited, so that fundamental human rights may be guaranteed.

b) Everyone shall have the right to participate, directly or indirectly in the administration of his country's public affairs. He shall also have the right to assume public office in accordance with the provisions of *Shari'ah*.

Article 24

All the rights and freedoms stipulated in this Declaration are subject to the Islamic *Shari'ah*.

Article 25

The Islamic *Shari'ah* is the only source of reference for the explanation or clarification of any of the articles of this Declaration.

Cairo, 14 Muharram 1411 H
5 August 1990

Annexure II

Muslim Population of Muslim Countries

A. Asia (Figures in thousands)

Country	Total Population	Muslim Population	Percentage
Afghanistan	19,062	18,871	99
Azerbaijan	7,283	5,972	82
Bahrain	533	528	99
Bangladesh	119,288	102,588	86
Brunei Darussalam	270	204	75
Indonesia	191,170	172,053	90
Iran	61,565	60,333	98
Iraq	19,290	18,326	95
Jordan	4,291	4,076	95
Kazakhstan	17,048	8,865	52
Kuwait	1,970	1,970	100
Kyrgyzistan	4,518	3,524	78
Lebanon	2,838	1,987	70
Malaysia	18,792	10,148	54
Maldives	227	227	100
Oman	1,637	1,637	100
Pakistan	124,773	121,030	97
Palestine	5,200	2,288	44
Qatar	453	453	100
Saudi Arabia	15,922	15,922	100
Syria	13,276	11,550	87
Tajikstan	5,587	4,917	88
Turkey	58,362	57,778	99
Turkmenistan	3,861	3,320	86
U.A.E.	1,670	1,670	100
Uzbekistan	21,453	18,450	86
Yemen	12,535	12,410	99
Total:	732,874	661,097	90.21

Muslim Population of Muslim Countries

B. Africa (Figures in thousands)

Country	Total Population	Muslim Population	Percentage
Algeria	26,346	25,819	98
Benin	4,918	2,459	50
Burkina Faso	9,513	5,327	56
Cameroon	12,198	6,099	50
Chad	5,846	4,676	80
Comoros	585	468	80
Djibouti	467	458	98
Egypt	54,842	50,455	92
Ethiopia	52,981	37,087	70
Gabon	1,237	619	50
Gambia	908	772	85
Guinea	6,116	5,810	95
Guinea Bissau	1,006	704	70
Ivory Coast	12,910	7,101	55
Libya	4,875	4,875	100
Malawi	10,356	5,178	50
Mali	9,818	9,033	92
Mauritania	2,143	2,143	100
Morocco	26,318	26,055	99
Mozambique	14,872	8,923	60
Niger	8,252	7,840	95
Nigeria	115,664	86,748	75
Senegal	7,736	7,504	97
Sierra Leone	4,376	3,063	70
Somalia	9,204	9,204	100
Sudan	26,656	22,658	85
Tanzania	27,829	19,480	70
Tunisia	8,401	8,149	97
Togo	3,763	2,070	55
Uganda	18,674	7,470	40
Total:	488,810	378,247	77.38

Muslim Population of Muslim Countries

C. Europe and America (OIC member/observer states)

(Figures in thousands)

Country	Total Population	Muslim Population	Percentage
Albania	3,300	2,475	75
Bosnia	4,366	2,050	47
(North) Cyprus	250	250	100
Guyana	808	161	20
Suriname	438	153	35
Turkey*	58,362	57,778	99
Total	67,524	62,867	

* Turkey appears both in Table A and Table C.

D. World Muslim Population

Muslim Population of Muslim Countries

(Figures in thousands)

Continent	Muslim Countries Total			Non-Muslim Countries Total			World Population Total		
	Muslims	Percentage		Muslims	Percentage		Muslims	Percentage	
Africa	470,386	371,022	78.88	211,336	30,348	14.36	681,722	401,370	58.88
Asia	732,874	661,097	90.21	2,577,954	263,065	10.20	3,310,828	924,162	27.91
America	–	–	–	739,709	7,923	1.07	739,709	7,923	1.07
Europe	3,315	2,652	80.00	725,053	41,799	5.76	728,368	44,451	6.1
Oceana	–	–	–	27,216	451	1.66	27,216	451	1.66
Total	**1,206,575**	**1,034,771**	**85.76**	**4,281,268**	**343,586**	**8.03**	**5,487,843**	**1,378,357**	**25.12**

Annexure III

A. Rabat Communiqué

(Issued at the conclusion of the 1st Islamic Summit at Rabat on 25 Sept. 1969)

I. The Heads of Islamic States and Governments of...met at the 1st Islamic Summit Conference held in Rabat from Sept. 22 to 25, 1969;

- Convinced that their common creed constitutes a powerful factor bringing their peoples closer together and fostering understanding between them;
- Resolved to preserve the spiritual, moral and socio-economic values of Islam which remain one of the essential factors for the achievement of progress by mankind.
- They affirm their unshakable faith in the precepts of Islam which proclaim the equality of rights among all men.
- They reaffirm their adherence to the Charter of the United Nations and Fundamental Human Rights, the purposes and principles of which establish a basis for fruitful cooperation among all peoples.
- Determined to strengthen the fraternal and spiritual bonds existing between their peoples and to safeguard their freedom and the heritage of their common civilization, founded in particular upon the principles of justice, tolerance and non-discrimination.
- Anxious to promote everywhere welfare, progress and freedom.
- Resolved to unite their efforts for the preservation of world peace and security.

To these ends hereby declare:

I. Their Governments shall consult together with a view to promoting between them, a policy of close collaboration and assistance in the economic, scientific, cultural and spiritual fields.

Their Governments undertake to settle their international disputes by peaceful means in such a manner that international peace and security, and justice, are not endangered.

Their Governments shall endeavor to contribute to the development of friendly relations among nations by promoting a better understanding of the precepts of Islam with a view to developing conditions conducive to peace, security and welfare.

Decide to consider establishing a Permanent Secretariat to ensure liaison between their Governments, in accordance with the spirit of this Declaration. The temporary headquarters of the Permanent Secretariat shall be in Jeddah, pending the liberation of Jerusalem.

II. Having considered the act of arson in the holy Al-Aqsa mosque, and the situation in the Middle East, the Heads of State and Government or their representatives hereby declare:

The grievous event of 21 August 1969 which caused extensive damage by arson to the sacred Al-Aqsa mosque, has plunged over six hundred million followers of Islam throughout the world in the deepest anguish.

This sacrilege against one of humanity's most venerated shrines and the acts of destruction and profanation of the holy places which have taken place under the military occupation by Israel of Al-Quds—the Holy City of Jerusalem, sacred to the followers of Islam, Christianity and Judaism, have exacerbated tensions in the Middle East and aroused indignation among peoples throughout the world.

The Heads of State and Government or their representatives declare that the continued threat upon the sacred shrines of Islam in Jerusalem is the result of the occupation of this City by the Israeli forces. The preservation of their sacred character and unimpeded access to them, require that the Holy City should be restored its status, previous to June 1967, which was established and sanctified by the history of thirteen hundred years.

They, therefore, declare that their Governments and peoples are firmly determined to reject any solution of the problem of Palestine which would deny Jerusalem the status it had before June 1967.

They urge all Governments particularly those of France, the Union of Soviet Socialist Republics, the United Kingdom, and the United States of America, to take into account the deep attachment of the followers of Islam to Jerusalem and the solemn resolve of their Governments to strive for its liberation.

The continued military occupation of Arab territories by Israel since June 1967, the refusal by Israel to pay the slightest heed to the calls by the Security Council and the General Assembly of the United Nations to rescind the measures purporting to annex the holy city of Jerusalem to Israel, have caused their peoples and their Governments the most profound concern.

Having considered this grave situation, the Heads of State and Government and representatives urgently and earnestly appeal to all members of the international community, and more particularly to the Great Powers which have a special responsibility to maintain international peace, to intensify their collective and individual efforts to secure the speedy withdrawal of Israeli military forces from all the territories occupied as a result of the war of June 1967, in accordance with the established principle of the inadmissibility of acquisition of territory by military conquest.

Moved by the tragedy of Palestine, they affirm their full support to the Palestinian people for the restitution of its usurped rights and in its struggle for national liberation.

They reaffirm their attachment to peace but peace based on honour and justice.

B. Lahore Declaration
(Approved by the 2nd Islamic Summit at Lahore on 24 Feb. 1974)

I

The Kings, Heads of State and Government and Representatives of...met at the Second Islamic Conference held in Lahore from 22 to 24 February, 1974.

II

The Kings, Heads of State and Government and the Representatives of the Islamic countries and Organizations proclaimed:

1. The conviction that their common Faith is an indissoluble bond between their peoples; that the solidarity of the Islamic peoples is based, not on hostility towards any other human communities nor on distinctions of race and culture, but on the positive and eternal precepts of equality, fraternity and dignity of man, freedom from discrimination and exploitation and struggle against oppression and injustice;
2. Their identification with the joint struggle of the peoples of Asia, Africa and Latin America for social and economic progress and prosperity of all nations of the world.
3. Their desire that their endeavors in promoting world peace based on freedom and social justice will be imbued with the spirit of amicability and cooperation with other Faiths, in accordance with the tenets of Islam.
4. Their determination to preserve and promote solidarity among Muslim Countries, to respect each other's independence and territorial integrity, to refrain from interference in each other's internal affairs, to resolve their differences through peaceful means in a fraternal spirit and, wherever possible to utilize the mediatory influence or good offices of fraternal Muslim State or States for such resolution.
5. Their appreciation of the heroic role played by the front-line States and the Palestinian Resistance in the Ramadhan war, as well as of the Arab effort and Muslim Solidarity which became more prominent at the decisive stage.
6. Their appreciation for the activities of the Islamic Conference and its Secretariat which will continue to be the vehicle for their dedication in promoting close and fraternal cooperation among themselves, and in their other joint endeavours.

III

Having considered the present situation in the Middle East they declared that:

1. The Arab cause is the cause of all countries which oppose aggression and will not suffer the use of force to be rewarded by territory or any other gains;
2. Full and effective support should be given to the Arab countries to recover, by all means available, all their occupied lands;
3. The cause of the people of Palestine is the cause of all those who believe in the right of a people to determine its own destiny by itself and by its free will;
4. The restitution of the full national rights of the Palestinian peoples in their homeland is the essential and fundamental condition for a solution to the Middle East problem and the establishment of lasting peace on the basis of justice.
5. The international community and particularly those States which sponsored the partition of Palestine in 1947, bear the heavy responsibility of redressing the injustice perpetrated on the Palestinian people;
6. Al-Quds is a unique symbol of the confluence of Islam with the sacred divine religions. For more

than 1300 years, Muslims have held Jerusalem as a trust for all who venerate it. Muslims alone could be its loving and impartial custodians for the simple reason that Muslims alone believe in all the three prophetic religions rooted in Jerusalem. No agreement, protocol or understanding which postulates the continuance of Israeli occupation of the holy city of Jerusalem or its transfer to any non-Arab sovereignty or makes it the subject of bargaining or concessions will be acceptable to the Islamic countries. Israeli withdrawal from Jerusalem is a paramount and unchangeable prerequisite for lasting peace in the Middle East;

7. The constructive efforts undertaken by the Christian Churches, all over the world and in the Arab countries, notably in Lebanon, Egypt, Jordan and Syria to explain the Palestinian question to the international public opinion and to the world religious conferences and to solicit their support for Arab sovereignty over Jerusalem and other holy places in Palestine should be appreciated.

8. Any measure taken by Israel to change the character of the occupied Arab territories and in particular of the holy city of Jerusalem is a flagrant violation of international law and is repugnant to the feelings of the member states of the Islamic Conference and of the Islamic World in general.

9. Those African and other countries which have taken an honourable and firm position in support of the Arab cause are worthy of the highest appreciation.

10. The present trends towards a just peace cannot but concentrate on the roots of the question and disengagement cannot be viewed but as a step towards the complete Israeli withdrawal from occupied Arab territories and the full restitution of the national rights of the Palestinian people.

IV

Having considered the world economic situation and in particular that obtaining in the Islamic countries in the light of the addresses made by the Heads of State and Government and specially those made by the President of the Summit Conference, the President of Algeria, and the President of Libya and realizing the need for

i. eradication of poverty, disease and ignorance from the member states;

ii. ending exploitation of developing countries by the developed countries;

iii. regulating the terms of trade between developed countries and developing countries in the matters

of supply of raw materials and import of manufactured goods and know-how;

iv. ensuring the sovereignty and full control of the developing countries over their natural resources;

v. mitigating the current economic difficulties of the developing countries due to recent increase in oil prices;

vi mutual economic cooperation and solidarity among the Muslim countries.

The member states established a Committee consisting of experts from Algeria, Egypt, Kuwait, Libya, Pakistan, Saudi Arabia, Senegal and United Arab Emirates with powers to coopt other interested Muslim countries, for devising ways and means for the attainment of the above objectives and for the welfare of the member countries. They directed that the Committee should commence its work immediately and submit its proposals to the next Conference of Foreign Ministers for immediate consideration and action.

This Committee will meet in Jeddah, at the invitation of the Secretary-General who shall fix a date for the meeting not later than one month after the conclusion of the present Summit Conference.

V

The Kings, Heads of State and Government and the Representatives approved resolutions on Jerusalem, Middle East and Palestinian cause, Islamic Solidarity Fund, Development and International Economic Relations and other matters. These are annexed to this Declaration and all form an integral part of it.

VI

In furtherance of these and other common objectives, they direct their representatives at the United Nations and other international bodies to consult together with a view to adopting joint and agreed positions.

C. Mecca Declaration
(Adopted by the 3rd Islamic Summit at Mecca on 25 January 1981)

We, the Kings, Presidents, Emirs and Heads of Government of the Member-States of the Organization of the Islamic Conference.

Assembled at the 3rd Islamic Summit Conference held in Mecca Al-Mukarramah, from 19–22 Rabi-ul-Awwal 1401 H, corresponding to 25–28 January 1981.

Bow in gratitude to Allah, the Almighty, who has, in His Infinite Grace, enabled us to congregate in this Sacred City, in the vicinity of the Holy Kaaba, venue of Divine Revelation and the Qibla of all Muslims, at the dawn of the new Hijra Century in an assembly which we consider to be a momentous event in the history of the Islamic Ummah and the beginning of an all-embracing Islamic resurgence, demanding of all Muslims to pause and take stock of their past, evaluate their present, and look forward with confidence to a better future in a spirit of Islamic solidarity in order to restore the unity in their ranks, work for their prosperity and advancement, and achieve, once again, an exalted position in the world community and human civilization.

Strict adherence to Islamic principles and values, as a way of life, constitutes the highest protection for Muslims against the dangers which confront them. Islam is the only path which can lead them to strength, dignity and prosperity and a better future. It is the pledge and guarantee of the authenticity of the Ummah safeguarding it from the tyrannical on-rush of materialism. It is the powerful stimulant for both leaders and peoples in their struggle to liberate their holy places and to regain their rightful place in this world so that they may, in concert with other nations, strive for the establishment of equality, peace and prosperity for the whole of mankind.

The belief of all Muslims in the eternal principles of liberty, justice, human dignity, fraternity, tolerance and compassion and their constant struggle against injustice and aggression, reinforce their determination to establish just peace and harmony among peoples, to ensure respect for human rights, and to work for the strengthening of international organizations based on humanitarian principles and peaceful co-existence among nations. Thus, a new age would dawn wherein relations between nations would be governed by principles and not by force, and wherein all forms of oppression, exploitation, domination, injustice, colonialism and neo-colonialism, as well as all kinds of discrimination on grounds of race, colour, creed or sex would be banished for ever from this earth.

We declare that only firm adherence to our faith will enable us to retain the strength of our social structures and help our communities to avoid succumbing to the disunity and degradation of the past when many Muslim homelands, particularly *Al-Quds Al-Sharif*—the first Qibla and the third holiest shrine of the world of Islam— fell prey to foreign domination. History is replete with instances where Muslim communities have fallen victim to injustice and aggression; their intellectual achievements eroded; their share of their own material resources diminished. Indeed the dawn of the century saw the Muslim world confronting dangers and

challenges to its independence, security, honour and dignity.

We are saddened to note that despite all its material and scientific and technological achievements mankind today suffers from poverty of the spirit, from moral and ethical decay and societies are marred by inequities, economies are crippled by severe crises and international political order is in constant danger of destabilization. The forces of evils are now on the march, multiplying the hotbeds of war, sowing the seeds of dissensions, threatening the security of the world, man's peace of mind, and jeopardizing human civilization.

We consider that the innate qualities of the Muslim Ummah point the way to unity and solidarity, to progress and advancement, to prosperity and power. It possesses the Book of God and the Sunnah of the Holy Prophet (PBUH). In them can be found a complete way of life leading us, guiding us along the path of goodness, righteousness, and salvation. This is our cultural heritage. It enables us to break the shackles of subservience and mobilises in us the spiritual strength to utilize to the fullest extent our inherent capabilities. It is our sheet anchor for a righteous life.

It is our conviction that the Ummah of 1000 million peoples, composed of various races, spread over vast areas of the globe and possessing enormous resources, fortified by its spiritual power and utilizing to the full its human and material potential, can achieve an outstanding position in the world and ensure for itself the means of prosperity in order to bring about a better equilibrium for the benefit of all mankind.

We meet today in this august assembly and in this Serene City at this momentous juncture in the annals of Islam, determined to reinforce our solidarity and set in motion the process of our renaissance. To this end, we make the following solemn declaration:

1. All Muslims, differing though they may be, in their language, colour, domicile or other conditions, form but one nation, bound together by their common faith, moving in a single direction, drawing on one common cultural heritage, assuming one mission throughout the world. Thus, they stand as a nation of moderation, rejecting alignment to any and all blocs and ideologies, steadfastly refusing to surrender to divisive influences or to conflicts of interest.

We are, therefore, determined to move forward to reinforce our solidarity, to overcome rifts and divisions and to settle in a peaceful manner all disputes that may arise amongst us on the basis of covenants and the principles of brotherhood, unity and inter-dependence and on our belief in the justice and compassion derived from the Holy Book of Allah and the Sunnah of His

Prophet (PBUH), which constitute for us the eternal source of justice.

In fulfilment of the aspirations of our peoples, we shall intensify consultations amongst ourselves and complement and coordinate our endeavours in the international field in order to better defend our common causes and thus to enhance our prestige and position in the world.

We are equally determined to engage in *Jihad* with all the means at our disposal, to liberate our occupied territories, to support one another in defending our independence and territorial integrity, in vindicating our rights and in eliminating the injustices wreaked on our nation, depending on our own strength and firm solidarity.

2.   Conscious that Muslims today are victims of innumerable injustices and are faced with multiple dangers due to the reign of force and aggression and the politics of violence in international behaviour;

Conscious also of the fact that Islam enjoins justice and equity both upon its followers and others and it also enjoins tolerance and magnanimity towards those who do not combat us, do not force us to leave our homes and do not violate our sacred values and which never take the side of wrongdoing, injustice or oppression;

We reaffirm our unflinching resolve to combat the Zionist usurpation by force of arms of Palestinian lands and other Arab territories and to frustrate all Zionist designs and actions in this regard. We condemn and reject the policies of those who assist this aggression by giving the Zionist entity political, economic, demographic and military support, we equally reject all initiatives that are not consistent with the Palestinian question, based on the realization of the inalienable national rights of the Palestinian people, including their right to return to their homeland, their right to self-determination, including the right to establish an independent Palestinian State in their homeland, under the leadership of Palestine Liberation Organization, the sole and legitimate representative of the Palestinian people. We also reject all attempts to exert pressure on us or on other countries of the world to accept a *fait accompli* and to surrender to unjust solutions. We affirm our resolve to confront this aggression and pressure with all the means at our disposal to prepare ourselves for Jihad in order to liberate the occupied Palestinian and Arab territories and the holy places and to recover the incontrovertible rights of the Palestinian people as recognized by International Law and the UN Resolutions relating to the question of Palestine.

The violations committed against the *Harem* of *Al-Quds Al-Sharif*, the aggression perpetrated against the people of Palestine and their established national and religious rights, and the continuation of aggression through the annexation of *Al-Quds Al-Sharif* leave us no choice but to firmly stand upto this aggression and to denounce its supporter. We, therefore, pledge to wage *jihad* with all the means at our disposal for the state liberation of *Al-Quds* and the occupied territories. We shall make this liberation struggle the prime Islamic cause of this generation until, God willing *Al-Quds Al-Sharif* and all the occupied Palestinian and Arab territories are restored to their legitimate owners.

Faced with the open invasion of the territory of Afghanistan, a sovereign Muslim State, and the violation of the right of Afghan people to freedom and self-determination and their right to preserve their Muslim identity, we are determined to continue to support the struggle of the people of Afghanistan and to feel deeply concerned over the situation created by the foreign military intervention in Afghanistan.

We reaffirm our determination to seek a political solution of this crisis, on the basis of an immediate and complete withdrawal of foreign forces from Afghanistan, respect for political independence and territorial integrity, as well as the non-aligned status of Afghanistan and respect for the inalienable rights of the heroic Afghan people to self-determination without any foreign intervention or pressure.

We declare our full solidarity with the people of Afghanistan who are engaged in a Jihad to attain their freedom and independence.

We express our deep concern over the increasing rivalry between the Super-powers, their competition for spheres of influence and their increasing endeavours to intensify their military presence in the areas near and adjacent to the states of the Islamic world, such as the Indian Ocean, the Arabian Sea, the Red Sea and the Gulf.

We affirm our common conviction that the peace and stability of the Gulf and the security of its sea lanes, is the exclusive responsibility of the Gulf States without any foreign interference.

The persecution of Muslim minorities and communities in many parts of the world constitutes a violation of human rights and is contrary to the dignity of man. We call upon all countries which have Muslim minorities to enable them to perform their religious rites in full freedom and to extend to them equal rights as citizens protected by the State, in accordance with the sanctity of Law.

3.   Taking note of the present state of international relations which are characterized by the evils of bigotry and racism, dominated by the rule of force and the arms race, by greed and injustice, colonialism and exploitation of weak nations, factors which threaten our civilization

and disturb social and material equilibrium of the world; desirous of seeing that the forces of good throughout the world establish the human values of fraternity, humanity and justice; we call upon all states and peoples of the world to rebuild it anew, through sincere and concerted efforts, so that peace may prevail and conflicts and wars may be avoided. We call for the disputes to be settled peacefully, and for relations to be conducted constructively, for man's capacities to be harnessed in the service of humanity, instead of being wasted in a race for the acquisition of armaments and of weapons of death and destruction. Should this come to pass, justice would prevail and human relations would be established on the basis of equality and fraternity, benevolence and compassion, and not on the basis of discrimination and injustice, thus would the oppressed peoples of the earth be liberated; thus would they avoid the mischief of warmongers; thus would mankind be blessed with peace, and basic human rights be once again triumphant.

We resolutely support, and call upon others to support, the United Nations Organization and all other inter-governmental institutions which provide a suitable framework for cooperation, an important platform for dialogue and understanding, and an instrument for settling disputes and resolving crises. We strongly denounce any tendency to impose tutelage on and obstruct the activity of the UN. We condemn Israel and the States which systematically violate the principles of the UN Charter. We confirm our loyalty to the principles and aims of non-alignment and support the League of Arab States and the Organization of African Unity, and our full solidarity with the countries of the Third World.

4.   Convinced of the need of our people to adhere strictly to their faith and to rely on their heritage in the building up of a society committed to faith, justice and morality, we confirm our determination to be guided by the Book of Allah and the *Sunnah* of the Holy Prophet (PBUH) in shaping our lives and our societies and in strengthening our relations with peoples and countries of the world. In this, we proceed from the belief that this is the best guarantee for the triumph of truth and virtue and for the establishment of justice and peace; it is also the surest path to dignity, prosperity and security for the Islamic Ummah.

We reiterate our desire to establish the practice of *Shura* (consultation) among all Muslims, to normalize this principle in all walks of life, in order that the doing of good deeds may be promoted and wrongdoing eliminated. Thus would solidarity be implanted in the collective conscience and people would participate in the running of their affairs putting an end to dissension and discord. We shall make every effort to facilitate contacts between individual Muslims and between specialized institutions in order to provide opportunities for continuous consultation. Inspired by the Book of God and the *Sunnah* of the Holy Prophet (PBUH) which are the basic course of guidance in this regard, we affirm our determination to protect human rights and dignity. We likewise affirm our determination to ensure the rights, freedoms and basic needs of mankind. We shall endeavor, to this end, to establish the basis and the means for the protection of rights and sacred values, for the removal of injustices for the triumph of all people struggling to achieve independence, freedom and justice and for the upholding of the principles of justice and dignity whenever they are violated, including Palestine and South Africa.

5.   Aware of our common interests, we declare our determination to eliminate poverty from which some of our peoples continue to suffer, by consolidating our economic cooperation on the basis of complimentarily and pooling of our resources to achieve coordinated development of our countries. We also declare our resolve in a spirit of Islamic solidarity, to promote economic development of the countries, which are least developed amongst us.

We further pronounce our resolve to rationalize our development policies in order to ensure balanced progress in both the material and spiritual domains.

We call for efforts to be made to establish economic relations in the world on bases of justice, interdependence and mutual interest, to ensure the disappearance of the wide gap separating the industrialized countries and the developing and poor countries, and the institution of a new economic order based on equity and solidarity, under which development policies are rationalized and integrated to eliminate, once and for all, famine and its dangers, as well as all kinds of deprivation and all forms of exploitation of peoples suffering under the effects of colonialism and backwardness and to ensure the development of these countries and the proper utilization of their resources. We reaffirm the right of States to have sovereignty over their natural resources and to control their exploitation.

6.   Believing the tenets of Islam which preach that the quest of knowledge is an obligation on all Muslims we declare ourselves determined to cooperate in spreading education more widely and strengthening educational institutions until ignorance and illiteracy have been eradicated and to take measures aimed towards the strengthening of Islamic educational curricula and to encourage research and *Ijtihad* among Muslim thinkers and *Ulema* while expanding the studies of modern sciences and technologies.

We also pledge ourselves to coordinate our efforts in the field of education and culture, so that we may draw on our religious and traditional sources in order to unite the Ummah, consolidate its culture and strengthen its solidarity, cleanse our societies of the manifestations of moral laxity and deviation by inculcating moral virtues, protecting our youth from ignorance and from exploitation of the material needs of some Muslims to alienate them from their religion.

Believing in the need to propagate the principles of Islam and the spread of its culture, glory throughout the Islamic societies and in the world as a whole and to emphasize its rich heritage, its spiritual strength, moral values and laws conducive to progress, justice and prosperity, we are determined to cooperate to provide the human and material means to achieve these objectives. We also pledge to exert further efforts in various cultural fields to achieve rapprochement in the thinking of Muslims and to purify Islamic thought of all that may be alien or divisive.

We further pledge ourselves, within a framework of cooperation and a joint progress to develop our mass media and information institutions, guided in this effort by the precepts and teachings of Islam, in order to ensure that these media and institutions will have an effective role in reforming society, in a manner that helps in the establishment of an international information order characterized by justice, impartiality and morality, so that our nation may be able to show to the world its true qualities, and refute the systematic media campaigns aimed at isolating, misleading, slandering and defaming our nation.

7. Recalling with satisfaction the establishment of the Organization of the Islamic Conference, and noting with pleasure the progressive development of this Organization, as well as its growing status in international forums symbol of the unity of Muslims and a framework of understanding and rapprochement among them, and noting also the establishment of other institutions emanating from the Organization, and the continuation of joint efforts in this direction, we commit ourselves to support and develop our Organization, and to provide it with appropriate skills and adequate resources, so that it may discharge the noble tasks assigned to it, and further to support the Islamic Solidarity Fund and Al-Quds Fund as well as other organs and projects of the Organization to ensure their success.

We jointly pledge to support all international and inter-governmental Islamic bodies and institutions which conform to the objectives of our Organization for the purpose of strengthening the bonds of brotherhood between Muslims, intensifying their cooperation in various fields and reinforcing their international role. We also jointly pledge to support non-official Islamic bodies and institutions which serve the purposes and principles of the Charter of our Organization in a manner that is not contrary to the legislation of the member states.

We appeal to our peoples to hold fast to the teaching and cultural values of our religion, to unify their forces so as to face the challenges that confront them and to support one another in improving their conditions and achieving strength, dignity and prosperity.

We appeal to all other States and peoples to reciprocate the sentiments of the Members states of the OIC and their peoples in a sincere spirit of human brotherhood. Let us banish all hatred, injustice and oppression so that we may together build a world fit for mankind and so that we may enhance the level of our spiritual and material life.

We pray to God to set us on the right path, to crown our efforts with success, and to lead us to a righteous life.

"Allah hath promised such of you as believe and do good works that He will surely make them to succeed (the present rulers) in the earth even as He caused those who were before them to succeed and that He will surely establish for them their religion which He hath approved for them, and will give them in exchange safety after their fear. They serve Me. They ascribe nothing as partner unto Me. Those who disbelieve henceforth, they are the miscreants".

D. Casablanca Charter
(Adopted by the 4th Islamic Summit at Casablanca on 19 January 1984)

The representatives of...attended the conference convened in Casablanca, in the Kingdom of Morocco, in January 1984. The Sovereigns, Heads of State and Government and Representatives of Countries and Governments, Members of the Organization of the Islamic Conference are deeply grateful to God Almighty for the realization of this meeting aimed at studying the various matters of great concern to leaders in all parts of the world, and for the precious opportunity which enabled them to consult with one another and exchange views regarding the measures and positions to take, in the light of the present situation and problems.

They are the more grateful to the Almighty for the divine assistance which, throughout this meeting of brotherhood, full concord and unanimity, crowned their persistent endeavours with success.

Confident that God Almighty never fails to reward men of good will, and praying Him to provide the Muslim Nation with the means of ensuring a prosperous present and a promising future, the Sovereigns, Heads of State and Representatives of Countries and Governments attending this conference hereby declare, with optimism, their commitment to the objectives, principles and means specified in the following Charter:

- Aware that the Islamic World has, for some time, been going through rather difficult moments strewn with unpredictable obstacles and challenges;
- Assured that such a situation facing them calls for a firm determination to act promptly on the basis of rigor, perseverance, greatness and wisdom;
- Convinced that such a harsh phase calls for constant caution as well as political serenity whereby the objectives, means and courses of action may be clearly defined;
- Aware that, in order for the Islamic Nation to fulfil its mission of serving its people, and humanity whole, the Muslim World should endeavour to dispel any impediment likely to hinder the will of achieving the high ideals and noble aspirations;
- Aware, likewise, that the marginal problems and issues of secondary importance may seriously endanger the conditions of the Islamic Nation and, if continuing to prevail, lead to regrettable ends, resulting in the negligence of what is really essential and affecting all endeavours and initiatives;
- Taking note of the exigencies of the present phase which is full of risks;
- Recognizing, therefore, that the action to be taken by the Islamic World should be of a particular as well as a general nature and geared towards two main areas and two directions, so as to synchronize the interests of the Islamic World with those of the International Community;
- Recognizing that neither the particular action on the level of the Islamic Community nor that undertaken internationally can be achieved to the fullest satisfaction, if not solidly founded and imbued with strong faith;
- Convinced that the surest and most reliable source of support is to be found in the Holy Qu'ran and the Prophet's Hadith, both of which containing commands, warnings, counselling, principles and values aimed at upholding the Islamic unity, warding off the threat of disunity and discord, consolidating the steps of righteousness, reinforcing the spirit of sincere brotherhood, cooperation, justice, peace and security, safeguarding human dignity and defending people's possessions, lives and honour; for Allah, the Most Just of Judges says, "Hold fast, all of you, onto Allah's rope, and do not separate"; He also says, "The believers are nothing but brothers; so bring about reconciliation between your brothers and fear Allah in piety, that you may be granted mercy"; He again says, "And let there spring amongst you a Nation that may invite to goodness, enjoin equity and forbid abominable deeds; such are the successful ones"; He also says, "And help one another in matters of righteousness and pious fear; do not help one another in matters of sin and hostility"; as to the Prophet Muhammad, he said, "None of you can be a true believer until he wishes for his brother what he wishes for himself"; he also said, "A Muslim is the one from whose tongue and hands other Muslims are safe"; and, "It is forbidden for a Muslim to make an attempt against any other Muslim's life, possessions or honour".
- Convinced that their objectives and aspirations are aimed at firmly realizing the Islamic solidarity and unity, promoting the means of achieving socio-economic development and prosperity, paving the way towards progress and emancipation, ensuring the necessary material and moral strength, paired with credibility among the nations of the world, defending and upholding the Islamic Creed, liberating the Islamic Holy Sites, preserving the Islamic cultural heritage and civilization identity, and performing the substantial and efficient role expected to be carried out on the international scene.
- Motivated by, and determined to clear, the Islamic moral principles and values thus far described and the necessities and imperatives formulated;
- Determined to clear the Islamic scene from all sources of discord and distress, and to see to it that the lives, the possessions and the honour of Muslims are preserved;
- Favouring the peaceful means and the genuinely Islamic approach in settling any eventual difference or disagreement among Muslims;

The Sovereigns, Heads of State and Representatives of Countries and Governments attending the Summit declare their full and unanimous agreement to entrust regional Reconciliation and Arbitration Commissions, consisting of representatives of Islamic states, with the task of settling disputes and differences.

For the sake of objectivity and impartiality of the work of the regional Reconciliation and Arbitration Commissions they hereby declare that each Commission shall be assigned to an area other than that to which any of the members may belong.

In conformity with this decision, they declare having defined the Regions on the basis of a geographic distribution of the Islamic World for the setting up of the Commissions, whose members they have also appointed as they declare having defined the prerogatives of each Commission and the procedures to be followed, as described in the Appendix of this Charter.

Confirming their steady commitment to the decisions and resolutions adopted at the previous Summit Conferences, particularly the third one, last held in the Kingdom of Saudi Arabia, the Sovereigns, Heads of State and Representatives of Countries and Governments Members of the Organization of the Islamic Conference declare the following objectives to be given absolute priority:

- To consolidate the bonds of solidarity, mutual assistance and cooperation among them;
- To settle differences through the above-mentioned means of reconciliation;
- To defend the Islamic Creed by facing, through every means possible, any aggressive act it may be the object of;
- To continue the struggle for the liberation of Al-Quds;
- To continue the struggle for the liberation of the occupied Arab and Islamic territories;
- To continue the support of the Palestinian struggle for the recovery of the Palestinian People's national rights, including that of return, that of self-determination and that of establishing a State under the leadership of the Palestine Liberation Organization, the sole and legitimate representative of the Palestinian People;
- To continue the endeavours aimed at achieving development and prosperity, and ensuring the necessary material and moral strength;
- To continue the endeavours aimed at widening the scope of knowledge and acquiring technology;

The Sovereigns, Heads of State and Governments of Islamic Countries reaffirm their commitment to the international conventions, their adherence to peace and justice, and their fervent desire to see peace and tranquillity prevail all over the world.

They appeal to all Muslims, wherever they may be to continue their endeavours, guided by the clear light of faith, holding fast onto Allah's solid rope, faithful to the Prophet's Message, and worthy of what God Almighty, who speaks only the Truth, has said about them, "You are the best Nation that has been raised up for mankind, enjoining equity, forbidding abominable deeds and believing in Allah."

E. Kuwait Communiqué
(Issued at the conclusion of the 5th Islamic Summit on 29 January 1987 at Kuwait)

1. At the gracious invitation extended by His Highness Sheikh Jabir Al-Ahmed Al-Sabah, the Amir of Kuwait and pursuant to the decision adopted by the 4th Islamic Summit Conference held in Casablanca, Kingdom of Morocco in 1984, the 5th Islamic Summit Conference, the Session of Islamic Solidarity, was held in Kuwait. The State of Kuwait from 26-29 Jumada Al Oula, 1407H, corresponding to 26–29 January, 1987.

2. The Kings, Heads of State, Amirs, Heads of Government and representatives of the following member states participated in the Conference...

[Paragraphs 3-20 have been omitted as they simply recount the speeches of the Chairman and the Secretary General of the OIC.]

21. The Summit approved the recommendation of the Foreign Ministers to declare the 5th Islamic Summit as the "Summit of Islamic Solidarity".

22. The Summit received the report of His Majesty King Hassan II, Chairman of the 4th Islamic Summit, and expressed thanks and appreciation to His Majesty for his efforts and achievements in the furtherance of joint Islamic action, solidarity and the unity of the Islamic Ummah during his term of office.

23. The Summit took note with appreciation of the report of the Secretary General of the Organization of the Islamic Conference regarding the work of the Organization for the period intervening between the 4th and 5th Islamic Summit Conference.

24. The Summit examined and approved the report of H.M. King Hassan II, Chairman of the Al-Quds Committee, the report of H.E. Sir Dawda Kairaba Jawara, Chairman of the Islamic Peace Committee, the report of H.E. President Zia-ul-Haq, Chairman of the Standing Committee on Scientific and Technological Cooperation, the report of H.E. President Abdou Diouf, Chairman of the Standing Committee on Information and Cultural Affairs, and the report of H.E. President Kenan Evren, Chairman of the Standing Committee on Economic and Commercial Cooperation.

25 The Summit heard with fraternal sentiments the statement of H.E. President Rauf Denktas who voiced the rightful cause of the Muslim people of Cyprus. The Summit reiterated its past resolutions on the question of Cyprus and expressed support for the efforts of the Secretary General of the United Nations to find a just and durable solution to the problem. The Summit commended the cooperation of the Muslim Turkish people of Cyprus with the efforts of the UN Secretary General culminating in his proposed framework agreement of March 1986, and reiterated its continued support for the efforts of the Muslim Turkish people of Cyprus to secure their just rights and regain equal status with Greek Cypriots. The Summit called for the strengthening of solidarity with the Turkish Muslims of Cyprus.

26. The Summit listened with sympathy and understanding to the statements made by Prof. Abdur Rab Rasool Sayaf, Representative of the Islamic Alliance of Afghan *Mujahideen* in which he referred to the just struggle of the Afghan people for the liberation of their occupied homeland and expressed appreciation for the support extended by the Islamic countries to the Afghan *Mujahideen*.

27. The Summit also heard a statement from Mr. Nur Misuari, Chairman of the Moro National Liberation Front, in which he informed the Summit of the agreement signed between MNLF and the Philippines Government under the auspices of the OIC on 3 January 1987, in Jeddah, Kingdom of Saudi Arabia, for the grant of full autonomy of the Bangsamoro homeland of Mindanao, Basilan, Sulu, Tawi-Tawi, and Palawan, through the democratic process. The Summit expressed the hope that the ongoing negotiations for full autonomy for the people of Mindanao and the Islands, will soon bear fruit. The Summit declared its continuous solidarity with the brotherly Bangsamoro people and its intention, both collectively and individually, to extend full cooperation to the Moro National Liberation Front for Bangsamoro autonomy.

28. During the general debate Heads of delegation spoke on issues and problems confronting the Islamic world and reiterated their solid support for Islamic causes. A number of suggestions and recommendations were also made to resolve some of the most important issues facing the Islamic Ummah.

Political Issues:

29. The Summit adopted a resolution pertaining to Palestine and the Middle East which reaffirmed that the Palestine question is the core of the Arab-Israeli conflict and that a just and comprehensive peace in the region can only be established on the basis of complete and unconditional withdrawal of the Zionist enemy from all occupied Palestinian and Arab territories, the restoration of the Palestinian people's inalienable rights including its right to return, to self-determination and to establish an independent Palestinian State on its national soil, with *Al-Quds Al-Sharif* as its capital, and under the leadership of the PLO, its sole legitimate representative. The Summit stressed that any solution to this conflict must be sought with the full participation of the Palestine Liberation Organization, on an equal and equitable footing with the other parties, in all international conferences, activities, and deliberations relating to the Palestine Question and the Arab-Zionist Conflict.

The resolution firmly rejected all separate agreements and initiatives and considered that Security Council resolution 242 of 1967 does not constitute an adequate basis for the solution of the Palestine and Middle East question. It called for resolute and continued action to implement the Arab Peace Plan and reaffirmed the need for the early convening of an International Conference on Peace in the Middle East under the auspices of the United Nations with the participation of all parties concerned including the PLO on an equal footing, and the participation of the permanent members of the Security Council to achieve a just and lasting settlement of the Palestine Question and the Middle East conflict. The resolution also called for the formation of a preparatory committee to facilitate the holding of the International Conference.

The Conference condemned the US policy of continued and unlimited support to the Zionist enemy in the political, military, economic and all other fields.

The Summit called upon member states to intensify their contacts with the European Economic Committee (EEC) with a view to inducing it to take more positive stands based on respect for international law, the UN Charter and resolutions Palestinian people.

The Conference reiterated that all Zionist legislations in *Al-Quds Al-Sharif*, the other occupied

Palestinian territories and the Heights are null and void.

It also considered that all the settlements set up or to be set up by the Zionist enemy in all occupied territories including *Al-Quds* are illegal and have no validity.

It hailed the steadfastness of the Lebanese people, and affirmed its strong resolve for the preservation of the independence, sovereignty, and territorial integrity of the land and people of Lebanon and its institutions, and demanded the immediate and complete withdrawal of all Israeli forces from Lebanon.

The Summit called on member states to abide by the principle of not establishing any form of direct or indirect relations with the Zionist enemy, and requested them to extend all forms of support and assistance to the Palestinian people so as to reinforce their steadfastness and enable them to attain their inalienable national rights. It called for continued issuance of the Palestine Stamp, the application of the provisions of Islamic boycott of the Zionist enemy, and to start teaching the course on the history and geography of Palestine on the basis of a unified syllabus and as a compulsory subject at all levels of school education. It expressed support for the efforts of the Islamic Bureau for Military Coordination with Palestine, and the efforts of the Committee for Monitoring the moves of the Zionist Enemy, and the Islamic Expert Committee on the Zionist settlements in Palestine.

It called on member states to redouble their efforts to stamp out racial discrimination and Zionism.

The Summit hailed the peoples of Namibia and South Africa and the friendly Third-World countries which advocate peace and equality, especially members of the Non-Aligned Movement and the Organization of African Unity.

30. The Summit adopted a resolution on the city of *Al-Quds Al-Sharif*, reaffirming total adherence to the provisions of the "Islamic Programme of Action" and all the resolutions adopted by Al-Quds Committee, regarding the Islamic Ummah's insistence on preserving the Arab-Islamic character of that holy city, and its commitment to work for liberating it. It called for effecting the twinning of Al-Quds Al-Sharif with all Islamic Capitals and Cities.

The Conference took note of the project for the establishment of an Arab hospital in Al-Quds to serve as a substitute for the Hospice Charity Hospital which has been closed down, without any justification, by the Israeli occupation authorities with a view to judaising Al-Quds. The Summit supported this humanitarian project and urged member states to participate in its realization.

31. The Conference adopted a resolution on the Syrian Golan Heights declaring Israel's occupation of the area and its decision to impose its laws and administration on the occupied Golan Heights as an act of aggression. It condemned the Zionist enemy's oppressive, terrorist measures against the Syrian citizens in that region.

32. The Conference adopted a resolution on the Strategic Alliance between the United States and Israel, declaring this alliance as contributing to the rising tension in the region, and called on member states to take effective measures to counter the dangers arising from it.

33. The Conference adopted a resolution on establishment of diplomatic relations with the Zionist enemy, condemning the resumption by some States of their diplomatic relations with the Zionist enemy and appealed to those States which intend to establish diplomatic relations with the enemy to desist from doing so, in pursuance of the resolutions of the Islamic Conference.

34. The Summit reaffirmed that Zionism is a form of racism and racial discrimination as stated in the UN General Assembly resolution 3370 (S-30) of 1975 and declared the Islamic States' resolve to coordinate their efforts in the United Nations to counter the US—Israeli campaign for rescinding that resolution.

35. The Summit adopted a resolution regarding the Al-Quds Fund and its *Waqf* which stressed the importance of the vital and effective role played by the Al-Quds Fund and its *Waqf* in supporting the steadfastness of the Palestinian people in the occupied territories. It called upon member states to fulfil their pledge to pay up the capitals of the Al-Quds Fund and its *Waqf* amounting to one hundred million dollars each.

36. The Summit adopted a resolution on the situation of the Palestinian camps in Lebanon, calling for immediate cease-fire and cessation of attacks on the Camps, the lifting of the siege laid to the camps and the return thereto of the displaced persons. It called for the support and follow up of the efforts of the League of Arab States in this regard.

F. Dakar Declaration

(Approved by the 6th Islamic Summit in Dakar on
11 December 1991)

We, the Sovereigns, Kings, Heads of State and Government of the member states of the Organization of the Islamic Conference met in Dakar, Republic of Senegal, from 3-5 Jumada II, 1412 H (9-11 December, 1991), for the 6th Islamic Summit Conference (Session of *Al-Quds Al-Sharif*, Concord and Unity). This Conference being held in Senegal, a country of the African continent assumes, therefore, special significance, as it confirms the importance of the African dimension in the Joint Islamic Action.

- Convinced that the African member states of the Organization of the Islamic Conference contribute in an effective and positive manner to the consecration in these different countries of the genuine principles of Islam, raising the banner of the true religion and spreading its noble precepts in the service of closer cooperation, greater solidarity among peoples and consolidation of the foundations of peace and security in the world.
- Firmly convinced that his Excellency President Abdou Diouf's Chairmanship of our prestigious Organization will be a fruitful and enriching period for the Islamic Ummah for its grandeur and the glory of our true religion at this crucial international juncture.
- Convinced also that his Excellency President Abdou Diouf's sagacity together with his deep knowledge of the activities of the Islamic Conference, his vast experience and his eminent international stature will be the firmest support for the fulfilment of the aspirations of the Islamic Ummah.
- Abiding by the noble teachings of Islam and in conformity with the objectives and principles of the Charter of the Organization of the Islamic Conference;
- Reaffirming our resolve to fulfil our solemn pledges contained in the Mecca Declaration to strengthen Islamic unity and solidarity by fostering Joint Islamic Action in different fields;
- Recognizing the importance of the current process of fundamental transformation in the system of international relations;
- Determined to contribute actively together with the international community toward the establishment of a New International Order based on peace and progress and respect for the international legality and capable of guaranteeing justice and equity for all;

- Emphasizing the importance of seeking solution to global issues through dialogue and cooperation among all nations of the World and adherence to the principles of international law;
- Recognizing the indivisible nature of the universal realization of the right of peoples to self-determination;
- Committed to the achievement of the objectives outlined in the Plan of Action to Strengthen Economic Cooperation among member states adopted by the 3rd Islamic Summit;
- Determined to foster further their cultural and information exchanges and to develop active cooperation in these fields;
- Convinced of the need to rationalize and revitalize the institutional mechanisms of the Organization of the Islamic Conference;
- Strongly attached to fundamental freedoms and human rights for all peoples of the world and determined to act together to safeguard and promote the dignity of all Muslims;
- Considering that solidarity must constitute a supreme value for guiding all development strategies established at the level of the Islamic Ummah.
- Committing ourselves, therefore, to make efforts to organize more strongly this solidarity, so that the immense material and human resources given to the Islamic Ummah by the Almighty Allah be perceived collectively as a manifestation of the Divine compassion for promoting the welfare of member states of the OIC.

We solemnly pledge to unite our efforts in defence of all Islamic causes, and in the first place the cause of *Al-Quds Al-Sharif*, the foremost cause of Islam, to ensure equity and justice in settling outstanding issues, conflicts and disputes, to banish poverty, misery and disease; and to develop the necessary scientific and technological capabilities through inter-Islamic cooperation; to further enrich our glorious Islamic heritage; and to work together with the international community in all domains to usher for the Islamic Ummah, and for the whole of mankind, a new era of peace, progress and prosperity.

In pursuance of the above, we, the leaders of the member states of the Organization of the Islamic Conference, solemnly commit ourselves to the following:

I

Political Cooperation

i. We reaffirm our resolve to face the Israeli occupation of Palestinian and other Arab territories occupied since 1967; as well our determination to continue to reject and oppose the pursuit of Israeli plans and practices. We also reject and denounce those policies which make this occupation possible by providing it political, economic, demographic and military support. We also reject any initiative that does not conform to a just solution of the question of Palestine based on the realization of the inalienable national rights of the Palestinian people including their right to return to their homeland, their right to self-determination and the establishment of an independent Palestinian State in their homeland. We reaffirm our resolve to confront this occupation and pressure with all the means at our disposal to mobilize ourselves to strive for the liberation of the occupied Palestinian and Arab territories and the Holy places and to recover the inalienable rights of the Palestinian people as recognized by International Law and the UN Resolutions relating to the question of Palestine.

The violations committed against the *Haram* of Al-Quds Al-Sharif, the aggression perpetrated against Islamic and Christian sanctities in occupied Palestine, and against the inalienable religious and national rights of the people of Palestine, as well as the continuation of the aggression through the decisions aimed at annexing Al-Quds Al-Sharif, and its usurpation from its legitimate owners prompt us to adopt a categorical stand in the face of this aggression and to denounce those who support or recognize it. Accordingly, we shall support efforts conducive to the liberation of Al-Quds and shall consider such liberation as the major Islamic cause and the responsibility of the present generation of our Ummah until such time, as Al-Quds and the occupied Palestinian and Arab territories are liberated and returned to their legitimate owners by the Grace of Allah.

ii. We welcome and support the peace process which is under way and which is aimed at establishing a just and comprehensive peace in the Middle East on the basis of Security Council Resolutions 242 and 338 and of the formula of land for peace and the inalienable national rights of the Palestinian people.

iii. We reaffirm resolution No. 2/20-P adopted by the 20th Islamic Conference of Foreign Ministers held in Istanbul concerning the occupied Syrian Golan. We further condemn Israel for persisting in the implementation of its settlement policies through the establishment of new settlement in the occupied Syrian Golan.

iv. We shall, within the framework of respect for the principles of international law and especially the principles of sovereign equality and respect for the rights inherent in the sovereignty, seek to develop further and consolidate our bilateral as well as multilateral relations.

v. We shall refrain in our mutual relations as well as in our international relations in general from the threat or use of force against the territorial integrity or political independence of any state.

vi. We reaffirm our unanimous condemnation of the phenomenon of terrorism which constitutes a violation of the teachings of the glorious Islamic religion, values, norms and traditions of our countries, which treat man with respect and dignity. We further affirm our unflinching determination to cooperate sincerely with the international community in its efforts within the framework of legality and respect of the principles of international law, with a view to eradicating international terrorism in all its forms and practices.

vii. We shall scrupulously abide by the principles of non-intervention and non-interference in the internal affairs of our respective countries.

viii. We consider as inviolable all the internationally recognized frontiers.

ix. We shall settle any dispute that might arise amongst ourselves by peaceful means. To this effect we shall use means as negotiations, good offices, inquiry, mediation, conciliation, arbitration, judicial settlement or other peaceful means to settle any dispute between us especially by using all possibilities offered in this regard by the Organization of the Islamic Conference.

x. We shall respect the equal rights of the peoples and their rights to self-determination, acting at all times in conformity with the purposes and principles of the Charters of the Organization of the Islamic Conference and of the United Nations. We shall join efforts to support the just struggle of the peoples under colonial domination or foreign occupation to enable them to exercise their right to self-determination.

xi. We shall consider any threat against any member state as directed against international peace and security, including of the member states. It is incumbent upon us to act individually and collectively within the framework of the Organization of the Islamic Conference, the United Nations and other international and regional organizations, to eliminate such a threat with a view to strengthening the security and stability of all member states through the adoption of appropriate measures aimed at consolidating our cooperation in these fields within the framework of international legality.

xii. We shall encourage, wherever appropriate, the initiation of confidence and security building measures among member states, bilaterally or at the sub-regional or regional levels in conformity with the provisions and principles of this Declaration.

xiii. We shall individually and collectively endeavor to protect and promote the rights of Muslim communities and minorities in non-member states as well as strengthen the means of action of the Organization of the Islamic Conference, in this regard.

xiv. We pledge to strengthen Joint Islamic Action in the humanitarian fields by consolidating actions of existing bodies in particular to alleviate the suffering of refugees and displaced persons as well as to meet the contingencies resulting from natural and other disasters.

II

Cooperation in the Field of Economics, Science and Technology

i. We shall promote the expansion of our mutual trade in goods and services by ensuring conditions in favour of such development. In this context we shall utilize the full potentials offered by the Organization of the Islamic Conference, in particular the Standing Committee on Commercial and Economic Cooperation, so as to conclude multilateral and intra-governmental and other agreements for the long-term development of intra-Islamic trade and highlight the important role which the private sector could play, and assist this sector to strengthen Joint Islamic Action, emphasizing the necessity of the member states to take appropriate measures to establish economic and commercial contacts between the firms, organizations, banks and enterprises and other Islamic institutions as well as businessmen in member states.

We shall endeavour to reduce or progressively eliminate all kinds of obstacles to the development of intra-Islamic trade and to encourage in the future the implementation of the principle of the Most Favoured Nation clause. In this regard we shall take appropriate measures, leading to the setting up of an Islamic common market.

ii. We shall consider measures for creating favourable conditions for the participation of private sector firms, organizations and enterprises of member states, for the development of intra-Islamic trade.

iii. We shall endeavour to organize either bilaterally or through the auspices of the Organization of the Islamic Conference an effective and efficient network of information relating to economic, commercial, financial and monetary matters so as to encourage economic contacts among member states.

iv. We shall endeavour to promote industrial cooperation bilaterally and multilaterally. In this context we shall consider establishment of joint industrial ventures including joint production and sale, specialization in production and sale, construction, adaptation and modernization of industrial plants and the exchange of technical information as well as of the pooling of the capital resources for such production.

v. We shall endeavour to build and improve efficient transportation and communication networks, wherever appropriate, including roads, rails and aviation facilities as well as shipping lines either bilaterally and or as part of sub-regional or regional cooperation, so as to improve economic and commercial exchange between the Islamic world.

vi. We shall give high priority to the human resources development and concert our efforts to achieve this development objective.

vii. We shall intensify our efforts to promote intra-Islamic cooperation in the scientific and technological fields bilaterally and multilaterally under the auspices of the OIC, and in the framework of the Standing Committee of Scientific and Technological Cooperation and Islamic Foundation for Science, Technology and Development.

We shall endeavour to establish mechanisms for exchange and dissemination of the results of scientific and technological research and ensure the intensification of the transfer of technology among member states.

viii. We shall ensure that in the following stage efforts will be intensified for the implementation of integrated development projects which help achieve economic growth in Africa and ensure to the Africans, better living standards and protection from the natural disasters to which they are exposed.

We have great hopes that the Committee of Islamic Solidarity with the Countries and the Peoples of the Sahel, will succeed in drawing up a consistent plan to protect African peoples and their economic potentialities against the disasters, drought and desertification that stand in the way of their development.

We are also aware that providing suitable conditions for such a development implies finding appropriate solutions to the problems of the indebtedness of African States. We consider that meeting the challenges of development in Africa necessarily imply a cultural plan based on the principles of our true religion which call for solidarity, tolerance and advancement to achieve the stability and security of our societies.

ix. We shall endeavour to take active part in the work of the United Nations Conference on Environment and Development to be held in June 1992 at Rio de Janeiro. We emphasize in this respect, the importance for this Conference to serve as an appropriate framework for promoting international cooperation in the field of environment and sustained development, requiring a multilateral sector-based approach, and taking into account the various components of the environment as well as the developmental priorities of the OIC member states.

III

Cooperation in the Social, Cultural and Information Fields

We affirm that belief in the same Islamic spiritual values is the very essence of the Organization of Islamic Conference, as such the cultural dimension of Joint Islamic Action asserts itself as a top priority. In this framework deeper mutual understanding between the people of the Islamic Ummah must be regarded as a basic objective. Proceeding from these major considerations we are determined to endeavour to:

i. Preserve and enhance the common Islamic heritage including monuments and arts related to Islamic culture and civilization in the member states as well as to promote the development of national and Islamic cultural values and to work for the strengthening of inter-Islamic cooperation within the framework of the OIC organs and institutions.

ii. Implement the OIC Cultural Strategy for the Islamic world as well as intensify our efforts to promote at the national level a better awareness among the Muslim youth, the noble values of Islam and to inculcate in them pride in the achievements of the glorious Islamic civilization, thus contributing to the development of understanding and tolerance among peoples and faiths through open mindedness.

iii. Provide the Organization of the Islamic Conference with the required resources in order to support and coordinate Islamic *Da'wa* efforts and to improve educational curricula and training programmes as well as to disseminate the teachings of Islam throughout the world, and also to instil the lofty Islamic values through the implementation of relevant programmes both in the educational institutions and through the media.

iv. Counter individually and collectively, any campaign of vilification and denigration waged against Islam and its sacred values, as well as the desecration of the Islamic places of worship.

v. Inform the whole world of the essence of Islamic civilization, culture and thought, so as to provide the best possible reflection of the true image of Islam, and to participate in the enrichment of universal civilization.

vi. Take appropriate measures to implement the Cairo Declaration on Human Rights in Islam taking into account the legislative procedures enforced by each member state.

vii. Concert our efforts to protect our societies from the evils of drug abuse.

viii. We insist that the survival, protection and full development of children should be of the highest priority in the national, regional and international programmes and reaffirm our commitment to implement in an effective manner the Declaration and Plan of Action of the World Summit for Children, held in New York in 1990.

ix. We reaffirm the importance of the role of women in the process of development of the Muslim societies and call for greater participation of women in the activities of economic and social development.

x. We shall endeavour to avail ourselves of the opportunities provided by the technological revolution in the fields of communications to develop and strengthen cooperation in the field of information. In this context, we shall undertake bilateral and multilateral cooperation to consolidate and encourage greater information flows among member states.

xi. We shall also provide full support required for the development and strengthening of the OIC institutions in the field of information and culture.

IV

Strengthening of the Effectiveness and Performance of the System of the Organization of the Islamic Conference

i. We are determined to fully utilize institutional mechanisms and structures of the OIC for further intensifying intra-Islamic cooperation in all fields.

ii. We hereby resolve to provide to the OIC institutions, requisite support so as to enable them to fulfil the noble tasks assigned to them.

iii. We also consider that the numerous changes and developments that have taken place on the international scene require readaptation of the Charter of the Organization of Islamic Conference so as to enable it to effectively benefit from the experience gained by the Organization in the various fields since the adoption of its Charter in 1971 to respond to the requirements of the coming phase.

V

Follow-Up and Implementation

We hereby entrust the Secretary General of the Organization of the Islamic Conference to pursue and follow up, the implementation of the provisions of this Declaration, and to regularly report thereon to the Chairman of the 6th Islamic Summit Conference, and to present a report to the 7th Islamic Summit Conference.

G. Casablanca Declaration

(Adopted by the 7th Islamic Summit on 14 December 1994 at Casablanca)

We the Kings, Heads of States and Governments of the member states of the Organization of the Islamic Conference, gathered in the City of Casablanca in the Kingdom of Morocco, on 11 and 13 Rajab 1415H (13 and 15 December 1994) for the 7th Islamic Summit (Session of fraternity and revival), which coincides with the 25th anniversary of the establishment of the Organization of the Islamic Conference at the First Islamic Summit, held in 1969 in the Kingdom of Morocco:

Proceeding from our adherence to the letter and spirit of the Islamic faith and our firm conviction of the good that ensues to humanity from the call and teachings of Islam;

Stressing our sincere determination to abide by the Charter of the Organization of the Islamic Conference

and to strengthen solidarity between the member states, and aware of the importance of the current world developments and of the need for our Ummah to adjust to them, while preserving its civilizational and cultural specifications;

Determined to contribute, together with the international community, to the establishment of a new world order, based on justice, equality, peace and the respect of international legality;

Adhering to the basic freedom and human rights of all peoples on Earth, to the preservation of the dignity of Muslims, and to the need of firmly meeting the challenges confronting the Islamic Ummah, as a result of the misrepresentations and misunderstandings, our true Islamic religion is being subjected to;

Relying on our total confidence in the wisdom of His Majesty, King Hassan II, his vast experience and the prominent position he occupies on the international scene, and on our conviction that His Majesty's chairmanship of our Organization will promote the fulfilment of the aspirations of our Islamic Ummah;

DECLARE our commitment to the following:

1. To make every effort to strengthen solidarity and join forces to defend all Islamic causes and protect the sanctity of Islam: to call for wisdom, good counsel and conciliatory dialogue.

And noting with satisfaction the ongoing peace process and the new developments in the Middle East Region, we believe that the progress achieved must be promptly followed by crucial steps forward on both the Syrian and Lebanese tracks with a view to establishing a just and comprehensive peace, on the basis of Security Council Resolutions 242, 338 and 425 and the principle of land for peace, and the restitution of all occupied Arab and Palestinian territories, including the City of *Al-Quds Al-Sharif*, the Syrian Golan and South Lebanon and the guaranteeing of the Palestinian people's sovereignty over their homeland and their right to return to self-determination and the setting up of their independent State with *Al-Quds Al-Sharif* as its capital. In this respect, we draw attention of the sponsors of the Peace Conference and international community to the danger of Israel's continued procrastination and dilatory attitude aimed at eluding the implementation of the resolutions of international legality.

2. To strive with due regard to international law, to develop and consolidate bilateral and multilateral relations, and to abide rigorously by the principles of non-interference in internal affairs and of settling conflicts between member states through peaceful means, while stressing the need to settle regional

disputes and conflicts in accordance with the principles of the UN Charter, the resolutions of international legality and the principles of justice and equity.

We consider that any threat to the security of any member state is a threat to world peace and security, which requires action within the framework of our Organization, of the United Nations and the other regional and international organizations, aimed at eliminating such threats in order to safeguard the peace and stability of all member states in accordance with international legality.

In the field of economic, scientific and technological cooperation, we encourage the expansion of commercial exchanges and creation of appropriate conditions for this development, including the possibility of reducing all kinds of obstacles to the development of trade within the Islamic World.

In the cultural and information fields, we declare our determination to preserve and enhance our common Islamic heritage, to intensify national efforts, to increase the awareness of Muslim Youth of the lofty values of Islam, and instil in them a sense of pride in the achievements of the glorious Islamic civilization, and to contribute to furthering understanding and tolerance among peoples and religions.

To this end we shall strive to coordinate the efforts of the Islamic *Da'wa*, develop educational curricula, and to disseminate the teachings of Islam throughout the world, with due regard for the sovereignty of nations and cooperation between them. We shall also attempt to propagate the values of Islam through the mass media, by developing information activities, and supporting the information institutions to counter the fierce campaign waged against Islam and to disseminate the true and honourable image of Islam and the essence of its eternal *Shariah,* in order to clear misunderstandings, and to expose ill-intentioned people who do wrong to Islam.

In this respect, we call for facing the reality of our modern times with an Islamic open-mindedness, based on the principles of the true Islamic religion, and far from all forms of extremism and fanaticism.

3. We reaffirm our denunciation of all forms of terrorism including state terrorism as they represent a total disregard of the teachings of the true Islamic religion, and a blatant violation of our values, our traditions, and our heritage. We also declare our firm determination to join, in a spirit of sincere cooperation, in international efforts, to eliminate all forms and practices of terrorism, with due regard to legality and the principles of international law without prejudice to the legitimate right of national resistance to rise up against occupation and secure national rights.

4. We pledge to strengthen joint Islamic action in all fields, especially, at the humanitarian level including support to those mechanisms which work towards alleviating the sufferings of refugees and displaced people, and which confront emergencies arising form natural disasters and others.

5. To work, at the individual and collective levels, towards protecting the rights of Muslim groups and minorities in non-member states.

6. To reaffirm human rights in Islam. In this context, we affirm the necessity of coordinating our efforts to protect our societies from the harmful effects of drug addiction and give great importance to the education and protection of children, to the role of women in Islamic society and their participation in activities related to economic and social development.

7. Aware of the need to upgrade our working methods in keeping with world developments and in order to meet the requirements of the next phase, we pledge to provide necessary support to the institutions, established within the framework of the Organization of the Islamic Conference so as to enable them to achieve the desired developments.

8. We commission the Secretary General of the Organization of the Islamic Conference to follow up the implementation of the provisions of this Declaration and report thereon, to the Chairman of the 7th Islamic Summit and to the member states.

H. Islamabad Declaration

(Text of Islamabad Declaration of the Extraordinary Session of the Islamic Summit held on 23rd March 1997)

We, the Sovereigns, Kings, Heads of State and Government of OIC States, assembled in Islamabad for the Extraordinary Session of the Islamic Summit Conference:

• Guided by the noble injunctions of Islam and imbued by the Quranic verse "Hold firm to the rope of Allah collectively and create no distensions" and "The believers are naught else than brothers; Therefore make peace between your brethren and fear Allah that happily ye may attain mercy."

• Reaffirming our resolve to fulfil our solemn pledges contained in the Mecca Declaration as well as the Declarations adopted by all previous Islamic Summit Conferences;

• Determined to strengthening Islamic solidarity and promoting cooperation among the OIC member states for the collective well-being of all Islamic nations and peoples in conformity with the principles and objectives of the OIC Charter;

- Cognisant of the processes of profound transformation in the global political, security, economic and commercial environment as mankind stands on the threshold of the new millennium;
- Emphasizing the need for forging a common vision of mankind's peace, progress and prosperity and ushering a new era of cooperation among nations to build a global society, based on shared values and founded on principles of equity, justice, law and respect for principles of sovereignty, territorial integrity and non-interference in internal affairs of states;
- Desirous of promoting harmony, tolerance and understanding among all peoples by consciously eschewing exclusivity, domination, religious, racial or cultural prejudice and extremism;
- Convinced that over 1 billion Muslims, across five continents, endowed by the Almighty Allah with tremendous spiritual, human and material resources, are destined to realize for themselves a glorious destiny;

In pursuance thereof we hereby solemnly declare that we shall:

Broaden and deepen cooperation among OIC member states in all spheres, augment unity and solidarity amongst us, harness our resources both human and material for the collective good of our societies and peoples.

Affirm that a just and comprehensive peace in the Middle East cannot be achieved without the implementation of Security Council Resolutions 242,338 and 425 and the principle of "land for peace", which guarantee Israel's total withdrawal from all Occupied Palestinian and Arab territories to the lines of 4 June 1967 including the city of *Al-Quds Al-Sheriff*, the Syrian Golan as well as occupied South Lebanon and Western Bekaa, occupied since 14 March 1978 and call upon Israel to reaffirm its adherence to the commitments, agreements and undertakings given by it during the negotiations and to resume the talks on the Syrian track from the point at which they stopped as well as enable the Palestinian people to regain their inalienable national right, including their rights to return, to self-determination and to the establishment of their independent State on their national soil, with *Al-Quds Al-Sharif* as its capital.

Reaffirm that *Al-Quds Al-Sharif* forms an integral part of the Palestinian territories occupied in 1967 and is subject to whatever is applicable to all the other occupied territories, call on the international community to compel Israel to abide by all international resolutions on the City of *Al-Quds Al-Sharif* to refrain from all measures, practices and decisions aimed at Judaising the city, intensifying Jewish settlements therein and expelling its Arab Palestinian inhabitants; and to desist from the desecration of Islamic shrines, including aggression against *Al-Quds Al-Sharif* and its threatened destruction, call for uniting all efforts to ensure the return of the city of *Al-Quds Al-Sharif* to its legitimate owners as capital of the State of Palestine and so as to guarantee for peace and security in the region;

Uphold the fundamental human rights of the people of Kashmir and the exercise of the right to self-determination in accordance with the relevant UN resolutions and condemn the massive violations of their human rights; and reaffirm that any political process/ election under foreign occupation cannot be a substitute to the exercise of the right of self-determination by the people of Jammu and Kashmir;

Affirm that a substantive dialogue is essential to resolve the Kashmir dispute which is the basic cause of tension between India and Pakistan and support the efforts of the Government of Pakistan to achieve a just and peaceful solution of the Jammu and Kashmir dispute and call upon the Government of India to respond positively;

Reaffirm the need to preserve the national unity, sovereignty, independence, territorial integrity and Islamic character of Afghanistan and in this respect emphasize the principles of non-intervention and non-interference and call upon all States to end immediately the supply of arms and ammunition to all Afghan parties;

Reiterate the need for early political reconciliation in Afghanistan and support the efforts of OIC and United Nations in this regard. It is also imperative that the international community provides adequate assistance for rehabilitation and reconstruction in Afghanistan including for the repatriation of Afghan refugees.

Reaffirm that it is imperative to preserve the unity, sovereignty, independence and territorial integrity of Bosnia Herzegovina in accordance with the provisions of the Dayton Agreements and call for all appropriate assistance to the Government of Bosnia-Herzegovina to secure the full implementation of these agreements;

Affirm the importance of the preservation of the independence, sovereignty, territorial integrity and unity of Albania and call for generous economic and humanitarian assistance to Albania;

Strongly oppose the aggression against Azerbaijan and call for the restitution of its territories under occupation;

Reaffirm solidarity with the Turkish Muslim Community of Kibris for the protection of its legitimate rights;

Emphasize the right of every Member State to defend its national security, sovereignty and territorial integrity,

Uphold the right of peoples under colonial or alien domination or foreign occupation to self-determination seek the liberation of all occupied territories and reach equitable and just solutions to all problems and disputes in the framework of respect for international legitimacy;

Renew our determination to promote and protect the rights of Muslim communities and minorities in non-member States on the basis of respect for their human rights and in accordance with the UN Charter.

Decide to establish between us relations of permanent consultation and coordinate our efforts on the international scene, within the framework of the UN Charter, particularly its provisions relating to collective security of Member States;

Uphold the principles of sovereignty, territorial integrity and non-interference in the internal affairs of states in accordance with the provisions of the Charter;

Resolve to strengthen joint Islamic action in the humanitarian field to alleviate the sufferings of refugees and displaced persons resulting from armed conflicts as well as those resulting from natural and other disasters;

Further promote the joint efforts in prevention of arms supply to zones of conflict as well as trafficking in illegal drugs;

Agree to cooperate in all efforts to eradicate the phenomenon of terrorism which constitutes a violation of the teachings of the glorious Islamic religion which enjoins compassion and moderation, as reflected in the OIC Code of Conduct to combat international terrorism, without prejudice to the legitimate struggle of people against foreign occupation and for realizing their right to self-determination;

Strengthen cooperation in the economic and commercial fields by encouraging and facilitating greater interaction among the private sector, progressively eliminating all obstacles to the development of intra-Islamic trade including reduction of tariff and non-tariff barriers, promote greater flow of investments, transfer of technology, undertake joint industrial projects, improve transportation and communication net works among the ports and cities of the Islamic World by land, air and sea, as appropriate, accord priority to the developmental needs of the African continent especially Sub-Saharan countries, endeavour to establish an Islamic common market and promote greater interaction among regional economic groupings in the Islamic World;

Commit ourselves to advance scientific and technological cooperation by harnessing our human and material resources to create Islamic institutions of higher learning throughout the Islamic world and by sharing expertise through all other means.

Support intensification of cooperation among Member States through the OIC Standing Committees on Economic and Commercial Cooperation (COMCEC), Science and Technology (COMSTECH) and Information and Culture (COMIAC) as well as through OIC and its subsidiary, specialized and affiliated bodies;

Agree to concert our policies and efforts for preserving and promoting the accomplishments, values and traditions of the Islamic civilization and inculcating in our younger generation high moral and ethical values and a sense of justifiable pride in Islam and Islamic culture;

Resolve to project the true essence of Islam universally especially its humane message of tolerance, justice, understanding, moderation, respect for human rights and dignity of human person and cooperate with peoples of the other religious faiths to build a better and more peaceful world free from strife, poverty, injustice and exploitation; and

Renew our determination to cooperate with the international community in promoting a world free from nuclear and other weapons of mass destruction and seeking effective solutions to common problems and contributing to ushering in a new era of peace, security, stability and progress for mankind.

We hereby entrust the OIC Secretary General with the follow-up of the implementation of this Declaration.

I. Tehran Declaration

(Approved by the 8th Islamic Summit in Tehran on 11 December 1997)

"And thus We have made you a justly balanced nation that you may be the bearers of witness to the people and (that) the Apostle may be a bearer of witness to you." (Quran; II: 143)

The Kings, Heads of State and the Government of the Member-States of the Organization of the Islamic Conference, assembled at the 8th Islamic Summit Conference, the Session of Dignity, Dialogue, Participation, held in Tehran, the Islamic Republic of Iran, from 8 to 10 Sha'aban 1418H, corresponding to 9-11 December 1997.

- Stressing their full adherence to *Al-Tawhid*, as the foundation for man's true freedom: and their devotion to the progressive percepts of Islam which provide a delicate balance between spiritual and material dimensions of human life, and between liberty and salvation, based on tolerance and compassion, wisdom, justice and participation.

- Affirming their strong determination to realize the purposes and principles of the Charter of the Organization of the Islamic Conference, in particular as regards the unity and solidarity of the Islamic Ummah, safeguarding of the Islamic values and principles.

- Determined to realize the legitimate aspirations of Islamic nations and peoples for peace and security as well as comprehensive, balance, and sustainable development through active participation and the realization of the fundamental right to self-determination of peoples under colonial or alien domination or foreign occupation.

- Recognizing the importance of preserving the identity of the Ummah and of holding fast to their tradition and historical heritage as the main factor in commenting the fabric of the society and enhancing social stability,

- Emphasizing the imperative of positive interaction, dialogue and understanding among cultures and religions; and rejecting the theories of clash and conflict which breed mistrust and diminish the grounds for peaceful interaction among nations.

- Noting the transitional international environment and the enormous capabilities and potentials of the Islamic Ummah to play a constructive role in shaping a more just, equitable and peaceful global order,

- Expressing their full confidence that Iran, under the leadership of His Eminence Ayatollah Khamene'i and the Presidency of His Excellency Khatami, will lead the OIC during its Chairmanship in the most able and constructive manner, further enhancing the role and participation of the Organization in international affairs,

Solidarity and Security in the Islamic World

1. Pledge solemnly to promote solidarity, peace and security within the Islamic world as their top priority, and to pursue consultations on a forum for security cooperation, and entrust the Inter-Government Expert Group on Solidarity and Security of Islamic States to study and recommend appropriate strategies and practical measures to achieve this objective.

2. Reaffirm their resolve to consolidate cooperation and coordination among the member states and their expectation from all regional organizations within the Islamic world to take effective practical measures in order to expand cooperation in all fields.

3. Emphasize that the goal of establishment of Islamic common market constitutes a significant step towards strengthening Islamic solidarity and enhancing the share of the Islamic world in global trade.

4. Condemn the continued occupation by Israel of Palestinian and other Arab territories including *Al-Quds Al-Sharif*, the Syrian Golan and Southern Lebanon; salute the steadfastness of the Palestinian, Lebanese and Syrian people in their resistance to the Israeli occupation; call for the liberation of all occupied Arab territories and restoration of the usurped rights of the Palestinian people; condemn the expansionist policies and practices by Israel, such as the establishment and expansion of Jewish settlements in the occupied Palestinian territory , as well as acts to change the demographic and geographic status of the Holy City of Al-Quds; and emphasize the need for Israel to desist from state-terrorism which it continues to practice in utter disregard for all legal and moral principles; call for making the Middle East a zone free of all nuclear weapons and weapons of mass destruction and the necessity for Israel to join the Non-Proliferation Treaty and to put all its nuclear installations under IAEA safeguards.

5. Underline their resolve and determination to regain the Holy City of Al-Quds and the noble sanctuary of *Masjid Al-Aqsa* and to restore the inalienable national rights of the Palestinian people, the exercise of the right of the Palestinians to return to their homes and property and the attainment and exercise of the right of the Palestinian people to self-determination and the establishment of the independent and sovereign Palestinian State with *Al-Quds Al-Sharif* as its capital, and their right to leave and return freely to their country.

6. Stress their solidarity with the Muslim people of Bosnia and Herzegovina and underscore their confidence that the Ministerial Contact Group will continue to actively pursue the process of peace and reconstruction.

7. Deplore continuation of conflict and violence in Afghanistan, and express their full support for inter-Afghan dialogue, formation of a board-based government, and activities at the regional and international level to stop the bloodshed and to establish lasting peace in Afghanistan.

8. Call for the rejection of aggression of the Republic of Armenia against the Republic of Azerbaijan and complete withdrawal of Armenian forces from all occupied territories and early and peaceful resolution of the Armenian-Azerbaijani conflict.

9. Reiterate their full support to the people of Jammu and Kashmir in the realization of their right to self-determination in accordance with UN resolution.

10. Strongly condemn terrorism in all its forms and manifestations while recognizing the right of peoples under colonial or alien domination or foreign occupation for self-determination, declare that the killing of innocent people is forbidden in Islam; reiterate their commitment to the provisions of the OIC Code of Conduct for combating international terrorism, and their resolve to intensify their efforts to conclude a treaty on this issue, and call on the international Community to deny asylum to terrorists, assist in bringing them to justice, and take all necessary measures to prevent or to dismantle support networks helpful in all forms of terrorism.

11. Pledge their commitment to extend full support to Muslim communities and minorities in non-Muslim countries in collaboration with their governments, and call upon all states to ensure their religious, political, civil, economic, social and cultural rights.

Revival of the Islamic Civilization and identity

12. Consider the revival of the Islamic civilization a peaceful global reality, express their concern at tendencies to portray Islam as a threat to the world, and emphasize that the Islamic civilization is firmly and historically grounded in peaceful coexistence, cooperation and mutual understanding among civilizations, as well as constructive discourse with other religions and thoughts.

13. Reaffirm the need to establish understanding and interaction among various cultures, in line with the Islamic teachings of tolerance, justice and peace, denounce various manifestations of cultural invasion, disregard for religious and cultural traditions of other nations particularly as regards Divine values and principles, and call for the speedy conclusion of an internationally binding document to prevent blasphemy in accordance with existing decisions.

14. Entrust the "Group of Experts on the Image of Islam" to formulate and recommend pragmatic and constructive steps to encounter negative propaganda, to remove and rectify mis-understandings, and to present the true image of Islam, the religion of peace, the liberty and salvation.

15. Welcome the increasing inclination towards the flourishing message of Islam in the world, and decide to take advantage of the technological achievements in the field of information and communications in order to present the rich culture and eternal principles of Islam to the whole of mankind.

Comprehensive, Balanced and Sustainable Development

16. Consider sustainable and balanced development in the moral, political, social, economic, cultural and scientific fields as vital for the Islamic world, and inspired by the noble principles and values of Islam, reaffirm their unwavering determination to ensure free exchange of ideas and the fullest participation of the broadest segments of the Islamic Ummah in the various activities of society; reiterate their support for the aims and principles of "The Cairo Declaration on Human Rights in Islam", and decide to undertake adequate measures to institutionalize and operationalize this declaration.

17. Invite Member Sates to make a collective effort towards substantial increase in trade and investments within the Islamic world and to put in place instruments including those decided within the context of COMCEC in order to expand the existing exchange of goods and services and transfer of technology and expertise.

18. Emphasize their full respect for the dignity and the rights of Muslim women and enhancement of their role in all aspect of social life in accordance with Islamic principles, and call in the General Secretariat to encourage and coordinate participation of women in the relevant activities of the OIC.

19. Underline the need for coordination among the Member States to enhance their role and participation in the global economic system and the international economic decision-making process; reject, at the same time, unilateralism and extraterritorial application of domestic law, and urge all States to consider the so-called D' Amato Law as null and void.

20. Stress the need for environmental cooperation among Islamic countries in various fields at the bilateral, regional and international levels to achieve sustained economic growth and sustainable development, as well as collaboration and

coordination of positions regarding these issues in international fora.

International Participation

21. Welcome the participation of the UN Secretary General, H.E. Kofi Annan, at the Tehran Summit as a sign of excellent relation and cooperation between the United Nations in a manner that ensures maximum democratization of the decision making within the UN system, and stress in this context, on the need for a more effective and equitable role and representation of the OIC membership in the UN organs, particularly the Security Council.

22. Emphasize that effective, constructive and meaningful participation of Islamic countries in the management of international affairs is essential for maintaining peace and security in the world, and establishing the new world order on the basis of equality, justice and shared prosperity and promoting morality and Divine values and, in this connection, all upon the General Secretariat to facilitate effective consultation and coordination among Islamic countries in all international fora.

Strengthening the Organization of the Islamic Conference

23. Recognize that concerted measures to strengthen and revitalize the Organization of the Islamic Conference is also imperative, and express their determination to provide all necessary support with strong conviction to the ongoing process of reform and restructuring of the Organization to reach higher levels of efficiency and competence and enhance its effectiveness, operationalize and implement its decisions, and to constantly adapt the Organization with evolving international circumstances; mandate the "Open-ended Expert Group", in coordination with the Secretary General and the Chairman of the Organization, to study this issue with a view to achieving practical solutions.

Follow-up

24. Request the Chairman of the Organization to carry out regular and substantive consultations with member-states and take all necessary measures to pursue the implementation of this Declaration with the cooperation of the Secretary General.

Bibliography

I. PERIODICALS

(i) Daily Newspapers

Al-Ahram (Arabic), Cairo, Egypt.
Dawn, Karachi, Pakistan.
Frontier Post, Peshawar, Pakistan.
Hindustan Times, New Delhi, India.
Jang, (Urdu), Rawalpindi, Pakistan.
Jordan Times, Amman, Jordan.
Kayhan International, Tehran, Iran.
Kuwait Times, Kuwait, Kuwait.
Le Monde (French), Paris, France.
New York Times, New York, USA.
Pakistan Observer, Islamabad, Pakistan.
Pakistan Times, Islamabad, Pakistan.
Tehran Times, Tehran, Iran.
The Muslim, Islamabad, Pakistan.
The Nation, Lahore, Pakistan.
The News, Islamabad, Pakistan.
Times of India, New Delhi, India.
Washington Post, Washington D.C., USA.

Note: Many of the newspapers are brought out from more than one city simultaneously. In the footnotes, the name of the city is mentioned just for the first reference in each chapter. For all later references of newspapers the city of publication should be taken as mentioned against each in this list, unless otherwise indicated.

(ii) Journals

Quarterly *American Journal of Islamic Social Sciences*, IIIT, Herndon, USA.
Quarterly *Call of Islam*, WSIC, Tripoli, Libya.
Quarterly *Foreign Affairs Pakistan*, Foreign Office, Islamabad, Pakistan.
Quarterly *IRCICA Newsletter*, Istanbul Centre, Istanbul, Turkey.
Monthly *Islam Today*, ISESCO, Rabat, Morocco.
Six-monthly *Journal of Economic Cooperation in Islamic Countries*, Ankara Centre, Ankara, Turkey.
Quarterly *Journal of Institute of Muslim Minority Affairs*, IMMA, Jeddah, Saudi Arabia.

Quarterly *Journal of Middle East Studies*, Institute of Middle East Studies, Washington, D.C., USA.
Quarterly *Journal of Palestine Studies*, Institute of Palestine Studies, Washington D.C., USA.
Monthly *MWL Journal*, MWL, Mecca, Saudi Arabia.
Quarterly *Pakistan Horizon*, PIIA, Karachi, Pakistan.
Quarterly *Periodica Islamica*, Jalan Riong, Kuala Lumpur, Malaysia.
Weekly *The Muslim World*, WMC, Karachi Pakistan.

(iii) Yearbooks/ Reference Books

Africa's Who's Who, London, African Books Ltd., 1981.
Europpa Year Book, London, Europpa Publications, Ltd., 1992–5.
Facts on File, New York, NY/ USA, Facts on File, Inc., 1968–98.
International Who's Who, London, Europpa Books Ltd., 1992.
Keesing's Contemporary Archives, Harlow, UK, Keesing's Publications Ltd./ Longman Group, 1965–1998.(Now renamed Keesing's Record of World Events.)
Statistical Yearbooks on Muslim Countries, Ankara, SESRTCIC, 1990–97.
World Muslim Gazetteer (Ten-yearly), Karachi, WMC, 1965—onward.
Yearbooks of Socio-Economic Indicators of Muslim Countries, Ankara, SESRTCIC, 1990–97.

II. OFFICIAL PUBLICATIONS, DOCUMENTS AND MEMOIRS

(i) Government Publications

Directorate of Films and Publications, Ministry of Information, Government of Pakistan, (Islamabad), *Report on the Second Islamic Summit*, (1974).
_____. *We Are One: Report on the first extra-ordinary session of ICFM*, (1980).
_____. *Report on the ICFM: Eleventh session, (1980).*
_____. *Pakistan and the OIC*, (1984).
_____. *Charter of the OIC*, (1993).

_____. *Introduction to the OIC*, (1993).

_____. *List of OIC members and conferences*, (1993)

_____. *OIC Resolutions on Afghanistan & Kashmir* (1993).

_____. *Declarations and Resolutions of the OIC Conferences held in Pakistan*, (1993).

_____. *Profiles of the member and Observer States of the OIC*, (1997).

_____. *Final Declaration of the Islamabad Islamic Summit*, (1997).

Government of Pakistan Publications (Karachi), *Foreign Policy of Pakistan: Speeches of Zulfiqar Ali Bhutto*, (1964).

Ministry of Foreign Affairs, Kingdom of Morocco (Rabat), *Al Quds Committee: Achievements and Perspectives*, (1984).

Ministry of Information, Kingdom of Saudi Arabia (Riyadh), *Saudi Arabia and its Place in the World*, (n.d).

_____. *King Faisal Speaks*, (n.d.).

_____. *Prince Faisal Speaks*, (n.d.).

Ministry of National Guidance, Information Administration, (Cairo), *The Philosophy of Revolution*, by President Gamal Abdul Nasser, (1954).

(ii) OIC General Secretariat Publications

Information Dept., OIC Secretariat (Jeddah), *The Islamic Conference*, (n.d.).

_____. *Final Declarations and Communiqués of the Islamic Summits* published from time to time.

_____. *Final Declarations and Communiqués of the Islamic Foreign Ministers' Conferences* published from time to time.

_____. *Declarations and Resolutions of the Islamic Summit and Ministers of Foreign Affairs Conferences: 1969-81*, (n.d.).

_____. *OIC Declarations and Resolutions on Economic Social and Cultural Affairs; 1969-81*, (n.d.).

_____. Secretary General's *Report on the condition of Cypriot Muslims presented to 23rd ICFM*, (1995).

_____. *OIC Plan of Action on Bosnia & Herzegovina* (July 1993).

_____. Secretary General's *Report on Jammu & Kashmir presented to the 21st ICFM*, (1993).

_____. Secretary General's *Report on Bosnia & Herzegovina presented to the 21st ICFM*, (1993).

_____. Secretary General's *Report on the condition of Bulgarian Muslims* presented to 17th ICFM, (1988).

(iii) Selected Official Publications of some Islamic Organizations

Al-Quds Committee: *Al-Quds: A Historical Document*, Jeddah, n.d.

ICCI & CE: *Islamic Chamber in Brief*, Karachi, 1996.

_____. *Report on Activities of the Islamic Chamber, 1996*.

ICPICH: *Islamic Commission for Preservation of Heritage*, Istanbul, n.d.

Islamic Development Bank: *20th Annual Report: 1415 A.H./1995 A.D.*, Jeddah, 1996.

_____. *Twenty-two Years in the Service of Development*, Jeddah, 1996.

_____. *IDB: Articles of Agreement*, Jeddah, 1984.

_____. *IDB: Information Bulletin*, Jeddah, 1984.

IFA: *The Declarations and Resolutions of the Islamic Fiqh Academy*, Jeddah, n.d.

IFSTAD: *Information Bulletin*, Jeddah, 1984.

_____. *Islam, Science, Technology and IFSTAD*, Jeddah, n.d.

_____. *Islamic Science, Technology and Development*, Jeddah, n.d.

IINA: *Background of the Islamic News Agency*, Jeddah, n.d.

IRCICA: Special Issue of the Newsletter on the *Achievements of the Istanbul Centre, No. 37*, Istanbul, 1995.

ISBO: *The Islamic States Broadcasting Services Organization*, Jeddah, 1981.

_____. *Ten Years Performance of ISBO*, Jeddah, 1987.

_____. *A Summary of ISBO Objectives and Activities*, Jeddah, 1995.

ISESCO: *Marching Ahead*, Rabat, n.d.

Islamic Solidarity Fund: *Islamic Solidarity Fund*, Jeddah, n.d.

Islamic University in Bangladesh: *Fact Sheet*, Dhaka, 1997.

Islamic University in Malaysia: *Graduate Prospectus: 1996*, Kuala Lumpur, 1996.

Islamic University in Uganda: *IUIU: Basic Information*, Mbale, 1997

ISSF: *Statute of the ISSF*, Riyadh, n.d.

_____. *Activity Report of ISSF*, Riyadh, 1997

MWL: *A brief history of Rabita*, Mecca, n.d.

_____. *Rabitah al-Alam al Islami: An Introduction,* Mecca, n.d.

OICC: *A March of Achievements and Progress* Jeddah, n.d.

OISA: *member states & Companies of the Islamic Shipowners Association,* Jeddah, n.d.

SESRTCIC: *Ankara Centre: Functions, Facilities, Activities,* Ankara, 1995.

WMC: *A Resume of the fifth World Muslim Conference; Baghdad–1962,* Karachi, n.d.

_____. *A brief description of sixth Conference; Mogadishu 1964,* Karachi, 1965.

_____. *A brief history of Mu'tamar al Alam al Islami Karachi,* 1985.

_____. *A bird's eye view of the Mu'tamar,* Karachi, 1988.

Note: See the List of abbreviations for the unknown acronyms.

III. BOOKS AND MONOGRAPHS

(i) Books on the OIC

Ahsan, Abdullah, *OIC: Introduction to an Islamic Political Institution,* Herndon, IIIT, 1988.

Baba, Noor Ahmad, *OIC: Theory and Practice of Pan-Islamic Cooperation,* Karachi, Oxford University Press, 1994.

Mehdi, Haider, *OIC: A review of its political and educational policies,* Lahore, Progressive Publishers, 1988.

Moinuddin, Hassan, *The Charter of the Islamic Conference,* Oxford, Clarendon Press, 1987.

OIC Secretariat Publication, '*Guide to the OIC*', Jeddah, OIC, 1995.

Pasha, Kamal, *India and the OIC,* New Delhi, Vikas, 1996.

Pirzada, Sharifuddin, *Speeches and Statements of H.E. Sharifuddin Pirzada as the OIC Secretary-General,* Karachi, n.p. 1989.

Selim, Mohammad el-Sayed (ed.), *The OIC in a Changing World,* Cairo, Cairo University, 1994.

Sarwar, Ghulam (Ed.) *OIC: Contemporary Issues of the Muslim World,* Rawalpindi, FRIENDS, 1997.

(ii) Books on International Organizations

Abi Saab, Georges (ed.), *The Concept of International Organization,* Paris, UNESCO, 1981.

Arbuthnott, Hugh and Geoffrey Edwards, *A Common Man's Guide to the Common Market: The European Community,* London, Macmillan for the Federal Trust, 1979.

Bennett, A. LeRoy, *International Organizations: Principles and Issues.* 3rd Ed., Englewood Cliffs, NJ, Prentice-Hall, 1984.

Boehr, P.R., *The United Nations: Reality and Ideal,* NY, Praeger, 1984.

Cox, Robert W. and others, *The Anatomy of Influence: Decision-making in International Organizations,* New Haven, Yale Univ. Press, 1973.

Coyle, David C., *The United Nations and How It Works.* Rev. Ed., New York, Columbia Univ. Pr., 1969.

Elmandjra, Mahdi, *The UN System: An analysis,* London, Faber, 1973.

Encyclopaedia of the United Nations and International Agreements, London, Taylor and Francis, 1985.

Feld, Warner J., et al., *International Organizations: A Comparative Approach,* NY, Praeger, 1983.

Gomaa. Ahmad M.. *The Foundation of the League of Arab States: Wartime Diplomacy and Inter-Arab Politics,* London. NY, Longman. 1977.

Jacobson, Harold K., *Networks of Interdependence: International Organizations and the Global Political System,* New York, Alfred A. Knopf. 1979.

Nye, Joseph, *Peace in Parts: Integration and Conflict in Regional Organization,* Boston, Little Brown, 1971.

(iii) Books on Islam and Politics

Abu Sulayman, Abul Hamid, *The Islamic Theory of International Relations: New Directions to Islamic Methodology and Thought,* Herndon, International Institute of Islamic Thought, 1987.

Agwani, M.S. *Politics in the Gulf* News Delhi, Vikas Publishing House, 1978.

Ahsan, Abdullah al, *Ummah or a Nation? Identity Crisis in the Modem Muslim World,* Leicester, Islamic Foundation, 1992.

Ajami, Fouad, *The Arab Predicament: Arab Political Thought and Practice Since 1967,* Cambridge, Cambridge University Press, 1981.

Ali, S. Amjad, *The Muslim World Today,* Islamabad, National *Hijra* Council, 1985.

Asad, Muhammad, *Islam at the Crossroads,* Islamabad, *Da'wa* Academy, 1990.

Ayoob, Mohammed, ed., *The Politics of Islamic Reassertion,* New York, St. Martin's Press, 1981.

Baloch, N.A., ed., *The World of Islam Today,* Islamabad, National Institute of Historical and Cultural Research, 1981.

Barkatullah, Mohammad, *The Khilafat,* Lahore, Accurate Press, n.d.

Bhutto, Zulfikar Ali, *The Great Tragedy,* Lahore, Jang Publishers, 1993.

_____. *If I am Assassinated,* New Delhi, Vikas, 1979.

_____. *Myth of Independence,* Karachi, Oxford University Press, 1969.

Bolitho, Hector, *Jinnah: Creator of Pakistan,* Peshawar, Maleeha Publications, n.d.

Canoy, Martin, *Education as Cultural Imperialism,* New York, David Mckay Inc., 1974.

Chapra, M. Umar, *Islam and the Economic Challenge,* Herndon, International Institute of Islamic Thought, 1992.

Curtis, Micheal (ed.), *Religion and Politics in the Middle East,* Boulder, Colourado, Westview Press, 1981.

Dawisha, Adeed, *Islam in Foreign Policy,* Cambridge, Cambridge University Press, 1983.

Dessouk, Ali E. Hillal (ed.), *Islamic Resurgence in the Arab World,* New York, Praeger, 1982.

Enayat, Hamid, *Modern Islamic Political Thought,* Austin, University of Texas Press, 1982.

Esposito, John L., *Islam and Politics,* Syracuse, Syracuse University Press, 1984.

_____. *Islam and Development: Religion and Socio-political Change,* Syracuse, Syracuse University Press, 1980.

Fromkin, David, *A Peace to End all Peace,* Henry Holt and Company, 1989.

Gauhar, Altaf, ed, *The Challenge of Islam,* London, Islamic Council of Europe, 1978.

Guillaume, Alferd, *Islam,* Harmondsworth, Pelican, 1976.

Hadavi, Sami, *Bitter Harvest: Palestine 1914-1979.* Rev. ed. , New York, The Caravan Books, 1979.

Haddad, Yvonne Y., (ed.) *The Muslims of America,* New York, Oxford University Press, 1991.

_____. *Contemporary Islam and the Challenge of History,* Albany, State University of New York Press, 1982.

Hodgson, Marshal G., *The Venture of Islam,* Chicago, University of Chicago Press, 1977.

Hudson, Michael, *Arab Politics: The Search for Legitimacy,* New Haven, Yale University Press, 1977.

Iqbal, Afzal, *Contemporary Muslim World,* Lahore, Institute of Islamic Culture, 1985.

_____. *Diplomacy in Islam,* 3rd Ed. Lahore, Institute of Islamic Culture, 1977.

Iqbal, Sheikh Mohammad, *The Arab Glory and the Arab Grief,* Delhi, Idrarah Adbiyat-i-Delhi, 1977.

Islamic Council of Europe, *The Muslim World and the Future Economic Order,* London, Islamic Council of Europe, 1979.

Ismael, Tareq, Y., ed., *Government and Politics of the Contemporary Middle East,* Homewood, Dorsey Press, 1970.

_____. *Government and Politics in Islam,* New York, St. Martin's Press, 1985.

Jansen, G.H., *Militant Islam,* London, Pan Brook Ltd., 1980.

Jinnah, Mohammad Ali, *Quaid-i-Azam Mohammad Ali Jinnah: Speeches and Statements as Governor General of Pakistan 1947–48,* Islamabad, Services Book Club, 1989.

Keddie, Nikki R., *Sayyid Jamal al-Din Al-Afghani: A Political Biography,* Los Angeles, University of California Press, 1972.

Kelly, Marjorie, ed., *Islam: The Religious and Political Life of a World Community,* New York, Praeger, 1984.

Kerr, Malcolm, *The Arab Cold War,* London, Oxford University Press, 1971.

Kettani, M. Ali, *Muslim Minorities in the Word Today,* Lahore, Services Book Club, 1990.

Khan, Chaudhri Nazir Ahmad, *Common Wealth of Muslim States: A Plea for Pan-Islamism,* Lahore, Al-Ahibba, 1972.

Landaue, Jacob, *The Politics of Pan- Islamism,* Oxford, Clarendon Press, 1990.

Lewis, Bernard, *Islam and the West,* Oxford, Oxford University Press, 1993.

_____. *The Political Language of Islam,* Chicago, The University of Chicago Press, 1988.

Malik, Zahid, ed., *Re-Emerging Muslim World,* Lahore, Pakistan National Centre, 1974.

Mawdudi. S.A.A., *Unity of the Muslim World,* Lahore, Islamic Publications Ltd., 1967.

McNeill, William H. and Waldman, M. Robinson (eds.). *The Islamic World,* Chicago, University of Chicago Press, 1973.

Memon, Abdul Fatah, *Invitation to a New Society.* Karachi, Inter Services Press Ltd., 1968.

Memon, Ali Nawaz, *The Islamic Nation and Future of Muslims in the New World Order,* Lahore, Vanguard, 1996.

Mohammed, Imam W. Deen, *Al-Islam Unity & Leadership,* Chicago, The Sense Maker, 1991.

Niazi, Maulana Kausar, *The Last Days of Premier Bhutto,* Lahore, Jang Publishers, 1989.

Piscatori, James P., *Islam in a World of Nation-States,* Cambridges Press Syndicate of the University of Cambridge, 1986.

Proctor, Harris, ed., *Islam and International Relations,* London, Full Hebb/ Pall Mall Press, 1965.

Qureshi, Mohammad Ibrahim, *World Muslim Minorities,* Islamabad, World Muslim Congress, 1993.

Rahman, Fazlur, *Islam,* 2nd Ed., Chicago, University of Chicago Press, 1979.

————. *Islam and Modernity,* Chicago, University of Chicago Press, 1982.

Rahman, Syed Tayyeb-ur, *Global Geo-Strategy of Bangladesh, OIC and Islamic Ummah,* Dhaka, Islamic Foundation Bangladesh, 1985.

Rashad, Adib, *Islam, Black Nationalism and Slavery: A Detailed History,* Beltsville, Writers Inc., 1995.

Rosenthal, Ervin.I.J., *Islam in the Modern National State,* Cambridge, Cambridge University Press, 1965.

Sadaat, Anwar al, *In Search of Identity: An autobiography,* New York, Harper Colon Books, Harper and Row, 1979.

Safdar, Ziauddin, *The Future of Muslim Civilization,* London, Croom Helm, 1979.

Schacht, Joseph and Bosworth, C.E., (eds.), *The Legacy of Islam,* Oxford: Oxford University Press, 1979.

Shari'ati, Ali, *On the Sociology of Islam,* translated by Hamid Algar, Oxford, Pergamon Press, 1980.

Siddique, Kaukab, *The Struggle of Muslim Women,* Kingsville, Maryland, American Society for Education & Religion, 1986.

Stoessinger, John G., *Why Nations Go to War,* New York, St. Martin's Press, 1982.

Stowasser, Barbera (ed.), *The Islamic Impulse,* Washington. D.C., Centre of Contemporary Arab Studies, Georgetown University, 1987.

Taylor, Allan R., *The Arab Balance of Power,* New York, Syracuse University Press, 1982.

Tirmizi, Amanullah Shah, *Energy in the Muslim Countries: A Pan-Islamic approach,* Islamabad, National Science Council, n.d.

Vatikiotis, P.J., *Islam and the State,* Beckenham, Kent, Croom Helm Ltd., 1987.

William, John Aden (ed.), *Themes of Islamic Civilization,* California, California University Press, 1971.

Wolpert, Stanley, *Bhutto: His Life and Times,* Karachi, Oxford University Press, 1993.

————. *Jinnah of Pakistan,* Karachi, Oxford University Press, 1990.

World Muslim Congress, *Studies on Commonwealth of Muslim Countries,* Karachi, Umma Publishing House, 1964.

Zia, Shakil Ahmed, *A History of Jewish Crimes,* Karachi, Asian Book Centre, 1969.

Index